Automatic Imitation

Oliver Genschow • Emiel Cracco
Editors

Automatic Imitation

Springer

Editors
Oliver Genschow
School of Management and Technology
Leuphana University Lüneburg
Lüneburg, Germany

Emiel Cracco
Department of Experimental Clinical
and Health Psychology
Ghent University
Ghent, Belgium

ISBN 978-3-031-62633-3 ISBN 978-3-031-62634-0 (eBook)
https://doi.org/10.1007/978-3-031-62634-0

This Springer imprint is published by the registered company Springer Nature Switzerland AG
The registered company address is: Gewerbestrasse 11, 6330 Cham, Switzerland

"Genschow and Cracco have compiled a remarkable collection of state-of-the-art research that spans a quarter of a century on how and why we imitate others, often automatically. Given the crucial role that automatic imitation plays in social interactions and bonding this book will become essential to researchers across the life and social sciences."

—Manos Tsakiris, *Professor of Psychology, Royal Holloway, University of London, UK*

"ChatGPT says that I coined the term 'automatic imitation'. I am not sure that is true, but I certainly admire this wide ranging volume. Drawing insights from cognitive, social, and affective psychology, the chapters give an overview of what is known, and what is yet to be discovered, about spontaneous mimicry—our tendency to copy the actions of others even when we do not want or intend to do so. This will make it a valuable resource for anyone interested in the topic."

—Cecilia Heyes, *Professor of Psychology, All Souls College, University of Oxford, UK*

Acknowledgments

This book was supported by two grants from the German Research Foundation (DFG; funding numbers: 246329797 and 497678237).

Contents

Chapter 1
Introduction to Automatic Imitation

Oliver Genschow and Emiel Cracco

Individuals have the tendency to automatically imitate a wide range of different behaviors such as facial expressions (e.g., Dimberg, 1982), characteristics of language (e.g., Cappella & Planalp, 1981), emotions (e.g., Hess & Fischer, 2014), postures (e.g., LaFrance, 1982), gestures (e.g., Cracco et al., 2018b), and simple movements (e.g., Brass et al., 2000; Genschow et al., 2013). In this respect, automatic imitation refers to the finding that the execution of an action is facilitated when observing compatible actions and impeded when observing incompatible actions (Cracco et al., 2018a; Genschow et al., 2017; Heyes, 2011). Research over the last two decades indicates that such imitative behavior fulfills an important social function as it bonds humans closely together by creating feelings of affiliation and fostering pro-social attitudes (for a review, see Duffy & Chartrand, 2015).

Interest in research on imitative behavior dates back to at least the eighteenth century when Adam Smith (1759) put forward the idea that spontaneous imitation can be regarded as a form of sympathy. Despite the longstanding theoretical interest, systematic investigations on imitative behavior did not start before the twentieth century when Hull (1933) discovered that participants unintentionally copied the body movements of an experimenter during a series of psychological tests. Later, Bandura (1962) linked imitative behavior to learning from others as part of his well-known social learning theory. It then took until the end of the 1990s and the beginning of the 2000s for research into automatic imitation to be carried out on a large scale. In this regard, a landmark finding was published by Chartrand and Bargh (1999). With reference to the so-called chameleon effect, the authors established a

O. Genschow (✉)
School of Management and Technology, Leuphana University Lüneburg, Lüneburg, Germany
e-mail: oliver.genschow@leuphana.de

E. Cracco
Department of Experimental Clinical and Health Psychology, Ghent University, Ghent, Belgium
e-mail: emiel.cracco@ugent.be

O. Genschow, E. Cracco (eds.), *Automatic Imitation*,
https://doi.org/10.1007/978-3-031-62634-0_1

social psychological paradigm on motor mimicry in which participants interacted with different confederates. The authors found that participants in this task touched their heads more often when a confederate touched their head as compared to when another confederate moved their foot. Conversely, participants moved their foot more often, when the confederate moved their foot, compared to when the confederate touched their head.

At a similar time point, Brass et al. (2000; see also Stürmer et al., 2000) applied the logic of stimulus-response compatibility (SRC) tasks—which are commonly used in cognitive psychological research—to investigate automatic imitation. In this task, which was later called the imitation-inhibition task, participants respond to one out of two imperative cues on the computer screen (e.g., number 1 or 2) with two different movements (e.g., lifting the index or middle finger). At the same time, participants either see another person lifting the same (congruent) or different (incongruent) finger. The typical finding in such a task is that participants respond faster and with fewer errors to congruent movements as compared to incongruent movements (Westfal et al., 2024). An adapted version of the imitation-inhibition task (Brass et al., 2000) has been recently developed and validated to investigate automatic imitation in online settings (Westfal et al., 2024). The following link provides resources for implementing the online task, analyzing its data, as well as a demo version of the task: https://www.automatic-imitation.com.

Over the last two decades, research on the chameleon effect and the imitation-inhibition task inspired many different disciplines including social and cognitive psychology, developmental psychology, clinical psychology, and neuroscience. The research in these disciplines furthered the understanding of the imitation phenomenon and fueled several debates. Despite comprehensive investigations, several important questions remain. In this book, well-known and esteemed experts across different research disciplines give an overview of the latest research on automatic imitation and review current debates in the literature. The book is divided into four parts. In the first part, the book provides an overview and comparison of different types of imitation. The second part then sheds light on the processes underlying automatic imitation. The third part reviews research investigating modulators of automatic imitation and shows under which conditions people tend to imitate others more (or less) strongly. Finally, in the fourth part of the book, the consequences of automatic imitation are reviewed and discussed.

Types of Imitation

In Chap. 2, Khemka and Catmur review a range of tasks for measuring the imitation of movements. The authors review and compare the advantages and disadvantages of passive action observation, kinematic measures of imitation, stimulus-response compatibility tasks, and naturalistic measures of mimicry and action synchrony.

Chapter 3 focuses on emotional mimicry—the imitation of nonverbal behaviors that signal emotions. In this chapter, Hess and Fischer first differentiate mimicry from other related phenomena, then give a historical overview of the research on emotional mimicry, and finally review different theories of emotional mimicry.

The first section on different types of imitation closes with Chap. 4 in which Adank and Wilt review research on speech imitation. In line with current theories of speech and language processing (Fadiga et al., 2002; Watkins & Paus, 2004), the authors incorporate research that connects speech perception and speech production to explain the underlying mechanisms of speech imitation. Moreover, the authors explain how SRC tasks can be used to study automatic imitation and then discuss which theories can explain the results obtained with such SRC tasks.

Processes Underlying Automatic Imitation

In the second part of this book, five chapters shed light on the processes of automatic imitation. In Chap. 5, Brass reviews functional theoretical accounts of automatic imitation by giving an overview of the historical context of the research on automatic imitation. In particular, he reviews theories that have been put forward to explain the "correspondence problem of imitation" (Brass & Heyes, 2005; Heyes, 2001), which refers to the question of how a perceptual representation of a movement can be transformed into a corresponding motor program.

In Chap. 6, Darda and Ramsey review neuroscientific research to explain the neurophysiological correlates that account for automatic imitation. When reviewing this literature, the authors take a critical view of dominant theories in the literature that explain the inhibition of imitation in terms of self-other distinction mechanisms that are tied to the theory-of-mind network (e.g., Brass et al., 2009). The authors argue that SRC tasks of automatic imitation engage in domain-general forms of control that are underpinned by the multiple-demand network.

While it is widely agreed that people have the automatic tendency to imitate others, the question of whether this imitative tendency is based on a goal- or movement-driven mechanism is part of a longstanding debate in the literature (e.g., Avikainen et al., 2003; Genschow et al., 2019; Wohlschläger et al., 2003). In Chap. 7, Hansen reviews the evidence for both mechanisms and then discusses potential processes that modulate the degree to which individuals engage in goal-based imitation versus movement-based imitation.

In Chap. 8, Pfister, Neszmélyi, and Kunde argue from an ideomotor perspective that automatic imitation is strongly influenced by anticipative processes. In essence, the authors argue that the social consequences of one's own behavior are readily integrated into human action representations, suggesting that imitation is strongly influenced by anticipative processes.

An interesting question is whether people's tendency to automatically imitate others is innate or learned. In Chap. 9, Farwaha and Slaughter review research on automatic imitation across the lifespan. This review reveals a significant disconnect between child and adult research on automatic imitation effects, which complicates developmental conclusions. To solve this issue, the authors put forward several promising avenues for future research.

Modulators of Automatic Imitation

The previous sections of this book may give the impression that in any situation and context, individuals automatically imitate whatever behavior they perceive. However, there is a rich literature suggesting that automatic imitation is a highly flexible behavior that can be modulated by different psychological factors. In Chap. 10, Cracco gives an overview of the research on imitation in the context of multiple agents and shows that automatic imitation varies as a function of group size. The reviewed literature demonstrates that automatic imitation is a complex process that takes into account regulatory processes to adjust cognitive control parameters as a function of both group size (Cracco & Brass, 2018) and the topographical relation between different observed actions (Cracco et al., 2022).

An often put-forward claim in the literature on automatic imitation is that imitative behavior as a social phenomenon should be modulated by social factors. In Chap. 11, Genschow and Cracco give an overview of theories that argue in favor of social modulation of automatic imitation and then critically reflect upon the idea of social modulation by reviewing social variables that have been repeatedly found to modulate automatic imitation and variables that seem not to influence automatic imitation. The authors conclude that the evidence for social modulation is rather mixed. Reasons for the mixed findings in the literature may especially be due to methodological shortcomings and imprecise theories.

In Chap. 12, Poliakoff and Gowen discuss whether and how different psychological pathologies facilitate or inhibit people's automatic tendency to imitate. Their review reveals that depending on the psychological condition, automatic imitation can either be increased, reduced, or intact. At the same time, the authors stress that these findings should not be overinterpreted as the reviewed literature includes rather small numbers of studies and participants.

Consequences of Automatic Imitation

The last part of the book sheds light on the consequences of being imitated. Chapters 13 and 14 review literature on the consequences of being behaviorally mimicked. In Chap. 13, Kulesza and Chartrand review mainly social psychological research findings showing that being mimicked by others has positive social consequences. Going one step further, the authors also discuss an often-neglected part of the motor mimicry literature by showing that under certain conditions, being mimicked can have negative social consequences as well.

While Kulesza and Chartrand review the social consequences of being mimicked, in Chap. 14, Wicher, Farmer, and Hamilton review different theories that explain these seminal findings. Their chapter highlights that the cognitive mechanisms underlying the effects of being mimicked are still unknown. The authors then discuss different possible neurocognitive models. Based on current evidence, they conclude that a domain-general model involving cognitive predictability and social learning is the most promising explanation for the effects of being mimicked.

Since imitating others has been found to have positive social consequences, scholars assumed that imitation could be a useful tool for psychotherapy. Interestingly, evidence for this claim is sparse as Salazar Kämpf and Exner conclude in Chap. 15. To deal with this issue, the authors present different theoretical approaches from which they derive new ideas on how imitative behavior might affect different psychological disorders and therapeutic processes.

The previous chapters in this book mainly focus on automatic imitation in dyadic interactions. Such a view neglects the fact that in many social situations, people are not interacting with another person in isolation, but are often witnessed by third-party observers. In Chap. 16, Powell and Winkielman review research about the inferences both children and adult observers draw from seeing other people imitate. The reviewed literature indicates that young observers typically draw positive inferences from imitative behaviors. However, as observers become more mature and more aware of social dynamics, they start taking into account more complex factors such as intention, mutual knowledge, social skills, theory of mind, and social strategies. As a consequence, adults not only form positive inferences but also negative inferences about people who imitate, depending on the situation.

Summary

Taken together, this book gives a comprehensive overview of the ubiquitous phenomenon of automatic imitation, by showing what and how people imitate. The chapters are written by esteemed experts from different psychological research fields who take a critical view of the research that has been carried out within the last two and a half decades. The reviewed research indicates that while there is strong evidence for several claims made in the literature, there is still an ongoing and lively debate for other research questions. We hope the chapters included in this book will be helpful for both scholars and students alike to get deep insights into an interesting social phenomenon and to develop new investigations to further the understanding of research questions that are currently part of ongoing debates.

References

Avikainen, S., Wohlschläger, A., Liuhanen, S., Hänninen, R., & Hari, R. (2003). Impaired mirror-image imitation in Asperger and high-functioning autistic subjects. *Current Biology, 13*, 339–341. https://doi.org/10.1016/s0960-9822(03)00087-3

Bandura, A. (1962). Social learning through imitation. In J. R. Marshall (Ed.), *Nebraska symposium on motivation* (pp. 211–274). University Press.

Brass, M., & Heyes, C. (2005). Imitation: Is cognitive neuroscience solving the correspondence problem? *Trends in Cognitive Sciences, 9*, 489–495. https://doi.org/10.1016/j.tics.2005.08.007

Brass, M., Bekkering, H., Wohlschläger, A., & Prinz, W. (2000). Compatibility between observed and executed finger movements: Comparing symbolic, spatial, and imitative cues. *Brain and Cognition, 44*, 124–143. https://doi.org/10.1006/brcg.2000.1225

Brass, M., Ruby, P., & Spengler, S. (2009). Inhibition of imitative behaviour and social cognition. *Philosophical Transactions of the Royal Society B: Biological Sciences, 364*, 2359–2367. https://doi.org/10.1098%2Frstb.2009.0066

Cappella, J. N., & Planalp, S. (1981). Talk and silence sequences in informal conversations III: Interspeaker influence. *Human Communication Research, 7*, 117–132. https://doi.org/10.1111/j.1468-2958.1981.tb00564.x

Chartrand, T. L., & Bargh, J. A. (1999). The chameleon effect: The perception-behavior link and social interaction. *Journal of Personality & Social Psychology, 76*, 893–910. https://doi.org/10.1037//0022-3514.76.6.893

Cracco, E., & Brass, M. (2018). The role of sensorimotor processes in social group contagion. *Cognitive Psychology, 103*, 23–41. https://doi.org/10.1016/j.cogpsych.2018.02.001

Cracco, E., Bardi, L., Desmet, C., Genschow, O., Rigoni, D., De Coster, L., … Brass, M. (2018a). Automatic imitation: A meta-analysis. *Psychological Bulletin, 144*, 453–500. https://doi.org/10.1037/bul0000143

Cracco, E., Genschow, O., Radkova, I., & Brass, M. (2018b). Automatic imitation of pro- and antisocial gestures: Is implicit social behavior censored? *Cognition, 170*, 179–189. https://doi.org/10.1016/j.cognition.2017.09.019

Cracco, E., Braem, S., & Brass, M. (2022). Observing conflicting actions elicits conflict adaptation. *Journal of Experimental Psychology: General, 151*, 493–505. https://doi.org/10.1037/xge0001089

Dimberg, U. (1982). Facial reactions to facial expressions. *Psychophysiology, 19*, 643–647.

Duffy, K. A., & Chartrand, T. L. (2015). Mimicry: Causes and consequences. *Current Opinion in Behavioral Sciences, 3*, 112–116. https://doi.org/10.1016/j.cobeha.2015.03.002

Fadiga, L., Craighero, L., Buccino, G., & Rizzolatti, G. (2002). Speech listening specifically modulates the excitability of tongue muscles: A TMS study. *European Journal of Neuroscience, 15*, 399–402. https://doi.org/10.1046/j.0953-816x.2001.01874.x

Genschow, O., Florack, A., & Wänke, M. (2013). The power of movement: Evidence for context-independent movement imitation. *Journal of Experimental Psychology: General, 142*, 763–773. https://doi.org/10.1037/a0029795

Genschow, O., van Den Bossche, S., Cracco, E., Bardi, L., Rigoni, D., & Brass, M. (2017). Mimicry and automatic imitation are not correlated. *PLoS One, 12*, e0183784. https://doi.org/10.1371/journal.pone.0183784

Genschow, O., Hansen, J., Wänke, M., & Trope, Y. (2019). Psychological distance modulates goal-based versus movement-based imitation. *Journal of Experimental Psychology: Human Perception and Performance, 45*, 1031–1048. https://doi.org/10.1037/xhp0000654

Hess, U., & Fischer, A. (2014). Emotional mimicry: Why and when we mimic emotions. *Social and Personality Psychology Compass, 8*, 45–57. https://doi.org/10.1111/spc3.12083

Heyes, C. (2001). Causes and consequences of imitation. *Trends in Cognitive Sciences, 5*, 253–261. https://doi.org/10.1016/s1364-6613(00)01661-2

Heyes, C. (2011). Automatic imitation. *Psychological Bulletin, 137*, 463–483. https://doi.org/10.1037/a0022288

LaFrance, M. (1982). Posture mirroring and rapport. In M. Davis (Ed.), *Interaction rhythms: Periodicity in communicative behavior* (pp. 279–298). Human Sciences Press.

Smith, A. (1759). *The theory of moral sentiments*. A. Miller.

Stürmer, B., Aschersleben, G., & Prinz, W. (2000). Correspondence effects with manual gestures and postures: A study of imitation. *Journal of Experimental Psychology: Human Perception and Performance, 26*, 1746–1759. https://doi.org/10.1037//0096-1523.26.6.1746

Watkins, K., & Paus, T. (2004). Modulation of motor excitability during speech perception: The role of Broca's area. *Journal of Cognitive Neuroscience, 16*, 978–987. https://doi.org/10.1162/0898929041502616

Westfal, M., Cracco, E., Crusius, J., & Genschow, O. (2024). *Validation of an online imitation-inhibition task*. Unpublished Manuscript.

Wohlschläger, A., Gattis, M., & Bekkering, H. (2003). Action generation and action perception in imitation: An instance of the ideomotor principle. *Philosophical Transactions of the Royal Society B: Biological Sciences, 358*, 501–515. https://doi.org/10.1098%2Frstb.2002.1257

Chapter 2
Measuring Movement Imitation

Divyush Khemka and Caroline Catmur

Introduction

In this chapter, we present a range of techniques for measuring the speed, accuracy, and extent of imitation of others' movements. In general, we define movement imitation as *the production of a configural body movement that matches the movement performed by another*. This definition comprises two components which are of particular importance when deciding whether a given technique can be said to be measuring imitation. The first is the focus on *configural* body movements. This states that it is the configuration of body parts with respect to other body parts that are of importance in deciding whether a response is imitative (cf. Heyes, 2021). The emphasis on body part configuration is important because it allows us to distinguish imitation from other social learning processes such as stimulus enhancement (where watching another's action focuses the observer's attention on a particular body part, increasing the likelihood to engage in movements with this body part) or effector matching (where the observer performs an action using the same effector—hand, foot, etc.—as that used by the actor; see Whiten et al., 2004, for further definitions of social learning). For example, when attempting to imitate a movement such as a swimming stroke, the observer must produce a movement that not only uses the same effectors as those used by the actor (e.g. the arm and hand) but also moves those effectors in the same way with respect to the rest of the body. Moving the arm and hand in a different configuration would be classified as effector matching rather

D. Khemka
Department of Psychiatry, University of Cambridge, Cambridge, UK
e-mail: dk707@cam.ac.uk

C. Catmur (✉)
Department of Psychology, Institute of Psychiatry, Psychology and Neuroscience, Kings College London, London, UK
e-mail: caroline.catmur@kcl.ac.uk

O. Genschow, E. Cracco (eds.), *Automatic Imitation*,
https://doi.org/10.1007/978-3-031-62634-0_2

than successful imitation: the observer has identified which part of the body to move, but not how to move it.

The second part of the definition focuses on the *matching* nature of the relationship between the actor's movements and the observer's movements. It is not enough for the observer to perform a configural body movement in response to the actor's movements: the observer's body movement must match that of the actor. This element of the definition of imitation may seem superfluous, but in fact it is not always trivial to determine whether two movements do indeed 'match'. For example, a child imitating an adult will produce movements that differ in size and velocity to those of the actor; in the swimming stroke example above, a full-body movement does not look the same, visually, when the observer watches the actor as when the observer produces it themselves. In general, then, matching refers to the visual similarity between the actor's and observer's movements when viewed from a third-person perspective. The visual similarity primarily refers to the form—i.e. the configuration—of the movement, but in some cases its size and velocity may also be relevant. We note that it could be argued that the *matching* component of the definition alone is enough to define imitation; however, as 'matching' can be defined in a variety of ways, the additional emphasis on *configural* body movements ensures that matching at the level of the effector alone is not sufficient for a response to be considered imitative.

In practice, for many of the techniques discussed in this chapter, the matching nature of the imitative response is indexed indirectly: by measuring the response in the muscle(s) that would be involved in performing the observed movement. In such cases (in particular for the techniques discussed in section "Measuring Movement Imitation Without Moving"), a matching response is indicated by a particular pattern of activity, such that the muscle that would be involved in performing the observed movement responds more when observing that movement than when observing another movement. However, such a pattern on its own does not demonstrate a matching relationship: it could be that there is a general, non-specific, increase in motor response when watching particular movements. To control for such a possibility, it is necessary to measure responses in at least two muscles while watching a variety of movements: some of which involve one of the measured muscles and some of which involve the other muscle. A *muscle-specific* pattern of responses must be observed in at least two muscles (for each muscle, greater response when observing movements involving that muscle than when observing movements involving the other muscle) in order to rule out the possibility that a general increase in motor response is producing the observed effects.

The majority of the techniques described in this chapter therefore index imitation via the presence of muscle-specific responses or other similar designs. Perhaps the clearest exception to this approach is in the final section where we discuss measures of *mimicry*. We define mimicry as a type of imitation that tends to occur in more naturalistic settings, often without awareness on the observer's part that they are imitating the actor (Chartrand & Bargh, 2002; although note that this definition does not preclude that some of the other measures discussed in this chapter may also index behaviours that take place without awareness). Studies of mimicry vary in the extent to which there is a matching relationship between the movements performed by the actor and the observer, and in many cases, these studies measure effector matching or sometimes purely temporal characteristics of the movement. We discuss the extent to which these measures can be considered truly imitative in section "Measuring Mimicry" of this chapter.

Finally, as this chapter is in the context of a volume on *automatic imitation*, we should note that we are deliberately excluding some techniques from this overview: we are not discussing measures of intentional or voluntary imitation nor of over-imitation (see, e.g., Keupp et al., 2018; Marsh et al., 2019).

Measuring Movement Imitation Without Moving

We start by considering methods that can be used to measure imitative activity during passive action observation. Since the discovery of 'mirror' neurons, neurons in sensorimotor brain areas that fire not only during action performance but also during observation of similar actions (di Pellegrino et al., 1992), a range of techniques have been developed that allow researchers to monitor motor activity while the observer is not themselves moving. Although such activity is not strictly imitative, in the sense of producing a motor output that matches the observed movement, it is generally considered that this motor activity reflects subthreshold motor responses (e.g. Maslovat et al., 2013). In this section, we focus on two techniques that, by virtue of being measured in the peripheral musculature, can show high muscle specificity compared to cortical measures of activity, allowing the researcher to verify that the response is produced in the muscle of the observer, which matches the muscle in the actor that is producing the observed movement.

Electromyographic Measures of Muscle Activity During Action Observation

Electromyography (EMG) involves measuring electrical activity in the muscle. In automatic imitation research, this is carried out non-invasively using surface electrodes. Electrodes are typically placed in a belly-tendon montage and the voltage difference between the two electrodes is displayed as the EMG signal, such that the electrical activity in the muscle itself can be isolated from surrounding electrical noise. The EMG signal therefore provides a relatively clean measure of the electrical activity created by the motor unit action potentials in the targeted muscle and as such can be considered a measure of the level of activation of that muscle. The EMG signal contains both positive and negative components and is therefore usually rectified (transforming all negative values to positive) before further data analysis is performed, allowing peak, total, and/or mean response values to be calculated (see Fig. 2.1).

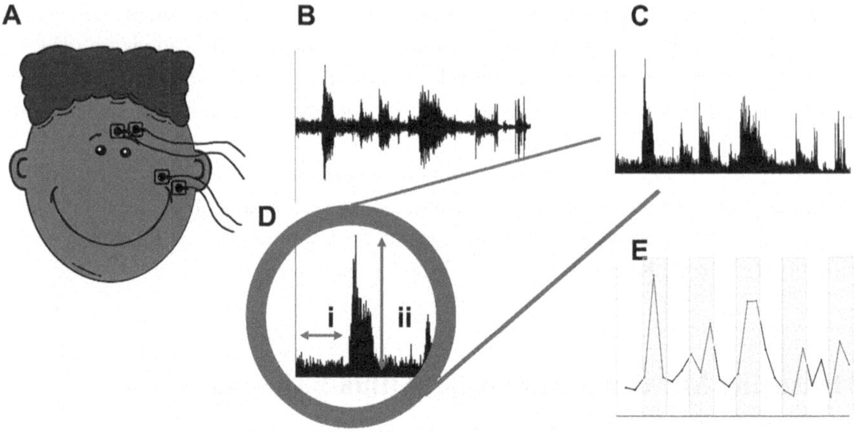

Fig. 2.1 (**a**) Indicative placement of surface electrodes for measurement of facial EMG from the corrugator (brow) muscle and zygomaticus (cheek) muscle. (**b**) Example of raw EMG signal (time runs left to right along the horizontal axis for panels B-E). (**c**) Rectified EMG signal. (**d**) Close-up from panel C illustrating (i) latency of first 'peak' in the EMG response; (ii) amplitude of first peak. (**e**) Illustration of 'epoch' approach, with signal averaged over adjacent time 'bins' and measured during certain time windows corresponding to different conditions, illustrated by the grey/ white bars

During action observation, the focus of this section, electromyography is performed in the muscle at rest. In many skeletal muscles, little electrical activity is recorded at rest, and action observation does not increase muscle activity to the point where motor unit action potentials can be detected with surface electrodes. However, in certain populations (e.g. infants and young children; Cattaneo et al., 2007; Turati et al., 2013) and for certain muscles (in particular those of the face and neck; e.g. Dimberg, 1982; Ruggiero & Catmur, 2018), it is possible to detect EMG signals during passive action observation. This permits the researcher to measure the level of activity in the recorded muscle(s) during various action observation conditions.

In principle, it is possible to measure a range of dependent variables from EMG during action observation, including latency of response and its magnitude. In practice, measuring latency is complicated by the need to define a threshold above which it can be considered that an EMG response is not just 'noise', with latency of onset then defined as the timepoint at which the EMG signal exceeds that threshold; however, during passive action observation the signal-to-noise ratio is low, and as such, latency measures are not commonly used in this literature. Another drawback of using latency measures in EMG recorded during action observation is that the observed movements unfold over time and as such—unlike with more punctate stimuli—there is not one clear timepoint from which latency can be measured. Instead, an 'epoch' approach is often used, with the signal during certain time windows (e.g. before or after a certain timepoint in the observed movement) being compared (Fig. 2.1). Typically, this signal will comprise the magnitude of the EMG response, which can be measured as either peak amplitude, or, more commonly, area under the curve—in effect a sum of activity—during a certain time window. Individual differences in a variety of factors (e.g. subcutaneous fat, which impedes signal detection from surface electrodes) can lead to wide variation in raw EMG signal magnitude, meaning it is important to control for this in group-level analyses, for example, by normalising each participant's EMG signal to their own mean (Halaki & Ginn, 2012).

As noted above, the use of EMG to measure muscle activity during passive action observation has on the whole been confined to head muscles. Studies using this technique to measure imitation have typically focused on imitation of emotional facial expressions, or of eating/swallowing movements (see also Chap. 3; this volume). Dimberg (1982) measured EMG responses in facial muscles during the observation of happy and angry facial expressions. Responses in the zygomaticus cheek muscle (involved in smiling) and in the corrugator brow muscle (involved in frowning) were each greater during the observation of the expression that used those muscles in the actor (i.e. during observation of happy and angry expressions, respectively), consistent with a muscle-specific imitative response to the observed expressions. Subsequent studies have used this technique to compare these imitative responses across different participant groups (e.g. McIntosh et al., 2006; Kaiser et al., 2017; Künecke et al., 2018; Scarpazza et al., 2018) and across different types of actors (e.g. human vs android; Hofree et al., 2014).

EMG responses during observation of eating movements are generally measured instead from the suprahyoid muscles just under the chin, which are involved in swallowing. Studies of responses to action observation in these muscles have focused on whether observers show an anticipatory imitative response when observing an object being grasped in order to be brought to the actor's mouth (grasp to eat) compared to when an object is being grasped in order to be placed at another location (grasp to place). Cattaneo et al. (2007) reported differential mylohyoid responses in neurotypical, compared to autistic, children when observing grasp-to-eat versus grasp-to-place movements; however, in this study the observed movement was confounded with the nature of the object being grasped, which may have driven the differential responses (Ruggiero & Catmur, 2018). Studies using the suprahyoid muscles also tend to record from one muscle only, making it hard to draw any conclusions regarding the muscle specificity of the response to the observed movements.

TMS-Evoked Measures of Motor Responses During Action Observation

The other key method to measure automatic imitation when participants are not moving utilises transcranial magnetic stimulation (TMS). TMS is well known in the cognitive neurosciences as a method for temporarily *disrupting* brain function (as a so-called virtual lesion technique; Walsh & Cowey, 1998; Pitcher et al., 2021), but it also has a long history in neurophysiological research and clinical settings, when combined with EMG, as a technique for *measuring* motor function (Chen et al., 2008); it is in this latter context that TMS is most relevant to the measurement of automatic imitation.

TMS is a method for inducing electrical current in the brain. When a TMS 'pulse' is fired, a strong and rapidly changing electrical current is passed through a coil consisting of copper wire wound around an iron core. Due to electromagnetic induction, the changing current generates a magnetic field which—when the TMS coil is placed against the head—passes through the skull and induces an electrical current in any electrical conductors within its range. In the case of TMS applied to the brain, the conductors are the axons of the neurons directly underneath the coil. If the TMS pulse is sufficiently strong, it depolarises these neurons, creating action potentials. In the case of TMS applied to the motor cortex, these action potentials are propagated down the corticospinal tract to the neuromuscular junction of the muscle which they innervate, creating a motor-evoked potential (MEP) in that muscle. The MEP can be detected and measured with surface electrodes in a similar fashion to EMG, as described in section "Electromyographic Measures of Muscle Activity During Action Observation" (see Fig. 2.2). Each individual participant will have a different 'resting motor threshold', the intensity of TMS that is required to induce MEPs in a particular muscle when the participant is at rest. In order to reliably induce MEPs on every trial during an experiment, TMS is usually delivered at an intensity just over (e.g. at 110% of) the participant's threshold.

When deciding on the dependent variable for MEP studies, some of the same considerations apply as mentioned above for EMG (see section "Electromyographic Measures of Muscle Activity During Action Observation"). The main choice is whether to use the area under the curve of the MEP or the peak-to-peak amplitude as the dependent variable. However, the MEP tends to be relatively larger and 'cleaner' (in terms of signal-to-noise) than the EMG signal; it is also more punctate as it occurs at a particular timepoint after the TMS pulse is delivered (usually around 20 ms for hand muscles, reflecting the conduction time between the brain and the hand musculature). As such, the magnitude of the MEP response is usually indexed

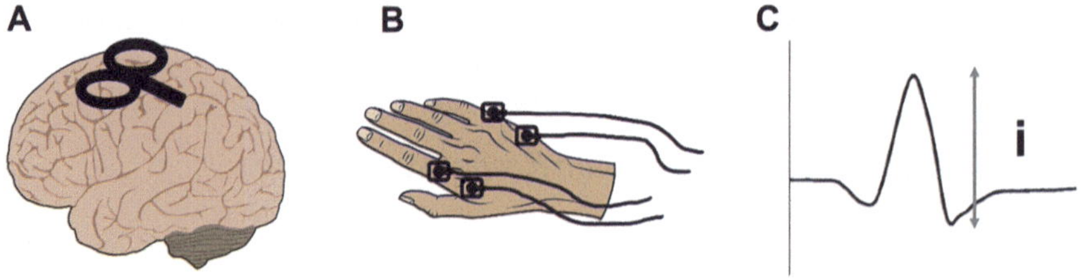

Fig. 2.2 (**a**) Illustration of TMS coil placement over the primary motor cortex hand area. (**b**) Indicative placement of surface electrodes for measurement of motor-evoked potentials from the first dorsal interosseus and abductor digiti minimi muscles. (**c**) Example of a motor-evoked potential, illustrating (i) peak-to-peak amplitude of MEP response

by the absolute amplitude (i.e. from the minimum peak to the maximum peak in a given time window), averaged over multiple trials from a given experimental condition.

Crucially for the present purposes, for a given strength of TMS pulse, the size of the MEP reflects the relative activation of the motor cortical representation stimulated by the TMS coil. Thus, MEPs generated in a particular muscle when the participant is at rest will be smaller than those recorded when the participant is activating that muscle (e.g. performing a movement or preparing to perform a movement). Critically, this increase in MEP size is also found when participants are at rest and merely observing others' movements. The utility of TMS-MEP measures for studies of action observation was first elucidated by Fadiga et al. (1995), who demonstrated that MEPs in hand muscles while participants were at rest but observing hand movements were greater than those recorded while the participants were observing other non-action stimuli such as dimming lights. A clearer demonstration of muscle specificity was subsequently reported by Strafella and Paus (2000), who showed greater MEPs in hand muscles while participants were watching hand movements compared to arm movements and vice versa for MEPs recorded from arm muscles. Subsequent studies have shown that the increased motor cortical activation is specific not only to the effector (hand vs. arm) but also to the muscle that would be involved in the observed movement (e.g. index finger vs. little finger muscle; Romani et al., 2005; Catmur et al., 2007). It should be noted that this specificity develops during the first few hundred milliseconds following the onset of the observed action: a comprehensive review of the TMS-MEP literature on motor responses to action observation (Naish et al., 2014) concluded that when observing others' actions, there is an initial non-specific increase in MEP amplitude, which occurs in the first 100 ms after the other's action. This cannot be considered an imitative response since it is not muscle-specific: instead, it suggests that—possibly due to a general attention-related or alerting mechanism—seeing other people's actions produces a general increase in motor activity in the observer. Naish et al. further reported that muscle-specific MEP responses start to develop around 200 ms after the onset of the observed action. Recall that these muscle-specific responses are found when participants are at rest, observing another person's action: as such, they are considered to be the neurophysiological signature of the tendency to automatically imitate other people's movements.

TMS-MEP measures have some significant advantages over other cognitive neuroscience methods when measuring motor responses to action observation: the temporal specificity of TMS is very high, allowing the timecourse of motor responses to be determined (as outlined by Naish et al., 2014); unlike most functional neuroimaging methods, the ability to record responses from multiple muscles permits the researcher to determine whether a response is muscle-specific or merely a reflection of generalised motor activity. It should, however, be noted that carefully designed behavioural studies of automatic imitation (see section "Stimulus-Response Compatibility Measures of Automatic Imitation") share many of these advantages; and there are some considerations to be taken into account when using TMS in this context. As noted above, actions unfold over time and this creates some difficulties when designing TMS-MEP studies of action observation: notably, if muscle-specific MEP responses develop from 200 ms after an observed action, one should not expect such responses to be exactly timelocked to the action that is being observed. Conversely, when observing ongoing actions (as opposed to single movements) the observer may be able to predict the outcome of the action, in which case the pattern of MEP response may be more closely aligned in time to the activity of the muscles involved in the observed movements. The observation of repeated actions (e.g. in a blocked design) may induce such predictive responses. Another consideration is how predictable the TMS pulse becomes during the course of the study: MEP amplitudes tend to reduce when the TMS pulse is predictable (e.g. occurring at a certain timepoint after a visual stimulus; Cavallo et al., 2014; Villiger et al., 2011), making it essential to control for pulse timing and predictability when comparing experimental conditions, especially when comparing to baseline when pulses may be less predictable than during stimulus presentation.

Finally, we should note that although single-pulse TMS, when used as outlined in this section, is a safe procedure, there are some contra-indications to TMS that make its use on certain populations problematic. The primary safety concern with TMS is the possibility of inducing a seizure in participants with a low seizure threshold; as such, TMS should not be used in people with a family or personal history of epilepsy. It is also not usually considered suitable for use in developmental studies with infant or child participants. Further details on best practice for ensuring the safety of TMS in neuroscience research can be found in Rossi et al. (2009, 2021).

Kinematic Measures of Movement Imitation

In this section, we consider how motion tracking can be used to measure movement imitation. This group of techniques uses motion trackers—physical or digital—to collect data on the location of one or more body parts in two- or three-dimensional space across time. Physical trackers are typically infrared reflectors (e.g. Kilner et al., 2003), or electromagnetic sensors (e.g. Forbes & Hamilton, 2017), which are attached to points on the participant's body while the participant carries out various movement tasks. Digital movement tracking instead uses techniques such as visual pattern recognition, or more laboriously, video coding, to identify the location, in images across time, of particular body parts (e.g. Niechwiej-Szwedo et al., 2018). For the purposes of this chapter, we will consider tasks where an observer is moving either while simultaneously observing an actor or shortly after observing an actor.

The data generated by these methods (location of body parts over time) are subjected to analyses that calculate values including the location, velocity, acceleration, and jerk (rate of change in acceleration) of each marker during a particular time window (see Fig. 2.3). Where more than one marker/location is recorded, the relative locations of multiple markers with respect to each other can also be calculated, along with the velocity, acceleration, and jerk of these markers with respect to each

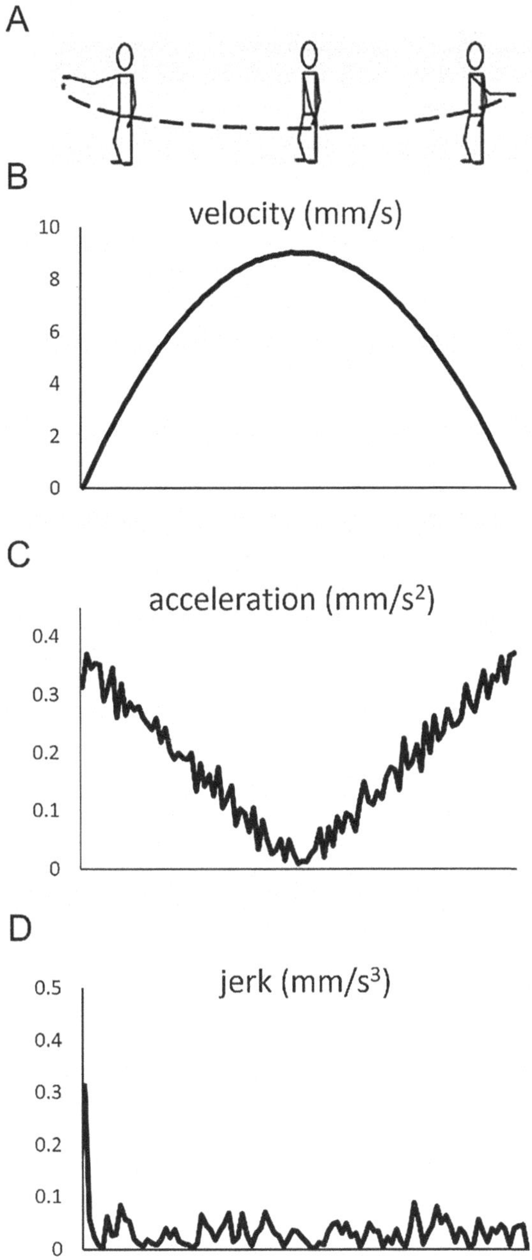

Fig. 2.3 (**a**) Illustration of participant performing a sinusoidal left-to-right movement in the horizontal plane. (**b**) Velocity of participant movement (time runs left to right along the horizontal axis for all panels). (**c**) Absolute acceleration of participant movement. (**d**) Jerk (rate of change in acceleration) of participant movement

other. These values can then be compared to equivalent values from the actor, across timepoints, and across experimental conditions.

To appreciate the wide range of research questions that can be addressed using such data, we provide an overview here of some of the most influential studies of imitation that have used kinematic measures. For a more detailed review, we refer the reader to Krishnan-Barman et al. (2017).

Kilner et al. (2003) used infrared motion tracking to measure the variance in participants' movements while they performed sinusoidal horizontal or vertical arm movements. Participants were asked to perform these movements at a speed of about 0.5 Hz while observing either a human actor or a robot actor performing the same type of movement in either the same or the other plane (i.e. horizontal or vertical) to the participant's own movement. The actor's observed movements interfered with those performed by the observer (i.e. resulted in greater variance) when the actor performed a movement in the other plane to that performed by the observer, even though the observed movements were incidental to those that the participant was performing. Furthermore, this interference was found only for biological motion and not for robotically observed movements. However, the robotically and human-observed movements varied in a number of ways: the velocity profiles were different (biological motion decelerates towards the end of the sinusoid to ensure a 'minimal jerk' velocity profile, whereas robotic motion has relatively constant velocity and thus greater change in acceleration at the end of each movement); the observed movements were performed live; thus, it is likely that the observed human movement was itself more variable than the observed robotic movement (see also Chap. 10 for a discussion on the moderators of automatic imitation). Follow-up studies demonstrated that the interference effect was indeed the result of the different velocity profiles of biological motion (Kilner et al., 2007); an intriguing series of studies by Cook et al. (2013, 2014) suggested that participants may demonstrate less interference from observed minimum jerk biological motion if they themselves move with less of a minimum jerk velocity profile. This latter finding is consistent with the idea that observed actions are represented in our own motor system as a result of sensorimotor experience in which we observe the visual consequences of our own actions (Heyes et al., 2005).

Kinematic techniques are not restricted to human participants. In an elegant study, Voelkl and Huber (2007) used motion analysis from video of marmosets who were attempting to open a small canister to retrieve a food reward. Observer marmosets were previously exposed to a model opening the canister with its mouth; non-observer marmosets did not receive this exposure. The head movements of the observer marmosets were consistently closer, in terms of a number of kinematic features, to the head movements of the model, compared to those of the non-observer marmosets. This study demonstrated high fidelity of movement imitation in non-human primates, casting doubt on previous claims that such high-fidelity imitation is specific to humans (see also Sartori et al., 2015 for a similar demonstration in dolphins).

Potentially 'irrational' imitation has also been revealed using motion tracking techniques. Forbes and Hamilton (2017) asked participants to touch a series of targets, copying the order in which an actor moved to their targets. The actor had to move around obstacles between their targets, but participants had no obstacles to avoid. Motion tracking was used to determine the peak height of participants' movements between their targets. These data demonstrated that despite the lack of obstacles, participants tended to imitate the actor's movement trajectory, even when this was excessively high and rated by other participants as an 'irrational' movement by the actor (even in the presence of an obstacle). It is not clear, however, whether this type of result reveals that participants are deciding to imitate the actor's irrational movements (e.g. due to perceived social desirability effects) or whether instead participants automatically imitate the actor's movements as a result of a more general process such as associative learning of the links between observed and performed actions, or spatial compatibility.

The rich data sets generated by motion tracking do have some drawbacks. In particular, they can lead to difficulties when generating a priori hypotheses regarding how an actor's movement may impact that of an observer. As there are so many potential parameters to compare, a potential multiple comparison problem arises, along with the possibility that 'fishing' in a large pool of possible parameters may lead the researcher to come up with hypotheses after the results are known (Krishnan-Barman et al., 2017; Kerr, 1998). Pre-registration of planned analyses and distinguishing these from exploratory analyses will be a helpful step in this regard.

Stimulus-Response Compatibility Measures of Movement Imitation

Stimulus-response compatibility tasks have been widely used to index both automatic imitation and the control processes required to suppress imitative tendencies. Such types of tasks are conducted mostly in laboratory settings (see Westfal et al., in preparation, for a recently validated online version of the task) and typically involve the measurement of response times (RTs) and error rates and, in some studies, kinematics (e.g. Kilner et al., 2003), during the performance of an instructed response while observing similar or dissimilar task-irrelevant movements (see Cracco et al., 2018, for a recent meta-analysis). Response times in these types of tasks can be recorded using various techniques including electromyography (e.g. Leighton et al., 2010), light sensors (e.g. Genschow et al., 2019), response boxes (e.g. Ainley et al., 2014), and keyboards (e.g. Sowden & Catmur, 2015). The current section will focus on stimulus-response compatibility tasks measuring RTs and error rates (see section "Kinematic Measures of Movement Imitation" for the measurement of kinematics in imitation). Stimulus-response compatibility tasks of imitation often involve action observation and execution of isolated and goalless movements such as finger lifts, finger abduction, and foot raises (but see Catmur & Heyes, 2019, for an example of automatic imitation of goal-directed actions). These tasks typically involve at least two conditions (see Fig. 2.4): (i.) compatible—when

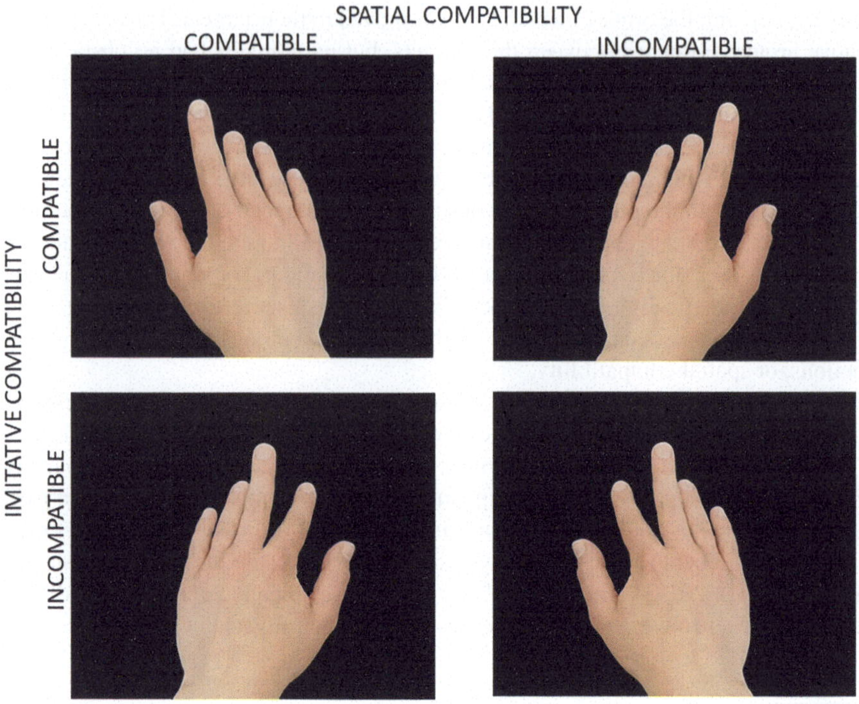

Fig. 2.4 Example of stimulus-response compatibility task stimuli involving hand movements. The 2 (imitative compatibility) × 2 (spatial compatibility) task design is illustrated for a trial when a right-hand index finger lift is the instructed response. When a right-hand middle finger lift is the instructed response, the levels of spatial and imitative compatibility are each reversed. (Adapted from Khemka et al., 2021)

the observed action is similar to the instructed response (e.g. see index finger, raise index finger, or see middle finger, raise middle finger); and (ii.) incompatible—when the observed action is dissimilar to the instructed response (e.g. see index finger, raise middle finger, or see middle finger, raise index finger). A decrease in response times and error rates during compatible trials provides an index of the tendency to automatically imitate observed movements. However, response times and error rates during incompatible trials are a more complex measure because they index not only the extent to which the observed action interferes with the instructed response but also the processes involved in controlling or overcoming this interference. As such, stimulus-response compatibility tasks have been used to measure both automatic imitation and imitation-inhibition, but as we discuss below, it is important to consider which aspects of these processes are being measured when interpreting the results of such studies.

Stimulus-Response Compatibility Measures of Automatic Imitation

The stimulus-response compatibility paradigm first used by Brass et al. (2000) has been widely used as a behavioural index of automatic imitation. In a forced choice response paradigm, participants were displayed an on-screen left-hand performing either an index or a middle finger lifting movement. Concurrently, a task-relevant symbolic cue (a number '1' or '2') was presented in between the index and middle fingers of the stimulus hand. Participants were instructed to lift either their own index or middle finger of their right hand in response to the symbolic cue, where the number '1' instructed participants to lift the index finger and the number '2' instructed them to lift the middle finger, thus making the on-screen finger lifts irrelevant to task performance. Contrasting conditions of compatibility between the observed action and the instructed response during each trial create compatible and incompatible conditions. A third trial type where the hand performed no movement was also included as a baseline. The results indicated that compared to baseline trials where the hand did not move, responses were faster and more accurate during compatible trials and slower and more inaccurate during incompatible trials. Similar effects have been found when using simple response tasks in which the response participants make is blocked (e.g. make hand opening movement throughout a block of trials) and the imperative stimulus, indicating when the participant should make their response, is an action that is either compatible or incompatible with the instructed response (Stürmer et al., 2000; Heyes et al., 2005). Studies utilising stimulus-response compatibility paradigms, whether choice or simple response tasks, have demonstrated that RTs are more sensitive to modulation compared to error rates since these paradigms typically report very low error rates (often as low as <5% of all trials; e.g. Brass et al., 2000; Stürmer et al., 2000).

The observation of an action likely activates the observer's own motor representation of that action, thereby facilitating compatible and interfering with incompatible trials (Brass et al., 2000; di Pellegrino et al., 1992). For example, the observation of a finger movement activates the motor representation of that specific movement in the observer. Participants demonstrate a tendency to copy movements regardless of whether the observed movements facilitate or interfere with response selection, which suggests that the imitation of movements in this task is, to a large extent, automatic. In compatible trials where the observed action and the instructed response lead to the activation of the same muscles, the observation of the same action as the instructed response facilitates action execution and speeds responses, which is taken as an index of automatic imitation of the observed action. The difference in RTs or error rates between compatible trials and baseline trials provides a measure of this facilitatory effect. However, although comparisons between compatible and baseline trials are useful to provide a specific measure of the facilitation of movement imitation, the setup of the baseline condition is a crucial consideration in stimulus-response compatibility tasks. Initial studies using these tasks used static images of limbs devoid of transient events as a baseline condition, as opposed to compatible and incompatible conditions, which involve transient changes in the stimuli. Wiggett et al. (2013) argued that it is important to control for the temporal alerting effects that are present in trials where a specific body part moves, which was lacking in previous versions of the task. In their study, Wiggett et al. used a baseline condition that involved body parts transiently reducing in size, eliciting similar temporal alerting effects as produced in the standard conditions, whilst allowing the measurement of RTs unadulterated by task-irrelevant actions. Another version of the baseline trial type, which also accounted for temporal alerting effects, was used by Sowden and Catmur (2015) where the presentation of a resting hand image was followed by the pixelation of the hand image. It is difficult, however, to design a 'true' baseline condition, since the magnitude of the alerting effect in the baseline condition will change as a function of the magnitude of visual change. As such, it is important to take into account the nature of the baseline or comparison condition that is used when one is considering stimulus-response compatibility studies of automatic imitation.

Stimulus-response compatibility tasks have been used in the literature to demonstrate the tendency of humans to spontaneously imitate (Brass et al., 2000, 2001; Stürmer et al., 2000), based on the premise that the compatibility effect (measured either as the difference between baseline and compatible trials, or between incompatible and compatible trials) is a reliable measure of imitation-specific processes (e.g. Genschow et al., 2017). However, this paradigm has been met with criticism in the past due to concerns that the compatibility effect is confounded by spatial compatibility (Aicken et al., 2007; Bertenthal et al., 2006; Catmur & Heyes, 2011; Jansson et al., 2007). Classic cognitive studies have shown that participants respond faster to visual stimuli when they are presented on the same side of space as the response effector (e.g. the participant's hand; Anzola et al., 1977; Simon, 1990). Thus, in choice RT tasks involving lateralised visual stimuli (e.g. the relative position of index and middle fingers of the on-screen hand) and lateralised responses (e.g. the fingers of the participant's hand), ipsilateral responses yield faster reaction times compared to contralateral responses. In the case of the imitation-inhibition paradigm developed by Brass et al. (2000, 2001), participants observed a left stimulus hand mirroring their right response hand. As a result, trials involving index finger lifts are not just imitatively compatible (e.g. see index finger lift, raise index finger), but are also spatially compatible (e.g. see left finger lift, raise left finger). Subsequent research demonstrated the independence of spatial compatibility and imitative compatibility effects and confirmed that the general compatibility effect previously used to index automatic imitation was confounded by spatial compatibility effects (Catmur & Heyes, 2011).

In their study, Catmur and Heyes (2011) modified the classic stimulus-response compatibility task to allow the measurement of each level of imitative compatibility (compatible, incompatible) at each level of spatial compatibility (compatible, incompatible). Participants performed index or little finger abduction movements with their right hand in response to a discriminative stimulus (i.e. colour of a circle), while concurrently observing a task-irrelevant right or left on-screen hand also performing index or little finger abduction movements. This task allowed the measurement of imitative compatibility since both the task-irrelevant stimuli and participants' responses involved configural body movements. Additionally, the inclusion of both left- and right-hand stimuli, presented in a first-person perspective, also allowed the measurement of spatial compatibility since both the task-irrelevant stimuli and participants' responses were oriented within the same (left-right) spatial dimension. In the case of the right-hand stimuli, the observed index finger movement was on the left side of space and the observed little finger movement was on the right side of space; in the case of the left-hand stimuli, the observed index finger movement was on the right side of space and the observed little finger movement was on the left side of space. Therefore, the use of both right- and left-hand stimuli while participants responded with their right hand allowed the manipulation of the spatial location of the stimulus independent of its finger identity (see Fig. 2.4). Catmur and Heyes demonstrated that both types of compatibility independently affected response times—participants were faster to respond when the moving stimulus was on the same side of space as their responding finger compared to when it was on the other side of space (spatial compatibility effect) and also when the moving stimulus comprised the same finger movement that they were making, compared to the other finger movement (imitative compatibility effect), but these two compatibility effects did not interact. They concluded that the 'general' compatibility effect measured in previous automatic imitation studies where spatial compatibility was not controlled for is a composite measure comprising both spatial and imitative compatibilities, illustrating the importance of measuring imitative compatibility independent of spatial compatibility. Further studies have demonstrated that these two effects may have distinct neural underpinnings (e.g., Marsh et al., 2016), making this an essential point to consider when designing or evaluating studies of automatic imitation.

Other studies involving stimulus-response compatibility measures of imitation have controlled for spatial compatibility by positioning the stimulus hand orthogonal to the participant's hand (Cook & Bird, 2011; Cook & Bird, 2012; Heyes et al., 2005; Press et al., 2005). This preserves imitative compatibility but controls for spatial compatibility since the stimulus hand is no longer positioned to mirror the participant's hand but instead points sideways instead of downward. However, a disadvantage of controlling for spatial compatibility by positioning the stimulus hand orthogonally is the reported tendency of participants to associate the 'lower' finger as the left finger and the 'upper' finger as the right finger, thereby only eliminating the influence of spatial compatibility if this orthogonal spatial compatibility effect is also controlled for (Weeks & Proctor, 1990).

Stimulus-response compatibility measures provide a robust measurement of automatic imitation and have been widely used to further our understanding of action imitation and the mechanisms that support this. Crucial considerations have been brought to light over the recent years concerning the influence of spatial compatibility effects in stimulus-response compatibility tasks of imitation and the importance of an appropriate baseline condition that has similar transient properties as the main trials to allow the measurement of purely facilitatory processes elicited by action observation. Further concerns regarding the relationship between stimulus-response compatibility measures of automatic imitation, and the 'real world' measures of mimicry described in Section "Measuring Mimicry", also remain to be addressed (e.g. Ramsey, 2018; but see also Cracco & Brass, 2019).

Stimulus-Response Compatibility Measures of Imitation-Inhibition

Stimulus-response compatibility tasks are complex in nature as they allow not just the measurement of response facilitation elicited by action observation, but also the processes required to control automatic imitation of the observed action. On trials where the observed action and the instructed cue activate competing motor representations (i.e. during incompatible trials where the observed action and the instructed response lead to the activation of opposing motor representations), the observer is required to inhibit the motor representation of the other person's action. The inhibition or regulation of the other's motor representation is cognitively demanding and, as such, takes time. Therefore, the response times and error rates on incompatible trials compared to compatible or baseline trials are higher. The difference in response times or error rates between incompatible and baseline trials allows a comparison between conditions where interference arising due to incompatible movements must be resolved and conditions where there is no action observation, thus indexing both inhibition and imitation.

In a range of studies, therefore, this type of stimulus-response compatibility task has been labelled an 'imitation-inhibition' task, and the response time or error rate difference between incompatible and either baseline or, more commonly, compatible trials has been considered to index the ability to inhibit imitation (Brass et al., 2001; Santiesteban et al., 2012). A larger response time difference (i.e. a larger imitative compatibility effect) reflects a greater tendency to imitate and, by extension, reflects weaker inhibition of such imitative tendencies. A smaller imitative compatibility effect is therefore thought to reflect the ability to successfully inhibit the motor representation evoked by the other's action and, instead, enhance one's own motor representation (Brass et al., 2001).

Previous studies have used the imitative compatibility effect (incompatible—compatible trial difference) as an index of imitation-inhibition or, in other words, the outcome of processes involved in controlling automatic imitative tendencies. However, as previously discussed, response time differences between imitatively incompatible and compatible trials index both response facilitation and inhibition. This raises an important question about which dimensions of this task measure automatic imitation and which of these measure imitation-inhibition. Furthermore, a small imitative compatibility effect could result from at least two sources: (a) a lack of automatic imitation of others' actions; or (b) intact automatic imitation alongside successful inhibition of imitation. Current studies rarely distinguish these two possibilities. One way to address this issue would be to consider the response time difference between baseline and compatible trials as a measure of pure facilitation and the response time difference between baseline and incompatible trials as a measure of inhibition and imitation. However, it is then crucial to incorporate appropriate baseline conditions that can help measure these separate processes that constitute imitation and the inhibition of imitation.

Overall, the literature often lacks clarity regarding the different processes measured by stimulus-response compatibility tasks (e.g. processes involved in imitation versus those involved in spatially compatible responding) and often fails to distinguish between the facilitative and inhibitory processes that contribute to the key effects measured using these tasks. The lack of consistent terminology for key effects (e.g. 'automatic imitation effect' and 'imitation-inhibition effect' are both described as the response time difference between incompatible and compatible trials; Heyes, 2011) has contributed to low specificity in describing the different effects emerging from the task. Future studies should aim to use appropriate baseline conditions together with consistent terminology that specifies the effect emerging from the task (e.g. 'imitative compatibility effect', 'spatial compatibility effect', or 'imitation-inhibition effect').

Measuring Mimicry

The final section of this chapter focuses on the measurement of mimicry, defined as a type of imitation that tends to occur in more naturalistic settings, often without awareness on the observer's part that they are imitating the actor (Chartrand & Bargh, 1999). Mimicry has previously been shown to play an important role in increasing affiliation and building interpersonal rapport (LaFrance & Broadbent, 1976; Chartrand & Bargh, 1999) and has thus been an important area of research into understanding social interactions in typical and atypical development. Research on mimicry has focused on two facets of mimicking behaviour: the mimicry of actions and the mimicry of action timing, also known as synchrony. Synchrony is generally considered as the tendency to perform repetitive actions (e.g. walking or rocking a chair) at the same rate as another person. Both motor mimicry and motor synchrony are important facets of interpersonal coordination and although synchronised actions are not necessarily imitative (i.e. synchrony may not involve the production of movements that are similar in form), it is often considered within the umbrella of the term 'imitation' in the literature (see Lakin, 2013 for review). This section will discuss the measures used in some of the most influential studies of automatic mimicry and synchronisation of actions.

Mimicking Actions

The empirical measurement of movement mimicry has previously been conducted during in-person dyadic interactions and during the observation of pre-recorded videos. For example, Chartrand and Bargh (1999, Experiment 1) recorded in-person interactions between participants and confederates, where the extent to which participants copied the confederate's movements was measured. Participants performed an unrelated 'photograph description' task together with two confederates, during two separate interactions. Each confederate was instructed to perform certain movements (e.g. either 'face-touching' or 'leg-shaking') during their interactions with the participant. Video recordings of these interactions were then coded to determine the frequency with which the participant performed the confederate's target movement, and the alternative movement, during each interaction. The frequency with which participants performed the confederate's movement during each interaction was compared to that at which the participant performed the alternative movement (i.e. that of the other confederate). An interaction effect, such that participants performed more face-touching movements while observing face-touching, and more leg-shaking movements while observing leg-shaking, demonstrates a tendency to mimic the observed actions, as was found in the study conducted by Chartrand and Bargh (1999). It should be noted that such mimicry tasks need to be structured in this way, with two different target movements, in order that similarity between the action performed by the confederate and that performed by the participant can be established. In contrast, tasks that measure mimicry of only one action could find what looks like mimicry (an increase in performance of a particular action when observing that action), but this could in principle result from a general increase in motor activity rather than from a specific activation of the motor representation of the target movement.

Although the naturalistic nature of this task provides high ecological validity and enables the study of mimicry during social interactions, it also leads to low experimental control, due to inevitable differences between conditions and across participants in terms of the precise movements performed by the confederates. Subsequent studies have therefore used a video-based variation of this mimicry paradigm to study important questions about top-down influences on movement mimicry including whether such mimicry can be modulated by group membership (Yabar et al., 2006), perceived similarity (Guéguen & Martin, 2009), and affiliative goals (Lakin & Chartrand, 2003). The video-based mimicry task typically involves participants observing video clips of a confederate performing an unrelated task such as reading a story or describing photographs, during which the confederate performs specific movements during regular intervals. The frequency with which participants perform similar movements is calculated by independent video coders to provide a measurement of movement mimicry. These studies using the video-based mimicry task did not use a two-action design as described by Chartrand and Bargh (1999), which makes it possible that the observed effects may reflect a general increase in motor activity, rather than mimicry. However, Genschow et al. (2017) utilised a video-based mimicry task involving the observation of two videos depicting two types of actions and demonstrated a mimicry effect, similar to the one found by Chartrand and Bargh.

Social psychologists have been able to answer a variety of questions about how individuals copy other people's movements during social interactions using the mimicry task paradigm. However, there are important methodological considerations associated with the measurement of movement mimicry. The foremost methodological concern is the manner in which mimicked actions are indexed. Video recordings of interactions between participants and confederates are subjectively rated post hoc, which can introduce measurement bias since the coders may be aware of the task condition (i.e. which movement is being manipulated in that condition) or may miss subtle movements, since unlike in automatic imitation tasks, there is no objective measurement of when a movement is executed, or of which movement is performed. Nevertheless, it is important to note that typically the video recording in mimicry tasks only shows the participant's and not the confederate's actions, which should remove one potential source of bias. Researchers have also aimed to reduce biases in the task by involving two independent coders and reporting the inter-rater reliability of coded actions, which is generally high. More generally, studies of mimicry tend to code actions at the level of the effector rather than the movement (e.g. coding any movement of the leg as a target 'leg-shaking' movement), meaning that such studies may be measuring effector matching rather than imitation of the other's configural body movements. Future advances in automated coding of video should allow closer investigation of the fidelity or precision of the imitation that occurs during naturalistic mimicry of others' actions.

Another concern relates to the reliability of this measure. Genschow et al. (2017) measured the internal consistency of mimicry performance in their study by calculating separate mimicry scores for even and odd minutes of the task. These scores showed a negative correlation, indicating low reliability. The low reliability of the mimicry task is difficult to address, however, due to the naturalistic nature of the task. Unlike measures of automatic imitation, the mimicry task does not involve a trial-by-trial measurement of mimicry, which makes it difficult to compare the characteristics of movements made during the experimental period. The lack of a trial-by-trial measurement of mimicry also limits the extent to which we can determine how each individual target movement influences the motor system of the observer. Since the frequency of movements is calculated across the entire task duration, rather than after each observed movement, it is possible that participants do not execute any movements for a vast majority of the task and may then execute multiple movements during a short span of time, which would increase the frequency of executed movements. However, this increase may be in response to a single observed movement, and that would not reflect a reliable mimicry effect. On a related note, the number of responses executed during mimicry tasks is typically very low (as low as five movements; Genschow et al., 2017), which raises concerns about the reliability of the effects interpreted based on a limited range of data, and also shows the infrequent nature of mimicry during naturalistic interactions. Furthermore, the complexity of the naturalistic interactions involved in the mimicry task may introduce additional variability from multiple sources. One such source is the irrelevant task that participants perform within this paradigm. Different studies involve participants describing various types of photographs, which introduces uncertainty regarding how the contents of the photographs may influence mimicry. For example, if certain stimuli evoke strong emotional responses, mimicry tendencies may be increased over and above action observation (Chartrand & Lakin, 2013). However, previous studies have tried to address these concerns by choosing neutral stimuli such as photographs of natural landscapes (Yabar et al., 2006). Additionally, characteristics of the confederate such as perceived similarity with the participant may also modulate the mimicry of actions. These considerations highlight the low suitability of the mimicry task for situations requiring multiple repeated trials for each experimental condition, such as when investigating the neurocognitive mechanisms underpinning the enhancement or control of perception-action links, but it is valuable in understanding the role of various social factors in modulating the tendency to mimic observed actions during more naturalistic social interactions.

Another naturalistic type of mimicry is contagious yawning, which refers to the onset of a yawn triggered by seeing, hearing, or even thinking about another person yawning (Platek et al., 2003, 2005; Provine, 1986; 1989). Although contagious yawning can be triggered even in the absence of perceptual inputs, the execution of a yawn in response to observing another person's yawn is often considered as a form of imitation. The way contagious yawning is measured in experimental settings is analogous to the way movement mimicry is measured. In one study, participants observed seven-second video recordings of a model in either a yawning, laughing, or neutral condition (Platek et al., 2003, Experiment 1). The inclusion of a laughing condition acts as a control to ensure that the yawning behaviour is not triggered by the observation of mouth-opening behaviour, whereas the inclusion of a neutral condition provides a baseline condition where no elicited yawns should be expected. The experimenter coded participants' behaviour (yawn, laugh, other, or no behaviour) and found that the incidence rate of evoked yawning (i.e. number of participants who yawned at least once) after watching yawning videos was 41.5%, while that after non-yawning videos was 9%. Furthermore, 60% of individuals who yawned at least once engaged in yawning more than once. The inclusion of a control condition is essential to determine the specificity of yawning behaviour, and not all studies include such control conditions (e.g. Helt et al., 2010). Previously discussed limitations of the measurement of movement mimicry such as low number of trials, lack of a trial-by-trial structure, and subjective measurement are also relevant to the measurement of contagious yawning. Nonetheless, previous research on contagious yawning has revealed several associations between contagious yawning and social cognitive performance. Platek et al. (2003) found that individuals who engaged in contagious yawning were quicker in identifying their own faces and better at inferring mental states, compared to those who did not engage in contagious yawning. It has also been hypothesised that contagious yawning may reflect a basic capacity for empathic processes such as emotion contagion (Palagi et al., 2020; Platek et al.,

2003, 2005). However, the evidence supporting a link between contagious yawning and empathy is inconclusive (Massen & Gallup, 2017; Gallup, 2021).

Mimicking Action Timing (Synchrony)

Synchrony has been defined as when individuals coordinate their movements (which may or may not be similar in form) to coincide with those of others in terms of timing or rhythm (Lakin, 2013). Although research on the synchronisation of actions is not as prevalent as research on the mimicry of actions, the measurement of synchronised actions has evolved from initial measures that relied on subjective ratings during the observation of interactions (e.g. Zivotofsky & Hausdorff, 2007) to more sophisticated methods such as motion capture systems, which can index the temporal organisation of movements and the dynamic characteristics of movement patterns. The current section focuses on the latter group of methods for measuring movement synchrony. There are two modes of movement coordination that are relevant to research on synchrony: in-phase and anti-phase. In-phase coordination refers to movements that are similar in both timing and form (e.g. two people walking together at the same rate of movement while performing the same right-left foot movement). Anti-phase coordination, on the other hand, refers to movements that are similar in timing but not in form (e.g. two people walking together at the same movement rate but one person performing a right-left foot movement while the other person performing a left-right foot movement or vice versa). Both in-phase coordination and anti-phase coordination reflect stable forms of synchrony.

The measurement of synchrony of actions typically involves two individuals performing a repetitive movement (e.g. walking on a treadmill, stepping on a standard exercise step, or tapping their fingers) while wearing a motion tracking system (see section "Kinematic Measures of Movement Imitation" for an overview of the different types of motion tracking systems). The key measure of interest in these tasks is the relative phase relationship between the movements of both individuals calculated separately to compare oscillatory end effectors (e.g. left-left and right-right leg movements). Relative phases are standardised to a range of 0–180°, reflecting in-phase and anti-phase coordination, respectively. For each participant, estimates of the time spent on each relative phase region (ranging in fixed intervals between 0° and 180°) are calculated when the participant and the other individual perform the key movement together. Synchrony between movements is indicated by a concentration of relative phase angles in the phase regions close to 0° and/or 180°. Another measure that enables the quantitative measurement of automatic synchronisation of actions is the power spectrum overlap between movements, which measures the percentage of movement frequencies common to interacting pairs.

The synchronisation of actions has previously been investigated with different types of movements. For example, in Miles et al. (2010), participants completed a task involving stepping on a standard exercise step where the movements of the participant and the confederate were measured using electromagnetic motion sensors attached to each leg above the knee. The exercise steps were aligned adjacent to each other with the confederate's exercise step positioned in front of the participant to provide participants a clear view of the confederate. Both individuals wore headphones where white noise was played for the participant and metronome tones were played for the confederate, which was used to time the steps. Movements were recorded during both a baseline stage (when only the participant was moving; used to account for chance coordination) and a test stage when both the participant and confederate were moving. Participants' movements were concentrated in the 0–20° range more during the test than during the baseline stage, suggesting that synchrony between the movements of the participant and the confederate during the test stage is attributable to the individuals coordinating their steps with each other. In a different study, participants walked on a treadmill with infrared reflectors attached to record movements of the left and right lower legs (van Ulzen et al., 2008). Participants with varying default stride frequencies walked side by side on the treadmill uninstructed while fixating their gaze on a white square, which provided a view of the other participant's leg in the peripheral view. This study demonstrated that individuals tend to synchronise their movements while walking together despite no instructions.

An important consideration while discussing the measurement of synchrony is the extent to which the interindividual coupling of movement timing and rhythm can be considered as imitative in nature. According to the definition of imitation provided at the start of this chapter, the production of a matching movement, at least in naturalistic settings, first requires the observation of another person's movement, which precludes executed movements to be synchronous with observed movements. However, there is evidence to suggest that imitative processes, in some cases, may be initiated even before the observation of the target movement (see also Chap. 8; this volume). This evidence comes from research on the anticipatory nature of imitation, which suggests that the matching of observed motor representations to one's own corresponding motor representation may be important to not just mirror observed movements but also anticipate the potential course of the other's action (Pfister et al., 2013). For example, Genschow and Brass (2015) demonstrated that observing an event in someone (e.g. nose wrinkling or hair falling on one's face) triggers the anticipated action in the observer (e.g. nose scratching or hair stroking). In this study, although participants did not observe the model perform the target movement (i.e. nose scratching or hair stroking), they were more likely to engage in nose scratching after observing nose wrinkling and hair stroking after observing hair falling. A subsequent TMS study revealed preliminary evidence showing that observing nose wrinkling leads to increased motor-evoked potentials in the biceps muscle, which suggests that anticipation of movements may elicit activity in the motor system in a similar manner as when perceived movements elicit neurophysiological activity in the corresponding muscle group (Genschow et al., 2018). Given that imitative processes may be initiated in anticipation of another person's movements, it is possible that imitation may be synchronous provided that the observer can anticipate the subsequent action. However, there is currently a gap in our understanding of the potential overlap between movement imitation and synchrony, from both behavioural and neuroscientific perspectives. Studies on automatic imitation and mimicry have predominantly focused on the copying of movements elicited by perceived movements and those investigating anticipatory imitation have not measured whether individuals tend to synchronise the target movements with those of the model. At the neural level, it is currently unclear whether automatic imitation and synchronisation of movements share overlapping mechanisms, which could provide insight into the relationship between imitation and synchrony. Nevertheless, within the existing parameters of what constitutes imitation and synchrony, it is unlikely that the execution of spontaneous movements elicited by observed movements can be synchronous. However, investigating whether individuals tend to synchronise the anticipated movements of the model would be interesting to uncover a potential overlap between imitation and synchrony.

Finally, although studies of synchrony tend to measure phase relationships between similar actions (e.g. similar leg movements in the case of walking speed), it may be that the similarity between the individuals' actions is less important than the synchrony (and thus that similar results would be obtained for the synchronisation of non-matching actions such as leg movements with arm movements; see Catmur & Heyes, 2013 for a related finding). As such, more research is needed to uncover the extent to which synchrony and mimicry share overlapping neurocognitive mechanisms.

Summary

This chapter has reviewed a range of different methods for measuring movement imitation. Researchers will wish to consider which methodology is most appropriate for their research question, depending on the requirements of their particular study (see Table 2.1 for a summary). Such considerations may relate to practicalities associated with data collection: whereas some methods (e.g. TMS) cannot be used outside of the research laboratory, other measures have been or are being adapted for use in online testing platforms (e.g. stimulus-response compatibility measures) and in more naturalistic settings (e.g. kinematic measures with subsequent video analysis). Other considerations relate to the type of stimuli for which one wishes to measure imitative responses: certain measures lend themselves to study designs involving more naturalistic interaction, whereas others require multiple trials for each experimental condition and, as such, trade-off ecological validity against experimental control. Finally, when designing studies of imitation or when reading and assessing such studies, it is essential to consider appropriate control conditions and the use of muscle-specific designs which allow one to draw conclusions regarding the specificity of the responses that are being recorded.

Table 2.1 Considerations regarding the use of the different imitation measures

Measure	Muscle–/action-specific?	Strengths	Weaknesses	When to use it	Other considerations
Electromyographic (EMG) measures of muscle activity	Yes, as long as at least two muscles are recorded from	Response can be averaged over time, allowing measurement during observation of ongoing movements; Can be used during observation of either live movements or recorded movements (e.g. video)	Can only be used in certain muscles (e.g. face and neck) where activity can be detected even at rest; Difficult to use outside of laboratory settings; Signal-to-noise ratio can be quite low	To measure activity in face and neck muscles during observation of ongoing movements involving those muscles	Important to control for individual differences in EMG signal magnitude
TMS-evoked measures of motor responses	Yes, as long as at least two muscles are recorded from; evoking *simultaneous* responses in two muscles is only possible if the motor cortical representations are very close (e.g. two hand muscles)	Pulses can be delivered at different times after the onset of observed actions to determine timecourse of motor responses; Can be used to measure responses to both single movements and ongoing actions, either live or recorded	Can only be used in laboratory settings which may lower ecological validity; Multiple trials of the same observed action are required for averaging	To measure motor activity in a wide range of muscles during observation of actions	Early responses (< c. 200 ms after observed action) are non-specific and likely reflect a general alerting mechanism; MEP amplitudes reduce when TMS pulses are predictable; Contra-indications to the use of TMS in certain populations
Kinematic measures	Can be, but studies are not always designed to look at action specificity	Suitable for both laboratory-based and more naturalistic studies; Generates rich datasets with large numbers of potential parameters	Video coding/motion analysis can be time-consuming; Rich datasets may lead to multiple comparison problems	To measure actions during naturalistic social interaction, in the laboratory and (via video coding) elsewhere	Pre-registration of planned analyses may help aid replicability of findings

Measure	Muscle–/action-specific?	Strengths	Weaknesses	When to use it	Other considerations
Stimulus-response compatibility (SRC) measures	Yes—In most cases, the task involves observing two types of movements and responding with corresponding actions/ muscles	High experimental control; Trial-by-trial design enabling the measurement of action execution elicited by specific movements	Generally, can only be used to measure responses to single movements, leading to low ecological validity; Multiple trials per condition required for averaging; Difficult to disentangle processes involved in imitation and imitation-inhibition	In controlled laboratory or online settings to investigate (neuro)-cognitive mechanisms underpinning automatic imitation and imitation-inhibition; Experimental studies to understand conditions under which perception-action links may be modulated	Appropriate baseline conditions are important to distinguish between facilitatory and inhibitory processes
Movement mimicry measures	Not usually—Mimicry tasks encode the copying of non-specific movements using similar body parts which may not be action–/ muscle-specific	High ecological validity; Allows measurement of imitation during in-person dyadic interactions that are more similar to real-life interactions compared to SRC tasks	Low experimental control; Imprecise measurement of mimicked actions; Poor (psychometric) reliability	To study conditions under which perception-action links are modulated using in-person dyadic interactions	Video versions of mimicry tasks provide increased experimental control but do not resolve the issues related to the imprecise measurement of mimicked responses
Action synchrony measures	Not usually—synchrony tasks rarely ask participants to perform more than one type of movement (e.g. walking)	Measured during in-person dyadic interactions; Motion trackers enable the measurement of the precise strength of synchronisation	Not necessarily imitative, limiting the extent to which findings involving such measures can be generalised to imitative behaviour	To measure movement coordination between individuals, in the laboratory and (via video coding) elsewhere	Unclear to what extent synchrony involves the same neurocognitive mechanisms as those involved in imitation

References

Aicken, M. D., Wilson, A. D., Williams, J. H. G., & Mon-Williams, M. (2007). Methodological issues in measures of imitative reaction times. *Brain and Cognition, 63*, 304–308. https://doi.org/10.1016/j.bandc.2006.09.005

Ainley, V., Brass, M., & Tsakiris, M. (2014). Heartfelt imitation: High interoceptive awareness is linked to greater automatic imitation. *Neuropsychologia, 60*, 21–28. https://doi.org/10.1016/j.neuropsychologia.2014.05.010

Anzola, G. P., Bertoloni, G., Buchtel, H. A., & Rizzolatti, G. (1977). Spatial compatibility and anatomical factors in simple and choice reaction time. *Neuropsychologia, 15*, 295–302. https://doi.org/10.1016/0028-3932(77)90038-0

Bertenthal, B. I., Longo, M. R., & Kosobud, A. (2006). Imitative response tendencies following observation of intransitive actions. *Journal of Experimental Psychology: Human Perception and Performance, 32*, 210–225. https://doi.org/10.1037/0096-1523.32.2.210

Brass, M., Bekkering, H., Wohlschläger, A., & Prinz, W. (2000). Compatibility between observed and executed finger movements: Comparing symbolic, spatial, and imitative cues. *Brain and Cognition, 44*, 124–143. https://doi.org/10.1006/brcg.2000.1225

Brass, M., Zysset, S., & von Cramon, D. Y. (2001). The inhibition of imitative response tendencies. *NeuroImage, 14*, 1416–1423. https://doi.org/10.1016/j.neuropsychologia.2004.06.018

Catmur, C., & Heyes, C. (2011). Time course analyses confirm independence of imitative and spatial compatibility. *Journal of Experimental Psychology: Human Perception and Performance, 37*, 409–421. https://doi.org/10.1037/a0019325

Catmur, C., & Heyes, C. (2013). Is it what you do, or when you do it? The roles of contingency and similarity in pro-social effects of imitation. *Cognitive Science, 37*, 1541–1552. https://doi.org/10.1111/cogs.12071

Catmur, C., & Heyes, C. (2019). Mirroring 'meaningful' actions: Sensorimotor learning modulates imitation of goal-directed actions. *Quarterly Journal of Experimental Psychology, 72*, 322–334. https://doi.org/10.1080/17470218.2017.1344257

Catmur, C., Walsh, V., & Heyes, C. (2007). Sensorimotor learning configures the human mirror system. *Current Biology, 17*, 1527–1531. https://doi.org/10.1016/j.cub.2007.08.006

Cattaneo, L., Fabbri-Destro, M., Boria, S., Pieraccini, C., Monti, A., Cossu, G., & Rizzolatti, G. (2007). Impairment of actions chains in autism and its possible role in intention understanding. *Proceedings of the National Academy of Sciences of the United States of America, 104*, 17825–17830. https://doi.org/10.1073/pnas.0706273104

Cavallo, A., Heyes, C., Becchio, C., Bird, G., & Catmur, C. (2014). Timecourse of mirror and counter-mirror effects measured with transcranial magnetic stimulation. *Social Cognitive and Affective Neuroscience, 9*, 1082–1088. https://doi.org/10.1093/scan/nst085

Chartrand, T. L., & Bargh, J. A. (1999). The chameleon effect: The perception–behavior link and social interaction. *Journal of Personality and Social Psychology, 76*, 893–910. https://doi.org/10.1037//0022-3514.76.6.893

Chartrand, T. L., & Bargh, J. A. (2002). Nonconscious motivations: Their activation, operation, and consequences. In A. Tesser, D. A. Stapel, & J. V. Wood (Eds.), *Self and motivation: Emerging psychological perspectives* (pp. 13–41). American Psychological Association. https://doi.org/10.1037/10448-001

Chartrand, T. L., & Lakin, J. L. (2013). The antecedents and consequences of human behavioral mimicry. *Annual Review of Psychology, 64*, 285–308. https://doi.org/10.1146/annurev-psych-113011-143754

Chen, R., Cros, D., Curra, A., Di Lazzaro, V., Lefaucheur, J. P., Magistris, M. R., Mills, K., Rösler, K. M., Triggs, W. J., Ugawa, Y., & Ziemann, U. (2008). The clinical diagnostic utility of transcranial magnetic stimulation: Report of an IFCN committee. *Clinical Neurophysiology: Official Journal of the International Federation of Clinical Neurophysiology, 119*, 504–532. https://doi.org/10.1016/j.clinph.2007.10.014

Cook, J., & Bird, G. (2011). Social attitudes differentially modulate imitation in adolescents and adults. *Experimental Brain Research, 211*, 601–612. https://doi.org/10.1007/s00221-011-2584-4

Cook, J. L., & Bird, G. (2012). Atypical social modulation of imitation in autism Spectrum conditions. *Journal of Autism and Developmental Disorders, 42*, 1045–1051. https://doi.org/10.1007/s10803-011-1341-7

Cook, J. L., Blakemore, S. J., & Press, C. (2013). Atypical basic movement kinematics in autism spectrum conditions. *Brain, 136*, 2816–2824. https://doi.org/10.1093/brain/awt208

Cook, J., Swapp, D., Pan, X., Bianchi-Berthouze, N., & Blakemore, S. J. (2014). Atypical interference effect of action observation in autism spectrum conditions. *Psychological Medicine, 44*, 731–740. https://doi.org/10.1017%2FS0033291713001335

Cracco, E., & Brass, M. (2019). Reaction time indices of automatic imitation measure imitative response tendencies. *Consciousness and Cognition, 68*, 115–118. https://doi.org/10.1016/j.concog.2019.01.001

Cracco, E., Bardi, L., Desmet, C., Genschow, O., Rigoni, D., De Coster, L., Radkova, I., Deschrijver, E., & Brass, M. (2018). Automatic imitation: A meta-analysis. *Psychological Bulletin, 144*, 453–500. https://doi.org/10.1037/bul0000143

di Pellegrino, G., Fadiga, L., Fogassi, L., Gallese, V., & Rizzolatti, G. (1992). Understanding motor events: A neurophysiological study. *Experimental Brain Research, 91*, 176–180. https://doi.org/10.1007/BF00230027

Dimberg, U. (1982). Facial reactions to facial expressions. *Psychophysiology, 19*, 643–647. https://doi.org/10.1111/j.1469-8986.1982.tb02516.x

Fadiga, L., Fogassi, L., Pavesi, G., & Rizzolatti, G. (1995). Motor facilitation during action observation: A magnetic stimulation study. *Journal of Neurophysiology, 73*, 2608–2611. https://doi.org/10.1152/jn.1995.73.6.2608

Forbes, P., & Hamilton, A. (2017). Moving higher and higher: Imitators' movements are sensitive to observed trajectories regardless of action rationality. *Experimental Brain Research, 235*, 2741–2753. https://doi.org/10.1007/s00221-017-5006-4

Gallup, A. C. (2021). On the link between emotional contagion and contagious yawning. *Neuroscience & Biobehavioral Reviews, 121*, 18–19. https://doi.org/10.1016/j.neubiorev.2020.11.023

Genschow, O., & Brass, M. (2015). The predictive chameleon: Evidence for anticipated social action. *Journal of Experimental Psychology: Human Perception and Performance, 41*, 265–268. https://doi.org/10.1037/xhp0000035

Genschow, O., van Den Bossche, S., Cracco, E., Bardi, L., Rigoni, D., et al. (2017). Mimicry and automatic imitation are not correlated. *PLoS One, 12*, e0183784. https://doi.org/10.1371/journal.pone.0183784

Genschow, O., Bardi, L., & Brass, M. (2018). Anticipating actions and corticospinal excitability: A preregistered motor TMS experiment. *Cortex, 106*, 81–92. https://doi.org/10.1016/j.cortex.2018.04.014

Genschow, O., Schuler, J., Cracco, E., Brass, M., & Wänke, M. (2019). The effect of money priming on self-focus in the imitation-inhibition task. *Experimental Psychology, 66*, 423–436. https://doi.org/10.1027/1618-3169/a000466

Guéguen, N., & Martin, A. (2009). Incidental similarity facilitates behavioral mimicry. *Social Psychology, 40*, 88–92. https://doi.org/10.1027/1864-9335.40.2.88

Halaki, M., & Ginn, K. (2012). Normalization of EMG signals: To normalize or not to normalize and what to normalize to? In G. R. Naik (Ed.), *Computational intelligence in electromyography analysis – A perspective on current applications and future challenges*. https://doi.org/10.5772/49957

Helt, M. S., Eigsti, I. M., Snyder, P. J., & Fein, D. A. (2010). Contagious yawning in autistic and typical development. *Child Development, 81*, 1620–1631. https://doi.org/10.1111/j.1467-8624.2010.01495.x

Heyes, C. (2011). Automatic imitation. *Psychological Bulletin, 137*, 463–483. https://doi.org/10.1037/a0022288

Heyes, C. (2021). Imitation. *Current Biology, 31*, R228–R232. https://doi.org/10.1016/j.cub.2020.11.071
Heyes, C., Bird, G., Johnson, H., & Haggard, P. (2005). Experience modulates automatic imitation. *Cognitive Brain Research, 22*, 233–240. https://doi.org/10.1016/j.cogbrainres.2004.09.009
Hofree, G., Ruvolo, P., Bartlett, M. S., & Winkielman, P. (2014). Bridging the mechanical and the human mind: Spontaneous mimicry of a physically present android. *PLoS One, 9*, e99934. https://doi.org/10.1371/journal.pone.0099934
Jansson, E., Wilson, A. D., Williams, J. H. G., & Mon-Williams, M. (2007). Methodological problems undermine tests of the ideo-motor conjecture. *Experimental Brain Research, 182*, 549–558. https://doi.org/10.1007/s00221-007-1013-1
Kaiser, J., Crespo-Llado, M. M., Turati, C., & Geangu, E. (2017). The development of spontaneous facial responses to others' emotions in infancy: An EMG study. *Scientific Reports, 7*, 17500. https://doi.org/10.1038/s41598-017-17556-y
Kerr, N. L. (1998). HARKing: Hypothesizing after the results are known. *Personality and Social Psychology Review: An Official Journal of the Society for Personality and Social Psychology, Inc, 2*, 196–217. https://doi.org/10.1207/s15327957pspr0203_4
Keupp, S., Behne, T., & Rakoczy, H. (2018). The rationality of (over)imitation. *Perspectives on Psychological Science, 13*, 678–687. https://doi.org/10.1177/1745691618794921
Khemka, D., Ahmadilari, N., Bird, G., & Catmur, C. (2021). Imitation in one's own presence: No specific effect of self-focus on imitation. *Acta Psychologica, 212*, 103194. https://doi.org/10.1016/j.actpsy.2020.103194
Kilner, J. M., Paulignan, Y., & Blakemore, S. J. (2003). An interference effect of observed biological movement on action. *Current Biology, 13*, 522–525. https://doi.org/10.1016/s0960-9822(03)00165-9
Kilner, J., Hamilton, A. F. D. C., & Blakemore, S. J. (2007). Interference effect of observed human movement on action is due to velocity profile of biological motion. *Social Neuroscience, 2*, 158–166. https://doi.org/10.1080/17470910701428190
Krishnan-Barman, S., Forbes, P., & Hamilton, A. (2017). How can the study of action kinematics inform our understanding of human social interaction? *Neuropsychologia, 105*, 101–110. https://doi.org/10.1016/j.neuropsychologia.2017.01.018
Künecke, J., Mokros, A., Olderbak, S., & Wilhelm, O. (2018). Facial responsiveness of psychopaths to the emotional expressions of others. *PLoS One, 13*, e0190714. https://doi.org/10.1371/journal.pone.0190714
LaFrance, M., & Broadbent, M. (1976). Group rapport: Posture sharing as a nonverbal indicator. *Group & Organization Studies, 1*, 328–333. https://psycnet.apa.org/doi/10.1177/105960117600100307
Lakin, J. L. (2013). Behavioral mimicry and interpersonal synchrony. In J. A. Hall & M. L. Knapp (Eds.), *Nonverbal communication* (pp. 539–575). De Gruyter Mouton. https://doi.org/10.1515/9783110238150.539
Lakin, J. L., & Chartrand, T. L. (2003). Using nonconscious behavioral mimicry to create affiliation and rapport. *Psychological Science, 14*, 334–339. https://doi.org/10.1111/1467-9280.14481
Leighton, J., Bird, G., Orsini, C., & Heyes, C. (2010). Social attitudes modulate automatic imitation. *Journal of Experimental Social Psychology, 46*, 905–910. https://psycnet.apa.org/doi/10.1016/j.jesp.2010.07.001
Marsh, L. E., Bird, G., & Catmur, C. (2016). The imitation game: Effects of social cues on 'imitation' are domain-general in nature. *NeuroImage, 139*, 368–375. https://doi.org/10.1016/j.neuroimage.2016.06.050
Marsh, L. E., Ropar, D., & Hamilton, A. (2019). Are you watching me? The role of audience and object novelty in overimitation. *Journal of Experimental Child Psychology, 180*, 123–130. https://doi.org/10.1016/j.jecp.2018.12.010
Maslovat, D., Chua, R., & Hodges, N. J. (2013). When unintended movements "leak" out: A startling acoustic stimulus can elicit a prepared response during motor imagery and action observation. *Neuropsychologia, 51*, 838–844. https://doi.org/10.1016/j.neuropsychologia.2013.01.016

Massen, J. J., & Gallup, A. C. (2017). Why contagious yawning does not (yet) equate to empathy. *Neuroscience & Biobehavioral Reviews, 80*, 573–585. https://doi.org/10.1016/j.neubiorev.2017.07.006

McIntosh, D. N., Reichmann-Decker, A., Winkielman, P., & Wilbarger, J. L. (2006). When the social mirror breaks: Deficits in automatic, but not voluntary, mimicry of emotional facial expressions in autism. *Developmental Science, 9*, 295–302. https://doi.org/10.1111/j.1467-7687.2006.00492.x

Miles, L. K., Griffiths, J. L., Richardson, M. J., & Macrae, C. N. (2010). Too late to coordinate: Contextual influences on behavioral synchrony. *European Journal of Social Psychology, 40*, 52–60. https://doi.org/10.1002/ejsp.721

Naish, K. R., Houston-Price, C., Bremner, A. J., & Holmes, N. P. (2014). Effects of action observation on corticospinal excitability: Muscle specificity, direction, and timing of the mirror response. *Neuropsychologia, 64*, 331–348. https://doi.org/10.1016/j.neuropsychologia.2014.09.034

Niechwiej-Szwedo, E., Gonzalez, D., Nouredanesh, M., & Tung, J. (2018). Evaluation of the leap motion controller during the performance of visually-guided upper limb movements. *PLoS One, 13*, e0193639. https://doi.org/10.1371/journal.pone.0193639

Palagi, E., Celeghin, A., Tamietto, M., Winkielman, P., & Norscia, I. (2020). The neuroethology of spontaneous mimicry and emotional contagion in human and non-human animals. *Neuroscience and Biobehavioral Reviews, 111*, 149–165. https://doi.org/10.1016/j.neubiorev.2020.01.020

Pfister, R., Dignath, D., Hommel, B., & Kunde, W. (2013). It takes two to imitate: Anticipation and imitation in social interaction. *Psychological Science, 24*, 2117–2121. https://doi.org/10.1177/0956797613489139

Pitcher, D., Parkin, B., & Walsh, V. (2021). Transcranial magnetic stimulation and the understanding of behavior. *Annual Review of Psychology, 72*, 97–121. https://doi.org/10.1146/annurev-psych-081120-013144

Platek, S. M., Critton, S. R., Myers, T. E., & Gallup, G. G., Jr. (2003). Contagious yawning: The role of self-awareness and mental state attribution. *Cognitive Brain Research, 17*, 223–227. https://doi.org/10.1016/S0926-6410(03)00109-5

Platek, S. M., Mohamed, F. B., & Gallup, G. G., Jr. (2005). Contagious yawning and the brain. *Cognitive Brain Research, 23*, 448–452. https://doi.org/10.1016/j.cogbrainres.2004.11.011

Press, C., Bird, G., Flach, R., & Heyes, C. (2005). Robotic movement elicits automatic imitation. *Cognitive Brain Research, 25*, 632–640. https://doi.org/10.1016/j.cogbrainres.2005.08.020

Provine, R. R. (1986). Yawning as a stereotyped action pattern and releasing stimulus. *Ethology, 72*, 109–122. https://doi.org/10.1111/j.1439-0310.1986.tb00611.x

Provine, R. R. (1989). Faces as releasers of contagious yawning: An approach to face detection using normal human subjects. *Bulletin of the Psychonomic Society, 27*, 211–214. https://doi.org/10.3758/BF03334587

Ramsey, R. (2018). What are reaction time indices of automatic imitation measuring? *Consciousness and Cognition, 65*, 240–254. https://doi.org/10.1016/j.concog.2018.08.006

Romani, M., Cesari, P., Urgesi, C., Facchini, S., & Aglioti, S. M. (2005). Motor facilitation of the human cortico-spinal system during observation of bio-mechanically impossible movements. *NeuroImage, 26*, 755–763. https://doi.org/10.1016/j.neuroimage.2005.02.027

Rossi, S., Hallett, M., Rossini, P. M., Pascual-Leone, A., & Safety of TMS Consensus Group. (2009). Safety, ethical considerations, and application guidelines for the use of transcranial magnetic stimulation in clinical practice and research. *Clinical Neurophysiology: Official Journal of the International Federation of Clinical Neurophysiology, 120*, 2008–2039. https://doi.org/10.1016/j.clinph.2009.08.016

Rossi, S., Antal, A., Bestmann, S., Bikson, M., Brewer, C., Brockmöller, J., Carpenter, L. L., Cincotta, M., Chen, R., Daskalakis, J. D., Di Lazzaro, V., Fox, M. D., George, M. S., Gilbert, D., Kimiskidis, V. K., Koch, G., Ilmoniemi, R. J., Lefaucheur, J. P., Leocani, L., & Lisanby, S. H. (2021). Safety and recommendations for TMS use in healthy subjects and patient populations, with updates on training, ethical and regulatory issues: Expert guidelines. *Clinical*

Neurophysiology: Official Journal of the International Federation of Clinical Neurophysiology, 132, 269–306. https://doi.org/10.1016/j.clinph.2020.10.003

Ruggiero, M., & Catmur, C. (2018). Mirror neurons and intention understanding: Dissociating the contribution of object type and intention to mirror responses using electromyography. *Psychophysiology, 55*, e13061. https://doi.org/10.1111/psyp.13061

Santiesteban, I., White, S., Cook, J., Gilbert, S. J., Heyes, C., & Bird, G. (2012). Training social cognition: From imitation to theory of mind. *Cognition, 122*, 228–235. https://doi.org/10.1016/j.cognition.2011.11.004

Sartori, L., Bulgheroni, M., Tizzi, R., & Castiello, U. (2015). A kinematic study on (un)intentional imitation in bottlenose dolphins. *Frontiers in Human Neuroscience, 9*, 446. https://doi.org/10.3389/fnhum.2015.00446

Scarpazza, C., Làdavas, E., & Cattaneo, L. (2018). Invisible side of emotions: Somato-motor responses to affective facial displays in alexithymia. *Experimental Brain Research, 236*, 195–206. https://doi.org/10.1007/s00221-017-5118-x

Simon, J. R. (1990). The effects of an irrelevant directional cue on human information processing. In R. W. Proctor & T. G. Reeve (Eds.), *Stimulus-response compatibility: An integrated perspective* (pp. 31–86). North-Holland.

Sowden, S., & Catmur, C. (2015). The role of the right temporoparietal junction in the control of imitation. *Cerebral Cortex, 25*, 1107–1113. https://doi.org/10.1093/cercor/bht306

Strafella, A. P., & Paus, T. (2000). Modulation of cortical excitability during action observation: A transcranial magnetic stimulation study. *Neuroreport, 11*, 2289–2292. https://doi.org/10.1097/00001756-200007140-00044

Stürmer, B., Aschersleben, G., & Prinz, W. (2000). Correspondence effects with manual gestures and postures: A study of imitation. *Journal of Experimental Psychology: Human Perception and Performance, 26*, 1746–1759. https://doi.org/10.1037/0096-1523.26.6.1746

Turati, C., Natale, E., Bolognini, N., Senna, I., Picozzi, M., Longhi, E., & Cassia, V. M. (2013). The early development of human mirror mechanisms: Evidence from electromyographic recordings at 3 and 6 months. *Developmental Science, 16*, 793–800. https://doi.org/10.1111/desc.12066

van Ulzen, N. R., Lamoth, C. J., Daffertshofer, A., Semin, G. R., & Beek, P. J. (2008). Characteristics of instructed and uninstructed interpersonal coordination while walking side-by-side. *Neuroscience Letters, 432*, 88–93. https://doi.org/10.1016/j.neulet.2007.11.070

Villiger, M., Chandrasekharan, S., & Welsh, T. N. (2011). Activity of human motor system during action observation is modulated by object presence. *Experimental Brain Research, 209*, 85–93. https://doi.org/10.1007/s00221-010-2522-x

Voelkl, B., & Huber, L. (2007). Imitation as faithful copying of a novel technique in marmoset monkeys. *PLoS One, 2*, e611. https://doi.org/10.1371/journal.pone.0000611

Walsh, V., & Cowey, A. (1998). Magnetic stimulation studies of visual cognition. *Trends in Cognitive Sciences, 2*, 103–110. https://doi.org/10.1016/s1364-6613(98)01134-6

Weeks, D. J., & Proctor, R. W. (1990). Salient-features coding in the translation between orthogonal stimulus and response dimensions. *Journal of Experimental Psychology: General, 119*, 355–366. https://doi.org/10.1037/0096-3445.119.4.355

Westfal, M., Cracco, E., Crusius, J., & Genschow, O. (in preparation). *Implementation of an online imitation inhibition task*. https://osf.io/q7fju/

Whiten, A., Horner, V., Litchfield, C. A., & Marshall-Pescini, S. (2004). How do apes ape? *Learning & Behavior, 32*, 36–52. https://doi.org/10.3758/bf03196005

Wiggett, A. J., Downing, P. E., & Tipper, S. P. (2013). Facilitation and interference in spatial and body reference frames. *Experimental Brain Research, 225*, 119–131. https://doi.org/10.1007/s00221-012-3353-8

Yabar, Y., Johnston, L., Miles, L., & Peace, V. (2006). Implicit behavioral mimicry: Investigating the impact of group membership. *Journal of Nonverbal Behavior, 30*, 97–113. https://psycnet.apa.org/doi/10.1007/s10919-006-0010-6

Zivotofsky, A. Z., & Hausdorff, J. M. (2007). The sensory feedback mechanisms enabling couples to walk synchronously: An initial investigation. *Journal of Neuroengineering and Rehabilitation, 4*, 1–5. https://doi.org/10.1186/1743-0003-4-28

Chapter 3
Emotional Mimicry

Ursula Hess and Agneta Fischer

The present chapter will focus on emotional mimicry, that is, the imitation of non-verbal behaviors that signal emotions. Emotional mimicry has been a focus of research and theorizing about empathy and mutual understanding since Lipps (1907) proposed a role for imitation for the understanding of others. Lipps suggested that people automatically adopt the behavior of others and that this imitation leads—via a feedback process—to shared mental states, thereby facilitating the recognition of these mental states in others. For Lipps, the mediating process was introspection. This general notion was taken up by Freud (1921) and entered the psychotherapy literature, where it was referred to as the role of empathy in the therapeutic process (e.g., Haase & Tepper, 1972). Given the focus on empathy and understanding, as well as the prevalent research interests of the time, emotional mimicry was referred to mainly in the clinical context.

In this vein, the importance of mimicry for therapy (for a detailed review, see Chap. 15; this volume) was also underlined by Carl Rogers and others (Rogers, 1957; Scheflen, 1964). They focused, however, more on the notion that the adoption of congruent nonverbal behaviors leads to increased rapport, because it signals rather than causes understanding à la Lipps. As such, these early views already laid the groundwork for two of the theoretical approaches to mimicry that are still relevant today: mimicry as a means to recognize the emotions of others and mimicry as a social signal of understanding and affiliation.

Much of the research discussed in this chapter will focus on the mimicry of emotions via facial expressions (Hess & Fischer, 2013), but we expect similar processes

U. Hess (✉)
Faculty of Life Sciences, Department of Psychology, Humboldt-University, Berlin, Germany
e-mail: Ursula.Hess@hu-berlin.de

A. Fischer
Faculty of Social and Behavioral Sciences, Department of Psychology, University of Amsterdam, Amsterdam, Netherlands
e-mail: a.h.fischer@uva.nl

O. Genschow, E. Cracco (eds.), *Automatic Imitation*,
https://doi.org/10.1007/978-3-031-62634-0_3

for other nonverbal channels, such as vocal expressions (Neumann & Strack, 2000) or emotional postures (Magnée et al., 2007). It is important to note that many behaviors, such as posture changes (Feese et al., 2012) and gestures (e.g., face touching; Chartrand & Bargh, 1999), can be mimicked, but not all carry emotional meaning. This is why we distinguish between behavioral mimicry and emotional mimicry. Although the antecedents and consequences of behavioral and emotional mimicry tend to overlap to some degree (Hess & Fischer, 2017), these two forms of mimicry also show considerable differences, which will be our focus in the present chapter.

In humans, emotional mimicry is a ubiquitous phenomenon that can be readily observed in everyday life. Interestingly, though, emotional mimicry is not restricted to humans. Primates also mimic facial expressions. For example, play-face mimicry has been observed in orangutans (Davila Ross et al., 2008) and in more egalitarian, but not in more "despotic," macaque species (Scopa & Palagi, 2016), suggesting a social context moderator. Mimicry of play signals has also been found in dogs (Palagi et al., 2015) and meerkats (Palagi et al., 2019). This common occurrence of mimicry in different species suggests that mimicry is a basic element of communication in species that overtly show emotions.

Because mimicry is defined as imitation or matching, the main criterion for the presence of mimicry implies that two (or more) individuals show the same behavior at (roughly) the same time. In emotional mimicry, there is usually a 300- to 500-ms delay between the visibility of the stimulus expression and the mimicry of that expression (Dimberg et al., 2002) although slightly longer lag times can also be observed. Yet, there are in fact many reasons why two people may show the same behavior, which we would not define as mimicry (Elfenbein, 2014). One example is when two people observe the same emotion-eliciting event and react in the same manner, without seeing each other's emotional expression (parallel emotional induction). In what follows, we will therefore first differentiate mimicry from other phenomena that may also result in matched behaviors. We will then briefly outline different theories of mimicry. Finally, we will discuss more recent theoretical approaches that focus on top-down effects on mimicry.

Theories of Mimicry

What Is Emotional Mimicry?

As noted above, both emotional and non-emotional behaviors are mimicked. The important difference between mimicry of emotional and non-emotional expressions, such as foot-tapping or face touching, is that the latter are not intrinsically meaningful. They tell us little about the person or their intentions, unless they are interpreted as an emotional signal, for example, as a sign of anxiousness.

Emotional signals are defined as behaviors that are perceived by an observer as signaling an emotional state. Although there is an ongoing debate about the degree to which emotional expressions are actually related to internal emotional states (e.g., Crivelli & Fridlund, 2019; Hassin et al., 2013; Hess, 2017), we argue that there is ample evidence based on the use of these expressions in the arts, films, and literature as well as scientific evidence that people infer emotions from such expressions and that they react in function of this understanding (see Niedenthal & Brauer, 2012). A given expression does not have to be perceived as emotional. For example, a frown can signal both concentration and irritation. When a nonverbal expression is appraised as an *emotional* signal, it carries information about the expresser's intentions toward the perceiver (or some other person), such as to back away, approach, attack, or ignore (see Scarantino et al., 2022, on the attributed meanings of emotional expressions). As we will outline below, only when this emotional signal is perceived as affiliative, will emotional mimicry be a likely consequence.

Furthermore, these signals have to be considered in context. For example, in general, happy expressions are considered affiliative and people who show happiness are judged positively; however, showing happiness at a funeral is not an affiliative signal and leads to a negative judgment and the reduction or absence of mimicry (Kastendieck et al., 2020). By contrast, some emotional expressions such as disgust are generally not considered to signal affiliation (Knutson, 1996) and these are not typically mimicked (see Hess & Fischer, 2013). Mauersberger et al. (2015) found that only a small group of participants in their study mimicked disgust and that this effect was moderated by individual differences such that participants higher in neuroticism were more likely to mimic disgust. Similarly to disgust, anger can be antagonistic (Knutson, 1996) and result in reduced mimicry, but this effect depends on the context—for example, when anger seems to be directed at a common foe it may support closeness rather than reduce it and hence be mimicked (Bourgeois & Hess, 2008).

Non-emotional signals do not have the property to foster affiliation, and even though emotionally meaningless behaviors such as face touching are mimicked, some of the interpersonal sequalae of emotional mimicry we discuss here do not apply.

Related Phenomena That Are Not Emotional Mimicry

A number of phenomena have been conceptualized as either causally linked to emotional mimicry or as forms of mimicry (with the associated overlapping terminology). We argue, however, that these phenomena should not be conflated with emotional mimicry.

Emotional Contagion

A phenomenon that is often confused with mimicry is emotional contagion, and in this vein, mimicry has sometimes been referred to as motor contagion (e.g., Becchio et al., 2007; Blakemore & Frith, 2005). Hatfield, Cacioppo, and Rapson (1993) define emotional contagion as the "catching" of someone else's emotional state, and they consider mimicry a causal antecedent to contagion. Yet, emotional contagion refers to a feeling state, whereas emotional mimicry refers to a (nonverbal) behavior. Hence, conceptually, the two are independent. In fact, whereas both mimicry and emotional contagion have been found in the same studies, they do not necessarily co-occur (e.g., Hess & Blairy, 2001; Lundqvist & Dimberg, 1995).

Synchrony

Another concept, which has especially been used in group contexts, is interpersonal synchrony. This is typically defined as the matching of behaviors and the coordination of movement between individuals in a temporally organized fashion during interpersonal communication (Bernieri et al., 1988; Miles et al., 2010; Vacharkulksemsuk & Fredrickson, 2012; Valdesolo & DeSteno, 2011). However, whereas in mimicry there is an initiator of the behavior—the mimicked person—followed by a time-locked response by the mimicker, synchrony can also refer to behaviors that occur simultaneously and does not depend on the time-locked matching of specific behaviors.

Automatic Imitation

Heyes (2011, p. 463) defines automatic imitation as "a type of stimulus-response compatibility effect in which the topographical features of task-irrelevant action stimuli facilitate similar, and interfere with dissimilar responses." A typical paradigm involves participants making a hand movement in response to a cue while at the same time observing another hand making the same or a different movement (Cracco et al., 2018). Notably, the mechanisms underlying automatic imitation (which focuses on the automatic effects of observing a movement on an intentional movement effectuated by the observer) and mimicry (which is an automatic reaction to an observed movement) are not the same. Specifically, mimicry is a direct automatic reaction to the movement, whereas automatic imitation is the modulation of an intentional movement. In addition, as mentioned above, the signal in automatic imitation does not carry emotional meaning. That said, there is nonetheless some overlap between these phenomena, as some moderators seem to operate similarly. For example, both phenomena can be found when the observed behavior is effectuated by an avatar (Pan & Hamilton, 2015; Weyers et al., 2006) and both are facilitated by social priming (Leighton et al., 2010; van Baaren et al., 2003). Mutual gaze can facilitate both emotional mimicry (Mauersberger et al., 2022a; Rychlowska et al., 2012) and automatic imitation (Wang et al., 2010), but this effect has not been consistently found (Carr et al., 2021). By contrast, whereas emotional mimicry is facilitated for in-groups (Bourgeois & Hess, 2008; van der Schalk et al., 2011), the same effect does not seem to be present for automatic imitation (Genschow et al., 2022a, b). As such, the degree of overlap between these phenomena remains uncertain.

Reactive Emotions

Finally, two people may show the same emotional expression in a time-locked manner, because one person reacts emotionally to the expression of the other. Thus, when person A shows an angry expression and person B feels insulted and reacts with anger as well, this is not an example of emotional mimicry, even though the expressions and timing might be very similar.

In sum, although the phenomena discussed so far all refer to matched behaviors, they differ in whether they constitute emotional signals, occur in reaction to one another, or result from an automatic tendency to synchronize. These differences are important, because they may imply different underlying processes and may therefore also occur in different contexts and have different boundary conditions.

Different Accounts of Mimicry

Over the years, a number of different accounts of the role and function, as well as the underlying processes related to mimicry, have been proposed. It is important to emphasize that these accounts are generally not contradictory. Rather, we argue that they focus on different aspects of mimicry.

Mimicry as Embodiment

The early account by Lipps (1907) proposed a model according to which individuals tend to imitate the emotional displays of their interaction partners, which induces a corresponding state that in turn informs, via introspection, the interaction partner about the other's emotional state. Modern-day accounts of embodied emotion recognition via mimicry (Niedenthal et al., 2017) focus on the action of mirror neurons rather than introspection. These accounts do not necessarily stipulate overt mimicry as a necessary component, but allow for a mediation via efferent copies (Goldman & Sripada, 2005). The basic notion is that when people make social judgments they simulate relevant aspects of the stimulus in a form of embodied cognition (Niedenthal et al., 2005). That is, when judging emotional expressions, such as a smile, people simulate this expression in sensorimotor cortex. If this simulation results in a motor output, this output would then be (facial) mimicry (for more detail, see Wood et al., 2016).

The notion of a simulation process that underpins social perception, in particular with regard to emotions, has been more recently supported by research on EEG mu responses. Specifically, the mu frequency band of the EEG, measured over sensorimotor cortex, is suppressed not only when a person performs a motor act but also when the person observes motor acts performed by someone else (Oberman et al., 2007a; Pineda, 2005). Based on this finding, the mu response has been linked to mirror neuron activity. A more recent study found a distinct mu suppression response during the observation of positively and negatively valenced emotional faces (Moore et al., 2012). These findings suggest a role for mirror neurons for the interpretation of social stimuli. However, there is some controversy as to whether mu suppression is indeed a reliable indicator of mirror neuron activity (Hobson & Bishop, 2017). In addition, mu suppression does not imply an actual motor output. Hence, the question of how mimicry is linked to these simulation processes and whether blocking mimicry can in fact hinder simulations remains open.

Mimicry as a Matched Motor Response

The standard view on behavioral mimicry is compatible with the mirror neuron account above (which, however, does not require an overt mimicry response). From this account, mimicry is an automatic, matched motor response, based on a perception-behavior link (Chartrand & Bargh, 1999; Preston & de Waal, 2002). Hess and Fischer (2013) refer to this idea as the Matched Motor Hypothesis, which assumes that merely perceiving a specific nonverbal display automatically entrains the same expression in the perceiver.

Various mechanisms have been proposed to underlie this link between perception and behavior, which include, in addition to mirror neurons, shared schemas (Barresi & Moore, 1996), shared representations (Prinz, 1997), or spreading activation (see Chartrand & Dalton, 2009). In either case, the perceptual activity is presumed to spread to behavioral representations, which in turn increases the probability of imitating that same behavior, without conscious awareness, control, or intent (Chartrand & Bargh, 1999). Emotional mimicry would then just be one instantiation of such motor behavior. Following the original Matched Motor Hypothesis, the movements in the face are thus spontaneously copied, independent of the intentions of the observer or expresser (see Chartrand & Bargh, 1999). More recent theorizing allows for some level of top-down social perception processes as a moderator (e.g., Chartrand & Lakin, 2013).

Mimicry as a Social Regulator

The Mimicry as Social Regulator view (Fischer & Hess, 2017; Hess, 2021; Hess & Fischer, 2013, 2014, 2017, 2022) is different from the Matched Motor Hypothesis in that it is based on the observation that the motivation to develop social bonds to fulfill our universal need to belong is one of the most powerful drivers of human behavior (Baumeister & Leary, 1995). Emotional mimicry is the unconscious process that serves this need by supporting our aim to establish social and emotional connections and to fulfill our basic need for shared understanding (Fischer & Hess, 2017). The core assumption of this view is that emotional mimicry has the function to foster affiliative interactions and is dependent on the goal to affiliate and to communicate with others that we understand them (see also Rogers, 1957; Bavelas et al., 1986).

This view implies that the mimicry of emotional signals requires a (rapid and usually automatic) appraisal of an emotional expression in the social context in which it occurs before it will be imitated. Is this an angry frown or concentration? Is this happy or malicious laughter? Whether mimicry follows or not will depend on this appraisal. This view is fundamentally different from the embodiment perspective (see Wood et al., 2016), which assumes that mimicry contributes to emotion decoding (see Wood et al., 2016), because the Mimicry as Social Regulator view sees mimicry as based on emotion understanding.

According to this view, emotional mimicry is not merely based on the perception of a facial display, but on the interpretation of the motives underlying this display in a specific context, and thus on understanding the emotion and its meaning in context (Hess & Fischer, 2013, 2014). Rather than merely seeing a movement of the corner of the lips, people may understand this movement to be playful amusement, or schadenfreude (the pleasure in the misfortune of others) or even sadistic pleasure, depending on the context, and whereas they mimic the perceived amusement, they do not mimic the identical expression when the movement is interpreted as sadistic pleasure (Mauersberger et al., 2022b). In other words, emotional mimicry requires the interpretation of signals as emotions, conveying emotional intentions in a specific context (Hess & Fischer, 2022). This is in line with one of the main functions of mimicry, namely smoothing social interactions and establishing or maintaining social bonds.

The Functions of Emotional Mimicry

Four different functions of emotional mimicry have been discussed in the literature, which are associated with the different theoretical accounts described above. Overall, these functions are not necessarily mutually exclusive. Rather, different theories focus more on the one or the other function.

Facilitating Emotion Understanding

The evidence on whether mimicry facilitates emotion understanding as proposed by embodiment theories of mimicry (see Wood et al., 2016) is complex. A number of well-controlled studies in which participants saw a series of standardized facial expressions found no relationship between mimicry and emotion recognition accuracy (Blairy et al., 1999; Bogart & Matsumoto, 2010; Hess & Blairy, 2001). There is some evidence that mimicry can speed up the emotion recognition process

(Niedenthal et al., 2001; Stel & van Knippenberg, 2008), but the reverse effect has also been found (Hawk et al., 2011).

The most consistent evidence on the facilitating role of mimicry on emotion recognition regards studies that demand subtle judgments regarding smiles, either because the smiles are weak (Oberman et al., 2007b) or because more difficult judgments are required, such as genuineness (Ipser & Cook, 2015; Maringer et al., 2011; Rychlowska et al., 2014). However, other studies found conflicting results (Hess et al., 1998; Stel et al., 2009). Most of these studies aimed to block mimicry by a variety of means and then compared accuracy in blocked versus unblocked trials. Interestingly, however, some of the methods used to block mimicry (such as holding a pen with puckered lips) do not actually block mimicry efficiently (Hess & Blaison, 2016; Hess et al., 2018), but block subvocalization. In this context, it is interesting that Ipser and Cook (2015) found that smile decoding accuracy was reduced when participants produced a vowel—a very efficient way to block subvocalization—but not necessarily one that would impede smiling. In short, the evidence favors no general effect of mimicry on emotion recognition, but points to the possibility that mimicry might be helpful for smile-related judgments in difficult decoding tasks.

Yet, there is evidence for the notion that mimicry may nonetheless contribute to a feeling of emotion understanding. For example, Yabar and Hess (2007) found that an interaction partner who shows congruent sad affect during an interaction is perceived as more understanding—even when the person is an out-group member. More recently, Mauersberger et al. (2015) found that the tendency to mimic sadness (an affiliative emotion) in a laboratory task predicted the positivity of daily interactions in a following diary task over 7 days. Conversely, the tendency to mimic disgust (which was much rarer) predicted negative interactions. These data suggest that indeed, one positive function of some forms of mimicry may be to create an atmosphere of mutual understanding, which then may well result in actual better understanding as suggested by Rogers (1957).

Mimicry Promotes Human Affiliation

Both motor mimicry (Chartrand & Lakin, 2013) and emotional mimicry (Hess & Fischer, 2013, 2014) have been shown to not only depend on affiliation but also foster affiliation. Hess and Fischer (2013, 2014) reviewed evidence that people mimic others' emotions more in contexts where participants have positive rather than negative attitudes toward each other (Likowski et al., 2008), or when they are similar rather than dissimilar (Olszanowski et al., 2022), or when they belong to the same group rather than a different group (Bourgeois & Hess, 2008; van der Schalk et al., 2011), or want to cooperate rather than compete with each other (Weyers et al., 2009). This is not only the case for emotional mimicry; Lakin and Chartrand (2013) also reported more behavioral mimicry when participants have a goal to affiliate. Thus, both behavioral mimicry and emotional mimicry are sensitive to the nature of the relationship with the mimickee. Whether, or at least the extent to which, people mimic emotional expressions depends on the perceived intentions of the expresser and on the observer's goals and values. These intentions can be inferred from the direction and type of the emotional signal, the relationship between observer and target, and the emotional state or disposition of the observer. Moreover, the relationship is not uni-directional, because emotional mimicry also serves to increase perceived similarity and liking (Hess et al., 1999; Stel et al., 2008; van der Schalk et al., 2011; Yabar & Hess, 2007).

Mimicry Enhances Social Standing

The STORM (social top-down response modulation) model (Wang & Hamilton, 2012) takes up the notions expressed above, in that it emphasizes the social function of mimicry and its dependence on social context. However, STORM sets a different emphasis for the function of mimicry. Here, mimicry is a Machiavellian strategy for enhancing one's social standing or a strategic intervention to change the social world for self-advancement. Wang and Hamilton base their model on the observation that people increase mimicry toward those who are important for their social welfare. Some of the evidence for this notion has also been adduced by the affiliation theories mentioned above, such that people preferentially mimic others who are nice (Likowski et al., 2008) or those who are in-group members (Bourgeois & Hess, 2008; van der Schalk et al., 2011). They also note that people increase mimicry when they feel that their social relationship is endangered such as when they fail to affiliate with other individuals (Lakin & Chartrand, 2003) or when they are ostracized by their group members (Brandenburg et al., 2022; Lakin et al., 2008).

However, much of the evidence for the model does not stem from research on mimicry (i.e., the imitation of nonverbal behaviors), but rather is based on a variant of the standard paradigm used in automatic imitation research (see above). In this variant, participants first learn social information about a hand, which then shows a finger movement that is either congruent or incongruent with one that the participant is required to perform. The degree of interference with the participant's movement is then a sign of imitation. Given the differences in mechanisms between automatic imitation and emotional mimicry, these findings offer at best circumstantial evidence. A later study on emotional mimicry by contrast (Carr et al., 2014) is more in line with Wang and Hamilton's argument in that they found emotion-specific effects of both observer and target power, congruent with the notion that social hierarchy influences mimicry in meaningful ways.

In essence, however, the main message of the model is that mimicry processes (and these include in this case automatic imitation) serve to regulate the social distance to socially attractive versus unattractive targets. As such, despite many differences in conceptualization, the model is surprisingly compatible with the Mimicry as Social Regulator model.

Mimicry Supports Implicit (Social) Learning

Another important potential function of mimicry regards (social) learning. This aspect is emphasized by Kavanagh and Winkielman (2016). In fact, one of the first reviews on mimicry by Hess et al. (1999) noted an older developmental literature that conceptualized mimicry as a "primitive motor code," which might be a primary cognitive medium for learning about other people during early development. That is, children imitate the behavior of adults and thereby learn the effects of that behavior on others. Similarly, Kavanagh and Winkielman (2016) consider mimicry as a tool for implicit social learning, because it leads to the acquisition of culturally appropriate bodily and emotional behaviors (see also Fischer, 2019). They emphasize that this learning process and the resulting knowledge are implicit. Thus, it cannot easily be rejected, criticized, revised, or employed by the learner in a deliberative or deceptive manner. The function of mimicry as a mechanism for social learning also explains why people generally preferentially mimic in-group members who by definition are more trusted to have the proper knowledge. As such, they conclude that mimicry can be considered an honest signal of group affiliation.

According to Kavanagh and Winkielman (2016), spontaneous mimicry can be costly when there is no focus on the in-group, because it would imply the learning of maladaptive behaviors. Given that the in-group is the group with the same values and priorities, it is likely that humans also share their feelings with this group and in-group members' feelings are thus considered more informative than that of out-group members. A child's fear of strangers emphasizes this point. Mimicry of in-group members therefore is beneficial to the mimickee and to the mimicker, because it supports not only mutual bonds but also the learning of culturally appropriate behaviors by the mimicker and the observation by the mimickee that new and appropriate behaviors are being learned. They further point out that mimicry that is too precise may become blatantly obvious to the mimickee and thus appear strategic and that the actual subtle and approximate expressions that are typically shown are more likely to serve as an honest signal. From this view, the fostering of affiliation is more of a side effect to the learning of appropriate group signals.

In sum, different theories of mimicry converge by highlighting two functions—mutual understanding and social affiliation. They differ in the emphasis given to each and in the exact processes that are presumed. For example, whereas embodiment theories consider mimicry a means for understanding via emotion recognition, the Mimicry as Social Regulator view presumes that emotion understanding precedes mimicry, but because mimicry signals understanding it invites a more open emotion communication.

Top-Down Influences

According to all theories described above, facial mimicry is an automatic process (Dimberg & Thunberg, 1998) that is difficult to suppress (Dimberg et al., 2002) and does not necessarily require explicit awareness of the stimulus (Dimberg et al., 2000). Theories that assume a matched motor response, based on a perception-behavior link (Chartrand & Bargh, 1999; Preston & de Waal, 2002), originally posited that merely perceiving a specific nonverbal display automatically entrains the same display in the perceiver. Nonetheless, there is mounting evidence for the influence of social context on both emotional mimicry and behavioral mimicry (for a review, see Chartrand & Lakin, 2013; Fischer & Hess, 2017; Hess & Fischer, 2013).

In line with this evidence, the Mimicry as Social Regulator model considers mimicry a social act that is influenced by the social context of the interaction and the social goals of the mimicker (Fischer & Hess, 2017; Hess, 2021; Hess & Fischer, 2013, 2014, 2017, 2022). It posits that mimicry is automatic but goal dependent. The goals that are served by mimicry are to communicate with others to foster affiliation and to regulate interpersonal closeness. Because of this, we do not mimic our enemies, people we do not like, or competitors. From this view, it is not the expression per se but the social interpretation of the expression in its context that drives mimicry. This strongly implies that emotional mimicry is shaped by top-down processes as well.

Specifically, there is increasing evidence that the meaning of a given expression in a given context impacts on mimicry. As noted above, smiles are generally considered to be affiliative and therefore smile mimicry often is preserved in contexts where other types of mimicry would be reduced or absent, for example, when the other is an out-group member or a disliked other (e.g., Bourgeois & Hess, 2008; Hess et al., 2017; Seibt et al., 2013; van der Schalk et al., 2011). However, there are many types of smiles (Niedenthal et al., 2010) that are not affiliative in nature (Hess et al., 2002). Thus, people may smile as an expression of schadenfreude—the pleasure in the misfortune of others—or as an expression of sadistic pleasure in another's pain (Mauersberger et al., 2022b). These smiles are malicious rather than affiliative, and the Mimicry as Social Regulator model predicts that such smiles would be mimicked to a lesser degree or not at all.

This notion was studied by Kastendieck et al. (2020), who showed participants videos of individuals who were embedded in an iconic social context associated with clear social norms regarding the prescribed emotional expressions: weddings and funerals. As expected, participants who smiled at weddings were mimicked, but those who smiled at funerals were mimicked less or not at all. The level of mimicry was mediated by perceived closeness, which in turn was mediated by the perceived appropriateness of the expression. To the degree that participants considered the expression inappropriate to the context, they felt more distant toward the expresser and mimicked their smiles to a lesser extent. Similarly, Mauersberger et al. (2022b) found that participants mimicked individuals who laughed at funny scenes more than those who laughed at schadenfreude scenes or disgusting scenes. Again, the level of mimicry was mediated by perceived closeness and appropriateness of the expression.

For the mimicry of sadness, the results seem less consistent. For example, Kastendieck et al. (2020) and Kastendieck et al. (2022b) found that mimicry of sad expressions does not depend on perceived closeness. This could be explained by the strong appeal to show empathy that is signaled by sad expressions (Scarantino et al., 2022). Still, another study has found an effect of context, showing that sad expressions are not mimicked when shown by disliked others (Likowski et al., 2008).

Also, some studies found that perceived contextual appropriateness may play a role for sadness expressions as well. For example, Fischer and Hess (2018) found that a sad face not showing tears was mimicked, but not when showing tears. This suggests that sad expressions that are too intense might not be mimicked (probably because they were deemed inappropriate as well). These findings also suggest an effect of contextual appropriateness, if we consider that the social signal conveyed by a sad expression is an appeal to empathize and to help (Scarantino et al., 2022). Tears, however, are often perceived as difficult to control or overwhelming. As such, a person who cries at a funeral may be forgiven for the "fault pas" and still liked, yet the sadness may reduce perceived closeness as people shy away from the social cost of helping that closeness may require of them.

In sum, there is evidence for top-down effects on emotional mimicry that depend on the perceived motives of the expresser and the resulting meaning that is attributed to the expression in a particular context. In fact, some of the studies referred to above, in which mimicry is reduced or absent, can be similarly interpreted even though these authors did not measure the mediating variables. For example, in a study by Lanzetta and Englis (1989) participants mimicked another person's smile only when they expected a collaboration with this person, but not when they expected competition. One explanation for the lack of mimicry in the competition condition could be that the smile of a competing other was interpreted as maliciousness or schadenfreude rather than as a signal of affiliation.

Future Perspectives

The conceptualization of mimicry has changed over time, from a view that understood mimicry of all behaviors—including emotional ones—as a process whereby "one's behavior passively and unintentionally changes to match that of others in one's current social environment" (Chartrand & Bargh, 1999, p. 893) to a process that heavily depends on the social context and the social motives of the interaction partners. Both emotional mimicry and behavioral mimicry act as "social glue" (Lakin et al., 2003), but for the most part only in contexts that are affiliative (Hess & Fischer, 2022; Lakin & Chartrand, 2013). Fortunately, for most interactions it seems that the default stance is one where affiliation is assumed. Only when there are clear signals of potential non-affiliation, such as the dislike or hostile intentions of an interaction partner (Likowski et al., 2008) or emotional deviance (Kastendieck et al., 2020), does mimicry fail.

Notably, as noted in the introduction, the effects of affiliation and social context on mimicry are most clearly evidenced for emotional mimicry, in comparison with behavioral mimicry, and even though some effects observed for mimicry—such as eye-gaze effects (Wang & Hamilton, 2014) or task relevance of the mimicked behavior (Hemed et al., 2022)—apply also to automatic imitation, others such as the effect of in-group status do not (Genschow et al., 2022a, b). Such differences may be expected, given the different degrees of social engagement afforded by emotional expressions versus hand movements and the differences in social signal value between the two. This further supports the notion that these are different processes even though they do share some common ground.

What is an important lesson from the research and theorizing on emotional mimicry is that we should acknowledge that perceivers are not passive. People are not emotion readout machines who look at a face and attach a suitable label independent of the context and of whom the face belongs to. They also are not automatons who move the muscle they see someone else move regardless of circumstance. Rather, they engage in active sensemaking that takes into account the context and the presumed goals of the interaction partner (Hess & Hareli, 2019). Thus, people do not simply look at a face and label an expression as a smile and move the corners of their mouth in imitation, but they judge the expression in light of the context and what they know about the expresser. Thus, the same smile may be considered pleasant or malicious and evoke divergent reactions.

However, this does not mean that facial expressions do not have any intrinsic meaning. Rather, both context and expression contribute to the social judgment by the perceiver (Hess & Hareli, 2018). In fact, emotional expressions can actually provide information about context as well. In one study, participants were able to deduce the rules of a made-up ball game based on the facial responses of the "spectators" (Hareli et al., 2019). Instead of trying to decide whether facial expressions or context dominate the judgments of perceivers, it is more realistic to propose that observers engage in active sensemaking based on the available information. If information about the expression is available, perceivers may use this to draw conclusions about the situation, and when information about the situation is available, it can be used to predict the likely expression. When both are available, the information is integrated in a way that makes sense to the perceiver (Hess & Hareli, 2019).

This notion of an active perceiver—what for visual stimuli is referred to as social vision (Adams et al., 2010)—is central to emotion communication. This can be seen in parallel to the understanding of 4E cognition (see, e.g., Newen et al., 2018). That is, emotion perception is a process that is embodied, embedded, enacted, and extended. Of these 4 Es, emotion research has addressed most explicitly embodiment (Niedenthal et al., 2017). Calls to understand emotions from the context in which they occur address the notions of the importance of extrabodily processes that underlie the notions of embeddedness and extendedness. With regard to mimicry, research such as by Kastendieck and colleagues (Kastendieck et al., 2020, 2022a; Mauersberger et al., 2022b) that aims to study mimicry with stimuli that are embedded in a specific (and meaningful) context is the first step in that direction.

However, it is just as important to keep in mind that emotions are enacted as well—we decode the emotions of others not just for the sake of applying a label, but in order to successfully interact (Hess & Kafetsios, 2022). Future research should investigate the presumed motives of the expresser and the goals of the interaction.

Finally, mimicry research to date has, except for research on out-group mimicry, paid little attention to the question of who interacts with whom. This is in part a heritage of the notion that mimicry is a simple reflex-like automatism. Yet, when we consider the importance of context and the social knowledge that we have about our interaction partners, the situation becomes more complex. Only more recently have researchers started to be more explicitly concerned with the intersection of social group identities. Specifically, many social processes play out differently for members of different groups and people tend to be members of more than one group. This implies that the combination of groups that people belong to may result in very specific effects. This in turn limits generalization across groups. For example, emotion stereotypes suggest that Black men are aggressive, but this does not apply in the same way to black women (for a review, see Hedgecoth et al., 2023). On the perceptual level, the wrinkles and folds of old age reduce perceived attractiveness disproportionally for women compared to men. Attractiveness in turn correlates positively with liking and perceived closeness (Sutherland & Young, 2023). As such, it will be important for future research to consider not only the social identities of mimicker and mimickee but also their intersection.

Summary

The present chapter focuses on emotional mimicry, that is, the mimicry of nonverbal behaviors that signal emotions. Emotional mimicry differs from behavioral mimicry and automatic imitation in that the actual signal—the emotional expression—carries meaning that is relevant for the relationship between expresser and mimicker. This is important because emotional mimicry depends crucially on perceived closeness or affiliation. We reviewed different functions of emotional mimicry that have been proposed in the literature, such as facilitating affiliation, emotion recognition when signals are ambiguous, social standing, and more broadly social-cultural learning. In addition, we summarized research on top-down effects on emotional mimicry showing how social judgments and the interpretation of emotional signals in a given context influence perceived closeness and affiliation and in turn support emotional mimicry.

References

Adams, R. B., Jr., Ambady, N., Nakayama, K., & Shimojo, S. (2010). *The science of social vision*. Oxford University Press.

Barresi, J., & Moore, C. (1996). Intentional relations and social understanding. *Behavioral and Brain Sciences, 19*, 107–122. https://doi.org/10.1017/S0140525X00041790

Baumeister, R. F., & Leary, M. R. (1995). The need to belong: Desire for interpersonal attachments as a fundamental human motivation. *Psychological Bulletin, 117*, 497–529. https://doi.org/10.1037/0033-2909.117.3.497

Bavelas, J. B., Black, A., Lemery, C. R., & Mullett, J. (1986). "I show how you feel": Motor mimicry as a communicative act. *Journal of Personality and Social Psychology, 50*, 322–329. https://doi.org/10.1037/0022-3514.50.2.322

Becchio, C., Pierno, A., Mari, M., Lusher, D., & Castiello, U. (2007). Motor contagion from gaze: The case of autism. *Brain, 130*, 2401–2411. https://doi.org/10.1093/brain/awm171

Bernieri, F. J., Reznick, J. S., & Rosenthal, R. (1988). Synchrony pseudosynchrony and dissynchrony: Measuring the entrainment process in mother-infant interactions. *Journal of Personality and Social Psychology, 54*, 243–253. https://doi.org/10.1037/0022-3514.54.2.243

Blairy, S., Herrera, P., & Hess, U. (1999). Mimicry and the judgment of emotional facial expressions. *Journal of Nonverbal Behavior, 23*, 5–41. https://doi.org/10.1023/A:1021370825283

Blakemore, S.-J., & Frith, C. (2005). The role of motor contagion in the prediction of action. *Neuropsychologia, 43*, 260–267. https://doi.org/10.1016/j.neuropsychologia.2004.11.012

Bogart, K. R., & Matsumoto, D. (2010). Facial mimicry is not necessary to recognize emotion: Facial expression recognition by people with Moebius syndrome. *Social Neuroscience, 5*, 241–251. https://doi.org/10.1080/17470910903395692

Bourgeois, P., & Hess, U. (2008). The impact of social context on mimicry. *Biological Psychology, 77*, 343–352. https://doi.org/10.1016/j.biopsycho.2007.11.008

Brandenburg, J. C., Albohn, D. N., Bernstein, M. J., Soto, J. A., Hess, U., & Adams, R. B. (2022). Facing social exclusion: A facial EMG examination of the reaffiliative function of smiling. *Cognition and Emotion, 36*, 741–749. https://doi.org/10.1080/02699931.2022.2041404

Carr, E. W., Winkielman, P., & Oveis, C. (2014). Transforming the mirror: Power fundamentally changes facial responding to emotional expressions, 143, 997–1003. https://doi.org/10.1037/a0034972

Carr, E. W., Bird, G., Catmur, C., & Winkielman, P. (2021). Dissociable effects of averted "gaze" on the priming of bodily representations and motor actions. *Acta Psychologica, 212*, 103225. https://doi.org/10.1016/j.actpsy.2020.103225

Chartrand, T. L., & Bargh, J. A. (1999). The chameleon effect: The perception-behavior link and social interaction. *Journal of Personality and Social Psychology, 76*, 893–910. https://doi.org/10.1037/0022-3514.76.6.893

Chartrand, T. L., & Dalton, A. N. (2009). Mimicry: Its ubiquity, importance, and functionality. In *Oxford handbook of human action* (pp. 458–483). Oxford University Press. https://doi.org/10.1093/oso/9780195309980.003.0022

Chartrand, T. L., & Lakin, J. L. (2013). The antecedents and consequences of human behavioral mimicry. *Annual Review of Psychology, 64*, 285–308. https://doi.org/10.1146/annurev-psych-113011-143754

Cracco, E., Bardi, L., Desmet, C., Genschow, O., Rigoni, D., De Coster, L., Radkova, I., Deschrijver, E., & Brass, M. (2018). Automatic imitation: A meta-analysis. *Psychological Bulletin, 144*, 453–500. https://doi.org/10.1037/bul0000143

Crivelli, C., & Fridlund, A. J. (2019). Inside-out: From basic emotions theory to the behavioral ecology view. *Journal of Nonverbal Behavior, 43*, 161–194. https://doi.org/10.1007/s10919-019-00294-2

Davila Ross, M., Menzler, S., & Zimmermann, E. (2008). Rapid facial mimicry in orangutan play. *Biology Letters, 4*, 27–30. https://doi.org/10.1098/rsbl.2007.0535

Dimberg, U., & Thunberg, M. (1998). Rapid facial reactions to emotional facial expressions. *Scandinavian Journal of Psychology, 39*, 39–45. https://doi.org/10.1111/1467-9450.00054

Dimberg, U., Thunberg, M., & Elmehed, K. (2000). Unconscious facial reactions to emotional facial expressions. *Psychological Science, 11*, 86–89. https://doi.org/10.1111/1467-9280.00221

Dimberg, U., Thunberg, M., & Grunedal, S. (2002). Facial reactions to emotional stimuli: Automatically controlled emotional responses. *Cognition and Emotion, 16*, 449–472. https://doi.org/10.1080/02699930143000356

Elfenbein, H. A. (2014). The many faces of emotional contagion: An affective process theory of affective linkage. *Organizational Psychology Review, 4*, 326–362. https://doi.org/10.1177/2041386614542889

Feese, S., Arnrich, B., Tröster, G., Meyer, B., & Jonas, K. (2012). Quantifying behavioral mimicry by automatic detection of nonverbal cues from body motion. In *2012 International Conference on Privacy, Security, Risk and Trust and 2012 International Conference on Social Computing*.

Fischer, A. (2019). Learning from others' emotions. In D. Dukes & F. Clement (Eds.), *Foundations of affective social learning: Conceptualizing the social transmission of value* (pp. 165–184). Cambridge University Press. https://doi.org/10.1017/9781108661362.008

Fischer, A., & Hess, U. (2017). Mimicking emotions. *Current Opinion in Psychology, 17*, 151–155.

Fischer, A., & Hess, U. (2018, April 4–5). *Facial mimicry of crying*. Paper presented at the CERE 2018, Glasgow, UK.

Freud, S. (1921). Group psychology and the analysis of the ego. In *The standard edition of the complete works of Sigmund Freud* (Vol. 18, pp. 65–143). The Hogart Press.

Genschow, O., Pauels, E., Krugmann, K., & Winter, A. (2022a). Group membership does not modulate goal-versus movement-based imitation. *Quarterly Journal of Experimental Psychology, 76*, 827–837. https://doi.org/10.1177/17470218221132842

Genschow, O., Westfal, M., Cracco, E., & Crusius, J. (2022b). Group membership does not modulate automatic imitation. *Psychological Research, 86*, 780–791. https://doi.org/10.1007/s00426-021-01526-1

Goldman, A., & Sripada, C. S. (2005). Simulationist models of face-based emotion recognition. *Cognition, 94*, 193–213. https://doi.org/10.1016/j.cognition.2004.01.005

Haase, R. F., & Tepper, D. T. (1972). Nonverbal components of empathic communication. *Journal of Counseling Psychology, 19*, 417–424. https://doi.org/10.1037/h0033188

Hareli, S., Elkabetz, S., & Hess, U. (2019). Drawing inferences from emotion expressions: The role of situative informativeness and context. *Emotion, 19*, 200–208. https://doi.org/10.1037/emo0000368

Hassin, R. R., Aviezer, H., & Bentin, S. (2013). Inherently ambiguous: Facial expressions of emotions, in context. *Emotion Review, 5*, 60–65. https://doi.org/10.1177/1754073912451331

Hatfield, E., Cacioppo, J. T., & Rapson, R. L. (1993). Emotional Contagion. *Current Directions in Psychological Science, 2*, 96–100. https://doi.org/10.1111/1467-8721.ep10770953

Hawk, S. T., Fischer, A. H., & Van Kleef, G. A. (2011). Taking your place or matching your face: Two paths to empathic embarrassment. *Emotion, 11*, 502–513. https://doi.org/10.1037/a0022762

Hedgecoth, N., Strand, N., & Adams, R. B., Jr. (2023). The intersection of race, gender/sex, and age in emotion perception from faces and bodies. In U. Hess, R. B. Adams Jr., & R. B. Kleck (Eds.), *Emotion communication by the aging face and body* (pp. 106–139). Cambridge University Press. https://doi.org/10.1017/9781009209656.006

Hemed, E., Mark-Tavger, I., Hertz, U., Bakbani-Elkayam, S., & Eitam, B. (2022). Automatically controlled: Task irrelevance fully cancels otherwise automatic imitation. *Journal of Experimental Psychology: General, 151*, 996–1017. https://doi.org/10.1037/xge0001117

Hess, U. (2017). Emotion categorization. In C. Lefebvre & H. Cohen (Eds.), *Handbook of categorization in cognitive science* (2nd ed., pp. 107–126). Elsevier. https://doi.org/10.1016/B978-0-08-101107-2.00005-1

Hess, U. (2021). Who to whom and why: The social nature of emotional mimicry. *Psychophysiology, 58*, e13675. https://doi.org/10.1111/psyp.13675

Hess, U., & Blairy, S. (2001). Facial mimicry and emotional contagion to dynamic emotional facial expressions and their influence on decoding accuracy. *International Journal of Psychophysiology, 40*, 129–141. https://doi.org/10.1016/S0167-8760(00)00161-6

Hess, U., & Blaison, C. (2016). *Blocking mimicry—Or not?* In 56th Annual Meeting of the Society for Psychophysiological Research, Minneapolis, Minnesota, September 21–25.

Hess, U., & Fischer, A. (2013). Emotional mimicry as social regulation. *Personality and Social Psychology Review, 17*, 142–157. https://doi.org/10.1177/1088868312472607

Hess, U., & Fischer, A. (2014). Emotional mimicry: Why and when we mimic emotions. *Social and Personality Psychology Compass, 8*, 45–57. https://doi.org/10.1111/spc3.12083

Hess, U., & Fischer, A. (2017). The role of emotional mimicry in intergroup relations. In H. Giles & J. Harwood (Eds.), *Oxford encyclopedia of intergroup communication.* Oxford University Press.

Hess, U., & Fischer, A. (2022). Emotional mimicry as social regulator: Theoretical considerations. *Cognition and Emotion, 36*, 785–793. https://doi.org/10.1080/02699931.2022.2103522

Hess, U., & Hareli, S. (2018). On the malleability of the meaning of contexts: The influence of another person's emotion expressions on situation perception. *Cognition and Emotion, 32*, 185–191. https://doi.org/10.1080/02699931.2016.1269725

Hess, U., & Hareli, S. (2019). The emotion-based inferences in context (EBIC) model. In *The social nature of emotion expression* (pp. 1–5). Springer. https://doi.org/10.1007/978-3-030-32968-6_1

Hess, U., & Kafetsios, K. (2022). Infusing context into emotion perception impacts emotion decoding accuracy. *Experimental Psychology, 68*, 285–294. https://doi.org/10.1027/1618-3169/a000531

Hess, U., Philippot, P., & Blairy, S. (1998). Facial reactions to emotional facial expressions: Affect or cognition? *Cognition and Emotion, 12*, 509–532. https://doi.org/10.1080/026999398379547

Hess, U., Philippot, P., & Blairy, S. (1999). Mimicry: Facts and fiction. In P. Philippot & R. S. Feldman (Eds.), *The social context of nonverbal behavior. Studies in emotion and social interaction* (pp. 213–241). Cambridge University Press.

Hess, U., Beaupré, M. G., & Cheung, N. (2002). Who to whom and why – Cultural differences and similarities in the function of smiles. In M. Abel & C. H. Ceia (Eds.), *An empirical reflection on the smile* (pp. 187–216). The Edwin Mellen Press.

Hess, U., Blaison, C., & Dandeneau, S. (2017). The impact of rewards on empathic accuracy and emotional mimicry. *Motivation and Emotion, 41*, 107–112. https://doi.org/10.1007/s11031-016-9590-6

Hess, U., Blaison, C., Hosemann, J., & Niebrügge, N. (2018, April 4–5). *Blocking mimicry? The effects of blocking facial movement on decoding accuracy.* Paper presented at the CERE 2018, Glasgow, UK.

Heyes, C. (2011). Automatic imitation. *Psychological Bulletin, 137*, 463–483. https://doi.org/10.1037/a0022288

Hobson, H. M., & Bishop, D. V. M. (2017). The interpretation of mu suppression as an index of mirror neuron activity: Past, present and future. *Royal Society Open Science, 4*, 160662. https://doi.org/10.1098/rsos.160662

Ipser, A., & Cook, R. (2015). Inducing a concurrent motor load reduces categorization precision for facial expressions. *Journal of Experimental Psychology: Human Perception and Performance.* https://doi.org/10.1037/xhp0000177

Kastendieck, T., Mauersberger, H., Blaison, C., Ghalib, J., & Hess, U. (2020). Laughing at funerals and frowning at weddings: Top-down influences of context-driven social judgments on emotional mimicry. *Acta Psychologica, 212*, 103195. https://doi.org/10.1016/j.actpsy.2020.103195

Kastendieck, T., Huppertz, D., Mauersberger, H., & Hess, U. (2022a). Does it matter where I need you? Mimicry of young and old faces shown in pleasant and unpleasant places. *Manuscript in Preparation.* https://doi.org/10.1098/rstb.2021.0188

Kastendieck, T., Zillmer, S., & Hess, U. (2022b). (Un)mask yourself! Effects of face masks on facial mimicry and emotion perception during the COVID-19 pandemic. *Cognition and Emotion, 36*, 59–69. https://doi.org/10.1080/02699931.2021.1950639

Kavanagh, L. C., & Winkielman, P. (2016). The functionality of spontaneous mimicry and its influences on affiliation: An implicit socialization account. *Frontiers in Psychology, 7*, 458. https://doi.org/10.3389/fpsyg.2016.00458

Knutson, B. (1996). Facial expressions of emotion influence interpersonal trait inferences. *Journal of Nonverbal Behavior, 20*, 165–182. https://doi.org/10.1007/BF02281954

Lakin, J. L., & Chartrand, T. L. (2003). Using nonconscious behavioral mimicry to create affiliation and rapport. *Psychological Science, 14*, 334–339. https://doi.org/10.1111/1467-9280.14481

Lakin, J. L., & Chartrand, T. L. (2013). Behavioral mimicry as an affiliative response to social exclusion. In *The Oxford handbook of social exclusion* (pp. 266–274). Oxford University Press. https://doi.org/10.1093/oxfordhb/9780195398700.013.002

Lakin, J. L., Jefferis, V. E., Cheng, C. M., & Chartrand, T. L. (2003). The Chameleon effect as social glue: Evidence for the evolutionary significance of nonconscious mimicry. *Journal of Nonverbal Behavior, 27*, 145–162. https://doi.org/10.1023/A:1025389814290

Lakin, J. L., Chartrand, T. L., & Arkin, R. M. (2008). I am too just like you: Nonconscious mimicry as an automatic behavioral response to social exclusion. *Psychological Science, 19*, 816–822. https://doi.org/10.1111/j.1467-9280.2008.02162

Lanzetta, J. T., & Englis, B. G. (1989). Expectations of cooperation and competition and their effects on observers' vicarious emotional responses. *Journal of Personality and Social Psychology, 56*, 543–554. https://doi.org/10.1037/0022-3514.56.4.543

Leighton, J., Bird, G., Orsini, C., & Heyes, C. (2010). Social attitudes modulate automatic imitation. *Journal of Experimental Social Psychology, 46*, 905–910. https://doi.org/10.1016/j.jesp.2010.07.001

Likowski, K. U., Mühlberger, A., Seibt, B., Pauli, P., & Weyers, P. (2008). Modulation of facial mimicry by attitudes. *Journal of Experimental Social Psychology, 44*, 1065–1072. https://doi.org/10.1016/j.jesp.2007.10.007

Lipps, T. (1907). Das Wissen von fremden Ichen. In T. Lipps (Ed.), *Psychologische Untersuchungen* (Vol. 1, pp. 694–722). Engelmann. https://doi.org/10.1515/9783110674194-012

Lundqvist, L. O., & Dimberg, U. (1995). Facial expressions are contagious. *Journal of Psychophysiology, 9*, 203–211.

Magnée, M. J. C. M., Stekelenburg, J. J., Kemner, C., & de Gelder, B. (2007). Similar facial electromyographic responses to faces, voices, and body expressions. *Neuroreport: For Rapid Communication of Neuroscience Research, 18*, 369–372. https://doi.org/10.1097/WNR.0b013e32801776e6

Maringer, M., Krumhuber, E. G., Fischer, A. H., & Niedenthal, P. M. (2011). Beyond smile dynamics: Mimicry and beliefs in judgments of smiles. *Emotion, 11*, 181–187. https://doi.org/10.1037/a0022596

Mauersberger, H., Blaison, C., Kafetsios, K., Kessler, C.-L., & Hess, U. (2015). Individual differences in emotional mimicry: Underlying traits and social consequences. *European Journal of Personality, 29*, 512–529. https://doi.org/10.1002/per.2008

Mauersberger, H., Kastendieck, T. M., & Hess, U. (2022a). I looked at you, you looked at me, I smiled at you, you smiled at me – The impact of eye contact on mimicry. *Frontiers in Psychology, 13*, 970954. https://doi.org/10.3389/fpsyg.2022.970954

Mauersberger, H., Kastendieck, T. M., Hetmann, A., Schöll, A., & Hess, U. (2022b). The different shades of laughter: When do we laugh and when do we mimic other's laughter? *Philosophical Transactions of the Royal Society London B, 377*, 20210188. https://doi.org/10.1098/rstb.2021.0188

Miles, L. K., Griffiths, J. L., Richardson, M. J., & Macrae, C. N. (2010). Too late to coordinate: Contextual influences on behavioral synchrony. *European Journal of Social Psychology, 40*, 52–60. https://doi.org/10.1002/ejsp.721

Moore, A., Gorodnitsky, I., & Pineda, J. A. (2012). EEG mu component responses to viewing emotional faces. *Behavioural Brain Research, 226*, 309–316. https://doi.org/10.1016/j.bbr.2011.07.048

Neumann, R., & Strack, F. (2000). "Mood contagion": The automatic transfer of mood between persons. *Journal of Personality and Social Psychology, 79*, 211–223. https://doi.org/10.1037/0022-3514.79.2.211

Newen, A., De Bruin, L., & Gallagher, S. (2018). 4E cognition: Historical roots, key concepts, and central issues. In *The Oxford handbook of 4E cognition* (Vol. 1, pp. 3–15). Oxford University Press.

Niedenthal, P. M., & Brauer, M. (2012). Social functionality of human emotion. *Annual Review of Psychology, 63*, 259–285. https://doi.org/10.1146/annurev.psych.121208.131605

Niedenthal, P. M., Brauer, M., Halberstadt, J., & Innes-Ker, A. H. (2001). When did her smile drop? Facial mimicry and the influences of emotional state on the detection of change in emotional expression. *Cognition and Emotion, 15*, 853–864. https://doi.org/10.1080/02699930143000194
Niedenthal, P. M., Barsalou, L. W., Winkielman, P., Krauth-Gruber, S., & Ric, F. (2005). Embodiment in attitudes, social perception, and emotion. *Personality and Social Psychology Review, 9*, 184–211. https://doi.org/10.1207/s15327957pspr0903_1
Niedenthal, P. M., Mermillod, M., Maringer, M., & Hess, U. (2010). The simulation of smiles (SIMS) model: Embodied simulation and the meaning of facial expression. *Behavioral and Brain Sciences, 33*, 417–433. https://doi.org/10.1017/S0140525X10000865
Niedenthal, P. M., Wood, A., Rychlowska, M., & Korb, S. (2017). Embodied simulation in decoding facial expression. In J.-M. Fernández-Dols & J. A. Russell (Eds.), *The science of facial expression* (pp. 397–414). Oxford University Press.
Oberman, L. M., McCleery, J. P., Ramachandran, V. S., & Pineda, J. A. (2007a). EEG evidence for mirror neuron activity during the observation of human and robot actions: Toward an analysis of the human qualities of interactive robots. *Neurocomputing, 70*, 2194–2203. https://doi.org/10.1016/j.neucom.2006.02.024
Oberman, L. M., Winkielman, P., & Ramachandran, V. S. (2007b). Face to face: Blocking facial mimicry can selectively impair recognition of emotional expressions. *Social Neuroscience, 2*, 167–178. https://doi.org/10.1080/17470910701391943
Olszanowski, M., Lewandowska, P., Ozimek, A., & Frankowska, N. (2022). The effect of facial self-resemblance on emotional mimicry. *Journal of Nonverbal Behavior, 46*, 197–213. https://doi.org/10.1007/s10919-021-00395-x
Palagi, E., Nicotra, V., & Cordoni, G. (2015). Rapid mimicry and emotional contagion in domestic dogs. *Royal Society Open Science, 2*, 150505. https://doi.org/10.1098/rsos.150505
Palagi, E., Marchi, E., Cavicchio, P., & Bandoli, F. (2019). Sharing playful mood: Rapid facial mimicry in Suricata suricatta. *Animal Cognition, 22*, 719–732. https://doi.org/10.1007/s10071-019-01269-y
Pan, X., & Hamilton, A. F. d. C. (2015). Automatic imitation in a rich social context with virtual characters. *Frontiers in Psychology, 6*. https://doi.org/10.3389/fpsyg.2015.00790
Pineda, J. A. (2005). The functional significance of mu rhythms: Translating "seeing" and "hearing" into "doing". *Brain Research Reviews, 50*, 57–68. https://doi.org/10.1016/j.brainresrev.2005.04.005
Preston, S. D., & de Waal, F. B. M. (2002). Empathy: Its ultimate and proximate bases. *Behavioral and Brain Sciences, 25*, 1–20. https://doi.org/10.1017/s0140525x02000018
Prinz, W. (1997). Perception and action planning. *European Journal of Cognitive Psychology, 9*, 129–154. https://doi.org/10.1080/713752551
Rogers, C. R. (1957). The necessary and sufficient conditions of therapeutic personality change. *Journal of Consulting Psychology, 21*, 95–103. https://doi.org/10.1037/h0045357
Rychlowska, M., Zinner, L., Musca, S. C., & Niedenthal, P. M. (2012). From the eye to the heart: Eye contact triggers emotion simulation. In *Proceedings of the 4th Workshop on Eye Gaze in Intelligent Human Machine Interaction*, Santa Monica, CA.
Rychlowska, M., Cañadas, E., Wood, A., Krumhuber, E. G., Fischer, A., & Niedenthal, P. M. (2014). Blocking mimicry makes true and false smiles look the same. *PLoS One, 9*, e90876. https://doi.org/10.1371/journal.pone.0090876
Scarantino, A., Hareli, S., & Hess, U. (2022). Emotional expressions as appeals to recipients. *Emotion, 22*, 1856–1868. https://doi.org/10.1037/emo0001023
Scheflen, A. E. (1964). The significance of posture in communication systems. *Psychiatry, 27*, 316–331. https://doi.org/10.1080/00332747.1964.11023403
Scopa, C., & Palagi, E. (2016). Mimic me while playing! Social tolerance and rapid facial mimicry in macaques (*Macaca tonkeana* and *Macaca fuscata*), 153–161. https://doi.org/10.1037/com0000028
Seibt, B., Weyers, P., Likowski, K. U., Pauli, P., Mühlberger, A., & Hess, U. (2013). Subliminal interdependence priming modulates congruent and incongruent facial reactions to emotional displays. *Social Cognition, 31*, 613–631. https://doi.org/10.1521/soco.2013.31.5.613

Stel, M., & van Knippenberg, A. (2008). The role of facial mimicry in the recognition of affect. *Psychological Science, 19*, 984–985. https://doi.org/10.1111/j.1467-9280.2008.02188.x

Stel, M., van Baaren, R. B., & Vonk, R. (2008). Effects of mimicking: Acting prosocially by being emotionally moved. *European Journal of Social Psychology, 38*, 965–976. https://doi.org/10.1002/ejsp.472

Stel, M., van Dijk, E., & Olivier, E. (2009). You want to know the truth? Then don't mimic! *Psychological Science, 20*, 693–699. https://doi.org/10.1111/j.1467-9280.2009.02350

Sutherland, C., & Young, A. (2023). Youth and beauty: Age-based trait impressions from faces. In U. Hess, R. B. Adams Jr., & R. B. Kleck (Eds.), *Emotion communication by the aging face and body: A multidisciplinary view* (pp. 171–196). Cambridge University Press.

Vacharkulksemsuk, T., & Fredrickson, B. L. (2012). Strangers in sync: Achieving embodied rapport through shared movements. *Journal of Experimental Social Psychology, 48*, 399–402. https://doi.org/10.1016/j.jesp.2011.07.015

Valdesolo, P., & DeSteno, D. (2011). Synchrony and the social tuning of compassion. *Emotion, 11*, 262–266. https://doi.org/10.1037/a0021302

van Baaren, R. B., Maddux, W. W., Chartrand, T. L., de Bouter, C., & van Knippenberg, A. (2003). It takes two to mimic: Behavioral consequences of self-construals. *Journal of Personality and Social Psychology, 84*, 1093–1102. https://doi.org/10.1037/0022-3514.84.5.1093

van der Schalk, J., Fischer, A., Doosje, B. J., Wigboldus, D., Hawk, S., Rotteveel, M., & Hess, U. (2011). Convergent and divergent responses to emotional displays of ingroup and outgroup. *Emotion, 11*, 286–298. https://doi.org/10.1037/a0022582

Wang, Y., & Hamilton, A. F. d. C. (2012). Social top-down response modulation (STORM): A model of the control of mimicry in social interaction. *Towards a Neuroscience of Social Interaction, 6*, 153. https://doi.org/10.3389/fnhum.2012.00153

Wang, Y., & Hamilton, A. F. d. C. (2014). Why does gaze enhance mimicry? Placing gaze-mimicry effects in relation to other gaze phenomena. *The Quarterly Journal of Experimental Psychology, 67*, 747–762. https://doi.org/10.1080/17470218.2013.828316

Wang, Y., Newport, R., & Hamilton, A. F. d. C. (2010). Eye contact enhances mimicry of intransitive hand movements. *Biology Letters*. https://doi.org/10.1098/rsbl.2010.0279

Weyers, P., Mühlberger, A., Hefele, C., & Pauli, P. (2006). Electromyographic responses to static and dynamic avatar emotional facial expressions. *Psychophysiology, 43*, 450–453. https://doi.org/10.1111/j.1469-8986.2006.00451.x

Weyers, P., Mühlberger, A., Kund, A., Hess, U., & Pauli, P. (2009). Modulation of facial reactions to avatar emotional faces by nonconscious competition priming. *Psychophysiology, 46*, 328–335. https://doi.org/10.1111/j.1469-8986.2008.00771.x

Wood, A., Rychlowska, M., Korb, S., & Niedenthal, P. M. (2016). Fashioning the face: Sensorimotor simulation contributes to facial expression recognition. *Trends in Cognitive Sciences, 20*, 227–240. https://doi.org/10.1016/j.tics.2015.12.010

Yabar, Y., & Hess, U. (2007). Display of empathy and perception of out-group members. *New Zealand Journal of Psychology, 36*, 42–50.

Chapter 4
Common Coding of Speech Imitation

Patti Adank and Hannah Wilt

Background

Speech perception and speech production have traditionally been viewed as separate processes that operate largely independently from each other. For instance, in the Wernicke-Lichtheim-Geschwind model (Tremblay & Dick, 2016), listening to speech and producing speech are localized in different areas of the brain. When listening to speech, sound waves ascend through the auditory system to the primary auditory cortex (Heschl's Gyrus), before words and sentences being processed in posterior temporal areas including posterior superior temporal gyrus (STG, "Wernicke's area"). When speaking, semantic information was thought to be sent from posterior STG through the arcuate fasciculus to "Broca's area" (the pars opercularis and pars triangularis of the Inferior Frontal Gyrus, IFG). From IFG, instructions for the speech to be produced are sent through to premotor and motor cortex. This traditional model has fallen out of fashion for a variety of reasons, one of which is the lack of appreciation of the close relationship between mechanisms to produce and perceive speech.

Most current speech scientists regard speech perception and production to be tightly linked (Fadiga et al., 2002; Watkins & Paus, 2004). It is uncontroversial to presume that speech production links closely to, and even relies crucially on, speech perception (Hickok & Poeppel, 2007; Rauschecker & Scott, 2009; Tourville & Guenther, 2011). A clear example of the reliance of speech production on speech perception is provided by auditory feedback paradigms. In an auditory feedback paradigm (Guenther et al., 2004), a speaker's speech output is altered in real time; e.g., the fundamental frequency is lowered. In response, the speaker will quickly compensate by changing their fundamental frequency of their voice to counteract

P. Adank (✉) · H. Wilt
Department of Speech, Hearing & Phonetic Sciences, University College London, London, UK
e-mail: p.adank@ucl.ac.uk; hannah.wilt.15@ucl.ac.uk

O. Genschow, E. Cracco (eds.), *Automatic Imitation*,
https://doi.org/10.1007/978-3-031-62634-0_4

the perceived change to their voice. The converse relationship, namely that speech perception is closely linked to and even relies crucially on speech production, is less accepted and the causal role of speech production is still being debated, despite substantial evidence demonstrating this relationship. For instance, Meister et al. (2007) used a brain stimulation method (transcranial magnetic stimulation, TMS), to demonstrate the reliance of speech perception on production. TMS is a neuro-stimulation method that can be used to examine causal links between task performance and the targeted brain area. It does so by temporarily disrupting processing in the brain area under study (Devlin & Watkins, 2006). Meister et al. presented participants with spoken syllables in background noise before and after applying 1-Hz TMS (a stimulation protocol associated with inhibition of task performance, Devlin & Watkins, 2006) to the left ventral premotor cortex, a brain area associated with speech production. They report poorer syllable perception performance after TMS compared to pre-TMS, thus showing a causal link between speech perception and a speech production brain area. Others have reported similar effects on speech perception after targeting other areas in the speech motor system (Möttönen & Watkins, 2009; Nuttall et al., 2016, 2017; Smalle et al., 2014; Watkins & Paus, 2004). Therefore, it seems highly implausible that speech perception, especially speech perception in challenging listening conditions such as background noise, relies entirely on auditory processing (Pulvermüller & Fadiga, 2010; Skipper et al., 2017; Stokes et al., 2019).

Behaviorally, the link between speech perception and production can be evaluated using a paradigm originally developed in cognitive psychology, the stimulus-response compatibility (SRC) paradigm (Brass et al., 2000), which is thought to measure covert, or *automatic*, imitation (Heyes, 2011). In a typical SRC task (for a review, see Chap. 2; this volume), participants are instructed to perform a manual action in response to a prompt (e.g., lift index finger when a written "1" appears, lift a middle finger when "2" appears). The prompt is presented superimposed on a distractor: an image or video of a hand lifting the index or middle finger. When the prompt is presented superimposed on a compatible distractor ("1" with a video of a lifting index finger), participants are faster to execute the prompted action than when the prompt is presented together with an incompatible distractor ("1" with a video of a lifting middle finger). It is assumed that action observation leads to a covert imitative response; i.e., it engages or primes motor patterns for performing the prompted action, thus reducing response times (RTs). Incompatible distractors are thought to result in competition between the motor patterns activated by observing the distractor and those required to produce the prompted response, leading to slower RTs. A larger *automatic imitation effect* (i.e., a larger RT difference between incompatible and compatible prompt-distractor stimulus pairs) indicates that motor mechanisms were more activated during observation of the distractor, signifying more imitation.

While most studies investigating the relationship between action perception and action production using the SRC task employed manual stimuli and manual responses (Cracco et al., 2018), a small but growing set of studies investigated the link between perception and production of speech using the SRC task. In a speech SRC paradigm (Table 4.1), a participant produces a speech response (e.g., "ba")

Table 4.1 Overview of speech SRC studies

Authors	Year	Study	N	Prompt	Distractors	Compatibility effect
Kerzel and Bekkering	2000	1	8	Written "Ba" and "Da"	Silent video recordings of a male speaker saying ba or da	35 ms
		2	8	Written "##" and "&&"	Silent video recordings of a male speaker saying ba or da	42 ms
		3	8	Written "Ba" and "Da"	Silent video recordings of a male speaker saying ba or da (with negative SOAs of 1000 ms)	17 ms
		4	8	Written "Ba" and "Da"	Silent video recordings of the male speaker saying ba or da (with white lines on lips, control for spatial effects)	Not significant
Galantucci et al.	2009	1	24	Written "##" and "&&"	Audio-only stimuli of the female speaker saying ba, da, pa, ta, ma, na (voiced, unvoiced, nasal)	Voiced: 10 ms Unvoiced: 10 ms Nasal: ns
		2	42	Written "##" and "&&"	Audio-only stimuli of male speaker saying ba, da, and ga (baseline), vocal and manual task, no distractor	28 ms (vocal task)
		3	24	Written "##" (same response per trial)	Audio-only stimuli of male speaker saying ba, da, and ga (baseline), vocal and manual task, no distractor	4 ms (vocal task)

(continued)

Table 4.1 (continued)

Authors	Year	Study	N	Prompt	Distractors	Compatibility effect
Jarick and Jones	2009	1	42	Written "BA" and "GA"	Video-only, audiovisual, or audio-only recording of male speaker saying aba or aga, hand, or vocal responses	~25–30 ms (vocal task, estimated from) ns (manual task)
Roon and Gafos	2015	1	38	Written "==" and "&&" (for ta, da, ka, or ga)	Audio-only stimuli of the female speaker saying pa, and ba, tone, or no distractor	Not significant
		2	35		Audio-only stimuli of the female speaker saying pa, ba, ga, tone, or no distractor	15 ms (individual articulator effects not significant)
Klein et al.	2015	1	40	## and ** for /ta/ or /ka/	Audio-only female speaker saying /ta/ and /ka/ stimuli, subsequently manipulated subphonemic feature (voice onset time differences from 45 to 120 ms in 15 ms steps)	Overall compatibility effect of 7 ms, no compatibility effects given of modulation of VOT
Adank et al.	2018	1	66 (3 * 22)	Written "Hood" and "Heed"	Video-only, audiovisual, or audio-only recording of the female speaker saying hood or heed	13 ms (no modality-specific differences)
		2	24	Written "Hood" and "Heed"	Video-only, audiovisual, or audio-only recording of the female speaker saying hood or heed	7 ms (no modality-specific differences)

(continued)

Table 4.1 (continued)

Authors	Year	Study	N	Prompt	Distractors	Compatibility effect
Virhia et al.	2019	1	40	Written "OO," "EE," "HAPPY," or "ANGRY"	Video-only recordings of the female speaker producing emotional (happy or angry) or neutral AA or OO	Larger compatibility effect when producing an emotional a neutral prompt (42 ms vs. 30 ms)
Wu et al.	2019	1	62 (2 * 31)	Written "##" and "&&"	Video-only recording of the female speaker saying ba or da, between-group design with mirror and counter-mirror training	Compatible group increased the effect from 42 ms to 61 ms after training.
Ghaffarvand Mokari et al.	2020	1	38	Written "**" and "##" (for /e/ and /u/)	Audio-only recordings of the female speaker producing /e/, /i/, /o/, /u/ extracted from /dVk/ context	Compatibility effects of 7 ms for phonemic incompatibility, parametric modulation of compatibility effects per increase in phonological feature between distractor and prompt (increase of 3 ms per phonological feature), for /u/ responses only
Ghaffarvand Mokari et al.	2021	1	24	Written "**" and "##" (for /dek/ and /duk/)	Audio-only recordings of the female speaker producing /e/, /i/, /o/, /u/ in /dVk/ context	Compatibility effects of 7 ms for phonemic incompatibility, parametric modulation of compatibility effects per increase in phonetic feature (3 ms), parametric modulation of 1 ms per ERB of acoustics distance between prompt and distractor

(continued)

Table 4.1 (continued)

Authors	Year	Study	N	Prompt	Distractors	Compatibility effect
Wilt et al.	2023	1 (online)	32	Written "£" and "&"	Audio-only stimuli of male speaker and synthetic (computer-generated) saying ba, da	Comparable compatibility effects of 15 ms for the human stimuli and 11 ms for the synthetic stimuli
Wilt et al.	2024	1	50	Written "&", "£", "%", "#"	Videos with audio of the female speaker saying /ba/, /la/, /ʙɑ/ /ʒɑ/	49 ms
		2 (online)	??	Written "&," "£", "%," "#"	Videos with audio of the female speaker saying /ba/, /la/, /ʙɑ/ /ʒɑ/	55 ms

following a written or auditory prompt (e.g., ba) while ignoring a distractor (e.g., a video of someone saying "da") (Kerzel & Bekkering, 2000). The results from speech SRC studies are similar to those from manual SRC studies; i.e., RTs for compatible prompt-distractor stimulus pairs are faster than RTs for incompatible pairs, thus showing automatic imitation. As can be seen in Table 4.1, speech SRC studies have addressed how a variety of factors affected the automatic imitation effect, including mode of presentation of the distractor (Adank et al., 2018; Jarick & Jones, 2009), emotional valence (Virhia et al., 2019), effect of sensorimotor training (Wu et al., 2019), speech feature overlap (Galantucci et al., 2009; Ghaffarvand Mokari et al., 2020, 2021), and biological status of the distractor (Wilt et al., 2023). However, it is unclear to which extent the effects in Table 4.1 can be explained by current theories for speech processing.

Current speech, language, and dialogue processing models assume an interdependence between speech production and speech perception (Pickering & Garrod, 2013; Schwartz et al., 2012). These models have incorporated a formalized control mechanism in the form of online predictive forward and/or inverse processing mechanisms that are reliant on close collaboration between speech perception and production systems. In Pickering and Garrod's integrated theory of language production and comprehension ("integrated theory" for short), the connection between speech perception and production is governed by forward models (Kawato, 1999; Wolpert, 1997). A forward model predicts the likely outcomes of motor commands. When planning to execute a speech action, a set of motor (articulatory) commands is formulated. At the same time as the motor command, two control signals are generated. First, a perceptual signal processes the proprioceptive (and/or visual/auditory) experience in the speech production system of the action being executed. This perceptual signal is used as sensory, or re-afferent, feedback of the action. Second, an efference copy is created, which is an internally generated signal consisting of the motor command generated by the motor system. This efference copy causes the forward model to generate a set of predictions regarding the outcome of the articulatory motor command, which in turn leads the forward model to construct a predicted percept of the experience of producing the planned utterance. Importantly, this efference copy is processed faster than the articulatory motor command. The perceptual feedback signal and the predicted percept are compared in real time during action execution. Whenever a discrepancy is detected, an error signal is sent to the action planning mechanism, so it can update the motor plans.

When perceiving speech, a similar mechanism is presumed; except in this case, a forward model generates a set of predictions regarding the upcoming sensory signal. When the speaker is familiar or similar to the listener, and/or listening conditions are favorable, listeners are thought to use a process of covert imitation to generate a forward perceptual model that is built upon the listener's simulations of the speech utterance (the simulation route). Garrod and Pickering propose that the simulation route facilitates joint action, especially in dialogue. Through the use of action simulation, joint action can be successful because conversation partners can effectively integrate and align their own action execution with their perception of their conversation partner's action. The perceptual system compares the forward perceptual model with the perceived speech signal in real time. When the speech or speaker is dissimilar, unfamiliar, or ambiguous (e.g., when noise is present), the system will use the association route, in which incoming speech patterns are analyzed predominantly using auditory mechanisms. In sum, the integrated theory therefore predicts that perception relies more on production processes when the speech is largely similar to past experience, familiar, or easy to process and that listening to dissimilar, unfamiliar, or harder-to-process speech signals relies more on perceptual processing systems.

The integrated theory can account for automatic imitation effects as measured using a standard speech SRC task. When observing an audio-only, video-only, or audiovisual distractor stimulus, the integrated theory predicts that the simulation route, and therefore, speech production substrates will be engaged, provided the stimulus is familiar and produced clearly. Indeed, results from speech SRC studies using familiar stimulus materials have shown an automatic imitation effect as predicted by the integrated theory (Adank et al., 2018; Galantucci et al., 2009; Jarick & Jones, 2009; Kerzel & Bekkering, 2000; Klein et al., 2015; Wu et al., 2019). However, if the distractor is less similar/familiar to the listener, for instance, when the distractor stimulus syllable is computer-generated as in (Wilt et al., 2023), the integrated theory predicts less engagement of motor substrates, as the association route will be used, which does not engage production mechanisms, and thus predicts a smaller automatic imitation effect. This prediction was not borne out, as Wilt et al. report nonsignificantly different automatic imitation effects for their human-produced and computer-generated speech stimuli. Moreover, the integrated theory does not make specific predictions regarding the engagement of speech production mechanisms for the emotional valence of the speech stimuli (Virhia et al., 2019) or more sophisticated phenomena, such as articulatory feature-specific effects (Ghaffarvand Mokari et al., 2020, 2021; Roon & Gafos, 2015).

In summary, it is unclear how speech perception and production processes are linked, how these connections are forged and maintained, and whether and how the potential interdependence of speech perception and production processing varies depending on the interactive situation. In this chapter, we will evaluate the results of speech SRC studies within a framework developed in cognitive psychology, namely the theory of event coding (Hommel, 2019; Hommel et al., 2001). TEC is a framework for action planning and action perception based on the ideomotor principle and common coding principles of action and perception. TEC offers a flexible framework for evaluating the link between action perception and action production but has to date not been applied to speech processing. Indeed, Pickering and Garrod (2013) propose that TEC might offer a mechanism through which speech and language perception and speech and language production link together. Nevertheless, the integrated theory has thus far not systematically exploited TEC's potential explanatory power, with respect to subphonemic effects, connections, emotional valence effects, or processing unfamiliar and/or non-native stimuli. In this chapter, we will review and evaluate the results of speech SRC studies within TEC, to establish whether this framework for action planning and action perception based on the ideomotor principle and common coding principles of action and perception can be extended to speech processing.

The Theory of Event Coding

The theory of event coding (TEC) was first formalized in 2001 as a response to cognitive frameworks seeking to study action perception and production independently (Hommel, 2019; Hommel et al., 2001). It was updated in 2019 with several conceptual changes, although its basic principles remained the same. As described in Hommel (2019), TEC currently consists of three general and five specific assumptions. Only assumptions immediately relevant for speech processing are discussed in this review, for in-depth discussion of TEC and its assumptions; see Hommel (2019) and Hommel et al. (2001).

TEC assumes (1) that action and perception share a *common code* and action and perception are represented by the same feature codes and (2) that these codes refer to the *distal* (i.e., environmental) features of the represented event. Furthermore, five specific assumptions are as follows: (i) Event features are *multimodal* in nature, (ii) there is a distinction between the *activation and integration* of feature codes, (iii) the coding of events is modulated by *intentional/attentional* factors, (iv) *stimulus and response codes share a common code* and differ only with respect to the role they play in a task, and (v) *feature codes are grounded in sensorimotor experience*. Below we outline how these concepts are implemented in TEC.

TEC's definition of "an event" is flexible and can be redefined to range from producing an individual speech sound to an entire narrative. Specifically, an event is defined to encompass at minimum a single goal-directed action, such as pushing a button in response to a prompt or producing a spoken syllable, but it has been presumed that it can also encompass a series of more complicated actions (Hommel, 2019; Hommel et al., 2001). However, for the purposes of this review and its focus on speech, we define *an event* as a single perceived and/or spoken syllable (e.g., "ba" or "heed"). TEC's assumptions relevant to speech processing are discussed in detail below.

TEC: General Assumptions

Assumption 1 holds that action and perception share a *common code* and are grounded in the ideomotor principle (Prinz, 1997). This principle states that actions are defined in terms of their sensory consequences. Executing an action is thought to trigger an adaptive process that results in the integration of motor patterns with the sensory, re-afferent, information that the action generates, such as the proprioceptive experience of moving one's hand, or auditory effects related to speaking. The re-afferent information is thus directly linked to the actual motor plans and can be engaged to activate or prime these patterns. Therefore, action (motor patterns) and perception (re-afferent sensory information) can facilitate or inhibit each other's function because they overlap in their representations. TEC's first general assumption can, as is the case for the integrated theory, account for all basic speech SRC effects, including all studies in Table 4.1. Table 4.1 shows automatic imitation effects displaying faster responses for compatible prompt-distractor pairs ranging between 4 ms (Galantucci et al., 2009) and 61 ms (Wu et al., 2019).

TEC's assumption 2 predicts that event codes comprise feature codes that reflect aspects of the perceived and planned event, such as perceiving and planning to produce a speech sound. It is this aspect of TEC explaining sophisticated speech perception and action links that cannot be explained by the integrated theory. In contrast to most manual actions (with the exception of sign language signs), speech sounds are coded phonetically in terms of the articulatory movements involved in their production, as formalized in the International Phonetic Alphabet (IPA, 1999).

TEC proposes an integrating mechanism that combines all features in an event code, linked through general feature binding processes (Treisman, 1996). TEC presumes that event codes consist of feature codes encoding the characteristics of the perceived or planned event. Hommel (2001) suggests that perceiving a cherry results in the activation of feature codes that are linked to the characteristics RED, ROUND, and SMALL, among others. Moreover, TEC presumes that activating any feature code will prime all events it shares features with. Thus, observing the cherry will facilitate perceiving other RED, ROUND, and SMALL objects or performing actions in which objects are manipulated possessing these features. Therefore, selecting the features of a to-be-executed action facilitates the perception and the production of other events, when these events share features. Feature integration or feature binding is proposed as the mechanism that creates event codes (Treisman, 1996). Feature binding allows sets of features to be combined into isolated perceived or planned events. This mechanism allows the observer to allocate appropriate features to their linked events. For instance, if a cherry is observed together with an apple, certain features will be shared across both perceptual events. An apple is also ROUND, but not RED and not necessarily as SMALL. Observing the apple should instead lead to activation of the feature codes GREEN, ROUND, and BIG (relatively speaking). Observing both objects together would therefore mean that five feature codes would be activated (RED, GREEN, ROUND, BIG, and SMALL). Feature binding is the coupling or synchronization mechanism through which RED, ROUND, and SMALL are attributed to the cherry and GREEN, ROUND, and BIG to the apple.

TEC presumes that feature activation is achieved before feature integration. This assumption has implications for predicting effects a perceived or planned event has on the perception or planning of other events. Activated—but not yet bound—feature codes will prime (or facilitate) all representations that include this specific feature code in a cross-modal way. Thus, seeing something red will also facilitate saying "red." Once the feature code is bound into a more integral event code, this feature code will interfere with perception or planning of other feature-overlapping events (Stoet & Hommel, 1999). Hommel (2001) explains this interference as follows. First, observing an object might result in binding two feature codes (RED and ROUND). Processing of another object will be facilitated if it has the same feature combination (RED and ROUND) or a different feature combination (GREEN and SQUARE), but predicts that it is difficult to process an object with partially overlapping features (ROUND and GREEN). Hommel states that feature integration leads to associations between feature codes and activating one feature of the emerging event code will spread activation to the other elements. This process develops in a facilitating manner when there is complete overlap (or no overlap), but interferes when there is only partial overlap. Re-applying an event code or forming two unrelated ones is not problematic but forming two overlapping codes is and results in interference. Hommel predicts a similar mechanism for action planning: If distinctive features of two responses R1 (e.g., "move LEFT and FORWARD") and R2 ("move LEFT and BACK") overlap, execution of R2 should be inhibited as the critical feature code (LEFT) is already associated to R1 and less available for R2, resulting in response inhibition for R2.

Several studies already demonstrated that these principles of features overlap during verbal planning using speeded syllable production experiments (Meyer & Gordon, 1985; Yaniv et al., 1990). In both studies, participants were instructed to plan a speed verbal production of one of two syllables (e.g., "ut"). They were then instructed to either produce the prepared syllable or to utter the other syllable (e.g., "up"). The results were in accordance with TEC's predictions, as pairs that showed post-vocalic consonants that overlapped in the voicing feature (e.g., "up" and "ut," which both have a voiceless final consonant) produced longer re-planning times than parings that showed no overlap (e.g., "up" and "ud" or "ut" and "ub").

Under these assumptions, the results from experiments on automatic imitation of speech using stimulus materials including consonantal distinctions (e.g., ba, da, ga syllables, e.g., Kerzel & Bekkering, 2000) can be explained as follows. Observing a spoken /b/ will result in the activation of those feature codes that represent the

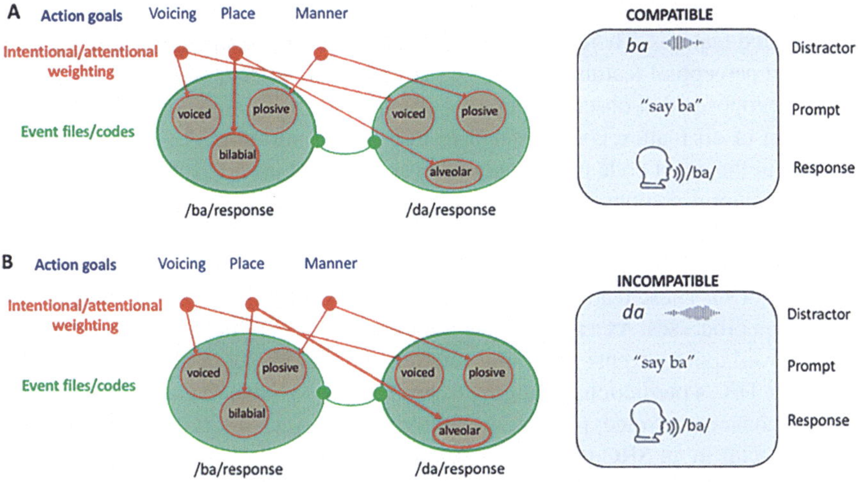

Fig. 4.1 Automatic imitation of speech per the predictions of TEC. Event files (left) for compatible (top) and incompatible (bottom) speech SRC trials (right). (**a**) In the compatible trial, participants are instructed to produce the syllable "ba" following a prompt, and they are also presented with a spoken (audio-only, audiovisual, or video-only) distractor of the same or a different syllable. When the prompt and distracter are the same (A), it is presumed that the action goals (in blue) consist of producing a consonantal voiced, bilabial, plosive sound (/b/) followed by a vowel /a/ (which is the same for both responses and not shown here). In TEC, attentional/intentional weighting refers to the relative contribution of each feature code to the representation of an event. Feature codes on dimension relevant to the task will have a stronger impact on the task than feature codes for irrelevant dimensions. The attentional/intentional weighting (in red) is strongest (indicated by a thicker red line) for features that allow this event file to contrast with others in the same response set, indicated by thicker lines for place. Overall facilitation of the prompted response is indicated by the thickness of the green lines surrounding the three event files, with thicker lines representing relative facilitation and thinner lines representing relative inhibition. The event file contains representations of both the planned response and the perceptual event (the distractor). The event file associated with the /ba/ response is facilitated, as indicated by the thick green line surrounding the event file. The event file for the /da/ response is neither facilitated nor inhibited. (**b**) shows event files for an incompatible distractor /da/ for the response /ba/. Here, the event file for the /da/ response is facilitated relative to the /ba/ response due to the increased *intentional*/attentional weighting of the alveolar feature because of the alveolar distractor, resulting effectively in interference and slower production of the response

(phonetic) attributes of this phoneme (symbols between forward slashes "/ /" indicate a broad phonetic transcription per IPA). The consonant /b/ is followed by the vowel /a/ for all consonant studies in Table 4.1. Following IPA, consonants are classified depending on their voicing, place of articulation, and manner of articulation. For example, /b/ is a voiced consonantal, bilabial, plosive sound. These three features are identical for perception and production of the /b/ phoneme and, per TEC's assumptions, bundled into the same event code (Fig. 4.1). Conversely, planning to produce the sound /d/ activates feature codes that represent the attributes for a voiced consonantal, alveolar, or plosive sound. Thus, where /b/ is produced by moving both lips together (bilabial), /d/ is produced by moving the tongue toward the alveolar ridge behind the teeth. Activating any feature in an event code will prime other shared features. Therefore, planning to produce the sound /d/ will also activate its shared perceptual features for /d/ (i.e., consonantal, voiced, and plosive).

TEC proposes that observation of the stimulus /b/ will first result in the parallel activation of all feature codes related to that speech stimulus. Also, if one of the features in the event code has already been activated or used to form another event code, behavioral responses related to this activated event code are also facilitated per TEC's predictions as outlined above. Planning to produce the sound /b/ will invoke a similar process. Second, all feature codes are integrated into a new event code (Fig. 4.1). These feature codes are then no longer available for other coding or integration processes. As a result, "Integration facilitation of processes operating on feature-overlapping events turns into interference" (Hommel et al., 2001. p. 883). Thus, per TEC's predictions, planning to produce the syllable /ba/ activates the features of consonant, voice, plosive, and bilabial. However, observing a syllable /da/ as a distracter in an SRC task, the features consonant, voice, plosive, and alveolar are activated. As the features for /da/ partially overlap with those of /ba/, this combination of promoted syllable and distracter syllable leads to interference and slower response times.

As illustrated in Fig. 4.1, in a speech SRC task, when prompted to produce the syllable "ba," the event code for the /ba/response will activate the features relevant for producing the initial voiced, bilabial, plosive consonant. A compatible distractor (/ba/) will further strengthen the activation of the event code for /ba/. This strengthening will result behaviorally in facilitated response times for compatible ba-ba prompt-distractor pairs. In contrast, when instructed to produce the syllable "ba" in the presence of an incompatible distractor "da," the response feature set for "da" (voiced, alveolar, plosive) will present interference as the features for /ba/ (voiced, bilabial, plosive) partially overlap with those for /da/ (voiced, alveolar, plosive). This interference will result in slower response times for incompatible pairs, as the action production system will have to correct for the erroneous activation of a motor pattern involving the tongue (vs. the lips) for producing "da."

Ghaffarvand-Mokari et al. (2020, 2021) exploited IPA's feature-based classification of vowels to establish if and how automatic imitation effects for speech are modulated by phonetic featural overlap between the stimulus and response in two studies. In IPA, vowels are classified in terms of the position of the jaw, tongue, and lips during production. These features tend to be explained for the cardinal vowels, i.e., the vowels at the extreme articulatory configurations in relation to each other, in particular /i/, /u/, /a/. /i/ is a produced with an almost closed jaw and therefore with a raised tongue position, with the tongue tip position close to the teeth (fronted tongue position) and unrounded lips. /u/ is produced with an almost closed jaw position, with the tongue pulled back and with rounded lips. /a/ is produced with the jaw more open and thus a lower tongue position, with lips neither rounded nor rounded and with the tongue in a neutral position in the mouth. In IPA terminology, /i/ is described as a close, front, unrounded vowel, /u/ as a close, back, rounded vowel, and /a/ as an open front, unrounded vowel. Two studies have exploited the featural composition of vowels to evaluate the sensitivity of the speech processing system to these subphonemic features (Ghaffarvand Mokari et al., 2020, 2021).

In Ghaffarvand-Mokari et al. (2020), native German participants were presented with audio-only distractors consisting of an isolated vowel /e/ (a close-mid unrounded front vowel), /i/, /o/ (a close-mid back rounded vowel), or /u/. All isolated vowels were extracted from a /dVk/ consonantal context. Participants were instructed to either produce "ee" (/e/) or "uu" ("ee" and "uu" are produced as /e/ and /u/ in German) following a written prompt. Ghaffarvand-Mokari et al. report a general automatic imitation effect of 7 ms when contrasting incompatible with compatible distractors. Moreover, they report modulation of the size of the automatic imitation effect depending on the overlap between the distractor and response in terms of phonetic features. When the distractor and response overlapped in all features (e.g., when an /u/ response was paired with an /u/ distractor), automatic imitation effects were the largest. Automatic imitation effects for /u/-/i/ were the smallest, as these two vowels share the least phonetic features. Further analysis of the results showed a subtle parametric modulation of automatic imitation effects per increase in phonological feature between distractor and prompt, i.e., an increase of 3 ms per phonetic/phonological features, for /u/ responses only.

Ghaffarvand Mokari et al. (2021) conducted a follow-up study and further explored the effects of feature overlap between vowel stimuli and responses in terms of phonetic features. Here, they also explored the effects of acoustic overlap. They used the same audio-only recordings of /e/, /i/, /o/, /u/ in /dVk/ context as Ghaffarvand Mokari et al. (2020), except in this experiment they were presented in their original /dVk/ context. Participants again produced /e/ or /u/ responses. Results for the overall automatic imitation effect replicated the previous study (7 ms) and showed parametric modulation per increase in phonetic feature (3 ms), for both /e/ and /u/ responses. In addition, the study reported small but significant effects of acoustic distance showing parametric modulation of 1 ms per ERB (Equivalent Rectangular Bandwidth, Moore & Glasberg, 1983) of acoustics distance between response and distractor. The results from both Ghaffarvand Mokari et al. (2020) and Ghaffarvand Mokari et al. (2021) thus show the effects of stimulus-driven modulation in line with TEC's predictions. When there is less featural overlap between response and distractor, there will be less interference due to the co-activation of response codes related to the distractor, resulting in smaller automatic imitation effects. TEC therefore can explain sophisticated subphonemic effect that cannot be accounted for by the integrated theory.

TEC: Specific Assumptions

Event Features Are Multimodal

TEC's first specific assumption that event features are multimodal in nature stems from its general assumption that action and perception features are distally coded. Distal coding of events implies that action perception and generation are modality general, as the coding mechanism is not restricted by physical or physiological characteristics (e.g., the resolution of the auditory system). Automatic imitation effects for speech have predominantly been reported for video-only or audio-only distractor stimuli (Table 4.1). Overall, it appears that automatic imitation effects for video-only distractors are overall larger than those measured for audio-only distractors. However, two of the studies listed in Table 4.1 compared whether automatic imitation effects are modulated by the modality of the distractor directly. Jarick and Jones (2009) presented participants with video-only, audio-only, and audiovisual distractors that consisted of spoken consonant-vowel (CV) syllable in which the consonant varied (/b/ or /g/) and the vowel remained stable (/a/), resulting in two distractor stimuli (BA and GA) that differed in the place of articulation and thus their primary articulator (lips for BA, tongue for GA). Participants were presented with the stimuli in a within-subject design with three blocks (video-only, audio-only, and audiovisual distractors). They once completed the experiment with vocal responses and once with manual responses for the same stimuli. The results showed automatic imitation effects for the vocal responses only, thus demonstrating that the automatic imitation effect is effector-specific. Second, similar effects were found for all three modalities.

In both experiments in Adank et al. (2018), distractor stimuli consisted of spoken consonant-vowel-consonant (CVC) syllables in which the vowel varied (/e/ or /u/) and the consonants remained the same (/h/ and /d/), resulting in two written distractor stimuli (HEED and HOOD) that differed mostly in vowel (lip) rounding (/e/ is unrounded, /u/ is rounded). In Experiment 1, participants were tested in a between-subject design split by modality condition (video-only, audio-only, and audiovisual distractors), while participants in experiment 2 completed all conditions in a within-subject design. The results followed a similar pattern as in Jarick and Jones: Automatic imitation effects were reported (albeit smaller than in Jarick and Jones), but these were not modulated by modality. The results from both these studies confirm TEC's specific assumption that event features are multimodal in nature as no modality-specific differences were reported for either study.

Intentional/Attentional Processing Modulates Event Coding

TEC's event coding is modulated by attentional and/or intentional processing. It is predicted that features are given differential weighting in perception and production depending on their relevance to the task. In action perception, feature weighting is regarded as an attentional process, while in action production it can be seen as an intentional process. Due to its inclusion of feature weighting, TEC can explain a wide range of phenomena, including effects of top-down features such as task instructions. However, thus far only the results from a single study unequivocally support this prediction (Longo et al., 2008).

Longo et al. tested TEC's assumption in a manual SRC study in which participants pressed a key with either their index or middle finger following a written prompt. The distractor stimuli were either animations of possible or impossible actions. In the possible distractor stimuli, a hand was shown without any modifications, executing the index or middle finger movement. The impossible actions showed a modified hand in which the finger bent inwards, thus displaying an impossible movement. In Experiment 1, participants were presented with both types of stimuli. The results showed automatic imitation effects for both possible and impossible stimuli of 7 ms. In experiment 2, participants were informed that the impossible stimuli were artificially created and could not be performed, thus focusing participants' attention on the feasibility of the actions. The results for experiment 2 showed a difference from those of experiment 1, as no automatic imitation effect was found for the impossible stimuli, while an automatic imitation effect of 9 ms was reported for the possible stimuli. These results suggest that focusing participants' attention on stimulus-specific features affects the extent to which stimulus-related event codes interfere with responses.

In contrast, other manual SRC studies did not support TEC's prediction that top-down manipulations affect the saliency of specific features (Cracco et al., 2018; Press et al., 2005, 2006). Press et al. (2005) presented participants with stimuli representing an opening or closing hand. The stimuli were produced by a human or a robot (and therefore no top-down or belief manipulation was included) or were naturalistic or schematic, in a factorial design. RTs were measured using electromyography to the participants' right first dorsal interosseus muscle, while participants made a prespecified response per stimulus block by either opening or closing their hand, in two sessions spaced a day apart. Press et al. found larger automatic imitation effects for the human stimuli (33 ms) versus robotic stimuli (6 ms). The authors found no effect of the schematic versus naturalistic manipulation of the stimuli. Press concludes that lower automatic imitation effects for the robotic stimuli show that human movement stimuli may be more effective visuomotor primes than robotic movement stimuli.

Press et al. (2006) manipulated stimuli depicting a human hand by adding a metal wire wrist and informed participants that these stimuli were produced by a robot. Participants in Experiment 1 produced a prespecified response (hand opening or closing) for compatible and incompatible distractors, while RTs were measured as in Press et al. (2005). They report no significant difference between SRC effects for the human (16 ms) and robotic stimuli (26 ms). In Experiment 2, participants were tested in a between-group design aiming to disentangle beliefs about the stimuli from stimulus animacy. Participants were shown either a genuine human or robotic hand (blue animated silhouettes) producing the actions; participants presented with the genuinely human stimulus were told that the hand was either human or robotic in the two sessions of testing. Experiment 2 removed the confound between the belief manipulation (informing participants that the stimuli with the added wrist were robotic) and a stimulus-driven (or bottom-up manipulation) manipulation (changing the stimuli by adding a wrist). In experiment 2, the belief manipulation was genuine and not implemented by changing the visual stimulus materials, while the bottom-up manipulation (stylization and the blue color) was applied to both types of stimuli. Participants who were presented with the genuinely robotic stimulus were told that the movement was generated by either human or robotic movement. The participants who were shown the genuine human stimuli displayed 15 ms automatic imitation effects for the stimuli they were told were human and 14 ms for the stimuli they were told were robotic. The group of participants who were shown the genuine robotic stimuli showed automatic imitation effects of 5 ms for the stimuli they were told were human and the same for the stimuli they were told were robotic. Neither experiment showed evidence that beliefs (or top-down effects) affect the size of the automatic imitation effect, but Experiment 2 demonstrated that stimulus properties (bottom-up effects) can modulate automatic imitation effects, with greater effects for stimuli that were genuinely robotic (and that might have been less effective distractor stimuli than the human stimuli). In their meta-analysis, Cracco et al. (2018) reported no effect of top-down manipulations on automatic imitation effects for manual actions. However, Cracco et al. mentioned also that the number of studies investigating top-down manipulations is overall too low to reach definite conclusions and that it may be a possibility that automatic imitation effects do not differ when the nonhuman stimuli are too human-like.

We conducted a study to establish if the effects reported by Longo et al. or those by Press et al. replicate speech stimuli. Wilt et al. (2023) aimed to establish how automatic imitation effects for vocal actions are affected by the biological status of these actions. We conducted an online speech SRC task in which we presented participants with speech stimuli ("ba" and "da") produced by a male human speaker and computer-generated using a speech synthesizer. We informed participants which stimuli were human-produced and which were computer-generated. The results showed an automatic imitation effect for both types of stimuli, and that this effect was statistically identical for the human (15 ms) and computer-generated (11 ms) stimuli. Therefore, while the results showed a trend toward a smaller automatic imitation effect for the computer-generated stimuli, including the interaction between automatic imitation and biological status in the statistical model did not improve model fit. This pattern in the results was reported despite a small, but significant, difference in intelligibility of the human (99%) and computer-generated stimuli (97%). Therefore, the results from Wilt et al. did not replicate the effects reported in Press et al., where non-biological stimuli evoked smaller automatic imitation effects, nor did they replicate Longo et al.'s results with respect to their top-down belief manipulation. Instead, speech stimuli seem to evoke automatic imitation effects regardless of their biological status and stimulus characteristics.

A second study from our group showed effects that appeared to partially support TEC's predictions regarding attentional weighting (Virhia et al., 2019), but only when attention was directed toward the production of the prompt. Virhia et al. explored the independent effects of the emotional valence of the distractor and the observer's emotional state on speech production. Participants completed an SRC paradigm for visual-only speech stimuli, consisting of emotional (happy or angry) or neutral AA (/a/ or OO (/o/) isolated vowels. Participants completed a series of eight SRC tasks in total (see Fig. 4.1 in Virhia et al. for more details), in which they produced the /a/ or /o/ in a neutral tone of voice or in a happy or angry tone of voice. They did so in the presence of video-only distractor stimuli either displaying a female speaker producing a neutral /a/ or /o/ or a happy or angry version of both sounds. Results from the eight tasks were combined into a 2x2 factorial analysis that aimed to untangle the effects of the emotional valence of the response from the emotional valence of the distractor stimuli. Results showed that automatic imitation effects were larger whenever participants produced an emotional response (42 ms) vs. when they produced a neutral response (30 ms). TEC predicts that the emotional valence of the stimulus materials would have to increase automatic imitation effects, as specific feature codes, namely the emotional status of the distractor stimulus, would have had an increased intentional/attentional weighting. However, the emotional valence of the distractor did not modulate automatic imitation effects. TEC's prediction was thus not confirmed for the distractor stimuli. Results instead show that attentional focus on one's own actions modulated the intentional/attentional weighting of the prompt. However, it is unclear how TEC can account for the increase in the automatic imitation effect, as it predicts that attentional focus should increase automatic imitation effects. TEC's prediction is based on manipulations of the distracter and does not consider changes to the execution of the prompt or response.

Wilt et al. (2024) aimed to establish whether automatic imitation effects could be modulated by the familiarity of speech sounds presented in audiovisual distractors. In a within-subjects laboratory-based experiment (experiment 1) and its online replication (experiment 2), participants performed an SRC task with native sounds (/ ba/ and /la) and an SRC task with non-native sounds (voiced bilabial trill /ʙɑ/ and voiced alveolar lateral fricative /ɮɑ/). Results across experiments demonstrated larger automatic imitation effects in the non-native task (64 ms in experiment 1 and 66 ms in experiment 2) than in the native task (36 ms in experiment 1 and 45 ms in experiment 2). As participants consistently perceived and produced either native or non-native sounds, the study was unable to disentangle whether the enhanced automatic imitation effects in the non-native tasks were driven by perceiving or by producing unfamiliar speech actions/sounds. Both options are in line with TEC's predictions/claims. Research on accent intelligibility suggests that non-native speech patterns are less well recognized and processed more slowly than native speech sounds (Adank et al., 2009; Floccia et al., 2009; Van Wijngaarden, 2001). Hence, it is possible that in the non-native task in Wilt et al. (2023), participants attended more closely/strongly to the distractor stimuli than in the native task, thereby enhancing automatic imitation effects. It is also possible that the effort and the attentional focus required to produce novel speech actions modulated the intentional/attentional weighting of the non-native distractors, yet these two possibilities are not mutually exclusive.

Studies conducted thus far seem to converge on the notion that top-down manipulations such as the biological origin of the action do not enhance automatic imitation effects, as predicted by TEC. Instead, top-down manipulations generally do not affect automatic imitation effects. No other SRC studies using speech stimuli have thus far manipulated top-down or attentional factors. However, it seems plausible that attentional weighting may be able to explain effects related to the production of the prompted action, as reported for emotional prompts (Virhia et al., 2019), or prompts with a non-native initial consonant (Wilt et al., 2023).

Feature Codes Are Grounded in Sensorimotor Experience

TEC proposes that feature codes are grounded in sensorimotor experience. This assumption is interpreted as that feature codes are created through associations between sensory and motor events. TEC also suggests that these associations are flexible and can be modified through experience. This assumption thus proposes essentially that the creation of new and maintenance of existing codes relies on domain-general associative learning principles and is closely linked to Pavlovian/operant condition principles (Heyes, 2011). Several manual SRC studies demonstrated that sensorimotor links themselves are indeed flexible and can be selectively modified using targeted training (Bird & Heyes, 2005; Heyes, 2005). We conducted a replication of these studies to establish if speech sounds are similarly flexible (Wu et al., 2019). In Wu et al., participants performed a standard speech SRC task, in which they produced CV syllables following a written prompt articulation (BA or DA) in the presence of a compatible or incompatible video-only distractor. Next, they were split into two groups and received either mirror training ("say /ba/ when the speaker says /ba/" and likewise for /da/) or counter-mirror training ("say /da/ when the speaker silently says /ba/" and vice versa). The next day, they repeated the initial speech SRC task. Automatic imitation effects were enhanced from 42 ms to 61 ms following mirror training, but not significantly reduced following counter-mirror training. These results confirm, in part, the proposal that sensorimotor links are flexible for speech sounds as well. However, the result indicated that sensorimotor training was only able to enhance existing sensorimotor links, but not weaken them. This difference between manual sensorimotor training studies and Wu et al.'s results could be due to the differences between the types of actions used. Manual studies tend to use hand opening and closing, while speech studies use complex linguistic structures. In addition, consonant pairs such as /p/ and /b/ are also categorically perceived (Liberman et al., 1957). Manual movements, such as hand opening and closing, are generally not categorically perceived, unless these movements are signs in a signed language and produced by a native signer (Emmorey et al., 2003). Perhaps actions with a more complex structure are less susceptible to counter-mirror training. This possibility will need to be explored in more detail in future research.

Nevertheless, the results reported in Wilt et al. (2023) discussed TEC's attentional/intentional processing assumption above do not support TEC's prediction that having had more sensorimotor experience with an action will increase the automatic imitation effects associated with that action. Wilt et al. report smaller automatic imitation effects for native prompt-distractors pairs than for non-native pairs. It thus seems to be plausible that attentional/intentional effects might facilitate the event file for the non-native response more compared to relative to sensorimotor experience's facilitation of the native response.

Conclusion

This chapter aimed to establish to which extent TEC's assumptions can explain results for speech SRC studies. The results discussed in this chapter present a mixed picture. With respect to TEC's general assumptions, the literature review showed the following. TEC assumes that perception and production share a common code where both processes are represented by feature codes. The speech SRC studies discussed all confirm this assumption, as all studies in Table 4.1 show a basic automatic imitation effect, ranging between 4 ms (Galantucci et al., 2009) and 62 ms (Wu et al., 2019). TEC's feature-based approach makes it especially suited to studying speech perception-action links. This assumption was explored in detail in Fig. 4.1, and we argued that TEC can explain all feature-based results in Table 4.1. This pattern in our results is despite Hommel et al. (2001) explicitly excluding speech stimuli from the scope of TEC (although this caveat was not present in the 2019 follow-up paper). However, Hommel et al. propose another restriction on the use of feature coding; i.e., TEC makes an exception for highly overlearned actions, thus proposing that its predictions do not apply to overlearned actions, potentially including phonemes in our native language.

Native phonemes can be considered to exist in an already integrated event code and thus do not have to be integrated into a new event code every time they are perceived or produced. If this assumption was valid, TEC's predictions with respect to feature integration and event coding would not apply. However, it appears that native phonemes are treated by the perception and production system as sets of features instead of as integrated events. TEC's proposed mechanism of feature coding was shown to be overall applicable to speech events as defined in this chapter. TEC can effectively explain results for speech SRC studies manipulating subphonemic features between their distractors (Galantucci et al., 2009; Ghaffarvand Mokari et al., 2020, 2021; Roon & Gafos, 2015).

Overall TEC's first specific prediction regarding the multimodal status of the distal stimuli fits with results reported for speech SRC studies comparing automatic imitation effects across audio-only, video-only, and audiovisual distractor modalities (Adank et al., 2018; Jarick & Jones, 2009). The second specific assumption that there is a distinction between activation and integration for feature codes was previously supported for two speech production studies using speech stimuli (Meyer & Gordon, 1985; Yaniv et al., 1990). However, this assumption has not yet been tested using a speech SRC experiment and is not discussed in detail in the present chapter. TEC's third specific assumption predicted that intentional/attentional modulation toward aspects of the distractor stimulus would positively modulate automatic imitation effects. The results from two of our studies did not confirm this assumption, Wilt et al. (2023) found a null effect on the biological status of the distractor stimulus, and Virhia et al. (2019) found a null effect on the emotional valence of the distractor stimulus, yet reported an increase in automatic imitation effects for conditions in which participants were to speak with an emotional tone of voice. The final specific assumption states that feature codes are grounded in sensorimotor experience. This assumption was partially confirmed for speech, as Wu et al. showed that sensorimotor training was able to enhance existing sensorimotor links, but not weaken them. Also, results from Wilt et al. (2023) contradict TEC's assumption that sensorimotor experience enhances automatic imitation effects, as participants showed larger effects for stimuli that had had less experience with (non-native speech sounds). Wilt et al.'s results suggest that attentional/intentional factors might 'overrule' effects on event codes from enhanced sensorimotor experience.

Summary and Outlook

Taken together, the results discussed above imply that, compared to the integrated theory, TEC is largely able to account for more sophisticated effects, including effect of subphonemic and sensorimotor training effects. There are two obvious ways forward. First, Pickering & Garrod's (2013) integrated theory cannot explain effects in Table 4.1 beyond the basic automatic imitation effect, but interestingly, explicitly alluded to TEC as a possible synthesis for how sensory and action features are connected. The integrated theory could be extended with the common coding approach to explain how speech events are treated by the model. Second, TEC could be updated to (more) explicitly incorporate speech events and with a mechanism that accommodated feature codes of the prompted response. For manual actions, response codes are not generally required, as it is not straightforward to focus attention on specific response features, with the exception of response force or delay. Speech stimuli, however, can vary widely in their response features, e.g., by varying the emotional valence, intonation of the response, loudness, or by producing non-native speech sounds. In conclusion, the integrated theory and TEC both represent an improvement on traditional unimodal theories of speech production and offer the potential to provide a comprehensive model for the link between speech perception and production.

Acknowledgments This work was supported by a Project Grant to Patti Adank by the Leverhulme Trust under project number RPG-2018-043, *"Mechanisms governing imitation of speech."*

References

Adank, P., Evans, B. G., Stuart-Smith, J., & Scott, S. K. (2009). Comprehension of familiar and unfamiliar native accents under adverse listening conditions. *Journal of Experimental Psychology Human Perception and Performance, 35*. https://doi.org/10.1037/a0013552

Adank, P., Nuttall, H. E., Bekkering, H., & Maegherman, G. (2018). Effects of stimulus response compatibility on covert imitation of vowels. *Attention, Perception & Psychophysics, 80*, 1290–1299. https://doi.org/10.3758/s13414-018-1501-3

Bird, G., & Heyes, C. (2005). Effector-dependent learning by observation of a finger movement sequence. *Journal of Experimental Psychology: Human Perception and Performance, 31*, 262–275. https://doi.org/10.1037/0096-1523.31.2.262

Brass, M., Wohlsläger, A., Bekkering, H., & Prinz, W. (2000). Compatibility between observed and executed finger movements: Comparing symbolic, spatial and imitative cues. *Brain and Cognition, 44*, 124–143. https://doi.org/10.1006/brcg.2000.1225

Cracco, E., Bardi, L., Desmet, C., Genschow, O., Rigoni, D., De Coster, L., Radkova, I., Deschrijver, E., & Brass, M. (2018). Automatic imitation: A meta-analysis. *Psychological Bulletin, 144*, 453–500. https://doi.org/10.1037/bul0000143

Devlin, J. T., & Watkins, K. E. (2006). Investigating language organisation with TMS. In E. Wasserman, C. Epstein, U. Ziemann, S. Lisanby, T. Paus, & V. Walsh (Eds.), *Oxford handbook of transcranial stimulation*. Oxford University Press.

Emmorey, K., McCullough, S., & Brentari, D. (2003). Categorical perception in American sign language. *Language and Cognitive Processes, 18*, 21–45. https://doi.org/10.1080/01690960143000416

Fadiga, L., Craighero, L., Buccino, G., & Rizzolatti, G. (2002). Speech listening specifically modulates the excitability of tongue muscles: A TMS study. *European Journal of Neuroscience, 15*, 399–402. https://doi.org/10.1046/j.0953-816x.2001.01874.x

Floccia, C., Butler, J., Goslin, J., & Ellis, L. (2009). Regional and foreign accent processing in English: Can listeners adapt? *Journal of Psycholinguistic Research, 38*, 379–412. https://doi.org/10.1007/s10936-008-9097-8

Galantucci, B., Fowler, C. A., & Goldstein, L. (2009). Perceptuomotor compatibility effects in speech. *Attention, Perception & Psychophysics, 71*, 1138–1149. https://doi.org/10.3758/APP.71.5.1138

Ghaffarvand Mokari, P., Gafos, A., & Williams, D. (2020). Perceptuomotor compatibility effects in vowels: Beyond phonemic identity. *Attention, Perception, & Psychophysics, 82*, 2751–2764. https://doi.org/10.3758/s13414-020-02014-1

Ghaffarvand Mokari, P., Gafos, A., & Williams, D. (2021). Perceptuomotor compatibility effects in vowels: Effects of consonantal context and acoustic proximity of response and distractor. *JASA Express Letters, 1*, 015204. https://doi.org/10.1121/10.0003039

Guenther, F. H., Perkell, J. S., Maassen, B., Kent, R. D., & Peters, H. F. M. (2004). A neural model of speech production and its application to studies of the role of auditory feedback in speech. *Speech Motor Control in Normal and Disordered Speech*, 29–49. https://doi.org/10.1093/oso/9780198526261.003.0002

Heyes, C. (2005). Imitation by association. In S. Hurley & N. Chater (Eds.), *Perspectives on imitation: From neuroscience to social science* (pp. 157–176). MIT Press.

Heyes, C. (2011). Automatic Imitation. *Psychological Bulletin, 137*, 463–483. https://doi.org/10.1037/a0022288

Hickok, G., & Poeppel, D. (2007). The cortical organization of speech processing. *Nature Reviews Neuroscience, 8*, 393–402. https://doi.org/10.1038/nrn2113

Hommel, B. (2019). Theory of event coding (TEC) V2. 0: Representing and controlling perception and action. *Attention, Perception, & Psychophysics, 81*, 2139–2154. https://doi.org/10.3758/s13414-019-01779-4

Hommel, B., Müsseler, J., Aschersleben, G., & Prinz, W. (2001). The Theory of Event Coding (TEC): A framework for perception and action planning. *Behavioural and Brain Sciences, 24*, 849–937. https://doi.org/10.1017/S0140525X01000103

IPA. (1999). *Handbook of the international phonetic association: A guide to the use of the international phonetic alphabet*. Cambridge University Press.

Jarick, M., & Jones, J. A. (2009). Effects of seeing and hearing speech on speech production: A response time study. *Experimental Brain Research, 195*, 175–182. https://doi.org/10.1007/s00221-009-1765-x

Kawato, M. (1999). Internal models for motor control and trajectory planning. *Opinion in Neurobiology, 9*, 718–727. https://doi.org/10.1016/S0959-4388(99)00028-8

Kerzel, D., & Bekkering, H. (2000). Motor activation from visible speech: Evidence from stimulus response compatibility. *Journal of Experimental Psychology: Human Perception and Performance, 26*, 634–647. https://doi.org/10.10371/0096-1523.26.2.634

Klein, E., Roon, K. D., & Gafos, A. I. (2015). Perceptuo-motor interactions across and within phonemic categories. In *ICPhS*.

Liberman, A. M., Harris, K., Hoffman, H. S., & Griffith, B. (1957). The discrimination of speech sounds within and across phoneme boundaries. *Journal of Experimental Psychology, 54*, 358–368. https://doi.org/10.1037/h0044417

Longo, M. R., Kosobud, A., Berthenthal, B., & I. (2008). Automatic imitation of biomechanically possible and impossible actions: Effects of priming movements versus goals. *Journal of Experimental Psychology: Human Perception and Performance, 34*, 489–501. https://doi.org/10.1037/0096-1523.34.2.489

Meister, I. G., Wilson, S. M., Deblieck, C., Wu, A. D., & Iacoboni, M. (2007). The essential role of premotor cortex in speech perception. *Current Biology, 17*, 1692–1696. https://doi.org/10.1016/j.cub.2007.08.064

Meyer, D. E., & Gordon, P. C. (1985). Speech production: Motor programming of phonetic features. *Journal of Memory and Language, 24*, 3–26. https://doi.org/10.1016/0749-596X(85)90013-0

Moore, B. C., & Glasberg, B. R. (1983). Suggested formulae for calculating auditory-filter bandwidths and excitation patterns. *The Journal of the Acoustical Society of America, 74*, 750–753. https://doi.org/10.1121/1.389861

Möttönen, R., & Watkins, K. E. (2009). Motor representations of articulators contribute to categorical perception of speech sounds. *Journal of Neuroscience, 5*, 9819–9825. https://doi.org/10.1523/JNEUROSCI.6018-08.2009

Nuttall, H. E., Kennedy-Higgins, D., Hogan, J., Devlin, J. T., & Adank, P. (2016). The effect of speech distortion on the excitability of articulatory motor cortex. *NeuroImage, 128*, 218–226. https://doi.org/10.1016/j.neuroimage.2015.12.038

Nuttall, H. E., Kennedy-Higgins, D., Devlin, J. T., & Adank, P. (2017). The role of hearing ability and speech distortion in the facilitation of articulatory motor cortex. *Neuropsychologia, 94*, 13–22. https://doi.org/10.1016/j.neuropsychologia.2016.11.016

Pickering, M. J., & Garrod, S. (2013). An integrated theory of language production and comprehension. *Behavioral and Brain Sciences, 36*, 329–347. https://doi.org/10.1017/S0140525X12001495

Press, C., Bird, G., Flach, R., & Heyes, C. (2005). Robotic movement elicits automatic imitation. *Cognitive Brain Research, 25*, 632–640. https://doi.org/10.1016/j.cogbrainres.2005.08.020

Press, C., Gillmeister, H., & Heyes, C. (2006). Bottom-up, not top-down, modulation of imitation by human and robotic models. *European Journal of Neuroscience, 24*, 2415–2419. https://doi.org/10.1111/j.1460-9568.2006.05115.x

Prinz, W. (1997). Perception and action planning. *European Journal of Cognitive Psychology, 9*, 129–154. https://doi.org/10.1080/713752551

Pulvermüller, F., & Fadiga, L. (2010). Active perception: Sensorimotor circuits as a cortical basis for language. *Nature Reviews Neuroscience, 11*, 351–360. https://doi.org/10.1038/nrn2811

Rauschecker, J. P., & Scott, S. K. (2009). Maps and streams in the auditory cortex: Nonhuman primates illuminate human speech processing. *Nature Neuroscience, 12*, 718–724. https://doi.org/10.1038/nn.2331

Roon, K. D., & Gafos, A. I. (2015). Perceptuo-motor effects of response-distractor compatibility in speech: Beyond phonemic identity. *Psychonomic Bulletin & Review, 22*, 242–250. https://doi.org/10.3758/s13423-014-0666-6

Schwartz, J. L. K., Basirat, A., Menard, L., & Sato, M. (2012). The Perception-for-Action-Control Theory (PACT): A perceptuo-motor theory of speech perception. *Journal of Neurolinguistics, 25*, 336–354. https://doi.org/10.1016/j.jneuroling.2009.12.004

Skipper, J., Devlin, J. T., & Lametti, D. R. (2017). The hearing ear is always found close to the speaking tongue: Review of the role of the motor system in speech perception. *Brain and Language, 164*, 77–105. https://doi.org/10.1016/j.bandl.2016.10.004

Smalle, E. H., Rogers, J., & Mottonen, R. (2014). Dissociating contributions of the motor cortex to speech perception and response bias by using transcranial magnetic stimulation. *Cerebral Cortex, 25*, 3690–3698. https://doi.org/10.1093/cercor/bhu218

Stoet, G., & Hommel, B. (1999). Action planning and the temporal binding of response codes. *Journal of Experimental Psychology: Human Perception and Performance, 25*, 1625–1640. https://doi.org/10.1037/0096-1523.25.6.1625

Stokes, R. C., Venezia, J. H., & Hickok, G. (2019). The motor system's [modest] contribution to speech perception. *Psychonomic Bulletin & Review, 26*, 1354–1366. https://doi.org/10.3758/s13423-019-01580-2

Tourville, J. A., & Guenther, F. H. (2011). The DIVA model: A neural theory of speech acquisition and production. *Language and Cognitive Processes, 26*, 952–981. https://doi.org/10.1080/01690960903498424

Treisman, A. (1996). The binding problem. *Current Opinion in Neurobiology, 6*, 171–178. https://doi.org/10.1016/s0959-4388(96)80070-5

Tremblay, P., & Dick, A. S. (2016). Broca and Wernicke are dead, or moving past the classic model of language neurobiology. *Brain and Language, 162*, 60–71. https://doi.org/10.1016/j.bandl.2016.08.004

Van Wijngaarden, S. J. (2001). Intelligibility of native and non-native Dutch speech. *Speech Communication, 35*, 103–113. https://doi.org/10.1016/S0167-6393(00)00098-4

Virhia, J., Kotz, S. A., & Adank, P. (2019). Emotional valence of the response increases automatic imitation of visual speech. *Quarterly Journal of Experimental Psychology, 72*, 2833–2847. https://doi.org/10.1177/1747021819867856

Watkins, K., & Paus, T. (2004). Modulation of motor excitability during speech perception: The role of Broca's area. *Journal of Cognitive Neuroscience, 16*, 978–987. https://doi.org/10.1162/0898929041502616

Wilt, H., Wu, Y., Evans, B. G., & Adank, P. (2024). Automatic imitation of speech is enhanced for non-native sounds. *Psychonomic Bulletin & Review, 31*, 1114–1130. https://doi.org/10.3758/s13423-023-02394-z

Wilt, H., Wu, Y., Trotter, A., & Adank, P. (2023). Automatic Imitation of Human and Computer-generated Vocal Stimuli. *Psychonomic Bulletin & Review, 30*, 1093–1102. https://doi.org/10.31234/osf.io/64erf

Wolpert, D. M. (1997). Computational approaches to motor control. *Trends in Cognitive Sciences, 1*, 209–216. https://doi.org/10.1016/S1364-6613(97)01070-X

Wu, Y., Evans, B., & Adank, P. (2019). Sensorimotor training modulates automatic imitation of visual speech. *Psychonomic Bulletin & Review, 26*, 1711–1718. https://doi.org/10.3758/s13423-019-01623-8

Yaniv, I., Meyer, D. E., Gordon, P. C., Huff, C. A., & Sevald, C. A. (1990). Vowel similarity, connectionist models, and syllable structure in motor programming of speech. *Journal of Memory and Language, 29*, 1–26. https://doi.org/10.1016/0749-596X(90)90007-M

Chapter 5
Automatic Imitation and the Correspondence Problem of Imitation: A Brief Historical Overview of Theoretical Positions

Marcel Brass

Automatic Imitation and the Correspondence Problem of Imitation: A Brief History

Imitation is considered one of the major tools for social learning (Boyd & Richerson, 1996). It allows infants and adults to acquire new motor skills. Furthermore, it contributes to smooth social interactions (Chartrand & Bargh, 1999). Importantly, imitation might also be a useful mechanism for artificial agents to acquire and transmit behaviour and to create social bonds with human agents (Breazeal & Scassellati, 2002; see also Chaps. 13 and 14; this volume). Therefore, understanding the functional mechanisms underlying imitation is extremely important. Intuitively, imitation is a very simple act: you do what you see. However, on closer inspection, this rather intuitive description becomes less plausible. Already in the eighteenth century, Tetens (1979) described the functional problem of imitation: he wondered how an action that we observe can be imitated, given that we only observe the 'outside' (the effect) of the action but not the 'inside'. In other words, when we observe a body movement, we do not perceive the muscle activation underlying that movement but rather the external consequences of the movement. So how can the observer know which muscle activation will lead to the observed movement? This problem has been called the correspondence problem of imitation (Brass & Heyes, 2005; Heyes, 2001), and various solutions to this problem have been proposed ranging from an innate ability to associative learning. In the following, I will give a brief historical overview of potential solutions to the correspondence problem.

M. Brass (✉)
Berlin School of Mind and Brain/Department of Psychology, Humboldt-Universität zu Berlin, Berlin, Germany

Cluster of Excellence 'Science of Intelligence', Berlin, Germany

Department of Experimental Psychology, Universiteit Gent, Ghent, Belgium
e-mail: marcel.brass@hu-berlin.de

O. Genschow, E. Cracco (eds.), *Automatic Imitation*,
https://doi.org/10.1007/978-3-031-62634-0_5

A Historical Perspective

Research on imitation has a long history in psychology, and the functional mechanisms underlying imitation have intrigued researchers for a long time (see Scheerer & Schönpflug, 1984). Theories of imitation provide a mirror to the scientific 'Zeitgeist' at the time they were developed and similar solutions to the correspondence problem have reemerged in psychology over the centuries.

Imitation as a Conditioned Reflex

Early views on imitation assumed it to be an instinct (e.g. James, 1890). Only in in the nineteenth century, this perspective was called into question and alternative views developed. Bain (1855), for example, put forward a number of arguments against the instinctive nature of imitation. He argued that imitation only develops relatively late in ontogeny. Furthermore, he argued that the correspondence between the behaviour of the model and the behaviour of the imitator does not occur instantaneously. His most convincing argument, however, was that imitation as an instinct would require an infinite number of innate links between observed and executed behaviours. Bain (1855) concluded that imitation must be based on acquired associations between observed and executed behaviours. This already set the stage for a learning theoretical approach to imitation. Thorndike (1911) argued that imitative behaviour does not differ from any other learned behaviour equalling imitation with any other habit. This position was further developed by Humphrey (1921). He describes the basic mechanisms underlying a conditioned reflex approach to imitation. First, imitation is based on a circular reflex (Baldwin, 1894) where a specific stimulus leads to an action that serves as a trigger for that same action. The example he gives is the crying of a baby. A painful stimulus triggers a baby to cry. Then, however, hearing the crying becomes a conditioned stimulus that triggers further crying so that the unconditioned stimulus is not required anymore for the crying to continue. Moreover, also hearing another baby crying will trigger the baby to cry. The second basic mechanism that explains imitation from a conditioning perspective is simultaneously observing and executing a specific movement. If an unconditioned stimulus leads the baby to smile while observing the mother smiling, the smiling of the mother becomes the conditioned stimulus for the smiling of the baby. Both principles raise fundamental questions. The circular reflex idea raises the question of how it can be stopped. If the effect of an action activates the action which produces the effect, this leads to an infinite regress. Furthermore, the idea that imitation is based on an accidental co-occurrence of the executed action with an identical observed action is problematic, because such a mechanism should produce all kinds of weird associations between random environmental events with specific behaviour. Furthermore, these approaches require an unconditioned stimulus to allow imitative behaviour to occur. Accordingly, Mowrer (1960) concludes that the idea of imitation as a conditioned reflex is a '...feeble fabrication witch is neither logically consistent nor empirically well supported' (s. 104).

Imitation Explained by Operant Conditioning

Miller and Dollard (1941) tried to explain imitation with operant conditioning. Like the conditioned reflex explanation, they assumed that the acquisition of imitative behaviour does not differ from the acquisition of any other learned behaviour. If a behaviour is accidentally imitated and the imitative act is rewarded, the observed behaviour becomes a discriminative stimulus for the executed behaviour. Assume that a mother smiles and the baby accidentally also smiles at the same time and is rewarded for this smile by the attention of the mother. This would lead to learning of an imitative act via operant conditioning. Like the explanation of imitation as a conditioned reflex, the operant conditioning interpretation raises the question of why imitation is so dominant compared to other forms of behaviour. Furthermore, the question arises whether it is plausible to assume that all imitative acts are acquired through extrinsic reward.

Modern Associative Learning Approaches

The idea that imitation is acquired via general learning mechanisms is far from being dead. Rather modern associative learning theories such as the associative sequence learning model of imitation (ASL) by Heyes (2001) try to explain imitation with general learning principles (Cook et al., 2014). The ASL model assumes that imitation is made possible by an excitatory link between a sensory representation of the observed movement and a matching motor representation (matching vertical associations). These associations are formed through the experience of concurrent activation of sensory and motor representations. In addition to these direct vertical associations, vertical associations can also be formed indirectly via verbal mediation. Learning of novel behaviour via imitation is achieved by a formation of links between sensory representations (horizontal associations) which have matching vertical associations. Assume that a dancer needs to learn a new sequence of dance moves. The single dance moves are already in the motor repertoire of the dancer, and their perceptual representation is associated with a specific motor program (i.e. a vertical association). Learning then requires linking the existing sensory representations of the single dance moves (i.e. forming horizontal associations). The ASL model emphasizes the similarity of imitative and non-imitative stimulus-response (S-R) associations. The privileged role of imitative compared to non-imitative S-R associations is simply due to the fact that the likelihood of forming matching vertical associations is high, because movement execution is often associated with perceiving the sensory consequences of the own movement. This model can account for the imitation of opaque movements (i.e. movements where the visual sensory consequences of the movement are not visible by the agent) via the experience of mirrors or verbal mediation. Furthermore, it can deal with the diversity of imitative phenomena. However, it has to address the question of what in particular makes imitative S-R associations so powerful for the acquisition of motor skills and language compared to non-imitative S-R associations.

The Revival of Imitation as an Innate Mechanism

While the idea of imitation as an instinctive behaviour was dismissed in the nineteenth century, the finding of neonatal imitation in the late 1970s led to a revival of the innate imitation hypothesis (Meltzoff & Moore, 1977). In contrast to the instinct interpretation of imitation, such accounts do not assume that all imitative acts are innate but rather that there is an innate mechanism specifically dedicated to imitation that provides the basis for imitative learning. The most prominent theory of this kind is the active intermodal matching model (AIM) by Andy Meltzoff (Meltzoff, 2002). While this model was primarily developed to explain neonatal imitation of simple facial acts, it has been extended to account for imitative phenomena in general. The AIM model assumes that the visual input is matched to the motor output via a supramodal representation. This matching is possible because it is assumed that infants at birth possess a very primitive body scheme on which they can map organ relations. As already outlined above, the strongest support for this model comes from neonatal imitation of facial gestures (Meltzoff & Moore, 1977). This finding is, however, very controversial (e.g. Anisfeld, 1996; Oostenbroek et al., 2016). Furthermore, the model assumes that a dedicated mechanism for imitation exists. One question that has not received much attention in the literature is whether there is neuropsychological evidence for such an imitation mechanism.

Another theory that assumes an innate mechanism for imitation is the mirror neuron theory of imitation (for an extensive discussion see Cook et al., 2014). Mirror neurons have been found in the ventral premotor cortex and the inferior parietal cortex of the macaque brain (di Pellegrino et al., 1992). These neurons are active when the monkey observes an action and also when it executes the same action. Therefore, they can be seen as a single-cell correlate of transforming observed into executed action. This makes mirror neurons a plausible candidate for a neural correlate of imitation. It has been argued that mirror neurons are an evolutionary adaptation (Ferrari et al., 2009). This hypothesis comes in different degrees. Some argue that the mirror system itself is innate. Some have argued that mirror neurons are the result of Hebbian learning but that a bias to associate observed on executed behaviour is genetically determined (Del Giudice et al., 2009; Keysers et al., 2014). However, one might argue that evidence for an innate mirror neuron system is sparse. For long, the mere existence of mirror neurons has been taken as evidence for their phylogenetic origin. However, all learning or motor control theories of imitation predict the existence of mirror neurons as well (M. Brass & Heyes,

2005; Cook et al., 2014). There is an additional problem with the idea that imitation is based on an innate mirror neuron system, namely that mirror neurons have been found in general-purpose motor control areas intermingled with neurons that do not have mirror neuron properties. First, the species in which mirror neurons have been identified does not really imitate (Visalberghi & Fragaszy, 2002).

An Ideomotor Approach to Imitation

Throughout the history of research on the functional problem of imitation, theories of imitation have struggled with two seemingly contradictory properties of imitative behaviour. First, imitation seems to be a special phenomenon that differs from other forms of learned behaviour and has a specific status in motor learning and social behaviour. These specific properties of imitative behaviour have led to the assumption that imitation must be based on an innate dedicated mechanism. Second, imitative behaviour describes a very broad class of behavioural phenomena, ranging from very simple motor primitives to complex social behaviour. This breadth of imitative phenomena has led researchers to assume that it must be based on general-purpose learning mechanisms (Heyes, 2001). Various attempts have been made to account for both aspects of imitation, either by assuming that an innate mechanism guides or biases general-purpose learning (e.g. Del Giudice et al., 2009) or by assuming that imitative behaviour is specific because it is based on self-observation which by its nature constitutes a specific type of sensorimotor mapping. Interestingly, a very old theory of motor control, the so-called ideomotor theory (James, 1890), addresses these seemingly contradictory properties of imitation. However, it took a long time before ideomotor theory was considered as a solution to the correspondence problem of imitation (Prinz, 2005).

The ideomotor principle goes back to the nineteenth century (James, 1890) and was developed to explain voluntary control of behaviour. The crucial question was how we can control our movements without having access to the workings of our motor system because movements seem to be primarily represented by their sensory consequences. The solution to this problem was to assume that actions are controlled by an anticipation of their sensory consequences. In other words, if I want to lift my arm, I anticipate how it looks like or feels to lift the arm. This 'idea' of the movement triggers the associated 'motor' command (hence ideomotor). However, the ideomotor principle was dismissed by behaviourism because the idea that behaviour was controlled by anticipations of the sensory consequences seemed superfluous. Only in the seventieth of the twentieth century, Anthony Greenwald (Greenwald, 1970a, b, 1972) revived the ideomotor principle and developed the 'Theory of Ideomotor Action'. This theory was based on two assumptions: first, actions are represented by an anticipation of their sensory consequences; second, these anticipatory images are used to control behaviour. While these two assumptions reformulate the old ideomotor principle, Greenwald (1970b) made the connection to imitative behaviour and proposed ideomotor theory as an extension of

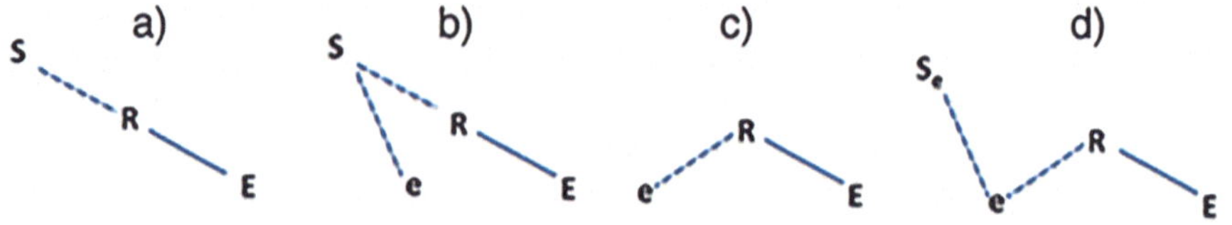

Fig. 5.1 Acquisition of an ideomotor representation. (Adapted from Greenwald, 1970). (**a**) A stimulus (S) triggers a specific response (R) that leads to a sensory effect (E). (**b**) After learning, the stimulus will activate an anticipation (e) of the effect that precedes the response. (**c**) This anticipation (e) becomes conditioned to the response and allows for control of the response. (**d**) Priming by action observation: a stimulus that resembles the effect of the action (Se) primes the ideomotor representation (e) which activates the response. (Brass & Muhle-Karbe, 2014, p. 195)

classical S-R learning (see Fig. 5.1). The basis for ideomotor representations is the circular reflex, where a motor output triggers a sensory consequence that becomes associated with the motor output and subsequently triggers this motor output. While the circular reflex idea can be sufficiently explained from a simple associative learning perspective, the ideomotor interpretation of the circular reflex adds an additional representational level. Through learning, an anticipation of the sensory consequence is formed. Now, observing a behaviour executed by someone else can trigger the anticipation of the sensory consequence of the movement which is associated with the motor command (Fig. 5.1).

Such a conceptualization of the circular reflex has a crucial advantage; namely, it solves the problem of how self-imitation can be stopped. Greenwald (1970b) writes, 'The ideo-motor mechanism avoids the circular reflex mechanism's difficulty in explaining cessation of action by attributing a facilitatory function to the image of feedback from an action rather than to the feedback itself. Thus, only a simple ability to discriminate image from actual feedback is required to enable the organism to cease an action initiated by the former on reception of the latter' (p. 86). One of the major advantages of the ideomotor principle is that it leads to a 'natural' solution to the correspondence problem. Because actions are controlled by an anticipatory image of their sensory consequences, observing an action activates or primes this anticipatory image via similarity. Consequently, one of the key predictions of the ideomotor theory of action is that action observation should 'automatically' prime the corresponding action in the observer.

Automatic Imitation and Ideomotor Compatibility

Since the 1950s (Fitts & Deininger, 1954; Fitts & Seeger, 1953), research has been concerned with the question of how properties of stimuli are related to response selection and initiation. This field was called stimulus-response compatibility research (e.g. Hommel & Prinz, 1997; Kornblum et al., 1990) and demonstrated that similarity plays a crucial role in stimulus-response compatibility (SRC; for a review, see Chap. 2; this volume). However, this research tradition focused primarily on similarity relations of specific features of the stimulus and the response such as the spatial location of the stimulus and the response (Simon & Rudell, 1967). Greenwald (1970a) related SRC phenomena to the ideomotor principle and argued that '…it may be suggested that S-R compatibility facilitates response selection by minimizing the time required for access to an image of the correct response' (Greenwald, 1970b, p. 91). He labelled this phenomenon ideomotor compatibility and defined it as '…the dimension denoting the extent to which a stimulus corresponds to sensory feedback from its required response' (Greenwald, 1970a, p. 52). While this concept can be applied to SRC phenomena, in general, it clearly paves the way to investigate and understand imitative behaviour: in imitative situations, ideomotor compatibility is extremely strong because there is a strong correspondence between the observed behaviour and the response image that is used to control the corresponding behaviour.

Empirically Investigating Ideomotor Compatibility

Already in the fiftieth of the twentieth century, studies were carried out that can retrospectively be interpreted as an indirect test of ideomotor compatibility. These studies investigated the influence of S-R compatibility on the increase of reaction time as a function of response alternatives, the so-called Hick's law (Hick, 1952). Usually, reaction times increase as a function of response alternatives. However, Leonard (1959) could show that this law applies to a much lesser degree when participants respond to vibro-tactile stimuli. So, if participants had to respond with a key press to a vibrotactile stimulation of the fingertip, the usual relationship between a number of choice alternatives and RT only showed the difference between a simple and a two-choice response but vanished when more response alternatives were required. From an ideomotor perspective, one can argue that responding with a key press to a vibrotactile stimulation of the fingertip is a high ideomotor compatibility, because the sensory consequence of a key press is the tactile sensation on the fingertip. In another study, Broadbent and Gregory (1962) compared Donders' b reactions (two stimuli and two responses) with Donders' c reactions (two stimuli but only one response to one of the stimuli). Usually, RT are faster for the c reaction compared to the b reaction, because participants have to select a response in the b reaction but not in the c reaction. They compared two types of mappings between stimuli and responses: in the compatible mapping, the response modality was congruent to the stimulus modality (verbal responses to auditory stimuli, key presses to vibrotactile stimuli); in the incompatible mapping, the stimulus and response modality did not match. They found the expected difference between b reaction and c reaction only for the incompatible mapping but not for the compatible mapping indicating that in compatible mappings the response is more directly specified by the stimulus.

Greenwald (1970a) also investigated ideomotor compatibility by manipulating the match of the modality between stimulus and response. He presented the stimuli either written or auditorily and tested the response either by letting participants write or say the response. In accordance with his assumption, he found an interaction between stimulus and response modality, showing faster responses if the stimulus and the response modality were congruent compared to an incongruent mapping. Interestingly, after Greenwald, the research tradition to explicitly manipulate ideomotor compatibility was not continued. More than 15 years later Prinz (1992), this approach was again taken up by Wolfgang Prinz and his group to investigate his common coding approach (M. Brass et al., 2000, 2001a; Stürmer et al., 2000). The common coding approach can be understood as an extension of ideomotor theory, with the main assumption that perceptual and motor events share a common representational basis (Prinz, 1997). This approach was later developed into the Theory of Event Coding (Hommel et al., 2001). Interestingly, while SRC research was very active at this time, it was primarily based on very simple stimulus-response relations and it was considered unnecessary to investigate more complex stimuli.

Automatic Imitation

In a seminal study, Stürmer et al. (2000) used a classical S-R compatibility approach to investigate the relationship between observing one of two hand gestures and executing the same or a different hand gesture (for a review, see Chap. 2; this volume). They used opening and closing the hand as hand gestures and measured the response with electromyography. In a series of experiments, they could show a strong compatibility effect between observed and executed actions. Furthermore, they provided the first evidence against a spatial compatibility interpretation of the results. Finally, they also demonstrated that the effect also occurred when only the end position of the hand gesture was shown. In a series of follow-up experiments, Brass et al. (2000) simplified the paradigm by asking participants to either lift their index and middle finger in response to an imperative cue while observing congruent or incongruent movements of a videotaped hand on the computer screen. This simplification allowed the investigation of automatic imitation with a simple key release. They replicated the congruency effect and also showed that it could not be reduced to spatial compatibility. In another set of experiments, Brass et al. (2001a) investigated automatic imitation in a simple response task, reviving the idea that ideomotor-compatible stimulus-response arrangements circumvent response selection and can directly specify the response. The results demonstrated that compatibility effects could be found when participants have to respond with a predefined finger movement to a congruent or incongruent observed finger movement. This is in contrast to spatial compatibility effects which only occur when participants establish both response alternatives (Hommel, 1996). In 2003 a 'kinematic' variant of the automatic imitation paradigm was developed (Kilner et al., 2003). In this paradigm, participants were asked to carry out either horizontal or vertical arm movements while observing congruent or incongruent horizontal or vertical movements. Kilner et al. (2003) found that variance in the movements was larger when participants observed incongruent compared to congruent movements, supporting the idea that participants were affected by the irrelevant observed movement.

In a recent meta-analysis, E. Cracco et al. (2018) provided a broad quantitative overview of research on automatic imitation. The aim of the following paragraphs is therefore not to reiterate this review but to outline some seminal studies that further specified the nature of automatic imitation.

Automatic Imitation and Spatial Compatibility

Early studies using the automatic imitation paradigm further investigated whether automatic imitation can be explained by spatial compatibility (e.g. Bertenthal et al., 2006). Bertenthal et al. (2006) introduced a clever manipulation in which they used a similar setup to the original experiment by Brass et al. (2000) but presented either a hand that looked like a mirrored hand of participants (a front view of the left hand) or a front view of the same hand the participant was using (the right hand, non-mirrored). While in the original setup of Brass et al. (2000) the hand on the computer screen looked like a mirrored hand of the participant, in this setup the hand on the computer screen was sometimes non-mirrored. Importantly, this puts spatial compatibility (i.e. position of the finger that moves) and finger compatibility (i.e. which finger moves) in opposition. If spatial compatibility would be solely responsible for the effect, one would expect a reversal of the effect in the non-mirrored condition. However, what they observed was an elimination of the effect, suggesting that both spatial compatibility and imitative compatibility contribute to the effect. With this setup, they could manipulate whether only the spatial position was compatible, only the finger that was moved or both. Thus, they were able to decompose the different contributions to automatic imitation.

Automatic Imitation and Properties of the Observed Agent

Another question that was addressed in early work on automatic imitation was whether automatic imitation is restricted to the observation of human biological agents (Kilner et al., 2003; Press et al., 2006) and whether kinematically non-plausible movements also lead to imitation (Longo et al., 2008). Press et al. (2006) demonstrated automatic imitation effects for a robotic hand. However, the effect was much smaller than for a schematic human hand, indicating that the similarity of the observed agent to a human agent matters. In a very intriguing design, Longo et al. (2008) investigated automatic imitation for biomechanically impossible movements. In their first experiment, they demonstrated that automatic imitation occurs, regardless of whether the observed movement is biomechanically possible or not. In a second experiment, they explicitly mentioned that the observed movement was biomechanically impossible. With this explicit instruction, the automatic imitation effect disappeared, suggesting that top-down beliefs about the nature of the observed behaviour can modulate automatic imitation. In another study, Longo and Bertenthal (2009) more explicitly investigated whether beliefs about the nature of the observed agent have an influence on automatic imitation. They demonstrated that automatic imitation effects were modulated by drawing attention to the artificial nature of a hand. Similar effects were also found by Liepelt and Brass (2010). Another study investigated whether it mattered for automatic imitation if people believed that an observed movement was an active or a passive movement (Liepelt et al., 2008). These experiments also indicated that beliefs about the nature of the observed agent have an influence on automatic imitation. However, one has to be aware that these experiments usually used small participant numbers. Using larger samples, recent research was not able to replicate this (Cracco et al., 2024) and similar findings (e.g. De Souter et al., 2021).

Non-Matching Associations Between Observed and Executed Behaviours

A major assumption of the ideomotor interpretation of automatic imitation is that this effect is mediated by the activation of a response image. Such response images result from a long history of self-observation and thus differ from short-term S-R associations. In a series of experiments, Heyes and colleagues challenged this view by showing that relatively brief training of non-matching associations between observed and executed actions can reverse automatic imitation effects (Catmur et al., 2007, 2008). After such training, observing an action activated the alternative motor response even when no instruction was given and response tendencies were assessed with motor TMS (Catmur et al., 2007). Such a finding is difficult to reconcile with an ideomotor interpretation of automatic imitation because, as outlined above, the ideomotor approach assumes that automatic imitation is a result of a long learning process of actions and outcomes. However, one could argue that these counter-imitation effects are based on a completely different mechanism than classical automatic imitation effects and reflect short-term stimulus-response learning. It is well known that we can learn new stimulus-response mappings in a few trials. In the counter-imitation example, one would associate the non-matching action effect with an action. Such a learned association would temporarily counteract the automatic imitation effect but would operate via a completely different mechanism. One approach to dissociate such different accounts would be to investigate temporal properties of counter-imitation. From the ideomotor perspective, one would assume that activation of the non-matching association should disappear after a certain amount of time and make place for classical matching automatic imitation effects. Another possibility would be to look at the anticipatory effects of motor preparation. Kunde (2001) could show that participants are slower in initiating an action when the anticipated outcome is incompatible with the initiated action (e.g. a left key press leads to a right action effect). The ideomotor interpretation of this effect is that in the incompatible mapping a conflict arises between the anticipated 'natural' action effect (the response image that is acquired throughout the lifetime) and the actual action effect (the incompatible action effect). The question is whether this relationship could be reversed through counter-imitation training. If counter-imitation is based on simple S-R associations, one would not expect these effects to occur or at least to be much weaker.

Automatic Imitation and Self-Other Distinction

The ideomotor interpretation of automatic imitation leads to another unique prediction, namely that inhibition of automatic imitation is related to self-other distinction (Brass et al., 2001b, 2009; Greenwald, 1970b; Spengler et al., 2009). If movement observation leads to an activation of a corresponding motor representation in the observer and this representation is also used to initiate voluntary behaviour, the question arises as to how the observer can distinguish between these externally triggered motor representations and their own motor intentions given that both have the same representational basis (Hurley, 2008). The first indirect evidence for such a role of self-other distinction in automatic imitation stems from early imaging work showing a network of brain regions being involved in automatic imitation (incongruent versus congruent trials) that has been related to self-other distinction and social-cognition rather than motor inhibition per se (Brass et al., 2001b, 2005). Follow-up training research and brain imaging work on inhibiting imitative response tendencies further supported the idea that suppressing automatic imitative response tendencies might be related to social cognitive processes involving self-other distinction (Brass et al., 2009; Santiesteban et al., 2012; Spengler et al., 2009). However, recently, the early imaging work has been difficult to replicate, challenging a basic piece of evidence for the idea that self-other distinction is crucially involved in automatic imitation (Darda & Ramsey, 2019). Given that this idea has gained support from other sources (e.g. Santiesteban et al., 2012), further research is needed to clarify the role of self-other distinction in automatic imitation.

Summary and Conclusions

The chapter provides a short history of theoretical accounts of the correspondence problem of imitation. Throughout the history of research on imitation, learning accounts were contrasted with accounts that assume an innate mechanism underlying imitation. These opposing accounts tried to accommodate two crucial observations related to imitation: first, the imitative behaviour seems to constitute a specific class of sensorimotor mappings that differ from other kinds of stimulus-response mappings; second, the imitation is extremely flexible spanning from simple facial gestures to complex patterns of behaviour. An ideomotor interpretation of imitation easily accommodates both observations. From an ideomotor perspective, imitative behaviour is the result of learning but is at the same time based on a specific mechanism that distinguishes it from other forms of S-R learning. The ideomotor interpretation of imitation has motivated a specific experimental approach that developed into the automatic imitation paradigm: if actions are controlled by an anticipation of their sensory consequences, perceiving the sensory consequences of an action should activate the corresponding motor representation in the observer.

Research on automatic imitation over the last almost 25 years has established the paradigm as a reliable experimental approach that cannot be reduced to more basic phenomena such as spatial compatibility. This research has investigated moderators of automatic imitation and how automatic imitation is related to other social-cognitive phenomena. It has stimulated new experimental approaches, has generated new hypotheses about the nature of social cognition and has fuelled the debate on the correspondence problem of imitation.

References

Anisfeld, M. (1996). Only tongue protrusion modelling is matched by neonates. *Developmental Research, 16*, 149–161. https://doi.org/10.1006/drev.1996.0006

Bain, A. (1855). *The senses and the intellect*. John W. Parker and Sons. https://doi.org/10.1037/12115-000

Baldwin, J. M. (1894). Imitation: A chapter in the natural history of consciousness. *Mind, 3*, 25–55. https://doi.org/10.1016/S0273-2297(03)00004-2

Bertenthal, B. I., Longo, M. R., & Kosobud, A. (2006). Imitative response tendencies following observation of intransitive actions. *Journal of Experimental Psychology: Human Perception and Performance, 32*, 210–225, https://doi.org/10.1037/0096-1523.32.2.210

Boyd, R., & Richerson, P. J. (1996). Why culture is common but cultural evolution is rare. *Proceedings of the British Academy, 88*, 77–93.

Brass, M., & Heyes, C. (2005). Imitation: Is cognitive neuroscience solving the correspondence problem? *Trends in Cognitive Sciences, 9*, 489–495. https://doi.org/10.1016/j.tics.2005.08.007

Brass, M., & Muhle-Karbe, P. S. (2014). More than associations: An ideomotor perspective on mirror neurons. *Behavioral and Brain Sciences, 37*, 195–196. https://doi.org/10.1017/S0140525X13002239

Brass, M., Bekkering, H., Wohlschlager, A., & Prinz, W. (2000). Compatibility between observed and executed finger movements: Comparing symbolic, spatial, and imitative cues. *Brain and Cognition, 44*, 124–143. https://doi.org/10.1006/brcg.2000.1225

Brass, M., Bekkering, H., & Prinz, W. (2001a). Movement observation affects movement execution in a simple response task. *Acta Psychologica, 106*, 3–22. https://doi.org/10.1016/s0001-6918(00)00024-x

Brass, M., Zysset, S., & von Cramon, D. Y. (2001b). The inhibition of imitative response tendencies. *NeuroImage, 14*, 1416–1423. https://doi.org/10.1006/nimg.2001.0944

Brass, M., Derrfuss, J., & Von Cramon, D. Y. (2005). The inhibition of imitative and overlearned responses: A functional double dissociation. *Neuropsychologia, 43*, 89–98. https://doi.org/10.1016/j.neuropsychologia.2004.06.018

Brass, M., Ruby, P., & Spengler, S. (2009). Inhibition of imitative behaviour and social cognition. *Philosophical Transactions of the Royal Society of London. Series B, Biological Sciences, 364*, 2359–2367. https://doi.org/10.1098/rstb.2009.0066

Breazeal, C., & Scassellati, B. (2002). Robots that imitate humans. *Trends in Cognitive Sciences, 6*, 481–487. https://doi.org/10.1016/s1364-6613(02)02016-8

Broadbent, D. E., & Gregory, M. (1962). Donders' B-and C-reactions and SR compatibility. *Journal of Experimental Psychology, 63*, 575–578, https://doi.org/10.1037/h0044674

Catmur, C., Walsh, V., & Heyes, C. (2007). Sensorimotor learning configures the human mirror system. *Current Biology, 17*, 1527–1531. https://doi.org/10.1016/j.cub.2007.08.006

Catmur, C., Gillmeister, H., Bird, G., Liepelt, R., Brass, M., & Heyes, C. (2008). Through the looking glass: Counter-mirror activation following incompatible sensorimotor learning. *European Journal of Neuroscience, 28*, 1208–1215. https://doi.org/10.1111/j.1460-9568.2008.06419.x

Chartrand, T. L., & Bargh, J. A. (1999). The chameleon effect: The perception-behavior link and social interaction. *Journal of Personality and Social Psychology, 76*, 893–910. https://doi.org/10.1037/0022-3514.76.6.893

Cook, R., Bird, G., Catmur, C., Press, C., & Heyes, C. (2014). Mirror neurons: From origin to function. *The Behavioral and Brain Sciences, 37*, 177–192. https://doi.org/10.1017/S0140525X13000903

Cracco, E., Bardi, L., Desmet, C., Genschow, O., Rigoni, D., De Coster, L., … Brass, M. (2018). Automatic imitation: A meta-analysis. *Psychological Bulletin, 144*, 453–500, https://doi.org/10.1037/bul0000143

Cracco, E., Liepelt, R., Brass, M., & Genschow, O. (2024). Top-down modulation of motor priming by belief about animacy: A registered replication report. *Experimental Psychology, 70*, 355–365. https://doi.org/10.1027/1618-3169/a000605

Darda, K. M., & Ramsey, R. (2019). The inhibition of automatic imitation: A meta-analysis and synthesis of fMRI studies. *NeuroImage, 197*, 320–329. https://doi.org/10.1016/j.neuroimage.2019.04.059

De Souter, L., Braem, S., Genschow, O., Brass, M., & Cracco, E. (2021). Social group membership does not modulate automatic imitation in a contrastive multi-agent paradigm. *Quarterly Journal of Experimental Psychology, 74*, 746–759. https://doi.org/10.1177/1747021820986528

Del Giudice, M., Manera, V., & Keysers, C. (2009). Programmed to learn? The ontogeny of mirror neurons. *Developmental Science, 12*, 350–363. https://doi.org/10.1111/j.1467-7687.2008.00783.x

di Pellegrino, G., Fadiga, L., Fogassi, L., Gallese, V., & Rizzolatti, G. (1992). Understanding motor events: A neurophysiological study. *Experimental Brain Research, 91*, 176–180. Retrieved from https://doi.org/10.1007/BF00230027

Ferrari, P. F., Bonini, L., & Fogassi, L. (2009). From monkey mirror neurons to primate behaviours: Possible 'direct' and 'indirect' pathways. *Philosophical Transactions of the Royal Society of London. Series B, Biological Sciences, 364*, 2311–2323. https://doi.org/10.1098/rstb.2009.0062

Fitts, P. M., & Deininger, R. L. (1954). SR compatibility: Correspondence among paired elements within stimulus and response codes. *Journal of Experimental Psychology, 48*, 483–492, https://doi.org/10.1037/h0054967

Fitts, P. M., & Seeger, C. M. (1953). SR compatibility: Spatial characteristics of stimulus and response codes. *Journal of Experimental Psychology, 46*, 199–210, https://doi.org/10.1037/h0062827

Greenwald, A. G. (1970a). A choice reaction time test of ideomotor theory. *Journal of Experimental Psychology, 86*, 20–25. https://doi.org/10.1037/h0029960

Greenwald, A. G. (1970b). Sensory feedback mechanisms in performance control: With special reference to the ideo-motor mechanism. *Psychological Review, 77*, 73–99. https://doi.org/10.1037/h0028689

Greenwald, A. G. (1972). On doing two things at once: Time sharing as a function of ideomotor compatibility. *Journal of Experimental Psychology, 94*, 52–57. Retrieved from https://doi.org/10.1037/h0032762

Heyes, C. (2001). Causes and consequences of imitation. *Trends in Cognitive Sciences, 5*, 253–261. Retrieved from https://doi.org/10.1016/s1364-6613(00)01661-2

Hick, W. E. (1952). On the rate of gain of information. *Quarterly Journal of Experimental Psychology, 4*, 11–26. https://doi.org/10.1080/17470215208416600

Hommel, B. (1996). SR compatibility effects without response uncertainty. *The Quarterly Journal of Experimental Psychology Section A, 49*, 546–571. https://doi.org/10.1080/713755643

Hommel, B., & Prinz, W. (1997). *Theoretical issues in stimulus-response compatibility.* Paper presented at the Symposium on the Theory of SR Compatibility, June, 1995, Benediktbeuern, Munich, Germany; The contributions to this book are the fruits of the aforementioned conference. https://doi.org/10.1017/S0140525X01000103

Hommel, B., Müsseler, J., Aschersleben, G., & Prinz, W. (2001). The theory of event coding (TEC): A framework for perception and action planning. *Behavioral and Brain Sciences, 24*, 849–878.

Humphrey, G. (1921). Imitation and the conditioned reflex. *Pedagogical Seminary, 28*, 1–21. https://doi.org/10.1017/S0140525X07003123

Hurley, S. (2008). The shared circuits model (SCM): How control, mirroring, and simulation can enable imitation, deliberation, and mindreading. *Behavioral and Brain Sciences, 31*, 1–22.

James, W. (1890). *The principles of psychology*. Holt. https://doi.org/10.1037/10538-000

Keysers, C., Perrett, D. I., & Gazzola, V. (2014). Hebbian learning is about contingency, not contiguity, and explains the emergence of predictive mirror neurons. *The Behavioral and Brain Sciences, 37*, 205–206. https://doi.org/10.1017/S0140525X13002343

Kilner, J. M., Paulignan, Y., & Blakemore, S.-J. (2003). An interference effect of observed biological movement on action. *Current Biology, 13*, 522–525. https://doi.org/10.1016/s0960-9822(03)00165-9

Kornblum, S., Hasbroucq, T., & Osman, A. (1990). Dimensional overlap: Cognitive basis for stimulus-response compatibility – A model and taxonomy. *Psychological Review, 97*, 253–270, https://doi.org/10.1037/0033-295X.97.2.253

Kunde, W. (2001). Response-effect compatibility in manual choice reaction tasks. *Journal of Experimental Psychology: Human Perception and Performance, 27*, 387–394, https://doi.org/10.1037/0096-1523.27.2.387

Leonard, J. A. (1959). Tactual choice reactions: I. *Quarterly Journal of Experimental Psychology, 11*, 76–83. https://doi.org/10.1080/17470215908416294

Liepelt, R., & Brass, M. (2010). Top-down modulation of motor priming by belief about animacy. *Experimental Psychology, 57*, 221–227, https://doi.org/10.1027/1618-3169/a000028

Liepelt, R., von Cramon, D. Y., & Brass, M. (2008). What is matched in direct matching? Intention attribution modulates motor priming. *Journal of Experimental Psychology: Human Perception and Performance, 34*, 578 –591, https://doi.org/10.1037/0096-1523.34.3.578

Longo, M. R., & Bertenthal, B. I. (2009). Attention modulates the specificity of automatic imitation to human actors. *Experimental Brain Research, 192*, 739–744. https://doi.org/10.1007/s00221-008-1649-5

Longo, M. R., Kosobud, A., & Bertenthal, B. I. (2008). Automatic imitation of biomechanically possible and impossible actions: Effects of priming movements versus goals. *Journal of Experimental Psychology: Human Perception and Performance, 34*, 489–501, https://doi.org/10.1037/0096-1523.34.2.489

Meltzoff, A. N. (2002). Imitation as a mechanism of social cognition: Origins of empathy, theory of mind, and the representation of action. In U. Goswami (Ed.), *Blackwell handbook of childhood cognitive development* (pp. 6–25). Blackwell Publishers.

Meltzoff, A. N., & Moore, M. K. (1977). Imitation of facial and manual gestures by human neonates. *Science, 198*, 74–78. Retrieved from https://doi.org/10.1126/science.897687

Miller, N. E., & Dollard, J. (1941). *Social learning and imitation*. Yale University Press.

Mowrer, O. H. (1960). *Learning theory and behavior*. Wiley. https://doi.org/10.1037/10802-000

Oostenbroek, J., Suddendorf, T., Nielsen, M., Redshaw, J., Kennedy-Costantini, S., Davis, J., … Slaughter, V. (2016). Comprehensive longitudinal study challenges the existence of neonatal imitation in humans. *Current Biology, 26*, 1334–1338. https://doi.org/10.1016/j.cub.2016.03.047

Press, C., Gillmeister, H., & Heyes, C. (2006). Bottom-up, not top-down, modulation of imitation by human and robotic models. *European Journal of Neuroscience, 24*, 2415–2419. https://doi.org/10.1111/j.1460-9568.2006.05115.x

Prinz, W. (1992). Why don't we perceive our brain states? *European Journal of Cognitive Psychology, 4*, 1–20. https://doi.org/10.1080/09541449208406240

Prinz, W. (1997). Perception and action planning. *European Journal of Cognitive Psychology, 9*, 129–154. https://doi.org/10.1080/713752551

Prinz, W. (2005). An ideomotor approach to imitation. In S. Hurley & N. Chater (Eds.), *Perspectives on imitation: From neuroscience to social science* (Vol. 1, pp. 141–156). MIT Press.

Santiesteban, I., White, S., Cook, J., Gilbert, S. J., Heyes, C., & Bird, G. (2012). Training social cognition: From imitation to Theory of Mind. *Cognition, 122*, 228–235. https://doi.org/10.1016/j.cognition.2011.11.004

Scheerer, E., & Schönpflug, U. (1984). Nachahmung. In J. Ritter & K. Gründer (Eds.), *Historische Wörterbuch der Philosophie*. Schwabe & Co.

Simon, J. R., & Rudell, A. P. (1967). Auditory SR compatibility: The effect of an irrelevant cue on information processing. *Journal of Applied Psychology, 51*, 300. https://doi.org/10.1037/h0020586

Spengler, S., von Cramon, D. Y., & Brass, M. (2009). Control of shared representations relies on key processes involved in mental state attribution. *Human Brain Mapping, 30*, 3704–3718. https://doi.org/10.1002/hbm.20800

Stürmer, B., Aschersleben, G., & Prinz, W. (2000). Correspondence effects with manual gestures and postures: A study of imitation. *Journal of Experimental Psychology: Human Perception and Performance, 26*, 1746–1759. https://doi.org/10.1037/0096-1523.26.6.1746

Tetens, J. N. (1979). *Philosophische Versuche über die menschliche Natur und ihre Entwicklung (Nachdruck der Ausgabe Leipzig, 1777)*. Olms.

Thorndike, E. L. (1911). *Animal intelligence*. Macmillan Co.

Visalberghi, E., & Fragaszy, D. (2002). "Do monkeys ape?": Ten years after. In *Imitation in animals and artifacts* (pp. 471–499). Boston Review.

Chapter 6
The Promise and Pitfalls of Studying the Neurophysiological Correlates of Automatic Imitation

Kohinoor M. Darda and Richard Ramsey

Few areas of current research have shed as much light on human social cognition as studying the cognitive and neurophysiological mechanisms of human imitation. Be it copying the posture, body language, or accent of someone we like—our ability to imitate others has been argued to build social connection between people (for a review, see Chaps. 13 and 14; this volume). Indeed, many researchers suggest that copying behaviours are at the very heart of being human and may have contributed to our species' survival success (Henrich, 2015; Legare & Nielsen, 2015; Nagy & Molnar, 2004; Wood, 2020). While a simple conceptualisation of imitation as "monkey see, monkey do" implies copying as a simple motor act with no social consequences, it is now generally accepted that imitation is a much more complex and multi-dimensional phenomenon that serves important social functions across multiple species. We often think of imitation as intentional (such as when learning a new skill), but people also tend to copy others without their conscious awareness, a process referred to as "automatic imitation" (Heyes, 2011).

Automatic imitation has been argued to be an adaptive and flexible behaviour that is central to social cognition, which strengthens social bonds between interacting partners and thus provides a functional benefit that can help guide social interactions (Chartrand & van Baaren, 2009; Kavanagh & Winkielman, 2016; Wang & Hamilton, 2012). Given the ubiquitous influence of imitation on our daily lives, it is not surprising that researchers have studied automatic imitation across a range of interconnected disciplines including cognitive science, social psychology,

K. M. Darda
Penn Center for Neuroaesthetics, University of Pennsylvania, Philadelphia, PA, USA

ARISA (Advancement and Research in the Sciences and Arts) Foundation, Pune, India

R. Ramsey (✉)
Department of Health Sciences and Technology, ETH Zürich, Zürich, Switzerland

Department of Humanities, Social and Political Sciences, ETH Zürich, Zürich, Switzerland
e-mail: richard.ramsey@hest.ethz.ch

O. Genschow, E. Cracco (eds.), *Automatic Imitation*,
https://doi.org/10.1007/978-3-031-62634-0_6

evolutionary biology, and cognitive neuroscience (Byrne & Russon, 1998; Chartrand & Bargh, 1999; Meltzoff & Prinz, 2002). This convergence across multiple disciplines has allowed for a range of perspectives on imitation to emerge, further empowered by neuroimaging advances in the last two decades.

Across these research domains, a variety of methods that vary in ecological validity have been adopted to index automatic imitation and its underlying cognitive and neural mechanisms. These methods include observation of live social interactions, as well as reaction-time measures based on stimulus-response compatibility (SRC) paradigms (Brass et al., 2000; Chartrand & Lakin, 2013). However, as in any domain of psychological research, drawing links between real-world behaviours, such as imitation, and laboratory-based measurements is fundamentally challenging and requires considerable validation for it to be meaningful (Ramsey, 2018; Scheel et al., 2021; Vazire et al., 2022).

Much like psychological research in general (Vazire et al., 2022), concerns about validity (i.e., whether the research study measures what it intends to measure) in the field of automatic imitation have not been at the forefront of the research programme until recently (Cracco & Brass, 2019; Ramsey, 2018). For example, tasks that index so-called "automatic imitation" are routinely used that claim to be "social" in the sense that they index cognitive processes that are specifically tied to the control of social interactions (Brass et al., 2009; de Guzman et al., 2016; Sowden & Shah, 2014; Steinbeis, 2016; Wang & Hamilton, 2012). However, such claims are substantially undercut by a lack of evidence for important dimensions of validity (Ramsey, 2018; but see Cracco & Brass, 2019 for a different view).

In the current chapter, therefore, we outline the promise and pitfalls of studying the neurophysiological correlates of automatic imitation. First, we consider the promise that this field has to offer by reviewing recent evidence across disciplines on the cognitive and neurophysiological mechanisms underlying automatic imitation. Second, we consider the pitfalls of this field by evaluating the evidence in the context of four types of validity: construct validity, internal validity, external validity, and statistical-conclusion validity (Shadish et al., 2002; Vazire et al., 2022). The conclusion we reach is that there is much promise to taking a cognitive neuroscience approach to studying automatic imitation, as it holds the potential to study key mechanisms of social cognition. However, there are also considerable pitfalls, which include a lack of validity for some of the claims being made. The good news is that there are many avenues for future research that could lead to a more robust and cumulative science of automatic imitation that would help the field realise its considerable potential, and we outline these future research directions throughout the chapter.

Our approach is to focus on one particular task, which has been influential and widely used in cognitive neuroscience research on imitation due to its ease of use in a wide variety of contexts, including neuroscientific investigation. We think it is valuable to provide a detailed test-case of the types of claims being made regarding the neurophysiological correlates of imitation, rather than provide a more comprehensive overview, as others have already done so (Heyes & Catmur, 2022; Iacoboni, 2009). At the same time, we recognise that there are many forms and types of imitation, such as imitation of speech, gestures, and emotions, some of which are covered in other chapters within this book. Importantly, however, many of the themes covered in this chapter, such as a lack of evidence for validity, are widespread and well-documented across psychological science in general (Vazire et al., 2022). Therefore, the conclusions from this chapter are likely to be applicable to the many other forms of imitation covered in this book, as well as the wider social and cognitive neuroscience community.

The Promise: Automatic imitation as a Window into Understanding Mechanisms of Social Cognition

In social psychology, automatic imitation, also termed as mimicry, has been studied in naturalistic social interactions (Chartrand & Bargh, 1999; Chartrand & Lakin, 2013). These paradigms involve recording overt copying behaviours. In contrast, in cognitive psychology and cognitive neuroscience, SRC tasks of automatic imitation have been argued to measure covert processes involved in controlling our tendency to automatically imitate using reaction time (RT) measures or kinematics (Heyes, 2011; for a review on different behavioural tasks to measure automatic imitation, see Chap. 2, this volume). In automatic imitation research, the first SRC paradigms indexing automatic imitation were developed by Brass et al. (2000) and Stuermer and colleagues (2000) using finger and hand stimuli, respectively. Since then, different versions of the initially developed SRC paradigms have been widely used in order to index imitative processes, and involve finger movements (Bertenthal et al., 2006; Brass et al., 2000; Catmur & Heyes, 2011), hand opening/closing movements (Heyes et al., 2005; Press et al., 2008), or arm movements in vertical or horizontal planes (Kilner et al., 2003; Stanley et al., 2007).

In a typical SRC task indexing automatic imitation, participants are instructed to respond to an imperative cue while also viewing an action on screen that is either compatible or incompatible to their own response. For example, participants may be instructed to lift their index finger when they see a number "1" on the screen and lift their middle finger when they see a number "2" on the screen. Simultaneously, they either view an index or middle finger movement on the screen. In compatible trials, the movement they see and execute are the same, whereas in incompatible trials the movement they see and execute are different. Results from these experiments consistently show that features irrelevant to the task (the index and middle finger movements that participants view) influence reaction time performance. Participant reaction times are longer in the incompatible condition compared to the compatible condition, and this reaction time difference has been argued to be a measure of imitation control (Heyes et al., 2005; Heyes, 2011).

As with other SRC measures using reaction times, SRC measures of automatic imitation are typically far removed from imitative behaviour "in-the-wild" and involve computerised testing procedures in laboratory settings, which provide a higher degree of experimental control. These tasks, therefore, lend themselves well to neuroimaging investigations where movement is restricted such as in functional magnetic resonance imaging (fMRI) studies. Neurophysiological investigations across social and cognitive neuroscience on automatic imitation have therefore mostly used different versions of the SRC task to index the control of automatic imitation and its underlying neural mechanisms (Bien et al., 2009; Brass et al., 2009; Darda et al., 2018).

At least two processes are involved during compatible and incompatible trials on the SRC task: action representation and action control or selection (Ramsey, 2018). First, observed actions in both compatible and incompatible conditions are perceived and represented. Second, a particular action needs to be selected and executed, dependent on the task instructions. Task demands on compatible and incompatible trials are different—on compatible trials, the action control or selection mechanism is assisted by observing the same action that needs to be executed, whereas on incompatible trials, action selection is challenging as it requires an additional effort to inhibit the observed action and execute the correct one. Consequently, it has been argued that the difference between incompatible and compatible trials, termed the compatibility effect, partly indexes control over our tendency to automatically imitate, such that incompatible actions are suppressed and one's motor intentions are prioritised (Brass & Heyes, 2005; Heyes, 2011).

A related interpretation suggests that the compatibility effect indexes a process of self-other distinction wherein motor intentions of one's own actions need to be distinguished from the motor intentions of another's actions (Brass et al., 2009). According to this interpretation, the control of imitative behaviour as indexed by the compatibility effect can also be considered as a measure of online control of self-other representations (Brass & Heyes, 2005; Santiesteban et al., 2012). A self-other distinction mechanism is thought to be a key process underlying many other socio-cognitive processes including empathy and our ability to attribute mental states to ourselves and others (de Guzman et al., 2016; Sowden & Shah, 2014; Steinbeis, 2016).

Several human neuroimaging and patient studies have investigated the underlying neural mechanisms of representation and control in the context of automatic imitation (Fig. 6.1). Representation of actions is likely to involve both perceptual and motor representations. For example, visual perception of others in our environment involves person perception processes such as the representation of faces, bodies, and biological motion that span the ventral visual stream and occipitotemporal cortices (for a review, see Kanwisher, 2010), as well as brain regions associated with motor performance in dorsolateral frontoparietal cortex (Bonini et al., 2023; Caspers et al., 2010; Cross et al., 2009, 2012; Hardwick et al., 2018; Iacoboni, 2009; Molenberghs et al., 2012; Rizzolatti & Craighero, 2004). Such findings are robust in the sense that they have been demonstrated in hundreds of experiments and across thousands of participants, as well as in meta-analyses, and across different methods and species (Bonini et al. 2023; Caspers et al., 2010; Kanwisher, 2010; Hardwick et al., 2018).

One dominant view is that a sub-part of the action representation system, which spans frontoparietal cortex and has been labelled the mirror neuron system, is

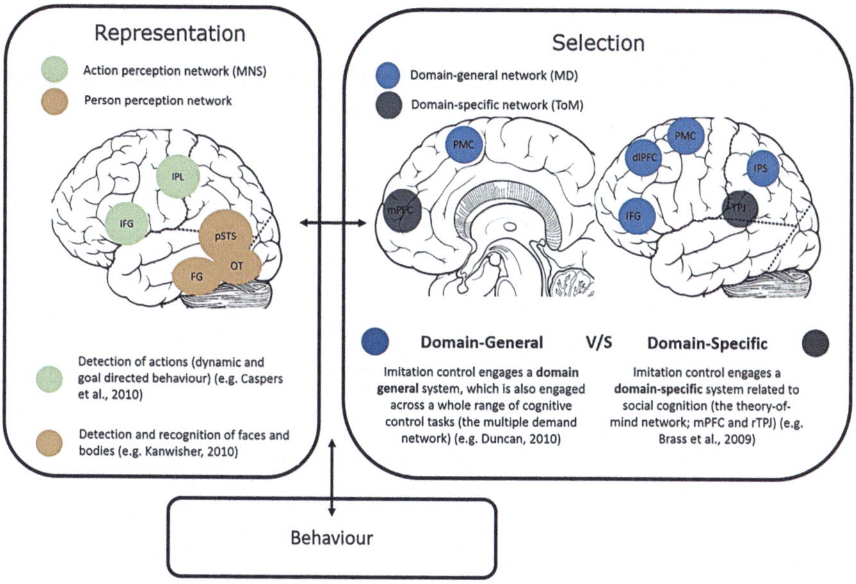

Fig. 6.1 Graphical illustration of action perception and representation, and a domain-specific (theory-of-mind network) and domain-general (multiple demand network) account of action control and selection in the context of automatic imitation. (Fig. 6.1 is taken from Darda & Ramsey, 2019)

involved in imitation (Heyes & Catmur, 2022; Iacoboni, 2009; Rizzolatti et al., 2001). The mirror neuron system is defined by cells (or macroscopic brain areas) that respond to the observation, as well as the execution, of action (Rizzolatti & Craighero, 2004). Given such neurophysiological properties and that imitation is defined by observing and performing actions, it seems intuitive that such a system would be involved in imitation in some way. However, we do not think it is intrinsically interesting that such cells exist or that they play some role in imitation. We think it could be interesting if studies were able to show what these particular cells do during imitative contexts, but that is very hard in human participants because of the reliance on non-invasive neuroscientific techniques that have poor spatial resolution relative to single-cell recordings. Nonetheless, for the purposes of this chapter, the main point to underscore here is that it seems highly likely that such a visuomotor action representation system plays some role in imitation as part of a distributed and multi-system neural network (Heyes & Catmur, 2022).

In contrast, the neurophysiological mechanisms underlying the control and selection of actions in the context of automatic imitation are less clear. In the following section, we outline two proposed accounts of control and selection in the context of imitation, which make divergent predictions: (1) Domain-specific control that relies on the theory-of-mind (ToM) network and a process of self-other distinction, and (2) Domain-general control, which relies on the multiple-demand network and general mechanisms of attention.

The first account, which is dominant in the literature, proposes that action control and selection in the context of automatic imitation rely on a domain-specific brain circuit related to social cognition and a mechanism of self-other distinction (Brass et al., 2009). The initial evidence supporting a domain-specific neural circuit underlying this process comes mainly from patient and neuroimaging studies, and points to the engagement of two candidate brain regions—the anterior medial prefrontal cortex (mPFC) and the right temporoparietal junction (rTPJ) (Brass et al., 2001, 2009; Brass & Heyes, 2005; Spengler et al., 2009). mPFC and rTPJ have been consistently identified as key nodes in the theory-of-mind (ToM) network, which is a brain network that is engaged in a wide range of social cognition tasks (Frith & Frith, 2010, 2012; Van Overwalle, 2009). Furthermore, there is a proposed functional dissociation between mPFC and rTPJ. The rTPJ is thought to differentiate between the self and the other, whereas the mPFC selects and enforces the correct action according to task demands (Brass et al., 2009). The functional division between mPFC and rTPJ is consistent with the interpretation that this particular compatibility effect indexes a process of self-other distinction.

The involvement of mPFC and rTPJ has been further supported by studies that demonstrated that patients with focal lesions show impaired imitation control (Brass et al., 2003; Spengler et al., 2010). Similarly, inhibiting rTPJ activity by transcranial magnetic stimulation (TMS) further impaired imitation control (Sowden & Catmur, 2015), whereas the impact of transcranial direct current stimulation on rTPJ was less clear (Hogeveen et al., 2015). More generally, mPFC and rTPJ have also been found to be engaged in other socio-cognitive tasks that are thought to rely on self-other control, including empathy, perspective taking, and attributing beliefs, desires, and attitudes to oneself and others (Frith & Frith, 2010, 2012; van Overwalle, 2009). Therefore, it is argued that the engagement of mPFC and rTPJ in this SRC task reflects the function of a neural network that is central to social cognition—the ToM network—and which is specifically engaged in regulating social interactions with other people (Brass et al., 2009; Sowden & Shah, 2014; de Guzman et al., 2016; Steinbeis, 2016; Wang & Hamilton, 2012).

A second account suggests that action selection and control in the context of automatic imitation may rely on a more domain-general neural circuit that is not specific to social contexts. That is, the control and selection mechanisms involved in SRC tasks with human action stimuli may not differ from mechanisms of control that are involved in resolving conflict in any other SRC task with pre-potent tendencies (Ramsey & Ward, 2020b). Cognitive control tasks such as the Stroop, Simon, and Flanker tasks require the control of automatic and overlearned response tendencies as well, similar to the SRC measure of automatic imitation, and these tasks have been found to engage dorsolateral frontoparietal cortices (Aron et al., 2014; Bunge et al., 2002; Nee et al., 2007; Wager et al., 2005).

This domain-general network that spans dorsolateral frontoparietal cortices has been labelled the multiple demand (MD) network because it is engaged across multiple mental operations that are deployed across a diverse range of stimuli and contexts (Duncan, 2010). For example, the same set of frontal and parietal brain regions were involved across 7 different, cognitively demanding tasks, which spanned a range of processes (reading, arithmetic, working memory, inhibition, and selection) and stimuli, such as words, numbers, colours, and spatial locations (Fedorenko et al., 2013). To further contextualise this brain system, the MD network shares functional and structural overlap with the frontoparietal brain circuit that is involved in a range of domain-general executive functions including processes such as filtering, selection, and inhibition, which can be applied to a range of inputs, both social and non-social (Corbetta et al., 2008; Petersen & Posner, 2012; Ptak, 2012).

In line with this domain-general account, some studies investigating the control of automatic imitation show engagement of the MD network (Bien et al., 2009; Crescentini et al., 2011; Cross et al., 2013; Darda et al., 2018; Marsh et al., 2016; Mengotti et al., 2012). For example, using fMRI, Darda et al. (2018) first identified MD and ToM brain areas with independent functional localiser scans. They then showed that there were no effects of compatibility in ToM regions, even though it was a high-power, multi-experiment study that involved 75+ participants. In contrast, there were clear and obvious compatibility effects in the MD network. This result is important because while the MD network was robustly engaged, there was not even suggestive evidence for the engagement of the ToM network, which overturns the original research that used considerably smaller sample sizes (e.g., Brass et al., 2001, 2009). Moreover, in a meta-analysis of all fMRI studies investigating automatic imitation using the SRC task, Darda and Ramsey (2019) found engagement of regions associated with the domain-general MD network for the imitative compatibility effect, but not mPFC or rTPJ (Darda & Ramsey, 2019). Together, these more recent and methodologically rigorous fMRI results suggest that the SRC effect using finger stimuli reflects a domain-general process of control and action selection rather than one tied to operations within the ToM network.

In summary, in both accounts of action control and selection in the context of automatic imitation, the visual input to the control or selection system is the same, i.e., the observed person and action. Moreover, the evidence identifying the neural circuits involved in person and action representation have been consistently reported in many studies. The neural circuits involved in person and action perception span the ventral visual stream, as well as lateral frontoparietal cortex (Caspers et al., 2010; Hardwick et al., 2018; Kanwisher, 2010). However, evidence from cognitive neuroscience regarding the selection or control mechanism that underlies the inhibition or control of automatic imitative tendencies is much more mixed. Initial evidence suggested the mechanisms might be domain-specific but later evidence has more strongly favoured a domain-general viewpoint. Of course, in principle, it could involve a combination of both types of control systems.

These mixed findings, especially the relatively weak evidence for domain-specific or "social" forms of control, raise questions about the validity of the claims being made. Based on decades of research studying cognitive control in similar SRC tasks, which do *not* have social dimensions (Duncan, 2010; Petersen & Posner, 2012), it would be quite striking if control and selection in the SRC imitation task requires such a departure from a standard "non-social" control model of executive function. In our view and the view of many others, such a departure from conventional models would require clear validation to empirically substantiate the novel claims being made (Flake & Fried, 2020; Ramsey, 2018; Ramsey & Ward, 2020b; Vazire et al., 2022). The novel claim being made by domain-specific, "social" control accounts is that this task indexes cognitive control processes that are specifically and uniquely tied to controlling interactions with other people and underpinned through the operation of the ToM network and a self-other distinction mechanism. Although this is plausible in principle, it needs empirical validation to be meaningful. To this end, in the next section, we evaluate the SRC automatic imitation task across a range of different types of validity.

The Pitfalls: A Lack of Validity Undercuts Some of the Specific Claims Being Made Regarding the Cognitive Mechanisms Underlying Automatic Imitation

Irrespective of the cognitive interpretation placed on the compatibility effect, and the underlying neural systems that are proposed to be engaged, almost all studies use the SRC paradigm as an index of automatic imitation. If the SRC paradigm is a laboratory equivalent of overt copying behaviours, as has been suggested (Heyes, 2011), the validity of the SRC task is a crucial component when evaluating evidence for domain-specificity for the control of automatic imitation.

Before turning to consider validity in more depth, however, we will quickly consider the reliability of the SRC measure of automatic imitation. Interference effects using hand or finger stimuli and an SRC paradigm appear to be reliably generated (Genschow et al., 2017). Genschow et al. (2017) used a split-half reliability approach to show that the congruency effect had high levels of reliability (Spearman-Brown coefficient $\rho^* = 0.86$ for the congruency effect). Also, Cracco and colleagues (2018a) performed a meta-analysis, which showed robust SRC effects across a range of labs, stimuli, and participants. Therefore, these results are promising, as reliable measures that replicate across samples are essential features of good measurement tools.

At this juncture, we want to make an obvious point: measures can be reliable without also being valid. For example, the SRC task with hand or finger stimuli could reliably generate an interference to reaction time *without* indexing covert imitative response tendencies, which are uniquely tied to social interactions and rely on a self-other distinction mechanism, as well as the ToM network. It is something very different to demonstrate with empirical evidence that a reaction time cost indexes covert imitative response tendencies, rather than some more general conflict resolution system. As such, in the following sub-sections, we now consider current evidence regarding the SRC automatic imitation task against four different types of validity outlined by Vazire et al. (2022) that span construct, internal, external, and statistical-conclusion validities. Whenever relevant, we also outline possible avenues for future research.

Before we do so, however, we also want to clarify the claim we are evaluating here. In the below analysis of validity, we focus on the conjoint claim that the congruency effect in this task indexes imitative tendencies and is resolved by a self-other mechanism that is underpinned by the ToM. This is because that is the claim that has been made and re-used by many other researchers to somehow verify (or reify) that this task indexes "social" processes in some way, rather than indexing general cognitive control mechanisms. It is also because this claim is, in part, based on neuroscientific evidence and this is a chapter about the neurophysiological correlates of imitation.

Construct Validity

Construct validity refers to the degree to which inferences about the construct of interest can be appropriately made from measured or manipulated measures. Simply put, it refers to the extent to which a test or variable measures what it is supposed to measure, and whether an experimental manipulation manipulates what it is supposed to manipulate (Cronbach & Meehl, 1955; Vazire et al., 2022; Wilson et al., 2010). Does the SRC measure of automatic imitation measure the construct it is meant to represent?

Like other behavioural assessments of cognitive or social processes, such as the dot-probe task (Parsons et al., 2019) or the reading the mind in the eyes task (Higgins et al., 2022, 2023), most researchers use the SRC measure of automatic imitation without reporting reliability metrics and without clear evidence of validity. This common practice is problematic because defining constructs and establishing the construct validity of measures is essential for valid inferences to be drawn about the cognitive and neural underpinnings of these constructs (Bringmann et al., 2022; Flake & Fried, 2020; Scheel et al., 2021). Moreover, such concerns are not restricted to cross-sectional research that use self-report measures, as they also apply to experimental designs that manipulate variables (Chambers & Tzavella, 2022; Chester & Lasko, 2021; Ejelöv & Luke, 2020; Fiedler et al., 2021; Gruijters, 2022).

To date, only one peer-reviewed study that we know of has attempted to provide evidence of construct validity for the SRC measure of automatic imitation. If the SRC measure of automatic imitation is related to overt imitative behaviours, evidence that the compatibility effect is correlated with overt copying behaviours can provide one measure of construct validity. However, a study by Genschow et al. (2017) addressing the reliability and validity of the SRC measure of imitation control found that overt copying behaviours did not correlate with the compatibility effect on the SRC task. Therefore, the relationship between imitation control as measured by the SRC task and imitation in real life seems to be more complex than has been previously suggested. Moreover, the measure of overt copying was found to be unreliable using a split-half test of reliability, which throws further caution on using demonstrably poor measurement tools to validate other tools. Subsequent work, which has just been published, has followed this up by re-analysing an existing dataset that used a different design (Cracco et al., 2024). However, this work remains exploratory and only permits suggestive inferences, as it lacks large scale replications where the relevant analysis plan is pre-registered in advance and where the experiments use well-justified and a priori sample size planning. In short, much more work is needed, in terms of defining and evidencing the construct that the SRC task is trying to tap into, before clear and obvious inferences can be drawn about the underlying neural systems that may support performance on this task.

Internal Validity

Internal validity refers to whether a causal relationship exists between the findings and manipulated variables that cannot be explained by other factors (McDermott, 2011). That is, internal validity is the validity of causal inferences and is dependent on whether alternative explanations are convincingly ruled out, and assumptions on which causal inferences are made are adequately justified (Vazire et al., 2022).

As previously stated, it has been claimed that the SRC imitation task relies on a self-other distinction mechanism that engages the ToM network (including anterior mPFC and rTPJ) and is uniquely tied to regulating social interactions with others by controlling imitative tendencies (Brass et al., 2009; Sowden & Shah, 2014; Spengler et al., 2009; Wang & Hamilton, 2012). Are there plausible alternative explanations that undermine this claim? Yes. Have plausible alternative explanations been convincingly ruled out? No. We detail a few of these alternatives below.

The first and most obvious alternative explanation that has *not* been convincingly ruled out is that control processes in this task are domain-general in nature. Much like other tasks that require executive functions, this task requires the inhibition of pre-potent responses, along with the selection and prioritisation of alternative responses (Duncan, 2010; Petersen & Posner, 2012; Ptak, 2012). As we have previously outlined in some detail, we see no reason why this task could not also rely on such a domain-general control architecture (Ramsey, 2018; Ramsey & Ward, 2020b). In fact, the most comprehensive fMRI work to date suggests that the control processes in this task are domain-general and not domain-specific (Darda et al., 2018; Darda & Ramsey, 2019). This means that not only has a compelling alterative explanation not been ruled out, but a growing body of evidence also suggests that it is highly likely to be involved.

Further evidence for a domain-general account has emerged using an empirical and computational modelling approach (Hemed et al., 2022). Hemed et al. (2022) found that automatic imitation occurs only when the others' actions are in the current response set, and not for otherwise familiar but task-irrelevant actions. The authors suggest that like other "automatic" processes such as perception or implicit learning, automatic imitation can be unintentionally "controlled". Thus, the task at best measures *conditional* imitation control and might reflect general S-R compatibility effects rather than mimicry or overt copying behaviours per se.

One way to make more progress establishing internal validity in the future would be to first use methods that aid theory development and require researchers to be more formal and explicit about the way parts of a system are thought to relate to each, such as by building computational models (Hintzman, 1991; Smaldino, 2017; Yarkoni, 2022) and causal graphs (Pearl, 1995, 2018). For example, mathematical formulations would make it easier to falsify and disagree with each other by making explicit the specific predictions that different accounts make, which would aid in the development of more mature theories (Nosek et al., 2022). We agree with others that there is currently too much wriggle room with verbally specified theories in general in psychology (Yarkoni, 2022), and specifically in relation to SRC measures of automatic imitation, which restricts more precise theory development.

We, therefore, very much welcome the few computational models that have been put forward to account for effects observed within this automatic imitation task (Cooper et al., 2013; Cracco & Cooper, 2019) or how the task is influenced by motor training (Cooper et al., 2013). However, like many other areas of psychology and human neuroscience research, we feel that the role of computational models needs expanding, in order to develop more mature theories (Proulx & Morey, 2021; Nosek et al., 2022). For example, and of particular relevance to this chapter, our lab has recently built a working computational model that clearly shows how the task could be solved by largely domain-general control and selection processes (Ward & Ramsey, 2024). If anyone is curious about the details of the computational model, then download it and run the model yourself, as it is freely available online and runs in the R programming language.

To give a further concrete example of how computational models can help clarify debate and organise future research, we consider evidence for "top-down modulation" of the SRC task by social factors (Ramsey & Ward, 2020a). Some authors seem to imply that if other social factors impact the size of the SRC effect, then it suggests that the cognitive processes involved in the task are "social" or "imitative" in some sense. In terms of empirical evidence, findings are mixed for this claim, with some studies showing modulation (Chiavarino et al., 2013; Cracco et al., 2018b; Genschow & Schindler, 2016) and others not (Galang & Obhi, 2020; Genschow et al., 2022; Rauchbauer et al., 2020).

In principle, however, we do not find this kind of argument at all convincing because the task itself lacks internal validity. That is, it seems to ignore the obvious, which is that social factors can impact mechanisms of attention (of which there are many), rather than anything specifically tied to imitation, and this could influence the size of the interference effect. Therefore, even if robust evidence emerges that some social factors can modulate the SRC task, without sufficient evidence for the internal validity of the task, it remains completely unknown and unproven if such modulation to interference reflects an impact on domain-general aspects of attention. As such, there is a very large evidence-based alternative explanation, which looms in the background and needs to be tackled head-on rather than avoided. And we think computational modelling can play a useful role in helping to elucidate the predictions that follow from different accounts of the underlying cognitive processes involved. In other words, computational models and causal graphs provide a more formal way to specify your hypotheses and assumptions, which can in turn be interrogated by others.

External Validity

External validity refers to whether observed effects are generalisable beyond the specific context of the study (Vazire et al., 2022). Can a given set of findings apply to a broader context?

As demonstrated in a recent meta-analysis, the SRC task of automatic imitation has been widely used across different samples, contexts, and stimulus groups (Cracco et al., 2018a). Therefore, the general compatibility effect as measured with reaction times appears to be quite robust in that it generalises across different sample characteristics and stimuli. However, the general compatibility effect that was measured in the majority of studies in the meta-analysis by Cracco, Bardi, and colleagues (2018a) is confounded by spatial effects. Indeed, only 54 out of 205 studies independently separated spatial from imitative effects. For instance, it is common for the observed hand to be a left hand and for participants to respond with their right hand. This experimental setup means that in compatible conditions, the observed finger is the same as the one that participants use (i.e., imitatively compatible), but the finger is also on the same side of space (i.e., spatially compatible).

An imitative compatibility effect that does not have the spatial confound can be measured by presenting both right and left hands to the participants (Catmur & Heyes, 2011), and calculating an effect of incompatible finger identity (rather than an incompatible spatial location). However, this so-called "imitative" effect is considerably smaller than the general compatibility effect, and more variable in the direction of the effect across people such that many individual participants show a negative imitative compatibility effect (Fig. 6.2). A negative compatibility effect shows that incompatible conditions facilitate, rather than interfere, with reaction times. So, even though the group average effect may consistently be above zero, a substantial minority of participants (approx. 25%) show the opposite of an imitative compatibility effect (compared to approx. 4% of participants who show the opposite of a spatial compatibility effect). Whilst we appreciate that the general approach in experimental psychology is to largely focus on group average effects (rather than individual differences), it does seem curious to us that if automatic imitation is so central to social life and this SRC task provides a signature of that process, then why do so many individuals not show an imitative effect? We feel that this would be worthy of addressing in future research.

Across psychology and cognitive neuroscience research more broadly, the generalisability of findings has also been questioned. For example, recent studies suggest that more than 50% of neuroimaging findings are likely to be false positives, and more than 40% of study findings do not replicate due to problems with small sample sizes, statistical power, p-hacking, and publication bias, as

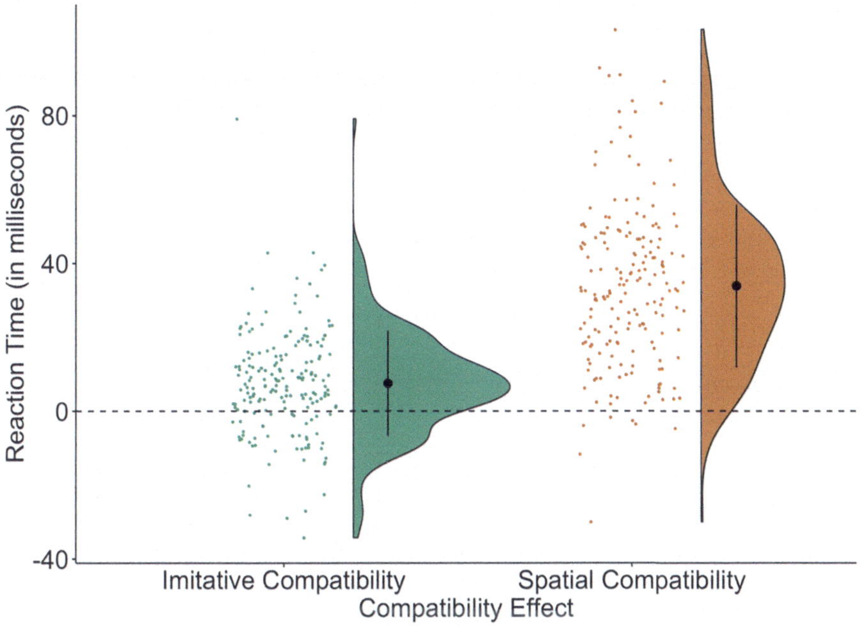

Fig. 6.2 Imitative and spatial compatibility effects as measured by reaction time. Error bars indicate standard deviation. The figure is based on data from Darda et al. (2020), Experiment 3, with $N = 189$ participants. (The data can be found on the Open Science Framework repository: https://osf.io/fsh9b/)

well as a lack of data sharing (Button et al., 2013; Hong et al., 2019; Munafò et al., 2017; Szucs & Ioannidis, 2017).

The generalisability and replicability of human neuroscience findings in the field of automatic imitation are also likely to be compromised given the low sample sizes of the original work and lack of pre-registered replication studies. The initial patient, fMRI, and neurostimulation studies, which are considered seminal in the field, have been used to evidence a role for the ToM network (mPFC and rTPJ) in controlling imitative tendencies (Brass et al., 2009; Spengler et al., 2009; Santiesteban et al., 2012). However, until pre-registered replication studies have been performed that use well-justified sample sizes and statistical approaches, we should remain very cautious about these results, given the wider landscape of irreproducible research and questionable research practices that plagues psychology and human neuroscience research in general (Munafò et al., 2017; Nosek et al., 2022; Simmons et al., 2018). As such, just like any other aspect of science, it is essential that modest claims are drawn before the reliability, validity, and generalisability of measures and findings can be evidenced (Ramsey, 2021).

Moreover, to our knowledge, neuroimaging studies of this SRC automatic imitation task have almost exclusively focused on Western populations, which means that one way of increasing external validity would be to generalise the findings across different populations underrepresented in research samples (Henrich et al., 2010).

Once more evidence for the basic validity of the task is established, it would then be interesting to see which components, if any, vary as a function of cultural background. If the task is shown to index domain-specific and domain-general forms of control, then it would be interesting to see if either of these vary across cultures. For example, maybe more "individualistic" cultures might show reduced interference compared to cultures known to be "collectivist", as has been evidenced in other socio-cognitive processes such as self-recognition and social orientation (Sui et al., 2009; Varnum et al., 2010). Such a proposal is speculative at the moment, however, and would necessarily require evidence for the validity of the basic task first.

Statistical-conclusion validity

Statistical-conclusion validity is the validity of statistical inferences. Due to low sample sizes (e.g., <20) and noisy signals, early fMRI work in general has been demonstrably proven to show poor statistical-conclusion validity (Cremers et al., 2017). This likely explains why the initial fMRI evidence using the SRC task (Brass et al., 2001) could not be replicated when it was submitted to a much more rigorous test using larger sample sizes with higher statistical power, multiple experiments, and functional localisers (Darda et al., 2018). The original work had 10 participants and used a fixed-effects analysis, which makes it hard to generalise beyond the data itself (Brass et al., 2001). It also makes chance variation and sampling error more likely.

The same lack of evidence for statistical-conclusion validity also applies to the patient and neurostimulation research using this task (Brass et al., 2003; Spengler et al., 2010; Hogeveen et al., 2015; Sowden & Catmur, 2015). Such work has been used to provide so-called "causal" evidence for the domain-specific, "social" control hypothesis. Like the fMRI work using this SRC task, the claims in these studies are based on one-off experiments with relatively small sample sizes. Pre-registered, larger-scale replication studies have not been completed to date. This is important to highlight because neurostimulation research, for example, has well-documented difficulties reproducing past findings, as well as the use of questionable research practices (Héroux et al., 2015; Jalali et al., 2017; Medina & Cason, 2017).

We want to make something clear here: we are not being critical of the sample sizes used in fMRI, patient or TMS studies in the late 1990s or early 2000s, as it was consistent with the industry standard of the time. We also do not want to deny that when technological innovations occur, which tend to be expensive, it might not be feasible to run studies that collect an optimal amount of data. We are firm believers that when such opportunities for novel research directions come along, researchers should not be afraid to be creative and pursue novel collaborations and exploit new techniques and methods. However, we do think that far too much emphasis was placed on these early results before the requisite confirmatory research was completed. It would have been extremely valuable to show in comprehensive follow-up research that these initial findings were robust and that the measurement tools were reliable and licensed valid inferences. As such, we think that researchers should adopt a more cautious attitude to science, especially when evaluating novel findings (Ramsey, 2021).

In the future, we see this as a good opportunity to embrace meta-science and open science best-practices (Munafo et al., 2017), as well as the routine completion of much more preparatory groundwork before moving towards a confirmatory "test" of a hypothesis (Scheel et al., 2021). For example, researchers can pre-register the main question and specific analysis pipeline to reduce "p-hacking" and weak statistical inferences. Furthermore, making the data available (even large fMRI datasets) would allow others to use it to guide future research plans, as well as perform alternative analyses and meta-analyses. There are plenty of resources available for making data available and for using externally validated processing scripts (Esteban et al., 2019; Poldrack & Gorgolewski, 2014, 2017; Yarkoni et al., 2011).

Summary and Implications

We have reviewed cognitive neuroscience claims associated with the SRC automatic imitation task across four different types of validity. We find that it lacks clear and comprehensive evidence for each kind of validity. Of course, this does not mean that the SRC task does not measure imitation control at all, or that imitation does not rely on a self-other distinction mechanism. It just means that such claims are currently unproven. It might be measuring one component of a more complex and multi-component process of imitation (Genschow et al., 2017), which we currently do not understand well. However, it might also only reflect domain-general cognitive control mechanisms that are applied to social stimuli (hands, fingers). The current state of the evidence suggests that alternative domain-general interpretations exist and are well-evidenced. In contrast, when subjected to a more methodologically rigorous test, there was not even suggestive evidence that the ToM network (mPFC and rTPJ) was engaged during imitation control (Darda et al., 2018; Darda & Ramsey, 2019). Therefore, until solid evidence for the validity of the SRC task can be established, and credible alternative explanations ruled out, we suggest that the task should *not* be used as an index of self-other distinction that is uniquely tied to social interactions through the control of imitation.

If the task lacks evidence of validity, why do researchers keep using it? We understand why many researchers would not want to discard this laboratory task. It has many appealing practical advantages. It is quick and easy to administer, and it reliably demonstrates an interference effect, which some say can address questions in social cognition. Therefore, it is appealing. And there may not be any reason to discard it, if it can be used in such a manner that it licenses empirically justifiable and valid claims. To put this in a wider context, validity is lacking from many paradigms, not just this one (Vazire et al., 2022). So, this reflects a more general problem that extends well beyond this task alone, which should not be ignored, otherwise we will spend another 20 years or more doing research with paradigms that lack conventional evidence for the validity of the underlying claims.

A further reason why the task has been widely used despite a lack of validity is that publishing, grant allocation, and hiring incentives are not aligned with first doing "boring but necessary" work (Scheel et al., 2021). Therefore, a research culture has developed that has downplayed or completely ignored the importance of good measurement (Flake & Fried, 2020). If it is simply not necessary to do this kind of work before you publish it in mainstream journals, why bother doing it?

A final reason is that some researchers argue that the SRC task already has sufficient evidence of internal validity to make claims that are specifically tied to automatic imitative tendencies (Cracco & Brass, 2019). Consequently, it has been suggested that there is no need to provide further empirical validation for the SRC automatic imitation task against the conventional types of validity outlined above (Cracco & Brass, 2019). Instead, Cracco & Brass (2019) suggest that measuring reaction time interference in an experimental task that involves observing and responding with the same or different body part is already sufficient evidence to validate the claims being made regarding automatic imitative tendencies. We (and many others) disagree and suggest that measurement quality is at the very heart of good science, which makes providing comprehensive evidence of the validity of measurement tools an essential component in making meaningful inferences from data (Chester & Lakso, 2021; Fiedler et al., 2021; Flake & Fried, 2020; Scheel et al., 2021). Moreover, we have so far seen no special reasons why this same logic of good measurement and validation should not be applied to the SRC automatic imitation task, or any other measure of imitation for that matter.

The minimalist validity position taken by Cracco and Brass (2019) leaves open the very real possibility that social stimuli (fingers, hands, etc.) could be driving a response conflict that is resolved by a domain-general response conflict system. Therefore, using this type of SRC task could be probing the operations of a domain-general response conflict system, just with social stimuli. As such, based on the evidence reviewed here, there seems to be a misalignment between the current empirical validation of the experimental design and the inference about the nature of cognitive systems being tested. To go beyond this position and make a more specific claim about the type of control being measured here, one that is *not* domain-general, would need clear validation, just like any other task or measure in any other aspect of psychology (Vazire et al., 2022).

If researchers want to proceed with using the SRC task without first establishing evidence for the types of validity that we have reviewed in this chapter, then the inferences drawn should be calibrated appropriately. That is, we feel it is no longer tenable to claim that the SRC task indexes automatic imitative tendencies that tap into a process of self-other distinction, which relies on the ToM network. Instead, the burden of proof is on researchers making these claims when using these tasks to provide the relevant evidence that validates their inferences. As with any task, however, in principle there are multiple ways that they can be used and many purposes that they may serve, which means it could still be valuable for addressing a range of research questions. For example, it might be informative to study domain-general cognition in this way, but it would need to be explicitly stated how. What are the theoretical and empirical contributions being made with such a paradigm? For the reasons outlined in this chapter, however, we do not see how that the task can be used to make claims about processes that are uniquely tied to regulating social interactions.

Limitations and Constraints on Generality

We have intentionally chosen to focus on one specific type of task here. Therefore, by definition, our analysis does not directly extend to all possible types of imitation tasks. However, although we use one task to provide a thorough test-case example, we think that a lack of evidence for validity has a high likelihood of being applicable to other imitation tasks, given the widespread validity issues in psychology (Vazire et al., 2022). While the identical validity issues may or may not arise in other imitative contexts, it is more that the principle and process of establishing validity and reliability, as well as other good measurement practices (Fiedler et al., 2021; Flake & Fried, 2020; Scheel et al., 2021), will almost certainly be applicable in other contexts. Moreover, the SRC imitation task has been used and cited widely (e.g., Brass et al., 2001 has 800+ citations), which means that it is having a substantial impact on various literatures, which is likely to influence the allocation of resources, such as grant funding and hiring decisions. As such, comprehensive validation of such work seems to be important, irrespective of whether the validity concerns raised here generalise to other imitation tasks or not.

We also chose to focus on evaluating the conjoint claim that that the congruency effect in this task indexes imitative tendencies and is resolved by a self-other mechanism that is underpinned by the ToM. However, we would also be curious to see what kind of evidence can be brought to bear on a claim about imitation in general. That is, what is the evidence that the congruency effect in this task, specifically, is related to automatic imitation? We are not talking about outlining assumptions that suggest that observing actions is likely to trigger imitative responses. We are also not talking about evidence that observing actions engages the motor system. They are not sufficient. Instead, we are talking about providing evidence for the validity of using the congruency effect in this task as an index of automatic imitative tendencies. Where is the evidence that shows the incongruent condition requires more automatic imitation than the congruent condition, rather than more attentional control, such as inhibition and selection? And how could researchers use this evidence to validate the inferences they make? For example, in the routine use of this task, how could an individual researcher or research group demonstrate that the congruency effect is actually indexing automatic imitative tendencies, rather than the cost of resolving conflict?

A basic task analysis easily shows that actions are being observed and performed and that there is a cost to response times when these are in conflict. That much we can all agree upon. But, as we outline in some detail elsewhere (Ramsey & Ward,

2020b; Ward & Ramsey, 2024), what we cannot see from the evidence presented to date (e.g., Heyes, 2011; Cracco et al., 2018a), is how this reaction time cost is specifically tied to automatic imitative tendencies, rather than the cost of resolving conflict, just like other conflict tasks that do not involve social stimuli (e.g., stroop, flanker). In our view and assessment of the literature, the suggestion that automatic imitative tendencies drive this congruency effect is one possibility amongst many plausible alternatives. We therefore do not agree that evidence showing that movement execution is facilitated by compatible and impeded by incompatible observed movements can used to validate the claim that imitation "exists" (Cracco et al., 2018a; Heyes, 2011). As such, even if one only considers a less elaborate claim about automatic imitative tendencies, which ignores roles for a self-other distinction mechanism and the ToM network, there is still a gap between the measured congruency effect and the inference being made about information processing systems. We leave this claim about imitation in general for others to consider in future work.

A related point is that our focus has been on laboratory tasks that are amenable to study in controlled environments and with neuroscience equipment. They do use social stimuli, in that they depict human actions, but we are not talking about studies that even remotely approximate real-life social interaction. Consequently, there need not be a direct mapping between research in the lab and research in naturalistic settings or "in-the-wild" (Kingstone et al., 2008). For example, real-life social interactions may depend more upon socially specific forms of control than in lab experiments, although this is an empirical question. As such, evidence that validates the claims being made in field studies would still be required. There is simply a very different starting point, in terms of the richness of the social environment, between laboratory-based reaction time experiments and real-life social interactions. In summary, if very simplified social stimuli are going to be used to make inferences about socially specific forms of cognition, then there is a requisite need evidence for the validity of those claims. And furthermore, such claims may not generalise in a straightforward manner beyond the lab. With this said, the ever-growing development of mobile neuroimaging technologies should may make it easier to test neuroscientific questions in more real-world contexts (Redcay & Schilbach, 2019; Shamay-Tsoory & Mendelsohn, 2019).

We have also chosen to focus on the available evidence for the validity of the claims being made. A related discussion, which we do not have space to cover in this work, would concern the need for greater conceptual clarity in addition to providing evidence of validity (Bringmann et al., 2022; Scheel et al., 2021). With all the many and varied forms and possible component processes of imitation (Chartrand & Lakin, 2013; Heyes, 2011), this seems like a ripe avenue for future research. The overall aim would be to provide a clear and justified link between the type or component of imitation under scrutiny and the type of evidence of validity that would be required to substantiate the specific claims being made.

Conclusion

In this chapter, we have reviewed evidence regarding the neuroscientific foundations of imitation, specifically the SRC imitation task. We have shown that use of such a task to index processes relating to the control of automatic imitative tendencies, which rely on a self-other distinction mechanism that is uniquely tied to human social interaction and engages the theory-of-mind network, lacks essential evidence for various forms of validity. Instead, given current evidence, the best estimate is that this task engages domain-general forms of control that are underpinned by the multiple-demand network. For claims to be supported regarding socially specific forms of control when using this task, robust evidence for each of the four validities that we have outlined above would be required. Fortunately, with the emergence of the meta-science movement over the past 10 years (Munafo et al., 2017; Nosek et al., 2022), there are more resources than ever before available to help unlock the vast potential that social and cognitive neuroscience approaches can offer to understand the mechanisms of human social behaviour, including automatic imitation.

Acknowledgments We thank Robert Ross and Wendy Higgins, as well as the Editors of this book (Oliver Genschow and Emiel Cracco), for valuable comments on earlier versions of this work.

References

Aron, A. R., Robbins, T. W., & Poldrack, R. A. (2014). Inhibition and the right inferior frontal cortex: One decade on. *Trends in Cognitive Sciences, 18*, 177–185. https://doi.org/10.1016/j.tics.2013.12.003

Bertenthal, B. I., Longo, M. R., & Kosobud, A. (2006). Imitative response tendencies following observation of intransitive actions. *Journal of Experimental Psychology: Human Perception and Performance, 32*, 210–225. https://doi.org/10.1037/0096-1523.32.2.210

Bien, N., Roebroeck, A., Goebel, R., & Sack, A. T. (2009). The brain's intention to imitate: The neurobiology of intentional versus automatic imitation. *Cerebral Cortex, 19*, 2338–2351. https://doi.org/10.1093/cercor/bhn251

Bonini, L., Rotunno, C., Arcuri, E., & Gallese, V. (2023). The mirror mechanism: Linking perception and social interaction. *Trends in Cognitive Sciences, 27*, 220–221. https://doi.org/10.1016/j.tics.2022.12.010

Brass, M., & Heyes, C. (2005). Imitation: Is cognitive neuroscience solving the correspondence problem? *Trends in Cognitive Sciences, 9*, 489–495. https://doi.org/10.1016/j.tics.2005.08.007

Brass, M., Bekkering, H., Wohlschlager, A., & Prinz, W. (2000). Compatibility between observed and executed finger movements: Comparing symbolic, spatial, and imitative cues. *Brain and Cognition, 44*, 124–143. https://doi.org/10.1006/brcg.2000.1225

Brass, M., Zysset, S., & von Cramon, D. Y. (2001). The inhibition of imitative response tendencies. *NeuroImage, 14*, 1416–1423. https://doi.org/10.1006/nimg.2001.0944

Brass, M., Derrfuss, J., Matthes-von Cramon, G., & von Cramon, D. Y. (2003). Imitative response tendencies in patients with frontal brain lesions. *Neuropsychology, 17*, 265–271. https://doi.org/10.1037/0894-4105.17.2.265

Brass, M., Ruby, P., & Spengler, S. (2009). Inhibition of imitative behaviour and social cognition. *Philosophical Transactions of the Royal Society B: Biological Sciences, 364*, 2359–2367. https://doi.org/10.1098/rstb.2009.0066

Bringmann, L. F., Elmer, T., & Eronen, M. I. (2022). Back to basics: The importance of conceptual clarification in psychological science. *Current Directions in Psychological Science, 31*, 340–346. https://doi.org/10.1177/09637214221096485

Bunge, S. A., Hazeltine, E., Scanlon, M. D., Rosen, A. C., & Gabrieli, J. D. E. (2002). Dissociable contributions of prefrontal and parietal cortices to response selection. *NeuroImage, 17*, 1562–1571. https://doi.org/10.1006/nimg.2002.1252

Button, K. S., Ioannidis, J. P. A., Mokrysz, C., Nosek, B. A., Flint, J., Robinson, E. S. J., & Munafo, M. R. (2013). Power failure: Why small sample size undermines the reliability of neuroscience. *Nature Reviews. Neuroscience, 14*, 365–376. https://doi.org/10.1038/nrn3475

Byrne, R. W., & Russon, A. E. (1998). Learning by imitation: A hierarchical approach. *Behavioral and Brain Sciences, 21*, 667–684. https://doi.org/10.1017/s0140525x98001745

Caspers, S., Zilles, K., Laird, A. R., & Eickhoff, S. B. (2010). ALE meta-analysis of action observation and imitation in the human brain. *NeuroImage, 50*, 1148–1167. https://doi.org/10.1016/j.neuroimage.2009.12.112

Catmur, C., & Heyes, C. (2011). Time course analyses confirm independence of imitative and spatial compatibility. *Journal of Experimental Psychology: Human Perception and Performance, 37*, 409–421. https://doi.org/10.1037/a0019325

Chambers, C. D., & Tzavella, L. (2022). The past, present and future of registered reports. *Nature Human Behaviour, 6*, 29–42. https://doi.org/10.1038/s41562-021-01193-7

Chartrand, T. L., & Bargh, J. A. (1999). The chameleon effect: The perception-behavior link and social interaction. *Journal of Personality and Social Psychology, 76*, 893–910. https://doi.org/10.1037/0022-3514.76.6.893

Chartrand, T. L., & Lakin, J. L. (2013). The antecedents and consequences of human behavioral mimicry. *Annual Review of Psychology, 64*, 285–308. https://doi.org/10.1146/annurev-psych-113011-143754

Chartrand, T. L., & van Baaren, R. (2009). Human mimicry, Chapter 5. In P. Z. Mark (Ed.), *Advances in experimental social psychology* (Vol. 41, pp. 219–274). Academic. https://doi.org/10.1016/s0065-2601(08)00405-x

Chester, D. S., & Lasko, E. N. (2021). Construct validation of experimental manipulations in social psychology: Current practices and recommendations for the future. *Perspectives on Psychological Science, 16*, 377–395. https://doi.org/10.1177/1745691620950684

Chiavarino, C., Bugiani, S., Grandi, E., & Colle, L. (2013). Is automatic imitation based on goal coding or movement coding? *Experimental Psychology, 60*, 213–225. https://doi.org/10.1027/1618-3169/a000190

Cooper, R. P., Catmur, C., & Heyes, C. (2013). Are automatic imitation and spatial compatibility mediated by different processes?. *Cognitive Science, 37*, 605–630. https://doi.org/10.1111/j.1551-6709.2012.01252.x

Corbetta, M., Patel, G., & Shulman, G. L. (2008). The reorienting system of the human brain: From environment to theory of mind. *Neuron, 58*, 306–324. https://doi.org/10.1016%2Fj.neuron.2008.04.017

Cracco, E., & Brass, M. (2019). Reaction time indices of automatic imitation measure imitative response tendencies. *Consciousness and Cognition, 68*, 115–118. https://doi.org/10.1016/j.concog.2019.01.001

Cracco, E., Genschow, O., & Brass, M. (2024). Covert and overt automatic imitation are correlated. *Psychonomic Bulletin & Review, 31*, 1348–1352. https://doi.org/10.3758/s13423-023-02420-0

Cracco, E., & Cooper, R. P. (2019). Automatic imitation of multiple agents: A computational model. *Cognitive Psychology, 113*, 101224. https://doi.org/10.1016/j.cogpsych.2019.101224

Cracco, E., Bardi, L., Desmet, C., Genschow, O., Rigoni, D., De Coster, L., Radkova, I., Deschrijver, E., & Brass, M. (2018a). Automatic imitation: A meta-analysis. *Psychological Bulletin, 144*, 453–500. https://doi.org/10.1037/bul0000143

Cracco, E., Genschow, O., Radkova, I., & Brass, M. (2018b). Automatic imitation of pro- and antisocial gestures: Is implicit social behavior censored? *Cognition, 170*, 179–189. https://doi.org/10.1016/j.cognition.2017.09.019

Cremers, H. R., Wager, T. D., & Yarkoni, T. (2017). The relation between statistical power and inference in fMRI. *PLoS One, 12*, e0184923. https://doi.org/10.1371/journal.pone.0184923
Crescentini, C., Mengotti, P., Grecucci, A., & Rumiati, R. I. (2011). The effect of observed biological and non biological movements on action imitation: An fMRI study. *Brain Research, 1420*, 80–92. https://doi.org/10.1016/j.brainres.2011.08.077
Cronbach, L. J., & Meehl, P. E. (1955). Construct validity in psychological tests. *Psychological Bulletin, 52*, 281–302. https://doi.org/10.1037/h0040957
Cross, E. S., Kraemer, D. J. M., Hamilton, A. F. d. C., Kelley, W. M., & Grafton, S. T. (2009). Sensitivity of the action observation network to physical and observational learning. *Cerebral Cortex, 19*, 315–326. https://doi.org/10.1093/cercor/bhn083
Cross, E. S., Liepelt, R., Hamilton, A. F. d. C., Parkinson, J., Ramsey, R., Stadler, W., & Prinz, W. (2012). Robotic movement preferentially engages the action observation network. *Human Brain Mapping, 33*, 2238–2254. https://doi.org/10.1002/hbm.21361
Cross, K. A., Torrisi, S., Reynolds Losin, E. A., & Iacoboni, M. (2013). Controlling automatic imitative tendencies: Interactions between mirror neuron and cognitive control systems. *NeuroImage, 83*, 493–504. https://doi.org/10.1016/j.neuroimage.2013.06.060
Darda, K. M., & Ramsey, R. (2019). The inhibition of automatic imitation: A meta-analysis and synthesis of fMRI studies. *NeuroImage, 197*, 320–329. https://doi.org/10.1016/j.neuroimage.2019.04.059
Darda, K. M., Butler, E. E., & Ramsey, R. (2018). Functional specificity and sex differences in the neural circuits supporting the inhibition of automatic imitation. *Journal of Cognitive Neuroscience, 30*, 914–933. https://doi.org/10.1162/jocn_a_01261
Darda, K. M., Butler, E. E., & Ramsey, R. (2020). Individual differences in social and non-social cognitive control. *Cognition, 202*, 104317. https://doi.org/10.1016/j.cognition.2020.104317
de Guzman, M., Bird, G., Banissy, M. J., & Catmur, C. (2016). Self–other control processes in social cognition: From imitation to empathy. *Philosophical Transactions of the Royal Society B: Biological Sciences, 371*. https://doi.org/10.1098/rstb.2015.0079
Duncan, J. (2010). The multiple-demand (MD) system of the primate brain: Mental programs for intelligent behaviour. *Trends in Cognitive Sciences, 14*, 172–179. https://doi.org/10.1016/j.tics.2010.01.004
Ejelöv, E., & Luke, T. J. (2020). "Rarely safe to assume": Evaluating the use and interpretation of manipulation checks in experimental social psychology. *Journal of Experimental Social Psychology, 87*, 103937. https://doi.org/10.1016/j.jesp.2019.103937
Esteban, O., Markiewicz, C. J., Blair, R. W., Moodie, C. A., Isik, A. I., Erramuzpe, A., Kent, J. D., Goncalves, M., DuPre, E., Snyder, M., Oya, H., Ghosh, S. S., Wright, J., Durnez, J., Poldrack, R. A., & Gorgolewski, K. J. (2019). fMRIPrep: A robust preprocessing pipeline for functional MRI. *Nature Methods, 16*, 1. https://doi.org/10.1038/s41592-018-0235-4
Fedorenko, E., Duncan, J., & Kanwisher, N. (2013). Broad domain generality in focal regions of frontal and parietal cortex. *Proceedings of the National Academy of Sciences, 110*, 16616–16621. https://doi.org/10.1073/pnas.1315235110
Fiedler, K., McCaughey, L., & Prager, J. (2021). Quo Vadis, methodology? The key role of manipulation checks for validity control and quality of science. *Perspectives on Psychological Science, 16*, 816–826. https://doi.org/10.1177/1745691620970602
Flake, J. K., & Fried, E. I. (2020). Measurement schmeasurement: Questionable measurement practices and how to avoid them. *Advances in Methods and Practices in Psychological Science, 3*, 456–465. https://doi.org/10.1177/2515245920952393
Frith, U., & Frith, C. D. (2010). The social brain: Allowing humans to boldly go where no other species has been. *Philosophical Transactions of the Royal Society B: Biological Sciences, 365*, 165–176. https://doi.org/10.1098/rstb.2009.0160
Frith, C. D., & Frith, U. (2012). Mechanisms of social cognition. *Annual Review of Psychology, 63*, 287–313. https://doi.org/10.1146/annurev-psych-120710-100449
Galang, C. M., & Obhi, S. S. (2020). Automatic imitation does not predict levels of prosocial behaviour in a modified dictator game. *Acta Psychologica, 204*, 103022. https://doi.org/10.1016/j.actpsy.2020.103022

Genschow, O., & Schindler, S. (2016). The influence of group membership on cross-contextual imitation. *Psychonomic Bulletin & Review, 23*, 1257–1265. https://doi.org/10.3758/s13423-015-0983-4

Genschow, O., van Den Bossche, S., Cracco, E., Bardi, L., Rigoni, D., & Brass, M. (2017). Mimicry and automatic imitation are not correlated. *PLoS One, 12*, e0183784. https://doi.org/10.1371/journal.pone.0183784

Genschow, O., Westfal, M., Cracco, E., & Crusius, J. (2022). Group membership does not modulate automatic imitation. *Psychological Research, 86*, 780–791. https://doi.org/10.1007/s00426-021-01526-1

Gruijters, S. L. K. (2022). Making inferential leaps: Manipulation checks and the road towards strong inference. *Journal of Experimental Social Psychology, 98*, 104251. https://doi.org/10.1016/j.jesp.2021.104251

Hardwick, R. M., Caspers, S., Eickhoff, S. B., & Swinnen, S. P. (2018). Neural correlates of action: Comparing meta-analyses of imagery, observation, and execution. *Neuroscience & Biobehavioral Reviews, 94*, 31–44. https://doi.org/10.1016/j.neubiorev.2018.08.003

Hemed, E., Mark-Tavger, I., Hertz, U., Bakbani-Elkayam, S., & Eitam, B. (2022). Automatically controlled: Task irrelevance fully cancels otherwise automatic imitation. *Journal of Experimental Psychology: General, 151*, 996–1017. https://doi.org/10.1037/xge0001117

Henrich, J. (2015). The secret of our success: How culture is driving human evolution, domesticating our species, and making us smarter. In *The secret of our success*. Princeton University Press. https://doi.org/10.1515/9781400873296

Henrich, J., Heine, S. J., & Norenzayan, A. (2010). The weirdest people in the world? *Behavioral and Brain Sciences, 33*, 61–83. https://doi.org/10.1017/S0140525X0999152X

Héroux, M. E., Taylor, J. L., & Gandevia, S. C. (2015). The use and abuse of transcranial magnetic stimulation to modulate corticospinal excitability in humans. *PLoS One, 10*, e0144151. https://doi.org/10.1371/journal.pone.0144151

Heyes, C. (2011). Automatic imitation. *Psychological Bulletin, 137*, 463–483. https://doi.org/10.1037/a0022288

Heyes, C., & Catmur, C. (2022). What happened to mirror neurons?. *Perspectives on Psychological Science, 17*, 153–168. https://doi.org/10.1177/1745691621990638

Heyes, C., Bird, G., Johnson, H., & Haggard, P. (2005). Experience modulates automatic imitation. *Cognitive Brain Research, 22*, 233–240. https://doi.org/10.1016/j.cogbrainres.2004.09.009

Higgins, W. C., Ross, R. M., Langdon, R., & Polito, V. (2022). The "Reading the Mind in the Eyes" test shows poor psychometric properties in a large, demographically representative U.S. sample. *Assessment*, 10731911221124342. https://doi.org/10.1177/10731911221124342

Higgins, W. C., Ross, R. M., Polito, V., & Kaplan, D. M. (2023). Three threats to the validity of the Reading the Mind in the Eyes test: A commentary on pavlova and Sokolov (2022). *Neuroscience & Biobehavioral Reviews, 147*, 105088. https://doi.org/10.1016/j.neubiorev.2023.105088

Hintzman, D. L. (1991). Why are formal models useful in psychology? In *Relating theory and data: Essays on human memory in honor of Bennet B. Murdock* (pp. 39–56). Lawrence Erlbaum Associates, Inc.

Hogeveen, J., Obhi, S. S., Banissy, M. J., Santiesteban, I., Press, C., Catmur, C., & Bird, G. (2015). Task-dependent and distinct roles of the temporoparietal junction and inferior frontal cortex in the control of imitation. *Social Cognitive and Affective Neuroscience, 10*, 1003–1009. https://doi.org/10.1093/scan/nsu148

Hong, Y.-W., Yoo, Y., Han, J., Wager, T. D., & Woo, C.-W. (2019). False-positive neuroimaging: Undisclosed flexibility in testing spatial hypotheses allows presenting anything as a replicated finding. *NeuroImage, 195*, 384–395. https://doi.org/10.1016/j.neuroimage.2019.03.070

Iacoboni, M. (2009). Imitation, empathy, and mirror neurons. *Annual Review of Psychology, 60*, 653–670. https://doi.org/10.1146/annurev.psych.60.110707.163604

Jalali, R., Miall, R. C., & Galea, J. M. (2017). No consistent effect of cerebellar transcranial direct current stimulation on visuomotor adaptation. *Journal of Neurophysiology, 118*, 655–665. https://doi.org/10.1152/jn.00896.2016

Kanwisher, N. (2010). Functional specificity in the human brain: A window into the functional architecture of the mind. *Proceedings of the National Academy of Sciences, 107*, 11163–11170. https://doi.org/10.1073/pnas.1005062107

Kavanagh, L. C., & Winkielman, P. (2016). The functionality of spontaneous mimicry and its influences on affiliation: An implicit socialization account. *Frontiers in Psychology, 7*. https://doi.org/10.3389/fpsyg.2016.00458

Kilner, J. M., Paulignan, Y., & Blakemore, S. J. (2003). An interference effect of observed biological movement on action. *Current Biology, 13*, 522–525. https://doi.org/10.1016/s0960-9822(03)00165-9

Kingstone, A., Smilek, D., & Eastwood, J. D. (2008). Cognitive ethology: A new approach for studying human cognition. *British Journal of Psychology, 99*, 317–340. https://doi.org/10.1348/000712607X251243

Legare, C. H., & Nielsen, M. (2015). Imitation and innovation: The dual engines of cultural learning. *Trends in Cognitive Sciences, 19*, 688–699. https://doi.org/10.1016/j.tics.2015.08.005

Marsh, L. E., Bird, G., & Catmur, C. (2016). The imitation game: Effects of social cues on 'imitation' are domain-general in nature. *NeuroImage, 139*, 368–375. https://doi.org/10.1016/j.neuroimage.2016.06.050

McDermott, R. (2011). Internal and external validity. Cambridge handbook of experimental political science, 27.

Medina, J., & Cason, S. (2017). No evidential value in samples of transcranial direct current stimulation (tDCS) studies of cognition and working memory in healthy populations. *Cortex, 94*, 131–141. https://doi.org/10.1016/j.cortex.2017.06.021

Meltzoff, A. N., & Prinz, W. (2002). *The imitative mind: Development, evolution and brain bases*. Cambridge University Press.

Mengotti, P., Corradi-Dell'Acqua, C., & Rumiati, R. I. (2012). Imitation components in the human brain: An fMRI study. *NeuroImage, 59*, 1622–1630. https://doi.org/10.1016/j.neuroimage.2011.09.004

Molenberghs, P., Cunnington, R., & Mattingley, J. B. (2012). Brain regions with mirror properties: A meta-analysis of 125 human fMRI studies. *Neuroscience & Biobehavioral Reviews, 36*, 341–349. https://doi.org/10.1016/j.neubiorev.2011.07.004

Munafò, M. R., Nosek, B. A., Bishop, D. V. M., Button, K. S., Chambers, C. D., Percie du Sert, N., Simonsohn, U., Wagenmakers, E.-J., Ware, J. J., & Ioannidis, J. P. A. (2017). A manifesto for reproducible science. *Nature Human Behaviour, 1*, 0021. https://doi.org/10.1038/s41562-016-0021

Nagy, E., & Molnar, P. (2004). Homo imitans or homo provocans? Human imprinting model of neonatal imitation. *Infant Behavior and Development, 27*, 54–63. https://doi.org/10.1016/j.infbeh.2003.06.004

Nee, D., Wager, T., & Jonides, J. (2007). Interference resolution: Insights from a meta-analysis of neuroimaging tasks. *Cognitive, Affective, & Behavioral Neuroscience, 7*, 1–17. https://doi.org/10.3758/cabn.7.1.1

Nosek, B. A., Hardwicke, T. E., Moshontz, H., Allard, A., Corker, K. S., Dreber, A., Fidler, F., Hilgard, J., Struhl, M. K., Nuijten, M. B., Rohrer, J. M., Romero, F., Scheel, A. M., Scherer, L. D., Schönbrodt, F. D., & Vazire, S. (2022). Replicability, robustness, and reproducibility in psychological science. *Annual Review of Psychology, 73*, 719–748. https://doi.org/10.1146/annurev-psych-020821-114157

Parsons, S., Kruijt, A.-W., & Fox, E. (2019). Psychological science needs a standard practice of reporting the reliability of cognitive-behavioral measurements. *Advances in Methods and Practices in Psychological Science, 2*, 378–395. https://doi.org/10.1177/2515245919879695

Pearl, J. (1995). Causal diagrams for empirical research. *Biometrika, 82*, 669–688. https://doi.org/10.1093/biomet/82.4.669

Pearl, J. (2018). *The book of why: The new science of cause and effect*. Basic Books.

Petersen, S. E., & Posner, M. I. (2012). The attention system of the human brain: 20 years after. *Annual Review of Neuroscience, 35*, 73–89. https://doi.org/10.1146/annurev-neuro-062111-150525

Poldrack, R. A., & Gorgolewski, K. J. (2014). Making big data open: Data sharing in neuroimaging. *Nature Neuroscience, 17*, 1510–1517. https://doi.org/10.1038/nn.3818

Poldrack, R. A., & Gorgolewski, K. J. (2017). OpenfMRI: Open sharing of task fMRI data. *NeuroImage, 144*, 259–261. https://doi.org/10.1016/j.neuroimage.2015.05.073

Press, C., Bird, G., Walsh, E., & Heyes, C. (2008). Automatic imitation of intransitive actions. *Brain and Cognition, 67*, 44–50. https://doi.org/10.1016/j.bandc.2007.11.001

Proulx, T., & Morey, R. D. (2021). Beyond statistical ritual: Theory in psychological science. *Perspectives on Psychological Science, 16*, 671–681. https://doi.org/10.1177/17456916211017098

Ptak, R. (2012). The frontoparietal attention network of the human brain: Action, saliency, and a priority map of the environment. *The Neuroscientist, 18*, 502–515. https://doi.org/10.1177/1073858411409051

Ramsey, R. (2018). What are reaction time indices of automatic imitation measuring? *Consciousness and Cognition, 65*, 240–254. https://doi.org/10.1016/j.concog.2018.08.006

Ramsey, R. (2021). A call for greater modesty in psychology and cognitive neuroscience. *Collabra: Psychology, 7*. https://doi.org/10.1525/collabra.24091

Ramsey, R., & Ward, R. (2020a). Challenges and opportunities for top-down modulation research in cognitive psychology. *Acta Psychologica, 209*, 103118. https://doi.org/10.1016/j.actpsy.2020.103118

Ramsey, R., & Ward, R. (2020b). Putting the nonsocial into social neuroscience: A role for domain-general priority maps during social interactions. *Perspectives on Psychological Science, 15*, 1076–1094. https://doi.org/10.1177/1745691620904972

Rauchbauer, B., Dunbar, R. I. M., & Lamm, C. (2020). Being mimicked affects inhibitory mechanisms of imitation. *Acta Psychologica, 209*, 103132. https://doi.org/10.1016/j.actpsy.2020.103132

Redcay, E., & Schilbach, L. (2019). Using second-person neuroscience to elucidate the mechanisms of social interaction. *Nature Reviews Neuroscience, 20*, 495–505. https://doi.org/10.1038/s41583-019-0179-4

Rizzolatti, G., & Craighero, L. (2004). The mirror-neuron system. *Annual Review of Neuroscience, 27*, 169–192. https://doi.org/10.1146/annurev.neuro.27.070203.144230

Rizzolatti, G., Fogassi, L., & Gallese, V. (2001). Neurophysiological mechanisms underlying the understanding and imitation of action. *Nature reviews neuroscience, 2*, 661–670.

Santiesteban, I., White, S., Cook, J., Gilbert, S. J., Heyes, C., & Bird, G. (2012). Training social cognition: From imitation to theory of mind. *Cognition, 122*, 228–235. https://doi.org/10.1016/j.cognition.2011.11.004

Scheel, A. M., Tiokhin, L., Isager, P. M., & Lakens, D. (2021). Why hypothesis testers should spend less time testing hypotheses. *Perspectives on Psychological Science, 16*, 744–755. https://doi.org/10.1177/1745691620966795

Shadish, W. R., Cook, T. D., & Campbell, D. T. (2002). *Experimental and quasi-experimental designs for generalized causal inference* (p. xxi, 623). Houghton, Mifflin and Company.

Shamay-Tsoory, S. G., & Mendelsohn, A. (2019). Real-life neuroscience: An ecological approach to brain and behavior research. *Perspectives on Psychological Science, 14*, 841–859. https://doi.org/10.1177/1745691619856350

Simmons, J. P., Nelson, L. D., & Simonsohn, U. (2018). False-positive citations. *Perspectives on Psychological Science, 13*, 255–259. https://doi.org/10.1177/1745691617698146

Smaldino, P. E. (2017). Models are stupid, and we need more of them. In R. R. Vallacher, S. J. Read, & A. Nowak (Eds.), *Computational social psychology* (pp. 311–331). Routledge. https://doi.org/10.4324/9781315173726-14

Sowden, S., & Catmur, C. (2015). The role of the right temporoparietal junction in the control of imitation. *Cerebral Cortex, 25*, 1107–1113. https://doi.org/10.1093/cercor/bht306

Sowden, S., & Shah, P. (2014). Self-other control: A candidate mechanism for social cognitive function. *Frontiers in Human Neuroscience, 8*, 789. https://doi.org/10.3389/fnhum.2014.00789

Spengler, S., von Cramon, D. Y., & Brass, M. (2009). Control of shared representations relies on key processes involved in mental state attribution. *Human Brain Mapping, 30*, 3704–3718. https://doi.org/10.1002/hbm.20800
Spengler, S., von Cramon, D. Y., & Brass, M. (2010). Resisting motor mimicry: Control of imitation involves processes central to social cognition in patients with frontal and temporo-parietal lesions. *Social Neuroscience, 5*, 401–416. https://doi.org/10.1080/17470911003687905
Stanley, J., Gowen, E., & Miall, R. C. (2007). Effects of agency on movement interference during observation of a moving dot stimulus. *Journal of Experimental Psychology Human Perception and Performance, 33*, 915–926. https://doi.org/10.1037/0096-1523.33.4.915
Steinbeis, N. (2016). The role of self–other distinction in understanding others' mental and emotional states: Neurocognitive mechanisms in children and adults. *Philosophical Transactions of the Royal Society B: Biological Sciences, 371*, 20150074. https://doi.org/10.1098/rstb.2015.0074
Stürmer, B., Aschersleben, G., & Prinz, W. (2000). Correspondence effects with manual gestures and postures: A study of imitation. *Journal of Experimental Psychology: Human Perception and Performance, 26*, 1746–1759. https://doi.org/10.1037/0096-1523.26.6.1746
Sui, J., Liu, C. H., & Han, S. (2009). Cultural difference in neural mechanisms of self-recognition. *Social Neuroscience, 4*, 402–411. https://doi.org/10.1080/17470910802674825
Szucs, D., & Ioannidis, J. P. A. (2017). Empirical assessment of published effect sizes and power in the recent cognitive neuroscience and psychology literature. *PLoS Biology, 15*, e2000797. https://doi.org/10.1371/journal.pbio.2000797
Van Overwalle, F. (2009). Social cognition and the brain: A meta-analysis. *Human Brain Mapping, 30*, 829–858. https://doi.org/10.1002/hbm.20547
Varnum, M. E. W., Grossmann, I., Kitayama, S., & Nisbett, R. E. (2010). The origin of cultural differences in cognition: Evidence for the social orientation hypothesis. *Current Directions in Psychological Science, 19*, 9–13. https://doi.org/10.1177/0963721409359301
Vazire, S., Schiavone, S. R., & Bottesini, J. G. (2022). Credibility beyond replicability: Improving the four validities in psychological science. *Current Directions in Psychological Science, 31*, 162–168. https://doi.org/10.1177/09637214211067779
Wager, T. D., Sylvester, C.-Y. C., Lacey, S. C., Nee, D. E., Franklin, M., & Jonides, J. (2005). Common and unique components of response inhibition revealed by fMRI. *NeuroImage, 27*, 323–340. https://doi.org/10.1016/j.neuroimage.2005.01.054
Wang, Y., & Hamilton, A. F. d. C. (2012). Social Top-down Response Modulation (STORM): A model of the control of mimicry in social interaction. *Frontiers in Human Neuroscience, 6*. https://doi.org/10.3389/fnhum.2012.00153
Ward, R., & Ramsey, R. (2024). Integrating Social Cognition Into Domain-General Control: Interactive Activation and Competition for the Control of Action (ICON). *Cognitive Science, 48*, e13415. https://doi.org/10.1111/cogs.13415.
Wilson, T. D., Aronson, E., & Carlsmith, K. (2010). The art of laboratory experimentation. In *Handbook of social psychology* (Vol. 1, 5th ed., pp. 51–81). Wiley. https://doi.org/10.1002/9780470561119.socpsy001002
Wood, C. (2020, January 14). *Being copycats might be key to being human*. The Conversation. http://theconversation.com/being-copycats-might-be-key-to-being-human-121932
Yarkoni, T. (2022). The generalizability crisis. *Behavioral and Brain Sciences, 45*, e1. https://doi.org/10.1017/S0140525X20001685
Yarkoni, T., Poldrack, R. A., Nichols, T. E., Van Essen, D. C., & Wager, T. D. (2011). Large-scale automated synthesis of human functional neuroimaging data. *Nature Methods, 8*, 8. https://doi.org/10.1038/nmeth.1635

Chapter 7
Levels of Imitation: Movements, Outcomes, and Goals

Jochim Hansen

Imitating other people is a phenomenon that ranges widely from imitating simple actions (such as yawning or face touching) to imitating complex behavior (such as food consumption, health-related behavior, or cooperation). In principle, any action that is imitated can be divided into a motor part (i.e., a movement) and a consequence produced by the movement (i.e., an outcome; Elsner, 2007; Elsner & Hommel, 2001; Hommel et al., 2001). That is, an observer may copy a model's body movements without necessarily considering the outcome or understanding the action goal (sometimes called *mimicry*), or he/she may copy the action outcome (or goal) by performing any movement from his/her own movement repertoire without necessarily executing the same movement as the model (sometimes called *goal emulation*). Both components (or levels of imitation) are typically related to each other because movements are usually performed to initiate desired changes in the environment and thus produce an outcome (e.g., Prinz, 1997). For instance, when watching a person eating, observers may imitate the movements (i.e., lifting the arm) to achieve the same outcome/goal (i.e., satisfying one's hunger). In this chapter, I discuss the different levels of imitation (i.e., movement imitation and outcome/goal imitation), introduce experimental paradigms that dissociate the levels from each other, and summarize conditions under which individuals show more or less movement imitation versus outcome imitation.

J. Hansen (✉)
Paris Lodron University of Salzburg, Salzburg, Austria
e-mail: jochim.hansen@plus.ac.at

O. Genschow, E. Cracco (eds.), *Automatic Imitation*,
https://doi.org/10.1007/978-3-031-62634-0_7

Different Levels of Imitation

One can differentiate between at least two levels that underlie imitation—the imitation of an outcome/goal and the imitation of its underlying movement. Fig. 7.1 illustrates the two levels of imitation: The dog in the drawing imitates the outcome of its owner's action (i.e., a wet tree) in the upper panel but imitates his movements in the lower panel (i.e., standing upright while urinating). Both components are combined in the middle panel.

To which degree imitation in general is a movement-based or an outcome/goal-based phenomenon is a matter of debate (Bouquet et al., 2011; Chiavarino et al., 2013; Cracco et al., 2018; Genschow, Hansen, et al., 2019; Hansen & Genschow, 2020; Liepelt et al., 2008, 2010; Press et al., 2008). Some scholars argue that imitation is a goal-directed process that involves decomposing observed actions into a hierarchy of features where the action goals (and outcomes) are more important

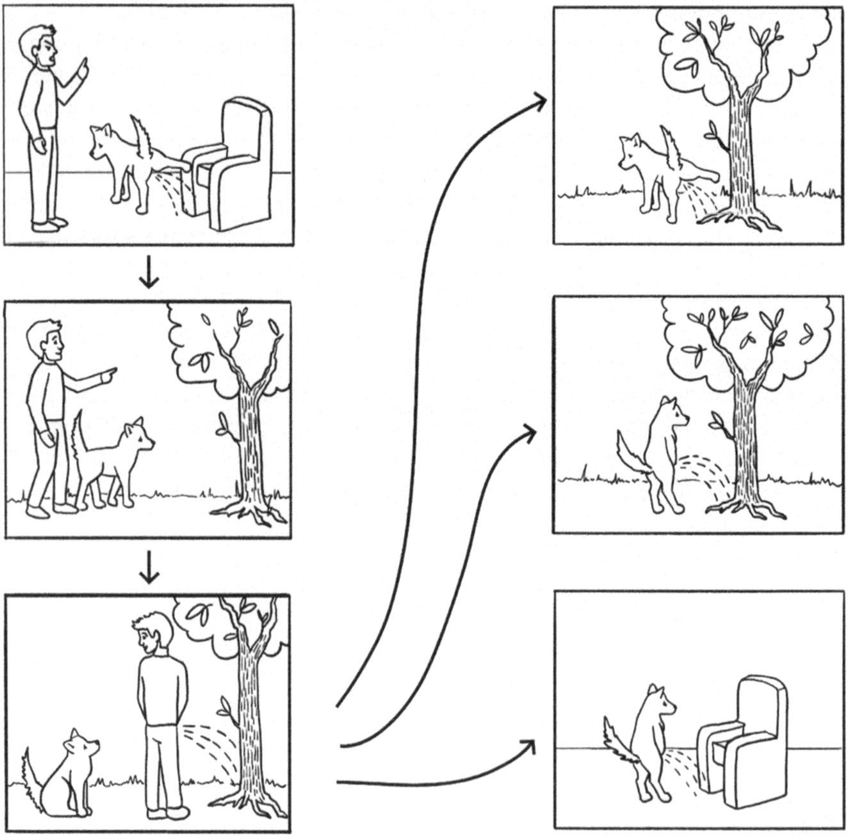

Fig. 7.1 Imitation of the outcome (upper panel on the right), the movements (lower panel on the right), or both (middle panel on the right)

than the process of how the outcomes are achieved (Wohlschläger et al., 2003). According to this view, children, as well as adults, prioritize the outcome/goal of an action over the means to achieve the outcome/goal when asked to imitate (Avikainen et al., 2003; Bekkering et al., 2000; Gattis et al., 2002; Gleissner et al., 2000; Want & Gattis, 2005). Other scholars ascribe the central role in the imitative process to the underlying movements. For instance, people imitate movements even without considering action goals (Chiavarino et al., 2013; Genschow & Florack, 2014; Genschow et al., 2013; Genschow & Schindler, 2016). Accordingly, automatic imitation occurs even when the movements of an observed person have no clear outcome or goal (Heyes et al., 2005; Press et al., 2008; Stürmer et al., 2000), or when the observed and executed movements are similar but fulfill different goals (Genschow et al., 2013; Genschow & Florack, 2014; Genschow & Schindler, 2016).

Importantly, both levels of imitation have been demonstrated in the literature and occur in real life, so it may be less important which level of imitation generally dominates but more important under which conditions which level dominates. For instance, participants who watch a video of a man eating a whole bowl of snack pretzels in a short period of time may imitate this behavior under certain conditions more than under others (e.g., Bischoff et al., 2020). In such a situation, a condition could have caused participants to adopt the model's goal of eating a large number of pretzels and creating the outcome of an empty bowl. Alternatively, it could have caused participants to imitate the model's movements of repeatedly grasping pretzels and raising them to the mouth. Many instances of imitation are consistent but not necessarily unique to movement-based or outcome/goal-based imitation. Thus, the crucial question is which level of imitative behavior is affected by which conditions.

At this point, it should be mentioned that in some situations outcome imitation can be differentiated from goal imitation (Call, 1999; Call & Carpenter, 2002; Carpenter & Call, 2002) because outcomes and goals sometimes differ from each other. For instance, when a demonstrator fails to attain his/her goals and ends up with a different outcome than intended, the observer can imitate either the (inferred but not observed) goal or the (observed) outcome. However, since action outcomes often are goals intended by an individual and goals can be defined as observable, physical outcomes (e.g., Fugazza et al., 2019; Leighton et al., 2010; Wohlschläger et al., 2003), I treat outcome imitation and goal imitation as roughly similar in the present chapter (see also Elsner, 2007). For instance, in the upper panel of Fig. 7.1, it is not clear whether the dog imitates the goal of his owner (i.e., wetting the tree instead of the chair) or the outcome (i.e., a wet tree). So, from an observer's perspective, imitation can be broken down into just two basic mechanisms: movement imitation (including mimicry) and outcome/goal imitation (including emulation and goal emulation).

Imitation of Movements

Imitation of movements can be understood as copying the body movement topography of a model and using the same appendage as a model. That is, the way that one part of the body moves relative to the rest of the body is imitated (Heyes, 2021). For instance, if a model uses his/her head to activate a light, movement imitation means that the observer is more likely to also use his/her head than his/her hand to activate a light.

The earliest theory explaining movement imitation is ideomotor theory (e.g., Brass et al., 2001; James, 1890; Prinz, 1997; Shin et al., 2010; see also Chap. 5). Ideomotor theory basically assumes that "every representation of a movement awakens in some degree the actual movement which is its object" (James, 1890). This is because perceived and executed actions are neurophysiologically very similar. Perceiving a motor action thus triggers a corresponding representation that facilitates a similar motor action. Research on mimicking simple motor actions such as foot shaking or face touching (e.g., Chartrand & Bargh, 1999; Chartrand & van Baaren, 2009; Dijksterhuis & Bargh, 2001) illustrates that this process can be automatic without involving inferences of the underlying action goals.

A special case of movement imitation is the movement of an object, for instance, if a person moves a hammer (Whiten et al., 2009). Imitating the movement of a hammer stroke includes several positions of the hammer which can be thought of as several (sub)outcomes regarding the position of the hammer and the movement of one's arm at the same time. To emphasize the similarity to body movement imitation, imitation of moving an object that is attached to one's appendage is labeled *object movement re-enactment* (Custance et al., 1999; Whiten et al., 2009). According to Whiten et al. (2009), one can imagine a causal continuum from body movements (e.g., lifting an arm) to object movements (e.g., using a hammer) to the outcomes caused by the movements (e.g., a broken cell phone). Movement imitation can be easiest attributed to the proximal end of the continuum while outcome imitation is clearest at the distal end of the continuum.

There is another situation in which movement and outcome imitation merge, that is when the movement itself is the outcome (or the goal), for instance, when learning to juggle or to dance. In these cases, it is obvious that the outcome or goal of the action is directly linked to the means or movements, and one cannot differentiate between movement and outcome imitation anymore (Hayes et al., 2008).

Imitation of Outcomes/Goals

Outcome/goal imitation (or *end-state emulation*, Whiten et al., 2009) can be defined as instances where individuals "achieve common goals to those modeled, but do so by using idiosyncratic means that were never observed" (Wood, 1989, p. 72). However, while observers may attain an outcome or achieve a goal in their own way, they might unintentionally choose the same movements as the model, which could thus be falsely recorded as movement imitation (Bekkering et al., 2000; Elsner, 2007; Gleissner et al., 2000; Wohlschläger & Bekkering, 2002).

Outcome/goal imitation has the function of fostering social learning, as "an observer learns simply that a particular goal can be achieved (…) and sets about achieving that goal by its own means" (Want & Harris, 2002, p. 3). As noted by Elsner (2007), this phenomenon is observable in animals and may be present in human infants, as well (Hurley & Chater, 2005).

The observation that children and adults often adopt a different movement pattern from that demonstrated by the model but still attain the same outcome or goal of an observed action is explained by the theory of goal-directed imitation (GOADI; Wohlschläger et al., 2003). According to GOADI, an observer cognitively decomposes and orders the observed action into a hierarchy of goals and subgoals (see Hayes et al., 2008). This hierarchy of goals follows the action's functionality, that is, observers give more importance to the end than to the means of the action. As a result, the goal of the action rather than the movements to achieve that goal is imitated (Bekkering et al., 2000; Wohlschläger et al., 2003). Several studies examining reaching and grasping movements provide support for GOADI (Wohlschläger et al., 2003). For instance, when preschool children are asked to imitate the gestures of a model who uses a contralateral arm movement to grasp an ear, they often grasp the ear by using an ipsilateral arm. When asked to imitate the gesture but to aim towards the open space beside the ear, they more likely correctly match the observed arm movements. It seems that reaching the open space next to the ear has a less salient outcome, and therefore the movement itself is put at the top of the hierarchy (Bekkering et al., 2000). Further, GOADI states that movements that resemble those of a model are more likely to be executed when imitating everyday actions (see Hayes et al., 2008). This is because here the means of the action already exist in an individual's motor repertoire (Wohlschläger et al., 2003): While imitating, the choice of the movement is determined by the motor program that is most strongly associated with the achievement of the goal (i.e., the ideomotor principle of movement control; Prinz, 1997) and not the model's movement pattern per se.

As should be clear by now, imitation of outcomes often involves imitation of an *intended* outcome (i.e., an inferred goal). Accordingly, imitation of general goal states (or *goal contagion*), such as imitation of achievement goals or cooperation goals, has been investigated, as well (Aarts et al., 2004, 2008; Aarts & Hassin, 2005; Dik & Aarts, 2007; Loersch et al., 2008; Wessler & Hansen, 2016). Goal contagion is much more complex than a simple imitation of movement outcomes, as it involves more psychological subprocesses (Laurin, 2016): The observer needs (a) to infer a goal from the observed behavior, (b) to adopt the goal (i.e., to desire to obtain the goal), (c) to choose the behavioral means to reach the goal (i.e., know how to obtain the goal), and (d) to execute the respective behavior. This may be the reason for the very weak effects of goal contagion, which is barely detectable even in meta-analyses (Brohmer et al., 2021).

Taken together, an action consists of two observable components: a movement and an outcome produced by the movement (Elsner, 2007; Elsner & Hommel, 2001;

Hommel et al., 2001). Because the goals of others need to be inferred from the observable action components (Call & Carpenter, 2002; Gattis, 2002; Song & Baillargeon, 2008), it is important to represent both the movements and the outcomes to understand and imitate the actions of a model and to control own actions (Elsner, 2007).

Methods to Assess Movement and Outcome Imitation

With different experimental paradigms, the amount of movement imitation and/or outcome/goal imitation can be estimated, and it can be tested whether specific conditions moderate the two levels of imitation. Some paradigms focus only on movement imitation, some focus only on outcome/goal imitation, and some include both.

Movement Imitation (Without Considering Outcome/Goal Imitation)

To measure automatic imitation of movements, stimulus-response compatibility paradigms are typically used (e.g., Bach et al., 2007; Brass et al., 2000, 2001; Catmur & Heyes, 2010; Gillmeister et al., 2008; Gowen et al., 2008; Kilner et al., 2003, 2007; Leighton & Heyes, 2010; see also Chap. 2; this volume). In these paradigms, participants are asked to respond to imperative cues across many trials with a movement (e.g., movement of fingers, arms, feet, or mouth) while watching either a congruent movement or an incongruent movement. For instance, participants are asked to open their hands in response to a red color cue and to close it in response to a blue color cue (or vice versa) while observing an opening or closing hand movement (Stürmer et al., 2000). Correct responses are usually started faster when the irrelevant action stimulus (i.e., the hand in the video) is response-compatible (e.g., when the hand has to be opened in the presence of an opening hand movement) than when the irrelevant action stimulus is response-incompatible (e.g., when the hand has to be opened in the presence of a closing hand movement). The difference between the response times in the compatible trials and the incompatible trials is considered an indicator of movement imitation (Heyes, 2011).

Genschow and colleagues (Genschow & Florack, 2014; Genschow et al., 2013; Genschow & Schindler, 2016) tested movement imitation in more complex behavior, such as drinking behavior. In this paradigm, participants are asked to taste a drink while watching a cross-contextually compatible or incompatible movement in a video. Participants are provided with ten plastic cups filled with an ice-tea-flavored drink and they were allowed to taste from the cups as much as they wanted until the video finished. Drinking from the cups involves repeated arm-lifting movements. Participants in the compatible movement condition watch a video of an athlete in a gym lifting a barbell from his waist toward his head. Participants in the incompatible movement condition watch the same athlete pushing the barbell away from his body. In both conditions, the athlete shows a behavior (and follows a goal) that has nothing to do with the situation of the participants who execute the drinking task so that only movement imitation can be observed. Still, watching the lifting movement usually activates compatible movements in participants—that is, lifting the cup to the mouth—which, in turn, results in increased drink intake. Watching the pushing movement, in contrast, activates a movement incompatible with drinking, usually decreasing drink intake. The amount of drunken liquid can be used as a measure of movement imitation across contexts.

Since movements are a crucial part of gestures, gesturing can be used to examine movement imitation, as well. One study, for instance, used an experimental paradigm in which participants are led to believe that they take part in a study on conducting job interviews (Wessler & Hansen, 2017). Participants are assigned to the role of a job interviewer who talks to an applicant for an internship. Their tasks include asking several interview questions that are provided by the experimenter as well as shortly summarizing the applicant's answers to these questions. Additionally, participants are asked to imitate the applicant's gestures during these summaries to "make the applicant feel more comfortable and reduce her nervousness." Unknown to the participants, the applicant is a confederate of the experimenter who has been instructed to use specific relevant and irrelevant gestures according to a predefined script. For instance, he/she taps the fingers on the table when talking about the impatience of others or rolls the arms when talking about swapping tasks with coworkers. The number of gestures imitated by the participants during their summaries can be used to assess movement imitation and to study conditions under which movement imitation is more or less prevalent. In contrast to the stimulus-response compatibility paradigms and the drinking task summarized above, movement imitation in this gesture task is explicitly instructed and thus not automatic. If one is interested in whether awareness of imitation affects the amount of imitation under certain conditions, different paradigms might be used and compared.

Goal-Directed Movement Imitation

In developmental psychology, several experimental paradigms have been created to investigate imitation of goal-directed movements (e.g., Abravanel & Gingold, 1985; Abravanel et al., 1976; Barr et al., 1996; Killen & Uzgiris, 1981; Meltzoff, 1988a). For instance, in a classic study by Meltzoff (1988a), the following paradigm was introduced (see also Gergely et al., 2002). Participants (in this case, 14-month-old children) observe an adult who is bending at the waist and touching his/her head to a panel which results in turning on a light. Typically, participants engage in imitation of such an unusual movement even though it would be easier for them to simply push the panel with the hand.

Likewise, movement imitation can be examined by presenting participants (i.e., children) with a puzzle box that has movable parts and contains a reward (e.g., Horner & Whiten, 2005; Lyons et al., 2011). In this paradigm, an experimenter demonstrates several actions on a box (see Keupp et al., 2018). Some of the actions are necessary to obtain the reward (e.g., the door hiding the reward must be opened), whereas others are unnecessary (e.g., tapping on the box and moving attachments on the outside of the box). When it is their turn to operate the box, children less than 2 years of age typically engage in the necessary actions only and ignore the unnecessary ones, but older children imitate also the irrelevant movements (e.g., McGuigan & Whiten, 2009).

A similar paradigm has been introduced for adults (Hansen et al., 2016). Participants learn a new activity—that is, creating a dog out of towels—by watching an instruction video. The model in the video performs the activity in a particular way, including several unnecessary steps. For instance, she rolls one of the towels first from the right and then from the left side, flattens the towel at specific points in the video, and folds the ear of the dog in a certain way. After watching the video, participants are asked to recreate the dog. To assess movement imitation, their behavior is coded for how closely their movements match those of the model. Typically, participants imitate also the irrelevant movements to a considerable amount.

The paradigms in the present subsection have been criticized because it is difficult to tease apart movement and outcome/goal imitation when movements come along with outcomes/goals (Want & Harris, 2002). In these paradigms, it is always possible that participants understand the observed behavior in terms of a goal (i.e., the model has the goal and then chooses the movements to reach it from among other possible movements) and imitate that goal by choosing the same movements. One solution to circumvent this problem is using a paradigm that contrasts outcomes/goals with movements, as introduced in the next subsection.

Contrasting Movement Imitation with Outcome/Goal Imitation

Movement-based and outcome/goal-based imitation can be contrasted in a paradigm developed by Genschow, Hansen, et al. (2019, Exp. 1). In this paradigm, participants are asked to watch a model who indicates his/her decision to either drink a lot of cups or only a few drinks by moving cups to the right side or the left side on a table. Participants likewise choose how much they would like to drink by placing cups on their right or left side (see Fig. 7.2). The degree to which participants imitate the outcome/goal of the model's action can be assessed by the chosen amount of cups, that is the number of cups placed on the "drink" field. Conversely, the degree to which participants imitate the movements can be assessed by the amount of right and left movements that matched those of the model. Crucially, the experimental setup is arranged in such a way that participants have to engage in movements as opposed to the model's movements when imitating the model's outcome/

Fig. 7.2 Participants choose drinks and place them on a field that says "TRINK" (drink) or "WEG" (away) while the model moves either a few or many cups to the right or left side

goal. Likewise, when imitating the model's movements, participants achieved the opposite of the model's outcome. In this way, the paradigm allows one to disentangle movement-based from outcome/goal-based imitation.

If interested in the relative proportion of movement-based versus outcome/goal-based imitation, this paradigm can be useful. However, a limitation of the paradigm is that movement-based imitation and outcome/goal-based imitation are confounded in such a way that more outcome/goal imitation means less movement imitation and vice versa. Thus, paradigms that allow one to dissociate movement-based from outcome/goal-based imitation may be useful if one is interested in the independent estimates of the two levels of imitation, as introduced in the next subsection.

Assessing Movement and Outcome/Goal Imitation Independently of Each Other

Studies in developmental psychology compare several experimental conditions with each other to assess whether participants (usually infants or young children) imitate movements (actions) and/or outcomes/goals (e.g., Bellagamba & Tomasello, 1999; Huang et al., 2002; Meltzoff, 1985, 1988b). Across different conditions, participants are provided with different amounts of information about a target action (see Elsner, 2007). In a baseline condition, participants receive an object (e.g., an unfamiliar toy) without having a model demonstrating a target action (e.g., pulling the toy apart and putting it together again in a different way) or an outcome of the action (e.g., the reassembled toy). This condition can be used to assess the spontaneous production of the target action. In another movement-only condition, the model performs arbitrary actions on the object that do not cause any salient outcome. This condition can be used to rule out the possibility that participants' actions just result from being attracted to the same object as the model as well as to test whether participants imitate outcome-independent movements. In the emulation condition, participants are presented with the outcome of an action (e.g., the reassembled toy) but not with the movement that caused the outcome. This condition can be used to test whether participants create the outcome without having observed a movement causing the outcome. The different conditions can be compared to a full-demonstration condition in which the model demonstrates both movements and outcomes. This allows one to tease apart which information is needed for the reproduction of the target actions and/or the movements in different age groups (Elsner, 2007). A common finding in such paradigms is that movement imitation develops in the second half of the first year of life and outcome/goal imitation develops at the beginning of the second year (see below).

The paradigms outlined in the previous paragraph have been criticized because they confound the level of imitation (movement vs. outcome) with the amount of given information since presenting a sequence of movements usually includes more information than presenting just the outcome (Heyes, 2021). So, it is not clear whether differences between the experimental conditions are driven by the content or the amount of given information. To circumvent such a confound, one could use paradigms that minimize the amount of movement information, such as in the pen-and-cups task (Bekkering et al., 2000; Wohlschläger et al., 2003).

In the pen-and-cups task (Bekkering et al., 2000; Wohlschläger et al., 2003), across multiple trials, three action components are manipulated: object selection, effector selection, and grip selection. On each trial, observers (usually children) see a model moving a pen into one of two colored cups (object), using the right or the left hand (effector) while grasping the pen with the thumb pointing up or down (grip). Participants are asked to imitate the behavior across several trials. Imitation of the outcome (object selection: In which cup is the pen at the end?) and imitation of the effector and grip (movement selection: How is the pen moved?) can be assessed.

Recently, a computerized and speeded version of the pen-and-cups task has been introduced that can be used with adult participants (Genschow, Hansen, et al., 2019, Exp. 2 and 3). In this paradigm, participants are watching on a computer screen the hands of a model pressing one of two keys on a keyboard by using either the right or the left hand across multiple trials. Participants are instructed to imitate the observed actions (i.e., they are asked to press the same key with the same hand as the model) as fast as possible. Imitation errors of hand use as well as of key presses are measured, and the inversion of the error rates can be used as indicators of movement imitation and outcome imitation, respectively.

In the pen-and-cups task as well as the computerized and speeded version, respectively, it has been shown that observers typically make fewer cup errors than hand errors and fewer hand errors than grip errors (Avikainen et al., 2003; Leighton et al., 2008; Wohlschläger & Bekkering, 2002), or fewer key errors than hand errors, respectively (Genschow, Hansen, et al., 2019). This pattern of goal-based imitation may mainly be due to the fact that the goal is more salient than the movements in these paradigms (Bird et al., 2007). If attention is shifted to the movements, participants are more likely to imitate the movements.

Dissociating Outcomes and Goals

So far, I treated outcome imitation and goal imitation as more or less similar because the action outcome does usually reflect the action goal. However, there are situations in which it is important to differentiate between outcome and goal since an outcome of an action does not always correspond to the intended goal of the action.

To disentangle outcome imitation and goal imitation, one can demonstrate failed attempts where a participant observes a model trying but failing to produce an action outcome. For example, a model could be shown trying to pull a dumbbell-shaped toy apart, but her fingers slip off the ends (Meltzoff, 1995, 2007). If participants engage in different means to produce the intended outcome rather than faithfully imitating the same failed movement that produced no outcome (or an unintended outcome), one can assume that the action goal rather than the outcome was imitated. It has been shown that 17- to 19-month-old (but not 12-month-old) children usually produce what the adult tried but failed to do (i.e., they imitate the goal) in such a condition. That is, the children are more likely to produce the intended outcome when an intention could be inferred than when an intention could not be inferred. In fact, children who have observed a trying but failing model show as many intended outcomes as children in a full-demonstration group where the model successfully demonstrates the intended outcome (Bellagamba & Tomasello, 1999; Huang & Charman, 2005; Huang et al., 2002; Meltzoff, 1995).

A slightly different paradigm was introduced by Carpenter et al. (1998a). In this paradigm, a model demonstrates a series of two-step actions on objects that make interesting results occur. The demonstrator vocally marks some of the actions as intentional ("There!") and others as accidental ("Whoops!"). After each action, participants are given a chance to produce the outcome. Typically, children imitate a lot more of the adult's intentional actions than his/her accidental ones, indicating imitation of goals instead of outcomes. It might be interesting to combine paradigms, for instance including the "There!"/"Whoops!" manipulation in the pen-and-cups task to examine if participants' cup selection reflects imitation of an outcome or imitation of a goal.

In summary, different experimental paradigms have been introduced to investigate outcome imitation and goal imitation. Some paradigms are more suitable for children, whereas others are more suitable for adults. Evidence for both movement imitation and outcome/goal imitation has been found. Although outcome/goal imitation seems to dominate in many cases, this is not always the case. Therefore, an interesting question is the following: Under which conditions do individuals give movement imitation more weight relative to outcome/goal imitation? The next section summarizes some variables that moderate the relative degree of movement imitation versus outcome/goal imitation.

Variables Moderating the Relative Degree of Movement and Outcome Imitation

Research has identified variables that increase or decrease imitation of movements or outcomes. Most notably, age and its associated knowledge about movement–outcome relations have been investigated as moderating factors. Additionally, situational context factors such as the salience of the outcome, the apparent causal relationship between movement and outcome, and situational constraints of the model's behavior affect the relative degree to which one engages in movement versus outcome imitation. Additionally, social group membership and psychological (particularly spatial) distance have been related to movement versus outcome imitation.

Imitation in Infancy: Knowledge About Movement–Outcome Relations

One of the best-researched moderators of imitation is the age at which different mechanisms of imitation develop (for reviews, see Elsner, 2007; Want & Harris, 2002; see also Chap. 9; this volume). In infancy, the capacity to encode and remember information develops as infants grow older, which helps in processing information provided by a model who is demonstrating an action. Thus, this information can be better and better related to one's growing knowledge about actions and movement–outcome relations. This, in turn, influences imitation of an action, which becomes increasingly flexible with age.

It has been demonstrated that movement imitation develops from about 6 to 13 months of age whereas outcome/goal imitation develops from 13 months onwards (Call & Carpenter, 2002; Want & Harris, 2002). It has been shown that 9-month-olds do not learn movement-outcome relations by observation, whereas 12-month-olds do (Carpenter et al., 1998b; Elsner & Aschersleben, 2003; Provasi et al., 2001). By 12 months, infants can even reproduce movements that do not lead to a salient outcome (although movements accompanied by a salient outcome are imitated more often, see below). By 14 months, infants can adjust their imitation to several aspects of the demonstration, such as verbal cues or situational constraints present during the demonstration, and show more and more outcome imitation (Carpenter et al., 1998a; Gergely et al., 2002).

In one study with infants aged between 9 and 15 months (Carpenter et al., 1998b), the paradigm of Meltzoff (1988a, b) was used, that is, the infants observed a model who was bending at the waist and touching her head to a panel resulting in a light turning on. Infants below 13 months engaged in movement imitation, that is, they imitated the movements without paying attention to the outcome of the action. Infants older than 13 months also engaged in movement imitation but additionally looked at the light to check whether their actions produced the same outcome as the model. Furthermore, 14-month-olds used their hand instead of their forehead to touch a box and turn on a light (see also Gergely et al., 2002), indicating that infants increasingly rely on their action-effect knowledge in imitative contexts the older they become and choose a simpler action from their own repertoire to reproduce observed outcomes (see also Huang et al., 2002).

The ability to predict goals or to infer unseen movements from incomplete demonstrations of goal-directed actions evolves over the second year of life. By 17 months, infants can infer the goals of "failed-attempts" movements (Bellagamba & Tomasello, 1999; Huang et al., 2002; Meltzoff, 1995). For instance, 18-month-old children who were presented with failed attempts to achieve a goal (e.g., pulling a toy apart or putting a stick in a hole) re-enacted the intended actions rather than the actual failed actions (Meltzoff, 1995) whereas 12-months-olds did not (Bellagamba & Tomasello, 1999). Likewise, children between 14 and 18 months were more likely to imitate actions that are vocally marked as intentional (i.e., the model exclaimed "There!" after having produced them) than actions vocally marked as accidental (i.e., the model exclaimed "Whoops!" after having produced them; Carpenter et al., 1998a), indicating that children of this age group start to imitate actions based on goals and not just outcomes (see Want & Harris, 2002).

In sum, the ability to learn movement–goal relations by observation emerges at the beginning of the second year and is regarded as the crucial factor for the changes in the imitation of incomplete demonstrations. Likewise, the ability to reproduce outcomes without seeing any movement that caused the outcome develops at the end of the second year. Growing knowledge about movement–outcome relations helps infants to infer the movements that are necessary to produce the observed outcome (Elsner, 2007).

Related to age, there is an interesting phenomenon called *over-imitation*. In over-imitation, individuals imitate causally irrelevant movements when observing a goal-directed action despite clear evidence that those actions are unnecessary to accomplish the task at hand (Hoehl et al., 2019; Keupp et al., 2018; Whiten et al., 2009). So, over-imitation is an inefficient form of imitation that stands in contrast to rational, selective imitation. It is particularly puzzling that over-imitation emerges at later ages: While infants and even chimpanzees (Horner & Whiten, 2005) can engage in more effective imitation (i.e., they ignore any causally irrelevant actions and choose efficient means when imitating outcomes), older children (3- to 5-year-olds; McGuigan et al., 2007) and even adults (Hansen et al., 2016; McGuigan et al., 2011) often faithfully imitate any kind of behavior and thus jeopardize efficient task performance (Horner & Whiten, 2005; for a review see Whiten et al., 2009).

In one study, for instance, 3- to 4-year-old children and young chimpanzees were presented with a puzzle box that contained a hidden reward (Horner & Whiten,

2005). A model engaged in both causally necessary and unnecessary movements to retrieve the reward. When the box was opaque, both chimpanzees and children copied the unnecessary movements to retrieve the reward. When the box was transparent, in contrast, chimpanzees only imitated the necessary movements and omitted the unnecessary ones, whereas human children imitated all (including the unnecessary) movements (see also Lyons et al., 2007).

Several explanations for such apparently irrational behavior have been proposed (for reviews, see Allen et al., 2021; Keupp et al., 2018; Schleihauf & Hoehl, 2020; Whiten et al., 2009). First, over-imitation may be a byproduct of causal learning. By imitation, individuals gain knowledge about the functioning of tools and other artifacts. Faithful movement imitation is a useful strategy because it helps in the learning process, particularly when individuals can "copy all now" and "refine/correct later" (Whiten et al., 2009). So, over-imitation may be adaptive because it provides a strategy that can be easily used when faced with novel tasks with unknown causalities. Accordingly, over-imitation may be a form of automatic imitation (Brass et al., 2009; Catmur et al., 2009; Massen & Prinz, 2009).

Second, over-imitation may emerge because individuals are motivated to affiliate with others (Nielsen, 2006; Nielsen & Blank, 2011; Over & Carpenter, 2012). By imitating movements exactly, an imitator signals sameness or a shared group membership with the demonstrator and thus establishes and strengthens a social bond with the demonstrator. Accordingly, it has been shown that over-imitation is more likely when the demonstrator and the observer share the same group (Buttelmann et al., 2013; Gruber et al., 2019).

Third, over-imitation may result from a motivation to conform to others and follow norms (Kenward, 2012; Kenward et al., 2011; Keupp et al., 2013; Legare & Nielsen, 2015). In this sense, over-imitation is a consequence of individuals' desire to learn how they ought to interact with a tool (Kenward et al., 2011). Accordingly, imitation includes not only the causally necessary but also the normatively "necessary" movements. Supporting evidence for this explanation comes from studies showing that the model's perceived reliability (Allen et al., 2021) and knowledgeableness (Buchsbaum et al., 2011) increase over-imitation.

Together, there seems to be agreement that neither of the suggested underlying psychological mechanisms alone is sufficient to explain over-imitation (Hoehl et al., 2019). An overall perspective on over-imitation was offered by Schleihauf and Hoehl (2020) who suggest using a dual-process framework to integrate the different explanations. According to their framework, cognitive resources determine which psychological processes cause over-imitation. With few cognitive resources, blanket copying (i.e., automatic movement imitation) based on type 1 processing is likely. With more cognitive resources, deliberate considerations about whether or not to faithfully imitate all movements come into play, based on type 2 processing. Here, it depends on the observer's goal in a given situation whether he/she over-imitates or not.

Situational Factors: Salience of the Outcome/Goal and Situational Constraints

Several contextual or situational factors modulate whether people imitate more or less on the basis of movements versus outcomes/goals. In addition to task and domain knowledge (that develops during infancy), the saliency of the outcome or the goal, respectively, and situational constraints recognized in the model's action have been identified as moderating variables that shift the degree to which movements are imitated more or less strongly than outcomes.

Related to the general capacity to recognize the goals of others' actions (which develops with age, see the previous subsection), it has been shown that the availability and salience of the outcome (or goal, respectively), affect movement versus outcome imitation. If the outcome (or goal) is salient, it is imitated more faithfully than the movements leading to the outcome (e.g., Bekkering et al., 2000; Carpenter et al., 2005; Schachner & Carey, 2013; Southgate et al., 2009; Williamson & Markman, 2006; Wohlschläger et al., 2003). In a study by Carpenter et al. (2005), for instance, 12- and 18-month-olds watched a model moving (i.e., hopping or sliding) a toy mouse on a table. In half of the trials, the action ended in one of two toy houses. In the other half of the trials, no toy houses were present, and the movements ended at some position on the table. When the mouse was moved to a house, participants imitated the movement's outcome more often and the observed movement less often than when there was no final destination for the mouse. Likewise, when adults and children were asked to imitate a model who moved his/her hand and touched a table, their imitation of the movement (i.e., the choice of the hand) was more precise when the table was unmarked than when it is marked with two dots (Bekkering et al., 2000; Wohlschläger et al., 2003). In line with GOADI (Wohlschläger et al., 2003), these findings indicate that the salience of an action outcome changes participants' encoding of a demonstration: When an outcome (e.g., the disappearance of the mouse or the touching of a dot) is salient, the movement is just a means to the outcome, and its specific features are not encoded. When the outcome is not salient or even absent, the movement itself becomes important and is imitated, in turn (see also Bird et al., 2007).

Relatedly, the causal relationship between the movement and the outcome may be a factor influencing which type of imitation takes place (Horner & Whiten, 2005). When a critical causal relationship is apparent to the observer, outcome imitation occurs, whereas movement is preferred when the causal relationship is less clear. In one study, for instance, the availability of information about the causal relationship was varied in a tool use task with young children and chimpanzees as participants (Horner & Whiten, 2005, see also Fugazza et al., 2019, for similar findings in dogs). Participants observed actions performed to obtain a reward inserted either into a transparent or an opaque box. When the reward was in the transparent box, the causal relationship between the movements performed with the tool and the outcome was visible; when the reward was in the opaque box, the causal relationship was not visible so participants could not see that some actions were irrelevant to solve the task. The findings showed that participants adjusted their behavior according to the situation and engaged in more outcome imitation in the first condition or relatively more movement imitation in the latter.

Besides the causal link between the movement and the outcome, situational constraints recognized in the model's action modulate whether people's imitation is more based on movement or more on outcomes. Specifically, individuals will imitate movements that represent unusual means to reach a goal only if the model does not have an apparent situational constraint to perform the strange movement. For instance, participants (in this case, 14-month-old children) imitated the movements of an adult who is bending at the waist and touching her head to a panel which results in turning on a light only when the model had her hands free (Gergely et al., 2002). Participants were more likely to use their hands instead of their head when the model was constrained to perform the strange movement, for instance when her hands were occupied by holding a blanket. In the hands-free condition, participants presumably inferred that the model deliberately chose to use her head, and they preferentially imitated the head movement. In the hands-occupied condition, in contrast, the model was not able to use her hands whereas the participants' hands were free to be used (for similar findings in adults, see Genschow & Brass, 2015). Accordingly, participants did not need to imitate the unusual head movement and could reach the same outcome by different means. Similar findings have also been shown for chimpanzees (Buttelmann et al., 2007) and dogs (Range et al., 2007).

Social Group Membership

In addition to situational factors, shared group membership of the observer and the model can increase the imitation of movements. For instance, stronger automatic imitation of movements has been found for human actions than for nonhuman actions (Cracco et al., 2018; Liepelt et al., 2008; Liepelt & Brass, 2010). Similarly, research on mimicry found that the movements of ingroup members are more strongly mimicked than the movements of outgroup members (Bourgeois & Hess, 2008; Cheng & Chartrand, 2003; Mondillon et al., 2007; Yabar et al., 2006). Relatedly, exclusion from one's ingroup (which increases the affiliation goal and the motivation to seek social proximity with the ingroup) causes participants to mimic an ingroup member more than an outgroup member (Lakin et al., 2008).

Likewise, the movements of ingroup members are more strongly imitated than the movements of outgroup members in a cross-contextual imitation paradigm. In one study, for instance, the experimenter told the participants that they would taste a new sports drink that was designed for consumption during workouts (Genschow & Schindler, 2016). Furthermore, it was stated that a video of an athlete exercising with a barbell would be presented to simulate the context of working out. Participants were provided with ten plastic cups filled with an ice-tea-flavored drink and they were allowed to taste from the cups as much as they wanted until the video finished. Drinking from the cups involves repeated arm-lifting movements. In the compatible movement condition, participants observed the athlete standing upright lifting a barbell from his waist to his chest. In the incompatible movement condition, the same athlete was laying on his back pushing the barbell up from his chest. The findings showed that participants who were motivated to affiliate with ingroup members imitated the compatible movements of the athlete more when the athlete was introduced as an ingroup member than when he was introduced as an outgroup member. Thus, one could conclude that social group membership increases movement imitation even across contexts.

However, several recent studies could not replicate the influence of group membership on imitation. For instance, group membership did influence imitation neither in imitation-inhibition tasks (De Souter et al., 2021; Genschow et al., 2022b) nor in the computerized and speeded pen-and-cups task (Genschow et al., 2022a). Future research may specify the exact conditions under which social group membership affects imitation.

Psychological Distance

Social group membership can be regarded as one dimension of psychological distance. That is, because of their familiarity and possibly shared goals, ingroup members are usually construed as socially closer than outgroup members. In addition to social distance, other distance dimensions affect imitation, too (for a review, see Hansen & Genschow, 2020). In particular, temporal and spatial distance has been investigated, which varies, for instance, when the model's behavior is shown in a video that has been recorded at a spatially near or far-away place (spatial distance) or has been recorded recently versus long ago (temporal distance). Construal level theory (Trope & Liberman, 2003, 2010; Trope et al., 2021) states that—independently of the specific distance dimension—psychological distance causes people to construe an activity more abstractly, that is, in terms of its more high-level elements (such as outcomes or goals), whereas psychological proximity causes people to construe an activity more concretely, that is, in terms of its low-level movements. Thus, outcomes and goals may be relatively more salient than movements when an action is perceived from the distance. The respective salient information, in turn, is likely to be imitated.

Research investigating the effect of psychological distance on movement-based imitation has shown that individuals reproduce near behavior, compared with distant behavior, in a more literal action-by-action manner (Hansen et al., 2016). In one study, for instance, participants learned a new activity—that is, creating a dog out of towels—by watching an instruction video in which a model demonstrated the activity in a particular way. Temporal distance from the model was manipulated by telling half of the participants that the video was made more than 10 years ago versus this year (Hansen et al., 2016, Exp. 1). When analyzing how closely participants' movements matched those of the model, it was found that the model's movements were more likely to be imitated when participants believed the model was temporally near than when they believed the model was temporally distant. A similar effect was found when spatial distance was manipulated (Hansen et al., 2016, Exp. 2). Participants more likely imitated the model's movements when they believed that the instruction video was produced in the city where the study was conducted (near) than when they believed that the video was produced in a city that was 3000 miles away (distant). These studies indicate that specifically movement-based imitation is facilitated when temporal and spatial distance is low (see also Hansen et al., 2020).

Additionally, spatial distance has been identified as a variable that dissociates between movement imitation and outcome imitation. In a series of studies (Genschow, Hansen, et al., 2019), participants performed the computerized and speeded pen-and-cups task that measures movement-based imitation independently of outcome-based imitation. Across multiple trials, participants watched on a computer screen the hands of a model pressing one of two keys on a keyboard by using either the right or the left hand. Participants were instructed to imitate the observed action as fast as possible (i.e., they were asked to press the same key with the same hand as the model). Errors of hand use (i.e., movement imitation) and errors of key presses (i.e., outcome imitation) were measured. The spatial distance was manipulated by presenting the model's action at either a spatially proximal or a spatially distant location on the screen. This was done by presenting the model's actions in broad arrows that pointed to either a spatially near or a spatially distant location on a picture (see Bar-Anan et al., 2007; Hansen & Wänke, 2010). The findings showed that participants made relatively more outcome errors (i.e., pressed the wrong key) when the actions were presented at a proximal compared with a distant location. This finding supports the idea that spatial distance causes participants to focus more strongly on the outcome than on the underlying movement, facilitating outcome imitation. One would expect that temporal distance, too, increases outcome/goal imitation relative to movement imitation, which however has not been tested empirically so far.

For future research, construal level theory offers a fruitful path, as many "real-world" context factors that affect the level of construal may also affect movement versus outcome imitation. For instance, it has been shown that good mood (Gasper & Clore, 2002), social power (Smith & Trope, 2006), thoughts about money (Hansen et al., 2013), motivational states (Hansen & Steinmetz, 2019), and musical sound patterns (Hansen & Melzner, 2014) can influence how abstractly individuals process information. These variables may also increase outcome imitation at the expense of movement imitation (see, for instance, Genschow, Schuler, et al., 2019, for the attenuating effect of money on movement imitation).

Summary and Future Directions

An observed action consists of at least two components that can be imitated—movements and outcomes. When imitating, observers sometimes additionally differentiate between the observable outcome and the underlying goal of the demonstrator. Different psychological subdisciplines have investigated movement imitation and outcome/goal imitation, ranging from cultural, animal, and developmental psychology to cognitive and social psychology. Evidence for both forms of imitation has been found with different experimental paradigms.

So, one can conclude that the different forms of imitation are not separate phenomena but should be considered on a continuum from lower-level movement imitation to higher-level goal imitation. When imitating an observed action, its components are usually perceived as hierarchically ordered with the means/movements being interpreted only after the outcome/goal is recognized (Leighton et al., 2010). This implies that the salience of an outcome or goal modulates imitation, with outcome/goal imitation dominating over movement imitation the more salient the outcome/goal becomes. Other factors found to modulate the two levels of imitation include social, spatial, and temporal distance that typically decrease movement imitation.

In future research, it would be interesting to investigate combinations of the different factors that different subdisciplines have identified as moderators of imitation. For instance, would situational constraints and salience of outcomes affect imitation also in more cognitive experimental paradigms, corroborating the comprehensive findings of developmental and cultural psychology? And may the level of construal be an alternative explanation for over-imitation? One could hypothesize that a low construal level or a low psychological (temporal, spatial, or social) distance may increase over-imitation because it causes individuals to more strongly focus on movements instead of outcomes. Methods with which construal levels can be manipulated in children (e.g., Liberman et al., 2012) may be useful to investigate such questions in experimental imitation paradigms of developmental psychology. Likewise, exclusion from an ingroup (triggering affiliation motivation) may increase over-imitation. And construal level manipulated in children may additionally affect the performance in the pen-and-cups task.

In sum, the relevance of both movements and outcomes/goals in imitation is supported by the findings highlighted in the present chapter. Future research may gain from considering the different perspectives of the different psychological subdisciplines to complete our understanding of the role of movements, outcomes, and goals in imitation.

References

Aarts, H., & Hassin, R. R. (2005). Automatic goal inference and contagion: On pursuing goals one perceives in other people's behavior. In S. M. Latham, J. P. Forgas, & K. D. Williams (Eds.), *Social motivation: Conscious and unconscious processes* (pp. 153–167). Cambridge University Press. https://doi.org/10.1017/CBO9780511735066.011

Aarts, H., Gollwitzer, P. M., & Hassin, R. R. (2004). Goal contagion: Perceiving is for pursuing. *Journal of Personality and Social Psychology, 87*, 23–37. https://doi.org/10.1037/0022-3514.87.1.23

Aarts, H., Dijksterhuis, A., & Dik, G. (2008). Goal contagion: Inferring goals from others' actions – And what it leads to. In J. Y. Shah & W. L. Gardner (Eds.), *Handbook of motivation science* (pp. 265–280). The Guilford Press.

Abravanel, E., & Gingold, H. (1985). Learning via observation during the second year of life. *Developmental Psychology, 21*, 614–623. https://doi.org/10.1037/0012-1649.21.4.614

Abravanel, E., Levan-Goldschmidt, E., & Stevenson, M. B. (1976). Action imitation: The early phase of infancy. *Child Development, 47*, 1032–1044. https://doi.org/10.2307/1128440

Allen, J. W. P., Sümer, C., & Ilgaz, H. (2021). Cultural affordances: Does model reliability affect over-imitation in preschoolers. *Cognitive Development, 57*, 100999. https://doi.org/10.1016/j.cogdev.2020.100999

Avikainen, S., Wohlschläger, A., Liuhanen, S., Hänninen, R., & Hari, R. (2003). Impaired mirror-image imitation in Asperger and high-functioning autistic subjects. *Current Biology, 13*, 339–341. https://doi.org/10.1016/S0960-9822(03)00087-3

Bach, P., Peatfield, N. A., & Tipper, S. P. (2007). Focusing on body sites: The role of spatial attention in action perception. *Experimental Brain Research, 178*, 509–517. https://doi.org/10.1007/s00221-006-0756-4

Bar-Anan, Y., Liberman, N., Trope, Y., & Algom, D. (2007). Automatic processing of psychological distance: Evidence from a Stroop task. *Journal of Experimental Psychology: General, 136*, 610–622. https://doi.org/10.1037/0096-3445.136.4.610

Barr, R., Dowden, A., & Hayne, H. (1996). Developmental changes in deferred imitation by 6- to 24-month-old infants. *Infant Behavior and Development, 19*, 159–170. https://doi.org/10.1016/S0163-6383(96)90015-6

Bekkering, H., Wohlschläger, A., & Gattis, M. (2000). Imitation of gestures in children is goal-directed. *The Quarterly Journal of Experimental Psychology: Section A, 53*, 153–164. https://doi.org/10.1080/713755872

Bellagamba, F., & Tomasello, M. (1999). Re-enacting intended acts: Comparing 12- and 18-month-olds. *Infant Behavior and Development, 22*, 277–282. https://doi.org/10.1016/S0163-6383(99)00002-8

Bird, G., Brindley, R., Leighton, J., & Heyes, C. (2007). General processes, rather than "goals," explain imitation errors. *Journal of Experimental Psychology: Human Perception and Performance, 33*, 1158–1169. https://doi.org/10.1037/0096-1523.33.5.1158

Bischoff, C., Reutner, L., & Hansen, J. (2020). The snacking chameleon: Psychological proximity increases imitation of food intake independently of brand choice. *Food, 9*, 228. https://doi.org/10.3390/foods9020228

Bouquet, C. A., Shipley, T. F., Capa, R. L., & Marshall, P. J. (2011). Motor contagion: Goal-directed actions are more contagious than non-goal-directed actions. *Experimental Psychology, 58*, 71–78. https://doi.org/10.1027/1618-3169/a000069

Bourgeois, P., & Hess, U. (2008). The impact of social context on mimicry. *Biological Psychology, 77*, 343–352. https://doi.org/10.1016/j.biopsycho.2007.11.008

Brass, M., Bekkering, H., Wohlschläger, A., & Prinz, W. (2000). Compatibility between observed and executed finger movements: Comparing symbolic, spatial, and imitative cues. *Brain and Cognition, 44*, 124–143. https://doi.org/10.1006/brcg.2000.1225

Brass, M., Bekkering, H., & Prinz, W. (2001). Movement observation affects movement execution in a simple response task. *Acta Psychologica, 106*, 3–22. https://doi.org/10.1016/S0001-6918(00)00024-X

Brass, M., Ruby, P., & Spengler, S. (2009). Inhibition of imitative behaviour and social cognition. *Philosophical Transactions of the Royal Society B: Biological Sciences, 364*, 2359–2367. https://doi.org/10.1098/rstb.2009.0066

Brohmer, H., Eckerstorfer, L. V., van Aert, R. C. M., & Corcoran, K. (2021). Do behavioral observations make people catch the goal? A meta-analysis on goal contagion. *International Review of Social Psychology, 34*, 3. https://doi.org/10.5334/irsp.428

Buchsbaum, D., Gopnik, A., Griffiths, T. L., & Shafto, P. (2011). Children's imitation of causal action sequences is influenced by statistical and pedagogical evidence. *Cognition, 120*, 331–340. https://doi.org/10.1016/j.cognition.2010.12.001

Buttelmann, D., Carpenter, M., Call, J., & Tomasello, M. (2007). Enculturated chimpanzees imitate rationally. *Developmental Science, 10*, F31–F38. https://doi.org/10.1111/j.1467-7687.2007.00630.x

Buttelmann, D., Zmyj, N., Daum, M., & Carpenter, M. (2013). Selective imitation of in-group over out-group members in 14-month-old infants. *Child Development, 84*, 422–428. https://doi.org/10.1111/j.1467-8624.2012.01860.x

Call, J. (1999). Levels of imitation and cognitive mechanisms in orangutans. In S. T. Parker, R. W. Mitchell, & H. L. Miles (Eds.), *The mentalities of gorillas and orangutans* (pp. 316–341). Cambridge University Press. https://doi.org/10.1017/CBO9780511542305.017

Call, J., & Carpenter, M. (2002). Three sources of information in social learning. In K. Dautenhahn & C. L. Nehaniv (Eds.), *Imitation in animals and artifacts* (pp. 211–228). Boston Review.

Carpenter, M., & Call, J. (2002). The chemistry of social learning. *Developmental Science, 5*, 22–24. https://doi.org/10.1111/1467-7687.00199

Carpenter, M., Akhtar, N., & Tomasello, M. (1998a). Fourteen- through 18-month-old infants differentially imitate intentional and accidental actions. *Infant Behavior and Development, 21*, 315–330. https://doi.org/10.1016/S0163-6383(98)90009-1

Carpenter, M., Nagell, K., & Tomasello, M. (1998b). Social cognition, joint attention, and communicative competence from 9 to 15 months of age. *Monographs of the Society for Research in Child Development, 63*, 176. https://doi.org/10.2307/1166214

Carpenter, M., Call, J., & Tomasello, M. (2005). Twelve and 18-month-olds copy actions in terms of goals. *Developmental Science, 8*, F13–F20. https://doi.org/10.1111/j.1467-7687.2004.00385.x

Catmur, C., & Heyes, C. (2010). Time course analyses confirm independence of automatic imitation and spatial compatibility effects. *Journal of Experimental Psychology: Human Perception and Performance, 37*, 409–421. https://doi.org/10.1037/a0019325

Catmur, C., Walsh, V., & Heyes, C. M. (2009). Associative sequence learning: The role of experience in the development of imitation and the mirror system. *Philosophical Transactions of the Royal Society B: Biological Sciences, 364*, 2369–2380. https://doi.org/10.1098/rstb.2009.0048

Chartrand, T. L., & Bargh, J. A. (1999). The chameleon effect: The perception-behavior link and social interaction. *Journal of Personality and Social Psychology, 76*, 893–910. https://doi.org/10.1037/0022-3514.76.6.893

Chartrand, T. L., & van Baaren, R. (2009). Human mimicry. *Advances in Experimental Social Psychology, 41*, 219–274. https://doi.org/10.1016/S0065-2601(08)00405-X

Cheng, C. M., & Chartrand, T. L. (2003). Self-monitoring without awareness: Using mimicry as a nonconscious affiliation strategy. *Journal of Personality and Social Psychology, 85*, 1170–1179. https://doi.org/10.1037/0022-3514.85.6.1170

Chiavarino, C., Bugiani, S., Grandi, E., & Colle, L. (2013). Is automatic imitation based on goal coding or movement coding? A comparison of goal-directed and goal-less actions. *Experimental Psychology, 60*, 213–225. https://doi.org/10.1027/1618-3169/a000190

Cracco, E., Bardi, L., Desmet, C., Genschow, O., Rigoni, D., De Coster, L., … Brass, M. (2018). Automatic imitation: A metaanalysis. *Psychological Bulletin, 144*, 453–500. https://doi.org/10.1037/bul0000143.

Custance, D. M., Whiten, A., & Fredman, T. (1999). Social learning of artificial fruit processing in capuchin monkeys (Cebus apella). *Journal of Comparative Psychology, 113*, 13–23. https://doi.org/10.1037/0735-7036.113.1.13

De Souter, L., Braem, S., Genschow, O., Brass, M., & Cracco, E. (2021). Social group membership does not modulate automatic imitation in a contrastive multi-agent paradigm. *Quarterly Journal of Experimental Psychology, 74*, 746–759. https://doi.org/10.1177/1747021820986528

Dijksterhuis, A., & Bargh, J. A. (2001). The perception–behavior expressway: Automatic effects of social perception on social behavior. *Advances in Experimental Social Psychology, 33*, 1–40. https://doi.org/10.1016/S0065-2601(01)80003-4

Dik, G., & Aarts, H. (2007). Behavioral cues to others' motivation and goal pursuits: The perception of effort facilitates goal inference and contagion. *Journal of Experimental Social Psychology, 43*, 727–737. https://doi.org/10.1016/j.jesp.2006.09.002

Elsner, B. (2007). Infants' imitation of goal-directed action: The role of movements and action effects. *Acta Psychologica, 124*, 44–59. https://doi.org/10.1016/j.actpsy.2006.09.006

Elsner, B., & Aschersleben, G. (2003). Do I get what you get? Learning about the effects of self-performed and observed actions in infancy. *Consciousness and Cognition: An International Journal, 12*, 732–751. https://doi.org/10.1016/S1053-8100(03)00073-4

Elsner, B., & Hommel, B. (2001). Effect anticipation and action control. *Journal of Experimental Psychology: Human Perception and Performance, 27*, 229–240. https://doi.org/10.1037/0096-1523.27.1.229

Fugazza, C., Petro, E., Miklósi, Á., & Pogány, Á. (2019). Social learning of goal-directed actions in dogs (Canis familiaris): Imitation or emulation? *Journal of Comparative Psychology, 133*, 244–251. https://doi.org/10.1037/com0000149

Gasper, K., & Clore, G. L. (2002). Attending to the big picture: Mood and global versus local processing of visual information. *Psychological Science, 13*, 34–40. https://doi.org/10.1111/1467-9280.00406

Gattis, M. (2002). Imitation is mediated by many goals, not just one. *Developmental Science, 5*, 27–29. https://doi.org/10.1111/1467-7687.00201

Gattis, M., Bekkering, H., & Wohlschläger, A. (2002). Goal-directed imitation. In A. N. Meltzoff & W. Prinz (Eds.), *The imitative mind: Development, evolution, and brain bases* (pp. 183–205). Cambridge University Press. https://doi.org/10.1017/CBO9780511489969.011

Genschow, O., & Brass, M. (2015). The predictive chameleon: Evidence for anticipated social action. *Journal of Experimental Psychology: Human Perception and Performance, 41*, 265–268. https://doi.org/10.1037/xhp0000035

Genschow, O., & Florack, A. (2014). Attention on the source of influence reverses the impact of cross-contextual imitation. *Journal of Experimental Psychology: Human Perception and Performance, 40*, 904–907. https://doi.org/10.1037/a0035430

Genschow, O., & Schindler, S. (2016). The influence of group membership on cross-contextual imitation. *Psychonomic Bulletin & Review, 23*, 1257–1265. https://doi.org/10.3758/s13423-015-0983-4

Genschow, O., Florack, A., & Wänke, M. (2013). The power of movement: Evidence for context-independent movement imitation. *Journal of Experimental Psychology: General, 142*, 763–773. https://doi.org/10.1037/a0029795

Genschow, O., Hansen, J., Wänke, M., & Trope, Y. (2019). Psychological distance modulates goal-based versus movement-based imitation. *Journal of Experimental Psychology: Human Perception and Performance, 45*, 1031–1048. https://doi.org/10.1037/xhp0000654

Genschow, O., Schuler, J., Cracco, E., Brass, M., & Wänke, M. (2019). The effect of money priming on self-focus in the imitation-inhibition task. *Experimental Psychology, 66*, 423–436. https://doi.org/10.1027/1618-3169/a000466

Genschow, O., Pauels, E., Krugmann, K., & Winter, A. (2022a). Group membership does not modulate goal-versus movement-based imitation. *Quarterly Journal of Experimental Psychology, 76*, 827–837. https://doi.org/10.1177/17470218221132842
Genschow, O., Westfal, M., Cracco, E., & Crusius, J. (2022b). Group membership does not modulate automatic imitation. *Psychological Research, 86*, 780–791. https://doi.org/10.1007/s00426-021-01526-1
Gergely, G., Bekkering, H., & Király, I. (2002). Rational imitation in preverbal infants. *Nature, 415*, 755. https://doi.org/10.1038/415755a
Gillmeister, H., Catmur, C., Liepelt, R., Brass, M., & Heyes, C. M. (2008). Experience-based priming of body parts: A study of action imitation. *Brain Research, 1217*, 157–170. https://doi.org/10.1016/j.brainres.2007.12.076
Gleissner, B., Meltzoff, A. N., & Bekkering, H. (2000). Children's coding of human action: Cognitive factors influencing imitation in 3-year-olds. *Developmental Science, 3*, 405–414. https://doi.org/10.1111/1467-7687.00135
Gowen, E., Stanley, J., & Miall, R. C. (2008). Movement interference in autism-spectrum disorder. *Neuropsychologia, 46*, 1060–1068. https://doi.org/10.1016/j.neuropsychologia.2007.11.004
Gruber, T., Deschenaux, A., Frick, A., & Clément, F. (2019). Group membership influences more social identification than social learning or overimitation in children. *Child Development, 90*, 728–745. https://doi.org/10.1111/cdev.12931
Hansen, J., & Genschow, O. (2020). Psychological distance and imitation. *Social and Personality Psychology Compass, 14*, e12564. https://doi.org/10.1111/spc3.12564
Hansen, J., & Melzner, J. (2014). What you hear shapes how you think: Sound patterns change level of construal. *Journal of Experimental Social Psychology, 54*, 131–138. https://doi.org/10.1016/j.jesp.2014.05.002
Hansen, J., & Steinmetz, J. (2019). Motivated level of construal: How temperature affects the construal level of state-relevant stimuli. *Motivation and Emotion, 43*, 434–446. https://doi.org/10.1007/s11031-018-09750-w
Hansen, J., & Wänke, M. (2010). Truth from language and truth from fit: The impact of linguistic concreteness and level of construal on subjective truth. *Personality and Social Psychology Bulletin, 36*, 1576–1588. https://doi.org/10.1177/0146167210386238
Hansen, J., Kutzner, F., & Wänke, M. (2013). Money and thinking: Reminders of money trigger abstract construal and shape consumer judgments. *Journal of Consumer Research, 39*, 1154–1166. https://doi.org/10.1086/667691
Hansen, J., Alves, H., & Trope, Y. (2016). Psychological distance reduces literal imitation: Evidence from an imitation-learning paradigm. *Journal of Experimental Psychology: Human Perception and Performance, 42*, 320–330. https://doi.org/10.1037/xhp0000150
Hansen, J., Michelbach, J., & Stabenow, M. (2020). Imitation of counter-goal behavior: The role of psychological distance and level of construal. *Acta Psychologica, 210*, 103164. https://doi.org/10.1016/j.actpsy.2020.103164
Hayes, S. J., Ashford, D., & Bennett, S. J. (2008). Goal-directed imitation: The means to an end. *Acta Psychologica, 127*, 407–415. https://doi.org/10.1016/j.actpsy.2007.07.009
Heyes, C. (2011). Automatic imitation. *Psychological Bulletin, 137*, 463–483. https://doi.org/10.1037/a0022288
Heyes, C. (2021). Imitation. *Current Biology, 31*, R228–R232. https://doi.org/10.1016/j.cub.2020.11.071
Heyes, C., Bird, G., Johnson, H., & Haggard, P. (2005). Experience modulates automatic imitation. *Cognitive Brain Research, 22*, 233–240. https://doi.org/10.1016/j.cogbrainres.2004.09.009
Hoehl, S., Keupp, S., Schleihauf, H., McGuigan, N., Buttelmann, D., & Whiten, A. (2019). Overimitation – A review and appraisal of a decade of research. *Developmental Review, 51*, 90–108. https://doi.org/10.1016/j.dr.2018.12.002
Hommel, B., Müsseler, J., Aschersleben, G., & Prinz, W. (2001). The theory of event coding (TEC): A framework for perception and action planning. *Behavioral and Brain Sciences, 24*, 849–937. https://doi.org/10.1017/S0140525X01000103

Horner, V., & Whiten, A. (2005). Causal knowledge and imitation/emulation switching in chimpanzees (*Pan troglodytes*) and children (*Homo sapiens*). *Animal Cognition, 8*, 164–181. https://doi.org/10.1007/s10071-004-0239-6

Huang, C.-T., & Charman, T. (2005). Gradations of emulation learning in infants' imitation of actions on objects. *Journal of Experimental Child Psychology, 92*, 276–302. https://doi.org/10.1016/j.jecp.2005.06.003

Huang, C.-T., Heyes, C., & Charman, T. (2002). Infants' behavioral reenactment of "failed attempts": Exploring the roles of emulation learning, stimulus enhancement, and understanding of intentions. *Developmental Psychology, 38*, 840–855. https://doi.org/10.1037/0012-1649.38.5.840

Hurley, S., & Chater, N. (Eds.). (2005). *Perspectives on imitation: From neuroscience to social science: Vol. 2. Imitation, human development, and culture*. MIT Press. https://doi.org/10.7551/mitpress/5331.001.0001

James, W. (1890). *The principles of psychology* (Vol. 2). Dover. (Reprinted 1950).

Kenward, B. (2012). Over-imitating preschoolers believe unnecessary actions are normative and enforce their performance by a third party. *Journal of Experimental Child Psychology, 112*, 195–207. https://doi.org/10.1016/j.jecp.2012.02.006

Kenward, B., Karlsson, M., & Persson, J. (2011). Overimitation is better explained by norm learning than by distorted causal learning. *Proceedings of the Royal Society B: Biological Sciences, 278*, 1239–1246. https://doi.org/10.1098/rspb.2010.1399

Keupp, S., Behne, T., & Rakoczy, H. (2013). Why do children overimitate? Normativity is crucial. *Journal of Experimental Child Psychology, 116*, 392–406. https://doi.org/10.1016/j.jecp.2013.07.002

Keupp, S., Behne, T., & Rakoczy, H. (2018). The rationality of (over)imitation. *Perspectives on Psychological Science, 13*, 678–687. https://doi.org/10.1177/1745691618794921

Killen, M., & Uzgiris, I. C. (1981). Imitation of actions with objects: The role of social meaning. *The Journal of Genetic Psychology: Research and Theory on Human Development, 138*, 219–229. https://doi.org/10.1080/00221325.1981.10534136

Kilner, J. M., Paulignan, Y., & Blakemore, S. J. (2003). An interference effect of observed biological movement on action. *Current Biology, 13*, 522–525. https://doi.org/10.1016/S0960-9822(03)00165-9

Kilner, J. M., Hamilton, A. F., & Blakemore, S. J. (2007). Interference effect of observed human movement on action is due to velocity profile of biological motion. *Social Neuroscience, 2*, 158–166. https://doi.org/10.1080/17470910701428190

Lakin, J. L., Chartrand, T. L., & Arkin, R. M. (2008). I am too just like you: Nonconscious mimicry as an automatic behavioral response to social exclusion. *Psychological Science, 19*, 816–822. https://doi.org/10.1111/j.1467-9280.2008.02162.x

Laurin, K. (2016). Interpersonal influences on goals: Current and future directions for goal contagion research. *Social and Personality Psychology Compass, 10*, 668–678. https://doi.org/10.1111/spc3.12289

Legare, C. H., & Nielsen, M. (2015). Imitation and innovation: The dual engines of cultural learning. *Trends in Cognitive Sciences, 19*, 688–699. https://doi.org/10.1016/j.tics.2015.08.005

Leighton, J., & Heyes, C. M. (2010). Hand to mouth: Automatic imitation across effector systems. *Journal of Experimental Psychology: Human Perception and Performance, 36*, 1174–1183. https://doi.org/10.1037/a0019953

Leighton, J., Bird, G., Charman, T., & Heyes, C. (2008). Weak imitative performance is not due to a functional "mirroring" deficit in adults with Autism Spectrum Disorders. *Neuropsychologia, 46*, 1041–1049. https://doi.org/10.1016/j.neuropsychologia.2007.11.013

Leighton, J., Bird, G., & Heyes, C. (2010). "Goals" are not an integral component of imitation. *Cognition, 114*, 423–435. https://doi.org/10.1016/j.cognition.2009.11.001

Liberman, N., Polack, O., Hameiri, B., & Blumenfeld, M. (2012). Priming of spatial distance enhances children's creative performance. *Journal of Experimental Child Psychology, 111*, 663–670. https://doi.org/10.1016/j.jecp.2011.09.007

Liepelt, R., & Brass, M. (2010). Top-down modulation of motor priming by belief about animacy. *Experimental Psychology, 57*, 221–227. https://doi.org/10.1027/1618-3169/a000028

Liepelt, R., von Cramon, D. Y., & Brass, M. (2008). What is matched in direct matching? Intention attribution modulates motor priming. *Journal of Experimental Psychology: Human Perception and Performance, 34*, 578–591. https://doi.org/10.1037/0096-1523.34.3.578

Liepelt, R., Prinz, W., & Brass, M. (2010). When do we simulate non-human agents? Dissociating communicative and noncommunicative actions. *Cognition, 115*, 426–434. https://doi.org/10.1016/j.cognition.2010.03.003

Loersch, C., Aarts, H., Payne, B. K., & Jefferis, V. E. (2008). The influence of social groups on goal contagion. *Journal of Experimental Social Psychology, 44*, 1555–1558. https://doi.org/10.1016/j.jesp.2008.07.009

Lyons, D. E., Young, A. G., & Keil, F. C. (2007). The hidden structure of overimitation. *Proceedings of the National Academy of Sciences of the United States of America, 104*, 19751–19756. https://doi.org/10.1073/pnas.0704452104

Lyons, D. E., Damrosch, D. H., Lin, J. K., Macris, D. M., & Keil, F. C. (2011). The scope and limits of overimitation in the transmission of artefact culture. *Philosophical Transactions of the Royal Society B: Biological Sciences, 366*, 1158–1167. https://doi.org/10.1098/rstb.2010.0335

Massen, C., & Prinz, W. (2009). Movements, actions and tool-use actions: An ideomotor approach to imitation. *Philosophical Transactions of the Royal Society B: Biological Sciences, 364*, 2349–2358. https://doi.org/10.1098/rstb.2009.0059

McGuigan, N., & Whiten, A. (2009). Emulation and "overemulation" in the social learning of causally opaque versus causally transparent tool use by 23- and 30-month-olds. *Journal of Experimental Child Psychology, 104*, 367–381. https://doi.org/10.1016/j.jecp.2009.07.001

McGuigan, N., Whiten, A., Flynn, E., & Horner, V. (2007). Imitation of causally opaque versus causally transparent tool use by 3- and 5-year-old children. *Cognitive Development, 22*, 353–364. https://doi.org/10.1016/j.cogdev.2007.01.001

McGuigan, N., Makinson, J., & Whiten, A. (2011). From over-imitation to super-copying: Adults imitate causally irrelevant aspects of tool use with higher fidelity than young children. *British Journal of Psychology, 102*, 1–18. https://doi.org/10.1348/000712610X493115

Meltzoff, A. N. (1985). Immediate and deferred imitation in fourteen- and twenty-four-month-old infants. *Child Development, 56*, 62–72. https://doi.org/10.1111/j.1467-8624.1985.tb00086.x

Meltzoff, A. N. (1988a). Infant imitation after a 1-week delay: Long-term memory for novel acts and multiple stimuli. *Developmental Psychology, 24*, 470–476. https://doi.org/10.1037/0012-1649.24.4.470

Meltzoff, A. N. (1988b). Infant imitation and memory: Nine-month-olds in immediate and deferred tests. *Child Development, 59*, 217–225. https://doi.org/10.2307/1130404

Meltzoff, A. N. (1995). Understanding the intentions of others: Re-enactment of intended acts by 18-month-old children. *Developmental Psychology, 31*, 838–850. https://doi.org/10.1037/0012-1649.31.5.838

Meltzoff, A. N. (2007). Infants' causal learning: Intervention, observation, imitation. In A. Gopnik & L. Schulz (Eds.), *Causal learning: Psychology, philosophy, and computation* (pp. 37–47). Oxford University Press. https://doi.org/10.1093/acprof:oso/9780195176803.003.0003

Mondillon, L., Niedenthal, P., Gil, S., & Droit-Volet, S. (2007). Imitation of in-group versus out-group members' facial expression of anger: A test with a time perception task. *Social Neuroscience, 2*, 223–237. https://doi.org/10.1080/17470910701376894

Nielsen, M. (2006). Copying actions and copying outcomes: Social learning through the second year. *Developmental Psychology, 42*, 555–565. https://doi.org/10.1037/0012-1649.42.3.555

Nielsen, M., & Blank, C. (2011). Imitation in young children: When who gets copied is more important than what gets copied. *Developmental Psychology, 47*, 1050–1053. https://doi.org/10.1037/a0023866

Over, H., & Carpenter, M. (2012). Putting the social into social learning: Explaining both selectivity and fidelity in children's copying behavior. *Journal of Comparative Psychology, 126*, 182–192. https://doi.org/10.1037/a0024555

Press, C., Bird, G., Walsh, E., & Heyes, C. (2008). Automatic imitation of intransitive actions. *Brain and Cognition, 67*, 44–50. https://doi.org/10.1016/j.bandc.2007.11.001

Prinz, W. (1997). Perception and action planning. *European Journal of Cognitive Psychology, 9*, 129–154. https://doi.org/10.1080/713752551

Provasi, J., Dubon, C. D., & Bloch, H. (2001). Do 9-and 12-month-olds learn means-ends relation by observing? *Infant Behavior and Development, 24*, 195–213. https://doi.org/10.1016/S0163-6383(01)00072-8

Range, F., Viranyi, Z., & Huber, L. (2007). Selective imitation in domestic dogs. *Current Biology, 17*, 868–872. https://doi.org/10.1016/j.cub.2007.04.026

Schachner, A., & Carey, S. (2013). Reasoning about "irrational" actions: When intentional movements cannot be explained, the movements themselves are seen as the goal. *Cognition, 129*, 309–327. https://doi.org/10.1016/j.cognition.2013.07.006

Schleihauf, H., & Hoehl, S. (2020). A dual-process perspective on over-imitation. *Developmental Review, 55*, 100896. https://doi.org/10.1016/j.dr.2020.100896

Shin, Y. K., Proctor, R. W., & Capaldi, E. J. (2010). A review of contemporary ideomotor theory. *Psychological Bulletin, 136*, 943–974. https://doi.org/10.1037/a0020541

Smith, P. K., & Trope, Y. (2006). You focus on the forest when you're in charge of the trees: Power priming and abstract information processing. *Journal of Personality and Social Psychology, 90*, 578–596. https://doi.org/10.1037/0022-3514.90.4.578

Song, H.-J., & Baillargeon, R. (2008). Infants' reasoning about others' false perceptions. *Developmental Psychology, 44*, 1789–1795. https://doi.org/10.1037/a0013774

Southgate, V., Chevallier, C., & Csibra, G. (2009). Sensitivity to communicative relevance tells young children what to imitate. *Developmental Science, 12*, 1013–1019. https://doi.org/10.1111/j.1467-7687.2009.00861.x

Stürmer, B., Aschersleben, G., & Prinz, W. (2000). Correspondence effects with manual gestures and postures: A study of imitation. *Journal of Experimental Psychology: Human Perception and Performance, 26*, 1746–1759. https://doi.org/10.1037/0096-1523.26.6.1746

Trope, Y., & Liberman, N. (2003). Temporal construal. *Psychological Review, 110*, 403–421. https://doi.org/10.1037/0033-295X.110.3.403

Trope, Y., & Liberman, N. (2010). Construal-level theory of psychological distance. *Psychological Review, 117*, 440–463. https://doi.org/10.1037/a0018963

Trope, Y., Ledgerwood, A., Liberman, N., & Fujita, K. (2021). Regulatory scope and its mental and social supports. *Perspectives on Psychological Science, 16*, 204–224. https://doi.org/10.1177/1745691620950691

Want, S. C., & Gattis, M. (2005). Are "late-signing" deaf children "mindblind"? Understanding goal directedness in imitation. *Cognitive Development, 20*, 159–172. https://doi.org/10.1016/j.cogdev.2004.12.003

Want, S. C., & Harris, P. L. (2002). How do children ape? Applying concepts from the study of non-human primates to the developmental study of 'imitation' in children. *Developmental Science, 5*, 1–13. https://doi.org/10.1111/1467-7687.00194

Wessler, J., & Hansen, J. (2016). The effect of psychological distance on automatic goal contagion. *Comprehensive Results in Social Psychology, 1*, 51–85. https://doi.org/10.1080/23743603.2017.1288877

Wessler, J., & Hansen, J. (2017). Temporal closeness promotes imitation of meaningful gestures in face-to-face communication. *Journal of Nonverbal Behavior, 41*, 415–431. https://doi.org/10.1007/s10919-017-0256-1

Whiten, A., McGuigan, N., Marshall-Pescini, S., & Hopper, L. M. (2009). Emulation, imitation, over-imitation and the scope of culture for child and chimpanzee. *Philosophical Transactions of the Royal Society of London. Series B, Biological Sciences, 364*, 2417–2428. https://doi.org/10.1098/rstb.2009.0069

Williamson, R. A., & Markman, E. M. (2006). Precision of imitation as a function of preschoolers' understanding of the goal of the demonstration. *Developmental Psychology, 42*, 723–731. https://doi.org/10.1037/0012-1649.42.4.723

Wohlschläger, A., & Bekkering, H. (2002). The role of objects in imitation. In M. I. Stamenov & V. Gallese (Eds.), *Mirror neurons and the evolution of brain and language* (pp. 101–113). John Benjamins Publishing Company. https://doi.org/10.1075/aicr.42.09woh

Wohlschläger, A., Gattis, M., & Bekkering, H. (2003). Action generation and action perception in imitation: An instance of the ideomotor principle. *Philosophical Transactions of the Royal Society of London Series B, Biological Sciences, 358*, 501–515. https://doi.org/10.1098/rstb.2002.1257

Wood, D. (1989). Social interaction as tutoring. In M. H. Bornstein & J. S. Bruner (Eds.), *Interaction in human development* (pp. 59–80). Lawrence Erlbaum. https://doi.org/10.4324/9781315808277

Yabar, Y., Johnston, L., Miles, L., & Peace, V. (2006). Implicit behavioral mimicry: Investigating the impact of group membership. *Journal of Nonverbal Behavior, 30*, 97–113. https://doi.org/10.1007/s10919-006-0010-6

Chapter 8
Anticipated Imitation

Roland Pfister, Bence Neszmélyi, and Wilfried Kunde

Experimental research in psychology and related fields has traditionally followed a straightforward agenda that we will call the stimulus-response paradigm here. The stimulus-response paradigm involves creating certain situations and measuring the behavior of humans and other animals in these situations. This paradigm offers an elegant blueprint for empirical studies on cognition and behavior, as it follows directly from attempts to introduce experimental methodology into the discipline of psychology (Ueberwasser, 1787; see also Schwarz & Pfister, 2016).

Against the background of the stimulus-response paradigm, it seems intuitive to manipulate clearly perceivable stimulus characteristics and measure behavior (i.e., responses) as a function of these characteristics. This approach already developed in the early days of psychological inquiry, when initial experimental studies approached human perception from the perspective of psychophysics (Fechner, 1877; Weber, 1851, cf. Kingdom & Prins, 2016). Other lines of inquiry quickly adopted similar methods such as early studies with response time measurements (Donders 1869), and this paradigm continues to be a major component of the methodological toolkit of contemporary psychological research.

Applying the stimulus-response agenda to the scientific study of imitation entails a straightforward roadmap for devising experimental setups. Imitation involves at least two agents, a model and an imitator. Because the model action has to precede the imitator action, it is natural to assign the model's behavior to the stimulus side of the experimental design (often using pictures or videos of the model action), and to assign the imitator's behavior to the response side. This assignment has enabled a series of relevant discoveries. One example concerns research on automatic

R. Pfister (✉)
General Psychology, University of Trier, Trier, Germany
e-mail: roland.pfister@uni-trier.de

B. Neszmélyi · W. Kunde
Department of Psychology, University of Würzburg, Würzburg, Germany
e-mail: bence.neszmelyi@uni-wuerzburg.de; wilfried.kunde@uni-wuerzburg.de

O. Genschow, E. Cracco (eds.), *Automatic Imitation*,
https://doi.org/10.1007/978-3-031-62634-0_8

imitation (Heyes, 2011) as studied experimentally via motor priming effects (Brass et al., 2000, 2001; Cracco et al., 2018). In studies on motor priming, participants are shown a stimulus on every trial, and this stimulus includes an action of an imitation model, e.g., lifting the index finger of the left hand. They are asked to respond to each stimulus with clearly defined responses, e.g., also lifting the left index finger. These setups reliably produce compatibility effects in the sense that response times and error rates of the imitator are lower if the model action matches the required response (compatible or imitation trials) as compared to mismatches between model action and imitator response (incompatible or counter-imitation trials). This occurs even if participants do not have to attend to the model action, e.g., when responding to a stimulus shape that is superimposed on the model action. Research on motor priming therefore suggests that perceiving the movement of another agent primes similar responses in the observer (Fadiga et al., 1995, but see Hemed et al., 2022).

An elegant way to explain motor priming effects is in terms of the ideomotor principle of action control (Brass & Heyes, 2005). The ideomotor principle assumes that agents represent and access their behavioral repertoire by means of the perceivable changes to be produced by the movement, i.e., in terms of its action effects (Harleß, 1861; Herbart, 1824; James, 1890 Washburn, 1908; for historical perspectives, see Stock & Stock, 2004; Pfister & Janczyk, 2012). Re-encountering any of these effects can therefore prime the associated movements by means of bidirectional associations between actions and their ensuing effects. For a simple finger movement, these effects include the proprioceptive and tactile changes triggered by the moving body, as well as the visual image of the moving finger (e.g., Pfister, 2019). This is precisely the kind of stimulus that triggers imitative tendencies in a typical experiment on motor priming. In this view, therefore, motor priming is a social manifestation of a general and basic property of action representations. The mechanisms proposed by ideomotor theorizing also extend seamlessly to other modalities so that they can account for automatic imitation of complex behaviors such as gestures (Bernieri, 1988; Cracco et al., 2018) and facial expressions (Dimberg, 1982; Seibt et al., 2015). It further accounts for a number of classic findings in the field. For instance, motor priming is affected by how similar model and imitator are (Brass et al., 2001; Liepelt & Brass, 2010; Longo & Bertenthal, 2009; Genschow et al., 2013, 2021; Vogt et al., 2003; see also Schütz-Bosbach & Prinz, 2007). It also captures changes of action priming through novel motor-effect contingencies (Gillmeister et al., 2008; Wiggett et al., 2011). In an ideomotor view, perceiving a model action can re-activate of existing action–effect associations to the extent that there are shared features between model and imitator action. As increased similarity implies increasingly many shared features, ideomotor accounts imply that imitative tendencies should vary with model-imitator similarity.

In the following, we argue that the ideomotor account offers even more than providing an elegant and parsimonious explanation of motor priming effects. Moreover, experimental paradigms that play a central role in studying ideomotor mechanisms of human action control allow to expand the field of study beyond simple reactions to external events. That is: Applying similar experimental approaches to the study of imitation shifts the focus away from the imitator and towards the psychological processes operating in the action model, thus opening a new look at a classic phenomenon. To motivate this claim, we will first discuss several key aspects of studying ideomotor action control outside the field of imitation, and we then show how this line of thinking has stimulated so-called "sociomotor" research on imitation and social actions in general (Kunde et al., 2017; Neszmélyi et al., 2022).

Ideomotor Action Control: The Role of Sensory Anticipations

Ideomotor action presupposes that agents can acquire bidirectional associations between the neural activity that generates overt movements and incoming sensory effects that are triggered by this movement (Harleß, 1861; Herbart, 1824). Once established, these bidirectional associations allow for goal-directed actions because mentally recollecting, i.e., anticipating, the effects will then spread activation across the available associations and thus initiate a movement. It is this anticipative component that renders the ideomotor mechanism particularly relevant for understanding how the human mind represents and produces actions (Kunde, 2006; Kunde et al., 2004).

Empirically studying effect anticipations poses a profound challenge to common experimental designs that follow the general stimulus-response agenda, however. It requires measuring how a stimulus that occurs only after action execution affects the very action that is going to produce the effect in the first place. Instead of varying perceivable characteristics of the current situation, experiments thus need to manipulate future but predictable events and probe for their impact on behavior.

One way to implement a structured manipulation of to-be-produced action effects is the response-effect compatibility paradigm (Kunde, 2001). In this paradigm, participants perform simple responses such as keypresses and each response produces a particular, foreseeable effect such as a visual event on the computer screen. If the experimental design implements responses and effects that vary on a shared dimension, e.g., left versus right, this setup can include compatible trials such that a left keypress triggers an effect on the left-hand side, and incompatible trials such that a left keypress triggers an effect on the right-hand side. Crucially, compatibility here relates to how action features map onto features of later action effects, i.e., events that are not yet present during action execution. Still, responses are usually observed to be faster in compatible trials than in incompatible trials (Pfister & Kunde, 2013; Pfister et al. 2014a; Wirth et al., 2016; Shin & Proctor, 2012). Similarly, the way actions are produced changes with the features of upcoming stimulation so that an action will be less forceful if it triggers a high-intensity effect as compared to a low-intensity effect or no effect at all (Horváth et al., 2018; Kunde et al., 2004; Neszmélyi & Horváth, 2017; Thébault et al., 2020). These findings clearly suggest that participants anticipate upcoming action effects, and that such effect anticipations are functionally relevant for action planning and control.

Even though technically still a stimulus-response paradigm (for the fact of implementing a controlled experimental design), research on response-effect compatibility offers an elegant perspective on imitation by highlighting the model's side of the process as the first part of an action–effect sequence (with the "action" in "action–effect" being the model's action and "effect" being the imitator's response). Understanding whether and how action models are affected by imitation requires a shift in focus towards measuring rather than manipulating the behavior of action models. What needs to be manipulated instead is the later response by the imitator, which also needs to be sufficiently predictable to allow the model to form meaningful anticipations. The following section covers this type of research.

Focusing on the Imitation Model

Imitation can affect the action model in two ways. First, experiencing another person imitate one's own actions may change later cognition and behavior of the model. This is true especially for affective consequences of imitation such as liking of the imitator (Chartrand & Bargh, 1999; De Coster et al., 2013; Dignath et al., 2018; van Baaren et al., 2004; for an overview see Chaps. 13 and 14; this volume). Second, expecting another agent to imitate one's own actions may even affect how models represent, plan, and control their actions in the first place. In this sense, imitative behavior of another person can be seen as an action effect of the model action. Ideomotor theorizing therefore suggests that predictable imitation should facilitate action control as compared to predictably mismatching responses (counter-imitation), and also compared to situations with unpredictable responses of a social interaction partner. Figure 8.1 shows a summary of the assumed processes underlying anticipated and reactive imitation.

Initial evidence for this hypothesis comes from a response-effect compatibility experiment that assessed the impact of anticipated action effects on how facial muscles are controlled (Kunde et al., 2011). Participants were asked to perform facial gestures by either contracting the zygomaticus major muscle (generating a smiling expression) or by contracting the corrugator supercilii muscle (generating a frowning expression). Each response further triggered the image of either a smiling or frowning face on the computer screen. Different blocks of the experiment implemented either a predictably compatible mapping (smiling response triggers smiling face) or a predictably incompatible mapping (smiling response triggers frowning face). Generating a correct facial gesture was indeed faster if predictably followed by a compatible rather than incompatible action effect. These findings are in line with the idea that social effects enter action representations in addition to other (e.g., body-related) effects so that anticipated imitation directly primes corresponding model responses.

In a second, direct test of the anticipated imitation hypothesis, we asked two participants to act in leader–follower, i.e., model–imitator dyads (Pfister et al., 2013). They sat face to face at a table and operated one response key each, with both

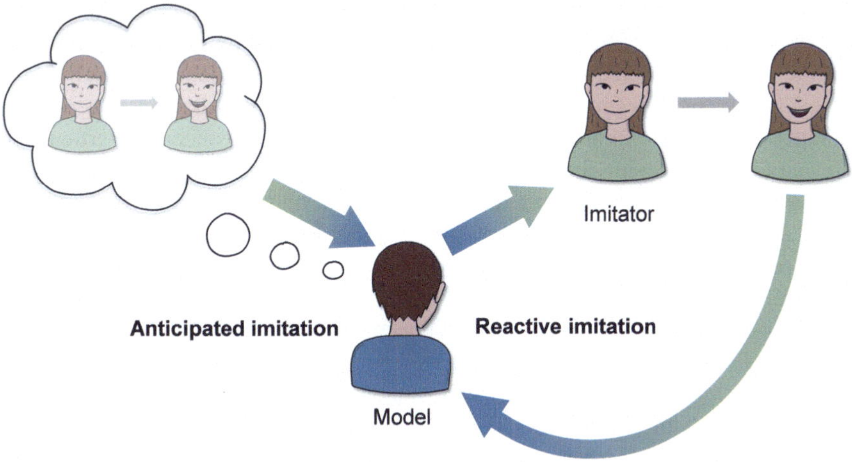

Fig. 8.1 Interplay of anticipated and reactive imitation when a model's smile (depicted from behind) makes the imitator smile back. Even before actually perceiving an imitative response (reactive imitation), models may anticipate likely imitative behavior which, in turn, triggers imitative tendencies on the model's side (anticipated imitation; for a corresponding theoretical framework, see Kunde et al., 2018). Such tendencies can be shown experimentally by having the imitator predictably imitate or counter-imitate a model action (e.g., Pfister et al., 2013; Müller, 2016)

keys placed close to each other on the table. The leader observed a computer screen on each trial and performed either a short or a long keypress in response to the screen background changing from black to either red or green. In different conditions, the follower was asked to consistently imitate or counter-imitate the leader's action. In the imitation condition, the follower would thus perform a short keypress in response to a short keypress of the leader, whereas the counter-imitation condition would call for long keypresses of the follower in response to a short keypress of the leader (see Kunde, 2003, for a blueprint of this setup with physical action effects). The experimental conditions were again manipulated across blocks so that the leader could predict the likely follower response to his or her action on each trial. Crucially, this manipulation did indeed affect the leader's behavior in that their responses were faster in the imitation condition as compared to the counter-imitation condition. These imitation effects on the leader were smaller than the imitation effects of directly perceived stimuli as observed with the follower but, crucially, both were highly reliable across experiments. The same held true when comparing the imitation condition to a control condition with unpredictable follower responses. Further work extended the approach to larger-scale movements such as moving virtual objects on a multi-touch table (Müller, 2016). These findings again suggest that models built up anticipations of upcoming imitator responses, thus boosting performance if these anticipations overlapped with the currently required response.

Carefully inspecting the setup and design of the latter two studies highlights a potential shortcoming, however (Lelonkiewicz & Gambi, 2017). Because the experimental conditions varied across blocks, each imitation trial also follows another imitation trial in the imitation condition, and each counter-imitation trial always follows other counter-imitation trials in the counter-imitation condition. Any systematic effects between conditions may therefore relate to anticipations as hypothesized above, or they might be due to after-effects of just having experienced imitation or counter-imitation in the preceding trial(s). This concern is particularly relevant for designs with direct interactions of actual participants, i.e., if not relegating either the model or the imitator side to picture or video stimuli (e.g., Pfister et al., 2013). In cases of direct interactions, imitators of course also show typical motor priming effects so that the imitator's responses are systematically delayed in the counter-imitation condition as compared to the imitation condition (Brass et al., 2001). One way to assess concerns related to the blocked experimental design is to manipulate imitation conditions on a trial-by-trial level. This design choice only requires an additional cue on every trial to enable the model to predict the imitator's response. The issue of different temporal delays during imitation and counter-imitation, by contrast, is best addressed by using virtual agents as imitator, which allows controlling the interval between the model's and the imitator's movements. Studies that applied such modifications to the original setup still replicated the previously observed impact of anticipated imitation, thus supporting the above reading in terms of actual anticipations (Lelonkiewicz et al., 2020; see also Pfister et al., 2017).

Predictable Imitation

The processes occurring during anticipated imitation are tied to the model actually predicting a social partner to imitate (see Fig. 8.1). But are such predictions actually warranted in the real world? They are warranted in the context of a psychological experiment as discussed above, because the imitator is explicitly asked to produce imitation actions in certain conditions. Imitation can indeed be expected also in many real-world interactions, however. Smiling at another person routinely triggers this person to smile back, greeting another person will also make this person greet back, though not necessarily using the same phrase. Many innocuous movements are also copied readily by others, such as scratching one's noes, crossing one's legs, and the like.

A familiar everyday instance of imitation is the tendency to copy the body posture of other people during a meeting. Imitation also occurs frequently when interacting with children or during interactions among children (Agnetta & Rochat, 2004). Imitative games between caregivers and children can involve extended loops of mutual provoking and performing imitative responses. Deliberately provoking imitation therefore enables early, pre-verbal forms of interaction and communication, thus serving a crucial role in ontogenetic development (Nagy, 2006; Nagy & Molnar, 2004).

Motor priming through anticipated imitation arguably facilitates these crucial interactions. Specifically, imitation is a kind of win-win situation for the imitator and the model alike. The benefits for imitators are pretty obvious (e.g., Heyes, 2013). For example, while it may sometimes be hard to explain a complicated body movement to another person verbally, e.g., performing a certain dance move or eating with cutlery, this is much more easily done by demonstrating the action to another person and asking him or her to do the same. Imitation drives the imitator towards doing the right thing in such demonstration scenarios. Yet, the foreseeable imitation is beneficial for the models as well, namely to generate the to-be-imitated behavior in the first place. Think of it: it is easier to demonstrate a certain movement to another person that most likely will imitate, as compared to demonstrating the same movement to, let us say to a wardrobe, that most likely will not imitate. Only in the former case can the model build reasonable anticipations of upcoming imitative responses. Motor priming by expected imitation from a social partner thus facilitates model behavior directly.

Despite imitation being likely and predictable on many occasions, direct interactions will also include situations in which corresponding expectations are violated. That is, a model might sometimes anticipate their interaction partner to imitate while the partner actually fails to do so. Reasons for such failures may be inattention to the model's action, error commission while actually aiming to imitate, or deliberate omission of an imitative response. Unexpectedly observing a social partner not to mirror one's behavior has been shown to trigger immediate neurophysiological and behavioral responses (Pfister et al., 2020; Weller et al., 2017), suggesting that action models monitor the behavior of their interaction partners closely.

Imitating Anticipated Actions

The discussion so far had centered on the model's perspective. Anticipation might also play a crucial role for the observing imitator. More precisely, when observing others, humans tend to predict future behavior of their social partners (Bach et al., 2011; Bach & Schenke, 2017). Following the logic of ideomotor theorizing, such predictions or anticipations might induce similar imitative tendencies as in the case of anticipated imitation. This is indeed the case: If participants can reasonably predict another agent to perform an action, they are biased towards performing precisely this predicted action (Genschow & Brass, 2015; Genschow et al., 2018). Watching someone wrinkle their nose, for instance, is predictive of this event being followed by nose scratching. Participants observing a model performing the first action (nose wrinkling) are indeed likely to perform the predicted follow-up action (nose scratching) themselves even if the model does not execute the second action at all. Moreover, merely drawing attention to a certain body part of others does not induce similar action tendencies (Genschow & Groß-Bölting, 2021). Participants therefore form a prediction of a specific action and likely activate own actions with similar features in much the same way as imitation models are primed by anticipating the imitator's response (Genschow & Brass, 2015; Pfister et al., 2013).

Findings on imitation of anticipated actions (Genschow & Brass, 2015) find a non-social counterpart in ideomotor-inspired research on motor priming by merely intended events (De Maeght & Prinz, 2004, Knuf et al., 2001; Prinz et al., 2005). In these experiments, participants watched the trajectory of a rolling ball that steered towards a target area. Each movement lasted several seconds and the ball appeared to miss the target if participants did not intervene early on in the trajectory. During the later phases of the trajectory, participants knew that they could no longer affect the ball movements. Still, they consistently continued to perform actions that would have steered the ball in the intended direction. This mirrors imitation of anticipated actions in that motor priming only derived from anticipated or intended events. In case these anticipated events are actions of another partner, however, this priming is additionally boosted by the strong resemblance of predicted partner actions and the observer's own motor repertoire (Colton et al., 2018).

Anticipating Imitation Versus Actually Imitating

The findings discussed so far suggest striking similarities between the impact of anticipated imitation and the processes occurring when actually performing an imitative response to a currently perceivable stimulus, i.e., reactive imitation. Both seem to come with a similar behavioral signature and both can be explained by the same ideomotor mechanism. This mirrors the relationship of stimulus–response and response–effect associations in ideomotor theorizing. Both types of associations are assumed to rely on the very same linkage between efferent activity and (re)afferent signals, regardless of the temporal order of the perceptual and motor events. Whenever action models expect or anticipate an imitative response of a social partner, this process effectively blurs who imitates whom: Even though the second person to physically respond is clearly triggered by observing the first action, this first action is already biased by imitative tendencies due to anticipated imitation. Expecting another person to return a smile thus makes us smile back before actually perceiving the imitative smile.

Several notable differences qualify the observed similarities of anticipated and reactive imitation, however. For instance, reactive imitation has been suggested to be moderated by group membership, with stronger imitation effects for in-group members than for outgroup members (Bourgeois & Hess, 2008; McIntosh, 2006; Yabar et al., 2006), specifically when groups were framed as competing with one another (Gleibs et al., 2016). This effect of group membership was further reported to depend on the imitator's motivation to affiliate with social partners, with reliable effects of group membership emerging particularly for participants with a high motivation to affiliate (Genschow & Schindler, 2016). The observation of limited imitation of out-group members resonates with a range of findings outside the imitation literature indicating that the impact of social partners on an agent's performance is relatively small or even absent when construing the other as belonging to an out-group (Aquino et al., 2015; Iani et al., 2011; McClung et al., 2013; Müller et al., 2011). The available evidence for anticipated imitation, by contrast, does not support a role of social group (Weller et al., 2020). Here, four participants were invited to each session and were split into two groups of two participants each. Group membership was consistently reinforced by colored t-shirts to be worn throughout the experiment (red for one group, blue for the other). Participants were further informed that one group would win an additional reward based on the combined performance of the group members to instill a competitive context. Participants then interacted with in-group members and out-group members in an imitation setup with short versus long keypresses of a leader and a follower as sketched above (Pfister et al., 2013). This study showed anticipated and reactive imitation for all participants and groups in two separate experiments, suggesting that anticipated imitation is not particularly sensitive to group membership. These conclusions have to be taken with caution for several reasons, however. For one, neither of the two experiments on anticipated imitation replicated common effects of group membership on the imitator's side and they also did not yield any effects of the group manipulation on closeness ratings to ingroup and outgroup members (Weller et al., 2020). For another, recent re-assessments of the effect of group membership on reactive imitation have questioned earlier findings (De Souter et al., 2021; Genschow et al., 2022, 2023).

A major difference between anticipated imitation and imitation of physically perceivable stimuli, however, is the role of different features that become represented in both situations. The experiments discussed up to now do not address such a question because each experiment focused on one single feature to distinguish different actions, i.e., facial expression (Kunde et al., 2011), duration (Lelonkiewicz et al., 2020; Pfister et al., 2013), or spatial location (Müller, 2016). Research on automatic imitation, by contrast, has shown that motor priming relies on rich representations that cover different features of the model's action if multiple features were included in the experimental design (Boyer et al., 2012).

When participants perceive the model action of lifting the left index finger, this movement obviously comprises spatial features relating to the location and direction of the movement in allocentric coordinates. It also comprises anatomical features of which body part moves, and temporal features relating to movement kinematics. Each of these features can be expected to trigger motor priming in its own right. Empirical studies have confirmed this prediction (Bertenthal et al., 2006; Boyer et al., 2012; Catmur & Heyes, 2011). One way to disentangle different features is to manipulate two or more features orthogonally across conditions. Figure 8.2 shows an exemplary setup for corresponding studies. When two participants sit face to face at a table and each have their index and middle finger rest on two adjacent keys, a study can implement spatially compatible or spatially incompatible conditions by asking the imitator to respond with operating the key that spatially corresponds or does not correspond to the key operated by the action model. Assuming that the model operates their pair of keys with the right hand, asking the imitator to use the left hand will result in a joint variation of spatial compatibility and anatomical compatibility in the sense that a spatially compatible condition will also be anatomically compatible. For example, lifting the left finger from the

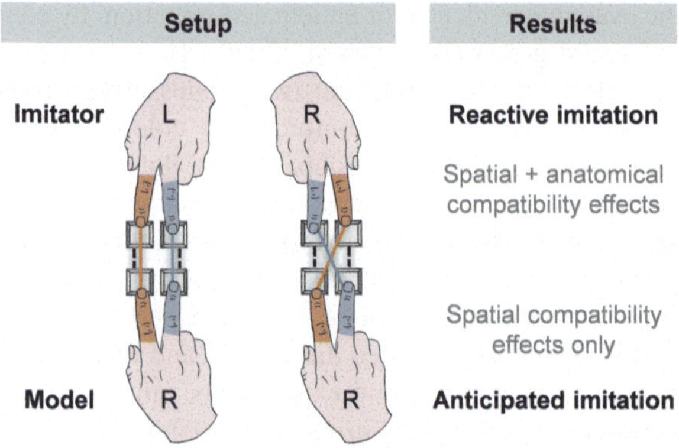

Fig. 8.2 Experimental setup for contrasting spatial coding (dashed lines) and anatomical coding (solid lines) with corresponding results. Models and imitators sit face to face at a table. They both operate a pair of keys with index and middle finger of one hand. If the model uses the right hand for operating the keys, spatial and anatomical compatibility go hand in hand if the imitator uses the left hand. Both are pitted against each other if the imitator uses the right hand, however. Studies in this design shows a joint influence of spatial and anatomical features for reactive imitation (Bertenthal et al., 2006; Boyer et al., 2012; Catmur & Heyes, 2011) whereas anticipated imitation has been observed to draw only on spatial features (Weller et al., 2019)

left key as a model will make the imitator lift the left finger from the key on the same side during imitation, whereas the imitator would lift the right finger from the key on the opposite side in the counter-imitation condition. Asking the imitator to use the right hand, by contrast, renders spatially compatible mappings anatomically incompatible, and vice versa. Evidence suggests that spatial and anatomical features both contribute to motor priming (Bertenthal et al., 2006; Boyer et al., 2012; Catmur & Heyes, 2011). Observing a movement to the right thus primes imitative responses to the same spatial location just as observing a movement of the index finger primes imitative responses with that same body part.

Anticipated imitation, by contrast, shows a distinct picture that seems to rely entirely on spatial coding (Weller et al., 2019). That is, expecting the imitator to respond at the same spatial location will expedite action planning for the model, irrespective of whether this movement is made with the same or a different effector. These experiments further replicated a role of anatomical compatibility for imitators in the same experimental setup, so that imitator responses with the same finger as the model were faster than responses with another finger. It is an open question whether anatomical features may affect anticipated imitation for more extended, salient movements. In any case, the available data indicate that anticipated imitation is less sensitive to anatomical features than reactive imitation. Anticipating imitation therefore cannot be equated directly with actually imitating when it comes to priming motor actions.

Imitative Versus Non-social Action Effects

Differences in the role of spatial and anatomical features in anticipated imitation and in reactive imitation mirror findings from the literature on ideomotor action control in non-social settings. Whereas empirical studies on anticipated imitation find a non-social counterpart in research in the response-effect compatibility paradigm, research on motor priming resembles spatial stimulus-response compatibility paradigms in various characteristics (Boyer et al., 2012). The Simon effect, for instance, describes the observation that making spatial responses to a non-spatial stimulus attribute is facilitated if the stimulus appears at a compatible spatial location (Simon & Rudell, 1967; Hommel, 2011). In a simple version, making a left or right response to the color of a stimulus that appears either on the left or right is easier if stimulus and response location match as compared to when they differ. Interestingly, the spatial stimulus location also primes anatomical features so that observing a stimulus on the right not only primes responses to that side, but also responses with the right hand (Heister et al. 1990; Klapp et al. 1979; Riggio et al. 1986; Simon et al., 1970). These conclusions emerged from experiments with crossed hands so that participants were asked to operate a left response key with their right hand and a right response key with their left hand. Spatial compatibility effects usually exceed anatomical compatibility effects by a substantial margin in these designs, but it is important note that both types of features are effective. Turning to response-effect compatibility designs, anticipating a spatial action effect was observed to prime responses at that spatial location while anatomical features in terms of left or right hand did not bear any relevance here (Pfister & Kunde, 2013; see also Hoffmann et al., 2009).

Viewing the evidence from studies on imitation and studies on compatibility effects in non-social settings side by side suggests that anticipations are surprisingly sparse in that they only draw on selected features of upcoming stimuli. Alternatively, the absent impact of anatomical features for anticipated stimuli might be explained by the overall lower effect sizes for anticipated as compare to perceived stimuli (Müller, 2016; Müller & Jung, 2018; Pfister et al., 2013). With a smaller overall effect size, detecting the weaker effects of anatomical as compared to spatial features would be more difficult and require more statistical power. Until such findings are available, however, we suggest that anticipations might actually be selective in what features become represented and what features are ignored. Crucially, these points suggest that different sensitivity of anticipated and reactive imitation derive from relatively broad differences between anticipation and perception.

The striking parallels between imitation and non-social compatibility effects raise the question whether effects related to imitation can be reduced to stimulus-response and response-effect compatibility effects in the non-social domain or if these should be regarded as separate phenomena. For reactive imitation, the empirical evidence shows a clear picture: Compatibility effects observed during imitation are stronger than stimulus-response compatibility effects obtained in paradigms where participants respond to non-social stimuli (Brass et al., 2000). Although these differences could also be a result of different stimulus properties in the social and non-social domain (Aicken et al., 2007; Jansson et al., 2007), other experimental methods that compared automatic imitation to other classes of stimulus-response compatibility, also found that the phenomena can be dissociated (Boyer et al., 2012). In the case of effect anticipation, the picture is less clear. Some studies that compared the influence of imitative and non-social action consequences found effects that could only be observed with imitative stimuli (Kunde et al., 2011; Flach et al., 2010). However, in these cases, the confounding effects of stimulus saliency or stimulus complexity were not controlled properly and more nuanced manipulations have not yet been used to assess the question. In the case of other (non-imitative) social effect types, recent results indicate that their influence on actions is surprisingly similar to the influence of non-social action consequences (Neszmélyi et al., 2022), but it has yet to be tested whether this also applies to imitative effects.

Imitative Versus Complementary Social Effects

One aspect that separates non-social and imitative effects is the possible role of shared representations for action observation and action execution (see also Chaps. 5 and 6; this volume). Using the same system for planning one's own action and for processing the observed actions might contribute particularly in the case of imitation (see the double route model of Sauser & Billard, 2006). However, shared representations could also contribute to the processing of the co-actor's actions if these are not identical with one's own actions, which raises questions about the relation between imitative interactions and other action–reaction-type interactions between two human agents. Again, this topic is better explored in the context of reacting to actually presented stimuli: It has been shown that seeing the execution of an action might not only activate identical actions in the observer but, depending on the context, it can also facilitate complementary dissimilar actions (Newman-Norlund et al., 2007). Although different neural populations are responsible for facilitating identical and complementary actions, the two systems are assumed to work in unison, and some findings suggest that when signaled by context or kinematic cues, people can seamlessly switch from imitating a movement to performing a dissimilar but complementary action (Sartori et al., 2012, 2013). A system that could enable facilitation of movements with varying levels of similarity between observed and performed action would be plausible: Although previously we mentioned several examples where imitation is relevant in everyday situations, a substantial majority of human interactions is based on complementary rather than on identical movements. Even such complementary actions usually share some of their features, thus, it is difficult to draw a clear line between imitative and non-imitative interactions (Flach et al., 2010). Rather than assuming a sharp distinction between identical and dissimilar actions, it might be more useful to conceptualize interactions on a continuum of shared features.

Studies on reactive as well as anticipated imitation can therefore be seen as providing a flexible empirical tool to study all kinds of social action representations, including those that are related to social interactions other than direct imitation. Anticipated imitation in particular highlights the goal-directed nature of many social interactions, in which an action aims at eliciting a response from an interaction partner. In more general terms, observing that human actions can become represented and controlled in terms of the social effects they produce offers an exciting approach to human action (Wolpert et al., 2003). We have previously dubbed such findings to reflect "sociomotor" action control, i.e., direct associations between one's own motor actions and the responses they evoke at social interaction partners (Kunde et al., 2018). As in the case of actual imitation, the ideomotor mechanism that we propose to underlie (anticipated) imitation could also handle interactions with smaller overlap between the initial action and the social response. But such ideas are yet to be explored.

The present ideomotor view on anticipating and producing social action effects is surprisingly non-social, however, in that it does not propose any mechanisms on top of what is needed to explain interactions with the non-social world (Neszmélyi et al., 2022). Nor are there any findings from anticipated imitation that would require any specifically social additions to the theoretical framework. This conclusion stands in contrast to how strongly human agents are attuned to processing social stimuli perceptually. The contrast to social perception becomes evident when considering the impact of biological motion (Johansson, 1973; Lacquaniti et al., 1983; Shiffrar & Freyd, 1990) such that even perceptually impoverished point-light walkers are easily identified as stemming from a human agent (Hudson et al., 2016). Similarly, tuning towards social stimuli has been proposed for faces (Oruc et al., 2019), eye-direction (Baron-Cohen, 1994), and language (Chomsky, 1980). Whether this tuning relates to dedicated, specialized mechanisms or whether it derives from extended learning experiences is debatable (Jarstorff et al., 2006; Vogelzang et al., 2017). In any case, social actions can leverage such capacities in principle, but it seems as if the impact of anticipated imitation is rooted deeply in basic mechanisms of human action control.

Open Questions

The available evidence for the impact of anticipated imitation raises several intriguing questions for future research. A first question relates to specific input–output modalities. Research on anticipated imitation has typically relied on manual tasks with only few notable exceptions (e.g., Kunde et al., 2011; Müller, 2020; Müller & Jung, 2018). Special input–output modalities that have been highlighted in research on social perception have not yet been targeted (e.g., Lacquaniti et al., 1983; Shiffrar & Freyd, 1990). These modalities come with several features that go beyond previous manipulations such as spatial or anatomical compatibility, especially in the case of language (e.g., pitch, phoneme duration, or semantics in the case of language; see also Chap. 4; this volume). Such features lend themselves to experimental manipulations in studies of anticipated imitation and may eventually reveal genuinely social components for such types of actions or social responses (note that many moderators of automatic imitation also still remain to be tested for anticipated imitation; for a summary of known moderators, see Cracco et al., 2018).

A second question concerns subjective agency for imitation, i.e., feelings of control over action outcomes. The sense of agency for interactions with the non-social world has attracted considerable interest across psychology and neuroscience in the last decades (Haggard & Tsakiris, 2009). It can be measured explicitly by asking for ratings of how strongly participants felt as if they had caused a certain event. Such ratings are often made on a visual analogue scale to elicit a graded response. In a typical imitation setting, the model clearly stimulates the imitator's response so that the model should strongly feel as causally responsible for the ensuing imitator response. Previous work has further tried to relate the perceptual illusion of temporal binding to agency. Temporal binding reflects a subjective compression of action–effect episodes, or cause–effect episodes in general, so that it can at least be expected to occur in imitation, even though its relation to agency is debatable (Schwarz et al., 2019). Crucially, explicitly reported agency and implicit temporal binding might be even stronger for imitation as compared to contingent but non-imitative responses. Because imitation draws on directly mirroring what the model is doing, the social consequence maps directly onto the model action so that the resulting overlap in perceptual features can be expected to boost binding. Despite first studies on agency in social context (Pfeiffer et al., 2012, 2014b; Grynszpan et al., 2019; for a review see Silver et al. 2021), there are currently no studies to assess subjective agency in the context of imitation. The question of subjective agency is also highly relevant on the imitator's end. Research on motor priming has shown that imitative responses are much more fluent than responding in a non-imitative or even counter-imitative way (Cracco et al., 2018). Fluency has been suggested to be a particularly strong cue to agency (Sidarus et al., 2013; Sidarus & Haggard, 2016), though here this cue accompanies those actions that arguably involve less control (and thus causation) for the imitator. Situations with a dynamic, real-time interaction may further yield particularly strong confusions as to who caused what during imitation. An everyday example for such confusion arises on pavements across the globe when two pedestrians approach each other. This situation will often trigger one person to step aside which, in turn, triggers the other person to perform an evasive action in the same direction, resulting in both pedestrians facing each other again. Going through two or three iterations of such imitative maneuvers blurs the difference of who is model and who is imitator, while each person aims not to be imitated in order to break the loop.

A third question pertains to direct and predictable imitation by virtual avatars (Böffel & Müsseler, 2018; Müsseler et al., 2022). Here, imitation can be seen as a major tool to embody such a virtual entity if the avatar's behavior maps sufficiently closely onto the behavior of the user (e.g., Eck et al., 2022; Kokkinara & Slater, 2014; Sanchez-Vives et al., 2010). Such virtual reality settings can further be construed in two ways: Imitative behavior of the avatar may either be seen as a direct extension of one's own behavior in the physical world, or the avatar may be expected to have some degree of autonomy while choosing to mirror what the human is doing. It is a relevant question for future research how such different ways to construe the same situation affect cognition and behavior in virtual environments.

A fourth question relates to situations in which a model is imitated by multiple imitators. This situation occurs frequently when instructing other people, say when a yoga teacher instructs his or her course. Arguably, having multiple imitators renders it difficult to build up anticipations of how the entire group is going to perform, so that it is an open question whether anticipated imitation actually occurs in these settings. At the same time, having multiple imitators might make imitation particularly salient. This effect has been demonstrated for reactive imitation (Cracco & Brass, 2018; Cracco et al., 2015). Exploring the role of multiple imitators for anticipated imitation will thus provide relevant insights into designing instructional interactions, including strategies of instructors on how to take advantage of positive effects of anticipated imitation while avoiding issues due to potential mismatches or prediction errors. Such work could also assess the transition of gradually merging imitative instruction-following to synchronized performance.

Conclusion

Just as it takes two to tango, imitation involves two agents that influence one another. While the impact of the imitation model on the imitator has been subject to extensive research, the role of the imitator's behavior for the action model has received comparatively little attention. Research on automatic imitation in direct, dyadic interactions indicates that model's incorporate upcoming imitative responses in their action representation. In turn, anticipated imitation shapes how models select and perform their action, showcasing a remarkably dynamic interplay of imitative tendencies during social interactions.

Author Note
Thank you to Emiel Cracco and Oliver Genschow for their guidance while preparing this chapter, and for all their helpful comments on earlier drafts. We are indebted to Lara Böhm for crafting Fig. 8.1. This work was funded by the German Research Foundation (Deutsche Forschungsgemeinschaft), projects PF 853/2-2 (313711646) and PF 853/10-1 (490925504).

References

Agnetta, B., & Rochat, P. (2004). Imitative games by 9-, 14-, and 18-month-old infants. *Infancy, 6*, 1–36. https://doi.org/10.1207/s15327078in0601_1

Aicken, M. D., Wilson, A. D., Williams, J. H., & Mon-Williams, M. (2007). Methodological issues in measures of imitative reaction times. *Brain and Cognition, 63*, 304–308. https://doi.org/10.1016/j.bandc.2006.09.005

Aquino, A., Paolini, D., Pagliaro, S., Migliorati, D., Wolff, A., Alparone, F. R., & Costantini, M. (2015). Group membership and social status modulate joint actions. *Experimental Brain Research, 233*, 2461–2466. https://doi.org/10.1007/s00221-015-4316-7

Bach, P., & Schenke, K. C. (2017). Predictive social perception: Towards a unifying framework from action observation to person knowledge. *Social and Personality Psychology Compass, 11*, e12312. https://doi.org/10.1111/spc3.12312

Bach, P., Bayliss, A. P., & Tipper, S. P. (2011). The predictive mirror: Interactions of mirror and affordance processes during action observation. *Psychonomic Bulletin & Review, 18*, 171–176. https://doi.org/10.3758/s13423-010-0029-x

Baron-Cohen, S. (1994). How to build a baby that can read minds: Cognitive mechanisms in mindreading. *Current Psychology of Cognition, 13*, 513–552.

Bernieri, F. J. (1988). Coordinated movement and rapport in teacher-student interactions. *Journal of Nonverbal Behavior, 12*, 120–138. https://doi.org/10.1007/BF00986930

Bertenthal, B. I., Longo, M. R., & Kosobud, A. (2006). Imitative response tendencies following observation of intransitive actions. *Journal of Experimental Psychology: Human Perception and Performance, 32*, 210–225. https://doi.org/10.1037/0096-1523.32.2.210

Böffel, C., & Müsseler, J. (2018). Perceived ownership of avatars influences visual perspective taking. *Frontiers in Psychology, 9*, 743. https://doi.org/10.3389/fpsyg.2018.00743

Bourgeois, P., & Hess, U. (2008). The impact of social context on mimicry. *Biological Psychology, 77*, 343–352. https://doi.org/10.1016/j.biopsycho.2007.11.008

Boyer, T. W., Longo, M. R., & Bertenthal, B. I. (2012). Is automatic imitation a specialized form of stimulus-response compatibility? Dissociating imitative and spatial compatibilities. *Acta Psychologica, 139*, 440–448. https://doi.org/10.1016/j.actpsy.2012.01.003

Brass, M., & Heyes, C. (2005). Imitation: Is cognitive neuroscience solving the correspondence problem? *Trends in Cognitive Sciences, 9*, 489–495. https://doi.org/10.1016/j.tics.2005.08.007

Brass, M., Bekkering, H., Wohlschläger, A., & Prinz, W. (2000). Compatibility between observed and executed finger movements: Comparing symbolic, spatial, and imitative cues. *Brain and Cognition, 44*, 124–143. https://doi.org/10.1006/brcg.2000.1225

Brass, M., Bekkering, H., & Prinz, W. (2001). Movement observation affects movement execution in a simple response task. *Acta Psychologica, 106*, 3–22. https://doi.org/10.1016/S0001-6918(00)00024-X

Catmur, C., & Heyes, C. (2011). Time course analyses confirm independence of imitative and spatial compatibility. *Journal of Experimental Psychology: Human Perception and Performance, 37*, 409–421. https://doi.org/10.1037/a0019325

Chartrand, T. L., & Bargh, J. A. (1999). The chameleon effect: The perception-behavior link and social interaction. *Journal of Personality and Social Psychology, 76*, 893–910. https://doi.org/10.1037/0022-3514.76.6.893

Chomsky, N. (1980). Remarks on nominalization. In R. Jacobs & P. Rosenbaum (Eds.), *Reading in English transformational grammar*. Georgetown University Press.

Colton, J., Bach, P., Whalley, B., & Mitchell, C. (2018). Intention insertion: Activating an action's perceptual consequences is sufficient to induce non-willed motor behavior. *Journal of Experimental Psychology: General, 147*, 1256–1263. https://doi.org/10.1037/xge0000435

Cracco, E., & Brass, M. (2018). Automatic imitation of multiple agents: Simultaneous or random representation? *Journal of Experimental Psychology: Human Perception and Performance, 44*, 729–740. https://doi.org/10.1037/xhp0000489

Cracco, E., de Coster, L., Andres, M., & Brass, M. (2015). Motor simulation beyond the dyad: Automatic imitation of multiple actors. *Journal of Experimental Psychology: Human Perception and Performance, 41*, 1488–1501. https://doi.org/10.1037/a0039737

Cracco, E., Bardi, L., Desmet, C., Genschow, O., Rigoni, D., de Coster, L., Radkova, I., Deschrijver, E., & Brass, M. (2018). Automatic imitation: A meta-analysis. *Psychological Bulletin, 144*, 453–500. https://doi.org/10.1037/bul0000143

de Coster, L., Verschuere, B., Goubert, L., Tsakiris, M., & Brass, M. (2013). I suffer more from your pain when you act like me: Being imitated enhances affective responses to seeing some-

one else in pain. *Cognitive, Affective, & Behavioral Neuroscience, 13*, 519–532. https://doi.org/10.3758/s13415-013-0168-4
De Maeght, S., & Prinz, W. (2004). Action induction through action observation. *Psychological Research, 68*, 97–114. https://doi.org/10.1007/s00426-003-0148-3
De Souter, L., Braem, S., Genschow, O., Brass, M., & Cracco, E. (2021). Social group membership does not modulate automatic imitation in a contrastive multi-agent paradigm. *Quarterly Journal of Experimental Psychology, 74*, 746–759. https://doi.org/10.1177/1747021820986528
Dignath, D., Lotze-Hermes, P., Farmer, H., & Pfister, R. (2018). Contingency and contiguity of imitative behaviour affect social affiliation. *Psychological Research, 82*, 819–831. https://doi.org/10.1007/s00426-017-0854-x
Dimberg, U. (1982). Facial reactions to facial expressions. *Psychophysiology, 19*, 643–647. https://doi.org/10.1111/j.1469-8986.1982.tb02516.x
Donders, F. C. (1869/1969). On the speed of mental processes (W. G. Koster, Trans.). Acta Psychologica, 30, 412–431. https://doi.org/10.1016/0001-6918(69)90065-1
Eck, J., Dignath, D., Kalckert, A., & Pfister, R. (2022). Instant disembodiment of virtual body parts. *Attention, Perception, & Psychophysics*, 2725–2740. https://doi.org/10.3758/s13414-022-02544-w
Fadiga, L., Fogassi, L., Pavesi, G., & Rizzolatti. (1995). Motor facilitation during action observation: A magnetic stimulation study. *Journal of Neurophysiology, 73*, 2608–2611. https://doi.org/10.1152/jn.1995.73.6.2608
Fechner, G. T. (1877). *In Sachen der Psychophysik*. Breitkopf und Hartel.
Flach, R., Press, C., Badets, A., & Heyes, C. (2010). Shaking hands: Priming by social action effects. *British Journal of Psychology, 101*, 739–749. https://doi.org/10.1348/000712609X484595
Genschow, O., & Brass, M. (2015). The predictive chameleon: Evidence for anticipated social action. *Journal of Experimental Psychology: Human Perception and Performance, 41*, 265–268. https://doi.org/10.1037/xhp0000035
Genschow, O., & Groß-Bölting, J. (2021). The role of attention in anticipated action effects. *Journal of Experimental Psychology: Human Perception and Performance, 47*, 323–330. https://doi.org/10.1037/xhp0000883
Genschow, O., & Schindler, S. (2016). The influence of group membership on cross-contextual imitation. *Psychonomic Bulletin & Review, 23*, 1257–1265. https://doi.org/10.3758/s13423-015-0983-4
Genschow, O., Florack, A., & Wänke, M. (2013). The power of movement: Evidence for context-independent movement imitation. *Journal of Experimental Psychology: General, 142*, 763–773. https://doi.org/10.1037/a0029795
Genschow, O., Klomfar, S., d'Haene, I., & Brass, M. (2018). Mimicking and anticipating others' actions is linked to social information processing. *PLoS One, 13*, e0193743. https://doi.org/10.1371/journal.pone.0193743
Genschow, O., Cracco, E., Verbeke, P., Westfal, M., & Crusius, J. (2021). A direct test of the similarity assumption – Focusing on differences as compared with similarities decreases automatic imitation. *Cognition, 215*, 104824. https://doi.org/10.1016/j.cognition.2021.104824
Genschow, O., Westfal, M., Cracco, E., & Crusius, J. (2022). Group membership does not modulate automatic imitation. *Psychological Research, 86*, 780–791. https://doi.org/10.1007/s00426-021-01526-1
Genschow, O., Paules, E., Krugmann, K., & Winter, A. (2023). Group membership does not modulate goal- versus movement-based imitation. *The Quarterly Journal of Experimental Psychology, 76*, 827–837. https://doi.org/10.1177/17470218221132842
Gillmeister, H., Catmur, C., Liepelt, R., Brass, M., & Heyes, C. (2008). Experience-based priming of body parts: A study of action imitation. *Brain Research, 1217*, 157–170. https://doi.org/10.1016/j.brainres.2007.12.076
Gleibs, I. H., Wilson, N., Reddy, G., & Catmur, C. (2016). Group dynamics in automatic imitation. *PloS one, 11*, e0162880. https://doi.org/10.1371/journal.pone.0162880

Grynszpan, O., Sahaï, A., Hamidi, N., Pacherie, E., Berberian, B., Roche, L., & Saint-Bauzel, L. (2019). The sense of agency in human-human vs human-robot joint action. *Consciousness and Cognition, 75*, 102820. https://doi.org/10.1016/j.concog.2019.102820

Haggard, P., & Tsakiris, M. (2009). The experience of agency. *Current Directions in Psychological Science, 18*, 242–246. https://doi.org/10.1111/j.1467-8721.2009.01644.x

Harleß, E. (1861). Der Apparat des Willens. *Zeitschrift für Philosophie und philosophische Kritik, 38*, 50–73.

Heister, G., Schroeder-Heister, P., & Ehrenstein, W. H. (1990). Spatial coding and spatio-anatomical mapping: Evidence for a hierarchical model of spatial stimulus-response compatibility. *Advances in Psychology, 65*, 117–143. https://doi.org/10.1016/S0166-4115(08)61220-0

Hemed, E., Mark-Tavger, I., Hertz, U., Bakbani-Elkayam, S., & Eitam, B. (2022). Automatically controlled: Task irrelevance fully cancels otherwise automatic imitation. *Journal of Experimental Psychology: General, 151*, 996–1017. https://doi.org/10.1037/xge0001117

Herbart, J. F. (1824). *Psychologie als Wissenschaft neu gegründet auf Erfahrung, Metaphysik und Mathematik*. August Wilhelm Unzer.

Heyes, C. (2011). Automatic imitation. *Psychological Bulletin, 137*, 463–483. https://doi.org/10.1037/a0022288

Heyes, C. (2013). What can imitation do for cooperation? In K. Sterelny, R. Joyce, B. Calcott, & B. Fraser (Eds.), *Cooperation and its evolution* (pp. 313–331). MIT Press.

Hoffmann, J., Lenhard, A., Sebald, A., & Pfister, R. (2009). Movements or targets: What makes an action in action-effect learning? *Quarterly Journal of Experimental Psychology, 62*, 2433–2449. https://doi.org/10.1080/17470210902922079

Hommel, B. (2011). The Simon effect as tool and heuristic. *Acta Psychologica, 136*, 189–202. https://doi.org/10.1016/j.actpsy.2010.04.011

Horváth, J., Bíró, B., & Neszmélyi, B. (2018). Action-effect related motor adaptation in interactions with everyday devices. *Scientific Reports, 8*, 6592. https://doi.org/10.1038/s41598-018-25161-w

Hudson, M., Nicholson, T., Simpson, W. A., Ellis, R., & Bach, P. (2016). One step ahead: The perceived kinematics of others' actions are biased toward expected goals. *Journal of Experimental Psychology: General, 145*, 1–7. https://doi.org/10.1037/xge0000126

Iani, C., Anelli, F., Nicoletti, R., Arcuri, L., & Rubichi, S. (2011). The role of group membership on the modulation of joint action. *Experimental Brain Research, 211*, 439–445. https://doi.org/10.1007/s00221-011-2651-x

James, W. (1890). *The principles of Psychology*. Henry Holt and Company.

Jansson, E., Wilson, A. D., Williams, J. H., & Mon-Williams, M. (2007). Methodological problems undermine tests of the ideo-motor conjecture. *Experimental Brain Research, 182*, 549–558. https://doi.org/10.1007/s00221-007-1013-1

Jarstorff, J., Kourtzi, Z., & Giese, M. A. (2006). Learning to discriminate complex movements: Biological versus artificial trajectories. *Journal of Vision, 6*, 791–804. http://dx.doi.org/10.1167/6.8.3

Johansson, G. (1973). Visual perception of biological motion and a model for its analysis. *Perception & Psychophysics, 14*, 201–211. https://doi.org/10.3758/BF03212378

Kingdom, F. A. A., & Prins, N. (2016). *Psychophysics: A practical introduction* (2nd ed.). Elsevier. https://doi.org/10.1016/C2012-0-01278-1

Klapp, S., Abbott, J., Coffman, K., Greim, D., Snider, R., & Young, F. (1979). Simple and choice reaction time methods in the study of motor programming. *Journal of Motor Behavior, 11*, 91–101. https://doi.org/10.1080/00222895.1979.10735177

Knuf, L., Aschersleben, G., & Prinz, W. (2001). An analysis of ideomotor action. *Journal of Experimental Psychology: General, 130*, 779–798. https://doi.org/10.1037/0096-3445.130.4.779

Kokkinara, E., & Slater, M. (2014). Measuring the effects through time of the influence of visuomotor and visuotactile synchronous stimulation on a virtual body ownership illusion. *Perception, 43*, 43–58. https://doi.org/10.1068/p7545

Kunde, W. (2001). Response-effect compatibility in manual choice reaction tasks. *Journal of Experimental Psychology: Human Perception and Performance, 27*, 387–394. https://doi.org/10.1037/0096-1523.27.2.387

Kunde, W. (2003). Temporal response-effect compatibility. *Psychological Research, 67*, 135–159. https://doi.org/10.1007/s00426-002-0114-5

Kunde, W. (2006). Antezedente Effektrepräsentationen in der Verhaltenssteuerung. *Psychologische Rundschau, 57*, 34–42. https://doi.org/10.1026/0033-3042.57.1.34

Kunde, W., Koch, I., & Hoffmann, J. (2004). Anticipated action effects affect the selection, initiation, and execution of actions. *The Quarterly Journal of Experimental Psychology, 57*, 87–106. https://doi.org/10.1080/02724980343000143

Kunde, W., Lozo, L., & Neumann, R. (2011). Effect-based control of facial expressions: Evidence from action-effect compatibility. *Psychonomic Bulletin & Review, 18*, 820–826. https://doi.org/10.3758/s13423-011-0093-x

Kunde, W., Weller, L., & Pfister, R. (2018). Sociomotor action control. *Psychonomic Bulletin & Review, 25*, 917–931. https://doi.org/10.3758/s13423-017-1316-6

Lacquaniti, F., Terzuolo, C., & Viviani, P. (1983). The law relating the kinematic and figural aspects of drawing movements. *Acta Psychologica, 54*, 115–130. https://doi.org/10.1016/0001-6918(83)90027-6

Lelonkiewicz, J. R., & Gambi, C. (2017). Spontaneous adaptation explains why people act faster when being imitated. *Psychonomic Bulletin & Review, 24*, 842–848. https://doi.org/10.3758/s13423-016-1141-3

Lelonkiewicz, J. R., Gambi, C., Weller, L., & Pfister, R. (2020). Action-effect anticipation and temporal adaptation in social interactions. *Journal of Experimental Psychology: Human Perception and Performance, 46*, 335–349. https://doi.org/10.1037/xhp0000717

Liepelt, R., & Brass, M. (2010). Automatic imitation of physically impossible movements. *Social Cognition, 28*, 59–73. https://doi.org/10.1521/soco.2010.28.1.59

Longo, M. R., & Bertenthal, B. I. (2009). Attention modulates the specificity of automatic imitation to human actors. *Experimental Brain Research, 192*, 739–744. https://doi.org/10.1007/s00221-008-1649-5

McClung, J. S., Jentzsch, I., & Reicher, S. D. (2013). Group membership affects spontaneous mental representation: Failure to represent the out-group in a joint action task. *PloS one, 8*, e79178. https://doi.org/10.1371/journal.pone.0079178

McIntosh, D. N. (2006). Spontaneous facial mimicry, liking and emotional contagion. *Polish Psychological Bulletin, 37*, 31–42.

Müller, R. (2016). Does the anticipation of compatible partner reactions facilitate action planning in joint tasks? *Psychological Research, 80*, 464–486. https://doi.org/10.1007/s00426-015-0670-0

Müller, R. (2020). How do partner reactions affect task set selection: Specific imitation or abstract tasks? *Quarterly Journal of Experimental Psychology, 73*, 2008–2025. https://doi.org/10.1177/1747021820937918

Müller, R., & Jung, M. L. (2018). Partner reactions and task set selection: Compatibility is more beneficial in the stronger task. *Acta Psychologica, 185*, 188–202. https://doi.org/10.1016/j.actpsy.2018.02.012

Müller, B. C. N., Kühn, S., van Baaren, R. B., Dotsch, R., Brass, M., & Dijksterhuis, A. (2011). Perspective taking eliminates differences in co-representation of out-group members' actions. *Experimental Brain Research, 211*, 423–428. https://doi.org/10.1007/s00221-011-2654-7

Müsseler, J., von Salm-Hoogstraeten, S., & Böffel, C. (2022). Perspective taking and avatar-self merging. *Frontiers in Psychology, 13*, 714464. https://doi.org/10.3389/fpsyg.2022.714464

Nagy, E. (2006). From imitation to conversation: The first dialogues with human neonates. *Infant and Child Development, 15*, 223–232. https://doi.org/10.1002/icd.460

Nagy, E., & Molnar, P. (2004). Homo imitans or homo provocans? Human imprinting model of neonatal imitation. *Infant Behavior and Development, 27*, 54–63. https://doi.org/10.1016/j.infbeh.2003.06.004

Neszmélyi, B., & Horváth, J. (2017). Consequences matter: Self-induced tones are used as feedback to optimize tone-eliciting actions. *Psychophysiology, 54*, 904–915. https://doi.org/10.1111/psyp.12845

Neszmélyi, B., Weller, L., Kunde, W., & Pfister, R. (2022). Social action effects: Representing predicted partner responses in social interactions. *Frontiers in Human Neuroscience, 16*, 837495. https://doi.org/10.3389/fnhum.2022.837495

Newman-Norlund, R. D., Noordzij, M. L., Meulenbroek, R. G. J., & Bekkering, H. (2007). Exploring the brain basis of joint action: Co-ordination of actions, goals and intentions. *Social Neuroscience, 2*, 48–65. https://doi.org/10.1080/17470910701224623

Oruc, I., Balas, B., & Landy, M. S. (2019). Face perception: A brief journey through recent discoveries and current directions. *Vision Research, 157*, 1–9. https://doi.org/10.1016/j.visres.2019.06.005

Pfeiffer, U. J., Schilbach, L., Jording, M., Timmermans, B., Bente, G., & Vogeley, K. (2012). Eyes on the mind: Investigating the influence of gaze dynamics on the perception of others in real-time social interaction. *Frontiers in Psychology, 3*. https://doi.org/10.3389/fpsyg.2012.00537

Pfister, R. (2019). Effect-based action control with body-related effects: Implications for empirical approaches to ideomotor action control. *Psychological Review, 126*, 153–161. https://doi.org/10.1037/rev0000140

Pfister, R., & Janczyk, M. (2012). Harleß' apparatus of will: 150 years later. *Psychological Research, 76*, 561–565. https://doi.org/10.1007/s00426-011-0362-3

Pfister, R., & Kunde, W. (2013). Dissecting the response in response-effect compatibility. *Experimental Brain Research, 224*, 647–655. https://doi.org/10.1007/s00221-012-3343-x

Pfister, R., Dignath, D., Hommel, B., & Kunde, W. (2013). It takes two to imitate: Anticipation and imitation in social interaction. *Psychological Science, 24*, 2117–2121. https://doi.org/10.1177/0956797613489139

Pfister, R., Janczyk, M., Wirth, R., Dignath, D., & Kunde, W. (2014a). Thinking with portals: Revisiting kinematic cues to intention. *Cognition, 133*, 464–473. https://doi.org/10.1016/j.cognition.2014.07.012

Pfister, R., Obhi, S., Rieger, M., & Wenke, D. (2014b). Action and perception in social contexts: Intentional binding for social action effects. *Frontiers in Human Neuroscience, 8*, 667. https://doi.org/10.3389/fnhum.2014.00667

Pfister, R., Weller, L., Dignath, D., & Kunde, W. (2017). What or when? The impact of anticipated social action effects is driven by action-effect compatibility, not delay. *Attention, Perception & Psychophysics, 79*, 2132–2142. https://doi.org/10.3758/s13414-017-1371-0

Pfister, R., Weller, L., & Kunde, W. (2020). When actions go awry: Monitoring partner errors and machine malfunctions. *Journal of Experimental Psychology: General, 149*, 1778–1787. https://doi.org/10.1037/xge0000748

Prinz, W., De Maeght, S., & Knuf, L. (2005). Intention in action. In G. W. Humphreys & M. J. Riddoch (Eds.), *Attention in action: Advances from cognitive neuroscience* (pp. 93–108). Psychology Press.

Riggio, L., de Gonzaga Gawryszewski, L., & Umilta, C. (1986). What is crossed in crossed-hand effects? *Acta Psychologica, 62*, 89–100. https://doi.org/10.1016/0001-6918(86)90006-5

Sanchez-Vives, M. V., Spanlang, B., Frisoli, A., Bergamasco, M., & Slater, M. (2010). Virtual hand illusion induced by visuomotor correlations. *PLoS One, 5*, e10381. https://doi.org/10.1371/journal.pone.0010381

Sartori, L., Cavallo, A., Bucchioni, G., & Castiello, U. (2012). From simulation to reciprocity: The case of complementary actions. *Social Neuroscience, 7*, 146–158. https://doi.org/10.1080/17470919.2011.586579

Sartori, L., Bucchioni, G., & Castiello, U. (2013). When emulation becomes reciprocity. *Social Cognitive and Affective Neuroscience, 8*, 662–669. https://doi.org/10.1093/scan/nss044

Sauser, E. L., & Billard, A. G. (2006). Parallel and distributed neural models of the ideomotor principle: An investigation of imitative cortical pathways. *Neural Networks, 19*, 285–298. https://doi.org/10.1016/j.neunet.2006.02.003

Schütz-Bosbach, S., & Prinz, W. (2007). Perceptual resonance: action-induced modulation of perception. *Trends in Cognitive Sciences, 11*, 349–355. https://doi.org/10.1016/j.tics.2007.06.005

Schwarz, K. A., & Pfister, R. (2016). Scientific psychology in the 18th century: A historical rediscovery. *Perspectives on Psychological Science: A Journal of the Association for Psychological Science, 11*, 399–407. https://doi.org/10.1177/1745691616635601

Schwarz, K. A., Weller, L., Klaffehn, A. L., & Pfister, R. (2019). The effects of action choice on temporal binding, agency ratings, and their correlation. *Consciousness and Cognition, 75*, 102807. https://doi.org/10.1016/j.concog.2019.102807

Seibt, B., Mühlberger, A., Likowski, K. U., & Weyers, P. (2015). Facial mimicry in its social setting. *Frontiers in Psychology, 6*, 1122. https://doi.org/10.3389/fpsyg.2015.01122

Shiffrar, M., & Freyd, J. J. (1990). Apparent motion of the human body. *Psychological Science, 1*, 257–264. https://doi.org/10.1111/j.1467-9280.1990.tb00210.x

Shin, Y. K., & Proctor, R. W. (2012). Testing boundary conditions of the ideomotor hypothesis using a delayed response task. *Acta Psychologica, 141*, 360–372. https://doi.org/10.1016/j.actpsy.2012.09.008

Sidarus, N., & Haggard, P. (2016). Difficult action decisions reduce the sense of agency: A study using the Eriksen flanker task. *Acta Psychologica, 166*, 1–11. https://doi.org/10.1016/j.actpsy.2016.03.003

Sidarus, N., Chambon, V., & Haggard, P. (2013). Priming of actions increases sense of control over unexpected outcomes. *Consciousness and Cognition, 22*, 1403–1411. https://doi.org/10.1016/j.concog.2013.09.008

Silver, C. A., Tatler, B. W., Chakravarthi, R., & Timmermans, B. (2021). Social agency as a continuum. *Psychonomic Bulletin & Review, 28*, 434–453. https://doi.org/10.3758/s13423-020-01845-1

Simon, J. R., & Rudell, A. P. (1967). Auditory S-R compatibility: The effect of an irrelevant cue on information processing. *The Journal of Applied Psychology, 51*, 300–304. https://doi.org/10.1037/h0020586

Simon, J. R., Hinrichs, J. V., & Craft, J. L. (1970). Auditory S-R compatibility: Reaction time as a function of ear-hand correspondence and ear-response-location correspondence. *Journal of Experimental Psychology, 86*, 97–102. https://doi.org/10.1037/h0029783

Stock, A., & Stock, C. (2004). A short history of ideomotor action. *Psychological Research, 68*, 176–188. https://doi.org/10.1007/s00426-003-0154-

Thébault, G., Pfister, R., Michalland, A.-H., & Brouillet, D. (2020). Flexible weighting of body-related effects in action production. *Quarterly Journal of Experimental Psychology, 73*, 1360–1367. https://doi.org/10.1177/1747021820911793 6

Ueberwasser, F. (1787). *Anweisungen zum regelmäßigen Studium der Empirischen Psychologie für die Candidaten der Philosophie zu Münster*. Friedrich Christian Theißing.

van Baaren, R. B., Holland, R. W., Kawakami, K., & van Knippenberg, A. (2004). Mimicry and prosocial behavior. *Psychological Science, 15*, 71–74. https://doi.org/10.1111/j.0963-7214.2004.01501012.x

Vogelzang, M., Mills, A. C., Reitter, D., van Rij, J., Hendriks, P., & van Rijn, H. (2017). Toward cognitively constrained models of language processing: A review. *Frontiers in Communication, 2*, 11. https://doi.org/10.3389/fcomm.2017.00011

Vogt, S., Taylor, P., & Hopkins, B. (2003). Visuomotor priming by pictures of hand postures: Perspective matters. *Neuropsychologia, 41*, 941–951. https://doi.org/10.1016/S0028-3932(02)00319-6

Washburn, M. F. (1908). *The animal mind: A textbook of comparative psychology*. Macmillan.

Weber, E. H. (1851). *Die Lehre vom Tastsinne und Gemeingefühle auf Versuche gegründet*. Friedrich Vieweg.

Weller, L., Kunde, W., & Pfister, R. (2017). Non-action effect binding: A critical re-assessment. *Acta Psychologica, 180*, 137–146. https://doi.org/10.1016/j.actpsy.2017.09.001

Weller, L., Pfister, R., & Kunde, W. (2019). Sociomotor actions: Anticipated partner responses are primarily represented in terms of spatial, not anatomical features. *Journal of Experimental Psychology: Human Perception and Performance, 45*, 1104–1118. https://doi.org/10.1037/xhp0000658

Weller, L., Pfister, R., & Kunde, W. (2020). Anticipation in sociomotor actions: Similar effects for in- and outgroup interactions. *Acta Psychologica, 207*, 103087. https://doi.org/10.1016/j.actpsy.2020.103087

Wiggett, A. J., Hudson, M., Tipper, S. P., & Downing, P. E. (2011). Learning associations between action and perception: Effects of incompatible training on body part and spatial priming. *Brain and Cognition, 76*, 87–96. https://doi.org/10.1016/j.bandc.2011.02.014

Wirth, R., Pfister, R., Foerster, A., Huestegge, L., & Kunde, W. (2016). Pushing the rules: Effects and aftereffects of deliberate rule violations. *Psychological Research, 80*, 838–852. https://doi.org/10.1007/s00426-015-0690-9

Wolpert, D. M., Doya, K., & Kawato, M. (2003). A unifying computational framework for motor control and social interaction. *Philosophical Transactions of the Royal Society of London: Biological Sciences, 358*, 593–602. https://doi.org/10.1098/rstb.2002.1238

Yabar, Y., Johnston, L., Miles, L., & Peace, V. (2006). Implicit behavioral mimicry: Investigating the impact of group membership. *Journal of Nonverbal Behavior, 30*, 97–113. https://doi.org/10.1007/s10919-006-0010-6

Chapter 9
Automatic Imitation in Infants and Children

Sumeet Farwaha and Virginia Slaughter

Introduction

The challenges in understanding the development of automatic imitation start with terminology. The term "imitation" has been used in the developmental psychology literature for decades, beginning with Piaget's classic observations (1962), to reference a wide array of copying behaviors. These run the gamut from preverbal infants' matching of others' actions and facial expressions to children's reproduction of complex action sequences. It is only recently that developmentalists have begun to use terminology that differentiates copying behaviors, but these are not always in line with the adult literature (see Verde-Cagiao et al., 2022; Rauchbauer & Grosbras, 2020).

Another challenge is methodology. Beginning with Piaget's classic experiments in the mid-twentieth century, "imitation" in infants and children has been assessed with a fairly standard paradigm. This is a naturalistic interaction where an experimenter captures the child's attention, then deliberately models a vocalization, body movement, or object-directed action. This model may be repeated several times. Following the model, the experimenter sits quietly while the child's behavior is observed during a response period which can be as short as 2 s or as long as several minutes. In the response period, the child may act spontaneously, or might be prompted to imitate, especially if initially nonresponsive. Imitation is credited when the child copies the model within the response period. Fidelity of match to the model is usually the primary indicator of imitation in these experiments, whereas speed of responding, number of matching responses or production of non-matching behaviors, is of secondary interest or ignored altogether. Although this approach has produced some findings relevant to automatic imitation, it does not map neatly onto the behavioral paradigms used to investigate the phenomenon in adults.

S. Farwaha · V. Slaughter (✉)
School of Psychology, University of Queensland, Brisbane, Australia
e-mail: s.farwaha@uq.edu.au; vps@psy.uq.edu.au

O. Genschow, E. Cracco (eds.), *Automatic Imitation*,
https://doi.org/10.1007/978-3-031-62634-0_9

In this chapter, we will focus on developmental psychology experiments that align with the notion of automatic imitation as defined in the adult literature. That is, motor matching to a model which is spontaneous rather than instructed, physically congruent with the model and occurring alongside or after the model. Others have already systematically reviewed relevant developmental findings (see Rauchbauer & Grosbras, 2020). Here we will selectively discuss this literature with a focus on understanding the similarities and differences across child and adult definitions and methodologies. Our discussion will be limited to research with infants and young children. This is not to imply that development of this behavior is complete by adolescence; it is because studies with adolescents already adopt the same methodologies as those used with adults. We will also limit our discussion to research involving typically developing children, because the literature is already complicated and studies with atypical children are relatively few.

To organize our discussion of automatic imitation in development, we will use Heyes' (2011) definitions of three related phenomena:

1. Motor mimicry is nonconscious, spontaneous matching of another's physical actions or vocal sounds during interpersonal interactions. This is assessed behaviorally via frequency and/or duration of matching actions during a specified interaction period. Motor mimicry has been contrasted with emotional mimicry, which includes matching facial expressions of emotion, contagious laughing, and crying (for more details, see Chap. 3; this volume). Motor mimicry involves matching actions which are subjectively neutral, whereas emotional mimicry involves activation of a congruent physiological and subjective state as well as matching another's motor movements. As such, the mechanisms involved in motor and emotional mimicry are thought to differ (Hess & Fischer, 2014). Motor mimicry is also contrasted with verbal mimicry, where the matching is across auditory rather than visuo-motor channels (Chartrand & Lakin, 2013). In this chapter, we will focus on the development of motor mimicry.
2. Automatic imitation is a laboratory phenomenon, assessed with experimental stimulus-response compatibility paradigms, most commonly the Automatic Imitation Task (AIT). During the AIT, participants perform simple motor movements while simultaneously viewing a matching or nonmatching model. Automatic imitation is evident in modulations to reaction times and/or accuracy in motor movement performance in the different model conditions. For the remainder of this chapter, the term "automatic imitation" will refer to the laboratory task. We will refer to "automatic imitation effects" when discussing the broader concept.
3. Mirror effects are neurophysiological indicators of motor potentiation or movement while passively watching others' motor movements. In the adult literature, these include EMG responses in matching muscle groups, mu suppression over the motor cortex as measured with EEG, TMS enhancement of motor cortex responses to viewed action models, and functional imaging of motor cortical activity during action observation (see Heyes, 2011 for review). Only the former two methods are suitable for infants and children.

In her review, Heyes (2011) suggested that these three phenomena are related. Motor mimicry occurs often during interpersonal interactions, its expression is modulated by a variety of individual and social factors, and it produces a range of social-affiliative outcomes. Automatic imitation is a form of motor mimicry elicited in a controlled laboratory setting. Both motor mimicry and automatic imitation are likely to be underpinned by activity of a mirror neuron system, which mirror effects are thought to index.

However, the question of whether automatic imitation and mimicry share the same underlying mechanism has since been debated. This debate is centered in methodological differences in the manifestation of these phenomena. First, the tasks used to index automatic imitation and motor mimicry in adults are inherently different. During the AIT, for example, participants are instructed to respond as quickly as possible to a visual cue while making a motor movement. The timing of the participant's response is so important in the AIT, that researchers make sure to exclude any premature or delayed responses, as they could indicate poor attention or lack of motivation during the task. This is in direct contrast with mimicry studies, where participants are not provided with any instructions (Genschow et al., 2017). Furthermore, participants' responses are coded differently in mimicry studies compared to automatic imitation studies. In the former, mimicry behavior occurring several seconds after observing the target action will still be counted for analysis, while in the latter, it would be excluded. As we discuss below, these sorts of differences are magnified in the developmental literature, where concessions for infants' and children's attention, memory, motivation, and motor development impact how these phenomena are measured.

In investigations with adults, automatic imitation and motor mimicry differ in terms of the specificity of copied actions. In the former, researchers take great care to match the observed actions with the response required by the participant. However, in the latter, there is a significant amount of variability in the overlap between the executed action and observed action. In many mimicry studies, non-matching (e.g., actions made using the opposite limb) mimicking behaviors are coded as equivalent to matching occurrences (e.g., actions made using the same limb; Casasanto et al., 2020). Researchers examining motor mimicry in adults have now distinguished between matching vs non-matching behaviors, by using terms like anatomical mimicry (i.e., mimicry of the action using the exact same limb) or specular mimicry (i.e., mimicry of the action using the opposite limb; Casasanto et al., 2020). These distinctions have not entered the developmental literature.

Thus, it is difficult to conclude that automatic imitation and mimicry share the same underlying mechanisms, since the respective studies vary significantly in terms of response time, specificity of the copied action, as well as how responses are coded (reaction time/error rate of imitation vs length/frequency of mimicry behavior). These issues are highlighted by recent evidence that in adults, mimicry and AI are not correlated (Genschow et al., 2017). This is a ripe area for developmental investigation because longitudinal assessments of theoretically related behaviors can shed light on whether or not there are shared underlying mechanisms driving development (e.g., Carpenter et al., 1998; Nielsen & Dissanayake, 2004).

Below, we discuss the evidence for motor mimicry, automatic imitation, and mirror effects in infants and children. We point out where there are terminological, methodological, and conceptual mismatches, where these differences lead to ambiguities in interpretation and where there are opportunities for future research.

Motor Mimicry

Motor mimicry is commonly observed in adults; this has come to be known as the Chameleon Effect (Chartrand & Bargh, 1999). The phenomenon is assessed in a naturalistic interaction whereby participants are invited to take part in a fun task (e.g., describing photographs or rating music) with an unassuming partner, who is typically a trained confederate of the study. During this session, the confederate performs specific actions (e.g., face touching, foot shaking, etc.) after a predetermined time (e.g., every 5 or 10 s) to assess whether the participant will nonconsciously mimic their actions. Covertly recorded videos of the interaction are coded for mimicry behavior, which is typically indexed by the frequency or duration of the participants' production of the target action, using a cross-target or baseline comparison method (Chartrand & Bargh, 1999; Hogeveen et al., 2015). This effect is modulated by a range of interpersonal factors, from similarity to and liking for the confederate, to the participant's own state of mind (see Duffy & Chartrand, 2015). Debrief interviews are conducted after the interaction to ensure that participants were unaware of the true purpose of the study. As van Baaren, Janssen, Chartrand, and Dijksterhuis (2009) explain, this paradigm is set up such that mimicry is a "by-product in the interaction" (p. 2382) rather than the focus. Few, if any, mimicry studies involving infants or children meet that criterion.

Neonatal Imitation and beyond

Although traditionally called "neonatal imitation," the phenomenon referenced in this literature broadly aligns with the contemporary concept of motor mimicry, that is, a spontaneous production of motor activity that matches another person's motor behavior, during face-to-face interaction. However as described below, some features of its presentation are not consistent with the adult definition of motor mimicry. It is assumed that neonates' copying behaviors are nonconscious, as is motor mimicry in adults, but this is based on theories about preverbal infants' capacity for self-awareness rather than evidence.

Much has been written about the 40-year controversy around neonatal imitation (see Oostenbroek et al., 2013; Leys, 2020; Ray & Heyes, 2011). In short, Meltzoff and Moore (1977) reported that newborns no older than 21 days spontaneously copy an adult's facial and manual actions. They reported two experiments in which an adult experimenter modelled face and hand actions to newborn infants in a close face-to-face format. In Experiment 1, the distinct actions of lip protrusion, mouth opening, tongue protrusion, and sequential finger movement were modelled to infants in separate blocks. The adult model performed each action four times for a duration of 15 s, followed by a 20 s response period. In Experiment 2, only the mouth opening and tongue protrusion actions were modelled, and the response period was extended to 150 s. Infant behavior while watching these face-to-face displays was videotaped. Later, trained observers coded the infants' spontaneous production of modelled actions. Using a "cross-target" comparison method, which compares the frequencies of infant actions to matching versus non-matching adult models, the researchers reported that newborns copied all the actions in both experiments. Meltzoff and Moore's (1977) findings were followed by a variety of independent replications and extensions (e.g., Heimann & Schaller, 1985; Reissland, 1988; see also Meltzoff & Moore, 1997 for a review).

This discovery changed the landscape of infancy research and is a standard reference for claims of an inborn human tendency to mimic underpinned by an innate mirror neuron system (Ferrari et al., 2009). However, the positive evidence for neonatal imitation has faced a significant amount of criticism. The most pressing problem is reliability: alongside the reported replications, numerous researchers dating back to Hayes and Watson (1981) failed to find evidence of imitation in newborns using a close variant of Meltzoff and Moore's (1977) procedure. To address the controversy, Davis et al. (2021) carried out a systematic review and meta-analysis to address whether neonatal imitation truly exists. Combining data from over 1000 infants under 6 weeks old, who were tested in 33 independent samples, Davis et al. (2021) found a significant overall effect ($d = 0.68$) but significant heterogeneity in the literature. Moderator analyses indicated that the effect is not influenced by any of the several factors that have been cited as essential for eliciting imitation in newborns, including the test setting, model presentation duration, infant response duration, infant testing position, or pre-exposure to the model. However, the size of the neonatal imitation effect was shown to vary significantly by research institution, with only 6 of 16 institutions finding effects that are statistically greater than zero (Davis et al., 2021).

If we adopt a generous interpretation of this literature and assume that newborn imitation is hard to capture but does exist, it is difficult to align with the concept of motor mimicry. First, it is evident that this is an unreliable behavior, both at the group and individual levels. Some researchers have argued for individual differences in neonatal imitation (e.g., Simpson et al., 2014) which, they suggest, mask the group level effect in some experiments. Yet, the only longitudinal study of neonatal imitation by Oostenbroek et al. (2016) found no intra-individual consistency of infants' imitative responses across four testing occasions between one and nine weeks of age. By contrast, although individual differences exist, motor mimicry in adults appears to be far more reliable (Duffy & Chartrand, 2015).

Another stumbling block to linking neonatal imitation with motor mimicry is that the interactions that elicit mimicry in newborns are not natural. In all of the experiments, modelling follows a pre-set timetable where the target action is repeated several times, often with the experimenter posing a passive and neutral facial expression between sets of actions. The idea is that newborns may be over-aroused by a moving face, interfering with their ability to generate a matching motor response. A "pause" period is included to give newborns time and space to marshal their imitative responses (Meltzoff et al., 2018). Relatedly, newborns' production of matching actions may not be evident for some time after the adult stops moving. Thus, newborns are credited with motor mimicry even if their social partners have stopped behaving for many seconds. Indeed, response periods in some of these studies have been as long as 2.5 min (see Davis et al., 2021). It has been argued that these features of repeated action modelling interspersed with stillness, and extended response periods, are crucial for eliciting motor mimicry in newborns (Meltzoff et al., 2018). This is at odds with our understanding of motor mimicry as a spontaneous, automatic matching of another's motor behavior.

Jones (2007) adopted a similar procedure to the neonatal imitation protocol, to investigate motor mimicry in infants aged between 6 and 20 months. In this study, infants' mothers were trained to model simple motor actions—manual, vocal, and facial actions—to their infants using a similar burst-pause procedure to that developed by Meltzoff and Moore (1977). Modelling of the target actions lasted up to 3 min and parents could encourage their infants to mimic. Although it makes a nice bridge to the neonatal imitation work, this procedure is a version of the standard paradigm pioneered by Piaget, which deviates from key features of adult motor mimicry studies. Jones (2007) found that mimicry first emerged around 8–12 months of age, which is consistent with the original observations of Piaget. Notably the target actions first mimicked had auditory components: tapping the table and "ah" vocalization. Simple motor acts without accompanying sounds including tongue protrusion, finger waving, and touching the hand to the head were not evident until infants were older than 12 months. This might indicate that motor mimicry emerges in the second year of life, but the same methodological criticisms as discussed above, plus the added issue of parental encouragement, cloud the picture.

Caregiver-Infant Interactions

In the large research literature investigating the structure and functions of face-to-face caregiver-infant interactions, motor mimicry by both participants is sometimes included as a dependent variable (see Cagiao et al., 2022 for a review). These interactions between caregivers and their infants (up to around 18 months of age) are natural and spontaneous, which brings them closer to adult investigations of motor mimicry. However, there are key differences. These studies invariably look at vocal and emotional mimicry as well as motor mimicry, and these forms are rarely analyzed separately. When they are separated, motor mimicry is less frequent than mimicry of vocalizations and emotional expressions (e.g., Masur & Rodemaker, 1999). Interestingly, these studies reveal that adult caregivers tend to mimic their infants around once every 2 min (see review in Ray & Heyes, 2011). This is similar to the rate at which adults nonconsciously mimic confederates in experimental studies (Chartrand & Bargh, 1999), which suggests a parallel, but the extent to which caregivers' mimicry of their infants is automatic and nonconscious, is not known.

Another difference is that caregivers' mimicry of their infants and infants' mimicry of their caregivers are highly correlated and synchronized (Moran et al., 1987; Masur & Rodemaker, 1999; Stern, 2002). The bidirectional and interdependent nature of these interactions makes it difficult to work out who is mimicking whom. Those researchers who have sought to disentangle caregiver and infant mimicry by coding initiation versus following roles find that caregivers copy their infants much more frequently than vice versa (Moran et al., 1987; see also Ray & Heyes, 2011). There is scope to generate novel experiments on the emergence of motor mimicry in the context of caregiver-infant interactions. For instance, caregivers could be instructed to interact with their infants naturally, while being surreptitiously cued to perform specific target actions similar to those generated by confederates in the adult studies.

Chameleon Effect in Children

Given the popularity of the Chameleon Effect in the adult literature, it is surprising that there are relatively few such studies with children. One possibility is that the effect is not present in young children interacting with an unfamiliar adult; indeed this was the conclusion drawn by Over and Carpenter (2009) in their paper on 5 year olds' imitation following ostracism priming. They reported results of a pilot study which they summarized as follows: "…when engaged in a conversation with an adult experimenter who repeatedly touched her face (as in Chartrand & Bargh, 1999), 5-year-old children did not increase their face touching above baseline levels" (p. F2). This is the only published report of a motor mimicry study testing children with the standard Chameleon Effect paradigm.

Soon after, van Schaik et al. (2013) reported positive findings of motor mimicry in children. They pioneered a novel approach which has similarities to the original Chameleon Effect paradigm, but also some important differences. For one thing, it is video-based, with children passively watching the confederate on screen, rather than engaging in a shared activity. In this adapted paradigm, children's motor mimicry is assessed while they are watching short video clips of an adult female modelling a specific target action such as yawning, laughing, frowning, scratching her cheek, rubbing her lips, and wiggling her head back and forth. Each 7-s video portrays a different target action. In the test, the action modelling videos are presented several times each, back-to-back, in a pseudo-random order. Children's performance of target actions throughout the video presentations is compared to their performance of the same actions spontaneously while watching a non-social baseline video.

Presenting the action models on video is argued to enhance control over the fidelity of the models, as well as allowing experimenters to assess children's attention to the models as a covariate of mimicry performance. It is also suggested that videos eliminate any interpersonal biases that could impact face-to-face interactions with children. However, it is difficult to draw developmental trajectories from these findings to the adult data, when something so fundamental differs between them, and while some mimicry studies with adults have found the effect during screen-based interactions (Genschow et al., 2017; Estow et al., 2007; Neufeld & Chakrabarti, 2016), children are subject to a "video deficit" effect, whereby learning from screens—including learning via directed imitation—is less effective than learning from a live model. The video deficit effect diminishes with age, but it is still apparent even for children over age 3 (Strouse & Samson, 2021).

Despite this threat to validity, van Schaik et al. (2013) found evidence for motor mimicry in 3-year-old children. This was concluded from the finding that children's performance of all the target actions, except laughing, was more frequent while watching the action modelling videos, compared to baseline. Furthermore, 23 of 26 children exhibited motor mimicry of at least one of the target actions. Data on timing of the mimicry were not reported, and this is an important omission because children were credited with mimicry if they performed a target action any time between its first presentation within the back-to-back video clips, to the end of the test. Thus, mimicry could be near simultaneous, or there could be a delay of many seconds between the modelled action and the child's mimicry response. This could mean that the child was credited with mimicry when performing an action, such as head scratching, at the same time that a different model, such as yawning, was visible on screen.

In this study, van Schaik et al. (2013) also investigated whether social evaluation of the confederates influenced children's motor mimicry, in line with such findings in the adult literature. This was accomplished by priming the children with separate videos of the confederates either helping or hindering another person, just prior to the presentation of the test. This manipulation had no effect. Finally, a nice addition to van Schaik et al.'s (2013) paradigm is the debrief: at the end of the procedure, children were asked if they remembered copying the model. Their answers to that question were unrelated to their performance in the test, suggesting that they were not conscious of mimicking.

A second study by van Schaik and Hunnius (2016) replicated the motor mimicry effect in children using a subset of the same action modelling videos (yawn, head shake, cheek scratch, and lip rub). Extending on their previous experiment, they found that 4- to 6-year-olds, as well as a new sample of 3-year-olds, exhibited motor mimicry. However, in this second study, only 45% of the 4- to 6-year-old children and 70% of the 3-year-olds performed any of the target actions during baseline or test. This was much lower than the 88% of children who did so in their initial study. Using a minimal-groups paradigm to prime in- and out-group identification, van Schaik and Hunnius (2016) found that in-group mimicry was significantly higher than out-group mimicry in this study, for the subset of children aged 4–6 years. This pattern replicates a common finding in the adult literature (Chartrand & Bargh, 1999).

In their next study, van Schaik and Hunnius (2018) developed a more naturalistic paradigm to further investigate how social factors modulate motor mimicry exhibited by 5-year-old participants. Here, two female confederates interacted with the child participant at the start of the experiment. One confederate shared one of two stickers with the child (i.e., the sharer) while the second kept both stickers for herself (i.e., the keeper). After this face-to-face social manipulation, children watched a video in which the two confederates each told a short children's story. For the experimental group, one of the confederates performed hand rubbing while the other performed face rubbing. For the control group, stories did not have accompanying face or hand rubbing. Results were contrary to expectation: children in the experimental group exhibited "negative mimicry" by performing the target behaviors significantly less frequently than children in the control group, and within the experimental group, there was no difference between mimicry of sharer versus keeper. On the positive side, this experiment revealed a significant correlation between children's social understanding, as reported by their parents, and mimicry in the hypothesized direction. Specifically, the higher the children's social understanding, the more motor mimicry they exhibited in the test.

So what do we make of all this? The Chameleon Effect is evidently hard to elicit in children, and the effect is fragile. The limited positive evidence points to its emergence in the preschool period, where the effect is similar to that seen in adults insofar as it can be modulated by social factors and it is linked to individual differences in social understanding. However, there are a lot of unanswered questions. Are we content to credit children with motor mimicry if it occurs minutes after the model, or if the child's action matches a previous model rather than the contemporaneous one? What is the impact of video versus live modelling by confederates? Most importantly, at what point in development is there continuity with motor mimicry effects commonly observed in adults? Here we clearly need longitudinal data that tests children and adults using the very same paradigm.

Contagious Yawning

Contagious yawning has also been a target of developmental studies investigating motor mimicry. Although some authors class contagious yawning as a form of emotional mimicry, its performance is associated more strongly with detection and attention to others' yawns, than by emotion-related factors (Gallup, 2021). Investigating its development, initial studies using videotaped yawn stimuli concluded that it was not evident until age 5 or 6 (e.g., Anderson & Meno, 2003). By contrast, Helt et al. (2010) adopted a live mimicry paradigm to investigate contagious yawning in children ranging in age from 1 to 15 years. They had children read a book together with a confederate who yawned four times over the 12-min session. Yawns that occurred within 90 s of the confederate's yawn were counted as instances of mimicry. The data indicated that contagious yawning was rare in children ages 1–3. At age 4, approximately 40% of children mimicked at least one of the confederate's yawns, and this level response was maintained through the higher ages. Recently an ethological study of children's contagious yawning in an Italian preschool (Cordoni et al., 2021) found evidence for the phenomenon as young as age 2; however, their operationalization included any yawns that occurred within 5 min of another's yawn. These studies highlight that video versus live modelling may not be equally effective at eliciting motor mimicry in children, although the small number of studies and vast differences across the methodologies limit what can be concluded.

The contagious yawning studies again bring up the problematic issue of timing. In the literature on motor mimicry in adults, there is no standard definition that references the time interval between model and mimicry (Hale & Hamilton, 2016). Rather, these studies calculate the frequency and/or duration of matching actions that participants produce while the model is intermittently displayed over an extended period, yet the definition of motor mimicry, as an automatic response, implies a relatively tight coupling between model and matching response. Some research on motor mimicry reverses the design and has the confederate copy the experimental participant; in those experiments, the mimicry manipulation occurs within several seconds (Chartrand & Bargh, 1999; Hale & Hamilton, 2016; van Baaren et al., 2009; Leander et al., 2012). In this context, most of the evidence for motor mimicry in infants and children is ambiguous, because timing is not reported, or the mimicry occurs so long after the model that it may not be automatic. These considerations point to the need for theoretically informed definitions of the time course of motor mimicry in infants, children, and adults.

Automatic Imitation in Children

Automatic imitation as defined by Heyes (2011) is difficult to assess in children due to the motivational and attentional demands inherent in tasks used to index this phenomenon. In adults, this has most commonly been via the AIT computer task where participants see a cue on-screen (e.g., a number or symbol) that prompts them to lift and re-press a specific key with their index or middle finger. Meanwhile, they can see an on-screen hand performing the same action as cued (i.e., congruent trials) or the opposite action (i.e., incongruent trials). Participants are told to ignore the on-screen hand, yet they are typically slower and less accurate on incongruent trials compared to congruent trials (Heyes, 2011). The difference between reaction times and error rates on congruent and incongruent trials is referred to as the interference effect. A large interference effect (i.e., greater susceptibility to imitating the on-screen action) is thought to be due to the automatic activation of the observed action in the observer (Heyes, 2011). This task is widely used with adults but has limited utility with young children because, among other things, they usually are unwilling to perform a dull finger-lifting task many times over.

With that said, one study has successfully implemented the standard AIT task with children, with the aim of establishing a proof of concept and assessing age-related differences (MacGowan et al., 2022). The only modification made to the standard AIT task for the sample of 6-year-olds they tested was to embed the finger-press response in a lemonade-making context whereby children pressed the "lemon" or "lime" colored key, as cued by the number on screen. This study revealed that the children were slower overall, as expected, but the error rate (i.e., number of mistakes made during the task) was comparable between undergraduate participants and children. Crucially, children exhibited reduced RT interference effects compared to their adult counterparts (MacGowan et al., 2022). In other words, the adult participants were more susceptible to imitating the incompatible on-screen actions during the task. While this finding is noteworthy, future work is encouraged to take additional steps to assess whether this age-related difference is due to imitative differences or whether children are simply less prone to congruency effects in stimulus-response compatibility tasks in general. On another note, it was also observed that shyness in 5-year-olds predicted higher automatic imitation 1 year later. The researchers suggested that this correlation could indicate that automatic imitation is enhanced in shy children both because they have more opportunities to observe others' behavior, and they may use it as an adaptive strategy to create and maintain affiliations within their social environments.

Although the AIT is considered a robust measure of automatic imitation, it is important to discuss some of its limitations. In the traditional version of the task, participants are required to make keypress and release actions using the "v" and "b" key on a standard computer keyboard using their index and middle finger, respectively. Meanwhile, the on-screen hand mirrors the exact position of the participant's resting hand on the keyboard. Some argue that this set-up makes it difficult to conclude whether observed interference effects are due to differences in automatic imitation, or whether they are a result of spatial compatibility effects whereby the cued response does not spatially correspond with the on-screen action (Jiménez et al., 2012). That is, participants may be slower or more error-prone during incongruent trials due to the mere presence of movement on the incompatible location. If so, that undermines the idea that this task solely captures imitative differences (Jiménez et al., 2012). Therefore, caution should be used when interpreting findings from the traditional version of the AIT. This concern is amplified when interpreting results from AIT tests with children, because they are significantly less capable of ignoring visual distractors compared to adults (Robinson et al., 2018).

In order to address the concern of spatial compatibility confounds during the AIT, researchers have moved away from presenting the on-screen hand on a horizontal plane (i.e., mirroring the participants hand) and have now rotated the stimuli 90° so that it is orthogonal to the position of the participant's hand at rest (Rauchbauer & Grosbras, 2020; Farwaha & Obhi, 2021; MacGowan et al., 2022). By implementing this change, researchers can ensure that left-left or right-right spatial compatibility effects do not interfere with the participants' responses. However, even with this change, other forms of orthogonal spatial compatibility (i.e., downward stimulus—leftward response, upward stimulus—rightward response) continue to exist (Cho & Proctor, 2004). Like in the traditional AIT, participants completing this version may simply be slower or make more mistakes during incongruent trials due to the mere presence of movement on the compatible side, which again undermines the idea that this task solely captures imitative differences. As such, recent work using the AIT has adopted a new configuration of stimuli to better control for these types of spatial compatibility effects (see Czekóová et al., 2021 for a detailed discussion).

In addition to spatial compatibility effects, there are other limitations of the AIT that should be noted. Although reaction time and error rate interference effects during this task can be seen as an index of an individual's susceptibility to imitate the actions of others, there may be other underlying factors driving this effect. For example, performance may be impacted by participants' ability to follow through with task instructions (i.e., ignore the on-screen hand) or by individual differences in attention to social stimuli (i.e., fixating on the on-screen hand more often). Again, these issues may be magnified when testing children, especially when trying to compare performance across age groups where such confounds may be subject to developmental effects of their own. Researchers are encouraged to incorporate other measures such as visual attention and executive function to help interpret children's performance on the AIT.

Other studies of automatic imitation in children have used more naturalistic paradigms. Marshall, Bouquet, Thomas, and Shipley (2010) developed clever adaption of the AIT for children. Participants were instructed to scribble horizontally or vertically on a screen using a stylus while the screen showed a model moving her arm congruently or incongruently with the child's scribble. Four-year-old children showed interference, with variability of the horizontal or vertical scribbles being significantly larger when the background movements were incongruent. The researchers demonstrated this interference effect when the models were adults (Experiment 1) and same-aged peers (Experiment 2). However, in Experiment 2, there was an overall stronger effect for the peer model, and the effect disappeared for the adult model. This difference is hard to interpret because the peer model could only be filmed performing horizontal movements, meaning that only half of the Experiment 1 design was replicated in the second experiment, in both the peer and adult model conditions. This difference might have explained the discrepancy in responses to the adult model across the two experiments. Using this same task, van Schaik et al. (2016) investigated group membership effects on children's automatic imitation. They partially replicated the effect in a sample of 4- to 6-year-olds; that is, the interference effect was present, but only for the out-group condition. No motor interference was evident for children in the in-group condition.

O'Sullivan et al. (2018) assessed automatic imitation in children with another naturalistic experimental paradigm. In this study, 3- to 7-year-olds sat across from a live experimenter and played a game where they were instructed to perform one of two hand actions, immediately after the experimenter had performed a matching or non-matching action. The hand actions were paired as follows: clapping and waving were deemed the "commonly imitated set" and finger pointing and hand closing were deemed the "rarely imitated set." The idea was that children naturally experience correlated visuo-motor input for the commonly imitated actions of clapping and waving since humans tend to do those in synchrony. This experience would facilitate imitation of the matching action and interfere with imitation of the non-matching action. The same effects would not be evident for the rarely imitated set. Results confirmed this hypothesis, showing that interference in the commonly imitated action set was significantly greater than in the rarely imitated set. This effect did not vary with age.

Thus overall, the developmental findings for automatic imitation are similar to those for motor mimicry. Automatic imitation can be elicited in preschool-aged children, with modifications to the standard paradigm. It seems to be less reliable in children compared to adults. There is some evidence that automatic imitation in children can be modulated by social factors; however, the evidence is extremely limited and must be reconciled with recent work questioning whether adults' automatic imitation is modulated by social factors (see Cracco et al., 2022 for a detailed discussion). The immaturity of children's attention, memory, and executive systems complicates comparisons with the adult findings; again, there is a need for longitudinal research.

Mirror Effects in Infants and Children

The behavioral effects of motor mimicry and automatic imitation are thought to rely, at least partially, on a mirror neuron system (Heyes, 2011; Rizzolatti et al., 2001). This system produces physiological motor resonance, whereby observation of another's motor movements automatically stimulates a matching neuro-motoric response in the observer. Developmental research on these effects has been thoroughly reviewed elsewhere (see Cuevas et al., 2014; Marshall & Meltzoff, 2014; Rauchbauer & Grosbras, 2020); here we will briefly summarize some key findings and considerations for future research.

Surface Electromyography (sEMG)

One technique for investigating mirror effects is via surface electromyography (sEMG), which is the recording of muscle electrical activity using non-invasive sticky electrodes affixed to the surface of the skin. This technique has long been used to examine timing or magnitude of muscle activity in infants and children while they perform various tasks or actions (Chowdhury et al., 2013; Hirschfeld, 1997; Sundermier et al., 2001). While sEMG has been used to study spontaneous mimicry in adults for many years (Dimberg, 1982; Carr and Winkielman, 2014), until recently, few researchers used sEMG for imitation studies with children (Hofree et al., 2015). This is surprising, as sEMG allows researchers to obtain a continuous recording of muscle activity and establish a reliable linkage between visual stimuli (e.g., action observation) and corresponding muscle activity (i.e., motor responses).

The youngest infants so far tested for mirror effects using sEMG were 4-month-olds. de Klerk et al. (2018) presented infants with a video-taped female model performing facial and manual actions including eyebrow raising, frowning, hand opening/closing, and finger movement. The experiment included two eye gaze conditions, whereby the model's eye gaze was either direct or averted during the action presentation, with the idea being that direct eye gaze, as a social signal, would enhance matching motor movements in the infants. Muscle potentiation was examined by placing electrodes over the infants' eyebrow region (i.e., frontalis), mouth region (i.e., masseter), and hand region (i.e., interosseous). This study found mirror effects, in that matching motor activation was evident during action observation; however, this was only for the eyebrow raising action in the direct gaze condition.

Another study by de Klerk et al. (2019) similarly explored mirror effects in 11-month-olds, using sEMG. Here, the social identity of the model was manipulated. Infants were presented with models that were initially presented speaking the infant's native language or an unfamiliar, foreign language. After this, they were shown modelling two facial actions of mouth opening and eyebrow raising. Results indicated greater activation of matching electrodes (placed on the eyebrow versus mouth region) in response to the familiar-language model. This finding fits with van Schaik and Hunnius (2016) who found greater production of overt motor matching in response to in-group models in 4- to 6-year-old children, although recall that they did not see the effect in 3 year olds.

de Klerk et al. (2020) explored whether a different social factor—ostracism—would enhance sEMG measures of mimicry in 30-month-old toddlers. Here, children observed a video depicting moving shapes, in which one shape appeared to be ostracized by the others. Next, toddlers watched eyebrow raising and mouth opening models on video. Matching muscle activation was greater for children in the ostracism condition, relative to those in a control condition.

These studies indicate that sEMG is a valuable tool for investigating the development of mimicry. However, researchers must be aware of its limitations especially with infant and child participants. Even with adults, it can be difficult to obtain muscle-specific activation during sEMG recordings, due to a significant amount of crosstalk from neighboring muscle groups. This problem is magnified with infants' and children's small bodies. Researchers have addressed this limitation by attributing muscle potentiation to general regions of interest rather than specific muscles (see Fridlund & Cacioppo, 1986; de Klerk et al., 2018). When testing infants, researchers must manage the participants' level of arousal which can influence data quality. Highly aroused infants may wiggle and squirm, producing motion artefacts that overrun the sEMG signal, and if infants become upset and cry before or during action observation, this can produce distress-related muscle fatigue that is a limiting factor for collecting meaningful physiological data. Indeed, in developmental sEMG studies, there tends to be a very high drop-out rate, sometimes close to 50%, because many infants and children do not tolerate the feeling of sticky electrodes. This may bias samples toward temperamentally easy, low-reactive individuals, which is a significant confound since this temperamental profile is associated with trait sociability (Kagan & Snidman, 2004). As such, researchers are encouraged to investigate the implications of these factors on the reliability and validity of sEMG, especially when used with infants and children.

Mu Suppression

Another technique for investigating mirror effects involves using EEG to record brain activity from regions of interest during action observation and/or action execution (for a review, see Hobson & Bishop, 2016). The resting mu-rhythm becomes suppressed when participants observe another individual performing an action and when they perform the action themselves (Hobson & Bishop, 2016; Hager et al., 2018). This brain-level matching of observed and performed actions has obvious parallels to automatic imitation, and some evidence suggests that mu suppression and motor mimicry are correlated (Hogeveen et al., 2015).

There are quite a few studies using mu-suppression as an index of mirror system activity in children, because it is relatively easy to implement even with young infants who do not mind wearing electrode caps, and it is robust to motion artefacts. This body of work indicates that mu suppression during action observation is first evident around 7–8 months of age (see Rauchbauer & Grosbras, 2020 for a summary). The effect is stronger, in children as well as adults, when viewing live as opposed to videotaped actions, and when viewing goal-directed actions such as grasping and lifting an object, as opposed to empty actions. Developmental studies on mu suppression have capitalized on the fact that infants vary in their motor skill development, using these individual differences to show that mu suppression is greater when the observed action is already within the child's motor repertoire (Cuevas et al., 2014).

A recent meta-analysis by Fox et al. (2016) has shown support for use of mu-suppression as an index of human mirror activity. Indeed, significant effect sizes for mu-suppression were observed during action observation and action execution across 85 studies and a total of 1508 participants (Fox et al., 2016). However, the use of mu-suppression as an index of mirror system activity has faced significant criticism in the extant literature. For example, Hobson and Bishop (2017) argue that most published mu-suppression work is generally underpowered, difficult to reproduce due to variability in the chosen frequency band for mu-suppression (e.g., 8–13 hz, 8–15 hz, or 10–14 hz), and the recorded brain activity is susceptible to crosstalk from neighboring areas. In addition, some researchers have also argued that mu-suppression may only index the mirroring of sensory information rather than motor responses (see Coll et al., 2017; Hobson & Bishop, 2017). As such, the mu-suppression findings from both adults and children should be interpreted with caution.

In sum, the developmental studies of mirror effects show that some forms of motor resonance are evident in the first year of life. However, there are significant limitations to data collection and interpretation when using these physiological tools with infants and children.

Competing Theories of the Origins of Automatic Imitation Effects

Based on their findings about newborn imitation, Meltzoff and Moore (1997) proposed a theory of Active Intermodal Mapping (AIM), which states that humans are equipped at birth with a shared supramodal representational system (Hurley & Chater, 2005; Meltzoff & Prinz, 2002) for mapping our own body movements to those of social partners. It is argued that this innate mirroring mechanism evolved to facilitate bonding between infants and their caregivers, at a time when the infant is still relatively helpless and otherwise unable to communicate (Ferrari et al., 2009; Meltzoff, 1988, 2007). Later, the AIM theory was expanded to include mirror neurons as the neurocognitive substrate for this matching. Ferrari et al. (2009) refined this theory with the idea that an inborn subcortical "direct mirror pathway" linking premotor and posterior parietal regions to primary motor cortex is responsible for neonatal imitation and automatic imitation effects in older children and adults. They also posit that a complementary "indirect mirror pathway" is responsible for later-developing, voluntary forms of imitation via connections with the prefrontal cortex (Ferrari et al., 2009). These theories claim that automatic imitation effects are present at birth, as a result of gene-based natural selection.

The alternative view is that automatic imitation effects are acquired through experience. The most influential theory on this side is Associative Sequence Learning (ASL; Cook et al., 2014), which holds that mirror neurons, which underpin matching behaviors, develop as a consequence of contingent and contiguous associations between visual and motor input over time (Ray & Heyes, 2011; Cook et al., 2014). For example, when a caregiver imitates their infant's facial action (e.g., eyebrow raising), the visual input received by the infant (e.g., caregiver's raised eyebrows) becomes associated with the infant's own motor activity, which then is strengthened over repeated experiences. Eventually, this forms a bi-directional relationship between sensory and motor neurons, whereby simply observing an action activates an internal motor representation of that action in the observer, which can then be indexed at the behavioral or physiological level (Ray & Heyes, 2011; Cook et al., 2014). These associations between sensory and motor neurons can also be built via experiences of self-observation (Ray & Heyes, 2011; Cook et al., 2014).

The emergence of learning models such as ASL has stimulated researchers to test this alternative view. For example, de Klerk et al. (2019) found that 4-month olds' duration of looking at their own hands during a 5-min unstructured observation was correlated with their manual EMG responses to modelled hand actions in an imitation test, although these hand responses did not reach behavioral criteria for motor mimicry. Rayson et al. (2017) similarly found an association between mothers' frequency of mirroring their 2-month-old infants' mouth opening and smiling, and infant motor cortex mu rhythm de-synchronization while observing those same two facial actions measured 7 months later. These findings are in line with the idea that co-experiences of action observation and execution produce mirror mechanisms during infancy.

The debate about the development of imitation is ongoing. Ultimately it is a nature-nurture question that turns on the status of neonatal imitation, but that literature is riddled with controversy in part because of methodological differences across investigating laboratories (see Davis et al., 2021). Physiological indicators may be more informative to reveal whether or not automatic imitation effects are evident at birth, but as yet those techniques have only been used with infants aged 4 months or older. As the technologies improve, researchers may be more willing to investigate mirror effects in newborn babies, although the practical constraints of collecting physiological data with such tiny participants, and challenges to interpretation, will still apply.

Conclusion

There has been a significant disconnect between the child and adult research on automatic imitation effects, making it difficult to draw developmental conclusions. Some gaps are unavoidable, because of the inherent constraints on testing infants and children, but others can be bridged. Developmental researchers should adopt more precise terminology and definitions, to align automatic imitation effects in children, with their adult manifestations. Relatedly, there needs to be a consensus on the timing of motor mimicry. Effort should go into developing experimental paradigms that work equally well with children and adults. That will enable longitudinal studies that are essential for understanding the development of these phenomena. Developmental studies have so far focused on the social factors that modulate automatic imitation in children, but it will be important in future to investigate other moderators such as live versus video modelling and individual differences including child temperament.

References

Anderson, J. R., & Meno, P. (2003). Psychological influences on yawning in children. *Current Psychology Letters, 11*, 1–6. https://doi.org/10.4000/cpl.390

Carpenter, M., Nagell, K., & Tomasello, M. (1998). Social cognition, joint attention, and communicative competence from 9 to 15 months of age. *Monographs of the Society for Research in Child Development, 63*, i–143.

Carr, E. W., & Winkielman, P. (2014). When mirroring is both simple and "smart": How mimicry can be embodied, adaptive, and non-representational. *Frontiers in Human Neuroscience, 8*, 505. https://doi.org/10.3389/fnhum.2014.00505

Casasanto, D., Casasanto, L. S., Gijssels, T., & Hagoort, P. (2020). The reverse chameleon effect: Negative social consequences of anatomical mimicry. *Frontiers in Psychology, 11*, 1876. https://doi.org/10.3389/fpsyg.2020.01876

Chartrand, T. L., & Bargh, J. A. (1999). The chameleon effect: The perception–behavior link and social interaction. *Journal of Personality and Social Psychology, 76*, 893–910. https://doi.org/10.1037/0022-3514.76.6.893

Chartrand, T. L., & Lakin, J. L. (2013). The antecedents and consequences of human behavioral mimicry. *Annual Review of Psychology, 64*, 285–308. https://doi.org/10.1146/annurev-psych-113011-143754

Cho, Y. S., & Proctor, R. W. (2004). Influences of multiple spatial stimulus and response codes on orthogonal stimulus – Response compatibility. *Perception & Psychophysics, 66*, 1003–1017. https://doi.org/10.3758/BF03194991

Chowdhury, R. H., Reaz, M. B., Ali, M. A. B. M., Bakar, A. A., Chellappan, K., & Chang, T. G. (2013). Surface electromyography signal processing and classification techniques. *Sensors, 13*, 12431–12466. https://doi.org/10.3390/s130912431

Coll, M. P., Press, C., Hobson, H., Catmur, C., & Bird, G. (2017). Crossmodal classification of mu rhythm activity during action observation and execution suggests specificity to somatosensory features of actions. *Journal of Neuroscience, 37*, 5936–5947. https://doi.org/10.1523/JNEUROSCI.3393-16.2017

Cook, R., Bird, G., Catmur, C., Press, C., & Heyes, C. (2014). Mirror neurons: From origin to function. *Behavioral and Brain Sciences, 37*, 177–192. https://doi.org/10.1017/s0140525x13000903

Cordoni, G., Favilli, E., & Palagi, E. (2021). Earlier than previously thought: Yawn contagion in preschool children. *Developmental Psychobiology, 63*, 931–944. https://doi.org/10.1002/dev.22094

Cracco, E., Genschow, O., & Baess, P. (2022). Top-down social modulation of perception-action coupling. *Acta Psychologica, 222*, 103481. https://doi.org/10.1016/j.actpsy.2021.103481

Cuevas, K., Cannon, E. N., Yoo, K., & Fox, N. A. (2014). The infant EEG mu rhythm: Methodological considerations and best practices. *Developmental Review, 34*, 26–43. https://doi.org/10.1016%2Fj.dr.2013.12.001

Czekóová, K., Shaw, D. J., Lamoš, M., Špiláková, B., Salazar, M., & Brázdil, M. (2021). Imitation or polarity correspondence? Behavioural and neurophysiological evidence for the confounding influence of orthogonal spatial compatibility on measures of automatic imitation. *Cognitive, Affective, & Behavioral Neuroscience, 21*, 212–230. https://doi.org/10.3758%2Fs13415-020-00860-y

Davis, J., Redshaw, J., Suddendorf, T., Nielsen, M., Kennedy-Costantini, S., Oostenbroek, J., & Slaughter, V. (2021). Does neonatal imitation exist? Insights from a meta-analysis of 336 effect sizes. *Perspectives on Psychological Science, 16*, 1373–1397. https://doi.org/10.1177/1745691620959834

de Klerk, C. C., Hamilton, A. F. D. C., & Southgate, V. (2018). Eye contact modulates facial mimicry in 4-month-old infants: An EMG and fNIRS study. *Cortex, 106*, 93–103. https://doi.org/10.1016%2Fj.cortex.2018.05.002

de Klerk, C. C., Bulgarelli, C., Hamilton, A., & Southgate, V. (2019). Selective facial mimicry of native over foreign speakers in preverbal infants. *Journal of Experimental Child Psychology, 183*, 33–47. https://doi.org/10.1016%2Fj.jecp.2019.01.015

de Klerk, C., Albiston, H., Bulgarelli, C., Southgate, V., & Hamilton, A. (2020). Observing third-party ostracism enhances facial mimicry in 30-month-olds. *Journal of Experimental Child Psychology, 196*, 104862. https://doi.org/10.1016/j.jecp.2020.104862

Dimberg, U. (1982). Facial reactions to facial expressions. *Psychophysiology, 19*, 643–647. https://doi.org/10.1111/j.1469-8986.1982.tb02516.x

Duffy, K. A., & Chartrand, T. L. (2015). Mimicry: Causes and consequences. *Current Opinion in Behavioral Sciences, 3*, 112–116. https://doi.org/10.1016/j.cobeha.2015.03.002

Estow, S., Jamieson, J. P., & Yates, J. R. (2007). Self-monitoring and mimicry of positive and negative social behaviors. *Journal of Research in Personality, 41*, 425–433. https://doi.org/10.1016/j.jrp.2006.05.003

Farwaha, S., & Obhi, S. S. (2021). The effects of socioeconomic status and situational power on self-other processing in the automatic imitation task. *Experimental Brain Research, 239*, 2519–2528. https://doi.org/10.1007/s00221-021-06152-2

Ferrari, P. F., Bonini, L., & Fogassi, L. (2009). From monkey mirror neurons to primate behaviours: Possible 'direct' and 'indirect' pathways. *Philosophical Transactions of the Royal Society of London. Series B, Biological Sciences, 364*, 2311–2323. https://doi.org/10.1098%2Frstb.2009.0062

Fox, N. A., Bakermans-Kranenburg, M. J., Yoo, K. H., Bowman, L. C., Cannon, E. N., Vanderwert, R. E., … & Van IJzendoorn, M. H. (2016). Assessing human mirror activity with EEG mu rhythm: A meta-analysis. *Psychological Bulletin, 142*, 291. https://doi.org/10.1037%2Fbul0000031

Fridlund, A. J., & Cacioppo, J. T. (1986). Guidelines for human electromyographic research. *Psychophysiology, 23*, 567–589. https://doi.org/10.1111/j.1469-8986.1986.tb00676.x

Gallup, A. C. (2021). On the link between emotional contagion and contagious yawning. *Neuroscience & Biobehavioral Reviews, 121*, 18–19. https://doi.org/10.1016/j.neubiorev.2020.11.023

Genschow, O., van Den Bossche, S., Cracco, E., Bardi, L., Rigoni, D., & Brass, M. (2017). Mimicry and automatic imitation are not correlated. *PLoS One, 12*, e0183784. https://doi.org/10.1371/journal.pone.0183784

Hager, B. M., Yang, A. C., & Gutsell, J. N. (2018). Measuring brain complexity during neural motor resonance. *Frontiers in Neuroscience, 12*, 758. https://doi.org/10.3389/fnins.2018.00758

Hale, J., & Hamilton, A. F. D. C. (2016). Testing the relationship between mimicry, trust and rapport in virtual reality conversations. *Scientific Reports, 6*, 1–11. https://doi.org/10.1038/srep35295

Hayes, L. A., & Watson, J. S. (1981). Neonatal imitation: Fact or artifact? *Developmental Psychology, 17*, 655–660. https://doi.org/10.1037/0012-1649.17.5.655

Heimann, M., & Schaller, J. (1985). Imitative reactions among 14–21 day old infants. *Infant Mental Health Journal, 6*, 31–39. https://doi.org/10.1002/1097-0355(198521)6:1<31::AID-IMHJ2280060106>3.0.CO;2-M

Helt, M. S., Eigsti, I. M., Snyder, P. J., & Fein, D. A. (2010). Contagious yawning in autistic and typical development. *Child Development, 81*, 1620–1631. https://doi.org/10.1111/j.1467-8624.2010.01495.x

Hess, U., & Fischer, A. (2014). Emotional mimicry: Why and when we mimic emotions. *Social and Personality Psychology Compass, 8*, 45–57. https://doi.org/10.1111/spc3.12083

Heyes, C. (2011). Automatic imitation. *Psychological Bulletin, 137*, 463–483. https://doi.org/10.1037/a0022288

Hirschfeld, H. (1997). Do infants have motor responses to sudden surface rotations in prone position? *Journal of Vestibular Research, 7*, 265–276.

Hobson, H. M., & Bishop, D. V. (2016). Mu suppression – Good measure of the human mirror neuron system? *Cortex, 82*, 290–310. https://doi.org/10.1016/j.cortex.2016.03.019

Hobson, H. M., & Bishop, D. V. (2017). The interpretation of mu suppression as an index of mirror neuron activity: Past, present and future. *Royal Society Open Science, 4*, 160662. https://doi.org/10.1098/rsos.160662

Hofree, G., Urgen, B. A., Winkielman, P., & Saygin, A. P. (2015). Observation and imitation of actions performed by humans, androids, and robots: An EMG study. *Frontiers in Human Neuroscience, 9*, 364. https://doi.org/10.3389/fnhum.2015.00364

Hogeveen, J., Chartrand, T. L., & Obhi, S. S. (2015). Social mimicry enhances mu-suppression during action observation. *Cerebral Cortex, 25*, 2076–2082. https://doi.org/10.1093/cercor/bhu016

Hurley, S. L., & Chater, N. (Eds.). (2005). *Perspectives on imitation: Imitation, human development, and culture* (Vol. 2). MIT Press.

Jiménez, L., Recio, S., Méndez, A., Lorda, M. J., Permuy, B., & Méndez, C. (2012). Automatic imitation and spatial compatibility in a key-pressing task. *Acta Psychologica, 141*, 96–103. https://doi.org/10.1016/j.actpsy.2012.07.007

Jones, S. S. (2007). Imitation in infancy: The development of mimicry. *Psychological Science, 18*, 593–599. https://doi.org/10.1111/j.1467-9280.2007.01945.x

Kagan, J., & Snidman, N. (2004). *The long shadow of temperament.* Belknap Press/Harvard University Press.

Leander, N. P., Chartrand, T. L., & Bargh, J. A. (2012). You give me the chills: Embodied reactions to inappropriate amounts of behavioral mimicry. *Psychological Science, 23*, 772–779. https://doi.org/10.1177/0956797611434535

Leys, R. (2020). *Newborn imitation: The stakes of a controversy (Elements in histories of emotions and the senses)*. Cambridge University Press.

MacGowan, T. L., Mirabelli, J., Obhi, S. S., & Schmidt, L. A. (2022). Observed shyness leads to more automatic imitation in early childhood. *Developmental Psychobiology, 64*, e22272. https://doi.org/10.1002/dev.22272

Marshall, P. J., & Meltzoff, A. N. (2014). Neural mirroring mechanisms and imitation in human infants. *Philosophical Transactions of the Royal Society of London. Series B, Biological Sciences, 369*, 20130620. https://doi.org/10.1098%2Frstb.2013.0620

Marshall, P. J., Bouquet, C. A., Thomas, A. L., & Shipley, T. F. (2010). Motor contagion in young children: Exploring social influences on perception-action coupling. *Neural Networks, 23*, 1017–1025. https://doi.org/10.1016/j.neunet.2010.07.007

Masur, E. F., & Rodemaker, J. E. (1999). Mothers' and infants' spontaneous vocal, verbal, and action imitation during the second year. *Merrill-Palmer Quarterly (1982–), 45*, 392–412. https://doi.org/10.1016%2Fj.infbeh.2008.04.005

Meltzoff, A. N. (1988). Infant imitation after a 1-week delay: Long-term memory for novel acts and multiple stimuli. *Developmental Psychology, 24*, 470–476. https://doi.org/10.1037%2F0012-1649.24.4.470

Meltzoff, A. N. (2007). 'Like me': A foundation for social cognition. *Developmental Science, 10*, 126–134. https://doi.org/10.1111%2Fj.1467-7687.2007.00574.x

Meltzoff, A. N., & Moore, M. K. (1977). Imitation of facial and manual gestures by human neonates. *Science, 198*, 75–78. https://doi.org/10.1126/science.897687

Meltzoff, A. N., & Moore, M. K. (1997). Explaining facial imitation: A theoretical model. *Early Development & Parenting, 6*, 179–192. https://doi.org/10.1002%2F(SICI)1099-0917(199709%2F12)6%3A3%2F4%3C179%3A%3AAID-EDP157%3E3.0.CO%3B2-R

Meltzoff, A. N., & Prinz, W. (Eds.). (2002). *The imitative mind: Development, evolution and brain bases* (Vol. 6). Cambridge University Press.

Meltzoff, A. N., Murray, L., Simpson, E., Heimann, M., Nagy, E., Nadel, J., ... & Ferrari, P. F. (2018). Re-examination of Oostenbroek et al. (2016): Evidence for neonatal imitation of tongue protrusion. *Developmental Science, 21*, e12609. https://doi.org/10.1111%2Fdesc.12609

Moran, G., Krupka, A., Tutton, A., & Symons, D. (1987). Patterns of maternal and infant imitation during play. *Infant Behavior and Development, 10*, 477–491. https://doi.org/10.1016/0163-6383(87)90044-0

Neufeld, J., & Chakrabarti, B. (2016). Empathy modulates the rewarding effect of mimicry. *Scientific Reports, 6*, 1–8. https://doi.org/10.1038/srep27751

Nielsen, M., & Dissanayake, C. (2004). Pretend play, mirror self-recognition and imitation: A longitudinal investigation through the second year. *Infant Behavior & Development, 27*, 342–365. https://psycnet.apa.org/doi/10.1016/j.infbeh.2003.12.006

O'Sullivan, E. P., Bijvoet-van den Berg, S., & Caldwell, C. A. (2018). Automatic imitation effects are influenced by experience of synchronous action in children. *Journal of Experimental Child Psychology, 171*, 113–130. https://doi.org/10.1016/j.jecp.2018.01.013

Oostenbroek, J., Slaughter, V., Nielsen, M., & Suddendorf, T. (2013). Why the confusion around neonatal imitation? A review. *Journal of Reproductive and Infant Psychology, 31*, 328–341. https://doi.org/10.1080/02646838.2013.832180

Oostenbroek, J., Suddendorf, T., Nielsen, M., Redshaw, J., Kennedy-Costantini, S., Davis, J., ... & Slaughter, V. (2016). Comprehensive longitudinal study challenges the existence of neonatal imitation in humans. *Current Biology, 26*, 1334–1338. https://doi.org/10.1016/j.cub.2016.03.047

Over, H., & Carpenter, M. (2009). Priming third-party ostracism increases affiliative imitation in children. *Developmental Science, 12*, F1–F8. https://doi.org/10.1111/j.1467-7687.2008.00820.x

Piaget, J. (1962). *Play, dreams and imitation in childhood.* Norton.

Rauchbauer, B., & Grosbras, M. H. (2020). Developmental trajectory of interpersonal motor alignment: Positive social effects and link to social cognition. *Neuroscience & Biobehavioral Reviews, 118*, 411–425. https://doi.org/10.1016%2Fj.neubiorev.2020.07.032

Ray, E., & Heyes, C. (2011). Imitation in infancy: The wealth of the stimulus. *Developmental Science, 14*, 92–105. https://doi.org/10.1111/j.1467-7687.2010.00961.x

Rayson, H., Bonaiuto, J. J., Ferrari, P. F., & Murray, L. (2017). Early maternal mirroring predicts infant motor system activation during facial expression observation. *Scientific Reports, 7*, 1–11. https://www.nature.com/articles/s41598-017-12097-w

Reissland, N. (1988). Neonatal imitation in the first hour of life: Observations in rural Nepal. *Developmental Psychology, 24*, 464–469. https://psycnet.apa.org/doi/10.1037/0012-1649.24.4.464

Rizzolatti, G., Fogassi, L., & Gallese, V. (2001). Neurophysiological mechanisms underlying the understanding and imitation of action. *Nature Reviews Neuroscience, 2*, 661–667. https://doi.org/10.1038/35090060

Robinson, C. W., Hawthorn, A. M., & Rahman, A. N. (2018). Developmental differences in filtering auditory and visual distractors during visual selective attention. *Frontiers in Psychology, 9*, 2564. https://doi.org/10.3389%2Ffpsyg.2018.02564

Simpson, E. A., Murray, L., Paukner, A., & Ferrari, P. F. (2014). The mirror neuron system as revealed through neonatal imitation: Presence from birth, predictive power and evidence of plasticity. *Philosophical Transactions of the Royal Society of London. Series B, Biological Sciences, 369*, 20130289. https://doi.org/10.1098%2Frstb.2013.0289

Stern, D. N. (2002). *The first relationship: Infant and mother*. Harvard University Press.

Strouse, G. A., & Samson, J. E. (2021). Learning from video: A meta-analysis of the video deficit in children ages 0 to 6 years. *Child Development, 92*, e20–e38. https://doi.org/10.1111/cdev.13429

Sundermier, L., Woollacott, M., Roncesvalles, N., & Jensen, J. (2001). The development of balance control in children: Comparisons of EMG and kinetic variables and chronological and developmental groupings. *Experimental Brain Research, 136*, 340–350. https://doi.org/10.1007/s002210000579

van Baaren, R., Janssen, L., Chartrand, T. L., & Dijksterhuis, A. (2009). Where is the love? The social aspects of mimicry. *Philosophical Transactions of the Royal Society of London. Series B, Biological Sciences, 364*, 2381–2389. https://doi.org/10.1098%2Frstb.2009.0057

van Schaik, J. E., & Hunnius, S. (2016). Little chameleons: The development of social mimicry during early childhood. *Journal of Experimental Child Psychology, 147*, 71–81. https://doi.org/10.1016/j.jecp.2016.03.003

van Schaik, J. E., & Hunnius, S. (2018). Modulating mimicry: Exploring the roles of inhibitory control and social understanding in 5-year-olds' behavioral mimicry. *PLoS One, 13*, e0194102. https://doi.org/10.1371%2Fjournal.pone.0194102

van Schaik, J. E, van Baaren, R., Bekkering, H., & Hunnius, S. (2013). Evidence for nonconscious behavior-copying in young children. In *Proceedings of the annual meeting of the cognitive science society, 35*. https://www.researchgate.net/publication/250615430_Evidence_for_nonconscious_behavior-copying_in_young_children

van Schaik, J. E., Endedijk, H. M., Stapel, J. C., & Hunnius, S. (2016). Young children's motor interference is influenced by novel group membership. *Frontiers in Psychology, 7*, Article 321. https://doi.org/10.3389/fpsyg.2016.00321

Verde-Cagiao, M., Nieto, C., & Campos, R. (2022). Mother-infant co-regulation from 0 to 2 years: The role of copy behaviors. A systematic review. *Infant Behavior and Development, 68*, 101749. https://doi.org/10.1016/j.infbeh.2022.101749

Chapter 10
Automatic Imitation of Multiple Agents

Emiel Cracco

Around the turn of the twenty-first century, a number of research groups more or less simultaneously provided the first unequivocal evidence for the longstanding suspicion (Smith, 1759) that humans spontaneously imitate each other (Brass et al., 2000; Chartrand & Bargh, 1999; Stürmer et al., 2000). This sparked a large literature on motor mimicry (Chartrand & Lakin, 2013), automatic imitation (Cracco et al., 2018a; Heyes, 2011), and related phenomena (e.g., Cook et al., 2014; Frischen et al., 2007) that substantially increased our knowledge of how other people's actions inform our own behavior. However, strikingly, research has largely been focused on imitating the actions of a single individual. In contrast, in real life, we often find ourselves surrounded by multiple people, all moving together (e.g., public transportation, family gatherings, concerts, etc.). This raises an important question: how does automatic imitation scale up from one to many? In this chapter, I will discuss recent research on automatic imitation in situations with not one but multiple agents and will present evidence that in multi-agent settings, humans spontaneously simulate the actions of multiple agents in their motor system, allowing action selection to be influenced by several people at once.

In the first part of this chapter, I will discuss recent advances in our understanding of how automatic imitation changes as a function of group size and how this allows for new insights into the mechanisms underlying social group phenomena like conformity (Bond, 2005; Latané, 1981) and rule breaking (Krause et al., 2021). In the second part, I will then go on to discuss automatic imitation in situations where multiple people perform different actions, as is often the case in daily life. In this part, I will also address the question of whether we integrate observed actions

E. Cracco (✉)
Department of Experimental Clinical and Health Psychology, Ghent University, Ghent, Belgium

Institute for Management and Organization, Leuphana University, Lüneburg, Germany
e-mail: emiel.cracco@ugent.be

O. Genschow, E. Cracco (eds.), *Automatic Imitation*,
https://doi.org/10.1007/978-3-031-62634-0_10

in the motor system, as appears to be the case for visual processing (Alvarez, 2011), or rather represent them separately, and the question of whether observing conflicting actions, like planning conflicting actions (Botvinick et al., 2001, 2004), elicits motor conflict and conflict adaptation (Braem et al., 2019). In the third part, I will consider two possible mechanisms underlying automatic imitation of multiple agents: a mechanism where multiple actions are processed simultaneously and a statistical facilitation mechanism where actions are processed randomly (Cracco & Brass, 2018a). Finally, in the last part of this chapter, I will talk about interactions between observing and being part of a group and will discuss how this influences automatic imitation and can help us understand how humans are able to so effortlessly coordinate their movements with other people to achieve common goals (Sebanz et al., 2003).

Does Automatic Imitation Depend on Group Size?

Though studies on automatic imitation have largely ignored the question of how group size influences spontaneous imitative behavior, at least two research lines suggest that such a relationship might exist. In one line of studies, researchers have investigated imitation fidelity in young children as they watch an individual or a group perform a certain action. For example, Herrmann et al. (2013) asked children to imitate an adult model performing an action sequence with a wooden mallet and a pegboard. Each child was assigned to one of four conditions. In the Single/Twice condition, one model performed the same action sequence twice. In the Successive/Twice condition, two models each performed the same action sequence once, one after the other. Finally, in the Synchronous/Once and Synchronous/Twice conditions, two models sitting next to each other performed the same action sequence either once or twice in a row. The results revealed that children imitated the observed action sequence more accurately in the Synchronous conditions than in the other two conditions. However, what this means in terms of motor representation is not entirely clear. Indeed, when asked why they acted like they did, children were more likely to provide convention explanations (e.g., "because I have to do exactly what she does") in the conditions with two actors than in the other condition. These results suggest that children may have imitated more accurately in the Synchronous conditions because they thought that two persons simultaneously doing something in the same way must mean that it is conventional to do so.

A different line of research hinting at a relationship between group size and automatic imitation is research on social group influence (Bond, 2005; Latané, 1981; Latané & Wolf, 1981). The central tenet of this research is the *lightbulb principle*, which states that social influence can be compared to the light emitted by a lightbulb and therefore is a function of the strength, immediacy, and number of sources acting on the individual. In other words, the lightbulb principle predicts that social influence will increase with group size. Applying this to imitation, Milgram et al. (1969) conducted a field experiment in which they manipulated the size of a group of confederates in a busy city street suddenly looking up at a 6th floor window. When analyzing the behavior of other people in the street, they found that passers-by often imitated this behavior and, crucially, were more likely to imitate as group size increased. This finding has since been replicated both in similar (Gallup et al., 2012) and in different contexts (Knowles & Bassett, 1976), in real life and in virtual reality (Jorjafki et al., 2018), and with different types of behavior such as queue formation (Mann, 1977), applause (Freedman & Birsky, 1980), and helping behavior (Darley & Latane, 1968; Fischer et al., 2011).

Interestingly, however, though clearly related to imitation, these findings are typically interpreted in reference to interpretative processes and social norms (Bond, 2005; Latané, 1981). Hence, like research on the imitation of groups in children, it is not clear what this research tells us in terms of motor processing. For example, Milgram et al. (1969) argued that individuals are more likely to follow the gaze of larger groups because they reason that when a large group of people looks in the same direction, they must be looking at something of interest. Similarly, Gallup et al. (2012) found that passers-by did not follow the gaze of a group more when the group could see them, leading them to conclude that gaze following behavior in these situations is not likely explained by some type of mindless conformity, but instead is probably driven by the goal of obtaining information. Finally, Jorjafki et al. (2018) found that participants sometimes did not look up even though they had seen the group, while other times they looked up multiple times. This, also, made them conclude that following the behavior of a group is a thoughtful rather than automatic process.

In sum, although initial research suggests an influence of group size on imitation, this effect has mostly been explained in terms of interpretative processes, leaving open whether groups may also have a more direct influence on motor processing and automatic imitation. To investigate this question, Cracco et al. (2015) decided to extend the well-known imitation-inhibition task of automatic imitation (Brass et al., 2000, 2001) from one agent to two agents (Fig. 10.1). In the original task, participants see a hand on the screen moving one of two fingers while simultaneously seeing a response cue instructing them to move either the same (congruent) or the other (incongruent) finger. Participants are usually faster to respond and make fewer errors on congruent than on incongruent trials, indicating that observing the movement triggered the execution of that same movement (Cracco et al., 2018a; Cracco & Brass, 2019; for an overview, see Chap. 2; this volume).

To test whether automatic imitation increases with group size, Cracco et al. (2015) showed not one but two hands and compared two conditions. In one condition, only one of the two hands performed a congruent or incongruent action, while the other hand remained still. In the other condition, both hands performed the same congruent or incongruent action. The results revealed a larger congruency effect in the latter compared to the former condition, supporting the hypothesis that the actions of both hands triggered the same imitative response and therefore produced a stronger automatic imitation effect. This was further supported by a transcranial magnetic stimulation (TMS) study showing that observing a particular action activates the muscles involved in that action (Fadiga et al., 2005; Naish et al., 2014)

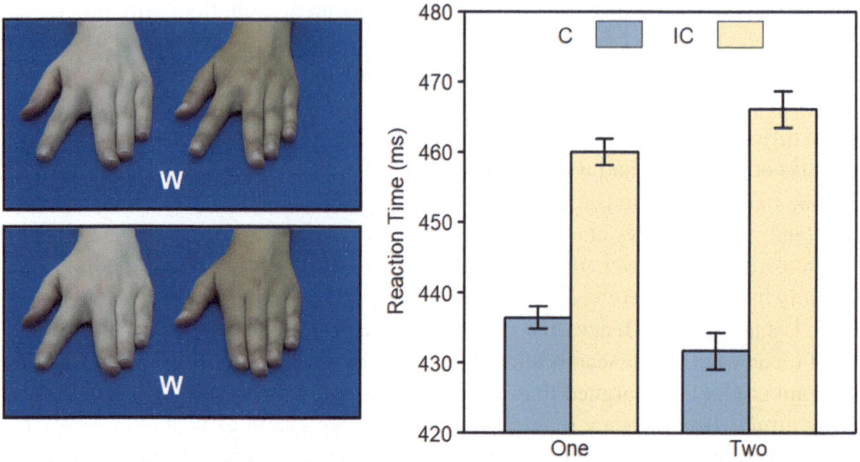

Fig. 10.1 Stimuli and results of Cracco et al. (2015). (Note: In Cracco et al. (2015), participants were asked to abduct their right index finger when the letter W was shown and their right little finger when the letter P was shown. At the same time, either one hand performed a congruent (C) or incongruent (IC) action or both hands performed the same congruent or incongruent action. An example is shown for both conditions of the number of movements manipulation. The results showed that reaction times were faster on congruent than on incongruent trials and that this congruency effect was larger when both stimulus hands performed an action than when only one hand performed an action)

more strongly when the action is performed by two agents compared with one agent (Cracco et al., 2016).

The studies by Cracco et al. (2015, 2016) suggest that group size can influence imitation not only indirectly, via inferential processes, but also directly, by modulating activity in motor areas of the brain. Indeed, in these studies, the hands not only perform meaningless actions (i.e., moving a finger), they are also irrelevant for the task (i.e., participants have to ignore the hands and respond to a symbolic cue). As a result, interpretative processes are unlikely to explain why automatic imitation increased with the number of agents in these tasks. Instead, a more plausible explanation is that group size had a more direct influence on motor excitability and that groups therefore exerted a stronger influence on behavior simply because their actions resonated louder in the motor system (Kemmerer, 2021). However, the studies by Cracco et al. (2015, 2016) included only two agents, whereas research in social group influence typically includes groups of larger sizes. To test whether automatic imitation also increases further as the group grows larger, Cracco and Brass (2018c) followed up on their initial research with another study in which they extended the number of stimulus hands from two to four. The results revealed that automatic imitation increased with the number of hands according to an asymptotic curve, mirroring what had previously been found in research on social group influence (Gallup et al., 2012; Jorjafki et al., 2018; Milgram et al., 1969).

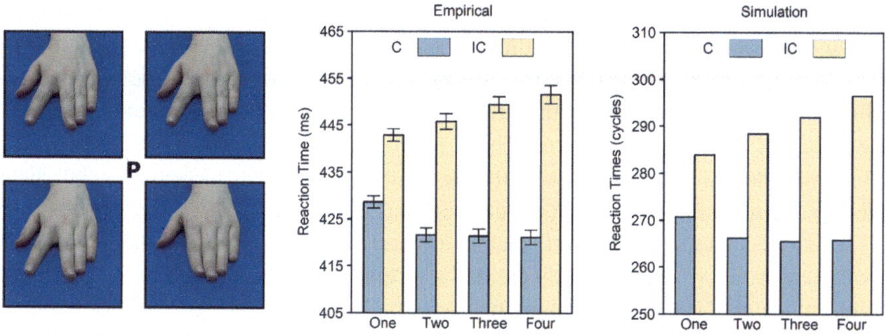

Fig. 10.2 Results of Cracco and Cooper (2019). (Note: Cracco and Cooper (2019) developed a computational model aimed at simulating the asymptotic curve found in Cracco and Brass (2018c) on congruent but not incongruent trials. In Cracco and Brass (2018c), participants were asked to abduct their right index finger when the letter W was shown and their right little finger when the letter P was shown. At the same time, either one hand, two hands, three hands, or four hands performed the same congruent (C) or incongruent (IC) action. An example of an incongruent trial is shown, together with the empirical results of Cracco and Brass (2018c) and the simulated results of Cracco and Cooper (2019))

Interestingly, however, splitting up the results for congruent and incongruent trials revealed that the asymptote was visible only when the required action was congruent to the observed actions. Based on this result, Cracco and Brass (2018c) argued that the reason why imitation reaches an asymptote with increasing group size may be that imitation is regulated by a flexible control mechanism that exerts more or less control depending on the amount of input (i.e., the size of the group) to prevent unwanted imitative responses, similar to what has been proposed in models of action selection (Houghton et al., 1996). In line with this idea, when only congruent trials were included and imitation was beneficial to task performance, the asymptote disappeared (Cracco & Brass, 2018c). A subsequent computational model further confirmed that input-based inhibition could indeed explain this pattern and that such a mechanism may be driven by differences in response conflict between tasks with both congruent and incongruent trials and tasks with only congruent trials (Cracco & Cooper, 2019; Fig. 10.2).

In sum, recent work suggests a close correspondence between findings on social group influence and on automatic imitation. However, there are also two important differences. First, research on social group influence usually looks at imitation of meaningful behavior such as gaze following, whereas research on automatic imitation typically studies imitation of meaningless actions such as lifting a finger. Second, research on social group influence studies imitation in ecologically valid settings, whereas research on automatic imitation instead mostly uses artificial computer tasks. To address the first point, recent studies have started to investigate the influence of group size on gaze following using similar paradigms as those used in research on automatic imitation (Capozzi et al., 2018, 2021; Sun et al., 2017). For example, Sun et al. (2017) asked participants to detect a target letter T appearing on the left or right side of the screen after seeing a group of ten avatars looking in the same or the opposite direction. Even though the group's gaze was not informative of the target's location, thereby limiting the role of inferential processes, participants were faster to respond when the group looked in the direction of the target than when the group looked in the other direction, and this effect again became larger as the group of agents grew in size. These results show that group size has a direct effect on automatic imitation not only for meaningless finger movements, but also for socially relevant behavior, like gaze following.

To address the second point, that automatic imitation research often has low ecological validity, a recent study created a virtual reality task based on the study of Milgram et al. (1969), but following the structure of automatic imitation tasks (Cracco et al., 2022a). In this study, participants stood in a city environment together with a group of ten virtual agents watching a cartoon movie (Fig. 10.3). The task was to detect a fire in the window of a building. That is, every so often, participants would hear an explosion, a collapsing structure, or glass breaking, cueing them to look either to the left or to the right (forced choice trials), or to choose where to look (free choice trials). When participants looked, they could see the fire they had to detect. Together with the sound, a variable number of virtual agents also looked to the left or to the right. As before, the gaze direction of the group was random. In addition, to further ensure that the group did not convey any meaningful information, the target fire was always present both left and right, and participants were made aware of this fact. Nevertheless, the results again revealed a clear relationship between group size and imitation, such that participants were more likely to follow the group's gaze as group size increased. Importantly, this was true not only when imitation was measured indirectly, as a congruency effect on forced choice trials, but also when it was measured directly, as the proportion of free choice trials where participants decided to follow the group.

In sum, research converges on the idea that group size has a direct influence on imitation, presumably because larger groups provide a stronger trigger to the motor system (Cracco et al., 2016) and therefore produce a strong urge to imitate (Capozzi et al., 2018; Cracco & Brass, 2018c; Sun et al., 2017). The fact that basic sensorimotor processes contribute to group influence does not necessarily mean that social norms and interpretative processes do not, however. Indeed, as mentioned, earlier research found clear evidence that they do (Gallup et al., 2012; Jorjafki et al., 2018). Similarly, Cracco et al. (2022a) found evidence that participants sometimes overturned their initial choice to follow the group. These changes of intention (Furstenberg et al., 2015) clearly show that reflexive imitative responses can be overturned by slower, top-down processes and thus suggest that imitation of groups is most likely driven by a two-step model, in which groups first elicit an automatic tendency to imitate, before strategic processes determine whether to act on this tendency. These strategic processes can be driven by task context, but also by social factors, such as whether the to-be-imitated behavior is socially appropriate (Cracco et al., 2018b; Kastendieck et al., 2021) or whether it is displayed by reliable and/or trustworthy individuals (Capozzi et al., 2016, 2021).

Although premature at this point, unraveling the role of imitation in group dynamics may have important real-world consequences for understanding how

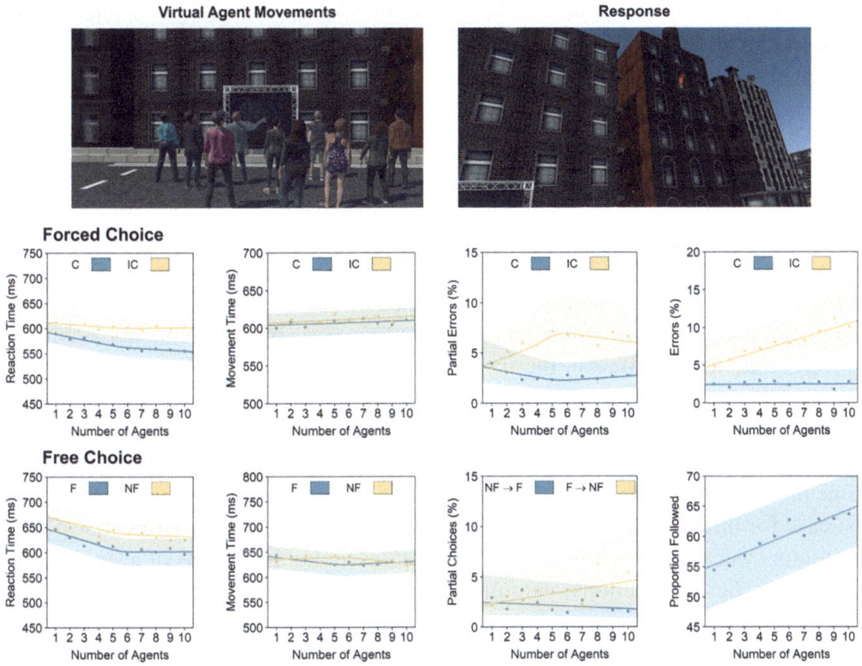

Fig. 10.3 Stimuli and results of Cracco et al. (2022a). (Note: In Cracco et al. (2022a), participants were in a virtual environment, watching a movie clip together with ten virtual agents. Occasionally, they heard a sound (i.e., an explosion, a collapsing structure, or glass breaking), telling them to look up to the left (forced choice), to look up to the right (forced choice), or to choose (free choice). In both locations, there was a fire. Participants' task was to detect the fire and to then look back at the screen. Together with the sound, a variable number (0–10) of virtual agents also looked left or right. The forced choice results revealed a congruency effect, with faster and more accurate responses on congruent (C) than on incongruent (IC) trials. For three of the four dependent measures (reaction time, partial errors, and errors), this congruency effect became larger as the number of virtual agents looking left or right increased. The free choice results revealed a decision effect, with faster responses when participants decided to follow the virtual agents (F) than when they decided not to follow them (NF). It also revealed that participants followed the virtual agents more than could be expected based on chance and that the probability of following them increased with group size. Finally, it revealed that participants sometimes changed their mind. Especially when participants initially followed the gaze of the group, they sometimes corrected their gaze in the other direction (partial choices). (The figures shown here were taken from Cracco et al. (2022a), where they were published under a CC-BY license))

societally relevant phenomena like rule breaking (Krause et al., 2021), violence (Hylander & Granström, 2010; Nassauer, 2019), and helping unfold (Darley & Latane, 1968; Fischer et al., 2011). Understanding these mechanisms, in turn, will be key to learn how a controlled group can be stopped from turning into an uncontrollable crowd. However, while research is now starting to address these questions, it is clear that much more work is still needed to reach this point and that extensive collaborations across relevant disciplines, such as psychology (e.g., Raafat et al., 2009; Tump et al., 2020), biology (e.g., Couzin, 2018; Sumpter, 2006), physics

(Dodds & Watts, 2004; Rahmani et al., 2020), and sociology (e.g., Hylander & Granström, 2010; Nassauer, 2019), will be needed to solve the complex puzzle of how group dynamics shape behavior.

Automatic Imitation of Multiple Different Actions

Though understanding the relationship between group size and automatic imitation is important to better understand the influence of social groups on behavior, very often, the people in our immediate surrounding perform different, not identical actions (e.g., when sitting in the train, you may see some people typing on their laptop and others chatting or on the phone). In terms of motor representation, representing multiple different observed actions is considerably more complex than representing multiple identical observed actions. Indeed, identical actions activate the same motor representation and can therefore be coded as a single action. This is not the case for different actions, however. As such, an important question arises: Can the motor system, which is geared towards representing the actions of a single individual (i.e., our own actions), simultaneously represent different actions of multiple agents?

To address this question, Cracco and Brass (2018b) adapted the imitation-inhibition task to contain not one but four hands (Fig. 10.4). They then compared

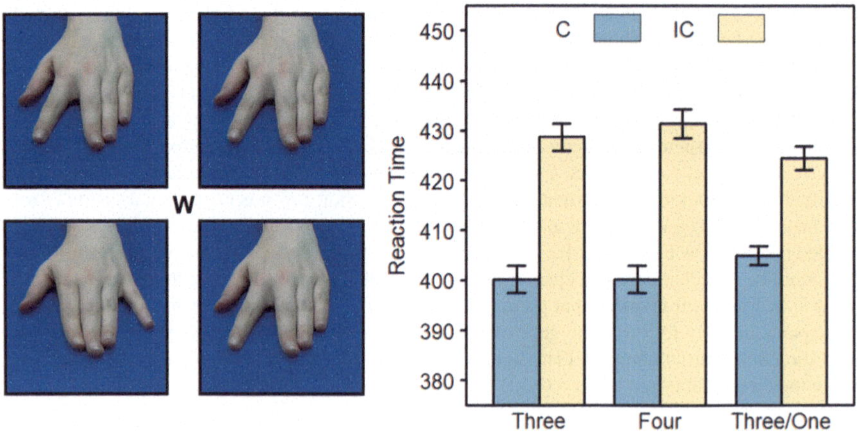

Fig. 10.4 Stimuli and results of Cracco and Brass (2018b). (Note: In Cracco and Brass (2018b), participants were asked to abduct their right index finger when the letter W was shown and their right little finger when the letter P was shown. Three conditions were compared. In the first condition, three hands all performed the same congruent (C) or incongruent (IC) action while the fourth hand did not move. In the second condition, all four hands performed the same congruent or incongruent action. In the third condition, three hands all performed the same congruent or incongruent action while the fourth hand performed the opposite action. An example of this last condition is shown in the figure. The results revealed that the congruency effect (calculated with respect to the majority) was reduced when one hand performed a different action than the other three hands)

three conditions. In the first condition, three hands performed the same action, while the fourth hand did not move. In the second condition, all four hands performed the same action. Finally, in the third and crucial condition, three hands performed one action while the fourth hand performed a different action. If in this last condition all four hands are represented motorically, three hands should trigger one response, whereas the fourth hand should trigger a different response. Hence, in this case, the overall congruency effect, determined with respect to the action performed by the majority, should be smaller in the mixed action condition than in the two control conditions. The results confirmed this hypothesis, suggesting that not just multiple identical but also multiple different observed actions can be simultaneously represented in the motor system.

But what if we see two actions that we cannot simultaneously execute? In their initial experiments, Cracco and Brass (2018b) showed hands moving either the index or little finger. In principle, however, it is possible to move both those fingers at the same time. Hence, perhaps the observed movements were represented as a single, compound action rather than as two different actions. To rule this out, Cracco and Brass (2018b) conducted an additional experiment in which they used the same task, but now with hands pointing either left or right. The rationale here is that even though it is possible to move two different fingers at the same time, it is not possible to simultaneously point the same finger in two directions. Nevertheless, the results revealed exactly the same pattern as before, confirming the hypothesis that even if two observed actions cannot be integrated, they are both represented in the motor system.

The fact that the motor system can simultaneously represent conflicting actions does not necessarily imply that it does not integrate non-conflicting actions into compound actions, however. Looking at research in visual perception, for instance, such integration seems likely. Indeed, research on ensemble processing suggests that humans automatically summarize complex social scenes with multiple agents by computing an average representation across those agents (e.g., Nguyen et al., 2021; Sweeny et al., 2013; Whitney & Leib, 2018). For example, Nguyen et al. (2021) briefly showed an array of 12 persons moving at variable speeds and asked participants to indicate the average speed of the crowd. Results revealed that participants could relatively accurately estimate the average speed despite short presentations (500 ms) and statistical simulations indicated that at least three to four agents were integrated in this period. Similarly, Sweeny et al. (2013) asked observers to indicate the average walking direction of a group of agents and found that participants were highly accurate in estimating the average walking direction of the group. In fact, accuracy in indicating the group's walking direction was better than accuracy in indicating the walking direction of an individual seen alone.

To investigate whether similar integration processes also occur at the motor level, a recent study adapted the imitation-inhibition task to measure imitation of compound movements (Cracco et al., 2022d). More specifically, in a first experiment, the authors showed a single hand lifting either the index finger, the middle finger, or both of these fingers, while asking participants to respond to a colored square requiring them to similarly lift their index finger, middle finger, or both of these fingers.

The results revealed that participants were faster to lift a single finger (index or middle finger) when the stimulus hand lifted a single finger, but faster to lift both fingers (i.e., index + middle finger; a compound response) when the stimulus hand lifted both fingers. In four additional experiments, the authors then investigated whether compound responses would also be triggered when seeing two hands of which one hand lifts the index finger and one hand lifts the middle finger. In contrast, two hands lifting two different fingers was found to activate the motor plan of lifting the fingers individually (i.e., lifting one finger), rather than together. These results thus suggest that the hands' actions were *not* integrated at the motor level but were represented independently instead.

What might drive these differences between visual and motor processing? One possibility is that motor representation mainly relies on input from visual areas with smaller receptive fields, which are less likely to integrate stimuli. Another possibility is that what is integrated are not actions but action parameters (i.e., the parameters that define *how* the action is performed). Indeed, an important difference with studies on ensemble processing is that ensemble processing research typically shows multiple agents performing the same action (Nguyen et al., 2021; Sweeny et al., 2013), whereas Cracco et al. (2022d) showed two agents performing different actions. As a result, a possible explanation for the diverging results is that ensemble processing is applied not to the actions themselves, but to action parameters like speed, movement direction, and force. In line with this idea, research suggests that different aspects of an action such as its goals and kinematics are indeed represented at different levels. However, whether this can explain the lack of motor integration will require further research.

In sum, concurrently observed actions are simultaneously represented in the motor system but are not integrated. What consequences does this have? According to dominant models of action representation, when two motor representations are simultaneously activated, this generates motor conflict (Botvinick et al., 2001, 2004). Although this assumption has received extensive support in the domain of action planning, whether seeing conflicting actions can also trigger motor conflict is not yet known. Initial evidence supporting this hypothesis comes from an fMRI study showing that seeing two different sign language gestures activates the anterior cingulate cortex (ACC; Cracco et al., 2019), a brain area well known to be involved in processing motor conflict (Botvinick et al., 2001, 2004; Braver et al., 2001; Ridderinkhof et al., 2004). However, just because the ACC is involved in motor conflict does not mean that ACC activity necessarily reflects motor conflict (e.g., Shackman et al., 2011; Vassena et al., 2017; Vermeylen et al., 2020). Therefore, to further test whether not just planning but also observing conflicting actions can elicit motor conflict, a recent study looked at the consequences of experiencing motor conflict, namely conflict adaptation (Cracco et al., 2022b).

Conflict adaptation is the phenomenon that conflict triggers changes in cognitive control (Braem et al., 2019). To test whether such adaptation also occurs after observing conflicting actions, Cracco et al. (2022b) conducted a series of experiments in which every trial consisted of two phases. In the first phase, participants saw two hands performing identical or conflicting gestures. Next, in the second phase, they did a prime-probe task (Weissman et al., 2014, 2015) in which they had to respond to a small arrow preceded by a big arrow pointing in the same or different direction. The results revealed that the prime-probe congruency effect, which is a measure of cognitive control, was larger after seeing conflicting gestures than after seeing identical gestures. This pattern is similar to what has been found in previous work on conflict adaptation across tasks (e.g., Braem et al., 2011; Brown et al., 2007; Freund & Nozari, 2018; Notebaert & Verguts, 2008; Scherbaum et al., 2011, 2016) and is usually taken to reflect that motor conflict increases cognitive control, but only in the task where it was experienced and at the cost of reducing control in other tasks (Verguts & Notebaert, 2008, 2009).

Thus, while much is still left to uncover, emerging research on automatic imitation in situations with multiple agents indicates that the brain simultaneously processes the actions of these agents, not just at the visual level but also at the motor level. Furthermore, this appears to be true even when they perform different actions, and even when those actions involve conflicting motor plans (Cracco et al., 2019; Cracco & Brass, 2018b). Yet, there are also important differences between visual and motor processing, as visual processing of scenes with multiple agents often involves integrative coding (Whitney & Leib, 2018), whereas no integration appears to take place at the motor level (Cracco et al., 2022d). Instead, processing multiple observed actions in the motor system seems to trigger a conflict signal (Cracco et al., 2019, 2022b). Although the function of this signal is still unknown, one possibility is that it leads people to process the scene more deeply so that they can resolve their conflict and choose the appropriate course of action (Shamay-Tsoory et al., 2019). Whatever the function (if any) may be, it is clear that extending research on automatic imitation from one to multiple agents opens up a host of new questions that, if studied, hold promise to substantially increase our knowledge on what, when, and why we imitate.

Simultaneous or Random Representation?

While extending the study of automatic imitation to multiple agents holds great promise, it also brings along important challenges. In particular, one key methodological issue in this type of research is the question what mechanism drives the effect of multiple agents on imitative behavior: simultaneous, or random representation? According to the simultaneous representation account, observers simultaneously represent the actions of multiple agents in their motor system and consequently can be influenced by multiple agents at once. In contrast, according to the random representation account, effects of multiple agents on automatic imitation are statistical artefacts that emerge not within but over trials as a result of a mechanism that randomly represents just one of the different observed agents at each time point.

To give an example, Cracco et al. (2015) found increased automatic imitation when participants observed two hands both making the same action compared to two hands of which only one hand made an action. According to the simultaneous representation account, this is because the actions of both hands were simultaneously represented in the motor system, therefore providing a stronger motor trigger and producing a stronger imitative response. In contrast, according to the random representation account, it is because participants on each trial randomly represented one of the two hands in their motor system. On trials where both hands performed an action, this means that they always represented an action. On trials where only one hand performed an action, however, it means that they represented an action only on half of the trials. Across trials, this becomes visible as increased automatic imitation in the condition where both hands performed an action, but only because in this condition, there was a higher probability that at least one action was represented (see Mooshagian et al., 2008, for a similar distinction between independent and interactive processing in the visual system).

To distinguish between both accounts, Cracco et al. (2018a) conducted two experiments in which they adapted previous research on automatic imitation of two hands (e.g., Cracco et al., 2015). In the first experiment, they changed the location of the response cue. More specifically, instead of putting it between the two hands, the cue was now put on top of one specific hand. Crucially, this hand always made a movement. At the same time, the other hand either did not move or made the same movement. According to the random representation account, this should have caused participants to always represent the hand on which the cue was positioned, because this was the location where their attention was directed. Because the cued hand always made a movement, this means that the random representation account expected no imitation of the second hand. In contrast, the simultaneous representation account assumes that participants always represent both hands and therefore still expected stronger automatic imitation when both hands made the same movement than when only the cued hand moved.

The result clearly supported the simultaneous representation account and this was further supported by an additional experiment in which participant were asked to imitate one hand while seeing another hand performing either the same action or a different action. Because intentional and automatic imitation rely on the same mechanisms (Bien et al., 2009; Brass & Heyes, 2005; Hamilton, 2015), the random representation account predicts that the motor system is "occupied" when imitating one hand and therefore no longer predicts an effect of the other hand. Nevertheless, response times where clearly faster when the other hand performed the same action as the to-be-imitated action than when it performed a different action.

In sum, research shows that the effects of multiple agents on automatic imitation are better explained by simultaneous than by random representation. This resonates with the work on conflict processing discussed earlier, as it is hard to see how conflicting actions could elicit motor conflict if only one action was processed at a time (Cracco et al., 2019, 2022b). Yet, these findings do not rule out that random representation never plays a role. Hence, it is important that (especially) new findings on the automatic imitation of multiple agents consider this possibility and rule it out either by experimental means or with control analyses.

Interactions Between Being in and Imitating a Group

So far, the research discussed in this chapter has focused on imitation *of* multiple agents. In the last section, I will instead turn to imitation *with* multiple agents. That is, in daily life, we often see groups of people. But, we are also often part of a group. As a result, an interesting question is whether being part of a group changes imitative behavior. To address this question, Tsai et al. (2011) designed a task in which participants sat on one side of a screen while seeing two hands of which either the hand on their side or both hands made a movement. Participants' task was to imitate the hand on their side as fast as possible, together with a confederate who sat on the other side of the screen and also imitated either the hand on their own side (compatible condition) or the hand on the participant's side, only when the hand on their own side did not move (incompatible condition). In the compatible condition, the number of required responses always matched the number of observed movements (i.e., when one hand moved, one person had to imitate, but when both hands moved, both persons had to imitate). In contrast, in the incompatible condition, the number of required responses never matched the number of observed movements (i.e., when one hand moved, both persons had to imitate, but when two hands moved, only one person had to imitate). The results revealed that participants were faster to imitate in the compatible condition than in the incompatible condition, but only when the two stimulus hands belonged to two different persons.

In other words, imitation was facilitated when the number of imitators matched the number of agents. This, in turn, suggests that actions performed together ("we-actions") are coded fundamentally different than actions performed alone ("me-actions") in the motor system. The results of Tsai et al. (2011) have since been replicated in adults, but intriguingly, not in young children (Essa et al., 2019). While speculative, this potentially indicates that the coding of actions in terms of "me" and "we" is a complex social process that develops only later in life. In another study, Ramenzoni et al. (2014) extended the study of Tsai et al. (2011) from discrete to continuous actions. In their study, participants saw two hands alternately tapping the index finger and were asked to tap their own index finger in synchrony with one of those two hands, either alone (solo condition) or together with another person synchronizing with the second hand (joint condition). In line with Tsai et al. (2011), the results revealed that synchrony in the joint condition was higher when the hands belonged to two different persons than when they belonged to the same person and vice versa in the solo condition.

Taken together, these findings show that when we act together with someone else, we integrate our own actions with those of the other person to form a higher-order "we-representation" (Gallotti & Frith, 2013) that is then used in action planning and determines how we process and respond to the actions of other people (Essa et al., 2019; Ramenzoni et al., 2014; Tsai et al., 2011). Such we-representations also have an important function in joint action, where they help individuals to coordinate their actions with other people to execute complex motor tasks that rely on the seamless cooperation of two or more persons (Kourtis et al., 2019). As such, they may form an essential component of social interaction more broadly.

Conclusion

We live in a complex social world. Navigating ourselves in this world critically requires us to adjust our own action plans to the actions of others. Automatic imitation and its underlying mechanisms play an important role in this process (Colling et al., 2013; Cracco et al., 2018a; Wilson & Knoblich, 2005). However, while social situations often involve many people, research on automatic imitation has mostly focused on dyadic situations. In this chapter, I discussed recent work that bridges this gap by investigating how automatic imitation varies as a function of group size (e.g., Capozzi et al., 2018; Cracco et al., 2015, 2022a; Sun et al., 2017), how it combines the actions of different people (Cracco et al., 2015, 2022d; Cracco & Brass, 2018b), and how it is affected by being part of a group oneself (e.g., Essa et al., 2019; Ramenzoni et al., 2014; Tsai et al., 2011). Overall, these studies indicate that automatic imitation is a complex process that takes into the account the actions of the different people in our surrounding (for a computational model, see Cracco & Cooper, 2019) and interacts with regulatory processes to adjust cognitive control parameters as a function of both group size (Cracco & Brass, 2018c) and the topographical relation between the different observed actions (Cracco et al., 2022b).

This research on automatic imitation goes hand in hand with an increasing interest in social perception beyond the dyad more generally. Discussing this latter research goes beyond the scope of this chapter, but recent years have seen many exciting advances in our understanding of how we process not just individuals but also the social relationships between individuals (e.g., Papeo, 2020; Papeo et al., 2017; Vestner et al., 2020) and their actions (e.g., Alp et al., 2017; Bellot et al., 2021; Cracco et al., 2022c), of how we summarize complex social scenes in the visual system (e.g., Elias et al., 2017; McHugh et al., 2010; Nguyen et al., 2021; Sweeny et al., 2013), and of how we go from processing actions to processing interactions (e.g., Ding et al., 2017; Isik et al., 2017; Oomen et al., 2022; Walbrin & Koldewyn, 2019; Yin et al., 2018). Going further along this path is sure to culminate in a better understanding of social cognition and of how we cope so effortlessly with the vast complexity that is social life.

References

Alp, N., Nikolaev, A. R., Wagemans, J., & Kogo, N. (2017). EEG frequency tagging dissociates between neural processing of motion synchrony and human quality of multiple point-light dancers. *Scientific Reports, 7*, 44012. https://doi.org/10.1038/srep44012

Alvarez, G. A. (2011). Representing multiple objects as an ensemble enhances visual cognition. *Trends in Cognitive Sciences, 15*, 3. https://doi.org/10.1016/j.tics.2011.01.003

Bellot, E., Abassi, E., & Papeo, L. (2021). Moving toward versus away from another: How body motion direction changes the representation of bodies and actions in the visual cortex. *Cerebral Cortex, 31*, 2670–2685. https://doi.org/10.1093/cercor/bhaa382

Bien, N., Roebroeck, A., Goebel, R., & Sack, A. T. (2009). The Brain's intention to imitate: The neurobiology of intentional versus automatic imitation. *Cerebral Cortex, 19*, 2338–2351. https://doi.org/10.1093/cercor/bhn251

Bond, R. (2005). Group size and conformity. *Group Processes & Intergroup Relations, 8*, 331–354. https://doi.org/10.1177/1368430205056464

Botvinick, M. M., Braver, T. S., Barch, D. M., Carter, C. S., & Cohen, J. D. (2001). Conflict monitoring and cognitive control. *Psychological Review, 108*, 3. 624–652. https://doi.org/10.1037/0033-295x.108.3.624

Botvinick, M. M., Cohen, J. D., & Carter, C. S. (2004). Conflict monitoring and anterior cingulate cortex: An update. *Trends in Cognitive Sciences, 8*, 539–546. https://doi.org/10.1016/j.tics.2004.10.003

Braem, S., Verguts, T., & Notebaert, W. (2011). Conflict adaptation by means of associative learning. *Journal of Experimental Psychology: Human Perception and Performance, 37*, 1662–1666. https://doi.org/10.1037/a0024385

Braem, S., Bugg, J. M., Schmidt, J. R., Crump, M. J. C., Weissman, D. H., Notebaert, W., & Egner, T. (2019). Measuring adaptive control in conflict tasks. *Trends in Cognitive Sciences, 23*, 769–783. https://doi.org/10.1016/j.tics.2019.07.002

Brass, M., & Heyes, C. (2005). Imitation: Is cognitive neuroscience solving the correspondence problem? *Trends in Cognitive Sciences, 9*, 489–495. https://doi.org/10.1016/j.tics.2005.08.007

Brass, M., Bekkering, H., Wohlschläger, A., & Prinz, W. (2000). Compatibility between observed and executed finger movements: Comparing symbolic, spatial, and imitative cues. *Brain and Cognition, 44*, 124–143. https://doi.org/10.1006/brcg.2000.1225

Brass, M., Bekkering, H., & Prinz, W. (2001). Movement observation affects movement execution in a simple response task. *Acta Psychologica, 106*, 1–2. https://doi.org/10.1016/S0001-6918(00)00024-X

Braver, T. S., Barch, D. M., Gray, J. R., Molfese, D. L., & Snyder, A. (2001). Anterior cingulate cortex and response conflict: Effects of frequency, inhibition and errors. *Cerebral Cortex, 11*, 825–836. https://doi.org/10.1093/cercor/11.9.825

Brown, J. W., Reynolds, J. R., & Braver, T. S. (2007). A computational model of fractionated conflict-control mechanisms in task-switching. *Cognitive Psychology, 55*, 37–85. https://doi.org/10.1016/j.cogpsych.2006.09.005

Capozzi, F., Becchio, C., Willemse, C., & Bayliss, A. P. (2016). Followers are not followed: Observed group interactions modulate subsequent social attention. *Journal of Experimental Psychology: General, 145*, 531–535. https://doi.org/10.1037/xge0000167

Capozzi, F., Bayliss, A. P., & Ristic, J. (2018). Gaze following in multiagent contexts: Evidence for a quorum-like principle. *Psychonomic Bulletin & Review, 25*, 2260–2266. https://doi.org/10.3758/s13423-018-1464-3

Capozzi, F., Bayliss, A. P., & Ristic, J. (2021). Standing out from the crowd: Both cue numerosity and social information affect attention in multi-agent contexts. *Quarterly Journal of Experimental Psychology, 74*, 1737–1746. https://doi.org/10.1177/17470218211013028

Chartrand, T. L., & Bargh, J. A. (1999). The chameleon effect: The perception-behavior link and social interaction. *Journal of Personality and Social Psychology, 76*, 893–910. https://doi.org/10.1037/0022-3514.76.6.893

Chartrand, T. L., & Lakin, J. L. (2013). The antecedents and consequences of human behavioral mimicry. *Annual Review of Psychology, 64*, 285–308. https://doi.org/10.1146/annurev-psych-113011-143754

Colling, L. J., Knoblich, G., & Sebanz, N. (2013). How does "mirroring" support joint action? *Cortex, 49*, 2964–2965. https://doi.org/10.1016/j.cortex.2013.06.006

Cook, R., Bird, G., Catmur, C., Press, C., & Heyes, C. (2014). Mirror neurons: From origin to function. *Behavioral and Brain Sciences, 37*, 177–192. https://doi.org/10.1017/S0140525X13000903

Couzin, I. D. (2018). Synchronization: The key to effective communication in animal collectives. *Trends in Cognitive Sciences, 22*, 844–846. https://doi.org/10.1016/j.tics.2018.08.001

Cracco, E., & Brass, M. (2018a). Automatic imitation of multiple agents: Simultaneous or random representation? *Journal of Experimental Psychology: Human Perception & Performance, 44*, 729–740. https://doi.org/10.1037/xhp0000489

Cracco, E., & Brass, M. (2018b). Motor simulation of multiple observed actions. *Cognition, 180*, 200–205. https://doi.org/10.1016/j.cognition.2018.07.007

Cracco, E., & Brass, M. (2018c). The role of sensorimotor processes in social group contagion. *Cognitive Psychology, 103*, 23–41. https://doi.org/10.1016/j.cogpsych.2018.02.001

Cracco, E., & Brass, M. (2019). Reaction time indices of automatic imitation measure imitative response tendencies. *Consciousness and Cognition, 68*, 115–118. https://psycnet.apa.org/doi/10.1016/j.concog.2019.01.001

Cracco, E., & Cooper, R. P. (2019). Automatic imitation of multiple agents: A computational model. *Cognitive Psychology, 113*, 101224. https://doi.org/10.1016/j.cogpsych.2019.101224

Cracco, E., De Coster, L., Andres, M., & Brass, M. (2015). Motor simulation beyond the dyad: Automatic imitation of multiple actors. *Journal of Experimental Psychology: Human Perception and Performance, 41*, 1488–1501. https://doi.org/10.1037/a0039737

Cracco, E., De Coster, L., Andres, M., & Brass, M. (2016). Mirroring multiple agents: Motor resonance during action observation is modulated by the number of agents. *Social Cognitive and Affective Neuroscience, 11*, 1422–1427. https://doi.org/10.1093/scan/nsw059

Cracco, E., Bardi, L., Desmet, C., Genschow, O., Rigoni, D., De Coster, L., Radkova, I., Deschrijver, E., & Brass, M. (2018a). Automatic imitation: A meta-analysis. *Psychological Bulletin, 144*, 453–500. https://doi.org/10.1037/bul0000143

Cracco, E., Genschow, O., Radkova, I., & Brass, M. (2018b). Automatic imitation of pro- and antisocial gestures: Is implicit social behavior censored? *Cognition, 170C*, 179–189. https://doi.org/10.1016/j.cognition.2017.09.019

Cracco, E., Keysers, C., Clauwaert, A., & Brass, M. (2019). Representing multiple observed actions in the motor system. *Cerebral Cortex, 29*, 3631–3641. https://doi.org/10.1093/cercor/bhy237

Cracco, E., Bernardet, U., Sevenhant, R., Vandenhouwe, N., Copman, F., Durnez, W., Bombeke, K., & Brass, M. (2022a). Evidence for a two-step model of social group influence. *IScience, 25*, 104891. https://doi.org/10.1016/j.isci.2022.104891

Cracco, E., Braem, S., & Brass, M. (2022b). Observing conflicting actions elicits conflict adaptation. *Journal of Experimental Psychology: General, 151*, 493–505. https://doi.org/10.1037/xge0001089

Cracco, E., Lee, H., van Belle, G., Quenon, L., Haggard, P., Rossion, B., & Orgs, G. (2022c). EEG frequency tagging reveals the integration of form and motion cues into the perception of group movement. *Cerebral Cortex, 32*, 2843–2857. https://doi.org/10.1093/cercor/bhab385

Cracco, E., Van Isterdael, C., Genschow, O., & Brass, M. (2022d). Concurrently observed actions are represented not as compound actions but as independent actions. *Journal of Experimental Psychology: Human Perception & Performance, 48*, 1172–1185. https://doi.org/10.1037/xhp0001043

Darley, J. M., & Latane, B. (1968). Bystander intervention in emergencies: Diffusion of responsibility. *Journal of Personality and Social Psychology, 8*, 377–383. https://doi.org/10.1037/h0025589

de Hamilton, A. F. C. (2015). The neurocognitive mechanisms of imitation. *Current Opinion in Behavioral Sciences, 3*, 63–67. https://doi.org/10.1016/j.cobeha.2015.01.011

Ding, X., Gao, Z., & Shen, M. (2017). Two equals one: Two human actions during social interaction are grouped as one unit in working memory. *Psychological Science, 28*, 1311–1320. https://doi.org/10.1177/0956797617707318

Dodds, P. S., & Watts, D. J. (2004). Universal behavior in a generalized model of contagion. *Physical Review Letters, 92*, 218701. https://doi.org/10.1103/PhysRevLett.92.218701

Elias, E., Dyer, M., & Sweeny, T. D. (2017). Ensemble perception of dynamic emotional groups. *Psychological Science, 28*, 193–203. https://doi.org/10.1177/0956797616678188

Essa, F., Sebanz, N., & Diesendruck, G. (2019). The automaticity of children's imitative group bias. *Cognitive Development, 52*, 100799. https://doi.org/10.1016/j.cogdev.2019.100799

Fadiga, L., Craighero, L., & Olivier, E. (2005). Human motor cortex excitability during the perception of others' action. *Current Opinion in Neurobiology, 15*, 213–218. https://doi.org/10.1016/j.conb.2005.03.013

Fischer, P., Krueger, J. I., Greitemeyer, T., Vogrincic, C., Kastenmüller, A., Frey, D., Heene, M., Wicher, M., & Kainbacher, M. (2011). The bystander-effect: A meta-analytic review on bystander intervention in dangerous and non-dangerous emergencies. *Psychological Bulletin, 137*, 517–537. https://doi.org/10.1037/a0023304

Freedman, J. L., & Birsky, J. (1980). Environmental determinants of behavioral contagion: Density and number. *Basic and Applied Social Psychology, 1*, 155–161. https://psycnet.apa.org/doi/10.1207/s15324834basp0102_4

Freund, M., & Nozari, N. (2018). Is adaptive control in language production mediated by learning? *Cognition, 176*, 107–130. https://doi.org/10.1016/j.cognition.2018.03.009

Frischen, A., Bayliss, A. P., & Tipper, S. P. (2007). Gaze cueing of attention: Visual attention, social cognition, and individual differences. *Psychological Bulletin, 133*, 694–724. https://doi.org/10.1037/0033-2909.133.4.694

Furstenberg, A., Breska, A., Sompolinsky, H., & Deouell, L. Y. (2015). Evidence of change of intention in picking situations. *Journal of Cognitive Neuroscience, 27*, 2133–2146. https://doi.org/10.1162/jocn_a_00842

Gallotti, M., & Frith, C. D. (2013). Social cognition in the we-mode. *Trends in Cognitive Sciences, 17*, 160–165. https://doi.org/10.1016/j.tics.2013.02.002

Gallup, A. C., Hale, J. J., Sumpter, D. J. T., Garnier, S., Kacelnik, A., Krebs, J. R., & Couzin, I. D. (2012). Visual attention and the acquisition of information in human crowds. *Proceedings of the National Academy of Sciences, 109*, 7245–7250. https://doi.org/10.1073/pnas.1116141109

Herrmann, P. A., Legare, C. H., Harris, P. L., & Whitehouse, H. (2013). Stick to the script: The effect of witnessing multiple actors on children's imitation. *Cognition, 129*, 536–543. https://doi.org/10.1016/j.cognition.2013.08.010

Heyes, C. (2011). Automatic imitation. *Psychological Bulletin, 137*, 463–483. https://doi.org/10.1037/a0022288

Houghton, G., Tipper, S. P., Weaver, B., & Shore, D. I. (1996). Inhibition and interference in selective attention: Some tests of a neural network model. *Visual Cognition, 3*, 119–164. https://doi.org/10.1080/713756733

Hylander, I., & Granström, K. (2010). Organizing for a peaceful crowd: An example of a football match. *Forum Qualitative Sozialforschung/Forum: Qualitative Social Research, 11*, 2. https://doi.org/10.17169/fqs-11.2.1462

Isik, L., Koldewyn, K., Beeler, D., & Kanwisher, N. (2017). Perceiving social interactions in the posterior superior temporal sulcus. *Proceedings of the National Academy of Sciences, 114*, E9145–E9152. https://doi.org/10.1073/pnas.1714471114

Jorjafki, E. M., Sagarin, B. J., & Butail, S. (2018). Drawing power of virtual crowds. *Journal of the Royal Society Interface, 15*, 20180335. https://doi.org/10.1098/rsif.2018.0335

Kastendieck, T., Mauersberger, H., Blaison, C., Ghalib, J., & Hess, U. (2021). Laughing at funerals and frowning at weddings: Top-down influences of context-driven social judgments on emotional mimicry. *Acta Psychologica, 212*, 103195. https://doi.org/10.1016/j.actpsy.2020.103195

Kemmerer, D. (2021). What modulates the mirror neuron system during action observation?: Multiple factors involving the action, the actor, the observer, the relationship between actor and observer, and the context. *Progress in Neurobiology, 205*, 102128. https://doi.org/10.1016/j.pneurobio.2021.102128

Knowles, E. S., & Bassett, R. L. (1976). Groups and crowds as social entities: Effects of activity, size, and member similarity on nonmembers. *Journal of Personality and Social Psychology, 34*, 837–845. https://doi.org/10.1037/0022-3514.34.5.837

Kourtis, D., Woźniak, M., Sebanz, N., & Knoblich, G. (2019). Evidence for we-representations during joint action planning. *Neuropsychologia, 131*, 73–83. https://doi.org/10.1016/j.neuropsychologia.2019.05.029

Krause, J., Romanczuk, P., Cracco, E., Arlidge, W., Nassauer, A., & Brass, M. (2021). Collective rule breaking. *Trends In Cognitive Sciences, 25*, 1082–1095. https://doi.org/10.1016/j.tics.2021.08.003

Latané, B. (1981). The psychology of social impact. *American Psychologist, 36*, 343–356. https://psycnet.apa.org/doi/10.1037/0003-066X.36.4.343

Latané, B., & Wolf, S. (1981). The social impact of majorities and minorities. *Psychological Review, 88*, 438–453. https://doi.org/10.1037/0033-295X.88.5.438
Mann, L. (1977). The effect of stimulus queues on queue-joining behavior. *Journal of Personality and Social Psychology, 35*, 437–442. https://psycnet.apa.org/doi/10.1037/0022-3514.35.6.437
McHugh, J. E., McDonnell, R., O'Sullivan, C., & Newell, F. N. (2010). Perceiving emotion in crowds: The role of dynamic body postures on the perception of emotion in crowded scenes. *Experimental Brain Research, 204*, 361–372. https://doi.org/10.1007/s00221-009-2037-5
Milgram, S., Bickman, L., & Berkowitz, L. (1969). Note on the drawing power of crowds of different size. *Journal of Personality and Social Psychology, 13*, 79–82. https://doi.org/10.1037/h0028070
Mooshagian, E., Kaplan, J., Zaidel, E., & Iacoboni, M. (2008). Fast visuomotor processing of redundant targets: The role of the right temporo-parietal junction. *PLoS One, 3*, e2348. https://doi.org/10.1371/journal.pone.0002348
Naish, K. R., Houston-Price, C., Bremner, A. J., & Holmes, N. P. (2014). Effects of action observation on corticospinal excitability: Muscle specificity, direction, and timing of the mirror response. *Neuropsychologia, 64*, 331–348. https://doi.org/10.1016/j.neuropsychologia.2014.09.034
Nassauer, A. (2019). *Situational breakdowns: Understanding protest violence and other surprising outcomes*. Oxford University Press. https://doi.org/10.1093/oso/9780190922061.001.0001
Nguyen, T. T. N., Vuong, Q. C., Mather, G., & Thornton, I. M. (2021). Ensemble coding of crowd speed using biological motion. *Attention, Perception, & Psychophysics, 83*, 1014–1035. https://doi.org/10.3758/s13414-020-02163-3
Notebaert, W., & Verguts, T. (2008). Cognitive control acts locally. *Cognition, 106*, 1071–1080. https://doi.org/10.1016/j.cognition.2007.04.011
Oomen, D., Cracco, E., Brass, M., & Wiersema, J. R. (2022). EEG frequency tagging evidence of social interaction recognition. *Social Cognitive and Affective Neuroscience, 17*, 1044–1053. https://doi.org/10.1093/scan/nsac032
Papeo, L. (2020). Twos in human visual perception. *Cortex, 132*, 473–478. https://doi.org/10.1016/j.cortex.2020.06.005
Papeo, L., Stein, T., & Soto-Faraco, S. (2017). The two-body inversion effect. *Psychological Science, 28*, 369–379. https://doi.org/10.1177/0956797616685769
Raafat, R. M., Chater, N., & Frith, C. (2009). Herding in humans. *Trends in Cognitive Sciences, 13*, 420–428. https://doi.org/10.1016/j.tics.2009.08.002
Rahmani, P., Peruani, F., & Romanczuk, P. (2020). Flocking in complex environments – Attention trade-offs in collective information processing. *PLoS Computational Biology, 16*, e1007697. https://doi.org/10.1371/journal.pcbi.1007697
Ramenzoni, V. C., Sebanz, N., & Knoblich, G. (2014). Scaling up perception–action links: Evidence from synchronization with individual and joint action. *Journal of Experimental Psychology: Human Perception and Performance, 40*, 1551–1565. https://doi.org/10.1037/a0036925
Ridderinkhof, K. R., Ullsperger, M., Crone, E. A., & Nieuwenhuis, S. (2004). The role of the medial frontal cortex in cognitive control. *Science, 306*, 443–447. https://doi.org/10.1126/science.1100301
Scherbaum, S., Fischer, R., Dshemuchadse, M., & Goschke, T. (2011). The dynamics of cognitive control: Evidence for within-trial conflict adaptation from frequency-tagged EEG. *Psychophysiology, 48*, 591–600. https://doi.org/10.1111/j.1469-8986.2010.01137.x
Scherbaum, S., Frisch, S., & Dshemuchadse, M. (2016). Switches of stimulus tagging frequencies interact with the conflict-driven control of selective attention, but not with inhibitory control. *International Journal of Psychophysiology, 99*, 103–107. https://doi.org/10.1016/j.ijpsycho.2015.11.012
Sebanz, N., Knoblich, G., & Prinz, W. (2003). Representing others' actions: Just like one's own? *Cognition, 88*, B11–B21. https://doi.org/10.1016/s0010-0277(03)00043-x
Shackman, A. J., Salomons, T. V., Slagter, H. A., Fox, A. S., Winter, J. J., & Davidson, R. J. (2011). The integration of negative affect, pain and cognitive control in the cingulate cortex. *Nature Reviews Neuroscience, 12*, 154–167. https://doi.org/10.1038/nrn2994

Shamay-Tsoory, S. G., Saporta, N., Marton-Alper, I. Z., & Gvirts, H. Z. (2019). Herding brains: A core neural mechanism for social alignment. *Trends in Cognitive Sciences, 23*, 174–186. https://doi.org/10.1016/j.tics.2019.01.002

Smith, A. (1759). *The theory of moral sentiments*. A. Miller. https://doi.org/10.1093/oseo/instance.00042831

Stürmer, B., Aschersleben, G., Prinz, W., Sturmer, B., Aschersleben, G., & Prinz, W. (2000). Correspondence effects with manual gestures and postures: A study of imitation. *Journal of Experimental Psychology-Human Perception and Performance, 26*, 1746–1759. https://doi.org/10.1037/0096-1523.26.6.1746

Sumpter, D. J. T. (2006). The principles of collective animal behaviour. *Philosophical Transactions of the Royal Society B: Biological Sciences, 361*, 5–22. https://doi.org/10.1098/rstb.2005.1733

Sun, Z., Yu, W., Zhou, J., & Shen, M. (2017). Perceiving crowd attention: Gaze following in human crowds with conflicting cues. *Attention, Perception, & Psychophysics, 79*, 1039–1049. https://doi.org/10.3758/s13414-017-1303-z

Sweeny, T. D., Haroz, S., & Whitney, D. (2013). Perceiving group behavior: Sensitive ensemble coding mechanisms for biological motion of human crowds. *Journal of Experimental Psychology: Human Perception and Performance, 39*, 329–337. https://doi.org/10.1037/a0028712

Tsai, J. C.-C., Sebanz, N., & Knoblich, G. (2011). The GROOP effect: Groups mimic group actions. *Cognition, 118*, 135–140. https://doi.org/10.1016/j.cognition.2010.10.007

Tump, A. N., Pleskac, T. J., & Kurvers, R. H. J. M. (2020). Wise or mad crowds? The cognitive mechanisms underlying information cascades. *Science Advances, 6*, eabb0266. https://doi.org/10.1126/sciadv.abb0266

Vassena, E., Holroyd, C. B., & Alexander, W. H. (2017). Computational models of anterior cingulate cortex: At the crossroads between prediction and effort. *Frontiers in Neuroscience, 11*, 316. https://doi.org/10.3389/fnins.2017.00316

Verguts, T., & Notebaert, W. (2008). Hebbian learning of cognitive control: Dealing with specific and nonspecific adaptation. *Psychological Review, 115*, 518–525. https://doi.org/10.1037/0033-295X.115.2.518

Verguts, T., & Notebaert, W. (2009). Adaptation by binding: A learning account of cognitive control. *Trends in Cognitive Sciences, 13*, 252–257. https://doi.org/10.1016/j.tics.2009.02.007

Vermeylen, L., Wisniewski, D., González-García, C., Hoofs, V., Notebaert, W., & Braem, S. (2020). Shared neural representations of cognitive conflict and negative affect in the medial frontal cortex. *Journal of Neuroscience, 40*, 8715–8725. https://doi.org/10.1523/JNEUROSCI.1744-20.2020

Vestner, T., Gray, K. L. H., & Cook, R. (2020). Why are social interactions found quickly in visual search tasks? *Cognition, 200*, 104270. https://doi.org/10.1016/j.cognition.2020.104270

Walbrin, J., & Koldewyn, K. (2019). Dyadic interaction processing in the posterior temporal cortex. *NeuroImage, 198*, 296–302. https://doi.org/10.1016/j.neuroimage.2019.05.027

Weissman, D. H., Jiang, J., & Egner, T. (2014). Determinants of congruency sequence effects without learning and memory confounds. *Journal of Experimental Psychology: Human Perception and Performance, 40*, 2022–2037. https://doi.org/10.1037/a0037454

Weissman, D. H., Colter, K., Drake, B., & Morgan, C. (2015). The congruency sequence effect transfers across different response modes. *Acta Psychologica, 161*, 86–94. https://doi.org/10.1016/j.actpsy.2015.08.010

Whitney, D., & Leib, A. Y. (2018). Ensemble perception. *Annual Review of Psychology, 69*, 105–129. https://doi.org/10.1146/annurev-psych-010416-044232

Wilson, M., & Knoblich, G. (2005). The case for motor involvement in perceiving conspecifics. *Psychological Bulletin, 131*, 460–473. https://doi.org/10.1037/0033-2909.131.3.460

Yin, J., Xu, H., Duan, J., & Shen, M. (2018). Object-based attention on social units: Visual selection of hands performing a social interaction. *Psychological Science, 29*, 1040–1048. https://doi.org/10.1177/0956797617749636

Chapter 11
Social Modulation of Imitative Behavior

Oliver Genschow and Emiel Cracco

As the saying goes "monkey see, monkey do," individuals have the automatic tendency to imitate a wide range of different behaviors such as facial expressions (e.g., Dimberg, 1982), characteristics of language (e.g., Cappella & Planalp, 1981), emotions (e.g., Hess & Fischer, 2014), postures (e.g., LaFrance, 1982), gestures (e.g., Cracco et al., 2018b), or simple movements (e.g., Genschow & Florack, 2014; Genschow et al., 2013; Genschow & Schindler, 2016). An often put-forward claim in the literature is that imitative behavior as a social phenomenon should be modulated by social factors. However, since some researchers find evidence for social modulation, but others do not, the current literature leaves open whether and how social factors actually influence imitative behavior (e.g., Cracco & Brass, 2018; Ramsey, 2018; Ramsey & Ward, 2020). In this chapter, we shed light onto the debate of whether and how social factors influence imitative behavior by reviewing current theories on social modulation of imitative behavior as well as the evidence in favor and against these theories. We will continue by discussing potential reasons for the mixed findings and then suggest potential paths for future research. In this chapter, we mainly focus on behavioral mimicry and automatic imitation, because social modulation has been tested especially for these two forms of imitative behavior.

O. Genschow (✉)
School of Management and Technology, Leuphana University Lüneburg, Lüneburg, Germany
e-mail: oliver.genschow@leuphana.de

E. Cracco
Department of Experimental Clinical and Health Psychology, Ghent University, Ghent, Belgium
e-mail: emiel.cracco@ugent.be

O. Genschow, E. Cracco (eds.), *Automatic Imitation*,
https://doi.org/10.1007/978-3-031-62634-0_11

Theories of Social Modulation

To assess imitative behavior, different tasks have been developed (for an overview, see Chap. 2; this volume). Cognitive psychologists measure *automatic imitation* with stimulus response compatibility (SRC) tasks, such as the imitation-inhibition task (Brass et al., 2000). In this task, participants respond in multiple trials to an imperative cue, such as the number "1" or "2," by lifting either the index or middle finger. In congruent trials, participants see another person's hand lifting the same finger, and in incongruent trials, they see the other person's hand lifting the other finger. Automatic imitation in such an SRC task refers to the finding that participants respond faster and with fewer errors to congruent than to incongruent trials (for reviews, see Cracco et al., 2018a; Heyes, 2011). To investigate imitative behavior in more natural settings, social psychologists measure *behavioral mimicry*. In a typical experiment (e.g., Chartrand & Bargh, 1999), participants interact with a confederate in two conversations. During each conversation, the confederate engages in one of two target actions, such as touching the face or moving the leg. The typical finding in mimicry experiments is that participants more often touch their face than move their leg when the confederate touches their face and vice versa when the confederate moves their legs. Regardless of the method used to assess imitative behavior, a frequent claim in the literature is that imitative behavior as a social phenomenon should be modulated by social factors. In the last two decades, two different theories have been put forward to explain such social modulation: motivational theories and self-other overlap theories.

Motivational Theories

Motivational theories of imitation (e.g., Chartrand & Dalton, 2009; Wang & Hamilton, 2012) postulate that people use imitation either consciously or unconsciously as a tool to affiliate with others. As a result, individuals are expected to imitate others more strongly when they have an affiliation goal. For example, the theory of social top-down response modulation (STORM; Wang & Hamilton, 2012) takes a kind of Machiavellian approach by stating that imitation is strategic and driven by the anticipated social consequences of the action. The basis for such a theoretical perspective comes from studies showing the positive social consequences of imitation (for an overview, see Chaps. 13 and 14; this volume). Such research suggests that being imitated leads individuals to like the imitator (e.g., Chartrand & Bargh, 1999; Kulesza et al., 2022; Sparenberg, Topolinski, et al., 2012), give more money to the imitator (van Baaren et al., 2003), increases prosocial orientation towards the imitator (Lakin et al., 2008; van Baaren et al., 2004), increases the feelings of affiliation with the imitator (Lakin & Chartrand, 2003), and increases the susceptibility of being persuaded by the imitator (Maddux et al., 2008).

Self-Other Overlap Theories

Self-other overlap theories (e.g., Brass & Heyes, 2005; Greenwald, 1970; Heyes, 2010; Prinz, 1990) suggest that imitative tendencies are learned responses that develop as a result of self-observation and interaction with other, often similar (Efferson et al., 2008), individuals (Brass & Heyes, 2005; Cook et al., 2014b; Heyes, 2010; Ray & Heyes, 2011). The observation of similar (as compared with dissimilar) individuals is assumed to elicit stronger activations of the corresponding motor plans (e.g., Press, 2011), thereby increasing imitative behavior (Cracco et al., 2018a). Recent support for this theory comes from a series of three experiments conducted in our lab (Genschow et al., 2021). In these experiments, participants run through a classical imitation-inhibition task (Brass et al., 2000). At the same time, participants were instructed to focus either on similarities or differences between the hand presented on the screen and their own hand. The results indicated that focusing on similarities (as compared to differences) increased perceived similarity and as a consequence automatic imitation.

Which Social Factors Modulate Imitative Behavior?

Although motivational and self-other overlap theories propose different underlying mechanisms of social modulation, both theories derive at similar predictions for the influence of most social factors. Interestingly, research testing whether these social variables influence imitative behavior produced rather mixed results. In the next section, we will review these results by firstly focusing on experimental manipulations and then on interindividual differences that are assumed to relate to imitative behavior. When evaluating the evidence for social modulation of imitative behavior, the evidence for social modulation can roughly be divided into five different categories (for an overview, see Table 11.1):

- *Strong evidence* means that there are several successful replications of an original finding and/or there is meta-analytical evidence in favor of social modulation.
- *Preliminary evidence* indicates that there is only a small number of studies that find support for social modulation. Often these studies are underpowered, meaning that only a small number of participants were tested. In the same time, there are no, or just a few, replication studies reported in the literature.
- *Mixed evidence* suggests that there are some studies finding support for social modulation, but also other studies that cannot replicate the original findings.
- *No evidence* means that besides some studies finding support for social modulation, there are several non-successful often high-powered replications and/or there is meta-analytical evidence for the null effect.
- *No data available* indicates that based on theory, it is assumed that social modulation should take place. However, there are no empirical studies actually testing this claim.

Table 11.1 Overview of social influences on imitative behavior

	Evidence for	
	Automatic imitation	Behavioral mimicry
Experimental manipulations		
Bottom-up animacy	[Strong evidence]	[No data available]
Top-down animacy	[Mixed evidence]	[No data available]
Self-other focus	[Mixed evidence]	[Preliminary evidence]
Pro- vs. anti-social mindset	[Mixed evidence]	[No data available]
Group membership	[No evidence]	[Preliminary evidence]
Affiliation goal	[No data available]	[Preliminary evidence]
Status & power	[No evidence]	[Preliminary evidence]
Eye gaze	[Mixed evidence]	[No data available]
Cooperation vs. competition	[Preliminary evidence]	[Preliminary evidence]
Perspective	[No evidence]	[No data available]
Liking	[Preliminary evidence]	[Preliminary evidence]
Interindividual differences		
Empathy	[No evidence]	[No evidence]
Perspective taking	[No evidence]	[No evidence]
Autism	[No evidence]	[No evidence]
Other interindividual factors*	[No evidence]	[No evidence]

Note.

Green	Yellow	Orange	Red	Grey
Strong evidence; e.g., based on multiple successful replications or meta-analytic evidence	Preliminary evidence; e.g., due to few replications and small sample sizes	Mixed evidence; e.g., due to successful as well as non-successful (conceptual) replications	No evidence; e.g., due to several failed replications, or meta-analytical evidence	No data available

*Other interindividual factors include among others narcissism, independent versus interdependent self-construal, individualism vs. collectivism, need to belong, and belief in free will

Experimental Manipulations

Human Versus Non-Human Actions With reference to the animacy effect, several experiments have tested whether individuals imitate human actions more strongly than non-human actions. More specifically, the literature can be divided into two lines of research. On the one hand, some researchers focus on *bottom-up* influences of animacy. That is, they test whether the actual observation of human actions leads to an increase in imitative responses, as compared to the observation of non-human actions (e.g., Bird et al., 2007; Kilner et al., 2003; Press et al., 2005; Press et al., 2006). For instance, Press et al. (2005) found stronger imitative responses in an automatic imitation task when participants observed actions performed by a human actor, as compared to actions performed by a robot. The idea that human actions are imitated more strongly in automatic imitation paradigms has been supported by several independent high-powered studies (Westfal et al., 2024) and a recent meta-analysis (Cracco et al., 2018a).

On the other hand, researchers investigate *top-down* modulations of animacy by testing whether merely believing that the presented stimulus is based on human, as compared to non-human agents, increases imitative tendencies. The literature on the influence of top-down animacy has produced rather mixed results. For example, Liepelt and Brass (2010) used the imitation-inhibition task and presented participants with hands in a glove that engaged in different finger lifting movements. While half of participants were made to believe that the observed finger movements were executed by a human, the other half of participants were made to believe that the movements were executed by a wooden hand. The results indicated that individuals imitate more strongly when they believe that they observe human actions. Despite this seminal demonstration, other researchers could not detect such effects. For example, Press et al. (2006) presented participants in an imitation-inhibition task either with robotic or human hand movements (bottom-up manipulation) or let participants believe that they saw human versus robotic hand movements (top-down manipulation). While the researchers found evidence for bottom-up animacy effects, they could not find support for top-down influences. Most recently, Cracco et al. (2023) were not able to successfully replicate the Liepelt and Brass (2010) finding.

There are no systematic investigations about the degree to which behavioral mimicry is modulated by animacy—most likely because it is difficult to create a social setting in which participants interact with actual humans and robots.

Self-Other Focus A crucial prerequisite for imitation to occur is attention to the other person's action. That is, the more attention is directed to an action, the stronger it is imitated (for a meta-analysis, see Cracco et al., 2018a). Based on this finding, researchers tested whether a focus on others, as compared to the self, increases imitative behavior. For example, in a seminal experiment, Spengler et al. (2010b) applied an evaluative task to manipulate participants' focus to the self. Specifically, participants in the self-focus condition were asked whether they agreed with a series of value-based statements. For example, participants had to indicate whether they thought that Leipzig (where the experiment was conducted) is a pleasant town. It is assumed that for forming such kind of judgments, participants need to retrieve and apply their internal value system (e.g., preferences, norms, aesthetic values, etc.) which then leads to a focus on the self (Amodio & Frith, 2006). In the control condition, participants engaged in a semantic memory retrieval task where they had to indicate whether a series of trivia statements were correct (e.g., Leipzig is the capital of Germany). Afterwards, the researchers administered the imitation-inhibition task. The results indicated that answering self-related questions decreased automatic imitation. In another experiment, the same authors manipulated participants' self-focus by letting them sit in front of two mirrors. In the control condition, the mirrors were turned so participants could not see themselves. The authors found smaller imitation indices when the mirrors faced participants as compared to when the mirrors were turned. It is important to note, however, that a recent study could not replicate this latter finding (Khemka et al., 2021). One potential reason for this is that sitting in front of a mirror is perhaps not the best and strongest manipulation of self-focus. Thus, it is somewhat unclear to which degree self-other focus influences automatic imitation.

There are only a few studies testing the influence of self-other focus on behavioral mimicry. Among the few studies, van Baaren et al. (2003) let participants either form sentences that included words related to the self (i.e., I, me, and mine) or sentences that included words related to others (i.e., he, him, and his). Afterwards, they assessed behavioral mimicry and found that participants mimicked more strongly when they focused on themselves. To the best of our knowledge, there are no other mimicry experiments testing similar effects, leaving open the degree to which this effect can be replicated.

Pro- versus Anti-social Mindset Several experiments assessing automatic imitation, but not behavioral mimicry, tested the hypothesis that a pro-social, as compared to an anti-social mindset, increases imitative behavior. The empirical evidence for this hypothesis is rather mixed. In a typical experiment, depending on the condition, participants either have to solve several pro-social scrambled sentences (e.g., "John gives Laura a warm and affectionate hug") or anti-social scrambled sentences (e.g., "Paul destroys Angelina's new toy train on purpose"). Some studies find that letting participants solve pro-social, as compared to an anti-social scrambled sentences, leads to larger congruency effects (Cook & Bird, 2011; Leighton et al., 2010). Interestingly, other authors could not replicate this finding. For example, in one experiment, Wang and Hamilton (2013) found the exact opposite meaning that participants in an anti-social context imitated more strongly than in a pro-social context. Most recently, when priming either a pro-social or a neutral mindset in participants, Newey et al. (2019) could not find any influence of the primed mindset on automatic imitation.

In another series of experiments, researchers tested whether the influence of pro- and anti-social primes on automatic imitation depends on certain boundary conditions. For example, Wang and Hamilton (2013) manipulated the self-relatedness of pro- and anti-social primes (i.e., whether the scrambled sentences are related to the self or others) and found that that pro-social primes increase automatic imitation only when the primes were related to the self, whereas anti-social primes increase automatic imitation only when the primes are unrelated to the self (Wang & Hamilton, 2015). In a more recent experiment, Cracco et al. (2018b) tested whether individuals imitate pro-social gestures more strongly than anti-social gestures. In line with their predictions, the authors found stronger congruency effects for pro-social, as compared to anti-social gestures. Additionally, the authors found in two experiments that this effect is stronger when participants are primed with a pro-social, as compared to an anti-social mindset.

Taken together, research on automatic imitation indicates that a pro-social (as compared to an anti-social) mindset per se may not increase automatic imitation. However, it could be that a pro-social mindset only increases automatic imitation under certain conditions, such as when the primes relate to the self (vs. others) or the imitated actions are pro-social (vs. anti-social).

Group Membership Being part of a social group and forming stable as well as cohesive relationships with its members plays a crucial role in people's life (e.g., Baumeister & Leary, 1995). As such, identifying someone as belonging to the same social or ethnic group influences how close people feel to that person (Fini et al., 2020) and triggers a desire to connect with them (Van Der Schalk et al., 2011). Based on such research, an often-alleged claim in the literature is that in-group members should be imitated more strongly than out-group members. In line with this assumption, Yabar et al. (2006) found that when assessing behavioral mimicry, individuals imitate in-group members more strongly than out-group members. Relatedly, Stel (2005) found that Dutch participants mimicked an out-group member (i.e., a Moroccan actor) less strongly than an in-group member (i.e., a Dutch actor) the more negative their attitudes towards Moroccans relative to Dutch were.

By applying a classical imitation-inhibition task, Gleibs et al. (2016) found that individuals imitate in-group members more strongly than out-group members when they believed that they have to cooperate with the other person later in the experiment. This effect was not present when participants believed that they have to compete against the other person later in the experiment (for similar findings, see Genschow & Schindler, 2016).

In contrast to these results, more recent studies could not find support for the basic idea that in-group members elicit stronger automatic imitation tendencies than out-group members. For example, in six high-powered experiments (total $N = 1538$). Genschow et al. (2022b) could not find an effect of group membership on imitative behavior in a classical imitation-inhibition task (for similar results, see De Souter et al., 2021; Genschow et al., 2022a). Rauchbauer et al. (2015) even found the opposite of previous research, meaning that individuals imitated out-group members in an imitation-inhibition task more strongly than in-group members (for similar results, see Rauchbauer et al., 2016).

Affiliation Goal Based on motivational theories of imitation (e.g., Chartrand & Dalton, 2009; Wang & Hamilton, 2012), one can derive the prediction that an affiliation goal increases imitative behavior. Experiments supporting this notion mainly measured imitation with behavioral mimicry tasks. For example, in one experiment, Lakin and Chartrand (2003) either presented participants with words related to affiliation (e.g., affiliate, friend, partner, and together) or with control words (e.g., neutral, background) and then measured imitation with a standard mimicry task (Chartrand & Bargh, 1999). The results indicated that letting participants read words related to affiliation increases behavioral mimicry.

People usually have an affiliation goal when they would like to belong to a group and social psychological research suggests that being socially excluded from a group increases the goal to affiliate with others (e.g., Mead et al., 2011). To test whether being excluded from a group increases imitative behavior, Lakin et al. (2008) either excluded or included participants from/to their in-group by letting them play a game of cyberball (Williams & Jarvis, 2006) and then assessed behavioral mimicry. The results indicated that after being excluded from their in-group, participants mimicked in-group members more strongly than out-group members, presumably because they had a stronger affiliation goal. By applying a paradigm similar to a classical imitation-inhibition task, Genschow and Schindler (2016) likewise found that having an affiliation goal with the in-group moderates the influence of group membership on imitation. That is, the more participants wanted to affiliate with the in-group, the more strongly they imitated in- compared with out-group members.

Status and Power Based on research on affiliation goals, it has often been argued that individuals imitate people high in power and status more than people low in power and status, because individuals have a stronger motivation to affiliate with high than with low power and status people (Chartrand & Dalton, 2009; Chartrand et al., 2005; Duffy & Chartrand, 2015). However, there is not much evidence that power and status itself actually influence imitative behavior. Among the few experiments, Cheng and Chartrand (2003) manipulated power and status of a confederate. In addition, they measured whether participants are self-monitors. The concept of self-monitoring reflects the extent to which individuals adapt their behavior to the behavior of their interaction partners. For high, but not low self-monitors, it is important how their interaction partner perceives them. As a consequence, high self-monitors tend to more assimilate to the behaviors of others. Cheng and Chartrand found that high power and status people are mimicked more than low power and status people only when the mimickers scored high on self-monitoring.

When using a classical imitation-inhibition task, Farmer et al. (2016) found that power and status itself does not modulate automatic imitation.

Eye Gaze Research on automatic imitation, but not on behavioral mimicry, investigated how the eye gaze of interaction partners modulates imitative behavior. Some studies found that directed (versus averted) eye gaze increases automatic imitation (Wang & Hamilton, 2014; Wang et al., 2011). In contrast, more recent investigations using similar paradigms could not replicate this finding, but found the exact opposite meaning that averted gaze increased automatic imitation (Carr et al., 2021).

Cooperation Versus Competition Several studies tested whether a cooperative mindset increases imitative behavior. For example, Lanzetta and Englis (1989) demonstrated that expecting a cooperative task leads participants to more strongly engage in behavioral mimicry as when expecting a competitive task (see also Weyers et al., 2009).

When using the imitation-inhibition task, Gleibs et al. (2016) found that participants who believed to engage in an cooperative task (as compared to participants who believed to engage in a competitive task) imitated in-group members more strongly than out-group members.

Perspective Research on automatic imitation investigated whether actions observed from the first-person perspective increase automatic imitation. In line with this idea, several studies found stronger automatic imitation for actions presented from a first-person perspective, as compared to a third-person perspective (Bortoletto et al., 2013; Genschow et al., 2013; Vogt et al., 2003). However, a recent meta-analysis (Cracco et al., 2018a) could not find support for this effect.

Liking The idea that likeability moderates imitative behavior has been studied with behavioral mimicry paradigms only (e.g., Stel et al., 2010a, b). For instance, Stel et al. (2010b) let participants read a background story about a confederate. The background story described the confederate as either likeable or not likeable. Afterwards, participants engaged in a classical behavioral mimicry task with the confederate. The authors found that participants mimicked the confederate more strongly when they believed to interact with a likeable person, as compared to a non-likeable person.

Interindividual Differences

Empathy A factor that is very often assumed to correlate with imitative behavior is empathy. Indeed, in early work, mimicry has been viewed as an expression of empathic concern (e.g., Maurer & Tindall, 1983). Over the last two decades, the link between empathy and mimicry has been studied using a variety of different tasks related to behavioral mimicry. For example, Platek et al. (2003) showed that people tend to engage in contagious yawning more often, the more empathic they are. Certainly, the most research on the empathy-mimicry link has been conducted with facial and emotional mimicry tasks. Most of these studies report a positive relation between empathy and mimicry (e.g., Drimalla et al., 2019; Perugia et al., 2020; Sonnby-Borgström et al., 2003; Sonnby-Borgström, 2002). However, there are also some studies that find rather small or no relations between empathy and facial mimicry (e.g., Kovalchuk et al., 2022). In line with such findings, a recent meta-analysis (Holland et al., 2021) concludes that "stronger facial mimicry responses are positively related to higher dispositions for empathy, but the weakness and variability of this effect suggest that this relationship is conditional on not-fully understood factors." (p. 150).

When using tasks that tap more strongly into behavioral mimicry, Müller et al. (2013) found that people imitate attractive, but not unattractive, persons more strongly, the more empathic they are. When applying a classical imitation-inhibition task, Haffey et al. (2013) found a positive correlation between empathy and automatic imitation. However, other studies could not successfully replicate this finding (Butler et al., 2015; Genschow et al., 2017). For instance, in a high-powered experiment, Genschow et al. (2017) were not able to detect a relation of empathy with neither behavioral mimicry nor with automatic imitation. Likewise, a meta-analysis on automatic imitation could not find a significant relation between empathy and automatic imitation either (Cracco et al., 2018a).

Perspective Taking While there is little evidence for the link between general forms of empathy and imitative behavior, researchers suggested that the link with imitative behavior might be specific to a subfactor of empathy—namely perspective taking. One of the first demonstration supporting this notion comes from Chartrand and Bargh (1999) who found that perspective taking abilities, but not other forms of empathy, correlate with mimicry behavior (for similar results, see Horton, 2014). Similar results have been detected when automatic imitation was assessed (Cracco & Brass, 2017; Cracco et al., 2015; Genschow et al., 2013). However, Genschow et al. (2017) could neither replicate the link between perspective taking and behavioral mimicry nor the link between perspective taking and automatic imitation. Similarly, Cracco et al.'s (2018a) meta-analysis could not detect a relation between perspective taking and automatic imitation either.

Autism Previous research has repeatedly studied imitative behavior in different clinical settings (for a review, see Chap. 12; this volume). In this respect, one of the most intensively investigated sample is autism. Research investigating a link between autism and imitative behavior mainly focused on automatic imitation. Interestingly, this research produced rather mixed results. On the one hand, some researchers found reduced automatic imitation in individuals with autistic spectrum disorder as compared to healthy controls (Cook et al., 2014a). In contrast to this result, other researchers found the exact opposite meaning that individuals with autistic spectrum disorder engaged in stronger automatic imitation (e.g., Spengler et al. 2010a), yet other researchers did not find any difference between autistic individuals and healthy controls (e.g., Gowen et al., 2008; Press et al., 2010; Sowden et al., 2015). In line with this latter null finding, a meta-analysis could not support the idea that autism is related automatic imitation (Cracco et al., 2018a). Also, when pursuing a correlational approach in a large healthy adult sample, Genschow et al. (2017) could find a relation of autistic traits neither with automatic imitation nor with behavioral mimicry (for similar results, see Butler et al., 2015).

Other Interindividual Factors Besides the above-mentioned well-studied factors, previous research has also investigated the relation of imitative behavior with several other interindividual factors. Among these factors, it has been found that automatic imitation is negatively related to narcissistic traits (Hogeveen & Obhi, 2013), an effect that could not be replicated by Butler et al. (2015). The latter authors could also not find a relation between automatic imitation and personality traits related to social behavior (i.e., extraversion and agreeableness), as well as autistic-like and schizotypal traits. In a similar vein, Genschow et al. (2017) could not find a relation of several personality traits related to social cognition (i.e., independent versus interdependent self-construal; individualism vs. collectivism; need to belong) with mimicry behavior and automatic imitation. Finally, when measuring higher order beliefs, Westfal et al. (2021) did not find a relation between belief in free will and automatic imitation.

Explanations for the Mixed Evidence

Taken together, the above-reviewed literature indicates that there is cumulative evidence only for a few social moderators of imitative behaviors. In particular, for automatic imitation, only bottom-up animacy has been repeatedly found to influence the congruency effect. For all other factors, there is either no evidence or only preliminary evidence of social modulation. For behavioral mimicry, there is at best preliminary evidence for some social modulators. An interesting observation across automatic imitation and behavioral mimicry tasks is that while there is at least some evidence for social modulation when reviewing the literature on experimental manipulations, there is no evidence for a relation between interindividual factors and imitative behavior on a correlational level. There are different explanations for these results that can roughly be divided into *methodological* and *theoretical* explanations.

Methodological Explanations

An interesting observation of the literature we reviewed here is that in the automatic imitation literature, there are several replications of previously published findings. In contrast, in the behavioral mimicry literature, there are just a few published empirical articles for each social factor and even fewer replications. Reasons for this are manifold. First, it might be that researchers were not interested in replicating previous findings, because they were afraid of conducting research that is not novel enough. Second, the few replications in the behavioral mimicry literature could be due to the fact that conducting mimicry experiments are rather effortful and costly. Thus, researchers might have decided to focus on other research questions that can be tested with less effort. Indeed, when reviewing the literature of the last two decades, an interesting observation is that since the so-called replication crises in (social) psychology, researchers started testing their predictions with larger sample sizes (e.g., Sassenberg & Ditrich, 2019). As mimicry experiments are very effortful and costly, experiments with large numbers of participants became less feasible, which may have reduced the published number of behavioral mimicry experiments. Third, the few published replication studies in the mimicry literature could hint to a file drawer problem, indicating that a few positive results were published, whereas several other experiments that do not support the original finding might not have been published.

For many social factors that are assumed to modulate imitative behavior, the present review finds either mixed or merely preliminary evidence. Besides the above-mentioned lack of replications, another explanation for this characteristic of the literature could be that previous research used rather small samples. A problem of such underpowered experiments is that the resulting effect sizes for significant findings are oftentimes overestimated especially when the true effect size is not large (e.g., Cumming, 2013). As a consequence, it might well be that when testing social modulation, researchers base their sample size on previous underpowered experiments, which leads to further underpowered experiments and as a result to inconclusive and difficult to interpret results.

An issue of many experiments testing the in influence of social factors on imitative behavior is that these experiments did not implement manipulation checks. That is, most of previous studies did not measure the degree to which the psychological factors they purported to manipulate were actually influenced. Thus, for many experiments, it remains open whether the implemented social manipulation actually worked. Note, only if the experimental manipulation actually influences the processes it aims to affect, one can expect social modulation of imitative behavior to occur. In addition, one would also predict that factors influencing the purported psychological variables the strongest should also influence imitative behavior the strongest. For example, it might be that letting participants sit in front of a small mirror leads participants to less strongly focus on themselves as compared with directly asking them to focus on themselves. As a consequence, one would expect stronger imitation effects when self-other focus is manipulated by directly asking participants to focus on themselves than by letting them sit in front of a mirror. Likewise, one could interpret the finding that bottom-up animacy manipulations lead to stronger effects than top-down manipulations (e.g., belief manipulations) with the notion that bottom-up manipulations influence perceived similarity more strongly. In sum, the lack of evidence for the influence of some social factors on imitative behavior could be due to the researchers applying manipulations that influence the assumed processes rather weakly.

The observation that interindividual differences do neither reliably correlate with automatic imitation nor with behavioral mimicry could be interpreted in different ways. First, one may argue that independent of any personality trait, different people have the same automatic tendency to imitate others. Second, it might be that there are some interindividual factors that relate to imitative behavior, but previous research has not studied them yet. Third, and probably most likely, the lack of evidence may be due to the psychometric properties of the tasks used to measure imitative behavior. A particular characteristic of classical imitation-inhibition tasks is that they produce very strong (Cracco et al., 2018a) and reliable (Genschow et al., 2017) effects in the sense that the congruency effect can be detected in almost every participant. As a consequence, automatic imitation tasks do not have much interindividual variability, which makes it difficult to find correlations with other measures (e.g., Goodwin & Leech, 2006). Behavioral mimicry tasks, on the other hand, are designed to detect imitative behavior in more natural settings. A disadvantage of these tasks is, however, that they do not measure imitative behavior in a very reliable manner (Genschow et al., 2017). Since unreliable measure are unlikely to correlate with other measures (Crocker & Algina, 1986; Cronbach, 1990), it is not surprising that previous research could not detect stable correlations between mimicry behavior and interindividual differences.

Theoretical Explanations

A specific characteristic of the literature on social modulation of imitative behavior is that researchers investigated social variables in a rather exploratory manner and just later explained the findings post hoc by putting forward different theories. In principle, two different theories have been proposed. Motivational theories (e.g., Chartrand & Dalton, 2009; Wang & Hamilton, 2012) assume that social modulation is due to differences in affiliation goals, whereas self-other overlap theories (e.g., Brass & Heyes, 2005; Greenwald, 1970; Heyes, 2010; Prinz, 1990) suggest that social modulation takes place based on differences in perceived similarity. Strikingly, previous research has neglected to rigorously test the degree to which these two processes (i.e., affiliation goals vs. perceived similarity) directly contribute to automatic imitation and mimicry behavior and whether the social factors assumed to modulate imitative behavior actually influence perceived similarity and affiliation goals.

Popper (1934/2005) argues that a theory can be evaluated based on two criteria: *universality* and *precision*. The level of *universality* (Allgemeinheit) specifies how many situations a theory can be applied to. The degree of *precision* (Bestimmtheit) specifies how accurate a theory can predict a certain outcome. Previous theories on the social modulation of imitative behavior score relatively high on universality as any factor that influences affiliation and/or similarity is assumed to increase imitative behavior. At the same time, these theories lack precision, because several crucial aspects remain unclear. First, previous theories on social modulation of imitative behavior leave open which social variables influence similarity and the goal to affiliate how strongly. Second, these theories also do not allow predicting which measures of imitative behavior will be influenced by which social factors. Third, previous theories do not specify whether perceived similarity and affiliation goals influence imitative behavior equally strong and whether the combination of both processes influences imitative behavior more strongly.

With respect to the latter, an interesting observation of the literature is that in several cases, researchers tested whether the combination of different social factors influences imitative behavior. For example, Gleibs et al. (2016) found that in-group members are only imitated more strongly than out-group members if participants believe to be cooperating with the other person. Likewise, Cracco et al. (2018b) found that the influence of a pro- vs. anti-social mindset on automatic imitation depends on whether participants imitate pro-social or anti-social gestures. Based on this research, it might be that social modulation of imitative behaviors hinges on crucial boundary conditions that are not specified by previous theories.

In sum, an explanation of why the literature on the impact of social factors on imitative behavior produced rather mixed findings can be explained by the imprecision of existing theories.

Avenues for Future Directions

Taken together, previous research on the social modulation of imitative behavior resulted in largely mixed results with few experiments finding support for the influence of some social variables and other experiments finding no influence for other variables. Based on the reasons for these mixed results reviewed-above, we can derive several potential directions for future research that will allow investigating which social factors influence imitative behavior based on which processes with more precision.

First, from a methodological point of view, there is the need to conduct more direct replications to test whether the variables for which is currently preliminary or mixed evidence influence imitative behavior. Such kind of replications will allow drawing a clearer picture about the degree to which imitative behavior is socially modulated. Another (or additional) way to assess the strength to which different social variables modulate imitative behavior is to carry out meta-analyses. While there are already some informative meta-analyses for automatic imitation (Cracco et al., 2018a; Genschow, Schuler et al., 2019), the literature currently lacks a meta-analysis on behavioral mimicry. Given that the literature might have a file drawer problem, researchers carrying out meta-analyses should take into account publication bias.

Second, as many previous experiments are underpowered, it is unclear to which degree they are replicable. Thus, when designing experiments to assess social modulation of imitative behavior, researchers are advised to conservatively calculate power analyses and to test larger samples.

Third, when testing the influence of social variables on imitation, future research should make sure that they use strong manipulations to detect potentially small effects. In addition, future research is advised to administer manipulation checks to test whether the applied manipulations influence the psychological variables the manipulations purported to manipulate. Additional manipulation checks should be implemented to assess the processes based on which social factors should influence imitative behavior. That is, based on previous theories, research may investigate the degree to which perceived similarity and affiliation goals mediate the influence of social factors on imitative behavior.

Fourth, since classical imitation-inhibition tasks (e.g., Brass et al., 2001; Brass et al., 2000) assess imitative behavior without much variance and behavioral mimicry tasks (Chartrand & Bargh, 1999) measure imitative behavior rather unreliably, future research should aim at developing and implementing other measures. In this respect, a potential direction could be to apply Virtual Reality to manipulate social factors (Cracco et al., 2022).

Fifth, based on the suggestions for future research made above, scholars may be able to derive at better theories that allow predicting social modulation with more precision. In line with the current call for formalized theories in psychology (e.g., Borsboom et al., 2021; Oberauer & Lewandowsky, 2019; West et al., 2019), future theories on social modulation of imitative behavior should be formulated in such a way that they are able to precisely predict which social factors influence how strongly what kind of imitation tasks based on which processes. These theories should also include potential boundary conditions under which social modulation can be expected.

Summary

Although different theories predict social modulation of imitative behavior, the evidence for social modulation is rather mixed in the sense that only for a few social factors, there is cumulative evidence in favor of social modulation. The reasons for the mixed findings are manifold, but may especially lay in several methodological shortcomings as well as imprecise theories. Future research may implement stronger methods which includes among other factors more replications, larger sample sizes, the integration of manipulation checks, as well as reliable measures that assess imitative behavior with more variability. In addition, scholars are advised to formalize more precise theories to better predict social modulation of imitative behavior.

References

Amodio, D. M., & Frith, C. D. (2006). Meeting of minds: The medial frontal cortex and social cognition. *Nature Reviews Neuroscience, 7*, 268–277. https://doi.org/10.1038/nrn1884

Baumeister, R. F., & Leary, M. R. (1995). The need to belong: Desire for interpersonal attachments as a fundamental human motivation. *Psychological Bulletin, 117*, 497–529. https://psycnet.apa.org/doi/10.1037/0033-2909.117.3.497

Bird, G., Leighton, J., Press, C., & Heyes, C. (2007). Intact automatic imitation of human and robot actions in autism spectrum disorders. *Proceedings of the Royal Society of London B: Biological Sciences, 274*, 3027–3031. https://doi.org/10.1098%2Frspb.2007.1019

Borsboom, D., van der Maas, H. L., Dalege, J., Kievit, R. A., & Haig, B. D. (2021). Theory construction methodology: A practical framework for building theories in psychology. *Perspectives on Psychological Science, 16*, 756–766. https://doi.org/10.1177/1745691620969647

Bortoletto, M., Mattingley, J. B., & Cunnington, R. (2013). Effects of context on visuomotor interference depends on the perspective of observed actions. *PLoS One, 8*, e53248. https://doi.org/10.1371/journal.pone.0053248

Brass, M., & Heyes, C. (2005). Imitation: Is cognitive neuroscience solving the correspondence problem? *Trends in Cognitive Sciences, 9*, 489–495. https://doi.org/10.1016/j.tics.2005.08.007

Brass, M., Bekkering, H., Wohlschläger, A., & Prinz, W. (2000). Compatibility between observed and executed finger movements: Comparing symbolic, spatial, and imitative cues. *Brain and Cognition, 44*, 124–143. https://doi.org/10.1006/brcg.2000.1225

Brass, M., Bekkering, H., & Prinz, W. (2001). Movement observation affects movement execution in a simple response task. *Acta Psychologica, 106*, 3–22. https://doi.org/10.1016/s0001-6918(00)00024-x

Butler, E. E., Ward, R., & Ramsey, R. (2015). Investigating the relationship between stable personality characteristics and automatic imitation. *PLoS One, 10*, e0129651. https://doi.org/10.1371/journal.pone.0129651

Cappella, J. N., & Planalp, S. (1981). Talk and silence sequences in informal conversations III: Interspeaker influence. *Human Communication Research, 7*, 117–132. https://psycnet.apa.org/doi/10.1111/j.1468-2958.1981.tb00564.x

Carr, E. W., Bird, G., Catmur, C., & Winkielman, P. (2021). Dissociable effects of averted "gaze" on the priming of bodily representations and motor actions. *Acta Psychologica, 212*, 103225. https://doi.org/10.1016/j.actpsy.2020.103225

Chartrand, T. L., & Bargh, J. A. (1999). The Chameleon effect: The perception-behavior link and social interaction. *Journal of Personality & Social Psychology, 76*, 893–910. https://doi.org/10.1037//0022-3514.76.6.893

Chartrand, T. L., & Dalton, A. N. (2009). Mimicry: Its ubiquity, importance, and functionality. In E. Morales, P. M. Gollwitzer, & J. A. Bargh (Eds.), *The psychology of action: Vol. 2. Mechanisms of human action* (pp. 893–910). Oxford University Press.

Chartrand, T. L., Maddux, W. W., & Lakin, J. L. (2005). Beyond the perception-behavior link: The ubiquitous utility and motivational moderators of nonconscious mimicry. In R. Hassin, J. Uleman, & J. A. Bargh (Eds.), *Unintended thoughts 2: The new unconscious* (pp. 334–361). Oxford University Press.

Cheng, C. M., & Chartrand, T. L. (2003). Self-monitoring without awareness: Using mimicry as a nonconscious affiliation strategy. *Journal of Personality and Social Psychology, 85*, 1170–1179. https://doi.org/10.1037/0022-3514.85.6.1170

Cook, J., & Bird, G. (2011). Social attitudes differentially modulate imitation in adolescents and adults. *Experimental Brain Research, 211*, 601–612. https://doi.org/10.1007%2Fs00221-011-2584-4

Cook, J., Swapp, D., Pan, X., Bianchi-Berthouze, N., & Blakemore, S.-J. (2014a). Atypical interference effect of action observation in autism spectrum conditions. *Psychological Medicine, 44*, 731–740. https://doi.org/10.1017%2FS0033291713001335

Cook, R., Bird, G., Catmur, C., Press, C., & Heyes, C. (2014b). Mirror neurons: From origin to function. *Behavioral and Brain Sciences, 37*, 177–192. https://doi.org/10.1017/s0140525x13000903

Cracco, E., & Brass, M. (2017). Motor simulation beyond the dyad: Automatic imitation of multiple actors. Retrieved from osf.io/eas4m

Cracco, E., & Brass, M. (2018). The role of sensorimotor processes in social group contagion. *Cognitive Psychology, 103*, 23–41. https://doi.org/10.1016/j.cogpsych.2018.02.001

Cracco, E., De Coster, L., Andres, M., & Brass, M. (2015). Motor simulation beyond the dyad: Automatic imitation of multiple actors. *Journal of Experimental Psychology: Human Perception and Performance, 41*, 1488–1501. https://doi.org/10.1037/a0039737. Empathy results retrieved from osf.io/eas1484m.

Cracco, E., Bardi, L., Desmet, C., Genschow, O., Rigoni, D., De Coster, L., … Brass, M. (2018a). Automatic imitation: A meta-analysis. *Psychological Bulletin, 144*, 453–500. https://doi.org/10.1037/bul0000143

Cracco, E., Genschow, O., Radkova, I., & Brass, M. (2018b). Automatic imitation of pro- and antisocial gestures: Is implicit social behavior censored? *Cognition, 170*, 179–189. https://doi.org/10.1016/j.cognition.2017.09.019

Cracco, E., Bernardet, U., Sevenhant, R., Vandenhouwe, N., Copman, F., Durnez, W., … Brass, M. (2022). Evidence for a two-step model of social group influence. *iScience, 25*, 104891. https://doi.org/10.1016/j.isci.2022.104891

Cracco, E., Liepelt, R., Brass, M., & Genschow, O. (2023). Top-down modulation of motor priming by belief about animacy: A registered replication report. *Experimental Psychology*, 70, 355–365. https://doi.org/10.1027/1618-3169/a000605

Crocker, L., & Algina, J. (1986). *Introduction to classical and modern test theory*. Holt, Rinehart, & Winston.

Cronbach, L. J. (1990). *Essentials of psychological testing* (5th ed.). Harper & Row.

Cumming, G. (2013). *Understanding the new statistics: Effect sizes, confidence intervals, and meta-analysis*. Routledge.

De Souter, L., Braem, S., Genschow, O., Brass, M., & Cracco, E. (2021). Social group membership does not modulate automatic imitation in a contrastive multi-agent paradigm. *Quarterly Journal of Experimental Psychology, 74*, 746–759. https://doi.org/10.1177/1747021820986528

Dimberg, U. (1982). Facial reactions to facial expressions. *Psychophysiology, 19*, 643–647.

Drimalla, H., Landwehr, N., Hess, U., & Dziobek, I. (2019). From face to face: The contribution of facial mimicry to cognitive and emotional empathy. *Cognition and Emotion, 33*, 1672–1686. https://doi.org/10.1080/02699931.2019.1596068

Duffy, K. A., & Chartrand, T. L. (2015). Mimicry: Causes and consequences. *Current Opinion in Behavioral Sciences, 3*, 112–116. https://doi.org/10.1016/j.cobeha.2015.03.002

Efferson, C., Lalive, R., & Fehr, E. (2008). The coevolution of cultural groups and ingroup favoritism. *Science, 321*, 1844–1849. https://doi.org/10.1126/science.1155805

Farmer, H., Carr, E. W., Svartdal, M., Winkielman, P., Hamilton, A. F., & d. C. (2016). Status and power do not modulate automatic imitation of intransitive hand movements. *PLoS One, 11*, e0151835. https://doi.org/10.1371/journal.pone.0151835

Fini, C., Verbeke, P., Sieber, S., Moors, A., Brass, M., & Genschow, O. (2020). The influence of threat on perceived spatial distance to out-group members. *Psychological Research, 84*, 757–764. https://doi.org/10.1007/s00426-018-1091-7

Genschow, O., & Florack, A. (2014). Attention on the source of influence reverses the impact of cross-contextual imitation. *Journal of Experimental Psychology: Human Perception and Performance, 40*, 904–907. https://doi.org/10.1037/a0035430

Genschow, O., & Schindler, S. (2016). The influence of group membership on cross-contextual imitation. *Psychonomic Bulletin & Review, 23*, 1257–1265. https://doi.org/10.3758/s13423-015-0983-4

Genschow, O., Florack, A., & Wänke, M. (2013). The power of movement: Evidence for context-independent movement imitation. *Journal of Experimental Psychology: General, 142*, 763–773. https://doi.org/10.1037/a0029795

Genschow, O., van Den Bossche, S., Cracco, E., Bardi, L., Rigoni, D., & Brass, M. (2017). Mimicry and automatic imitation are not correlated. *PLoS One, 12*, e0183784. https://doi.org/10.1371%2Fjournal.pone.0183784

Genschow, O., Schuler, J., Cracco, E., Brass, M., & Wänke, M. (2019). The effect of money priming on self-focus in the imitation-inhibition task. *Experimental Psychology, 66*, 423–436. https://doi.org/10.1027/1618-3169/a000466

Genschow, O., Cracco, E., Verbeke, P., Westfal, M., & Crusius, J. (2021). A direct test of the similarity assumption – Focusing on differences as compared with similarities decreases automatic imitation. *Cognition, 215*, 104824. https://doi.org/10.1016/j.cognition.2021.104824

Genschow, O., Pauels, E., Krugmann, K., & Winter, A. (2022a). Group membership does not modulate goal-versus movement-based imitation. *Quarterly Journal of Experimental Psychology, 76*, 827–837. https://doi.org/10.1177/17470218221132842

Genschow, O., Westfal, M., Cracco, E., & Crusius, J. (2022b). Group membership does not modulate automatic imitation. *Psychological Research, 86*, 780–791. https://doi.org/10.1007/s00426-021-01526-1

Gleibs, I. H., Wilson, N., Reddy, G., & Catmur, C. (2016). Group dynamics in automatic imitation. *PLoS One, 11*, e0162880. https://doi.org/10.1371%2Fjournal.pone.0162880

Goodwin, L. D., & Leech, N. L. (2006). Understanding correlation: Factors that affect the size of r. *The Journal of Experimental Education, 74*, 249–266. https://doi.org/10.3200/JEXE.74.3.249-266

Gowen, E., Stanley, J., & Miall, R. (2008). Movement interference in autism-spectrum disorder. *Neuropsychologia, 46*, 1060–1068. https://doi.org/10.1016%2Fj.neuropsychologia.2007.11.004

Greenwald, A. G. (1970). Sensory feedback mechanisms in performance control: With special reference to the ideo-motor mechanism. *Psychological Review, 77*, 73–99. https://psycnet.apa.org/doi/10.1037/h0028689

Haffey, A., Press, C., O'Connell, G., & Chakrabarti, B. (2013). Autistic traits modulate mimicry of social but not nonsocial rewards. *Autism Research, 6*, 614–620. https://psycnet.apa.org/doi/10.1037/h0028689

Hess, U., & Fischer, A. (2014). Emotional mimicry: Why and when we mimic emotions. *Social and Personality Psychology Compass, 8*, 45–57. https://psycnet.apa.org/doi/10.1111/spc3.12083

Heyes, C. (2010). Where do mirror neurons come from? *Neuroscience & Biobehavioral Reviews, 34*, 575–583. https://doi.org/10.1016/j.neubiorev.2009.11.007

Heyes, C. (2011). Automatic imitation. *Psychological Bulletin, 137*, 463–483. https://doi.org/10.1037/a0022288

Hogeveen, J., & Obhi, S. S. (2013). Automatic imitation is automatic, but less so for narcissists. *Experimental Brain Research, 224*, 613–621. https://doi.org/10.1007/s00221-012-3339-6

Holland, A. C., O'Connell, G., & Dziobek, I. (2021). Facial mimicry, empathy, and emotion recognition: A meta-analysis of correlations. *Cognition and Emotion, 35*, 150–168. https://doi.org/10.1080/02699931.2020.1815655

Horton, W. S. (2014). Individual differences in perspective taking and field-independence mediate structural persistence in dialog. *Acta Psychologica, 150*, 41–48. https://doi.org/10.1016/j.actpsy.2014.04.006

Khemka, D., Ahmadilari, N., Bird, G., & Catmur, C. (2021). Imitation in one's own presence: No specific effect of self-focus on imitation. *Acta Psychologica, 212*, 103194. https://doi.org/10.1016/j.actpsy.2020.103194

Kilner, J., Paulignan, Y., & Blakemore, S. (2003). An interference effect of observed biological movement on action. *Current Biology, 13*, 522–525. https://doi.org/10.1016/s0960-9822(03)00165-9

Kovalchuk, Y., Budini, E., Cook, R. M., & Walsh, A. (2022). Investigating the relationship between facial mimicry and empathy. *Behavioral Sciences, 12*, 250. https://doi.org/10.3390/bs12080250

Kulesza, W., Chrobot, N., Dolinski, D., Muniak, P., Bińkowska, D., Grzyb, T., & Genschow, O. (2022). Imagining is not observing: the role of simulation processes within the mimicry-liking expressway. *Journal of Nonverbal Behavior, 46*, 233–246. https://psycnet.apa.org/doi/10.1007/s10919-022-00399-1

LaFrance, M. (1982). Posture mirroring and rapport. In M. Davis (Ed.), *Interaction rhythms: Periodicity in communicative behavior* (pp. 279–298). Human Sciences Press.

Lakin, J. L., & Chartrand, T. L. (2003). Using nonconscious behavioral mimicry to create affiliation and rapport. *Psychological Science, 14*, 334–339. https://doi.org/10.1111/1467-9280.14481

Lakin, J. L., Chartrand, T. L., & Arkin, R. M. (2008). I am too just like you – Nonconscious mimicry as an automatic behavioral response to social exclusion. *Psychological Science, 19*, 816–822. https://doi.org/10.1111/j.1467-9280.2008.02162.x

Lanzetta, J. T., & Englis, B. G. (1989). Expectations of cooperation and competition and their effects on observers' vicarious emotional responses. *Journal of Personality and Social Psychology, 56*, 543–554. https://doi.org/10.1037/0022-3514.56.4.543
Leighton, J., Bird, G., Orsini, C., & Heyes, C. (2010). Social attitudes modulate automatic imitation. *Journal of Experimental Social Psychology, 46*, 905–910. https://awspntest.apa.org/doi/10.1016/j.jesp.2010.07.001
Liepelt, R., & Brass, M. (2010). Top-down modulation of motor priming by belief about animacy. *Experimental Psychology, 57*, 221–227. https://doi.org/10.1027/1618-3169/a000028
Maddux, W. W., Mullen, E., & Galinsky, A. D. (2008). Chameleons bake bigger pies and take bigger pieces: Strategic behavioral mimicry facilitates negotiation outcomes. *Journal of Experimental Social Psychology, 44*, 461–468. https://doi.org/10.1016/j.jesp.2007.02.003
Maurer, R. E., & Tindall, J. H. (1983). Effect of postural congruence on client's perception of counselor empathy. *Journal of Counseling Psychology, 30*, 158–163. https://doi.org/10.1037/0022-0167.30.2.158
Mead, N. L., Baumeister, R. F., Stillman, T. F., Rawn, C. D., & Vohs, K. D. (2011). Social exclusion causes people to spend and consume strategically in the service of affiliation. *Journal of Consumer Research, 37*, 902–919. https://doi.org/10.1086/656667
Müller, B. C., Leeuwen, M. L., Baaren, R. B., Bekkering, H., & Dijksterhuis, A. (2013). Empathy is a beautiful thing: Empathy predicts imitation only for attractive others. *Scandinavian Journal of Psychology, 54*, 401–406. https://doi.org/10.1111/sjop.12060
Newey, R., Koldewyn, K., & Ramsey, R. (2019). The influence of prosocial priming on visual perspective taking and automatic imitation. *PLoS One, 14*, e0198867. https://doi.org/10.1371%2Fjournal.pone.0198867
Oberauer, K., & Lewandowsky, S. (2019). Addressing the theory crisis in psychology. *Psychonomic Bulletin & Review, 26*, 1596–1618. https://doi.org/10.3758/s13423-019-01645-2
Perugia, G., Paetzel, M., & Castellano, G. (2020). On the role of personality and empathy in human-human, human-agent, and human-robot mimicry. Paper presented at the *Social Robotics: 12th International Conference, ICSR 2020, Golden, CO, USA, November 14–18, 2020*, Proceedings 12.
Platek, S. M., Critton, S. R., Myers, T. E., & Gallup, G. G., Jr. (2003). Contagious yawning: The role of self-awareness and mental state attribution. *Cognitive Brain Research, 17*, 223–227. https://doi.org/10.1016/s0926-6410(03)00109-5
Popper, K. R. (1934/2005). *Logik der Forschung* (11th ed.). Mohr Siebeck.
Press, C. (2011). Action observation and robotic agents: Learning and anthropomorphism. *Neuroscience & Biobehavioral Reviews, 35*, 1410–1418. https://doi.org/10.1016/j.neubiorev.2011.03.004
Press, C., Bird, G., Flach, R., & Heyes, C. (2005). Robotic movement elicits automatic imitation. *Cognitive Brain Research, 25*, 632–640. https://doi.org/10.1016/j.cogbrainres.2005.08.020
Press, C., Gillmeister, H., & Heyes, C. (2006). Bottom-up, not top-down, modulation of imitation by human and robotic models. *European Journal of Neuroscience, 24*, 2415–2419. https://doi.org/10.1111/j.1460-9568.2006.05115.x
Press, C., Richardson, D., & Bird, G. (2010). Intact imitation of emotional facial actions in autism spectrum conditions. *Neuropsychologia, 48*, 3291–3297. https://doi.org/10.1016%2Fj.neuropsychologia.2010.07.012
Prinz, W. (1990). A common coding approach to perception and action. In O. Neumann & W. Prinz (Eds.), *Relationships between perception and action* (pp. 167–201). Springer.
Ramsey, R. (2018). What are reaction time indices of automatic imitation measuring? *Consciousness and Cognition, 65*, 240–254. https://doi.org/10.1016/j.concog.2018.08.006
Ramsey, R., & Ward, R. (2020). Challenges and opportunities for top-down modulation research in cognitive psychology. *Acta Psychologica, 209*, 103118. https://doi.org/10.1016/j.actpsy.2020.103118
Rauchbauer, B., Majdandžić, J., Hummer, A., Windischberger, C., & Lamm, C. (2015). Distinct neural processes are engaged in the modulation of mimicry by social group-membership and emotional expressions. *Cortex, 70*, 49. https://doi.org/10.1016/j.cortex.2015.03.007

Rauchbauer, B., Majdandžić, J., Stieger, S., & Lamm, C. (2016). The modulation of mimicry by ethnic group-membership and emotional expressions. *PLoS One, 11*, e0161064. https://doi.org/10.1371/journal.pone.0161064
Ray, E., & Heyes, C. (2011). Imitation in infancy: The wealth of the stimulus. *Developmental Science, 14*, 92–105. https://doi.org/10.1111/j.1467-7687.2010.00961.x
Sassenberg, K., & Ditrich, L. (2019). Research in social psychology changed between 2011 and 2016: Larger sample sizes, more self-report measures, and more online studies. *Advances in Methods and Practices in Psychological Science, 2*, 107–114. https://doi.org/10.1177/2515245919838781
Sonnby-Borgström, M. (2002). Automatic mimicry reactions as related to differences in emotional empathy. *Scandinavian Journal of Psychology, 43*, 433–443. https://doi.org/10.1111/1467-9450.00312
Sonnby-Borgström, M., Jönsson, P., & Svensson, O. (2003). Emotional empathy as related to mimicry reactions at different levels of information processing. *Journal of Nonverbal Behavior, 27*, 3–23. https://doi.org/10.1023/A:1023608506243
Sowden, S., Koehne, S., Catmur, C., Dziobek, I., & Bird, G. (2015). Intact automatic imitation and typical spatial compatibility in autism spectrum disorder: Challenging the broken mirror theory. *Autism Research, 9*, 292–300. https://doi.org/10.1002/aur.1511
Sparenberg, P., Topolinski, S., Springer, A., & Prinz, W. (2012). Minimal mimicry: Mere effector matching induces preference. *Brain and Cognition, 80*, 291–300. https://doi.org/10.1016/j.bandc.2012.08.004
Spengler, S., Bird, G., & Brass, M. (2010a). Hyperimitation of actions is related to reduced understanding of others' minds in autism spectrum conditions. *Biological Psychiatry, 68*, 1148–1155. https://doi.org/10.1016/j.biopsych.2010.09.017
Spengler, S., Brass, M., Kühn, S., & Schütz-Bosbach, S. (2010b). Minimizing motor mimicry by myself: Self-focus enhances online action-control mechanisms during motor contagion. *Consciousness and Cognition, 19*, 98–106. https://doi.org/10.1016/j.concog.2009.12.014
Stel, M. (2005). *The social functions of mimicry: On the consequences and qualifiers of facial imitation*. PrintPartners Ipskamp. https://doi.org/10.1017/CBO9781107587595.003
Stel, M., Blascovich, J., McCall, C., Mastop, J., Van Baaren, R. B., & Vonk, R. (2010a). Mimicking disliked others: Effects of a priori liking on the mimicry-liking link. *European Journal of Social Psychology, 40*, 867–880. https://doi.org/10.1002/ejsp.655
Stel, M., van Baaren, R. B., Blascovich, J., van Dijk, E., McCall, C., Pollmann, M. M., … Vonk, R. (2010b). Effects of a priori liking on the elicitation of mimicry. *Experimental Psychology, 57*, 412–418. https://doi.org/10.1027/1618-3169/a000050
van Baaren, R. B., Maddux, W. W., Chartrand, T. L., De Bouter, C., & van Knippenberg, A. (2003). It takes two to mimic: Behavioral consequences of self-construals. *Journal of Personality and Social Psychology, 84*, 1093–1102. https://doi.org/10.1037/0022-3514.84.5.1093
Van Baaren, R. B., Holland, R. W., Kawakami, K., & Van Knippenberg, A. (2004). Mimicry and prosocial behavior. *Psychological Science, 15*, 71–74. https://doi.org/10.1111/j.0963-7214.2004.01501012.x
Van Der Schalk, J., Fischer, A., Doosje, B., Wigboldus, D., Hawk, S., Rotteveel, M., & Hess, U. (2011). Convergent and divergent responses to emotional displays of ingroup and outgroup. *Emotion, 11*, 286–298. https://doi.org/10.1037/a0022582
Vogt, S., Taylor, P., & Hopkins, B. (2003). Visuomotor priming by pictures of hand postures: Perspective matters. *Neuropsychologia, 41*, 941–951. https://doi.org/10.1016/s0028-3932(02)00319-6
Wang, Y., & Hamilton, A. (2013). Understanding the role of the 'self' in the social priming of mimicry. *PLoS One, 8*, e60249. https://doi.org/10.1371%2Fjournal.pone.0060249
Wang, Y., Newport, R., & Hamilton, A. F. d. C. (2011). Eye contact enhances mimicry of intransitive hand movements. *Biology Letters, 7*, 7–10. https://doi.org/10.1098/rsbl.2010.0279
Wang, Y., & Hamilton, A. F. d. C. (2012). Social top-down response modulation (STORM): A model of the control of mimicry in social interaction. *Frontiers in Human Neuroscience, 6*, 1–10. https://doi.org/10.3389/fnhum.2012.00153

Wang, Y., & Hamilton, A. F. d. C. (2014). Why does gaze enhance mimicry? Placing gaze-mimicry effects in relation to other gaze phenomena. *Quarterly Journal of Experimental Psychology, 67*, 747–762. https://doi.org/10.1080/17470218.2013.828316
Wang, Y., & Hamilton, A. F. d. C. (2015). Anterior medial prefrontal cortex implements social priming of mimicry. *Social Cognitive and Affective Neuroscience, 10*, 486–493. https://doi.org/10.1093/scan/nsu076
West, R., Godinho, C. A., Bohlen, L. C., Carey, R. N., Hastings, J., Lefevre, C. E., & Michie, S. (2019). Development of a formal system for representing behaviour-change theories. *Nature Human Behaviour, 3*, 526–536. https://doi.org/10.1038/s41562-019-0561-2
Westfal, M., Crusius, J., & Genschow, O. (2021). Imitation and interindividual differences: Belief in free will is not related to automatic imitation. *Acta Psychologica, 219*, 103374. https://doi.org/10.1016/j.actpsy.2021.103374
Westfal, M., Cracco, E., Crusius, J., & Genschow, O. (2024). Validation of an Online Imitation-Inhibition Task. *Unpublished manuscript.*
Weyers, P., Mühlberger, A., Kund, A., Hess, U., & Pauli, P. (2009). Modulation of facial reactions to avatar emotional faces by nonconscious competition priming. *Psychophysiology, 46*, 328–335.
Williams, K. D., & Jarvis, B. (2006). Cyberball: A program for use in research on interpersonal ostracism and acceptance. *Behavior Research Methods, 38*, 174–180.
Yabar, Y., Johnston, L., Miles, L., & Peace, V. (2006). Implicit behavioral mimicry: Investigating the impact of group membership. *Journal of Nonverbal Behavior, 30*, 97–113.

Chapter 12
Automatic Imitation of Hand Movements in Clinical and Neurodiverse Populations

Ellen Poliakoff and Emma Gowen

Introduction

Seeing someone else move can have a powerful effect on our own motor system, making us more likely to make the same movement even if we are not intending to do so. This *motor resonance* or *automatic imitation* is driven by overlapping representations between observed and executed action in fronto-parietal brain areas (e.g., Hardwick et al., 2018). This has historically been referred to as the "mirror neurone system" (e.g., Rizzolatti et al., 2009) or action observation network. These processes are thought to account for learning through observation (Buccino et al., 2004), as well as unconscious mimicry of movements and speech during social interactions (Iacoboni, 2009). It is also important to control automatic imitation, so that we do not copy everything we see. This top-down modulation of who and when to imitate is important for social bonding (Wang & Hamilton, 2012). Indeed, brain areas such as the medial prefrontal cortex and temporo-parietal area that inhibit automatic imitation are also involved in Theory of Mind processes (Spengler et al., 2010). These processes also require the ability to separate the representation of self and other (Spengler et al., 2010).

Given the involvement of motor and social-cognitive processes in automatic imitation, researchers have investigated how this process is affected in a range of clinical and neurodiverse populations. Indeed, "broken mirror neurone" accounts have been proposed for several conditions, including autism and schizophrenia (e.g., Mehta et al., 2014). These accounts suggest that impairments in the perception-action mapping attributed to mirror neurones could account for core symptoms, such as difficulties reading the intentions of other people. As will be outlined below, the motivation for studying automatic imitation differs between clinical groups,

E. Poliakoff (✉) · E. Gowen
Body Eyes and Movement (BEAM) Laboratory, Division of Psychology Communication & Human Neuroscience, School of Health Sciences, University of Manchester, Manchester, UK
e-mail: Ellen.Poliakoff@manchester.ac.uk; Emma.Gowen@manchester.ac.uk

O. Genschow, E. Cracco (eds.), *Automatic Imitation*,
https://doi.org/10.1007/978-3-031-62634-0_12

from investigating the control of actions or links to voluntary imitation (e.g., in schizophrenia, Simonsen et al., 2019) to using automatic imitation as a measure of social cognition (e.g., in Alzheimer's disease, Bisio et al., 2012). Moreover, reports of imitation behavior and utilization behavior, whereby patients imitate gestures or use objects apparently automatically, have been reported in patient populations such as those with frontal lobe damage (Lhermitte et al., 1986). It has also been argued that investigating the imitation of neutral hand actions could be a cleaner method of evaluating imitation, since there it does not involve processing emotions as is needed when using faces as stimuli (Simonsen et al., 2019). Furthermore, automatic imitation has also been employed as a simpler alternative to voluntary imitation which involves more cognitive processes such as understanding of the task, attention, and motor planning (e.g., Rudolph et al., 2022; Sowden et al., 2016).

Automatic imitation of hand movements has generally been investigated using two main types of task (for an overview, see Chap. 2; this volume). First, there are tasks based on the work of Brass and colleagues, where participants are required to make a particular finger response but ignore a concurrently viewed finger movement. They may be trying to move one finger, but primed to move a different finger (Brass et al., 2000) or moving in one direction (up/down) but primed to move in a different direction (Brass et al., 2001). Participants are slower in these *incompatible* trials than in *compatible* trials, where the moving finger matches the movement that they are trying to make (herein referred to as a *compatibility effect*; note that some authors use the terms congruent/incongruent to describe these conditions). To investigate the specificity of this effect for imitation, it is important to include a control condition to test for general spatial compatibility effects based on the location or direction of the stimulus. For example, some studies rotate the observed hand so the finger now moves left/right rather than up/down (e.g., Bek et al., 2018). Second, there are kinematic interference tasks where participants are asked to copy one element of an observed action (such as the timing or end point) but to ignore other elements such as the speed or orientation (horizontal/vertical; e.g., Albert et al., 2010). The measure of automatic imitation is the extent to which this task-irrelevant stimulus attribute affects their own movement. For both types of task, it can be informative to contrast biological (human) and non-biological (abstract moving shapes) stimuli (Gowen & Poliakoff, 2010) to explore the specificity of automatic imitation. Some variations include methods to investigate the modulation of automatic imitation, such as cueing participants to the origin of the hand (e.g., human or robotic/computer generated; Stanley et al., 2007) or manipulating the context of imitation (e.g., adding social cues; Cook & Bird, 2012).

In this review, we consider neurodegenerative conditions (Parkinson's, Alzheimer's), psychiatric or mental health conditions (schizophrenia, depression, eating disorders), and then neurodiverse/neurodevelopmental conditions (mirror touch synesthesia, autism, developmental coordination disorder, and Tourette's). We briefly introduce each condition and outline the motivations for investigating automatic imitation in that population before describing the key findings and tasks used. Identifying commonalities and differences across conditions is likely to be informative, particularly as there are mostly only a small number of studies per condition. This provides an opportunity to identify strengths and weaknesses in the methodologies and approaches, and to identify future research directions.

Alzheimer's Disease

Alzheimer's disease is a progressive neurodegenerative condition and the commonest cause of dementia. Given the visuomotor issues observed in Alzheimer's disease, such as control of fine finger movements (Yan et al., 2008) and the broad cortical damage, including the parietal cortex, it is important to investigate how automatic imitation of movements is affected in people with the condition. There are also earlier observations in the literature of spontaneous imitation of others in people with Alzheimer's disease, as well as those with frontal damage (Lhermitte et al., 1986, see section "Introduction").

Bisio et al. (2012) compared 25 people with mild-to-moderate Alzheimer's disease to 16 healthy older controls on a kinematic task where participants were asked to point to the end point of a moving (non-biological) target. Participants were not told whether the movement was computer or human-generated. Both groups were influenced by the velocity of the moving target, which the authors argue demonstrates motor resonance. However, the fact that the stimulus was non-biological means it is not conclusively automatic imitation. In addition, the Alzheimer's group made more anticipatory errors, beginning to move prior to the end of the stimulus movement. This suggests that the Alzheimer's group had greater difficulty in inhibiting observed motion, but future work will be needed to demonstrate whether this is a general effect or could be even stronger for human actions.

In summary, the study by Bisio et al. (2012) provides preliminary evidence that automatic imitation is intact in people with Alzheimer's disease. Importantly, if this is the case, it is relevant for therapeutic interventions that could circumvent the requirement for explicit instructions and relearning (Bisio et al., 2012). Skills such as communication could be addressed since the initiation and desire to communicate verbally and nonverbally can be reduced in people with Alzheimer's (Bisio et al., 2012). Moreover, people with Alzheimer's may forget to carry out healthy behaviors, such as drinking enough water, and such behaviors could be encouraged by providing imitative cues (see Nam & Shune, 2020 for a drinking intervention in healthy ageing).

Parkinson's Disease

Parkinson's disease is a neurodegenerative condition which is primarily a motor disorder associated with slower initiation of movement and lower amplitude of movements. These motor difficulties could mean that automatic imitation is impaired or reduced, or on the other hand, that this group could benefit from automatic imitation to facilitate their movements (Poliakoff, 2013). The first study to investigate automatic imitation in Parkinson's used a variant of the Brass task, where participants pressed a button in response to a go signal presented after observing either a finger or object moving downward (compatible) or upward (incompatible; Poliakoff et al., 2007). The control group ($N = 24$) exhibited a greater compatibility effect for the finger than object, while the Parkinson's group ($N = 24$), who were tested on their dopaminergic medication, exhibited equivalent compatibility effects for the two types of stimuli. This suggested that there could be a lack of specificity in their response; however, the size of compatibility effects was rather small overall. This is likely to be due to the go signal being presented after the moving stimulus so the effect of priming from the moving stimulus is reduced (see Gowen et al., 2010).

Albert et al. (2010) used an interference task where participants moved their hands horizontally or vertically, in time with an external stimulus. This stimulus was either a moving hand or a moving dot, which moved either in the same or opposite plane to the participant's own movement. They compared people with Parkinson's ($N = 10$) off medication to a group of controls ($N = 10$). Both groups exhibited a greater interference effect (from the stimulus moving in the mismatching plane) for the hand than for the dot, suggesting that automatic imitation is intact in people with Parkinson's. This contrasted with the findings of Poliakoff et al. (2007), which could potentially be because the movement was task-irrelevant in their study, while Albert et al. asked participants to attend to one aspect (timing) of the moving stimulus (see later discussion on the role of attention in automatic imitation).

Bek et al. (2018) set out to disentangle imitative compatibility from stimulus-response compatibility, by using a similar task to Poliakoff et al. (2007) but rotating the stimulus by 90° anti-clockwise such that a finger lift moved leftward on the screen and a finger press moved rightward. This meant that any general stimulus-response effects would work in the opposite direction to imitative compatibility. That is, the pressing finger moved rightward which was away from the responding (left) hand and in the opposite direction to orthogonal stimulus-response compatibility, whereby rightward and upward and leftward and downward movements are linked (Gowen et al., 2016). This allowed them to demonstrate imitative compatibility effects, that could not be accounted for by general stimulus-response compatibility, in both 23 people with mild to moderate Parkinson's (tested on medication) and 24 healthy controls. They also observed that response times for the incompatible finger movement correlated positively with level of motor symptoms in the Parkinson's group, suggesting greater difficulties in inhibitory control with increased symptom severity.

In summary, there is evidence for intact automatic imitation processes in Parkinson's, which has significance for therapeutic interventions. More basic cues (visual markers, metronomes) have been widely used to support movements in physiotherapy for Parkinson's (Nieuwboer, 2008) and evidence is now accumulating that action observation can be used to support interventions (for a review, see Temporiti et al., 2020). Observing another person's action (e.g., on video) can be used as a cue to elicit movements or to prompt motor imagery (mental simulation) of movements (Bek et al., 2019). Moreover, the urge to imitate can be capitalized on in interventions and activities such as dance classes which are popular with people with Parkinson's (Bek et al., 2020). It should be noted, however, that it is not yet known whether automatic imitation of biological moving stimuli is stronger than well-matched non-biological stimuli in people with Parkinson's. Moreover, although Albert et al. (2010) tested people with Parkinson's off their dopaminergic medication, no study to date has directly compared automatic imitation on and off medication.

Depression

Depression is characterized by low or depressed mood, anhedonia, and fatigue; motor slowing is also observed in some patients (e.g., Caligiuri & Ellwanger, 2000). In addition to emotional and physical symptoms, depression also involves impaired social functioning. Lhermitte (1993) reported both imitation and utilization behavior (see section "Introduction") in patients following major depression, which suggest a difficulty in inhibiting imitation. More recently, Bennabi et al. (2018) investigated this experimentally. They measured automatic imitation in 23 participants with unipolar depression and 11 controls using the same task that Bisio et al. (2012) used in people with Alzheimer's. Although the group with unipolar depression were slower to make pointing movements overall, they showed a similar influence of the target velocity to the controls; that is, automatic imitation of velocity of a non-biological stimulus. However, the group with depression produced more anticipatory errors; a similar pattern to that found for Alzheimer's (Bisio et al., 2012) and which the authors linked to general impairments in inhibitory processing and action monitoring.

In summary, there is only one study to date on depression and automatic imitation which suggests that it is intact. If motor resonance is intact in people with depression, this could potentially be capitalized on therapeutically to facilitate changes in behavior such as initiating healthy activities such as exercise and eating. However, as for the findings in Alzheimer's, the specificity of this effect to observed action (rather than any moving stimulus) is unclear.

Schizophrenia

Schizophrenia, a chronic mental health condition, typically emerges during adolescence with a breadth of possible symptoms including delusions, hallucinations, and cognitive impairment. In relation to imitation, "mimicry of movements" (echopraxia) has been reported in schizophrenia (e.g., Pridmore et al., 2008). It has also been hypothesized that mirror neurone system dysfunction might be associated with specific symptoms; impaired social cognition; negative symptoms (emotional blunting, motor slowing); and catatonic symptoms, such as being completely still for periods of time (for a review, see Mehta et al., 2014). Neurophysiological studies have shown both reduced and increased activity in frontro-parietal areas in people with schizophrenia during action observation (Mehta et al., 2014) and reduced voluntary imitation has been reported (Rudolph et al., 2022). Therefore, it is highly relevant to investigate automatic imitation in this population, which has been done in two recent studies with good sample sizes.

Simonsen et al. (2019) compared 39 individuals with a diagnosis of schizophrenia or schizoaffective disorder with 40 matched healthy controls. They used an automatic imitation task where participants moved their index or middle finger in response to a 1 or a 2, while simultaneously watching a compatible or incompatible finger movement. In addition, an effector priming control condition was used, where instead of the finger moving, the whole finger changed color (see Cook & Bird, 2012). The schizophrenia group were overall slower and made more errors. The authors contrasted the compatible moving finger versus primed (control) trials and found that both groups were faster with the moving finger, but this effect was larger for the schizophrenia group, suggesting increased automatic imitation. Furthermore, this effect was higher with increased antipsychotic dosage which was not accounted for by symptom severity. This is consistent with observations of stronger activity in putative mirror neurone system brain areas with greater doses of antipsychotic medication (Mehta et al., 2014). In the incompatible condition, there was no difference between conditions for either group. The authors conclude that inhibition of imitation is intact in the schizophrenia group. Nevertheless, it should be noted that a failure of inhibition could potentially explain the larger effect observed in the compatible condition. Nevertheless, the slightly unusual analysis approach—comparing across rather than within tasks—makes the interpretation of this study challenging (Rudolph et al., 2022).

Rudolph et al. (2022) compared 37 patients with schizophrenia with 36 matched controls. They used the same type of automatic imitation task (index versus middle finger) as Simonsen et al. (2019), but without the control condition. Based on previously observed null effects of social context on the performance of other tasks in people with schizophrenia, they also included a context imitation task based on Liepelt et al. (2009). In this task, participants also moved a finger according to whether they viewed a 1 or a 2, but they simultaneously viewed a static first-person image of a hand which had either congruent or incongruent fingers restrained. They found that reaction times were longer and errors higher in the schizophrenia group. In the automatic imitation task, there was a greater compatibility effect than in the control group (a very similar finding to that of Simonsen et al., 2019). They also reported that automatic imitation was not significantly affected by IQ, antipsychotic dosage, or positive/negative symptoms. For the context task, a smaller effect of action context (viewing a constrained hand) was found in the schizophrenia group compared to the controls. This suggests that the top-down control of imitation is affected in schizophrenia.

In summary, two studies have investigated automatic imitation in schizophrenia. Although the tasks and analysis approaches differ, both found evidence for increased automatic imitation in the group with schizophrenia, indicating a difficulty in inhibiting imitation which could link to a difficulty in self-other representation. Rudolph et al. (2022) also observed reduced top-down control of automatic imitation in their study. Difficulty modulating one's motor system in different contexts is likely to have social consequences for people with schizophrenia and could link to changes in processes such as empathy and theory of mind.

Mirror Touch Synesthesia

Individuals with mirror touch synesthesia experience tactile sensations on their own body, when they observe someone else being touched (Banissy & Ward, 2013). It is thought that approximately 1.8% of people experience mirror-touch synesthesia. It has been hypothesized that this may be due to a deficit in self-other representations, so Santiesteban et al. (2015) investigated how a group of 16 people with mirror touch synesthesia performed in an automatic imitation task in comparison to 16 controls. Participants were asked to move their index or second finger when they saw a 1 or 2 onscreen and ignore a concurrent video of another person's index or second finger moving. Importantly, they removed the three participants from the synesthesia group who reported experiencing touch sensations while observing the videos during the experiment, since this might have directly affected performance in the automatic imitation task. They found that the group with mirror-touch synesthesia were disproportionately slower than the controls in the incompatible (but not the compatible) condition, that is, an impairment in inhibiting automatic imitation. This is a very interesting initial finding; however, it would have been valuable to include a non-biological control task or a non-imitative inhibitory task to understand the specificity of the effect.

Eating Disorders

Feeding and eating disorders are psychiatric conditions associated with disruptions in eating behavior, including restricted eating and loss of control of eating. These conditions usually develop during adolescence, with up to 1 in 8 experiencing an eating disorder by age 20 (Stice et al., 2013). Social-cognitive processes, such as understanding the emotions and intentions of others (Oldershaw et al., 2011), have also been reported, so it is possible that automatic imitation may also be affected. In the first study of automatic imitation in eating disorders, Corsi et al. (2021) used an imitation-inhibition task where colored cues indicated whether to move the index or middle finger, at the same time as observing a video of an index or second finger moving. Importantly, they measured spatial as well as imitative compatibility by using both left and right hands (see Catmur & Heyes, 2011). They compared female participants with anorexia nervosa or bulimia nervosa ($N = 75$) to a control group ($N = 66$). The groups did not differ in spatial compatibility, but the eating disorder group exhibited lower imitative compatibility, as well as slower responses overall. There was also an influence of depression (but not anxiety) on imitative compatibility, but this did not account for the group difference.

In summary, a single study has found evidence for reduced automatic imitation in people with eating disorders. This finding clearly warrants replication and further investigation. In particular, the authors point out that participants were not screened for autism which could potentially account for the group difference (although see below, as automatic imitation has been found to be intact in autism). Indeed, as discussed below, co-morbidities are a salient issue across many of the conditions reviewed in this chapter. However, this study should be commended for statistically exploring the effects of anxiety and depression, using a good sample size and separating out spatial and imitative compatibility.

Autism

Compared to the other conditions reviewed, a relatively large number of studies have examined automatic imitation in autistic individuals. This particular focus on automatic imitation in autism is due to the link between imitation and social interaction, with difficulties in the latter being a key diagnostic criterion of autism. In particular, the "broken mirror neurone" theory of autism (e.g., Rizzolatti et al., 2009) suggests that automatic imitation should be reduced as it relies on activation of the observer's own motor system, a key function of the mirror neurone system. Although, it should be noted that little supporting evidence has been found for this theory (Southgate & Hamilton, 2008). Additionally, researchers have explored top-down regulation of automatic imitation in autism to understand whether contextual cues modulate the level of imitation in a similar manner between autistic and non-autistic individuals.

In contrast to initial predictions, the majority of studies show similar compatibility effects between autistic and non-autistic groups. This is across a range of paradigms including finger movement tasks (Cook & Bird, 2012; Grecucci et al., 2013; Schunke et al., 2016; Sowden et al., 2016; Gordon et al., 2020), hand movement tasks where participants must open or close their hand in response to viewing a compatible or incompatible opening/closing action (Bird et al., 2007; Forbes et al., 2017) and arm interference tasks (Gowen et al., 2008). This conclusion is supported by a meta-analysis (Cracco et al., 2018). Importantly, those studies that control for stimulus-response compatibility effects (Gordon et al. 2020; Sowden et al., 2016; Cook & Bird, 2012; Bird et al., 2007) confirm absent group differences, suggesting that imitative compatibility is intact in autistic individuals. Although, it should be noted that only Sowden et al. (2016) controlled for orthogonal spatial compatibility which has been shown to be influential (Czekóová et al., 2021). If basic motor resonance is intact in autism, this could be used within interventions, for example addressing the recently identified issue with inertia that involves difficulties with starting, stopping, or changing activities (Buckle et al., 2021). Participants who experienced inertia described that having other people around frequently helped them out of a "stuck" state, raising the possibility that observing the actions of others may facilitate appropriate movement during "stuck" states.

Regarding top-down regulation, a consistent pattern is that group differences in automatic imitation appear with the introduction of social primes or content, suggesting that while the basic mechanism of automatic imitation is intact in autistic individuals, modulation is affected. For example, non-autistic individuals show greater automatic imitation in the presence of socially relevant stimuli, such as direct compared to inverted gaze and social compared to non-social words, but for autistic individuals, this difference is absent (Bird et al., 2007; Forbes et al., 2017; although see Carr et al. 2021 for an absent effect of direct gaze in typical individuals). Gordon et al. (2020) directly tested top-down modulation by comparing compatibility effects between a block with mostly compatible trials and a block with mostly incompatible trials: modulation would be observed as lower compatibility effects for the block with mostly incompatible trials due to an increase in proactive inhibition. No group differences were observed. However, as regulation was assessed through proactive control of the task rather than social priming, it is possible that it could be specifically social top-down modulation that is altered. This remains to be tested within the same participants. Altered inhibitory regulation has also been used to explain occasional findings of increased compatibility effects for autistic compared to non-autistic groups (Bird et al., 2007; Spengler et al., 2010). However, it should be noted that stimulus-response compatibility effects were not fully controlled so it is unclear whether this represents increased imitative compatibility or general stimulus-response compatibility effects. As the level and location of attention influences automatic imitation (Gowen et al., 2010; Bach et al., 2007), it is possible that differences in attention between the groups lead to differences in automatic imitation and may explain rare findings of absent automatic imitation in autistic individuals (Cook et al., 2014).

In summary, it seems that the basic mechanism of automatic imitation is intact in autistic individuals but that top-down modulation in response to social cues and context may be reduced, potentially due to differences in attention to these cues. This would fit with findings of altered attention in voluntary imitation (Gowen et al., 2020) and it would be useful to investigate whether autistic individuals are able to modulate automatic imitation when attention is drawn to the social cues or primes.

Developmental Co-ordination Disorder/Dyspraxia

Developmental co-ordination disorder, or dyspraxia, is a developmental condition characterized by difficulties with performing and learning motor coordination skills at age-appropriate levels (Wilson et al., 2017). The rationale for studying automatic imitation in this group is to test the mirror neurone deficit hypothesis (Reynolds et al., 2015), which suggests that motor difficulties may arise due to observational learning and imitation being affected. Nobusako et al. (2018) used an interference task where 29 children with dyspraxia and 42 without made vertical movements using their index finger on a tablet, while observing an experimenter making vertical (compatible) or horizontal (incompatible) movements. In contrast to the group without dyspraxia, the dyspraxia group exhibited no compatibility effect. However, the dyspraxia group showed greater error (variability in the horizontal direction) for the compatible condition, which was correlated with manual dexterity. As the interference effect is calculated by subtracting compatible from incompatible conditions, this could have reduced any differences between the two conditions for the dyspraxia group, an idea supported by the observation that the incongruent condition was not significantly different between groups.

In contrast, Scott et al. (2019) observed intact automatic imitation in a small group of 12 children with and 12 children without dyspraxia. They used a task where participants performed a rhythmical action (e.g., face washing) which was preceded by a distractor action that was a different speed. Automatic imitation was measured by the effect of the distractor speed on the performed action.

Given the small participant numbers in the Scott et al. (2019) study and the potential confounding factor of greater error in the compatible condition for the Nobusako et al. (2018) study, the integrity of automatic imitation in dyspraxia remains unclear. Moving forward, it would be valuable to use more traditional finger type paradigms in this group, as well as comparing top-down modulation between dyspraxia and autistic groups using social primes to assess whether altered modulation in response to social context is unique to autistic groups.

Gille de Tourette's Syndrome

Gille de Tourette's Syndrome is a neuropsychiatric condition, involving motor and vocal tics, which typically appears in children under 10 years old. People with Tourette's often exhibit automatic imitation of behavior (e.g., gestures, facial movements) that they observe, known as echopraxia, as well as imitation of vocalizations (Ganos et al., 2012). Investigating, imitation may shed light on the relationship between echophenomena and tics (Ganos et al., 2012). Three studies have investigated automatic imitation of finger movements in Tourette's.

Jonas et al. (2010) compared a small sample of 11 adults with Tourette's, without medication or co-morbidities, to 10 healthy adults. Participants were required to lift their index finger or their little finger according to whether they heard a high or low auditory go signal presented at the start or end of a visual stimulus. This was either the movement of the compatible or incompatible finger, or a moving dot overlaid on the finger. Both groups exhibited a greater compatibility effect for the finger than the dot, when the auditory signal was presented early but not late. They found that the Tourette's group were slower for the finger than the dot for incompatible trials, while the controls were faster for the finger than the dot for compatible trials. The Tourette's group exhibited a slower mean response time which correlated with their level of tics. The authors suggest that a reduced level of motor excitability (i.e., slower response time) is a strategy for reducing tics and accounted for the slower incompatible finger response (see also Ganos et al., 2012).

Brandt et al. (2019) used the same task in 15 children with Tourette's (screened for Obsessive Compulsive Disorder or Attention Deficit Hyperactivity Disorder) and 15 control children. Both groups showed compatibility effects, but there was no difference between finger and dot conditions, showing a lack of specificity. The Tourette's group exhibited slower movements overall and a reduced compatibility effect. The authors again suggest that slower responses might be a strategy to compensate for the greater tendency to imitate through greater tonic inhibition, and this could also account for the reduced compatibility effect.

The final study by Quadrelli et al. (2021) investigated a larger number of child participants; they compared 32 with Tourette's, as well as other comorbidities (11 of whom had hand/arm tics) to 32 healthy controls. They used hand images from a first-person perspective (as if looking at one's own hand) and a slightly different task to previous work. Participants viewed the index finger or middle finger move and in separate blocks were instructed to either move the same finger or the opposite finger. Both groups were faster when they had to move the same compared to the opposite finger (compatibility effect), but the Tourette's group exhibited a smaller compatibility effect because they were faster than controls when moving the opposite finger and produced a greater number of errors overall. The increase in errors suggests a difficulty with motor inhibition, while in contrast, the reduced compatibility effect could suggest better inhibitory control in the incompatible condition. Alternatively, the authors argue it could reflect disinhibition of automatic imitation. Interestingly, the error rate was also associated with Attention Deficit Hyperactivity Disorder symptoms, suggesting that automatic imitation may be affected by Attention Deficit Hyperactivity Disorder. It is difficult to directly compare these findings with the previous studies given the difference in perspective of the hand and the task (where the finger that moved was relevant even in the incompatible block). Furthermore, presenting the conditions in different blocks may have influenced strategy, allowing participants to prepare in advance for compatible versus incompatible conditions.

In conclusion, the findings of automatic imitation in Tourette's remain inconclusive given the conflicting findings and different tasks used. However, the incompatible condition in the Quadrelli et al. (2021) study is particularly interesting whereby participants must attend to and perceive a moving finger, but subsequently inhibit this movement and choose to move the opposite finger. Considering response times and strategies is particularly relevant to this population, who adapt their motor systems through attempts to control the expression of their tics (Ganos et al., 2012). It would also be highly relevant to explore top-down control of automatic imitation in this population.

Discussion

The review of the literature demonstrates the relevance of investigating automatic imitation across a range of conditions with motor and social-cognitive consequences (see Table 12.1, for a summary). For most of the conditions reviewed, there are only a handful of studies, often with quite small participant numbers. Therefore, the integrity (or otherwise) of automatic imitation is not conclusive. As can be seen above, the range of tasks (and analysis approaches) can make comparisons of studies within and across conditions challenging. Throughout the review, we have highlighted some of the methodological strengths and weaknesses of studies and their approaches, which we briefly summarize below alongside suggestions for future research.

Table 12.1 Summary of main findings from each group

Group and number of studies	Findings	Future directions/questions
Alzheimer's Disease (1)	Possible *intact* automatic imitation of nonbiological kinematics Possible inhibitory difficulties	Replication needed Biological versus non-biological untested
Parkinson's Disease (3)	*Intact* automatic imitation Inhibitory difficulties may be associated with more severe symptoms	Biological versus non-biological inconclusive
Depression (1)	Possible *intact* automatic imitation of nonbiological kinematics Possible inhibitory difficulties	Replication needed Biological versus non-biological untested
Schizophrenia (2)	Possible *increased* automatic imitation Possible reduced effect of context (top-down modulation)	Replication needed with more standard tasks Further investigation of top-down modulation
Mirror-touch synesthesia (1)	Possible *increased* automatic imitation	Replication needed
Eating disorders (1)	Possible *reduced* automatic imitation	Replication needed
Autism (10)	*Intact* automatic imitation Possible reduced modulation of automatic imitation to social cues	Further investigation of top-down modulation
Developmental Discoordination Disorder (2)	*Inconclusive*	Further investigation needed
Tourette's (3)	*Inconclusive* Possible increased and reduced inhibitory control	Further investigation needed Need to accounting for changes in response time/strategy Relevant to investigate top-down modulation

We consider that the evidence is inconclusive for developmental coordination disorder and Tourette's. There is, however, some evidence of intact automatic imitation in several conditions: Parkinson's, Alzheimer's, depression, and autism. For autism, there are a reasonable number of studies, but for the other conditions, there are more limited numbers of studies. Importantly, if automatic imitation is preserved in a condition, then this process can be tapped into therapeutically. For example, in motor or behavioral interventions or within more complex interventions (e.g., dance or drama). This may be particularly valuable where there are issues with initiating movement or motor imagery (see section "Parkinson's Disease").

In contrast, increased automatic imitation effects have been observed in both schizophrenia and mirror-touch synesthesia (and possibly people with Parkinson's with more severe motor symptoms). This may reflect a difficulty in inhibiting automatic imitation and control of actions. Moreover, the top-down modulation of automatic imitation has been found to be affected in autism and in one study in schizophrenia. This suggests that these groups experience difficulty modulating social-motor behavior according to the context, and could account for inappropriate over-imitation. In contrast, reduced automatic imitation was observed in one study of eating disorders, which could suggest that interventions focussed on social cognition could be beneficial for this population.

In terms of task methodology, many studies did not include both biological and non-biological stimuli, which is essential to draw conclusions about the specificity of any observed effects to the automatic imitation of actions (for a review, see Gowen & Poliakoff, 2012). More basic stimulus-response compatibility effects should also be accounted for either by using a control condition or separating out imitative compatibility. Another element that varies between tasks is the task-relevance of the observed action, which might indicate when, how far or what finger the participant should move. If any features of the action are relevant, the participant is then required to selectively attend to one (or more) element of the observed action. Given that some level of attention to the stimulus is required to elicit automatic imitation (Gowen et al., 2010; Bach et al., 2007), differences in the attention toward the stimulus required by the task might account for differences between studies (Bek et al., 2018). Some studies have also separated the go signal from the observed action, for example using a flash (e.g., Poliakoff et al., 2007) or auditory tone (e.g., Jonas et al., 2010). This approach means the observed action is entirely task-irrelevant and allows the time-course of the automatic imitation effect to be explored, but it necessitates more complex stimuli. Using an auditory go signal may be beneficial because the go signal being presented in a separate sensory modality from the visual action stimulus potentially reduces selective attention demands. However, it introduces a multisensory component, which could be problematic for some participant groups (e.g., Poole et al., 2018).

More generally, the details of the task, as well as the broader laboratory context, might influence that extent to which attention is drawn to the to-be-ignored action. The instructions given to participants, particularly those in clinical or neurodiverse groups, are also critically important. In general, it is essential that participants understand the task and particularly what they need to focus their attention on. The

Bisio et al. (2012) study on Alzheimer's disease included other tasks to demonstrate that participants could follow the task instructions. For this, future researchers ought to consider collaborating with people affected by the condition to ensure that instructions and task are as clear as possible (e.g., Gowen et al., 2019). There is also opportunity to further investigate elements of the observed action(s) in these populations. First, the perspective of the observed action could be manipulated; most studies use the third-person perspective, with the first-person perspective being used in only a few studies (e.g., Quadrelli et al., 2021). This could inform how automatic imitation may be capitalized on within interventions, but may also be critical for investigating self-other processes. Motor resonance from object directed actions (Bek et al., 2018) or scenes involving multiple actors (Cracco et al., 2019) could also be explored. These are likely to be highly relevant in everyday social and action contexts (e.g., Rudoph et al., 2022). Researchers should also consider whether the observed actions and their kinematics are within the participant group's motor repertoire since this could account for altered effects of action observation (see Castiello et al., 2009 for discussion of this for voluntary imitation in Parkinson's).

In terms of analysis and interpretation, there is the challenge of accounting for group differences in response time (see Corsi et al., 2021) or motor performance (e.g., Nobusako et al., 2018), when examining differences between compatible and incompatible conditions. Indeed, in relation to Tourette's, it has been suggested that participants might slow down their overall response time as a strategy to allow greater control (e.g., Nobusako et al., 2018). This could be explored in future research by exploring sequential trial-by-trial effects on response time, such as slower responses post-error as has been investigated for the control of other stimulus-response compatibility effects (e.g., Praamstra & Plat, 2001). It should also be considered that automatic imitation effects increase with longer reaction times (Brass et al., 2001), so it is possible that participants who take longer to respond provide more opportunity for imitative effects to exert an influence on their response times. There was also variation between studies in their analysis approach; some focussed on comparing compatibility effects between groups, whereas others compared performance in the compatible or incompatible conditions between groups. Both approaches are potentially informative and ought to be reported. However, given the issue of overall response time mentioned above, future research could usefully include a neutral baseline condition (see Corsi et al., 2021), so that stronger conclusions can be drawn about facilitation versus inhibition in compatible and incompatible conditions (see Galpin et al., 2011 for a similar approach in relation to affordances). The inconsistent analysis approaches might also suggest that some of the analyses are exploratory and therefore should be interpreted cautiously. Future research ought to include pre-registration of the hypotheses and analysis.

In relation to participant characteristics, it is important to consider co-morbidities and other factors alongside the main condition of interest, for example accounting for age and depression (e.g., Corsi et al., 2021). It could also be important to screen for mirror-touch synesthesia, which could directly affect experience of the task itself (see above). While it might seem cleaner to exclude participants with comorbidities, this can reduce the generalizability of the findings to the broader population (Jonas et al., 2010), so ought to be used only with caution. Although gender was not observed to influence automatic imitation in a recent meta-analysis (Cracco et al., 2018), the gender balance of participant groups should also be considered, as there are observations of greater spatial interference in females (Darda et al., 2020). Many of the conditions also involve treatment using centrally acting medication (e.g., dopamine agonists or antagonists) and this should be documented (and included in the analysis) where possible. Interestingly, while symptoms of Attention Deficit Hyperactivity Disorder were found to affect error rate in one study (Quadrelli et al., 2021), we found no studies focussing on automatic imitation in people with this condition.

The relevance of automatic imitation across conditions indicates that it could be considered as transdiagnostic (e.g., Corsi et al., 2021). However, the variability in tasks and approaches used means it is currently difficult to compare across different studies and participant groups. Future research could usefully compare across groups within the same study or between studies using closely matched tasks. In particular, top-down modulation of automatic imitation has only been explored in a few conditions and it would be informative to investigate within and across conditions. It would also be valuable to measure automatic imitation longitudinally in some of the populations and to explore whether it is affected by changes in symptoms or interventions. For example, Mehta et al. (2014) hypothesize that changes in "mirror neurone" brain areas (involved in perception action mapping) could account for phasic changes of symptoms in schizophrenia. Finally, it is also important to consider automatic imitation of other motor processes, such as facial imitation (e.g., Simons et al., 2003) and imitation of posture (Pelosin et al., 2018), which were beyond the scope of this review but are of great importance for everyday social interaction and motor function.

Conclusion

In conclusion, there is clear justification to investigate automatic imitation and its modulation across a range of neurodegenerative, psychiatric, and neurodiverse conditions to inform both theory and the development of new intervention approaches. As summarized in Table 12.1, there is some evidence for increased, reduced, and intact automatic imitation in different conditions, but conclusions are often limited by small numbers of studies and participants. Future research ought to use tightly controlled tasks that control for general effects and pre-registered analyses to explore automatic imitation within and between groups, taking into account co-morbidities. Moreover, automatic imitation should be measured in different contexts, such as after social priming or using more complex stimuli.

References

Albert, N. B., Peiris, Y., Cohen, G., Miall, R. C., & Praamstra, P. (2010). Interference effects from observed movement in Parkinson's disease. *Journal of Motor Behavior, 42*, 145–149. https://doi.org/10.1080%2F00222891003612805

Bach, P., Peatfield, N. A., & Tipper, S. P. (2007). Focusing on body sites: The role of spatial attention in action perception. *Experimental Brain Research, 178*, 509–517. https://doi.org/10.1007/s00221-006-0756-4

Banissy, M. J., & Ward, J. (2013). Mechanisms of self-other representations and vicarious experiences of touch in mirror-touch synesthesia. *Frontiers in Human Neuroscience, 7*, 112. https://doi.org/10.3389/fnhum.2013.00112

Bek, J., Gowen, E., Vogt, S., Crawford, T. J., & Poliakoff, E. (2018). Action observation produces motor resonance in Parkinson's disease. *Journal of Neuropsychology, 12*, 298–311. https://doi.org/10.1111%2Fjnp.12133

Bek, J., Gowen, E., Vogt, S., Crawford, T. J., & Poliakoff, E. (2019). Combined action observation and motor imagery influences hand movement amplitude in Parkinson's disease. *Parkinsonism & Related Disorders, 61*, 126–131. https://doi.org/10.1016/j.parkreldis.2018.11.001

Bek, J., Arakaki, A. I., Lawrence, A., Sullivan, M., Ganapathy, G., & Poliakoff, E. (2020). Dance and Parkinson's: A review and exploration of the role of cognitive representations of action. *Neuroscience & Biobehavioral Reviews, 109*, 16–28. https://doi.org/10.1016/j.neubiorev.2019.12.023

Bennabi, D., Carvalho, N., Bisio, A., Haffen, E., & Pozzo, T. (2018). Motor resonance mechanisms during action imitation in depression. *Neuropsychiatry, 8*, 1503–1512. http://dx.doi.org/10.4172/Neuropsychiatry.1000484

Bird, G., Leighton, J., Press, C., & Heyes, C. (2007). Intact automatic imitation of human and robot actions in autism spectrum disorders. *Proceedings of the Royal Society B: Biological Sciences, 274*, 3027–3031. https://doi.org/10.1098%2Frspb.2007.1019

Bisio, A., Casteran, M., Ballay, Y., Manckoundia, P., Mourey, F., & Pozzo, T. (2012). Motor resonance mechanisms are preserved in Alzheimer's disease patients. *Neuroscience, 222*, 58–68. https://doi.org/10.3389%2Ffnagi.2016.00048

Brandt, V. C., Moczydlowski, A., Jonas, M., Boelmans, K., Bäumer, T., Brass, M., & Münchau, A. (2019). Imitation inhibition in children with Tourette syndrome. *Journal of Neuropsychology, 13*, 82–95. https://doi.org/10.1111/jnp.12132

Brass, M., Bekkering, H., Wohlschläger, A., & Prinz, W. (2000). Compatibility between observed and executed finger movements: Comparing symbolic, spatial, and imitative cues. *Brain and Cognition, 44*, 124–143. https://doi.org/10.1006/brcg.2000.1225

Brass, M., Bekkering, H., & Prinz, W. (2001). Movement observation affects movement execution in a simple response task. *Acta Psychologica, 106*, 3–22. https://doi.org/10.1016/s0001-6918(00)00024-x

Buccino, G., Vogt, S., Ritzl, A., Fink, G. R., Zilles, K., Freund, H. J., & Rizzolatti, G. (2004). Neural circuits underlying imitation learning of hand actions: An event-related fMRI study. *Neuron, 42*, 323–334. https://doi.org/10.1016/s0896-6273(04)00181-3

Buckle, K. L., Leadbitter, K., Poliakoff, E., & Gowen, E. (2021). "No way out except from external intervention": First-hand accounts of autistic inertia. *Frontiers in Psychology, 1592*. https://doi.org/10.3389/fpsyg.2021.631596

Caligiuri, M. P., & Ellwanger, J. (2000). Motor and cognitive aspects of motor retardation in depression. *Journal of Affective Disorders, 57*, 83–93. https://doi.org/10.1016/s0165-0327(99)00068-3

Carr, E. W., Bird, G., Catmur, C., & Winkielman, P. (2021). Dissociable effects of averted "gaze" on the priming of bodily representations and motor actions. *Acta Psychologica, 212*, 103225. https://doi.org/10.1016/j.actpsy.2020.103225

Castiello, U., Ansuini, C., Bulgheroni, M., Scaravilli, T., & Nicoletti, R. (2009). Visuomotor priming effects in Parkinson's disease patients depend on the match between the observed and the executed action. *Neuropsychologia, 47*, 835–842. https://doi.org/10.1016/j.neuropsychologia.2008.12.016

Catmur, C., & Heyes, C. (2011). Time course analyses confirm independence of imitative and spatial compatibility. *Journal of Experimental Psychology: Human Perception and Performance, 37*, 409–421. https://psycnet.apa.org/doi/10.1037/a0019325

Cook, J. L., & Bird, G. (2012). Atypical social modulation of imitation in autism spectrum conditions. *Journal of Autism and Developmental Disorders, 42*, 1045–1051. https://doi.org/10.1007/s10803-011-1341-7

Cook, J., Swapp, D., Pan, X., Bianchi-Berthouze, N., & Blakemore, S. J. (2014). Atypical interference effect of action observation in autism spectrum conditions. *Psychological Medicine, 44*, 731–740. https://doi.org/10.1017%2FS0033291713001335

Corsi, E., Cardi, V., Sowden, S., Coll, M. P., Cascino, G., Ricca, V., … & Monteleone, A. M. (2021). Socio-cognitive processing in people with eating disorders: Computerized tests of mentalizing, empathy and imitation skills. *International Journal of Eating Disorders, 54*, 1509–1518. https://doi.org/10.1002/eat.23556

Cracco, E., Bardi, L., Desmet, C., Genschow, O., Rigoni, D., De Coster, L., … & Brass, M. (2018). Automatic imitation: A meta-analysis. *Psychological Bulletin, 144*, 453–500. https://doi.org/10.1037/bul0000143

Cracco, E., Keysers, C., Clauwaert, A., & Brass, M. (2019). Representing multiple observed actions in the motor system. *Cerebral Cortex, 29*, 3631–3641. https://doi.org/10.1093/cercor/bhy237

Czekóová, K., Shaw, D. J., Lamoš, M., Špiláková, B., Salazar, M., & Brázdil, M. (2021). Imitation or polarity correspondence? Behavioural and neurophysiological evidence for the confounding influence of orthogonal spatial compatibility on measures of automatic imitation. *Cognitive, Affective, & Behavioral Neuroscience, 21*, 212–230. https://doi.org/10.3758%2Fs13415-020-00860-y

Darda, K. M., Butler, E. E., & Ramsey, R. (2020). Individual differences in social and non-social cognitive control. *Cognition, 202*, 104317. https://doi.org/10.1016/j.cognition.2020.104317

Forbes, P. A., Wang, Y., & de C Hamilton, A. F. (2017). STORMy interactions: Gaze and the modulation of mimicry in adults on the autism spectrum. *Psychonomic Bulletin & Review, 24*, 529–535. https://doi.org/10.3758%2Fs13423-016-1136-0

Galpin, A., Tipper, S. P., Dick, J. P., & Poliakoff, E. (2011). Object affordance and spatial-compatibility effects in Parkinson's disease. *Cortex, 47*, 332–341. https://doi.org/10.1016/j.cortex.2010.01.011

Ganos, C., Ogrzal, T., Schnitzler, A., & Münchau, A. (2012). The pathophysiology of echopraxia/echolalia: Relevance to Gilles de la Tourette syndrome. *Movement Disorders, 27*, 1222–1229. https://doi.org/10.1002/mds.25103

Gordon, A., Geddert, R., Hogeveen, J., Krug, M. K., Obhi, S., & Solomon, M. (2020). Not so automatic imitation: Expectation of incongruence reduces interference in both autism spectrum disorder and typical development. *Journal of Autism and Developmental Disorders, 50*, 1310–1323. https://doi.org/10.1007/s10803-019-04355-9

Gowen, E., & Poliakoff, E. (2012). How does visuomotor priming differ for biological and non-biological stimuli? A review of the evidence. *Psychological Research, 76*, 407–420. https://psycnet.apa.org/doi/10.1007/s00426-011-0389-5

Gowen, E., Stanley, J., & Miall, R. C. (2008). Movement interference in autism-spectrum disorder. *Neuropsychologia, 46*, 1060–1068. https://doi.org/10.1016%2Fj.neuropsychologia.2007.11.004

Gowen, E., Bradshaw, C., Galpin, A., Lawrence, A., & Poliakoff, E. (2010). Exploring visuomotor priming following biological and non-biological stimuli. *Brain and Cognition, 74*, 288–297. https://psycnet.apa.org/doi/10.1016/j.bandc.2010.08.010

Gowen, E., Bolton, E., & Poliakoff, E. (2016). Believe it or not: Moving non-biological stimuli believed to have human origin can be represented as human movement. *Cognition, 146*, 431–438. https://doi.org/10.1016/j.cognition.2015.10.010

Gowen, E., Taylor, R., Bleazard, T., Greenstein, A., Baimbridge, P., & Poole, D. (2019). Guidelines for conducting research studies with the autism community. *Autism Policy & Practice, 2*, 29.

Gowen, E., Vabalas, A., Casson, A. J., & Poliakoff, E. (2020). Instructions to attend to an observed action increase imitation in autistic adults. *Autism, 24*, 730–743. https://doi.org/10.1177/1362361319882810

Grecucci, A., Brambilla, P., Siugzdaite, R., Londero, D., Fabbro, F., & Rumiati, R. I. (2013). Emotional resonance deficits in autistic children. *Journal of Autism and Developmental Disorders, 43*, 616–628. https://doi.org/10.1007/s10803-012-1603-z

Hardwick, R. M., Caspers, S., Eickhoff, S. B., & Swinnen, S. P. (2018). Neural correlates of action: Comparing meta-analyses of imagery, observation, and execution. *Neuroscience & Biobehavioral Reviews, 94*, 31–44. https://doi.org/10.1016/j.neubiorev.2018.08.003

Iacoboni, M. (2009). Imitation, empathy, and mirror neurons. *Annual Review of Psychology, 60*, 653–670. https://doi.org/10.1146/annurev.psych.60.110707.163604

Jonas, M., Thomalla, G., Biermann-Ruben, K., Siebner, H. R., Muller-Vahl, K., Baumer, T.,…Munchau, A. (2010). Imitation in patients with Gilles de la Tourette syndrome–a behavioral study. *Movement Disorders, 25*, 991–999. https://doi.org/10.1002/mds.22994

Lhermitte, F. (1993) [Imitation and utilization behavior in major depressive states]. *Bulletin de l'Academie Nationale de Medecine, 177*, 883–890–892. https://doi.org/10.1136%2Fjnnp.61.4.396

Lhermitte, F., Pillon, B., & Serdaru, M. (1986). Human autonomy and the frontal lobes. Part I: Imitation and utilization behavior: A neuropsychological study of 75 patients. *Annals of Neurology, 19*, 326–334. https://doi.org/10.1002/ana.410190404

Liepelt, R., Ullsperger, M., Obst, K., Spengler, S., von Cramon, D. Y., & Brass, M. (2009). Contextual movement constraints of others modulate motor preparation in the observer. *Neuropsychologia, 47*, 268–275. https://doi.org/10.1016/j.neuropsychologia.2008.07.008

Mehta, U. M., Thirthalli, J., Aneelraj, D., Jadhav, P., Gangadhar, B. N., & Keshavan, M. S. (2014). Mirror neuron dysfunction in schizophrenia and its functional implications: A systematic review. *Schizophrenia Research, 160*, 9–19. https://doi.org/10.1016/j.schres.2014.10.040

Nam, S., & Shune, S. E. (2020). Behavioral mimicry as a strategy to increase drinking behaviors in older adults. *American Journal of Speech-Language Pathology, 29*, 1640–1649. https://doi.org/10.1044/2020_ajslp-19-00184

Nieuwboer, A. (2008). Cueing for freezing of gait in patients with Parkinson's disease: A rehabilitation perspective. *Movement Disorders, 23*, S475–S481. https://doi.org/10.1002/mds.21978

Nobusako, S., Sakai, A., Tsujimoto, T., Shuto, T., Nishi, Y., Asano, D., … & Nakai, A. (2018). Deficits in visuo-motor temporal integration impacts manual dexterity in probable developmental coordination disorder. *Frontiers in Neurology, 9*, 114. https://doi.org/10.3389/fneur.2018.00114

Oldershaw, A., Hambrook, D., Stahl, D., Tchanturia, K., Treasure, J., & Schmidt, U. (2011). The socio-emotional processing stream in anorexia nervosa. *Neuroscience & Biobehavioral Reviews, 35*, 970–988. https://doi.org/10.1016/j.neubiorev.2010.11.001

Pelosin, E., Bisio, A., Pozzo, T., Lagravinese, G., Crisafulli, O., Marchese, R., … & Avanzino, L. (2018). Postural stabilization strategies to motor contagion induced by action observation are impaired in Parkinson's disease. *Frontiers in Neurology, 9*, 105. https://doi.org/10.3389%2Ffneur.2018.00105

Poliakoff, E. (2013). Representation of action in Parkinson's disease: Imagining, observing, and naming actions. *Journal of Neuropsychology, 7*, 241–254. https://psycnet.apa.org/doi/10.1111/jnp.12005

Poliakoff, E., Galpin, A., Dick, J., Moore, P., & Tipper, S. P. (2007). The effect of viewing graspable objects and actions in Parkinson's disease. *Neuroreport, 28*, 483–487. https://doi.org/10.1097/wnr.0b013e32805867a1

Poole, D., Gowen, E., Warren, P. A., & Poliakoff, E. (2018). Visual-tactile selective attention in autism spectrum condition: An increased influence of visual distractors. *Journal of Experimental Psychology: General, 147*, 1309–1324. https://doi.org/10.1037/xge0000425

Praamstra, P., & Plat, F. M. (2001). Failed suppression of direct visuomotor activation in Parkinson's disease. *Journal of Cognitive Neuroscience, 13*, 31–43. https://doi.org/10.1162/089892901564153

Pridmore, S., Brüne, M., Ahmadi, J., & Dale, J. (2008). Echopraxia in schizophrenia: Possible mechanisms. *Australian & New Zealand Journal of Psychiatry, 42*, 565–571. https://doi.org/10.1080/00048670802119747

Quadrelli, E., Bartoli, B., Bolognini, N., Cavanna, A. E., Zibordi, F., Nardocci, N., … & Termine, C. (2021). Automatic imitation in youngsters with Gilles de la Tourette syndrome: A behavioral study. *Child Neuropsychology, 27*, 782–798. https://doi.org/10.1080/09297049.2021.1892050

Reynolds, J. E., Thornton, A. L., Elliott, C., Williams, J., Lay, B. S., & Licari, M. K. (2015). A systematic review of mirror neuron system function in developmental coordination disorder: Imitation, motor imagery, and neuroimaging evidence. *Research in Developmental Disabilities, 47*, 234–283. https://doi.org/10.1016/j.ridd.2015.09.015

Rizzolatti, G., Fabbri-Destro, M., & Cattaneo, L. (2009). Mirror neurons and their clinical relevance. *Nature Clinical Practice Neurology, 5*, 24–34. https://doi.org/10.1038/ncpneuro0990

Rudolph, A., Liepelt, R., Kaffes, M., Hofmann-Shen, C., Montag, C., & Neuhaus, A. H. (2022). Motor cognition in schizophrenia: Control of automatic imitation and mapping of action context are reduced. *Schizophrenia Research, 240*, 116–124. http://dx.doi.org/10.1016/j.schres.2021.12.024

Santiesteban, I., Bird, G., Tew, O., Cioffi, M. C., & Banissy, M. J. (2015). Mirror-touch synaesthesia: Difficulties inhibiting the other. *Cortex, 71*, 116–121. http://dx.doi.org/10.1016/j.cortex.2015.06.019

Schunke, O., Schöttle, D., Vettorazzi, E., Brandt, V., Kahl, U., Bäumer, T., … & Münchau, A. (2016). Mirror me: Imitative responses in adults with autism. *Autism, 20*, 134–144. https://dx.doi.org/10.1177/1362361315571757

Scott, M. W., Emerson, J. R., Dixon, J., Tayler, M. A., & Eaves, D. L. (2019). Motor imagery during action observation enhances automatic imitation in children with and without developmental coordination disorder. *Journal of Experimental Child Psychology, 183*, 242–260. https://doi.org/10.1016/j.humov.2020.102620

Simons, G., Ellgring, H., & Smith Pasqualini, M. (2003). Disturbance of spontaneous and posed facial expressions in Parkinson's disease. *Cognition & Emotion, 17*, 759–778. http://dx.doi.org/10.1080/02699930302280

Simonsen, A., Fusaroli, R., Skewes, J. C., Roepstorff, A., Campbell-Meiklejohn, D., Mors, O., & Bliksted. (2019). Enhanced automatic action imitation and intact imitation-inhibition in schizophrenia. *Schizophrenia Bulletin, 45*, 87–95. http://dx.doi.org/10.1093/schbul/sby006

Southgate, V., & Hamilton, A. F. D. C. (2008). Unbroken mirrors: Challenging a theory of autism. *Trends in Cognitive Sciences, 12*, 225–229. https://doi.org/10.1016/j.tics.2008.03.005

Sowden, S., Koehne, S., Catmur, C., Dziobek, I., & Bird, G. (2016). Intact automatic imitation and typical spatial compatibility in autism spectrum disorder: Challenging the broken mirror theory. *Autism Research, 9*, 292–300. https://doi.org/10.1002/aur.1511

Spengler, S., von Cramon, D. Y., & Brass, M. (2010). Resisting motor mimicry: Control of imitation involves processes central to social cognition in patients with frontal and temporo-parietal lesions. *Social Neuroscience, 5*, 401–416. https://doi.org/10.1080/17470911003687905

Stanley, J., Gowen, E., & Miall, R. C. (2007). Effects of agency on movement interference during observation of a moving dot stimulus. *Journal of Experimental Psychology: Human Perception and Performance, 33*, 915–926. https://doi.org/10.1037%2F0096-1523.33.4.915

Stice, E., Marti, C. N., & Rohde, P. (2013). Prevalence, incidence, impairment, and course of the proposed DSM-5 eating disorder diagnoses in an 8-year prospective community study of young women. *Journal of Abnormal Psychology, 122*, 445–457. https://doi.org/10.1037/a0030679

Temporiti, F., Adamo, P., Cavalli, E., & Gatti, R. (2020). Efficacy and characteristics of the stimuli of action observation therapy in subjects with Parkinson's disease: A systematic review. *Frontiers in Neurology, 11*, 808. https://doi.org/10.3389/fneur.2020.00808

Wang, Y., & Hamilton, A. F. D. C. (2012). Social top-down response modulation (STORM): A model of the control of mimicry in social interaction. *Frontiers in Human Neuroscience, 6*, 153. https://doi.org/10.3389%2Ffnhum.2012.00153

Wilson, P. H., Smits-Engelsman, B., Caeyenberghs, K., Steenbergen, B., Sugden, D., Clark, J., Mumford, N., & Blank, R. (2017). Cognitive and neuroimaging findings in developmental coordination disorder: New insights from a systematic review of recent research. *Developmental Medicine and Child Neurology, 59*, 1117–1129. http://dx.doi.org/10.1111/dmcn.13530

Yan, J. H., Rountree, S., Massman, P., Smith Doody, R., & Li, H. (2008). Alzheimer's disease and mild cognitive impairment deteriorate fine movement control. *Journal of Psychiatric Research, 42*, 1203–1212. http://dx.doi.org/10.1016/j.jpsychires.2008.01.006

Chapter 13
The Benefits—and Costs—of Behavioral Mimicry: Applications in Marketing, Sales, and Therapy

Wojciech Kulesza and Tanya Chartrand

Benefits Stemming from Mimicry: Liking of and Closeness to Other People and Groups

In 1999, the term "the chameleon effect" was introduced by Chartrand and Bargh (1999) on the basis of several experiments. Two of these experiments found that people automatically imitate a confederate's specific actions (e.g., smiling, rubbing the face). One of the experiments showed that this tendency to mimic depends on the level of perspective taking: the higher participants scored on perspective taking abilities (i.e., a form of cognitive), the greater their tendency to imitate (for a detailed and critical coverage of moderators of the chameleon effect, please see Chap. 11; this volume). More relevant for the current chapter on consequences of mimicry is an experiment reported in the same paper in which participants were (or were not) nonverbally imitated by a confederate. The results indicated that participants who were mimicked liked the confederate more strongly and perceived the interaction as smoother than participants who were not mimicked.

Subsequent research has deepened the understanding of the social consequences of nonverbal mimicry by going beyond the effects of liking and smooth interactions. For instance, in one study, participants were asked to interact with another person in such a way that one person watched a video clip and then reported its content to the other person (Stel & Vonk, 2010). The participants who were assigned the role of listener were told to either imitate their partner or to refrain from such behavior. The

W. Kulesza (✉)
SWPS University, Psychology Department, Warsaw, Poland
e-mail: wkulesza@swps.edu.pl

T. Chartrand
Duke University: The Fuqua School of Business, Durham, NC, USA
e-mail: tanya.chartrand@duke.edu

O. Genschow, E. Cracco (eds.), *Automatic Imitation*,
https://doi.org/10.1007/978-3-031-62634-0_13

results showed that the listener as well as the reporter indicated a greater sense of closeness when the listener imitated their partner.

The fact that closeness increased as a result of mimicry suggests that mimicry could be a useful tool in therapeutic settings when developing a relationship between a therapist and patient. Indeed, several studies focusing on clinical relationships support this idea (for a more extensive review, see Chaps. 12 and 15; this volume).

Taken together, research has demonstrated that mimicry changes the perception of the person with whom they are interacting as well as the perception of the interaction itself. Importantly, this positive effect spills over from dyadic interactions to the perception of the group that the mimicking partner represents. For example, in one experiment, an experimenter approached people who were just exiting a church after a service and asked them to have a conversation about their faith (Zgliniecka & Kulesza, 2014). The interviewer, after hearing the answer to the first question, responded "I personally am a non-believer, but I perfectly understand what you mean." Afterwards, she proceeded to mimic (or not) participants. Participants perceived the mimicking non-believer to be more honest, friendly, and modest, and they were liked more strongly. In a similar study, Inzlicht et al. (2012) found that instructing non-Black students to imitate a Black person led to a reduction of general bias against the Black outgroup.

While the above-reviewed literature indicates that being mimicked influences the perception of the mimicker and the group the mimicker represents, other research has demonstrated that mimicry can also affect the perception of the larger social environment. Stel et al. (2013), for instance, investigated whether mimicry influences the perception of the world as a fair place. Analyses of data obtained from men (comparisons for women showed no significant differences) showed that when they were asked to mimic a person on a computer screen (regardless of gender), they perceived the world as a fairer place compared to when they were not instructed to mimic. In another line of research, Stel and Harinck (2011) showed that mimicked persons perceived their bond with the social environment as stronger than those participants who were not mimicked.

Prosocial Behavior

Several studies found that being mimicked increases pro-social orientations. For example, Stel and Harinck (2011) found in their analysis of the influence of mimicry on political views that after being mimicked, individuals support pro-social activities undertaken by authorities more strongly (Stel & Harinck, 2011).

Other studies showed that being mimicked also increases helping behaviors. For example, van Baaren et al. (2004) let participants engage in a conversation with an experimenter. The experimenter either mimicked or did not mimic the participants' gestures. After the conversation, the experimenter asked the participants to fill in a set of questionnaires and then left the room. When re-entering the room, the experimenter dropped pens they were carrying on a pile of documents. The researchers were interested in how many pens the participants would pick up as a proxy of prosocial behavior. The results indicated that participants who had been mimicked previously picked up more pens than control participants. The second experiment found the same effects even when a person who was not the mimicker dropped the pens. In the third study, participants were asked to donate to a charitable cause. The person asking for a donation was either someone they had talked to previously or a stranger. The results showed that more participants in the mimicry condition donated a larger amount than participants in the control condition) irrespective of whether the mimicker or a stranger asked for donations. This indicates that the pro-social consequences of mimicry can spill over to other persons not involved in the social situation in which mimicry took place.

Changes in Self-perception

While the above-reviewed literature suggests that mimicry increases pro-social behavior, the question arises as to how this effect can be explained. Several researchers have proposed that changes in pro-social behavior could be due to a perception shift from "me" to "others." In other words, pro-social behavior could be explained by people perceiving themselves as more interdependent. Self-construal theory (Markus & Kitayama, 1991) puts forward that the type of culture in which individuals grow up (i.e., collective versus individualistic) influences how they perceive the social world around them (Cousins, 1989). For instance, research has shown that in collectivistic cultures, such as East Asian (in contrast to Western cultures), people perceive themselves as interdependent—that is, they define themselves in relation to other people. In contrast, Western countries define themselves as independent self-construal (Nisbett et al. 2001).

In a study, Redeker et al. (2011) tested whether being instructed to mimic others changes in participants' self-perception. The results indicated that participants who were asked to mimic others reported a more interdependent self-construal than participants who were not asked to mimic. Another study explored the link between mimicry and the perception of the social world (van Baaren et al., 2003). In this study, the researchers tested whether people of different cultural backgrounds (i.e., collective versus individualistic) differ in their tendency to mimic. Students at an American University who were either born in the USA (individualistic culture) or recently came from Japan (collectivist culture) were invited to participate in the experiment. The participants engaged in two conversations. During one conversation, they interacted with an American confederate, whereas they interacted with a Japanese confederate in the other conversation. During each conversation, the confederate touched her head or face. The results showed that the degree of imitation depended on the participants' culture, with Japanese students (interdependent self-construal) spending more time imitating than Americans (independent self-construal). Interestingly, this effect could be detected regardless of whether participants were interacting with a confederate from the same or a different culture.

To test whether self-construal accounts for the influence of mimicry on pro-social behavior, Ashton-James et al. (2007) conducted a series of experiments. The researchers found that being mimicked leads to interdependent self-perceptions. For example, in one experiment, Ashton-James et al. tested whether the relationship between mimicry and pro-social behavior is mediated by participants' self-perception. Participants were initially interviewed about their day. During this interview, the interviewer either mimicked or did not mimic the participants. After the interview, participants' self-construal was measured. At the end of the experiment, participants were asked if they would agree to help a PhD student by filling out additional questionnaires. The results showed that participants' willingness to help depended on prior mimicry: when being mimicked, more participants were willing to support the PhD student than when they were not mimicked. Furthermore, the results revealed a stronger interdependent self-construal in mimicked versus non-imitated persons. A mediation analysis showed that the relationship between helping behavior and mimicry was due to changes in self-construal.

Business Contexts: Retail and Negotiations

So far, we have reviewed literature showing that mimicry changes the perception of others (e.g., increased liking, tendency to provide help), and that self-perception shifts from "me" to "others," leading to enhanced prosocial behavior toward the mimicker. This suggests that mimicry may be a powerful element in persuasion, business, or retail settings because it increases susceptibility to social influence (Drury & van Swol, 2005; van Swol, 2003).

In early work testing this assumption, students were asked to rate to what extent they would support the idea of building a pub on a university campus and to offer a justification for their opinion (Drury & van Swol, 2005). The confederate's task was to express an opinion different from that of the participant and to mimic (or not) the participants. Results revealed that mimickers were considered by the participants to be more persuasive than non-mimickers. In a similar study, van Swol (2003) showed that participants perceived persons who nonverbally mimicked them as more persuasive than those who did not mimic them.

These results led researchers to explore possible business applications of this effect in several lines of research. For example, in a retail context, it was found that mimicry impacts the evaluation of products (Stel et al., 2011). Participants in this study were asked to mimic the people visible on a computer screen (presented as an advertisement), to refrain from mimicking, or were provided no instruction regarding mimicry. The authors found that the mimicking students liked commercials more than the non-mimicking ones. In another experiment, the researchers found that the instruction to imitate positively influenced the perception of advertised products, but did not change attitudes towards other, similar products. Willingness to buy was similarly affected; mimicking participants were willing to buy the advertised products more often, but only those that were featured in the advertisement, not other, similar products.

The influence of mimicry on mimickees and their consumer judgments was also analyzed by Tanner et al. (2008). The results of their study showed that after being mimicked by a person who introduced an isotonic drink, participants perceived the drink as more favorable. This study inspired Kulesza et al. (2017) to investigate whether mimicry changes initial perceptions to be more positive (i.e., if an initial assessment were negative, it would become more favorable after imitation), or whether mimicry simply strengthens whatever the initial perceptions are (i.e., if an initial assessment were negative, it would become even less favorable after mimicry). To investigate this question, experimenters gave participants a bad-tasting beverage to drink. Then, a confederate mimicked (or not) the participants. After mimicry took place, participants indicated their opinion about the beverage. The results demonstrated that being mimicked led to a more favorable opinion about the drink. Additionally, willingness to pay for the isotonic drink increased, leading to the conclusion that mimicry may lead to increased sales even if the beverage tastes bad.

Since the aforementioned studies were run in laboratories (far from a direct retail context), follow-up research tested applications of mimicry in natural settings. For instance, Kulesza et al. (2014) investigated the consequences of mimicry in a beauty supply store. While serving the customer, a saleswoman was instructed to either imitate or not the customer's gestures. Along with the manipulation of mimicry, the researchers also manipulated the attractiveness of the saleswoman by having her either wear make-up or not. The analysis showed that customers spent more money and were more satisfied with the service in the condition in which they were mimicked, as compared to the condition in which they were not mimicked. Interestingly, this effect increased when clients were mimicked by the attractive (as compared to the less attractive) saleswoman.

In more recent studies, the influence of mimicry on service satisfaction was explored in more detail by Kulesza et al. (2022a, b) who assessed customers of a cable TV provider who were mimicked (or not) by a technician. The results indicated that even short periods of mimicry impacted perceived service quality. In another experiment, Kulesza and colleagues (2018) investigated customers of a restaurant. Waitresses at a restaurant were instructed to mimic customers either at the beginning of the interaction when taking the order, at the end of the stay (when a survey was also administered), at both moments (i.e., at the beginning and at the end), or not at all. The results showed that mimicry increased the average tip the waitresses received. Interestingly, waitresses received the largest tip when they mimicked twice indicating that the amount of mimicry matters. Finally, two experiments conducted in a grocery shop and hotel showed an increase in the perceived quality of service after mimicry was performed by an employee (Kulesza et al., 2023). More specifically, the employee who mimicked the customers was perceived as kinder. In addition, the researchers discovered a spillover effect as customers who were mimicked gave the company higher ratings and reported a higher likelihood to return to the shop/hotel.

Based on the research reviewed so far, researchers tested whether increased susceptibility to social influence as a result of mimicry also impacts negotiations. Such research found that participants who were mimicked gave more truthful answers (Shaw et al., 2015). A more in-depth analysis of the link between mimicry and the tendency to share information as a basis for negotiations was recently reported in an interesting work combining verbal and nonverbal mimicry (Novotny et al., 2021). During an interview, a confederate verbally mimicked participants, nonverbally mimicked them, performed a combination of the two mimicry behaviors (verbal and nonverbal), or presented none of these behaviors. Results showed that participants were more willing to discuss personal topics when verbal mimicry was performed alone, versus in conjunction with nonverbal mimicry. The authors proposed two explanations for this effect. First: an "overdose effect" stemming from the communication accommodation theory (ACT; Giles & Ogay, 2007) postulating an optimal level of communicative accommodation among interacting dyads. Second: cognitive overload (which we will discuss below in this chapter) meaning that simultaneously employing two techniques made the interaction too difficult.

Sharing more information with others as a result of mimicry probably stems from the fact that mimicry increases trust and, on that basis, might be employed in negotiations. One experiment (Swaab et al., 2011) testing this explanation involved pairs of students who were randomly assigned to the role of a person applying for a job or a recruiter. The latter was instructed to mimic (or not) the "applicant's" words at the beginning or towards the end of the interaction. Higher gains (total number of points in a negotiation game) were achieved by persons who imitated at the beginning of the conversation (for the first 10 min). The overall scores in the negotiation game were higher when mimicry occurred early.

A similar result was found by Maddux et al. (2008). The results of a first experiment showed that mimicry led to higher gains in a negotiation game for both mimickers and mimickees (compared to the control condition). In another experiment, the authors found that in a situation where the buyer mimicked the seller, an agreement was reached in two-thirds of pairs. In comparison, only 2 out of 16 couples in the control condition reached an agreement. A mediation analysis showed that perceived trust in the seller (mimickee) accounted for the observed effect. In more recent studies on the relationship between mimicry, negotiations, and trust, researchers have explored the issue of verbal mimicry with trust, rapport, and liking (Muir et al., 2020). The results indicate that mimicry is associated with greater joint and individual gains, but also the perception of rapport by the mimicked partner.

Increase in Creativity

A final series of experiments investigated whether mimicry increases creativity. In one study (Ashton-James & Chartrand, 2009), a research assistant nonverbally mimicked (or not) participants during an interview. After the interview, the participants were asked to fill in a questionnaire measuring creative thinking. The results indicate that participants who had been imitated, scored higher in creative thinking. A second study by the same authors analyzed the influence of mimicry on creative thinking via a procedure that calls on the subject to name new products. The participants had at their disposal a set of already used names and were expected to come up with new, original ones using this list as an example. If the proposed name was similar to the existing ones, the result was coded as non-original and not creative. The analyses revealed that more creative names were invented by those participants who were mimicked.

Costs Stemming from Mimicry and Lack of Mimicry

Thus far, we have discussed benefits stemming from mimicry. In particular, the studies reviewed above suggest that mimicking others has positive consequences, whereas not mimicking others has neither benefits nor costs. This line of research, however, neglects that mimicry, as well as its absence, can also have negative consequences. Such costs of mimicry are broad and includes important consequences such as stress, lie detection, self-esteem, and cognitive resource functioning. Below, we loosely divide these negative consequences into four categories: emotional, perceptual, cognitive, and behavioral costs.

Emotional Costs

First, researchers have found negative emotional consequences in response to not being mimicked. The positive social-emotional consequences of being mimicked discussed earlier suggests that when not being mimicked, positive social-emotional consequences are absent. Going one step further, other researchers could show that not mimicking actually has negative emotional consequences, such as increased stress (Kouzakova et al., 2010a, b). In particular, individuals' cortisol level (a well-known marker of stress) significantly increases when they are not mimicked in an interaction, presumably because the affiliation mechanism—stemming from mimicry—was annulled from the interaction.

Perceptual Costs

There are a number of perceptual costs associated with mimicry. One of these costs is a more negative perception of one's close relationships. For example, students in a romantic relationship participated in a study during which mimicry either took place or did not (Kouzakova et al., 2010b). It turned out that non-mimicked (vs. mimicked) participants had a better evaluation of their current romantic relationship. Mediation analyses revealed that the link between mimicry and relationship evaluations was driven by increased belongingness needs, specifically for the non-mimicked participants.

A further perceptual cost for the mimicker is the decreased ability to detect lies in others (Stel et al., 2009). Participants were told that they would be assigned one of two roles: an observer or an actor. The actors were asked to donate to a charity. The experimenters then asked "actors" to take part in a conversation with an "observer." Depending on the experimental condition, the researchers asked the actors to tell the truth or lie about their own behavior regarding their donation. The observers were instructed to either mimic or not mimic the facial expressions of the person they were conversing with (or no instruction on mimicry was mentioned). The analysis of the results showed that the "observers" who were asked to refrain from mimicry more correctly read the actor's intentions (i.e., they were better at guessing the truth). Conversely, those who mimicked were less likely to detect the truth. The authors argue that the use of mimicry results in a poorer ability to discriminate when someone is lying and when they are telling the truth.

Another perceptual cost experienced by mimickers is related to emotion identification. In a study on the imitation of facial expressions (Kulesza et al., 2015), participants were asked to imitate (or not) the facial expressions of emotions presented by another person. After observing each emotion, participants were asked to identify it and write it down. The authors counted the number of emotion misidentifications, and also counted how many "empty" spaces participants had left on their lists as an indicator of cognitive process overload. It turned out that mimickers fared worse on both counts. This indicated that mimicry exhausted the cognitive resources of study participants (see also Dalton et al., 2010, discussed below). Such problems were not encountered by those who were told to refrain from mimicking. This suggests that intentional mimicry causes a deterioration of emotional perception.

Finally, mimicry can have negative consequences for self-perception, that is, a decrease in self-liking and self-esteem (Kot & Kulesza, 2016). After a nonverbal mimicry manipulation, participants completed questionnaires measuring their self-esteem, how much they liked the confederate, and how much they liked themselves. In line with Chartrand and Bargh's Experiment 2 (1999), the results revealed that the experimenter was liked better by those who were mimicked, compared to those who were not mimicked. Most interestingly, mimicked participants liked themselves less and had lower self-esteem compared to those who were not mimicked.

Cognitive Costs

Researchers have also found cognitive consequences of mimicry (or a lack thereof) in social interactions. That is, not being mimicked—or, in some conditions, being mimicked—can lead to depletion of one's cognitive resources (Dalton et al., 2010). When interacting with peers, the implicit expectation is that mimicry will take place, and when it does not, the person who is not mimicked will have fewer cognitive resources to spend on other tasks. However, in some situations, there is an implicit expectation that an individual will not be mimicked. For instance, someone with less power is less likely to be mimicked by someone with more power. When that implicit expectation is violated, it can lead to a depletion of resources as well. Based on four experiments supporting this theory, Dalton and colleagues concluded that cognitive resources are preserved when the amount of mimicry displayed by interacting individuals adheres to implicit social norms, while resources are depleted when these mimicry norms are violated.

Behavioral Costs

In terms of behavioral costs of mimicry, it is important to recall the experiments on lie detection reviewed earlier (Stel et al., 2009). In a recent experiment on the relationship between mimicry and lies, Muniak et al. (2021) focused not on the detection of lies, but rather on telling lies. In a first experiment, participants were either verbally mimicked or not during an interview. Participants who were mimicked were more likely to lie than those who were not mimicked. To test the generalizability of this effect, a nonverbal mimicry manipulation was employed in a second experiment. Again, a higher tendency to lie was present in the mimicry condition, showing that both verbal and nonverbal mimicry leads to a heightened tendency to lie to the mimicker. This somewhat surprising effect is currently being further explored by our research consortium.

Another behavioral consequence of mimicry is the tendency for mimickees to conform to stereotypical features. In an experiment, White, Asian, and African American students were enlisted to participate in a study (Leander et al., 2011). The composition of the participants was established on the basis of the stereotype that Asians perform particularly well in mathematics, whereas White people perform at an average level, and Black people perform somewhat worse. Upon arriving in a waiting room, the participants took part in a discussion that was arranged in such a way that the participant and a confederate (who nonverbally mimicking or not) pair had to switch between the role of interviewer and interviewee. Afterwards, each participant completed a math test. The results indicated that the stereotype that Asians perform the best at mathematics, followed by White people, with Black people performing the weakest, was confirmed only in the condition where the subjects had been mimicked. Importantly, such differences between ethnic groups were not significant when participants were not mimicked.

Conclusions and Critical Remarks

This chapter highlights the power of the chameleon effect as mimicry affects many domains of our lives, in multiple ways. In this respect, we showed that mimicry has, in contrast to the general accepted view, not only several benefits, but also multiple costs. Despite the large number of interesting findings, there are several limitations that need to be discussed and crucial questions to be asked.

First, currently, it is unclear what would happen if individuals in social interactions become aware that they are being mimicked. Would awareness of mimicry—just as with the vast majority of social influence techniques—not only reduce the impact of mimicry on a given outcome, but potentially backfire as predicted by the Persuasion Knowledge Theory (Friestad & Wright, 1994)? On the one hand, there are, indeed, some studies suggesting that awareness of mimicry may backfire (Genschow & Florack, 2014; Wessler et al., 2023). On the other hand, some research has also proposed that perhaps the mechanism underlying the chameleon effect is unique in the sense that becoming aware of mimicry does not change the result (Kulesza et al., 2016). Future research should shed further light on the question of whether and how awareness of mimicry can backfire.

Second, there is the question of what the purpose of mimicry actually is. While previous research suggests that mimicry plays an important role in learning (Bandura, 1971), more recent research indicates that mimicry fulfills an important social function as it has many pro-social consequences (e.g., Dijksterhuis, 2005; Lakin et al. 2003., Lakin & Chartrand et al., 2003). With respect to the latter, in this chapter, we presented a broad range of experiments, supporting the claim that mimicry has social benefits. However, the second part of our chapter reviewed a variety of studies finding negative social consequences of mimicry. This somehow challenges the general view that mimicry has only positive consequences. Future research should thus investigate under which specific conditions mimicry has positive and negative consequences with the goal to formulate a more fine-grained theory that allows better and more precise predictions to be derived regarding the outcome of mimicry.

Finally, there are important methodological caveats stemming from the reviewed experiments on mimicry. In particular, most of the experiments on the consequences on mimicry were conducted around 10 (and more) years ago. As is typical for the experiments at this time, the sample sizes were rather small (often less than 20 participants per experimental condition). Even more concerning, many of the reviewed findings have relatively high p-values (e.g., just below .05). The combination of small samples with high p-values calls for great caution when, for example, making recommendations or even considering the results as a pattern supporting theoretical implications. Therefore, future research should replicate previous experiments with larger samples to consolidate current theories and their supporting findings. Conducting such replications will be challenging, because most of the older research on mimicry was conducted without preregistration and published without making data or stimulus materials publicly available. Moreover, since mimicry studies are usually carried out in the lab with the involvement of confederates, assessing large samples is both costly and time-consuming. To deal with this challenge, future research may consider conducting multiple labs studies.

Taken together, in this chapter, we reviewed results showing that mimicry has not only positive, but also negative social consequences. The findings for negative consequences, in particular, challenge previous theories that argue that mimicry has mainly positive social outcomes. Future research should, thus, investigate boundary conditions for positive and negative social consequences with the aim to develop a more fine-grained theory of mimicry. Moreover, since previous research assessed mainly small sample sizes and detected rather high p-values, future research is encouraged to carry out high-powered and pre-registered replications.

References

Ashton-James, C. E., & Chartrand, T. L. (2009). Social cues for creativity: The impact of behavioral mimicry on convergent and divergent thinking. *Journal of Experimental Social Psychology, 45*, 1036–1040. https://doi.org/10.1016/j.jesp.2009.04.030

Ashton-James, C., van Baaren, R. B., Chartrand, T. L., Decety, J., & Karremans, J. (2007). Mimicry and me: The impact of mimicry on self-construal. *Social Cognition, 25*, 518–535. https://doi.org/10.1521/soco.2007.25.4.518

Bandura, A. (1971). *Social learning theory*. General Learning Press.

Chartrand, T. L., & Bargh, J. A. (1999). The chameleon effect: The perception-behavior link and social interaction. *Journal of Personality and Social Psychology, 76*, 893–910. https://doi.org/10.1037/0022-3514.76.6.893

Cousins, S. D. (1989). Culture and self-perception in Japan and the United States. *Journal of Personality and Social Psychology, 56*, 124–131. https://doi.org/10.1037/0022-3514.56.1.124

Dalton, A. N., Chartrand, T. L., & Finkel, E. J. (2010). The schema-driven chameleon: How mimicry affects executive and self-regulatory resources. *Journal of Personality and Social Psychology, 98*, 605–617. https://doi.org/10.1037/a0017629

Dijksterhuis, A. (2005). Why we are social animals: The high road to imitation as social glue. S. S. L. Hurley & N. Chater (Eds.), *Perspectives of imitation: From cognitive neuroscience to social science* (t. 2, pp. 207–220). MIT Press.

Drury, M. L., & van Swol, L. (2005). Are people who mimic others perceived as more friendly, likeable, persuasive, and knowledgeable? *Conference: The National Communication Association Annual Conference*, Boston.

Friestad, M., & Wright, P. (1994). The persuasion knowledge model: How people cope with persuasion attempts. *Journal of Consumer Research, 21*, 1–31. https://doi.org/10.1086/209380

Genschow, O., & Florack, A. (2014). Attention on the source of influence reverses the impact of cross-contextual imitation. *Journal of Experimental Psychology: Human Perception and Performance, 40*, 904–907. https://doi.org/10.1037/a0035430

Giles, H., & Ogay, T. (2007). Communication accomodation theory. In B. B. Whaley & W. Samter (Eds.), *Explaining communication: Contemporary theories and exemplars* (pp. 293–310). Lawrence Erlbaum.

Inzlicht, M., Gutsell, J. N., & Legault, L. (2012). Mimicry reduces racial prejudice. *Journal of Experimental Social Psychology, 48*, 361–365. https://doi.org/10.1016/j.jesp.2011.06.007

Kot, S., & Kulesza, W. (2016). The chameleon as a leech: The costs of mimicry for the mimickee. *Polish Psychological Bulletin, 47*, 131–135. https://doi.org/10.1515/ppb-2016-0014

Kouzakova, M., Karremans, J. C., van Baaren, R. B., & van Knippenberg, A. (2010a). A stranger's cold shoulder makes the heart grow fonder: Why not being mimicked by a stranger enhances longstanding relationship evaluations. *Social Psychological and Personality Science, 1*, 87–93. https://doi.org/10.1177/1948550609355718

Kouzakova, M., van Baaren, R., & van Knippenberg, A. (2010b). Lack of behavioral imitation in human interactions enhances salivary cortisol levels. *Hormones and Behavior, 57*, 421–426. https://doi.org/10.1016/j.yhbeh.2010.01.011

Kulesza, W., Szypowska, Z., Jarman, M., & Dolinski, D. (2014). Attractive chameleons sell: The mimicry-attractiveness link. *Psychology and Marketing, 31*, 549–561. https://doi.org/10.1002/mar.20716

Kulesza, W., Cislak, A., Vallacher, R. R., Nowak, A., Czekiel, M., & Bedynska, S. (2015). The face of the chameleon: The experience of facial mimicry for the mimicker and the mimickee. *Journal of Social Psychology, 155*, 590–604. https://doi.org/10.1080/00224545.2015.1032195

Kulesza, W., Dolinski, D., & Wicher, P. (2016). Knowing that you mimic me: The link between mimicry, awareness and liking. *Social Influence, 11*, 68–74. https://doi.org/10.1080/15534510.2016.1148072

Kulesza, W., Dolinski, D., Migon, M., Rizulla, A., Gamian-Wilk, M., & Grzyb, T. (2017). The use of mimicry to improve evaluation of unsought beverages. *Food Quality and Preference, 62*, 137–143. https://doi.org/10.1016/j.foodqual.2017.06.004

Kulesza, W., Dolinski, D., Szczęsna, K., Kosim, M., & Grzyb, T. (2018). Temporal aspects of the Chameleon Effect and hospitality: The link between mimicry, Its impact, and duration. *Cornell Hospitality Quarterly, 60*, 212–215. https://doi.org/10.1177/1938965518797075

Kulesza, W., Chrobot, N., Dolinski, D., Muniak, P., Bińkowska, D., Grzyb, T., & Genschow, O. (2022a). Imagining is not observing: The role of simulation processes within the mimicry-liking expressway. *Journal of Nonverbal Behavior, 46*, 233–246. https://doi.org/10.1007/s10919-022-00399-1

Kulesza, W., Dolinski, D., Kosim, M., Grzyb, T., Muniak, P., & Jemielniak, D. (2022b). The Chameleon Effect, the temporal aspects of mimicry and their impact on service measurement. *European Review of Applied Psychology, 72*, 100767. https://doi.org/10.1016/j.erap.2022.100767

Kulesza, W., Dolinski, D., Muniak, P., Borkowska, J., Bibikova, P., & Grzyb, T. (2023). The chameleon effect in customer relationship management: Experiments in natural settings. *Frontiers in Psychology, 14*, 1016125. https://doi.org/10.3389/fpsyg.2023.1016125

Lakin, J. L., & Chartrand, T. L. (2003). Using nonconscious behavioral mimicry to create affiliation and rapport. *Psychological Science, 14*, 334–339. https://doi.org/10.1111/1467-9280.14481

Lakin, J. L., Jefferis, V. E., Cheng, C. M., & Chartrand, T. L. (2003). The chameleon effect as social glue: Evidence for the evolutionary significance of nonconscious mimicry. *Journal of Nonverbal Behavior, 27*, 145–162. https://doi.org/10.1023/A:1025389814290

Leander, N. P., Chartrand, T. L., & Wood, W. (2011). Mind your mannerisms: Behavioral mimicry elicits stereotype conformity. *Journal of Experimental Social Psychology, 47*, 195–201. https://doi.org/10.1016/j.jesp.2010.09.002

Maddux, W. W., Mullen, E., & Galinsky, A. D. (2008). Chameleons bake bigger pies and take bigger pieces: Strategic behavioral mimicry facilitates negotiation outcomes. *Journal of Experimental Social Psychology, 44*, 461–468. https://doi.org/10.1016/j.jesp.2007.02.003

Markus, H., & Kitayama, S. (1991). Culture and the Self—implications for cognition, emotion, and motivation. *Psychological Review, 98*, 224–253. https://doi.org/10.1037/0033-295X.98.2.224

Muir, K., Joinson, A., Collins, E., Cotterill, R., & Dewdney, N. (2020). When asking "what" and "how" helps you win: Mimicry of interrogative terms facilitates successful online negotiations. *Negotiation and Conflict Management Research*. https://doi.org/10.1111/ncmr.12179

Muniak, P., Dolinski, D., Grzyb, T., Cantarero, K., & Kulesza, W. (2021). You want to know the truth? Then don't mimic! *Zeitschrift für Psychologie, 299*, 185–190. https://doi.org/10.1027/2151-2604/a000451

Nisbett, R. E., Peng, K., Choi, I., & Norenzayan, A. (2001). Culture and systems of thought: Holistic versus analytic cognition. *Psychological Review, 108*, 291–310. https://doi.org/10.1037/0033-295X.108.2.291

Novotny, E., Frank, M. G., & Grizzard, M. (2021). A laboratory study comparing the effectiveness of verbal and nonverbal rapport-building techniques in interviews. *Communication Studies, 72*, 819–833. https://doi.org/10.1080/10510974.2021.1975141

Redeker, M., Stel, M., & Mastop, J. (2011). Does mimicking others change your self-view? *The Journal of Social Psychology, 151*, 387–390. https://doi.org/10.1080/00224545.2010.481691

Shaw, D. J., Vrij, A., Leal, S., Mann, S., Hillman, J., Granhag, P. A., & Fisher, R. P. (2015). Mimicry and investigative interviewing: Using deliberate mimicry to elicit information and cues to deceit. *Journal of Investigative Psychology and Offender Profiling, 12*, 217–230. https://doi.org/10.1002/jip.1438

Stel, M., & Harinck, F. (2011). Being mimicked makes you a prosocial voter. *Experimental Psychology, 58*, 79–84. https://doi.org/10.1027/1618-3169/a000070

Stel, M., & Vonk, R. (2010). Mimicry in social interaction: Benefits for mimickers, mimickees, and their interaction. *British Journal of Psychology, 101*, 311–323. https://doi.org/10.1348/000712609X465424

Stel, M., van Dijk, E., & Olivier, E. (2009). You want to know the truth? Then don't mimic! *Psychological Science, 20*, 693–699. https://doi.org/10.1111/j.1467-9280.2009.02350.x

Stel, M., Mastop, J., & Strick, M. (2011). The impact of mimicking on attitudes toward products presented in TV commercials. *Social Influence, 6*, 142–152. https://doi.org/10.1080/15534510.2011.580978

Stel, M., van den Bos, K., Sim, S., & Rispens, S. (2013). Mimicry and just world beliefs: Mimicking makes men view the world as more personally just. *The British Journal of Social Psychology, 52*, 397–411. https://doi.org/10.1111/j.2044-8309.2011.02084.x

Swaab, R. I., Maddux, W. W., & Sinaceur, M. (2011). Early words that work: When and how virtual linguistic mimicry facilitates negotiation outcomes. *Journal of Experimental Social Psychology, 47*, 616–621. https://doi.org/10.1016/j.jesp.2011.01.005

Tanner, R. J., Ferraro, R., Chartrand, T. L., Bettman, J. R., & van Baaren, R. (2008). Of chameleons and consumption: The impact of mimicry on choice and preferences. *Journal of Consumer Research, 34*, 754–766. https://doi.org/10.1086/522322

van Baaren, R. B., Maddux, W. W., Chartrand, T. L., de Bouter, C., & van Knippenberg, A. (2003). It takes two to mimic: Behavioral consequences of self-construals. *Journal of Personality and Social Psychology, 84*, 1093–1102. https://doi.org/10.1037/0022-3514.84.5.1093

van Baaren, R. B., Holland, R. W., Kawakami, K., & van Knippenberg, A. (2004). Mimicry and prosocial behavior. *Psychological Science, 15*, 71–74. https://doi.org/10.1111/j.0963-7214.2004.01501012.x

van Swol, L. M. (2003). The effects of nonverbal mirroring on perceived persuasiveness, agreement with an imitator, and reciprocity in a group discussion. *Communication Research, 30*, 461–480. https://doi.org/10.1177/0093650203253318

Wessler, J., Loschelder, D. D., Fendel, J. C., & Friese, M. (2023). The too-much-mimicry effect: Strong (vs. subtle) mimicry impairs liking and trust in distributive negotiations. *Journal of Nonverbal Behavior*, 1–24. https://dx.doi.org/10.1007/s10919-023-00446-5

Zgliniecka, A., & Kulesza, W. (2014). The chameleon effect the stereotypes of non-believers held by religious persons. *Annals of Psychology, 17*, 185–197.

Chapter 14
Cognitive Mechanisms of Being Imitated

Paula Wicher, Harry Farmer, and Antonia Hamilton

Introduction

Imagine a social situation where Anna leans forward, scratches her eyebrow, and shifts her legs as she speaks, and shortly after Bob leans forward and scratches his eyebrow, and shifts his legs. Here, Bob mimics Anna's actions, probably without realizing he is doing so. A number of research studies suggest that this mimicry behavior is associated with liking and affiliation—that Bob and Anna will now feel closer and will like each other more. This chapter reviews this literature, with a focus on the methods used to study this and the parallels between mimicry of motor behavior and mimicry of more abstract choices. We consider both positive and negative effects specifically in the case of the person who is *being mimicked* (Anna in the example above).

To avoid confusion between discussion of mimicry (as performed by Bob) and the situation of being mimicked (as experienced by Anna), we will use the term *BeMim* to refer specifically to the experience of Anna, and to experimental conditions which create a situation where a participant is being mimicked. The term mimicry can describe the actions of Bob or the global dyadic interaction of both people. The idea that mimicry correlates with affiliation is found in Condon and Ogston (1966) and Scheflen (1964) but attention towards this phenomenon rapidly increased with the publication of Chartrand and Bargh's (1999) landmark study on the Chameleon effect. That paper includes an explicit and well controlled test of the effects of BeMim, where a naive participant took part in a conversation with a

P. Wicher (✉) · A. Hamilton
Institute of Cognitive Neuroscience, University College London, London, UK
e-mail: paula.wicher.20@ucl.ac.uk; a.hamilton@ucl.ac.uk

H. Farmer
School of Human Sciences, Institute of Lifecourse Development, University of Greenwich, London, UK
e-mail: h.farmer@greenwich.ac.uk

O. Genschow, E. Cracco (eds.), *Automatic Imitation*,
https://doi.org/10.1007/978-3-031-62634-0_14

confederate who copied some of the participant's gestures and movements. After the conversation, participants who experienced BeMim rated the confederates more positively than did participants who interacted with a non-mimicking confederate, providing evidence that there is a causal effect of the manipulation of the confederate's mimicry behavior on the social perception of the participant.

One key point to resolve before we review the literature around BeMim is what should count as of mimicry or imitation. For some researchers (Boesch & Tomasello, 1998; Fridland & Moore, 2015; Heyes, 1994), the direct matching of bodily movements is a definitional component that distinguishes imitation from other forms of social learning. However, as noted by Heyes (2021) the everyday use of imitation to refer to the copying of another's behavior in general has been retained by researchers in fields such as behavioral ecology and cultural evolution as well as in the wider vernacular. On this wider sense, we can consider the imitation of others occurring across a range of levels, moving from the matching of motor actions at the most direct level through the matching of the outcomes of motor actions (often referred to as emulation) and then into increasingly abstract areas such as the matching of preferences and values (which is commonly referred to within the literature on social influence). In all these cases, we can think of imitation occurring when one agent observes the behavior of another and subsequently shows the same behavior themselves and use BeMim to refer to the experience of being the copied agent. For example, if Anna says she likes Jazz and Bob replies that he does too, this might be perceived by Anna as a form of BeMim.

In recent decades, many different experimental methods have been used to explore the concept of being mimicked both at a motor level and an abstract level. BeMim is a challenging concept to study in the lab because it ideally requires a situation where person A spontaneously produces a distinctive behavior or preference, person B then copies (or does not copy) that behavior; afterwards the affiliation of A towards B can be measured. This can be characterized as a social learning task, as illustrated in Fig. 14.1, where A has an initial impression of B which might be changed by B's behavior (mimicking or not mimicking), and the new impression

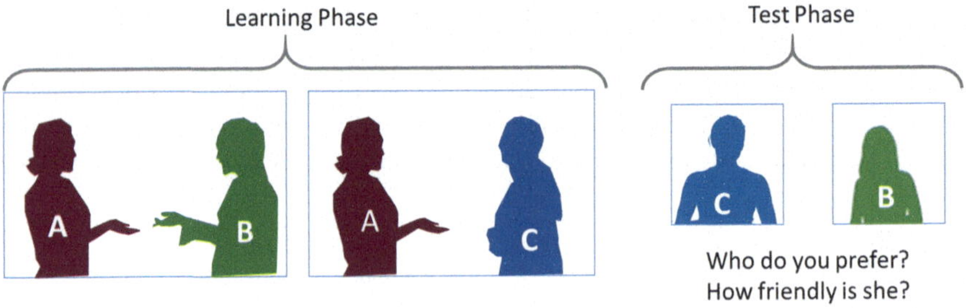

Fig. 14.1 Experimental design. A typical BeMim study has a learning phase where the participant (A) encounters confederates (B, C) who mimic (B) or do not mimic (C). After the learning phase is complete, the participant must evaluate the confederates in the test phase. This figure illustrates a within-subjects design but a between-subjects design, where each participant meets only one confederate who mimics or not, is also possible

can then be measured by the experimenter. Typically, such studies also require a control condition where A engages in the same behaviors but is not mimicked; this could be a within-subjects design (e.g., A encounters a new person, C, who does not mimic) or a between-subjects design (a new participant encounters B who is instructed not to mimic).

For an experimenter wishing to study the effects of BeMim, the challenge is to create a scenario where A can behave naturally and then to implement the actions of B in an ecologically valid fashion. In various studies, B has been implemented using a confederate, using a virtual human, using a deceptive video clip (where participants believe the video is a live confederate) or using an "ordinary" video clip (where participants are not deceived). In the study of shared preferences, there are also a range of different methods used. Some studies have examined shared preferences in the context of laboratory experiments in which participants simply learn about the traits of a target other without interacting with that target, while other studies involve examining levels of similarity within existing relationships (Montoya et al., 2008). Within laboratory studies, similarity of attitudes between self and other can be presented as having come about via chance (e.g., Farmer et al., 2019) or due to the confederate directly copying the participant (e.g., White & Argo, 2011). Finally, the growth of social media and other forms of networked communication has allowed for researchers to identify the effect of shared preferences on the formation of large-scale social networks "in the wild" (e.g., Ma & Hu, 2015)

In designing BeMim experiments, there are also some other important factors to consider. First, it is not always clear what is the most appropriate control condition. If a control condition is designed with reduced movement from the confederate in the interaction, that might feel unnatural to the participants. If a control condition has movements of a different limb that are not mimicry, that might also feel unnatural. So, it can be hard to find an appropriate control. Similarly, another issue is whether BeMim effects arise only when there is precise mimicry between participant and confederate (the same limb performing the same action) or if more general contingent responses with any limb are enough to lead to BeMim effects. Some previous studies suggest that merely responding to another person's movement might be enough to induce the BeMim liking effect, without the need to mimic the same movements (Sparenberg et al., 2012; Kulesza et al., 2022). The implications of these results for our theories will be considered in the section about BeMim neurocognitive mechanisms.

To organize this review, we will divide studies up into four overarching categories, as illustrated in Fig. 14.2. Some studies use tightly controlled interactions in the lab, such as moving in the same way as a person seen on video (Fig. 14.2C) or preferring the same piece of art as an unseen person (Fig. 14.2A). Others use live interaction between real (or virtual) humans who show similar motor movements (Fig. 14.2D) or similar abstract preferences (Fig. 14.2B). Each of these methods has advantages and disadvantages, and here we review work in each domain with a focus on evaluating methods. We do not provide an exhaustive review of all work using each method, but rather aim to highlight what can be done and what the

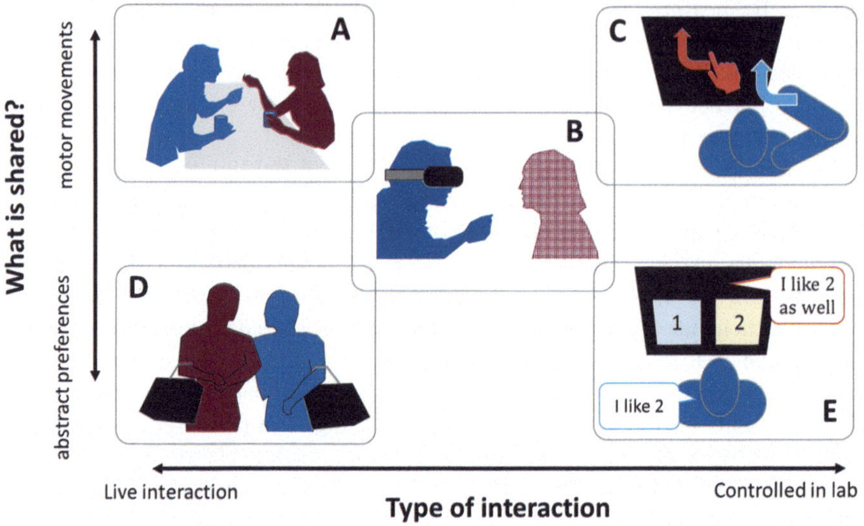

Fig. 14.2 Ways to study BeMim effects can vary according to what is shared (movements or preference) and the type of interaction (live or controlled). **A** illustrates a face-to-face conversation where movements are mimicked by a confederate (e.g., Chartrand & Bargh, 1999). **B** illustrates a virtual reality encounter where a participant is mimicked by a virtual agent. **C** illustrates controlled movement paradigms (e.g., Dignath et al., 2018). **D** illustrates consumer choices in live discussions. **E** illustrates controlled choices of abstract preferences (e.g., Farmer et al., 2019). In all cases, the blue figure represents the participant, and the red figure represents the confederate

limitations of each method are. In the second section of this chapter, we will then consider the broader implications and theories behind this work.

Varieties of Ways to Study Being Mimicked

Studying Motor Mimicry in Live Interactions

The prototypical case of motor mimicry is a live conversation where one person copies (or does not copy) the actions of the other. In the landmark study of Chartrand and Bargh (1999), participants were asked to have a 15-min conversation about pictures with another "participant" who was a confederate (a research assistant who is not aware of the hypothesis, but follows specific instructions on how to act). Here, the confederate was told to mimic the movements and posture of the participants during the conversation, and afterwards the participant's liking towards the confederate was measured using simple Likert-scale rating questions. Participants who were mimicked reported having a smoother interaction and liking the confederate more than participants in the control group who were not mimicked (for a review, see Chap. 13; this volume).

Numerous studies have recreated this type of confederate paradigm in in-lab or field research settings. For example, van Baaren and colleagues (2009) ran a similar study where each participant had a chat about advertisements with a confederate who mimicked (or not) their facial expressions, face/hair touching, and feet/arms movements. The interaction lasted specifically 5.5–6 min and the mimicry was performed with a 4-second delay. After the task, participants were shown two pictures and asked how similar they find them. The data showed that mimicked participants saw more similarities between random objects than the non-mimicked ones. The authors claim that BeMim influences similarity from various perspectives: it makes people feel more similar to others, behave more prosocial, but also see random objects as more similar.

Other researchers conducted a study with live corporate interviews in the US exploring cultural differences between Latino and Anglo managers to BeMim response (Sanchez-Burks et al., 2009). Participants' gestures were mimicked or not by a confederate who was asking them personal questions about their career. Participants who were mimicked rated that the interview was better, answered questions faster, and were evaluated as better than participants in the non-mimicry condition. In general, these results suggest that BeMim can provide a boost in confidence in a professional setting that results in actual better performance.

A very limited number of studies used a BeMim study design where anti-mimicry is included as a comparison. In a series of studies, researchers explored the role of physical attractiveness and BeMim in the sales context (Kulesza et al., 2014). The study was conducted in a cosmetic store, where the confederate pretended to be a salesperson who was welcoming and helping new clients. Confederates (with or without make-up) were instructed to mimic, stay still, or anti-mimic in relation to the participant's movements. Results showed that mimicry made participants spend and rate customer service more favorably. Eighteen out of 19 all participants who said that they do not want to return to the store for future purchases were from the less attractive (without make-up) and anti-mimicking condition. This study suggests that BeMim positively influences purchasing behavior and the effect is even stronger when the mimicker is physically attractive.

Another study explored whether BeMim creating motoric self-other overlap can be generalized to automatic imitation indices (Rauchbauer et al., 2020). During the picture description task, confederates mimicked or anti-mimicked participants' body movements with 3 to 6 second delay. They used participants' middle and index fingers in the Imitation-Inhibition task with congruent and incongruent trials to measure facilitation, inhibition, and interference of automatic imitation (for a review of such and similar tasks, see Chap. 2; this volume). Results showed only a decrease in inhibition index in a BeMim condition and an increase in an anti-mimicking condition; facilitation and interference index were not significant. Overall, this study showed that the self-other overlap after BeMim cannot be generalized to automatic imitation indices. This suggests that mimicry and automatic imitation are two separate cognitive processes.

There are both advantages and disadvantages to studying BeMim in live interactions. Conducting studies in these ecological settings allows researchers to study

BeMim in an environment close to (or in) natural conversations, and as a result participants can act in a relatively genuine and spontaneous fashion, even in experimental situations. Live interactions can reveal behavior patterns that would be impossible to study with more controlled experimental settings. It is especially relevant when it comes to studying the undefined unconscious nature of BeMim (e.g., Chartrand & Lakin, 2013; Chartrand et al., 2006). However, the biggest challenge of live studies is low experimental control—it is possible that other factors (besides motor mimicry) could influence the participant's affiliation feelings towards their interlocutor. Possible factors include the type and number of spontaneous (to-be-mimicked) actions produced by the participant, the background and training of the confederates, their knowledge of the hypothesis, and the other movements and speech of the confederates that are not mimicry.

An ideal confederate would be able to hold the same conversation with every participant (regardless of that participant's characteristics) while mimicking specific aspects of the participants actions and not changing her smiles, eye contact, tone of voice, or any other social cues. In practice, this is a very demanding task that requires excellent acting skills and self-control from confederates. Spontaneous behaviors like smiles or subtle differences in performing copying behavior might not be well controlled (Fox et al., 2009). Furthermore, the amount of mimicry in an interaction depends on the interlocutors' tendency to mimic others, on differences between unique dyads and on reciprocity (Salazar Kämpf et al., 2018). This means that confederates might find it easier to mimic some participants than others. The confederate's initial liking of the participant (McIntosh et al., 2006), group membership (Bourgeois & Hess, 2008; Lakin et al., 2008), or personality traits such as extraversion (Duffy & Chartrand, 2015), and interdependence (van Baaren et al., 2009) could also influence how much mimicking behavior confederates perform/produce.

Researchers can try to control these factors with manipulation checks such as using hypothesis blind video coders to capture differences in confederates' mimicry behavior, and by evaluating their friendliness or smiling across the studies (Sanchez-Burks et al., 2009). However, these checks seem subjective—for example how can one objectively rate "[confederate's] apparent liking for the participant based on the video recording"?

Confederates can also fail at performing naturally. In some studies, researchers reported participants' or observers' comments about the confederates' exaggerated behavior (Davydenko et al., 2020). This might cause participants to engage in atypical behavior or make them guess the goal of the study or the fact that they interact with confederates. Moreover, confederates cannot be blinded to the key experimental manipulation (mimic/do not mimic), and they might have prior expectations about the study outcome which could influence the results. When confederates know about the study hypothesis, they might unconsciously change their verbal backchannels or nonverbal cues such as facial micro expressions, tone of voice, pauses, or eye gaze in a way that biases participants (Doyen et al., 2012; Gilder & Heerey, 2018). Researchers can limit such cases by providing to the confederates as little information about the hypothesis and the study design as possible. Ideally, they should be blind to the study hypothesis, purpose, design, and if possible, how their behavior is related to the variables (Kuhlen & Brennan, 2013).

A further challenge is that the cognitive demands experienced by confederates focused on mimicking cause changes in some aspects of social interaction dynamics (Hale & Hamilton, 2016). A confederate who is explicitly copying actions may not act in the same way as people in a real spontaneous interaction where mimicry is related to establishing affiliative bonds (Chartrand & Bargh, 1999), ameliorating a negative social situation—to make peace with someone (Rauchbauer et al., 2016) or to deal with rejection (Lakin et al., 2008). This might have influence on the interaction dynamic and BeMim response.

It is also difficult to determine if participants were (not) aware of the manipulation since study debriefing (asking participants what is the study goal after the experiment) is based on their declaration which could be influenced by social bias, how the question was phrased, and the assumed expectations. Some researchers offer financial incentives to the participants after the study if they correctly guessed if their interlocutor was a confederate or just a participant (Keysar et al., 1998, 2000). However, this could make participants feel they have been treated unfairly if they do not guess the answer, which can discourage them from participating in future studies.

Finally, there is also a lack of consistency in terms of the non-mimicry condition. Most of BeMim research includes a control condition that assumes a neutral position throughout the task or/and a lack of copying behavior (e.g., Chartrand & Bargh, 1999; Sanchez-Burks et al., 2009). For example, in Kühn et al.'s (2010) study when participants crossed their legs the confederates folded their hands or touched their hair. The design which includes an increased mimicry in a BeMim condition and a decreased mimicry in a control condition might give confusing results. There is a possibility it doesn't feel natural, and as a result, this might be the main driving factor for the results. However, there are also studies that define non-mimicry as anti-mimicry when confederate does opposite movements to the ones performed by the participant (e.g., Hasler et al., 2014; Neufeld & Chakrabarti, 2016). For example, when a participant leans forward, the confederate reacts by leaning backward. These different non-mimicry conditions might have different effects; for example, people spend significantly more money, wanted to revisit the store, and gave higher customer service ratings when they interacted with the non-mimicking salesperson in comparison to the anti-mimicking one (Kulesza et al., 2014). However, there are limited number of studies on the anti-mimicry effects which could be a new direction for the future research. For example, the question whether anti-mimicry drives any negative feelings towards the interlocutor (to our knowledge) remains unanswered.

Overall, studies of BeMim effects which use live face-to-face interactions are the closest to real world conditions and can provide an ecologically valid test of whether and how BeMim might impact on social evaluations and social interactions. However, it is hard to implement appropriate controls and results may be rather inconsistent (Hale & Hamilton, 2016). Thus, some researchers turn to virtual reality or to more tightly controlled experimental designs to understand the cognitive mechanisms of BeMim.

Studying BeMim Using Virtual Reality

Virtual reality is an increasingly popular tool for gaming, real world jobs, and psychological research. Within this domain, the creation and manipulation of virtual humans (who may or may not be presented in an immersive virtual world) is also a growing area. Virtual humans are computer generated characters who look, move, and interact like real people. The creation and manipulation of virtual humans has massive potential for the study of social perception and affiliation, because the experimenter has absolute control of every aspect of the behavior and appearance of the virtual human. In particular, virtual humans' studies allow the experimenter to define what type of actions are copied and what precise delay is present between the actions of the participant and the mimicry by the virtual human, which can be very useful for building and testing theories. However, there are several important challenges to researchers in this domain (Pan & Hamilton, 2018).

One of the most important is how the virtual human is controlled. Some virtual humans are avatars, which means they are controlled in real time by a real person and simply provide a virtual representation of that person's actions. Others are agents, which means they are fully controlled by a computer with no human intervention. In the game PacMan, the ghost are agents, while PacMan is the avatar of the player. Some virtual humans can be partially controlled by a person and partially by a computer or may be controlled by a human but without the other interaction partner realizing this. This is called a Wizard of Oz setup (abbreviated to WoZ), because the participant believes they are speaking to or interacting with an autonomous virtual human (an agent) when in fact parts of the agent's behavior are controlled by another person (e.g., a PhD student) pressing buttons behind the scenes. WoZ setups are typically used when it is too complex to program naturalistic behavior into the virtual human, e.g., in conversations. These different control modes are important to the experimental design of BeMim studies and also have implications for how we interpret the studies.

The first study to create a virtual human who mimics a participant and use that virtual human to test for the impact of BeMim on social interaction was from Bailenson and Yee (2005). Their participants entered an immersive VR and saw a virtual human who gave a (prerecorded) persuasive message about campus safety and also mimicked (or did not mimic) the head movements of the participant with a 4 second delay. Participants who were not mimicked saw the virtual human make pre-recorded normal head movements. The group who experienced the BeMim condition rated the agent as more effective and had a more positive impression of the agent. Note that the 4 second delay was chosen based on a prior small study suggesting this was optimal to reduce detection of BeMim, but that 8 of 69 participants detected that the virtual human was mimicking (and were excluded).

Several other papers have examined whether BeMim from virtual humans leads to increased liking or affiliation. Hasler et al. (2021) created a detailed scenario where Israeli participants engaged in conversation with a virtual human who appeared to be Palestinian (i.e., outgroup member). The virtual human spoke in pre-recorded segments leaving time for the participant to reply, and also mimicked (or did not mimic) the posture of the participant (e.g., legs crossed/uncrossed). Both posture and speech timing were controlled by WoZ. After the interaction, participants who were mimicked reported more empathy, sympathy, and liking for the Palestinian character. This shows positive effects of BeMim even during interactions with outgroup members. Positive effects were also seen in a study from Aburumman et al. (2022) in which a virtual human performed head movement during a picture description task. Mimicry parameters were closely modelled on Hale et al. (2020) with a 600 msec delay between the participant's head movement and mimicry by the virtual human, and additional nodding from the virtual human when the participant was speaking. Participants interacted with two virtual humans and gave more positive ratings to the one who showed mimicry. These studies show that it is possible for well controlled mimicry of head movements by a virtual human to lead to increases in liking in a context where all other social parameters are held constant.

However, not all studies in this area have positive results. In one study, researchers created a virtual human who mimicked a participant's head movements while explaining the rules of an investment game. Participants who interacted with the mimicking agent did not show more trust in that agent during the investment game, unlike previous studies. However, they did like and trust the mimicking agent more in a second route-planning task (Verberne et al., 2013). Null results were found in a study from Hale and Hamilton (2016) which created a virtual human who could perform a "picture description task" with a participant, that is, the participant and the virtual human took turns to describe a picture to each other. During the task, the virtual human mimicked the participant's head movements (excluding large movements to look down at the picture) with a 1 or 3 second delay. Experiment one found marginal positive effects of BeMim on rapport ratings, and that 30% of participants detected the mimicry when the delay was set to 1 second, while only 4% detected it at 3 seconds. Experiment two was a pre-registered replication of this with an additional ingroup/outgroup manipulation which found null results. In a study from Choi et al. (2017), participants interacted with a telepresence robot who showed no mimicry or head movement mimicry (500 msec delay) among other conditions, but no positive effects of mimicry were found either. Ghazali et al. (2019) used an interactive robot who completed several tasks with a participant. During the tasks, the robot could show no mimicry, head movement mimicry, or head movement mimicry plus verbal praise. They found that participants had positive responses to the robot in the BeMim verbal praise condition but there was no clear difference between no mimicry and mimicry alone. The authors interpreted this in terms of increasingly rich social cues leading to increased liking.

To summarize, of seven published papers which directly examine BeMim effects using virtual humans, three report positive effects, two report mixed effects, and two report null effects. This suggests that BeMim effects in virtual humans are fragile and hard to study. One possible explanation could be that our ability to create believable virtual humans and have them interactively engage with participants is too limited, and that as we gain a better understanding of real-world mimicry and better generative models for human social behavior, we will be able to build virtual humans that show high quality mimicry behavior and observe the positive impacts on participants. Another explanation could be that BeMim alone is not enough to cause positive effects, and that many of the effects reported in real-life confederate studies might be false positives. Stronger pre-registered replications of the most robust BeMim paradigms would be very valuable.

Studying Motor BeMim with Controlled Movement Paradigms

Traditional cognitive psychology studies in which participants experience many similar trials of a computer-controlled paradigm provide an alternative approach to the study of BeMim. Here, in the learning phase, the participants perform an action (typically following the computers instructions) and then see an image or video of another person perform the same (or a different) action. A test phase involving questionnaires, or a more complex evaluation task, is then used to determine how the learning affected the participant's attitudes towards the images or social cognition in general. These tightly controlled studies allow experimenters to manipulate specific factors such as timing and contingency.

For example, Catmur and Heyes (2013) used computerized mimicry to study pro-social effects of BeMim and the role of similarity and contingency in it. The participant's task was to lift their hand or foot while seeing a video of a lifting hand or foot on the computer screen, and participants were placed in one of four groups with high/low contingency and high/low similarity. Those in the similar groups saw a hand movement on the screen being lifted when the participant lifted their hand; while those in the dissimilar groups saw a hand movement on the screen being lifted when the participant lifted their feet. Those in the contingent groups made a movement which was followed by an action on the screen in 100% of trials, while for those in the non-contingent groups, their own action was followed by an action on the screen in 50% of trials. Participants' attention was controlled by asking them to say "yes" when they saw a hand or foot rotated by 45°. After the task was completed, participants in contingent groups (regardless of similarity) enjoyed the task more, felt closer to a random other person, and were more willing to help the researcher (measured by asking to sign up to a follow-up experiment). This implies that the positive effects of BeMim arise because of a basic contingency between self-movement and the other's movement, regardless of whether that movement is actually mimicry. Other studies also showed similar effects indicating that merely responding to another person's movement might be enough to induce the liking effect, without the need to mimic the same movements (Sparenberg et al., 2012; Kulesza et al., 2022).

Controlled tasks can also be used to explore facial mimicry effects. In a series of studies from Neufeld and Chakrabarti (2016), participants were asked to perform happy or sad facial expressions followed by short clips of faces mimicking them or anti-mimicking (showing an opposite facial expression). EMG data recording was used to check if participants performed the correct facial expressions. Here, an implicit preferential looking task was used as an outcome measure of the social learning, rather than the more common questionnaire measures. First, participants were eye-tracked (baseline), and afterwards while seeing static faces of the two actors, one who previously mimicked their facial expressions and the other one who did not. Evidence for a learning effect was found because the gaze was biased towards mimicking faces and was also associated with positive evaluation through ratings of attractiveness and likeability. Moreover, after the conditioning task, participants with higher trait empathy showed greater gaze bias to the mimicking faces versus the anti-mimicking ones. The results reported here suggest that BeMim influences mimickee's gaze patterns and the effect is even stronger for people with high empathy traits.

The role of contingency was also tested in a study by Dignath and colleagues (2018). Here, participants saw a cue to action, performed an action, and then saw a video clip of another person performing the same (or a different) action, thus creating BeMim conditions. Different video confederates were present in different blocks and produced mostly matching actions or mostly mismatching actions. Results showed higher affiliation ratings towards video confederates who mimicked. A second experiment manipulated the delay between participant's actions and the video starting, ranging from 0 to 3 seconds and found higher affiliation ratings for short delays. These studies suggest that both contingency and temporal proximity are important for BeMim effects.

A similar experiment was conducted by De Coster (2014). It started with a resting phase, where the participant placed their right hand on a custom-made response box while watching a resting right hand on a video clip. Then, the action phase started, where a participant was asked to move one of their fingers which resulted in showing the video of a confederate doing the same movement in the mimicry block or a different movement in the non-mimicry blocks with no time delay. After each condition, a video clip showing a pain scenario was presented followed by empathy related questions. The results showed that participants felt more empathy for pain in the mimicry condition than in the non-mimicry block.

The studies of effects of BeMim in highly controlled environments allow researchers to focus on specific factors such as contingency or spatial features. Well-controlled BeMim designs allow researchers to eliminate numerous challenges that come with performing mimicking actions by confederates such as action quality and their number, their knowledge about the mimicry mechanism or the study, as described in detail earlier in this chapter. Many motor BeMim studies use within-subjects designs which can reduce individual differences and provide greater statistical power. Here, the study's success does not depend on human factors, but on upon the design of the experimental paradigm. Moreover, using video stimuli offers an opportunity to test numerous participants in an online setting (Kulesza et al., 2022). Getting a high-powered sample is challenging for live interactions, thus, using video paradigm online with large samples in highly controlled lab settings seems very promising for future BeMim research.

However, the spontaneity element is removed from these tasks which changes the social interaction dynamics. Often participants are instructed to perform a chosen action which could be mimicked, rather than having a free choice of many possible actions as in a conversation. This is especially challenging since BeMim is a spontaneous social mechanism. The question is whether researchers still study the same mechanisms if they remove participants from the social context and try to control behavior as much as possible with timings, number of repetitions, computer generated instructions, pictures, and videos. For example, in many of the studies reviewed above, the time delay between the participant's action and the BeMim action is very short and unlike natural social mimicry which has a much longer time course. As a result, these very fast events might tap into different cognitive mechanisms. For example, the studies using the Imitation-Inhibition task which is a potential controlled paradigm of BeMim showed that the automatic imitation and BeMim might tackle different cognitive processes (Rauchbauer et al., 2020). Another challenge with highly controlled environments is a risk of participants being aware of the manipulation. The tasks are performed outside of the social context (contrary to live interactions) which means it could be easier to guess the BeMim study design and the goal of the study.

Mimicry of Abstract Preferences

So far in this paper we have concentrated on forms of being mimicked that involve the direct copying of the motoric actions of others. In this section we discuss research into the cognitive mechanisms that underly the recognition of, and reaction to, imitation in this wider sense. In the rest of this section, we will focus on the literature around the more abstract cases of BeMim, particularly the imitation of preferences and values.

The issue of how we learn and are influenced by the similarity of others' preferences to our own is a key one for researchers in fields as diverse as psychology (Lee & Chung, 2022), evolutionary theory (Jones & DuVal, 2019), sociology (McPherson et al., 2001), and consumer marketing (Dholakia et al., 2004; Chloe Ki et al., 2022). In all these disciplines, there has been great interest in the question of social influence, how discovering the preferences of others can lead to a change in one's own, with a vast proliferation of research on the structure of social influence and the factors that increase influence (Izuma, 2013; Chloe Ki et al., 2022; Lee & Chung, 2022; Schnuerch & Gibbons, 2014). However, as with research around motor imitation, there has been much less interest in the effects of being the target of preference mimicry.

Unlike in the case of motor imitation, where it is usually possible to ascertain the direction of imitation due to the imitation being closely related in time, research on

BeMim in preference imitation is complicated by the fact that, it can often be hard to separate out the effects of direct social influence from that of homophily or "love for similar others." The presence of homophily complicates our understanding of how BeMim for preferences modulates social affiliation as it can be difficult to know whether any specific example of shared preferences is due to one partner in a dyad actively copying the other or whether the partners have affiliated together because they shared a pre-existing preference.

Controlled Studies of Abstract Preference Mimicry

To date relatively few studies have directly examined the effect of BeMim for preferences. However, several studies have sought to examine the effects of learning that others share our preferences via controlled studies that manipulate the degree of similarity between self and other. To the extent that such participants perceive the choices of others as being dependent on their own choices, these might be perceived as instances of BeMim.

Farmer et al. (2019) had participants learn the aesthetic preferences of two target others: one of who shared their own preferences 75% of the time and the other of whom differed from them 75% of the time during an fMRI scan. The authors then applied a reinforcement learning model to show that information about accumulated similarity was stored in an area of the dMPFC a region commonly linked to processing the relationship between self and other (Flagan & Beer, 2013). In line with findings of the positive effects of similarity, the similar target was also rated as more likeable and trustworthy than the different one.

While Farmer and colleagues examined how shared preference learning affects dyadic relationships between individuals, Gershman and colleagues (2017) used latent structure learning models to show that the effects of shared preferences on social bonds extend beyond dyadic interactions and plays a role in defining group boundaries. Gershman et al. demonstrated this in a series of studies in which participants first learnt about the film preference of two targets, one of whom shared 75% of their preferences (e.g., Alice) and the other of whom shared 25% (e.g., Bob). Participants then learnt about the preferences of a third person (e.g., Carl) who shared 50% of their preferences with the participant but 75% with one of the targets. They found that if this third person shared preferences with the similar target (e.g., Carl and Alice) then the participant treated them as an ingroup member while if they shared preferences with the target who had a different preference to the participant (e.g., Carl and Bob), they were treated as an outgroup member. Further studies have replicated this result for political views (Lau et al., 2018) and identified the right anterior insula as encoding the latent structure revealed by these different groups (Lau et al., 2020). Overall, these studies show that learning others share our preferences plays a role in the formation of social bonds at both the interpersonal and group level.

Other studies have examined factors that modulate the effect of shared preferences on affiliation. Several studies have found that learning that one's preferences are shared by disliked or dissimilar others can motivate a change in preferences either to as a means of signalling a distinct social identity (Berger & Heath, 2007; Berger & Heath, 2008) or to avoid being associated with an undesired reference group (Izuma & Adolphs, 2013; White & Dahl, 2006). For example, Izuma and Adolphs (2013) found that participants increased their preference for a t-shirt image when they learned that image was also liked by a liked group, i.e., students at the same university but reduced their preference when they learned the images was also liked by a disliked group, i.e., sex offenders. In addition, the degree of cognitive imbalance on different trials correlated with activations in a region of the dorsomedial prefrontal cortex (dmPFC) commonly linked with self-processing. The authors interpreted this finding in line with the theory of cognitive balance (Heider, 1946, 1958) which argues that our attitudes towards objects, other agents, and those agents' preferences towards the objects must be consistent.

In addition to the identity of the people or groups who share our preferences, our response to discovering shared preferences can also be modulated by the nature of the preference shared. Lab based studies manipulating the nature of shared preferences have found that people show greater affiliation to those who share rare, as opposed to commonly held preferences (Alves, 2018; Vélez et al., 2019). There is also evidence that the valence of the shared preference is relevant, with people reporting more positive attitudes towards those who liked the same things they liked than they did towards those who disliked the same things they disliked (Zorn et al., 2022). Finally, the basis for the effects of shared preferences in domains such as music on affiliation is driven by participants' assumption that shared preferences are an indicator of shared values more widely (Boer et al., 2011).

Studies of shared preferences using controlled designs typically involve a computerized task in which participants learn the preferences of target people who they do not directly interact with. This design allows researchers to have full control of the target's behavior and choices and to remove confounds such as past social interactions, knowledge of the target's wider preferences, and other aspects of their social identity. It also allows participants to precisely manipulate the number of shared preferences so as to explore different similarity levels. It is also easy to have a large number of different targets who are encountered and compare them. However, to date such learning have not directly manipulated cases where participants perceive the targets as simply happen to share their preferences from cases where targets are perceived as mimicking the participants responses. Future research that explicitly compares these two situations is needed to allow us to disentangle the effects of BeMim from those of homophily.

In contrast to body movements, cognitive abstract choices seem easier to control. One challenge is to quantify the similarity—for example, how much preference mimicry means "being highly similar"—70% or 90%? At the same time the greater the overlap in preference, the more likely it is that the participant will guess either the goal of the study or the manipulation, which might change the results, although at present, no study has directly measured this. Thus, there is a challenge to induce a feeling of similarity between the participant and the agent, but still not make the manipulation obvious to the participant. Moreover, similar to motor BeMim studies, it is difficult to study preference mimicry outside of a specific social context. Finally, these controlled studies could be criticized for being not social enough—participants do not see or interact with any real people and so might be more likely to use non-social mechanisms to make decisions.

Studying BeMim for Preferences "In the Wild"

As well as lab-based studies, other researchers have used observational data from real social groups to examine factors influencing the similarity-affiliation link. For example, Bahns et al. (2017) collected data on a range of personality traits, attitudes, and behaviors from over 1500 pre-existing interacting pairs. The authors found that the perceived importance of an attitude was a key moderator of the amount of dyadic similarity, i.e., how much similarity there was between that attitude for the individuals in each pair. This indicates that people are more likely to affiliate with others based on preferences they judge to be important. Indeed, an additional analysis showed that ratings of attitude importance were just as strong a predictor of dyadic similarity as were the actual attitudes themselves. Cullum and Harton (2007) found similar results when surveying college students living in halls of residence. They found that, across the semester, cohabiting participants increased their attitudinal similarity and that the greatest increase in similarity occurred for attitudes the participants considered the most important.

Finally, the growth of social media and large-scale communication networks since the turn of the millennium have given researchers access to a rich new source of data which can be used to study the links between shared preferences and affiliation. Ma et al. (2015) examined the purchasing and call data on caller ring-back tones (CBRT), a form of personalized dial tones heard by those calling the purchaser which are commonly used across Asia. So if Alice purchases a specific CBRT that plays a piece of music, then when Bob calls Alice, he will hear that music until she picks up. Ma et al. used the combination of purchase data, i.e., who paid to apply a particular CBRT, and caller data, i.e., which CBRTs people had heard when they called others, to model the role of both latent homophily and mimicry, in explaining similarity between consumers in their choice of CBRT purchase and found a considerable role for each. Other studies have used social media networks to similarly quantify levels of homophily and mimicry in social media use (Noe et al., 2016; Šćepanović et al., 2017).

This short review shows that there is correlational evidence for both homophily and social influence "in the wild." People tend to affiliate more with those who are similar and become more similar to those they affiliate with, but there is no specific evidence that preference BeMim alone causes liking. Indeed as we lay out in here, there might be various cofounding factors influencing these results making it difficult to specify cause and effect. Future studies in this area should aim to create realistic social situations in which a participant makes a choice and then is mimicked (or not) by another person and then measure the effects of that abstract mimicry on feelings of affiliation between the participant and this other person (Table 14.1).

Table 14.1 Summary of methods to study BeMim

Method	Description	Pros	Cons	Example research questions
Picture Description Task	A conversation about pictures with a confederate who is believed to be a participant. The confederate mimics (or not) the movements/posture of the participant	Ecological settings: participants can act spontaneously	Low experimental control, e.g., confederate's knowledge and acting skills	Does the BeMim effect arise in live interactions and why?
Virtual humans	Tasks that involve combining live tracking of participant's movements with virtually generated characters to allow those characters to imitate participant's actions	High experimental control—e.g., defining the type of actions copied and what precise delay is present between the participant's actions and the mimicry by the virtual human	Challenging to create believable virtual humans and have them interactively engage with participants; the results might differ from studies on humans	Does the strength of BeMim effects depend on the time delay in copied actions?
Video clips	The participant performs an action (typically following the computer's instructions) and then sees an image or video of another person copying (or not) the same action	High experimental control—all challenges connected to human factors are removed; Opportunity to test numerous participants in an online setting	The settings aren't social—participants cannot act spontaneously; The goal of the study might be more visible to the participants	What is the role of specific factors such as timing and contingency in BeMim effects?
Preference Indication	A computerized task where the participant makes a choice (e.g., about pictures) followed by a target's choice. The experimenter has control of the target's behavior and choices	High experimental control—precise control over the amount of similarity; Easy to implement	The settings aren't social—participants cannot act spontaneously; Hard to distinguish the effects of homophily from the BeMim effects	Does the strength of BeMim effects depend on the number of shared preferences?

(continued)

Table 14.1 (continued)

Method	Description	Pros	Cons	Example research questions
Large-scale social networks in the wild	Observational data (e.g. purchasing information, social media connections) from real social groups to examine factors influencing the choice similarity-affiliation link	Large samples of real-life data, strong ecological validity	Many confounding factors make it difficult to specify cause and effect	What are the links between shared preferences and affiliation?
Creative task	The participant performs a task with some creative element e.g., object customization or colouring in a shape and compares their work with that of confederates who complete the task after them	Naturalistic and ecologically valid task. Allows for variation in the extent of imitation	It can be hard to identify exactly which aspect of imitation produces the result	Does the BeMim effect arise in creative tasks?

Potential Neurocognitive Mechanisms of BeMim Effects

The review above describes a range of studies of BeMim effects which use a wide variety of methods. The range from naturalistic tasks such as conversation to tightly controlled tasks such as a single foot movement, and vary from copying of motor actions to copying of more abstract choices of art. While all of these can be described under the overarching concept of "being imitated," it is not clear if they all engage the same cognitive mechanisms, nor what those mechanisms might be. In this second half of the chapter, we lay out three distinct models of BeMim which vary in their amount of generality. Model 1 posits as specialized neurocognitive system attuned to motoric forms of BeMim while Model 2 considers the effects of both motor and abstract BeMim to be subcases of a wider form of social learning, Finally Model 3 takes the most domain general approach viewing the consequences of BeMim to depend upon universal mechanisms relating to stimuli predictability. We then consider empirical evidence that could distinguish between these models focusing on the how awareness of BeMim and timing and the cases where BeMim might have a negative impact on social interactions.

Model 1: A Specialized Mechanism for Motor Mimicry and BeMim

Implicit in many discussions of the link between motor mimicry and affiliation is that there must be a specialized cognitive mechanism that underlies this, a social glue that is specific to motor mimicry (Chartrand & Lakin, 2013). In terms of neural systems, the most plausible candidate would be the mirror neuron system (Rizzolatti et al., 2001; Rizzolatti & Craighero, 2004), which responds when a person sees an action and performs the same action (imitation). Given the properties of mirror neurons themselves, it seems sensible to suggest that this brain system might also be engaged if participants perform an action and later see the same action (BeMim), though this has rarely been directly tested. Indirect evidence comes from Kilner et al. (2009) who had participants see and do actions in different sequences and found overlapping engagement of inferior frontal gyrus in both.

One study (Hogeveen et al., 2015) used EEG recordings of the mu-rhythm, which is considered to be a marker of mirror neuron system (MNS) function, to examine BeMim effects (later studies showed that using mu-suppression to examine MNS is unreliable; Hobson & Bishop, 2016). Participants were asked to do a "music-rating" task in a dyad or alone on the computer. Specifically, they were assigned to one of the three conditions: interaction with a mimicking confederate, an anti-mimicking confederate, or no social interaction at all (doing the task on the computer). They recorded participants' brain activity before and after the task while they were watching a simple video showing action execution. Mu-rhythm suppression was taken as an indirect index of MNS activity. They found an increase in mu-suppression after the task in the mimicry condition in comparison to the no-interaction one; the anti-mimicry manipulation did not lead to a change in mu-suppression. This data suggests that BeMim during social interaction results in enhanced MNS activation afterwards, during subsequent action watching.

However, there is also evidence that brain regions outside the MNS are important in BeMim contexts. In a study from Brass and colleagues (2009), participants performed index finger or middle finger movements during fMRI and saw an image of a hand doing a congruent or incongruent finger movement after a short delay. Results showed engagement of temporoparietal junction and mPFC for delayed BeMim conditions, which the authors linked to self-other differentiation. In a neuroimaging study of BeMim in autistic and neurotypical participants, Okamoto and colleagues (2014) found engagement of extrastriate body area (EBA) when being imitated, with less activation in the autism group. EBA is localized within the occipito-temporal region and is activated when looking at the human body and its movements (Downing et al., 2001; Astafiev et al., 2004). Overall, there is not enough evidence to specifically localize BeMim effects to one particular brain system, and it might be more helpful to consider them as part of a wider network of regions engaged in social cognition and social interaction.

Model 2: BeMim as a Form of Social Learning

A second category of models suggests that there are general "like-me" mechanisms that apply only to other humans (not to cell-phones or cars or trees) and that people use to learn about others and to prefer other people who are more "like-me." Such systems are not restricted to motor mimicry but are part of a more general social learning system for acquiring knowledge about other people and other groups. In these models, detection of similarity between self and other would employ some shared systems across motor and non-motor domains and link into other neural systems involved in both domain general learning and social cognition. On this account, all studies of BeMim effects could be characterized as social learning studies, whereby participants experience particular actions of behaviors from a confederate or partner, and thereby learn to update their estimation of the character or self-similarity of the confederate.

An expansive version of this type of model is given by Haun and Over (2015), who survey a wide literature to argue that a general preference towards similar others, i.e., homophily, is an evolved innate trait that drives the development of key drivers of human cultural transmission including motor imitation, conformity, and the formation of psychological norms. In support of their position, they note evidence for the existence of homophily in non-human primates (Paukner et al., 2009) and for the early development of homophily in children with evidence that young children not only prefer similar others (Gerson et al., 2017; Mahajan & Wynn, 2012) but also expect others to show that same preference (Bian & Baillargeon, 2022; Liberman et al., 2021).

Additional evidence in support of this model can be found in studies that examine BeMim in relation to in learning and reward. Following on from the behavioral studies described above, Hsu and colleagues (2018) used their facial mimicry task to explore differences between participants with autism and neurotypical participants. They used a mimicry conditioning task, where participants were asked to perform happy or sad facial expressions followed by short clips of faces mimicking them or anti-mimicking (showing an opposite expression). In the test phase, participants saw static images of the same people with neutral faces in the MRI scanner. The neurotypical group showed higher likeability ratings and a higher ventral striatum response to mimicking faces in comparison to anti-mimicking faces. The autistic individuals had an opposite pattern: a reduced ventral striatum response to mimicking faces in comparison to the anti-mimicking ones. This study confirmed the link between BeMim and the reward system and showed how it is affected by autistic traits.

Studies investigating more abstract versions of similarity have also found evidence linking similarity learning to brain regions involved domain general reward processing and regions specialized for social cognition. Farmer et al. (2019) used fMRI to track brain activity in a context where participants could choose which painting, they prefer from a pair and then subsequently saw the art preferences of two agents, one of whom mostly had similar preferences and the other most dissimilar preferences. Brain activity patterns were modelled in terms of prediction errors for choices on each trial, that is, how well each agent conformed to the pattern of their previous preference similarity. Results showed that areas of the caudate linked to domain general reward learning were activated by positive prediction errors, i.e., when the agent made a choice that conformed to their overall pattern of preference similarity (either similar or different). By contrast when an agent made a choice that elicited a negative prediction error, i.e., that was more inconsistent with the agents' overall preference similarity to the self than predicted, this led to activations in a range of brain regions linked to social cognition including dmPFC and temporal-parietal junction (TPJ). Lau and colleagues (2020) also used computational modelling to map brain areas involved in similarity learning and linked similarity between self and other to the anterior cingulate cortex, a brain region that has been implicated in the learning of reward for both self and others (Apps et al., 2016).

To summarize, the social learning models of BeMim suggest that detecting and processing the similarity between self and others is a general feature of learning about people. Such mechanisms apply across a range of different types of mimicry (both motor mimicry and abstract choices) but are specific to learning about humans and could not be expected to apply to learning about objects or other physical events in the world.

Model 3: Universal Predictability

A third possible model for BeMim effects looks towards more general brain and cognitive mechanisms that apply across all domains, not just social interactions. Several lines of research suggest that events which are fluent or predictable are easier to process and potentially more rewarding than events which are disfluent or unpredictable (Oppenheimer, 2008; Reber et al., 1998). This applies to perceptual tasks (Reber et al., 1998) but also to motor tasks. For example, priming actions increases fluency and the sense of agency (Chambon & Haggard, 2012), and can even influence purchasing decisions (Chen & Lin, 2021). Even very young infants show a preference for performing actions which lead to a contingent predictable effect (Watson, 1972). It has been proposed that even young infants have a "contingency detection system" (Gergely & Watson, 1999) which allows them to determine which events in the world (both social and non-social) are caused by their own movements, and thus to learn to interact with and control the world. In adults, sense of agency over motor actions decays with delays of just 200 msec (Farrer et al., 2008), while if the participant performs an action and then an effect (a visual image) is delayed by more than 4 seconds, participants do not judge that they have caused the effect. This implies that predictability/fluency works best at very short timescales.

Under this type of model, people enjoy and find reward in actions which result in predictable effects, so if A's hand action causes B to move his hand, A will find B's action predictable (on a neural level) and thus more rewarding than if B were to do a different action. Crucially, the same mechanism would apply if A's finger action caused a predictable non-social effect (e.g., open an app on a touchscreen phone), which would be more rewarding than if the same action caused an unpredictable effect or no effect. The central claim here is that any predictable action-effects, both social and nonsocial, are linked to reward, and that BeMim effects can be subsumed within the much larger category of predictable effects. Evidence in favor of this comes from the study by Catmur et al., in which participants preferred contingent responses to their own movements to non-contingent responses regardless of the motor matching (Catmur & Heyes, 2013). Note that in this study, there was almost no delay between the action of the participant and the action-effect seen on the screen, whereas real-life mimicry effects typically have delays from 600 msec to 6 seconds. A strong version of the universal predictability model should suggest that shorter delays are always more predictable and thus are "better," but, as we will lay out below, it is not clear that this is the case for mimicry effects.

Predictability accounts of mimicry can also be extended to the case of shared preferences. Several models of social decision making have argued that the drive to affiliate with similar others can be linked to more fluent cognitive processing. For example, the anchoring and adjustment account of social inference argues that we use the self as a basis for inferences about the preferences of others leading it to take longer to process discrepancies between our own preferences and those of similar others (Tamir & Mitchell, 2013). Srivastava and Schrater (2011) designed a computational model of decision making in which cognitive agents naturally tend to affiliate and interact with other agents who share their "beliefs" due to the fact these agents are the easiest to predict the actions of and therefore cooperate with. Behavioral economic research has found that dyads whose members shared preferences ended up producing more optimal outcomes when playing economic games, even when the game required the dyad members to make different decisions. This provides evidence that participants have a real-world advantage when coordinating with others who they perceive as similar to them (Chierchia & Coricelli, 2015). These results show the potential for domain general processes based in cognitive fluency to result in an increased drive to affiliate with others who share one's preferences.

Distinguishing Between Models—Awareness and Timing

To potentially distinguish between these models and move the field of BeMim research forward, we suggest it is important to consider two subtle factors that could impact on people's experiences of being mimicked and their response to this. These factors interact and have rarely been studied systematically but have the potential to substantially affect our understanding of where BeMim effects come from and what they mean. First, we consider the case of awareness of being mimicked, and how that may rapidly reverse the positive, prosocial effects of BeMim. Second, we consider the impact of different time delays between the actions of a participant and the mimicker, and how this could link to both awareness and fluency effects. Third, we consider a few additional mediators such as the design of the control condition and the form of the agent's response to the mimicked person.

Awareness of Being Mimicked

In classic studies of BeMim effects in live interaction, there is an assumption (not always tested) that mimicry is an implicit effect. That is, the participants in the study are not aware that mimicry is the topic of investigation and are not aware that a confederate was mimicking their actions. In many studies, this is confirmed with a funnel-debrief interview after the main experimental task (Lakin & Chartrand, 2003; van Baaren et al., 2003), and it is common to exclude participants who guessed the goal of the study and/or realized that they were imitated. This choice by the experimenters is based on the intuition that participants would find being *explicitly* imitated to be a negative experience. Mimicry of (for example) political figures is a common form of mockery in popular entertainment (Filani, 2016), while in horror movies, excessive copying of a character's actions or choices is provided as evidence of ill intent (e.g., *Single White Female* movie (Schroeder, 1992)). However, we are aware of only one study which specifically tested the negative effects of awareness of motor BeMim.

Kulesza's team ran a study exploring the link between mimicry, awareness, and liking (Kulesza et al., 2016). University students were invited to the lab where they talked to a confederate who was introduced as an intern interviewer. The mimicry awareness was manipulated by the course description which students were supposed to read before the interview. There were four different conditions: participants did not get the module description (no awareness), they read general information about the mimicry (saying only that people mimic each other) or more developed information including either true (mimicking causes affiliation) or false (mimicking causes dislike) information about social consequences of being imitated. Then, participants were asked to share their thoughts about current university modules and the "potential new course" (the course information provided before the interview was the awareness manipulation). During the interview, the confederate mimicked or not the posture and gestures of the participant. The researchers found out that when participants were not aware of mimicry or were told general information without mentioning its consequences, they liked their mimicking interlocutor more in the mimicry condition. However, when they were informed about the social consequences of being imitated (either true or false), mimicry did not influence rapport. In addition, in the non-mimicry condition, being aware of the true or false effects of being imitated increased liking.

These examples of negative feelings and changes in liking with awareness of BeMim, suggest that being mimicked and knowing about it might make participants feel they have been deceived in their social interaction. According to deception theories, advantages are lost when the deception is detected (Zuckerman et al., 1981). When a mimicked participant knows about the imitation, they can interpret it as a manipulation by the mimicker who might be trying to take advantage of them. An alternative explanation of why mimicry awareness reduces the liking effect of BeMim was introduced by Kulesza's and colleagues (2016). They suggest that it might be explained by a boomerang effect or reactance—participants' freedom was threatened by the expectation that they would like their interlocutor more, so they prevented this and did not pay attention to the copying behavior. However, none of the participants reported being aware of the manipulation. It seems mimicry knowledge might not be the same as mimicry awareness. Would it change results if participants were aware of being imitated instead of having information about the manipulation in general? This is still unknown, and more research is needed.

As is the case with motor mimicry, very few studies have sought to directly examine the effect of awareness of BeMim for preferences. However, the limited studies suggest that people perceive deliberate copying as a negative act. We found two studies that directly investigated this question. The first study investigated the developmental trajectory of this dislike of being copied and found that adults and children as young as 5–6 years old disliked those who deliberately copied them when drawing, but that this was not the case for 3–4-year-olds (Olson & Shaw, 2011).

The second study by White and Argo (2011) examined how preferences for products were affected by deliberate copying. They found that participants were likely to want to dispose of or exchange a product, e.g., perfume if someone they knew deliberately copied them in using it. This was particularly the case if the mimicker was similar to the participant, if the product had high symbolic value, or if the participant had a high need for uniqueness or had been given an independent self-construal. Interestingly a recent study from D'Angelo et al. (2019) suggests that people are also aware of this dislike of obvious BeMim when they are in the role of potential mimicker. In D'Angelo's study, participants were shown examples of customized products created by individuals in their social circle and then asked to make their own custom version of the product. They found that participants tended to design their own version of the product to be less similar to that of others, particularly when that other was a close friend.

The role of social closeness in motivating both the negative reaction from targets of BeMim (White & Argo, 2011) and the avoidance of copying in potential mimickers (D'Angelo et al., 2019) suggests that these responses are, at least to some extent, driven by a need to distinguish oneself from similar others. Such an account fits in with the claims of optimal distinctiveness theory (Brewer, 1991; Leonardelli et al., 2010), which posits that we seek to balance a need to be included with the need for distinctiveness. This theory can thus explain why people are particularly averse to BeMim from close others where distinctiveness is already low. This optimal distinctiveness account may also explain the negative response to others we see as infringing on our uniqueness via deliberate motor or preference mimicry. While there are not many studies which have explored the impact of awareness on BeMim effects, the fact that some impact can be found argues for models which can incorporate awareness effects. That is, social learning models and dedicated BeMim models could both include awareness effects without changing the core model. For example, if social learning mechanisms lead people to like those who mimic them but also to dislike those who are too close, this is compatible with data on awareness of

BeMim. However, a domain-general predictability model might struggle to account for the impact of awareness on BeMim, because there is no obvious reason why awareness would change the impact of predictability across all domains.

Timing of Being Mimicked

The factor of timing in BeMim interactions is critically important for several reasons, and this can best be illustrated by considering some examples (illustrated in Fig. 14.3). First, we can consider the classic real-world motor mimicry situation where a participant performs an action, and this is imitated by a confederate after a suitable delay. This condition is likely to lead to the strongest affiliative effects (Fig. 14.3B). However, if the delay were substantially longer, for example the confederate imitated after 5 min, it seems unlikely that this action would impact much on the participant and it might not even register as mimicry. In contrast, if the confederate imitated very rapidly, the participant is more likely to explicitly detect "he is copying me" and the negative effects of being imitated might arise. A small number of studies have manipulated the timing of BeMim effects in different ways and can help us clarify when the positive and negative consequences arise.

In a set of pilot studies which explored different mimicry delay options, Bailenson et al. (2004) had participants sit in a virtual room with two agents: a human one

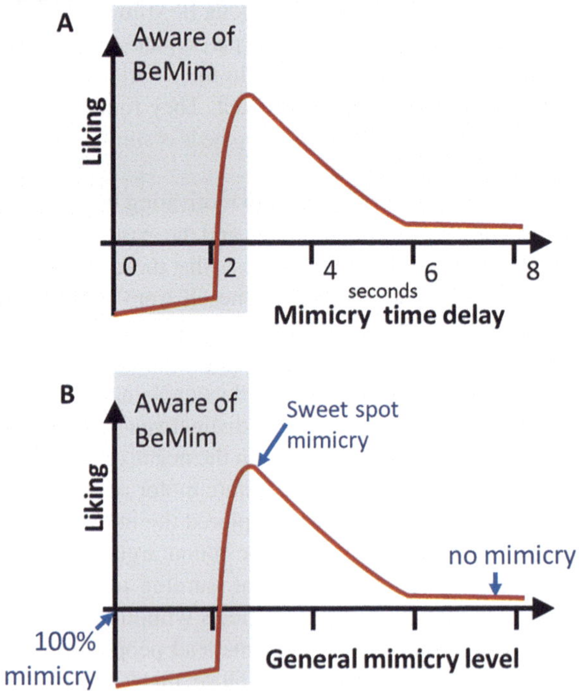

Fig. 14.3 Hypothesized mimicry effects. (**a**) The effects of time-delays on motor mimicry. As delays become shorter (from 6 to 3 seconds), motor mimicry has a positive effect on liking, but if the mimicry is detected (grey box), then participants may dislike the person mimicking them. (**b**) In the case of abstract mimicry, the parameter "time delay" could be replaced with a more general "mimicry level" parameter. Perfect mimicry could be detected and disliked, whereas the mimicry at the "sweet spot" level would lead to liking. This is similar to the idea of optimal distinctiveness

whose movements were controlled by a person in another room and a computer-generated agent who was mimicking participants' head movements either at 1, 2, 4, or 8 seconds' delay. Participants were told that one agent is a computer and is mimicking their head moves and their task was to identify a human agent. On average, only 60% of participants correctly guessed which avatar is a real person. Moreover, it was easy for them to identify the mimicker when the delay lasted 1 second, and then the longer the delay, the more difficult it was for them to identify the mimicker. These results suggest that the shorter the mimicry delay, the easier it would be for people to detect the imitation.

A few years later, the same authors carried out a similar study where (among other goals) they examined the effect of mimicry detection on social influence (Bailenson et al., 2008). Eleven percent of the sample detected head mimicry. In general, they found out that the mimicking agent was seen as more effective when participants did not realize that they were mimicked. When they detected mimicry, the agent was still evaluated well on the informativeness and agreement scale (more objective measures) but got a worse rating in terms of trustworthiness and warmth factors. The authors argue that the mimicking agent is seen as a liar by people detecting mimicry. As a result, participants give low ratings for warmth and credibility.

Using a similar method, Hale and Hamilton (2016) created a virtual human who carried out a picture-description task with a naive participant. The virtual human imitated the participant's head movements with either a 1 second delay or a 3 second delay (between subjects). Thirty percent of participants from the 1-second delay group detected the mimicry manipulation but only 4% of participants from the 3-second delay group detected it (Hale & Hamilton, 2016). In a follow-up, Hale and Ward captured head nodding motion from natural conversation and suggested that delays of only 600 msec are most common in real interactions (Hale et al., 2020). This is substantially shorter than used in most studies with artificial agents. A study with artificial agents used the natural BeMim delay of 600 msec in a picture description task and found that agents who showed this behavior were rated more positively than those who did not (Aburumman et al., 2022). An important new study examined the effects of timing in detail for facial expressions (Kroczek & Mühlberger, 2023). Participants were instructed to produce a smile or frown and then saw a smile or frown from a virtual agent and were asked to rate if the agent "was responding to me." Critically, facial EMG recordings from the participants were used to precisely calculate the delay between the participant's action and the agent's action on each trial. Results showed a clear non-monotonic effect, with peak ratings of "responsiveness" around 600–700 msec for both smiles and frowns; actions that occurred faster or slower than this time were rated as much less responsive. While this is not a direct measure of BeMim effects, the study does provide striking evidence that the timing of social behavior matters and that 600–700 msec may be an optimal time delay for perceiving interactivity.

Based on the results summarized above, the optimal timing for BeMim effects is still unclear. While some studies suggest delays should be as long as 3 to 7 seconds, others have found positive effects with delays as short as 600 msec. It is clear that short delays can also lead to more detection of BeMim, leading to the negative effects described above. This is hard to reconcile with a fluency/predictability model of BeMim, because under that model, movements with short delays should always be easier to predict and thus be more positive. In contrast, the conjunction of the timing and awareness studies suggest that predictability is not the only thing that matters for BeMim effects. Instead, BeMim may work best in a "sweet spot" that is similar but not too similar, in a pattern reminiscent of optimal distinctiveness effects.

However, the results described above for timing apply primarily to motor mimicry where each action is a distinct event that occurs at one time. In contrast, a preference normally lasts over a longer time (the painting I prefer on Monday will still be preferred on Tuesday), so it may not make sense to study mimicry timing in the context of shared preferences. It remains to be seen if there are other factors which behave in the same fashion as timing in the context of abstract mimicry—perhaps just the intensity of the mimicry matters. For example, copying one element of a complex item might be positive but copying all elements might be negative.

These results showing that both awareness and timing of BeMim can modulate its social effects help to give us some means of evaluating the three different models that we discussed above. As previously mentioned, studies showing that there is an optimal time frame for motor BeMim that is not directly linked to the predictability or fluency of response is a point against our Model 3 account which attributes the positive effects of BeMim purely to domain general fluency effects (Bailenson et al., 2004; Hale & Hamilton, 2016). In addition, findings suggesting a similar negative response to the detection of BeMim in both the motor and preference domains give some support to the Model 2 accounts that relate BeMims effects to a social but not motor specific, set of neurocognitive processes such as the desire for optimal distinctiveness or the detection of attempts to deceive or manipulate (Brewer, 1991; Bailenson et al., 2008).

Summary

To sum up, in the first part of this chapter, we presented an overview of BeMim methods. There are numerous approaches to study BeMim effects—researchers can choose from a spectrum of real-world (ecological, but not controlling cofounds) and controlled in the lab (less interactive but removing cofounds) paradigms. In general, using a wide range of methods is useful—it allows researchers to combine benefits of various approaches (e.g., adding more control to a live study paradigm using VR agents designed to perform with specific timing instead of human confederates). The choice is also to be made between motor movement and abstract preferences mimicry. However, it is still unknown whether various BeMim paradigms tap the same cognitive mechanisms. More carefully designed studies that bridge across methods will be needed to determine this, possibly including real-world neuroimaging methods.

The second part of this chapter covered cognitive mechanisms for processing BeMim. There are three possible main neurocognitive models which try to explain how BeMim could work: a specialized mechanism for BeMim, universal predictability, and social learning model. The first one labels mirror neuron systems (MNS) as a specialized cognitive mechanism that responds to performing an action and then seeing others doing the same action. The universal predictability is about more general, non-social mechanisms responding to BeMim: fluent or predictable events are easier to process and potentially more enjoyable than disfluent or unpredictable events. The social learning model claims that there is a general human social learning mechanism responsible for learning about others and having a preference for people similar to them, which applies to both motor mimicry and abstract preference sharing but not to non-human objects. In the last part of the chapter, we discussed awareness and timing of BeMim. The impacts of BeMim on social judgement and social affiliation are probably non-monotonic. That is, more mimicry is not always better. Both the awareness studies and the timing studies suggest that mimicry which is too close in time and space and form to the participant's action is judged negatively rather than positively.

Based on these ideas about awareness and timing, we suggest that the social learning model seems to be the strongest one. This is because data suggest that people prefer to be optimally distinctive to others, both in their abstract choices and their motor patterns, and this fits best with the social learning approach. Gaining a greater understanding of the links and parallels between BeMim for motor tasks and BeMim for abstract tasks will be useful to advance our theories in this area.

References

Aburumman, N., Gillies, M., Ward, J. A., & Hamilton, A. F. de C. (2022). Nonverbal communication in virtual reality: Nodding as a social signal in virtual interactions. *International Journal of Human-Computer Studies, 164*, 102819. https://doi.org/10.1016/j.ijhcs.2022.102819

Alves, H. (2018). Sharing rare attitudes attracts. *Personality and Social Psychology Bulletin, 44*, 1270–1283. https://doi.org/10.1177/0146167218766861

Apps, M. A. J., Rushworth, M. F. S., & Chang, S. W. C. (2016). The anterior cingulate gyrus and social cognition: Tracking the motivation of others. *Neuron, 90*, 692–707. https://doi.org/10.1016/j.neuron.2016.04.018

Astafiev, S. V., Stanley, C. M., Shulman, G. L., & Corbetta, M. (2004). Extrastriate body area in human occipital cortex responds to the performance of motor actions. *Nature Neuroscience, 7*, 542–548. https://doi.org/10.1038/nn1241

Bahns, A. J., Crandall, C. S., Gillath, O., & Preacher, K. J. (2017). Similarity in relationships as niche construction: Choice, stability, and influence within dyads in a free choice environment. *Journal of Personality and Social Psychology, 112*, 329–355. https://doi.org/10.1037/pspp0000088

Bailenson, J. N., & Yee, N. (2005). Digital chameleons: Automatic assimilation of nonverbal gestures in immersive virtual environments. *Psychological Science, 16*, 814–819. https://doi.org/10.1111/j.1467-9280.2005.01619.x

Bailenson, J. N., Beall, A. C., Loomis, J., Blascovich, J., & Turk, M. (2004). Transformed social interaction: Decoupling representation from behavior and form in collaborative virtual environments. *Presence: Teleoperators and Virtual Environments, 13*, 428–441. https://doi.org/10.1162/1054746041944803

Bailenson, J. N., Yee, N., Patel, K., & Beall, A. C. (2008). Detecting digital chameleons. *Computers in Human Behavior, 24*, 66–87. https://doi.org/10.1016/j.chb.2007.01.015

Berger, J., & Heath, C. (2007). Where consumers diverge from others: Identity signaling and product domains. *Journal of Consumer Research, 34*, 121–134. https://doi.org/10.1086/519142

Berger, J., & Heath, C. (2008). Who drives divergence? Identity signaling, outgroup dissimilarity, and the abandonment of cultural tastes. *Journal of Personality and Social Psychology, 95*, 593–607. https://doi.org/10.1037/0022-3514.95.3.593

Bian, L., & Baillargeon, R. (2022). When are similar individuals a group? Early reasoning about similarity and in-group support. *Psychological Science, 33*, 752–764. https://doi.org/10.1177/09567976211055185

Boer, D., Fischer, R., Strack, M., Bond, M. H., Lo, E., & Lam, J. (2011). How shared preferences in music create bonds between people: Values as the missing link. *Personality and Social Psychology Bulletin, 37*, 1159–1171. https://doi.org/10.1177/0146167211407521

Boesch, C., & Tomasello, M. (1998). Chimpanzee and human cultures. *Current Anthropology, 39*, 591–614. https://doi.org/10.1086/204785

Bourgeois, P., & Hess, U. (2008). The impact of social context on mimicry. *Biological Psychology, 77*, 343–352. https://doi.org/10.1016/j.biopsycho.2007.11.008

Brass, M., Ruby, P., & Spengler, S. (2009). Inhibition of imitative behaviour and social cognition. *Philosophical Transactions of the Royal Society B: Biological Sciences, 364*, 2359–2367. https://doi.org/10.1098/rstb.2009.0066

Brewer, M. B. (1991). The social self: On being the same and different at the same time. *Personality and Social Psychology Bulletin, 17*, 475–482. https://doi.org/10.1177/0146167291175001

Catmur, C., & Heyes, C. (2013). Is it what you do, or when you do it? The roles of contingency and similarity in pro-social effects of imitation. *Cognitive Science, 37*, 1541–1552. https://doi.org/10.1111/cogs.12071

Chambon, V., & Haggard, P. (2012). Sense of control depends on fluency of action selection, not motor performance. *Cognition, 125*, 441–451. https://doi.org/10.1016/j.cognition.2012.07.011

Chartrand, T. L., & Bargh, J. A. (1999). The chameleon effect: The perception–behavior link and social interaction. *Journal of Personality and Social Psychology, 76*, 893–910. https://doi.org/10.1037/0022-3514.76.6.893

Chartrand, T. L., & Lakin, J. L. (2013). The antecedents and consequences of human behavioral mimicry. *Annual Review of Psychology, 64*, 285–308. https://doi.org/10.1146/annurev-psych-113011-143754

Chartrand, T. L., Maddux, W. W., & Lakin, J. L. (2006). Beyond the perception-behavior link: The ubiquitous utility and motivational moderators of nonconscious mimicry. In R. R. Hassin, J. S. Uleman, & J. A. Bargh (Eds.), *The new unconscious* (pp. 334–361). Oxford University Press. https://doi.org/10.1093/acprof:oso/9780195307696.003.0014

Chen, M., & Lin, C.-H. (2021). What is in your hand influences your purchase intention: Effect of motor fluency on motor simulation. *Current Psychology, 40*, 3226–3235. https://link.springer.com/article/10.1007/s12144-019-00261-6

Chierchia, G., & Coricelli, G. (2015). The impact of perceived similarity on tacit coordination: Propensity for matching and aversion to decoupling choices. *Frontiers in Behavioral Neuroscience, 9*. https://doi.org/10.3389/fnbeh.2015.00202

Chloe Ki, C.-W., Park, S., & Kim, Y.-K. (2022). Investigating the mechanism through which consumers are "inspired by" social media influencers and "inspired to" adopt influencers' exemplars as social defaults. *Journal of Business Research, 144*, 264–277. https://doi.org/10.1016/j.jbusres.2022.01.071

Choi, M., Kornfield, R., Takayama, L., & Mutlu, B. (2017). Movement matters: Effects of motion and mimicry on perception of similarity and closeness in robot-mediated communication. In *Proceedings of the 2017 CHI conference on human factors in computing systems* (pp. 325–335). https://doi.org/10.1145/3025453.3025734

Condon, W. S., & Ogston, W. D. (1966). Sound film analysis of normal and pathological behavior patterns. *Journal of Nervous and Mental Disease, 143*, 338–347. https://doi.org/10.1097/00005053-196610000-00005

Cullum, J., & Harton, H. C. (2007). Cultural evolution: Interpersonal influence, issue importance, and the development of shared attitudes in college residence halls. *Personality and Social Psychology Bulletin, 33*, 1327–1339. https://doi.org/10.1177/0146167207303949

D'Angelo, J. K., Diehl, K., & Cavanaugh, L. A. (2019). Lead by example? Custom-made examples created by close others lead consumers to make dissimilar choices. *Journal of Consumer Research, 46*, 750–773. https://doi.org/10.1093/jcr/ucz019

Davydenko, M., Zelenski, J. M., Gonzalez, A., & Whelan, D. (2020). Does acting extraverted evoke positive social feedback? *Personality and Individual Differences, 159*, 109883. https://doi.org/10.1016/j.paid.2020.109883

De Coster, L., Andres, M., & Brass, M. (2014). Effects of being imitated on motor responses evoked by pain observation: Exerting control determines action tendencies when perceiving pain in others. *Journal of Neuroscience, 34*, 6952–6957. https://doi.org/10.1523%2FJNEUROSCI.5044-13.2014

Dholakia, U. M., Bagozzi, R. P., & Pearo, L. K. (2004). A social influence model of consumer participation in network- and small-group-based virtual communities. *International Journal of Research in Marketing, 21*, 241–263. https://doi.org/10.1016/j.ijresmar.2003.12.004

Dignath, D., Lotze-Hermes, P., Farmer, H., & Pfister, R. (2018). Contingency and contiguity of imitative behaviour affect social affiliation. *Psychological Research, 82*, 819–831. https://doi.org/10.1007/s00426-017-0854-x

Downing, P. E., Jiang, Y., Shuman, M., & Kanwisher, N. (2001). A cortical area selective for visual processing of the human body. *Science, 293*, 2470–2473. https://doi.org/10.1126/science.1063414

Doyen, S., Klein, O., Pichon, C.-L., & Cleeremans, A. (2012). Behavioral priming: It's all in the mind, but whose mind? *PLoS One, 7*, e29081. https://doi.org/10.1371/journal.pone.0029081

Duffy, K. A., & Chartrand, T. L. (2015). The extravert advantage: How and when extraverts build rapport with other people. *Psychological Science, 26*, 1795–1802. https://psycnet.apa.org/doi/10.1177/0956797615600890

Farmer, H., Hertz, U., & Hamilton, A. F. de C. (2019). The neural basis of shared preference learning. *Social Cognitive and Affective Neuroscience, 14*, 1061–1072. https://doi.org/10.1093/scan/nsz076

Farrer, C., Bouchereau, M., Jeannerod, M., & Franck, N. (2008). Effect of distorted visual feedback on the sense of agency. *Behavioural Neurology, 19*, 53–57. https://doi.org/10.1155/2008/425267

Filani, I. (2016). The use of mimicry in Nigerian stand-up comedy. *Comedy Studies, 7*, 89–102. https://doi.org/10.1080/2040610X.2016.1139810

Flagan, T., & Beer, J. (2013). Three ways in which midline regions contribute to self-evaluation. *Frontiers in Human Neuroscience, 7*. https://doi.org/10.3389%2Ffnhum.2013.00450

Fox, A. B., Rosen, J., & Crawford, M. (2009). Distractions, distractions: Does instant messaging affect college students' performance on a concurrent reading comprehension task? *Cyberpsychology & Behavior, 12*, 51–53. https://doi.org/10.1089/cpb.2008.0107

Fridland, E., & Moore, R. (2015). Imitation reconsidered. *Philosophical Psychology, 28*, 856–880. https://doi.org/10.1080/09515089.2014.942896

Gergely, G., & Watson, J. S. (1999). Early socio–emotional development: Contingency perception and the social-biofeedback model. In *Early social cognition: Understanding others in the first months of life* (pp. 101–136). Lawrence Erlbaum Associates.

Gershman, S. J., Pouncy, H. T., & Gweon, H. (2017). Learning the structure of social influence. *Cognitive Science, 41*, 545–575. https://doi.org/10.1111/cogs.12480

Gerson, S. A., Bekkering, H., & Hunnius, S. (2017). Do you do as I do?: Young toddlers prefer and copy toy choices of similarly acting others. *Infancy, 22*, 5–22. https://doi.org/10.1111/infa.12142

Ghazali, A. S., Ham, J., Barakova, E., & Markopoulos, P. (2019). Assessing the effect of persuasive robots interactive social cues on users' psychological reactance, liking, trusting beliefs and compliance. *Advanced Robotics, 33*, 325–337. https://doi.org/10.1080/01691864.2019.1589570

Gilder, T. S. E., & Heerey, E. A. (2018). The role of experimenter belief in social priming. *Psychological Science, 29*, 403–417. https://doi.org/10.1177/0956797617737128

Hale, J., & Hamilton, A. F. de C. (2016). Cognitive mechanisms for responding to mimicry from others. *Neuroscience & Biobehavioral Reviews, 63*, 106–123. https://doi.org/10.1016/j.neubiorev.2016.02.006

Hale, J., Ward, J. A., Buccheri, F., Oliver, D., & Hamilton, A. F. de C. (2020). Are you on my wavelength? Interpersonal coordination in dyadic conversations. *Journal of Nonverbal Behavior, 44*, 63–83. https://doi.org/10.1007/s10919-019-00320-3

Hasler, B. S., Hirschberger, G., Shani-Sherman, T., & Friedman, D. A. (2014). Virtual peacemakers: Mimicry increases empathy in simulated contact with virtual outgroup members. *Cyberpsychology, Behavior, and Social Networking, 17*, 766–771. https://doi.org/10.1089/cyber.2014.0213

Hasler, B. S., Landau, D., Hasson, Y., Schori-Eyal, N., Giron, J., Levy, J., Halperin, E., & Friedman, D. (2021). Virtual reality-based conflict resolution: The impact of immersive 360° video on changing view points and moral judgment in the context of violent intergroup conflict. *New Media & Society, 23*, 2255–2278. https://doi.org/10.1177/1461444821993133

Haun, D., & Over, H. (2015). Like me: A homophily-based account of human culture. In *Epistemological dimensions of evolutionary psychology* (pp. 117–130). Springer Science + Business Media. https://doi.org/10.1007/978-1-4939-1387-9_6

Heider, F. (1946). Attitudes and cognitive organization. *The Journal of Psychology, 21*, 107–112. https://doi.org/10.1080/00223980.1946.9917275

Heider, F. (1958). The naive analysis of action. In *The psychology of interpersonal relations* (pp. 79–124). Wiley. https://doi.org/10.1037/10628-004

Heyes, C. M. (1994). Social learning in animals: Categories and mechanisms. *Biological Reviews, 69*, 207–231. https://doi.org/10.1111/j.1469-185X.1994.tb01506.x

Heyes, C. (2021). Imitation and culture: What gives? *Mind & Language*, mila.12388. https://doi.org/10.1111/mila.12388

Hobson, H. M., & Bishop, D. V. (2016). Mu suppression–a good measure of the human mirror neuron system? *Cortex, 82*, 290–310. https://doi.org/10.1016/j.cortex.2016.03.019

Hogeveen, J., Chartrand, T. L., & Obhi, S. S. (2015). Social mimicry enhances mu-suppression during action observation. *Cerebral Cortex, 25*, 2076–2082. https://doi.org/10.1093/cercor/bhu016

Hsu, C.-T., Neufeld, J., & Chakrabarti, B. (2018). Reduced reward-related neural response to mimicry in individuals with autism. *European Journal of Neuroscience, 47*, 610–618. https://doi.org/10.1111/ejn.13620

Izuma, K. (2013). The neural basis of social influence and attitude change. *Current Opinion in Neurobiology, 23*, 456–462. https://doi.org/10.1016/j.conb.2013.03.009

Izuma, K., & Adolphs, R. (2013). Social manipulation of preference in the human brain. *Neuron, 78*, 563–573. https://doi.org/10.1016/j.neuron.2013.03.023

Jones, B. C., & DuVal, E. H. (2019). Mechanisms of social influence: A meta-analysis of the effects of social information on female mate choice decisions. *Frontiers in Ecology and Evolution, 7*. https://doi.org/10.3389/fevo.2019.00390

Keysar, B., Barr, D. J., Balin, J. A., & Paek, T. S. (1998). Definite reference and mutual knowledge: Process models of common ground in comprehension. *Journal of Memory and Language, 1*, 1–20. https://doi.org/10.1006/jmla.1998.2563

Keysar, B., Barr, D. J., Balin, J. A., & Brauner, J. S. (2000). Taking perspective in conversation: The role of mutual knowledge in comprehension. *Psychological Science, 11*, 32–38. https://doi.org/10.1111/1467-9280.00211

Kilner, J. M., Neal, A., Weiskopf, N., Friston, K. J., & Frith, C. D. (2009). Evidence of mirror neurons in human inferior frontal gyrus. *Journal of Neuroscience, 29*, 10153–10159. https://doi.org/10.1523/JNEUROSCI.2668-09.2009

Kroczek, L. O. H., & Mühlberger, A. (2023). Time to smile: How onset asynchronies between reciprocal facial expressions influence the experience of responsiveness of a virtual agent. *Journal of Nonverbal Behavior, 47*, 345–360. https://doi.org/10.1007/s10919-023-00430-z

Kuhlen, A. K., & Brennan, S. E. (2013). Language in dialogue: When confederates might be hazardous to your data. *Psychonomic Bulletin & Review, 20*, 54–72. https://doi.org/10.3758/s13423-012-0341-8

Kühn, S., Müller, B. C. N., van Baaren, R. B., Wietzker, A., Dijksterhuis, A., & Brass, M. (2010). Why do I like you when you behave like me? Neural mechanisms mediating positive consequences of observing someone being imitated. *Social Neuroscience, 5*, 384–392. https://doi.org/10.1080/17470911003633750

Kulesza, W., Szypowska, Z., Jarman, M. S., & Dolinski, D. (2014). Attractive chameleons sell: The mimicry-attractiveness link. *Psychology & Marketing, 31*, 549–561. https://doi.org/10.1002/mar.20716

Kulesza, W., Dolinski, D., & Wicher, P. (2016). Knowing that you mimic me: The link between mimicry, awareness and liking. *Social Influence, 11*, 68–74. https://doi.org/10.1080/15534510.2016.1148072

Kulesza, W., Chrobot, N., Dolinski, D., Muniak, P., Bińkowska, D., Grzyb, T., & Genschow, O. (2022). Imagining is not observing: The role of simulation processes within the mimicry-liking expressway. *Journal of Nonverbal Behavior, 46*, 233–246. https://doi.org/10.1007/s10919-022-00399-1

Lakin, J. L., & Chartrand, T. L. (2003). Using nonconscious behavioral mimicry to create affiliation and rapport. *Psychological Science, 14*, 334–339. https://doi.org/10.1111/1467-9280.14481

Lakin, J. L., Chartrand, T. L., & Arkin, R. M. (2008). I am too just like you: Nonconscious mimicry as an automatic behavioral response to social exclusion. *Psychological Science, 19*, 816–822. https://doi.org/10.1111/j.1467-9280.2008.02162.x

Lau, T., Pouncy, H. T., Gershman, S. J., & Cikara, M. (2018). Discovering social groups via latent structure learning. *Journal of Experimental Psychology: General, 147*, 1881–1891. https://doi.org/10.1037/xge0000470

Lau, T., Gershman, S. J., & Cikara, M. (2020). Social structure learning in human anterior insula. *eLife, 9*, e53162. https://doi.org/10.7554/eLife.53162

Lee, H., & Chung, D. (2022). Characterization of the core determinants of social influence from a computational and cognitive perspective. *Frontiers in Psychiatry, 13*, 846535. https://psycnet.apa.org/doi/10.3389/fpsyt.2022.846535

Leonardelli, G., Pickett, C., & Brewer, M. (2010). Chapter 2 – Optimal distinctiveness theory: A framework for social identity, social cognition, and intergroup relations. In *Advances in experimental social psychology* (pp. 63–113). Academic. https://psycnet.apa.org/doi/10.1016/S0065-2601(10)43002-6

Liberman, Z., Kinzler, K. D., & Woodward, A. L. (2021). Origins of homophily: Infants expect people with shared preferences to affiliate. *Cognition, 212*, 104695. https://doi.org/10.1016/j.cognition.2021.104695

Ma, Q., & Hu, Y. (2015). Beauty matters: Social preferences in a three-person ultimatum game. *PLoS One, 10*, e0125806. https://doi.org/10.1371/journal.pone.0125806

Ma, L., Krishnan, R., & Montgomery, A. L. (2015). Latent homophily or social influence? An empirical analysis of purchase within a social network. *Management Science, 61*, 454–473. https://dx.doi.org/10.1287/mnsc.2014.1928

Mahajan, N., & Wynn, K. (2012). Origins of "us" versus "them": Prelinguistic infants prefer similar others. *Cognition, 124*, 227–233. https://doi.org/10.1016/j.cognition.2012.05.003

McIntosh, D. N., Reichmann-Decker, A., Winkielman, P., & Wilbarger, J. L. (2006). When the social mirror breaks: Deficits in automatic, but not voluntary, mimicry of emotional facial expressions in autism. *Developmental Science, 9*, 295–302. https://doi.org/10.1111/j.1467-7687.2006.00492.x

McPherson, M., Smith-Lovin, L., & Cook, J. M. (2001). Birds of a feather: Homophily in social networks. *Annual Review of Sociology, 27*, 415–444. https://doi.org/10.1146/annurev.soc.27.1.415

Montoya, R. M., Horton, R. S., & Kirchner, J. (2008). Is actual similarity necessary for attraction? A meta-analysis of actual and perceived similarity. *Journal of Social and Personal Relationships, 25*, 889–922. https://doi.org/10.1177/0265407508096700

Neufeld, J., & Chakrabarti, B. (2016). Empathy modulates the rewarding effect of mimicry. *Scientific Reports, 6*, 1–27751. https://doi.org/10.1038/srep27751

Noe, N., Whitaker, R. M., & Allen, S. M. (2016). Personality homophily and the local network characteristics of facebook. In *2016 IEEE/ACM international conference on advances in social networks analysis and mining (ASONAM)* (pp. 386–393). https://doi.org/10.1109/ASONAM.2016.7752263

Okamoto, Y., Kitada, R., Tanabe, H. C., Hayashi, M. J., Kochiyama, T., Munesue, T., Ishitobi, M., Saito, D. N., Yanaka, H. T., Omori, M., Wada, Y., Okazawa, H., Sasaki, A. T., Morita, T., Itakura, S., Kosaka, H., & Sadato, N. (2014). Attenuation of the contingency detection effect in the extrastriate body area in autism spectrum disorder. *Neuroscience Research, 87*, 66–76. https://doi.org/10.1016/j.neures.2014.06.012

Olson, K. R., & Shaw, A. (2011). 'No fair, copycat!': What children's response to plagiarism tells us about their understanding of ideas. *Developmental Science, 14*, 431–439. https://doi.org/10.1111/j.1467-7687.2010.00993.x

Oppenheimer, D. M. (2008). The secret life of fluency. *Trends in Cognitive Sciences, 12*, 237–241. https://doi.org/10.1016/j.tics.2008.02.014

Pan, X., & Hamilton, A. F. de C. (2018). Why and how to use virtual reality to study human social interaction: The challenges of exploring a new research landscape. *British Journal of Psychology, 109*, 395–417. https://doi.org/10.1111/bjop.12290

Paukner, A., Suomi, S. J., Visalberghi, E., & Ferrari, P. F. (2009). Capuchin monkeys display affiliation toward humans who imitate them. *Science, 325*, 880–883. https://doi.org/10.1126/science.1176269

Rauchbauer, B., Majdandžić, J., Stieger, S., & Lamm, C. (2016). The modulation of mimicry by ethnic group-membership and emotional expressions. *PLoS One, 11*, e0161064. https://doi.org/10.1371/journal.pone.0161064

Rauchbauer, B., Dunbar, R. I. M., & Lamm, C. (2020). Being mimicked affects inhibitory mechanisms of imitation. *Acta Psychologica, 209*, 103132. https://doi.org/10.1016/j.actpsy.2020.103132

Reber, R., Winkielman, P., & Schwarz, N. (1998). Effects of perceptual fluency on affective judgments. *Psychological Science, 9*, 45–48. https://doi.org/10.1111/1467-9280.00008

Rizzolatti, G., & Craighero, L. (2004). The mirror-neuron system. *Annual Review of Neuroscience, 27*, 169–192. https://doi.org/10.1146/annurev.neuro.27.070203.144230

Rizzolatti, G., Fogassi, L., & Gallese, V. (2001). Neurophysiological mechanisms underlying the understanding and imitation of action. *Nature Reviews Neuroscience, 2*, 661–670. https://doi.org/10.1038/35090060

Salazar Kämpf, M., Liebermann, H., Kerschreiter, R., Krause, S., Nestler, S., & Schmukle, S. C. (2018). Disentangling the sources of mimicry: Social relations analyses of the link between mimicry and liking. *Psychological Science, 29*, 131–138. https://doi.org/10.1177/0956797617727121

Sanchez-Burks, J., Bartel, C. A., & Blount, S. (2009). Performance in intercultural interactions at work: Cross-cultural differences in response to behavioral mirroring. *Journal of Applied Psychology, 94*, 216–223. https://doi.org/10.1037/a0012829

Šćepanović, S., Mishkovski, I., Gonçalves, B., Nguyen, T. H., & Hui, P. (2017). Semantic homophily in online communication: Evidence from twitter. *Online Social Networks and Media, 2*, 1–18. https://doi.org/10.1016/j.osnem.2017.06.001

Scheflen, A. E. (1964). The significance of posture in communication systems. *Psychiatry, 27*. https://doi.org/10.1080/00332747.1964.11023403

Schnuerch, R., & Gibbons, H. (2014). A review of neurocognitive mechanisms of social conformity. *Social Psychology, 45*, 466–478. https://doi.org/10.1027/1864-9335/a000213

Schroeder, B. (Director). (1992). *Single white female* [Film]. Columbia Pictures.

Sparenberg, P., Topolinski, S., Springer, A., & Prinz, W. (2012). Minimal mimicry: Mere effector matching induces preference. *Brain and Cognition, 80*, 291–300. https://doi.org/10.1016/j.bandc.2012.08.004

Srivastava, N., & Schrater, P. R. (2011). Cognitive efficiency as a causal mechanism for social preferences. In *2011 IEEE third international conference on privacy, security, risk and trust and 2011 IEEE third international conference on social computing* (pp. 647–650). https://doi.org/10.1109/PASSAT/SocialCom.2011.224

Tamir, D. I., & Mitchell, J. P. (2013). Anchoring and adjustment during social inferences. *Journal of Experimental Psychology. General, 142*, 151–162. https://doi.org/10.1037/a0028232

van Baaren, R. B., Maddux, W. W., Chartrand, T. L., de Bouter, C., & van Knippenberg, A. (2003). It takes two to mimic: Behavioral consequences of self-construals. *Journal of Personality and Social Psychology, 84*, 1093–1102. https://doi.org/10.1037/0022-3514.84.5.1093

van Baaren, R., Janssen, L., Chartrand, T. L., & Dijksterhuis, A. (2009). Where is the love? The social aspects of mimicry. *Philosophical Transactions of the Royal Society B: Biological Sciences, 364*, 2381–2389. https://doi.org/10.1098/rstb.2009.0057

Vélez, N., Bridgers, S., & Gweon, H. (2019). The rare preference effect: Statistical information influences social affiliation judgments. *Cognition, 192*, 103994. https://doi.org/10.1016/j.cognition.2019.06.006

Verberne, F., Ham, J., Ponnada, A., & Midden, C. (2013). *Trusting digital chameleons: The effect of mimicry by a virtual social agent on user trust* (p. 245), 234–245. https://doi.org/10.1007/978-3-642-37157-8_28

Watson, J. S. (1972). Smiling, cooing, and "the game". *Merrill-Palmer Quarterly of Behavior and Development, 18*, 323–339.

White, K., & Argo, J. J. (2011). When imitation doesn't flatter: The role of consumer distinctiveness in responses to mimicry. *Journal of Consumer Research, 38*, 667–680. https://doi.org/10.1086/660187

White, K., & Dahl, D. W. (2006). To be or not be? The influence of dissociative reference groups on consumer preferences. *Journal of Consumer Psychology, 16*, 404–414. https://doi.org/10.1207/s15327663jcp1604_11

Zorn, T. J., Mata, A., & Alves, H. (2022). Attitude similarity and interpersonal liking: A dominance of positive over negative attitudes. *Journal of Experimental Social Psychology, 100*, 104281. https://doi.org/10.1016/j.jesp.2021.104281

Zuckerman, M., DePaulo, B. M., & Rosenthal, R. (1981). Verbal and nonverbal communication of deception. In *Advances in experimental social psychology* (Vol. 14, pp. 1–59). Elsevier. https://doi.org/10.1016/S0065-2601(08)60369-X

Chapter 15
Mimicry in Psychological Disorders and Psychotherapy

Maike Salazar Kämpf and Cornelia Exner

> The human is indissolubly linked with imitation: a human being only becomes human at all by imitating other human beings.
>
> —Theodo r W. Adorno

Imitation is an important part of human life. We learn by imitating others, but we also connect or distance ourselves through it: Imitation can signal group membership, for example by wearing similar clothes or a uniform, and it can also signal distance from others by exaggerating the imitation and parodying others (Arnold & Winkielman, 2020). Maybe you have noticed that in some conversations you unconsciously start to use certain verbal expressions that are typical for the region your friend is from, or that when observing people that are on a date, they start to sit in the same postures, leaning forward at the same time or scratching their noses almost simultaneously. This form of subtle imitation, which is linked to connecting with others, has been termed social mimicry (Chartrand & Bargh, 1999). Even though it can be easily observed, this unconscious imitation of an interaction partner is generally neither actively perceived by the ones who are imitated, nor by the ones who imitate.

Mimicry can occur in different ways. It can occur verbally, such as using similar words, accent echoing, intonation, or speech rate (for a review, see Chap. 4; this volume), and/or non-verbally like mirroring facial expressions, postures, or gestures (Chartrand & Lakin, 2013; see also Chaps. 2 and 3; this volume). Studies have shown that mimicry fosters the initiation (Salazar Kämpf et al., 2018) and maintenance of relationships (Lakin & Chartrand, 2003). Moreover, it increases closeness

The original version of the chapter has been revised. A correction to this chapter can be found at https://doi.org/10.1007/978-3-031-62634-0_17

M. Salazar Kämpf (✉)
Technical University Dresden, Dresden, Germany

C. Exner
University of Leipzig, Leipzig, Germany

O. Genschow, E. Cracco (eds.), *Automatic Imitation*,
https://doi.org/10.1007/978-3-031-62634-0_15

(Stel & Vonk, 2010) is connected to affective empathy (Sonnby-Borgström, 2002) and part of our everyday social communication (Hess & Fischer, 2022). When mimicry is hindered or disturbed, it can impair emotion recognition (Oberman et al., 2007) and a lack of mimicry has been linked to elevated stress reactions, as indicated by an enhanced need to belong by the counterpart (Kouzakova et al., 2010), and the crying of babies in the so called still face paradigm (Weinberg & Tronick, 1996).

Different theoretical approaches claim that mimicry plays an important role in social interactions. Problems in social interactions are both diagnostic criteria as well as risk factors of psychological disorders (De Silva et al., 2005; Eklund & Hansson, 2007). Mimicry behavior of people with psychological disorders might be different compared to people who are not suffering from a psychological disorder, and this may contribute to their problems in social interactions which in turn might worsen symptomatology (Geerts et al., 2006) and may have consequences for the therapeutic process (see also Chap. 12; this volume). Astonishingly, there are almost no studies on spontaneous mimicry and clinical populations (Salazar Kämpf et al., 2021). The fact that mimicry has not yet been studied extensively in clinical settings is surprising given the long recognition of the importance of imitation in psychotherapy (Charny, 1966; Scheflen, 1964; Tickle-Degnen & Rosenthal, 1990). As there have not been many studies on the subject matter, mimicry is still not part of treatment manuals, even though mimicry can be easily detected in ongoing therapy sessions and might have an important impact on improving the patients' social lives (Salazar Kämpf et al., 2021).

In this chapter we will first summarize existing studies on mimicry and akin phenomena in psychotherapy and related contexts (like counseling). As the evidence is sparse, we will present four theoretical approaches to mimicry, from which we will derive ideas on how mimicry might affect different psychological disorders and the therapeutic process. Afterwards, we will shortly recapitulate the evidence on mimicry in clinical populations. Finally, at the end of this chapter, we will suggest possible future research on mimicry in psychotherapy.

Existing Evidence for Mimicry in Psychotherapy

Mimicry has been described as a correlate of rapport and therefore important for therapy and counseling (Tickle-Degnen & Rosenthal, 1990). Existing evidence on imitation, which is related to mimicry, points towards the potentially important role of mimicry in psychotherapy. For example, consciously mirroring postures and mannerisms of clients has been investigated as a technique in therapy (Caldwell, 2006) and in counseling situations (Geerts et al., 2006; Maurer & Tindall, 1983; Sharpley et al., 2001).

Imitation has been used as therapeutic technique to create a connection with patients suffering from "communicative difficulties" (p. 275), like patients with severe autism (Caldwell, 2006). Caldwell found that the imitation performed by the therapist not only calmed the patients, but by copying the behavior of her patients, the therapist learned their language, which in turn shifted the patient's attention towards the interaction and reduced their distressed behavior. People with autism therefore seem to profit from imitation in therapy. Interestingly, Caldwell further suggests to enrich imitation with surprising elements. For example, instead of directly copying a repetitive hand movement, she sometimes switched the rhythm or sound of the hand movement. These elements of surprise captured the attention of her patients and shifted them from themselves towards the other person, in this case towards her, the therapist.

Mimicry also seems to play a role in people with former depression: The nonverbal behavior of formerly depressed patients while talking to an interviewer was assessed during a clinical interview (Geerts et al., 2006). The patients and interviewers were filmed while being seated approximately 1 m apart. The participants' gaze, gesticulations, and head movements were rated in terms of mimicry (body postures or speech was not part of the mimicry ratings, which would also have been interesting). The more the patients and interviewers mimicked each other, the more satisfied patients were with the interview and the lower was the risk of a new depressive episode during a 2-year follow-up period.

Another study found that career counselors who mirrored participants postures were perceived as more empathic (Maurer & Tindall, 1983). Fifteen-minute conversations between counselors and participants were videotaped. Depending on the experimental condition, the counselor either maintained congruent or noncongruent positions of arms and legs of the participant. The counselor changed position each time the participant changed position after 30 s but did not imitate shorter movements like scratching or gesturing. When the counselor's arm and leg positions were congruent compared to noncongruent, the participants rated the counselor's level of empathy higher. The authors highlight the importance of naturalistic settings to investigate the reciprocal nonverbal processes between clients and counselors and reference Scheflens idea (1964) that the congruence of body parts between two individuals is an indication of empathy, rapport, and mutual interest.

However, people affected by an eating disorder seem to react differently to being mimicked (Erwin et al., 2022). Eating disorders involve abnormal eating, and exaggerated preoccupation with food, body weight, or shape, which cannot be explained by other health conditions or the cultural context. Erwin et al. (2022) suggested that patients with eating disorders feel "triggered" when being mimicked. Since mimicry is linked to physical and emotional closeness, which as stated by the authors is feared by individuals with eating disorders, and that furthermore comparison and imitation is part of "learning" disordered eating, they argue that mimicry causes stress. To test their hypothesis, the authors compared patients with eating disorder to a non-clinical group. A confederate mimicked vs. did not mimic the mannerisms of each participant. Afterwards participants rated the confederate's likability and the smoothness of interaction. Interestingly, the authors hypothesis was confirmed and participants with an eating disorder who were not mimicked rated the confederate as slightly more likable and the interaction smoother than participants who were mimicked. A longer duration of the eating disorder was associated with lower liking of the mimicking confederate. This is fascinating, as it shows that the type of disorder might play a role in how mimicry affects social relationships and therapy.

Thus, for the most part, conscious imitation of patients by therapists seems to be a promising technique to create mutual understanding (Geerts et al., 2006), rapport (Sharpley et al., 2001) and empathy (Maurer & Tindall, 1983), thereby supporting the well-established idea that congruent body movements are important for psychotherapy (Charny, 1966; Scheflen, 1964)—but only for some disorders. The type of disorder might play a crucial role in how being mimicked by the therapist is perceived. Now we will take a closer look at the evidence of what effects it might have if patients are trained to imitate others.

Imitation as Intervention in Clinical Populations

If being able to imitate affects our social relationships, what about the effects of patients being trained to imitate others? We found two studies that investigated the effect of "practicing mimicry" with clinical populations. Koehne et al. (2016) did this through a dance/movement intervention for people with autism spectrum disorder and Pancotti et al. (2021) through a facial muscle training for participants with schizophrenia. Both studies report a positive effect on emotion recognition performance of patients through the training.

Koehne et al. (2016) compared a 10-week imitation- and synchronization-based dance/movement intervention to a control movement intervention in participants with high-functioning autism spectrum disorder. The 90-minute intervention, which was administered ten times over the course of 3 months, aimed at enhancing socio-cognitive and socio-affective processes. The intervention consisted of exercises which were either executed within dyads or within a bigger group of participants, focusing on movement imitation and synchronization with and without music (such as arm swings initiated by the other participant or dancing in circles in choreographed movement). Participants treated with the imitation- and synchronization-based dance/movement intervention showed a significantly larger improvement in emotion inference, but not empathic feelings, both measured with the Multifaceted Empathy Test, than those treated with the control intervention. Furthermore, the imitation- and synchronization-based dance/movement intervention increased the tendency to mimic others compared to the control condition. The authors suggest that the dance/movement intervention increases mimicry behavior, which fosters the increase in emotion inference.

In the second study, a facial muscle training (similar to a rehabilitation approach after facial paralysis) was tested for people with schizophrenia (Pancotti et al., 2021). People with schizophrenia often show impairments in expressing and perceiving social emotions, which as the authors suggest consequently leads to problems in their social lives. The authors hypothesized that the training would improve their ability to mimic and consequently improve facial expression recognition. Twelve participants with schizophrenia were assigned to an experimental group and 12 to a control group. The experimental group trained the mobilization of lip muscles, and the muscles around the eyes three times a week for 45 min over the period of 5 weeks. The participants in the control group meanwhile took part in activities instructed by the nursing home (which are not further specified in study). Before and after the training, both groups completed a facial expression categorization test. Results showed a positive impact in the recognition of others' facial emotions for those who had done the facial muscle training, specifically for the responses of "fear." The authors believe in the great potential of such interventions and advocate for incorporating therapeutic "approaches based on the body and its interaction with the environment" (p. 10) to treat psychological disorders. The evidence we presented so far focused on the effects of being mimicked, which involved a confederate, and on practicing mimicry. We will continue with presenting the evidence on spontaneous mimicry between therapists and patients.

Spontaneous Mimicry in Psychotherapy

We are only aware of three studies investigating spontaneous mimicry in psychotherapy. Avdi and Seikkula (2019) examined mimicry in a single case study of a psychoanalytic therapy session, focusing on both postural congruence or mimicry and the heart rate of therapist and patient. During their in-session research, they found that mimicry and heart rate synchrony were highest during alliance ruptures. This means that more mimicry was shown when verbal disjunction and tension threatened the therapeutic alliance. Hence, the authors suggest that the therapeutic dyad uses mimicry to regulate the tension. Patient and therapist mimic each other until this tension is resolved. Mimicry is therefore seen by the authors as a form of mutual regulation (Benecke et al., 2005).

Reinecke et al. (2021) examined the hand movements of 28 patient-therapist dyads at the beginning and end of a psychodynamic therapy (56 videos). Two independent raters analyzed the hand movements using the neuroges analysis system for nonverbal behavior (Lausberg, 2013). This system consists of an algorithm grouped into three modules. The authors used the first module "activation category," which measures four activation values (one for each hand of both therapist and patient). Subsequently, overlapping and simultaneous hand movements can be measured with the neuroges analysis system (Lausberg, 2013). Simultaneous hand movements correlated negatively with social anxiety symptoms and patients' right- hand movement with the therapeutic alliance. The authors suggest that mimicry is a process-sensitive parameter to measure therapeutic alliance and outcomes of psychotherapy.

We also conducted a study on mimicry, focusing on 64 patients with obsessive compulsive disorder and their therapists during a short-term cognitive-behavioral therapy (Salazar Kämpf et al., 2021). Two raters gave a global mimicry value to both the therapist and the patient during the first, middle, and last therapy session of a short-term therapy of twelve sessions. Our results suggest that the patients' mimicry behavior remains relatively stable over time and that mimicry at the beginning of therapy predicts the perceived working alliance by patients at the end of therapy.

Therapists adapted their mimicry levels to the patients. However, the therapists' mimicry did not influence the perceived working alliance by patients.

These three studies suggest that mimicry might take on the function of mutual regulation during conflicts (Avdi & Seikkula, 2019), is correlated with symptom decrease, and is an indicator of the therapeutic alliance (Reinecke et al., 2021). In addition, therapist and patient influence each other in their mimicry, which possibly influences their therapeutic alliance (Salazar Kämpf et al., 2021). Interestingly, even though the importance of imitation and mimicry in psychotherapy has been a topic for quite some time, (a) clear theoretical frameworks are missing on why this might be the case. Furthermore, as research on mimicry in psychotherapy is sparse, we do not know if (b) different clinical populations show distinct mimicry behavior.

What is known however is that people with psychological disorders often show rigid patterns in how they regulate their affects and relationships and show "a specific structure and form of their internal representations" (p. 83, Benecke et al., 2005). These repeated patterns of behavior have a powerful impact on a person's experience. We therefore suggest that mimicry behavior might be associated with specific patterns for each psychological disorder. Hence, we will now continue this chapter by presenting four possible theoretical approaches for mimicry in psychotherapy (a), which are borrowed from research in other areas of psychology, like social, developmental and personality psychology. Afterwards, we will present research on mimicry in clinical populations (b).

Theoretical Approaches to Mimicry

Different theoretical approaches, which we will now describe in more detail, give possible explanations why mimicry plays such an important role in our social life and might help to develop a theoretical background on mimicry in psychotherapy. We will present (1) the theory on perception-action-coupling, (2) the embodiment theory, (3) the social glue approach, and (4) the social regulator theory. Even though some of these theories overlap in their claims, the differences lead to divergent assumptions on what the role of mimicry might be in psychotherapy, for therapists and patients with different disorders.

Perception-Action-Coupling One approach to explain why humans mimic each other is the theory on *perception-action-coupling* (Vicaria & Dickens, 2016). According to this theory, unconscious mimicry, through simulating the observed behavior of others, leads to an inner representation of that behavior. This so-called perception-action-link has three theoretical claims on why social mimicry might have developed through human evolution:

The first claim is that perception-action-coupling increases chances of survival. It states that, for example, seeing one person run away from a dangerous situation automatically facilitates fleeing behavior in others. Imagine someone running away from a tiger. Instead of having to think it through ("Oh, why is this person running?

Oh, I can see a tiger. This might be dangerous. Maybe I should also run.") the perception-action-link is said to automatically activate "running" in our brains so we can react faster in potentially dangerous situations.

The second claim is that embodied representations facilitate emotional understanding and empathy (Varcin et al., 2010). If we listen to a friend who tells us a sad story, maybe cries, and has a sad expression on his or her face, we automatically imitate this sad expression. Maybe our eyes get teary or the corners of our mouth point down. This mirrored facial expression is said to facilitate feelings of sadness in oneself, thus to have a similar experience as the person we are observing. The perception-action-link suggests that even the mere observing of emotional expressions in others activates the same neural pathways that are activated when experiencing this emotion oneself. This activation is theorized to explain emotional contagion and thereby affective empathy (Sonnby-Borgström, 2002).

The third claim suggests, that mimicry creates social bonds. By resonating the others' behavior, we increase mutual resemblance, as if we would wear similar clothes. These similar movements seem to foster rapport (Lakin et al., 2003; Stel & Vonk, 2010) and mutual liking (Salazar Kämpf et al., 2018).[1]

Assuming the theory of perception-action-coupling was valid, we could derive different theoretical consequences for psychological disorders and psychotherapy. The fist claim refers to fight-or-flight situations, meaning that we can react faster through mimicry in dangerous situations. This is a claim which might be especially relevant for people who are under the impression that they might possibly be in a dangerous situation. If we think of psychological disorders as maladaptive behavioral patterns, this could mean that some mimic fear-relevant expressions in an exaggerated manner. In terms of psychological disorders, this should be true for all fear-related anxiety disorders, such as general anxiety disorder, social phobia, and specific phobia. According to the perception-action-coupling-theory, patients should mimic fear-relevant stimuli more and therefore process and react faster in fear-relevant situations. In line with this assumption, Derryberry and Tucker (1994) could show that fearful states direct attention away from the self and to the environment. Consequently, for example people with anxiety disorders should mimic, perceive, and process facial expressions that indicate danger faster than non-clinical populations.

The second claim on the relationship between empathy and mimicry goes beyond Scheflens' (1964) idea that mimicry is an indication of empathy and mutual interest. If mimicry as suggested creates empathy, it should be relevant for both therapists and patients, as therapists might use mimicry to put themselves in the patients' shoes and patients might be more or less empathic, depending on whether their type of disorder might be associated with more or less mimicry behavior. If the second claim is confirmed then mimicry might be a tool to regulate empathic responses (for

[1] Similarity is of course highly depended on context factors and can be represented on different levels, such as visual similarity, similarity because of gender, race and class etc.

patients and therapists alike), that is to enhance or reduce empathy depending on the context.

The third claim about mimicry creating social bonds is important for the patient-therapist-dyad during the therapeutic process and for the patients' social lives. As people with psychological disorders often have problems in their interpersonal relationships, it might be interesting to study whether low or inappropriate levels of social mimicry contribute to the problems in their interpersonal relationships and if so, if they can be improved through mimicry. Moreover, therapists might also be able to better the therapeutic relationship if trained to use mimicry. This would be in line with Caldwell's (2006) suggestion that a social bond is fostered by creating a mutual language through imitation.

Embodiment Theory The *embodiment theory* (Arnold & Winkielman, 2020) proposes that cognition is grounded in perceptual, somatosensory, and motor experiences. To support this claim, Arnold and Winkielman (2020) refer to studies on emotion recognition, where participants are asked to inhibit their own facial expression, which have shown to sometimes impair for example the distinction between true and false smiles. Supporting this assumption, lesions and temporary inactivation of sensory-motor areas can impair emotion recognition (e.g., Adolphs et al., 2000). Arnold and Winkielman (2020) claim that this type of motor activation is especially useful in subtler recognition of emotions—for example if the facial expression is ambiguous, complex, or brief. This is in line with Zwick and Wolkenstein's (2017) claim that facial mimicry is associated with an acceleration of the facial emotion recognition process. In sum, this theoretical approach suggests that mimicry helps us to perceive the world faster and more accurately by creating representations of the same experiences observed in others. However, some studies contradict this assumption (Blairy et al., 1999; Hess & Blairy, 2001). For example, some studies show that people suffering from facial paralysis perform normally on emotion recognition tasks (e.g., Rives Bogart & Matsumoto, 2010).

Theoretical consequences of the embodiment approach for psychological disorders and psychotherapy could be that disturbed cognitive processes are connected to disturbances in mimicry and vice versa. Specifically, the interpretation of social signals should generally be slower and ambiguous facial expressions harder to identify for people with psychological disorders. This theory would make it plausible that mimicry might be connected to attentional processes and that differences in mimicry should also be found whether the attention is more self-referential or focused on outward stimuli. Mimicry might further be a way for therapists to decrypt ambiguous facial expressions of patients in ambivalent situations.

Social Glue Approach This approach focuses on mimicry as a "powerful medium of affective communication" and key to create "feelings of rapport" (p. 288, Tickle-Degnen & Rosenthal, 1990): Lakin and Chartrand (2003) assume that the desire to affiliate may cause people to pay more attention to what occurs in their social environments and therefore to activate mimicry of any behavior (it doesn't matter if it is foot shaking or a facial expression), which in turn creates social bonds. Consequently, the desire to affiliate should influence the amount of mimicry shown and the more mimicry is shown the more the mutual liking should increase (Lakin et al., 2003; Seibt et al., 2015). This bidirectional link (liking increasing mimicry behavior and mimicry increasing linking) has been shown in one of our own studies, where people did not know each other before and talked to each other in a "speed-friending" setting (non-romantic speed-dating for friendships; Salazar Kämpf et al., 2018).

According to this approach, mimicry should be especially relevant for therapists at the beginning of therapy to create a bond with the patient. Improving the mimicry of patients during therapy should furthermore be a means to improve their social relationships. In terms of specific psychological disorders, disorders where people have a heightened desire to affiliate might show elevated levels of mimicry behavior, like histrionic personality disorder or people experiencing a manic episode. In the same vein, people suffering from psychological disorders associated with lower levels of desire to affiliate, like depression (known to be associated with social withdrawal), should show lower levels of mimicry. More research has to be done to know if this could be part of diagnostics or could serve as a process-sensitive parameter, as suggested by Reinecke et al. (2021), and what therapist can learn in terms of the therapeutic relationship if they monitor the patient's and their own mimicry behavior. Furthermore, according to this theory, it would be beneficial to include mimicry training as a part of the social skills training during therapy for those who show exaggerated or very low levels of mimicry.

Social Regulator Theory Hess and Fischer (2013, 2022) suggest that mimicry functions as social regulator. According to this theory, mimicry signals emotions back to the observer, which fosters affiliation by communicating to others that we feel with them (for a review, see Chap. 3; this volume). This view is embedding mimicry in a social context and differentiates emotional mimicry from imitating behaviors that do not carry any emotional signal (contrary to the social glue approach by Lakin and Chartrand). Hess and Fischer have three key assumptions: a) the intention to affiliate is key for mimicry behavior, b) behaviors that carry affiliation signals such as smiling are more likely to be imitated, and c) mimicry is context-dependent—smiling in socially inappropriate contexts might reduce mimicry, e.g., when something disgusting happens. According to the authors, this explains mixed results regarding the mimicking of sad faces. Furthermore, emotions that are too intense will also not be mimicked. Central to their theoretical suggestion is also the implication for measuring mimicry, as the focus lays on the communication of inner states, "that is, people mimic what they understand an emotion signal to mean – and not necessarily specific muscle movements." (p. 4). This implies that the valence (positive vs. negative emotion) and fit (is the emotion context appropriate) are key components of mimicking behavior. If the emotion that is mimicked does not fit the context, Hess and Fischer (2022) argue that this is not mimicry but rather a mere reaction to an emotional expression.

The social regulator theory could explain why mimicry might have an effect on the interpersonal life of patients: if they show abnormal mimicry behavior, they send unusual social signals to others which in turn might lead to misunderstandings in interpersonal contexts. For example, people with depression, as they show very little or sad facial expression, should be mimicked less and as they often withdraw socially, they should also mimic others less, according to the social regulator theory. Furthermore, if a person has less desire for social connection with others, or thinks that the other person might not be a valuable social contact, they should be less likely to mimic them.

Therapists could make this a target of psychotherapy, for example by analyzing videos of the sessions together with the patient or talking about the signals patients send versus what signal they actually want to send in the ongoing session. According to this theory, mainly context-appropriate positive emotions should be mimicked by the therapists to support patients. It is unclear if imitating sad expressions should therefore have contrary effects on affiliation and rapport in psychotherapy according to the social regulator approach or if imitating sad expressions is a way of signaling understanding what the other person is going through.

Now that we have gained an overview about the existing theories and their potential consequences for therapists, patients, and psychotherapy in general, we will summarize the existing evidence on mimicry and psychological disorders. Given the paucity of direct evidence of the impact of mimicry in psychotherapy, these results might help to develop specific hypotheses and ideas for future research.

Mimicry and Psychological Disorders

People with psychological disorders might show specific patterns of atypical mimicry behavior, which may in turn influence their social relationships. For example, some research shows that depressive states and anxiety decrease mimicry (Duffy & Chartrand, 2015; Likowski et al., 2011; van Baaren et al., 2006; Vrijsen et al., 2010) and some people with mental illnesses show lower levels of non-verbal output (Riehle & Lincoln, 2018), lower levels of mimicry than therapists (Salazar Kämpf et al., 2021), and atypical non-verbal reactions (Varcin et al., 2010). One could hypothesize that the specific type of disorder affects non-verbal behavior in different ways. For example, a disorder which is characterized by social isolation and an inward-focus, like depression, might lead to less mimicry behavior, whereas people experiencing a manic phase, which is often characterized by heightened mood and sociability, might show more mimicry behavior (Salazar Kämpf & Kanske, 2023). We will therefore shortly summarize the evidence clustered by each psychological disorder.

Depression

Studies have shown that sadness increases self-focused attention. Hence, one could assume people affected by psychological disorders accompanied by increased sadness or numbness, like depression, might have greater difficulties to direct their attention towards external social stimuli (Likowski et al., 2011). Consequently, they should show less mimicry behavior and be less receptive to mimicry behavior. This might contribute to a further understanding of the fact that people suffering from psychological disorders often have smaller social networks (e.g., for depression, Segrin, 2000). Indeed, people with depression (Wexler et al., 1994; Zwick & Wolkenstein, 2017), which is accompanied by lowering of mood and often a reduction of interest, energy, activity and concentration, mimic emotional stimuli less (pictures or videos) compared to non-clinical control groups. Even sub-clinical dysphoric participants react less to happy faces than non-dysphoric participants (Sloan et al., 2002). However, people with depression only mimic less during their depressive episodes and not during remission (Zwick & Wolkenstein, 2017). Reduced mimicry might be interpreted by others as a lack of affiliative tendencies, and thus lead to reduced liking (Chartrand & Bargh, 1999; Likowski et al., 2011; Salazar Kämpf et al., 2018), leading to avoidance of people with depression by others. This would point towards a vicious cycle with negative mood lowering mimicry behavior and thus enhancing social exclusion which in turn worsens symptomatology (Likowski et al., 2011).

Alexithymia

People with alexithymia (Franz et al., 2021), which is characterized by difficulties identifying feelings and emotions, were compared to a control group. All participants viewed video sequences of faces displaying fear, sadness, disgust, anger, and joy. The participants' facial mimicry responses were recorded via electromyography. The results suggest that people affected by alexithymia mimic emotional stimuli less than non-clinical participants.

Autism

There is a lively debate on autism, a neurodevelopmental disorder characterized by interactional difficulties and repetitive interests and behaviors, and mimicry. Some studies have found that people with autism hyperimitate (Spengler et al., 2010) and, as described above, it has been reported that they can be trained to mimic (Koehne et al., 2016). In contrast, other studies show mixed results (Hermans et al., 2009) or no differences between participants with autism and non-clinical participants (Sowden et al., 2015). Finally, some studies even found that people with autism mimic less (Forbes et al., 2016; Yoshimura et al., 2015) or more slowly and less precise (Drimalla et al., 2021). Although most studies on autism use rather small samples, they apply a wide range of methods to study mimicry, like virtual reality (Forbes et al., 2016). This methodological richness makes the studies difficult to compare but compelling for theoretical development.

Schizophrenia

Schizophrenia is defined by disturbances in thought, perception, volition, and affect, and is often accompanied by bizarre behavior. Similar to autism, mimicry behavior of people with schizophrenia has been studied with a wide range of methods, yielding mixed results. Some studies found no differences between non-clinical controls and participants with schizophrenia (Raffard et al., 2018; Riehle & Lincoln, 2018; Torregrossa et al., 2019). Other studies found that people with schizophrenia show less mimicry (Sestito et al., 2013; Walther et al., 2015) and atypical facial reactions towards emotional stimuli (Falkenberg et al., 2008; Varcin et al., 2010). Social functioning deficits in schizophrenia and schizoaffective disorder might partly be explained by these atypical facial reactions to emotional stimuli (Varcin et al., 2010). As described above, it might be possible to train people with schizophrenia to enhance mimicry behavior (Pancotti et al., 2021).

Social Anxiety

To experience excessive fear in one or more social situations is called social anxiety. Dimberg and Thunberg (2007) suggest that people with social anxiety show higher levels of mimicry, whereas Dijk et al. (2017) and Vrana and Gross (2004) found mixed results and Abbott et al. (2018) and Vrijsen et al. (2010) found that people with social anxiety show less mimicry.

Post-traumatic Stress Disorder

Post-traumatic stress disorder is a disorder which develops over the course of several weeks after a horrific event. The person afflicted re-experiences the traumatic event (flashbacks), avoids "triggers" of these flashbacks, and has a persistent perception of current threat. Participants with post-traumatic stress disorder showed no differences compared to traumatized participants without post-traumatic stress disorder and non-traumatized non-clinical participants in facial reactions during a facial emotion recognition task (Passardi et al., 2019).

Borderline Personality Disorder

Borderline personality disorder is characterized by being emotionally unstable and impulsive. We found three studies on mimicry and borderline personality disorder, all with different results. Pizarro-Campagna et al. (2020) found no group differences in mimicry between non-clinical participants and borderline participants. Hauschild et al. (2018) found that patients showed more mimicry. Finally, Matzke et al. (2013) found reduced mimicry behavior of positive social signals and increased mimicry to negative social signals by patients compared to non-clinical participants.

Psychopathic Traits

Psychopathic traits, characterized by dissociality and detachment, are said to be linked to less empathy. Therefore Künecke et al. (2018) hypothesized that individuals high on psychopathic traits would also show less mimicry. However, they did not find any group differences in mimicry of emotional stimuli between criminal offenders and controls. Kyranides et al. (2022) found that participants with higher psychopathic symptoms expressed more negative emotions and could be instructed to imitate. Finally, Deming et al. (2022) found that the criminal offenders in their study did not show any spontaneous mimicry of emotional video stimuli at all.

Disorder-Specific Mimicry Patterns

By summarizing these studies, we have gotten an overview over the existing research on mimicry and different psychological disorders. Studies on psychological disorders paint a complex picture. According to the existing data, it is difficult to describe a pattern for each psychological disorder, as mixed results (more, less, and no differences compared to non-clinical participants) can be found for participants with autism (Drimalla et al., 2021; Forbes et al., 2016; Hermans et al., 2009; Spengler et al., 2010; Sowden et al., 2015; Yoshimura et al., 2015), schizophrenia (Falkenberg et al., 2008; Raffard et al., 2018; Riehle & Lincoln, 2018; Sestito et al., 2013; Torregrossa et al., 2019; Varcin et al., 2010; Walther et al., 2015), social anxiety (Abbott et al., 2018; Dijk et al., 2017; Dimberg & Thunberg, 2007; Vrana & Gross, 2004; Vrijsen et al., 2010), borderline disorder (Hauschild et al., 2018; Matzke et al., 2013; Pizarro-Campagna et al., 2020), and psychopathic traits (Deming et al.,

2022; Künecke et al., 2018; Kyranides et al., 2022). One explanation on why the results might be mixed are the small sample sizes and the methodological approaches that are used. To make sense of the results, we will now combine them with the theoretical approaches we presented above.

Combining Theory and Disorder-Specific Results: Theoretical Implications for Mimicry in Psychotherapy

There is great potential to incorporate mimicry into current theories, research, and practice of psychotherapy. Until now, research on mimicry and psychotherapy has not been defined by a clear theoretical background. This is why in this chapter we presented four different mimicry theories (the theory on perception-action-coupling, the embodiment theory, the social glue approach and the social regulator theory), which have different claims on how and why mimicry is important for psychotherapy and may differ between psychological disorders.

The *theory of perception-action-coupling* suggests that facial expressions should be perceived and processed faster by people with anxiety disorders, especially when they signal some kind of danger. In regard to social anxiety, the results are mixed, but mostly do not support the claim that facial expressions are perceived and processed faster. Although Dimberg and Thunberg (2007) results indicate that people with higher social anxiety show higher levels of mimicry, Dijk et al. (2017) found that they foremostly mimic polite smiles. Abbott et al. (2018) and Vrijsen et al. (2010) found that people with social anxiety show less mimicry and explain this with a heightened self-focused attention. This could also mean that other anxiety related disorders, like generalized anxiety or specific phobias, show completely different results. However, there are no studies on the subject matter, yet.

The second (relationship between empathy and mimicry) and third claim (mimicry creates social bonds) cannot be evaluated in detail in regards to psychological disorders as only few studies investigated mimicry in a dyadic setting. Results by Spengler et al. (2010) point towards "hyperimitation" of participants with autism being *negatively* linked to Theory of Mind. It might therefore be possible that mimicry is negatively linked to cognitive empathy, but positively to affective empathy. However, considering the small sample size of this study, it is imperative that it is first replicated before any conclusions are drawn.

Regarding social bonds, Riehle and Lincoln (2018) found that participants reported to be less willing to interact with people with schizophrenia in the future, than to interact with non-clinical participants, yet this was not related to mimicry of smiles but maybe more to generally awkward non-verbal behavior. In terms of rapport in psychotherapy, Avdi and Seikkula (2019) suggested that mimicry might help fix ruptures in the alliance; however, they did not test this assumption directly. Further, Reinecke et al. (2021) found that simultaneous hand movements of therapists and patients negatively correlated with the patients' symptoms. We found only a small effect of mimicry levels of patients with obsessive-compulsive disorder and the therapeutic alliance (Salazar Kämpf et al., 2021). In sum, the evidence on mimicry in psychotherapy is not completely supportive of the claims on perception-action-coupling, more studies have to be done regarding the processing of stimuli, the focus of attention and in a dynamic setting.

According to the *embodiment approach*, disturbed cognitive processes should be connected to disturbances in social mimicry and vice versa. However, studies investigating samples afflicted with psychological disorders and mimicry have not focused on ambiguous facial or attentional processes yet. The only exception being the study by Abbott et al. (2018), which assessed self-focused attention and found that participants with increased self-focused attention mimicked the confederate less. We do not have evidence on other cognitive disturbances, attentional processes in therapists, or cognitive processes during psychotherapy. In people with psychopathic symptoms (Deming et al., 2022) and borderline personality disorder (Matzke et al., 2013), no link between emotion recognition accuracy and mimicry was found, yet Kyranides et al. (2022) found that when people with psychopathic symptoms were instructed to imitate facial expressions, they improved their emotion recognition performance, which is in line with the embodiment approach. In sum, there is still too little evidence on the subject matter.

In line with the *social glue approach,* mimicry should be especially relevant for creating rapport between patient and therapist, but also between patients and other people in general. As there are almost no studies investigating the social effects of mimicry in people with psychological disorders and the therapeutic context, we are excited to see future research dedicating more time and effort towards this topic, as for example examining if patients can improve their social relationships through mimicry. We did not find any studies regarding psychological disorders with a heightened desire to affiliate. In line with the core assumptions of the social glue approach, Zwick and Wolkenstein (2017) found that people with acute depression (known to be associated with social withdrawal) did show lower levels of mimicry. Be that as it may, studies on depression only focused on mimicry towards static pictures. Studying mimicry in social interactions will shed light on this phenomenon. Further, negative effects of mimicry, like people with eating disorders being "triggered" by imitative behavior, as suggested by Erwin et al. (2022), cannot be explained by this theoretical approach and have not been investigated sufficiently.

The *social regulator theory* states that non-affiliative expressions like anger and excessive sadness should be mimicked less. Most of the studies on psychological disorders recorded facial reactions towards emotional pictures and video stimuli. Interestingly, Sloan et al. (2002) and Zwick and Wolkenstein (2017) found that subclinical depressed patients and acutely depressed patients did not show differences in the mimicry of sad faces; however, they mimicked happy faces less. A similar but slightly enhanced pattern was found by Matzke et al. (2013) in patients with borderline personality disorder, which showed enhanced mimicry in reaction to angry, sad, and disgusted facial expressions, and lower mimicry in reaction to happy and surprised faces. According to the social regulator theory, this means that they do show less affiliative signals and this might impact their social relationships. This assumption (the effect of these affiliative signals on social relationships) could be fruitful for future research.

Moreover, people with alexithymia (Franz et al., 2021) and autism spectrum disorder (Drimalla et al., 2021; Yoshimura et al., 2015) showed lower, slower, or less precise mimicry reactions regardless of the affect, whereas Dimberg and Thunberg (2007) found that participants with high public speaking fear showed stronger mimicry of both happy and angry faces overall. This could indicate that there are appropriate levels of mimicry of affect depending on the context. Both too low or too high levels of mimicry might thus affect social interactions.

Riehle and Lincoln (2018) found that participants with schizophrenia did not differ in their mimicry of smiles, yet interaction partners still reported less willingness to interact with people with schizophrenia in the future. Falkenberg et al. (2008) found that patients with schizophrenia were more likely to display a smile as a reaction to a sad face and Varcin et al. (2010) found that participants with schizophrenia or schizoaffective disorder showed less mimicry regardless if happy or angry faces were shown. Even though these results are somehow conflicting, all of them could hint towards a mismatch between the mimicry reactions and the fit of the situation. In line with the social regulator theory, people with schizophrenia might show atypical facial reactions that do not fit the context and therefore cause irritation in their interaction partners.

It would be interesting to study how others react towards these patterns, as for now most the results are only drawn from patients watching video or picture stimuli and not from social interactions. Seibt et al. (2015) argue that social settings require different behaviors, as social norms and scripts influence our behavior in a setting and that most mimicry studies are impoverished compared to natural settings. For example, in laboratory settings, stimulation is reduced compared to a real social interaction: noises and visual stimulation are reduced to a minimum. Therefore, results obtained by studies with participants passively watching photos, computer-generated images, or short video sequences on a screen are not the same as a naturalistic interaction.

Conclusion and Future Directions

In this chapter, we have recapitulated the evidence on mimicry in psychotherapy. Mimicry is part of everyday social interactions and understanding and gives insight into the function and dysfunction of social cognition and behavior (Arnold & Winkielman, 2020), which might be helpful for the therapeutic process. Mimicry helps us to bond with others, which in turn increases well-being, safety, and access to resources. In his book "Atomic Habits" (2018), James Clear writes that one of the deepest desires of humankind is to belong and that therefore our earliest habits are the result of imitation and habits and form our identity. He writes "I find that I often imitate the behavior of those around me without realizing it (…) As a general rule, the closer we are to someone, the more likely we are to imitate some of their habits

(…) We soak up the qualities and practices of those around us." (p. 116, 117). If this is true, mimicry is the mechanism through which we form our identity. This in turn makes it an invaluable tool for the therapeutic practice.

Theoretical Approaches

We have taken a closer look on different theoretical approaches; however, an overarching theory is still missing and the evidence so far can neither confirm nor rule out any of those approaches. It is likely that mimicry has various functions (e.g., increasing liking, sending social signals, maybe aiding emotion recognition) and that it therefore has a special role during the therapeutic process. Generally speaking, mutual mimicry during therapy should lead to positive effects, like a deeper bond between therapist and patient (in line with the theory of perception-action-coupling, the social glue approach and social regulator theory). Mimicry can also help to explain why the environment we choose (e.g., friends) can have an important impact on our identity, as we tend to imitate those we are close to, which has implications on how patients might be able to change dysfunctional habits, if we learn to use it as a therapeutic tool.

But mimicry might not have positive effects during the therapeutic process at all times. The imitation of heightened negative emotions, which often occur during a therapeutic process, for example, might lead to irritation. According to the social regulator theory (Hess & Fischer, 2022), during those parts of the therapeutic process, the therapist has to find a way to signal understanding and compassion, but not to join in the despair.

Methodological Approaches

Mostly, facial electromyography in reaction to different pictures or video stimuli has been used to asses mimicry in psychological disorders. More specifically the activity of the facial muscles zygomaticus major in response to happy faces and corrugator supercilii in response to sad faces (e.g., Sloan et al., 2002; Wexler et al., 1994; Zwick & Wolkenstein, 2017). Using stimuli in the laboratory makes the input more comparable between subjects. However, those stimuli are often not representative of dynamic real-life situations. Studies that used a wider range of methods (as for example the studies on schizophrenia and autism) show that mixed results become more likely. This indicates that how one measures mimicry might be central for the outcome of the results.

Apart from measurement differences, most studies take a passive observer perspective: how much do participants mimic picture or video stimuli? Only one study by Erwin et al. (2022) focused on how being mimicked was perceived by people with eating disorders. Contrary to results with non-clinical participants (Stel &

Vonk, 2010), participants with an eating disorder who were *not* mimicked rated the confederate as more likable and the interaction smoother than participants who were mimicked. Reactions to video and picture stimuli are certainly very interesting to study specific subprocesses of mimicry and just like we do not study zebra behavior only in the zoo, we should study our own human behavior in real interpersonal encounters.

Future Directions

We are excited to see how the future of mimicry research develops. There are many interesting questions one could study. First and foremost, it seems crucial to study real therapeutic interactions. How does the therapist patient dyad interact? How do people interact in group therapy? What differences do we find between people with different disorders in these interactive settings? What differences can we find between therapists? Do we find differences between different therapeutic approaches? Taking into account the different perspectives (i.e., the effect of mimicking, the effect of being mimicked, and dyadic effects) might be fruitful to investigate for future research to get a clearer picture on the role of mimicry in psychotherapy.

Three main points become clear by summarizing the existing evidence on mimicry: (1) a common theoretical ground on mimicry in psychotherapy can still be developed. This is important, as it seems like mimicry could represent an important source for diagnostic and intervention in psychotherapy. (2) Psychotherapy is a dynamic interactional process between patient and therapist and it is unclear if the results of studies focusing on video or picture stimuli are transferable. Therefore, evidence on social mimicry needs to be broadened systematically in interactional psychotherapeutic settings with different clinical samples. (3) Imitation, mimicry, and bodily processes seem to be a promising area for psychotherapy research and practice.

Acknowledgments We would like to thank Annelie Mekelburg for her help in searching articles on mimicry and psychological disorders and Konrad Lehmann for his insightful comments and suggestions.

Disclosure Statement The authors report no conflict of interest.

References

Abbott, K. A., Kocovski, N. L., & Obhi, S. S. (2018). Impact of social anxiety on behavioral mimicry during a social interaction with a confederate. *Journal of Social and Clinical Psychology, 37*, 22–43. https://doi.org/10.1521/jscp.2018.37.1.22

Adolphs, R., Damasio, H., Tranel, D., Cooper, G., & Damasio, A. R. (2000). A role for somatosensory cortices in the visual recognition of emotion as revealed by three-dimensional lesion

mapping. *Journal of Neuroscience, 20*, 2683–2690. https://doi.org/10.1523/JNEUROSCI.20-07-02683.2000
Arnold, A. J., & Winkielman, P. (2020). The mimicry among us: Intra-and inter-personal mechanisms of spontaneous mimicry. *Journal of Nonverbal Behavior, 44*, 195–212. https://doi.org/10.1007/s10919-019-00324-z
Avdi, E., & Seikkula, J. (2019). Studying the process of psychoanalytic psychotherapy: Discursive and embodied aspects. *British Journal of Psychotherapy, 35*, 217–232. https://doi.org/10.1111/bjp.12444
Benecke, C., Peham, D., & Bänninger-Huber, E. (2005). Nonverbal relationship regulation in psychotherapy. *Psychotherapy Research, 15*, 81–90. https://doi.org/10.1080/10503300512331327065
Blairy, S., Herrera, P. & Hess, U. (1999). Mimicry and the judgment of emotional facial expressions. *Journal of Nonverbal Behavior 23*, 5–41. https://doi.org/10.1023/A:1021370825283
Caldwell, P. (2006). Speaking the other's language: Imitation as a gateway to relationship. *Infant and Child Development: An International Journal of Research and Practice, 15*, 275–282. https://doi.org/10.1002/icd.456
Charny, J. E. (1966). Psychosomatic manifestations of rapport in psychotherapy. *Psychosomatic Medicine, 28*, 305–315. https://doi.org/10.1097/00006842-196607000-00002
Chartrand, T. L., & Bargh, J. A. (1999). The chameleon effect: The perception–behavior link and social interaction. *Journal of Personality and Social Psychology, 76*, 893–910. https://doi.org/10.1037/0022-3514.76.6.893
Chartrand, T. L., & Lakin, J. L. (2013). The antecedents and consequences of human behavioral mimicry. *Annual Review of Psychology, 64*, 285–308. https://doi.org/10.1146/annurev-psych-113011-143754
De Silva, M. J., McKenzie, K., Harpham, T., & Huttly, S. R. (2005). Social capital and mental illness: A systematic review. *Journal of Epidemiology & Community Health, 59*, 619–627. https://doi.org/10.1136/jech.2004.02967
Deming, P., Eisenbarth, H., Rodrik, O., Weaver, S. S., Kiehl, K. A., & Koenigs, M. (2022). An examination of autonomic and facial responses to prototypical facial emotion expressions in psychopathy. *PLoS One, 17*, e0270713. https://doi.org/10.1371/journal.pone.0270713
Derryberry, D., & Tucker, D. M. (1994). Motivating the focus of attention. In P. M. Niedenthal & S. Kitayama (Eds.), *The heart's eye: Emotional influences in perception and attention* (pp. 167–196). Academic. https://doi.org/10.1016/B978-0-12-410560-7.50014-4
Dijk, C., Fischer, A. H., Morina, N., van Eeuwijk, C., & van Kleef, G. A. (2017). Effects of social anxiety on emotional mimicry and contagion: Feeling negative, but smiling politely. *Journal of Nonverbal Behavior, 42*, 81–99. https://doi.org/10.1007/s10919-017-0266-z
Dimberg, U., & Thunberg, M. (2007). Speech anxiety and rapid emotional reactions to angry and happy facial expressions. *Scandinavian Journal of Psychology, 48*, 321–328. https://psycnet.apa.org/doi/10.1111/j.1467-9450.2007.00586.x
Drimalla, H., Baskow, I., Behnia, B., Roepke, S., & Dziobek, I. (2021). Imitation and recognition of facial emotions in autism: A computer vision approach. *Molecular Autism, 12*, Article: 27. https://doi.org/10.1186/s13229-021-00430-0
Duffy, K. A., & Chartrand, T. L. (2015). Mimicry: Causes and consequences. *Current Opinion in Behavioral Sciences, 3*, 112–116. https://doi.org/10.1016/j.cobeha.2015.03.002
Eklund, M., & Hansson, L. (2007). Social network among people with persistent mental illness: Associations with sociodemographic, clinical and health-related factors. *International Journal of Social Psychiatry, 53*, 293–305. https://doi.org/10.1177/0020764006074540
Erwin, S. R., Liu, P. J., Datta, N., Nicholas, J., Rivera-Cancel, A., Leary, M., Chartrand, T. L., & Zucker, N. L. (2022). Experiences of mimicry in eating disorders. *Journal of Eating Disorders, 10*, 103. https://doi.org/10.1186/s40337-022-00607-9
Falkenberg, I., Bartels, M., & Wild, B. (2008). Keep smiling! Facial reactions to emotional stimuli and their relationship to emotional contagion in patients with schizophrenia. *European Archives of Psychiatry and Clinical Neuroscience, 258*, 245–253. https://doi.org/10.1007/s00406-007-0792-5

Forbes, P. A. G., Pan, X., & de Hamilton, A. F. C. (2016). Reduced mimicry to virtual reality avatars in autism Spectrum disorder. *Journal of Autism and Developmental Disorders, 46*, 3788–3797. https://doi.org/10.1007/s10803-016-2930-2

Franz, M., Nordmann, M. A., Rehagel, C., Schäfer, R., Müller, T., & Lundqvist, D. (2021). It is in your face—Alexithymia impairs facial mimicry. *Emotion, 21*, 1537–1549. https://doi.org/10.1037/emo0001002

Geerts, E., Van Os, T., Ormel, J., & Bouhuys, N. (2006). Nonverbal behavioral similarity between patients with depression in remission and interviewers in relation to satisfaction and recurrence of depression. *Depression and Anxiety, 23*, 200–209. https://doi.org/10.1002/da.20162

Hauschild, S., Winter, D., Thome, J., Liebke, L., Schmahl, C., Bohus, M., & Lis, S. (2018). Behavioural mimicry and loneliness in borderline personality disorder. *Comprehensive Psychiatry, 82*, 30–36. https://doi.org/10.1016/j.comppsych.2018.01.005

Hermans, E. J., van Wingen, G., Bos, P. A., Putman, P., & van Honk, J. (2009). Reduced spontaneous facial mimicry in women with autistic traits. *Biological Psychology, 80*, 348–353. https://doi.org/10.1016/j.biopsycho.2008.12.002

Hess, U., & Blairy, S. (2001). Facial mimicry and emotional contagion to dynamic emotional facial expressions and their influence on decoding accuracy. *International Journal of Psychophysiology, 40*, 129–141. https://doi.org/10.1016/S0167-8760(00)00161-6

Hess, U., & Fischer, A. (2013). Emotional mimicry as social regulation. *Personality and Social Psychology Review, 17*, 142–157. https://doi.org/10.1177/1088868312472607

Hess, U., & Fischer, A. (2022). Emotional mimicry as social regulator: Theoretical considerations. *Cognition and Emotion, 36*, 785–793. https://doi.org/10.1080/02699931.2022.2103522

Koehne, S., Behrends, A., Fairhurst, M. T., & Dziobek, I. (2016). Fostering social cognition through an imitation- and synchronization-based dance/movement intervention in adults with autism Spectrum disorder: A controlled proof-of-concept study. *Psychotherapy and Psychosomatics, 85*, 27–35. https://doi.org/10.1159/000441111

Kouzakova, M., Karremans, J. C., van Baaren, R. B., & Knippenberg, A. V. (2010). A stranger's cold shoulder makes the heart grow fonder: Why not being mimicked by a stranger enhances longstanding relationship evaluations. *Social Psychological and Personality Science, 1*, 87–93. https://doi.org/10.1177/1948550609355718

Künecke, J., Mokros, A., Olderbak, S., & Wilhelm, O. (2018). Facial responsiveness of psychopaths to the emotional expressions of others. *PLoS One, 13*, e0190714. https://doi.org/10.1371/journal.pone.0190714

Kyranides, M. N., Petridou, M., Gokani, H. A., Hill, S., & Fanti, K. A. (2022). Reading and reacting to faces, the effect of facial mimicry in improving facial emotion recognition in individuals with antisocial behavior and psychopathic traits. *Current Psychology, 42*, 14306. https://doi.org/10.1007/s12144-022-02749-0

Lakin, J. L., & Chartrand, T. L. (2003). Using nonconscious behavioral mimicry to create affiliation and rapport. *Psychological Science, 14*, 334–339. https://doi.org/10.1111/1467-9280.14481

Lakin, J. L., Jefferis, V. E., Cheng, C. M., & Chartrand, T. L. (2003). The chameleon effect as social glue: Evidence for the evolutionary significance of nonconscious mimicry. *Journal of Nonverbal Behavior, 27*, 145–162. https://doi.org/10.1023/A:1025389814290

Lausberg, H. (2013). *Understanding body movement: A guide to empirical research on nonverbal behaviour with an introduction to the NEUROGES® coding system*. Peter Lang GmbH, Internationaler Verlag der Wissenschaften.

Likowski, K. U., Weyers, P., Seibt, B., Stöhr, C., Pauli, P., & Mühlberger, A. (2011). Sad and lonely? Sad mood suppresses facial mimicry. *Journal of Nonverbal Behavior, 35*, 101–117. https://doi.org/10.1007/s10919-011-0107-4

Matzke, B., Herpertz, S. C., Berger, C., Fleischer, M., & Domes, G. (2013). Facial reactions during emotion recognition in borderline personality disorder: A facial electromyographys. *Psychopathology, 47*, 101–110. https://doi.org/10.1159/000351122

Maurer, R. E., & Tindall, J. H. (1983). Effect of postural congruence on client's perception of counselor empathy. *Journal of Counseling Psychology, 30*, 158–163. https://doi.org/10.1037/0022-0167.30.2.158

Oberman, L. M., Winkielman, P., & Ramachandran, V. S. (2007). Face to face: Blocking facial mimicry can selectively impair recognition of emotional expressions. *Social Neuroscience, 2*, 167–178. https://doi.org/10.1080/17470910701391943

Pancotti, F., Mele, S., Callegari, V., Bivi, R., Saracino, F., & Craighero, L. (2021). Efficacy of facial exercises in facial expression categorization in schizophrenia. *Brain Sciences, 11*, 825. https://doi.org/10.3390/brainsci11070825

Passardi, S., Peyk, P., Rufer, M., Wingenbach, T. S., & Pfaltz, M. C. (2019). Facial mimicry, facial emotion recognition and alexithymia in post-traumatic stress disorder. *Behaviour Research and Therapy, 122*, 103436. https://doi.org/10.1016/j.brat.2019.103436

Pizarro-Campagna, E., Terrett, G., Jovev, M., Rendell, P. G., Henry, J. D., & Chanen, A. M. (2020). Rapid facial mimicry responses are preserved in youth with first presentation borderline personality disorder. *Journal of Affective Disorders, 266*, 14–21. https://doi.org/10.1016/j.jad.2020.01.097

Raffard, S., Salesse, R. N., Bortolon, C., Bardy, B. G., Henriques, J., Marin, L., Stricker, D., & Capdevielle, D. (2018). Using mimicry of body movements by a virtual agent to increase synchronization behavior and rapport in individuals with schizophrenia. *Scientific Reports, 8*, 17356. https://doi.org/10.1038/s41598-018-35813-6

Reinecke, K. C. H., Joraschky, P., & Lausberg, H. (2021). Hand movements that change during psychotherapy and their relation to therapeutic outcome: An analysis of individual and simultaneous movements. *Psychotherapy Research, 32*, 104–114. https://doi.org/10.1080/10503307.2021.1925989

Riehle, M., & Lincoln, T. M. (2018). Investigating the social costs of schizophrenia: Facial expressions in dyadic interactions of people with and without schizophrenia. *Journal of Abnormal Psychology, 127*, 202–215. https://doi.org/10.1037/abn0000319

Rives Bogart, K., & Matsumoto, D. (2010). Facial mimicry is not necessary to recognize emotion: Facial expression recognition by people with Moebius syndrome. *Social Neuroscience, 5*, 241–251. https://doi.org/10.1080/17470910903395692

Salazar Kämpf, M., & Kanske, P. (2023). Mimicry and affective disorders. *Frontiers in Psychiatry, 13*, 1–7. https://doi.org/10.3389/fpsyt.2022.1105503

Salazar Kämpf, M., Liebermann, H., Kerschreiter, R., Krause, S., Nestler, S., & Schmukle, S. C. (2018). Disentangling the sources of mimicry: Social relations analyses of the link between mimicry and liking. *Psychological Science, 29*, 131–138. https://doi.org/10.1177/0956797617727121

Salazar Kämpf, M., Nestler, S., Hansmeier, J., Glombiewski, J., & Exner, C. (2021). Mimicry in psychotherapy–an actor partner model of therapists' and patients' non-verbal behavior and its effects on the working alliance. *Psychotherapy Research, 31*, 752–764. https://doi.org/10.1080/10503307.2020.1849849

Scheflen, A. E. (1964). The significance of posture in communication systems. *Psychiatry, 27*, 316–331. https://doi.org/10.1080/00332747.1964.11023403

Segrin, C. (2000). Social skills deficits associated with depression. *Clinical Psychology Review, 20*, 379–403. https://doi.org/10.1016/S0272-7358(98)00104-4

Seibt, B., Mühlberger, A., Likowski, K. U., & Weyers, P. (2015). Facial mimicry in its social setting. *Frontiers in Psychology, 6*, 1122. https://doi.org/10.3389/fpsyg.2015.01122

Sestito, M., Umiltà, M. A., De Paola, G., Fortunati, R., Raballo, A., Leuci, E., Maffei, S., Tonna, M., Amore, M., Maggini, C., & Gallese, V. (2013). Facial reactions in response to dynamic emotional stimuli in different modalities in patients suffering from schizophrenia: A behavioral and EMG study. *Frontiers in Human Neuroscience, 7*, 1–12. https://doi.org/10.3389/fnhum.2013.00368

Sharpley, C. F., Halat, J., Rabinowicz, T., Weiland, B., & Stafford, J. (2001). Standard posture, postural mirroring and client-perceived rapport. *Counselling Psychology Quarterly, 14*, 267–280. https://doi.org/10.1080/09515070110088843

Sloan, D. M., Bradley, M. M., Dimoulas, E., & Lang, P. J. (2002). Looking at facial expressions: Dysphoria and facial EMG. *Biological Psychology, 60*, 79–90. https://doi.org/10.1016/S0301-0511(02)00044-3

Sonnby-Borgström, M. (2002). Automatic mimicry reactions as related to differences in emotional empathy. *Scandinavian Journal of Psychology, 43*, 433–443. https://doi.org/10.1111/1467-9450.00312

Sowden, S., Koehne, S., Catmur, C., Dziobek, I., & Bird, G. (2015). Intact automatic imitation and typical spatial compatibility in autism spectrum disorder: Challenging the broken mirror theory. *Autism Research, 9*, 292–300. https://doi.org/10.1002/aur.1511

Spengler, S., Bird, G., & Brass, M. (2010). Hyperimitation of actions is related to reduced understanding of others' minds in autism spectrum conditions. *Biological Psychiatry, 68*, 1148–1155. https://doi.org/10.1016/j.biopsych.2010.09.017

Stel, M., & Vonk, R. (2010). Mimicry in social interaction: Benefits for mimickers, mimickees, and their interaction. *British Journal of Psychology, 101*, 311–323. https://doi.org/10.1348/000712609X465424

Tickle-Degnen, L., & Rosenthal, R. (1990). The nature of rapport and its nonverbal correlates. *Psychological Inquiry, 1*, 285–293. https://doi.org/10.1207/s15327965pli0104_1

Torregrossa, L. J., Bian, D., Wade, J., Adery, L. H., Ichinose, M., Nichols, H., Bekele, E., Sarkar, N., & Park, S. (2019). Decoupling of spontaneous facial mimicry from emotion recognition in schizophrenia. *Psychiatry Research, 275*, 169–176. https://doi.org/10.1016/j.psychres.2019.03.035

van Baaren, R. B., Fockenberg, D. A., Holland, R. W., Janssen, L., & van Knippenberg, A. (2006). The moody chameleon: The effect of mood on non–conscious mimicry. *Social Cognition, 24*, 426–437. https://doi.org/10.1521/soco.2006.24.4.426

Varcin, K. J., Bailey, P. E., & Henry, J. D. (2010). Empathic deficits in schizophrenia: The potential role of rapid facial mimicry. *Journal of the International Neuropsychological Society, 16*, 621–629. https://doi.org/10.1017/S1355617710000329

Vicaria, I. M., & Dickens, L. (2016). Meta-analyses of the intra-and interpersonal outcomes of interpersonal coordination. *Journal of Nonverbal Behavior, 40*, 335–361. https://doi.org/10.1007/s10919-016-0238-8

Vrana, S. R., & Gross, D. (2004). Reactions to facial expressions: Effects of social context and speech anxiety on responses to neutral, anger, and joy expressions. *Biological Psychology, 66*, 63–78. https://doi.org/10.1016/j.biopsycho.2003.07.004

Vrijsen, J. N., Lange, W. G., Becker, E. S., & Rinck, M. (2010). Socially anxious individuals lack unintentional mimicry. *Behaviour Research and Therapy, 48*, 561–564. https://doi.org/10.1016/j.brat.2010.02.004

Walther, S., Stegmayer, K., Sulzbacher, J., Vanbellingen, T., Müri, R., Strik, W., & Bohlhalter, S. (2015). Nonverbal social communication and gesture control in schizophrenia. *Schizophrenia Bulletin, 41*, 338–345. https://doi.org/10.1093/schbul/sbu222

Weinberg, M. K., & Tronick, E. Z. (1996). Infant affective reactions to the resumption of maternal interaction after the still-face. *Child Development, 67*, 905–914. https://doi.org/10.1111/j.1467-8624.1996.tb01772.x

Wexler, B. E., Levenson, L., Warrenburg, S., & Price, L. H. (1994). Decreased perceptual sensitivity to emotion-evoking stimuli in depression. *Psychiatry Research, 51*, 127–138. https://doi.org/10.1016/0165-1781(94)90032-9

Yoshimura, S., Sato, W., Uono, S. et al. (2015). Impaired overt facial mimicry in response to dynamic facial expressions in high-functioning autism spectrum disorders. *Journal of Autism and Developmental Disorders 45*, 1318–1328. https://doi.org/10.1007/s10803-014-2291-7

Zwick, J. C., & Wolkenstein, L. (2017). Facial emotion recognition, theory of mind and the role of facial mimicry in depression. *Journal of Affective Disorders, 210*, 90–99. https://doi.org/10.1016/j.jad.2016.12.022

Chapter 16
Watching Others Mirror: Explaining the Range of Third-Party Inferences from Imitation

Lindsey J. Powell and Piotr Winkielman

Imitation plays an important role in human social life. In this chapter, we focus on a subset of imitation we refer to as socially-oriented imitation, or for short "social imitation." Social imitation necessarily occurs in the context of an interaction between two or more actors. Contrary to learning-oriented imitation, or imitative acquisition of skills or preferences that are useful to the learner, social imitation often involves arbitrary behaviors only temporarily adopted by the imitator and/or model. Common examples of social imitation include copying a social partner's posture, actions, speech, or choices in an ongoing social interaction (for comprehensive reviews, see Chaps. 2, 3, and 4; this volume). In their own dyadic interactions, people respond, usually positively, to being imitated in this way (e.g., Carpenter et al., 2013; Chartrand & Bargh, 1999; Meltzoff, 1990; van Baaren et al., 2003; for comprehensive reviews, see Chaps. 12 and 13, this review). People also imitate their social partners in ways that suggest intended positive social effects: they increase imitation toward likable social partners or after being ostracized, and they imitate more when their social partners can see them (e.g., Bavelas et al., 1986; Lakin & Chartrand, 2003; Lakin et al., 2008; Over & Carpenter, 2009; Sinclair et al., 2005; Watson-Jones et al., 2016; for a review, see Chap. 11; this volume). There is a very rich literature on effects and mechanisms of mimicry when it involves the first party—direct participants in the interaction (for reviews, see Arnold & Winkielman, 2019; Chartrand & Lakin, 2013; Cracco et al., 2018; Duffy & Chartrand, 2015; Hess & Fischer, 2013; Heyes, 2011; Stel et al., 2016; Wang & Hamilton, 2012).

Importantly, people also make inferences from social imitation as third-party observers of interactions. Often these inferences seem uniformly positive, involving the attribution of prosocial traits and relationships to the imitator or dyad. Some studies, however, contradict this simple story, as observations of imitation lead participants to make negative social inferences about the imitator. Though the

L. J. Powell (✉) · P. Winkielman
Department of Psychology, University of California, San Diego, CA, USA
e-mail: ljpowell@ucsd.edu; pwinkielman@ucsd.edu

O. Genschow, E. Cracco (eds.), *Automatic Imitation*,
https://doi.org/10.1007/978-3-031-62634-0_16

empirical literature is not as rich, social as well as developmental psychology is in need of a comprehensive explanation of how people extract social information from the patterns of imitation they observe. This explanation can shed light not only on inferences from third-party imitation, but also on first-party dyadic mimicry, and also more generally on social inferences guiding our interpersonal interactions.

We first review evidence for third-party inferences from imitation across the lifespan, from infancy to adulthood. We then make a proposal regarding the social cognitive processes that support inferences from observed imitation. We discuss how a simple concept of social affiliation, embedded in an intuitive theory of psychology, can account for basic, positive inferences from observations of imitation beginning in human infancy. We then describe how similar processes can support a wider range of nuanced inferences and evaluations in mature observers.

A Review of Third-Party Inferences from Imitation

Developmental Methods

In order to understand how perceivers think about imitation, it is useful to take a lifespan perspective. After all, social thinking begins early, develops rapidly, and shapes important early social interactions (Csibra & Gergely, 2009; Heyman & Legare, 2013; Kuhl, 2007; Wellman & Gelman, 1992). Developmental psychologists use a range of methods to study social inferences and evaluations in infants and young children. Obviously, infant research cannot use verbal measures, and thus often relies on systematic differences in looking behavior that can be elicited via a variety of experimental designs (Aslin, 2007). Some of such studies aim to test infants' expectations. The "violation-of-expectation" method typically involves familiarizing or habituating infants to a set of similar events designed to evoke expectations from infants about what else might happen in the same context. Test trials then show events that either do or do not meet the target expectations, with the hypothesis that infants will look longer if the "unexpected" event does trigger their surprise (Stahl & Kibbe, 2022). Other studies on early expectations measure infants' ability to anticipate where an event will occur, or bias in where they look for the source of an ongoing stimulus, such as a speech pattern (e.g., Fawcett & Liszkowski, 2012; Kudrnova et al., 2024; Thomas et al., 2022).

Other infant study paradigms are designed to measure infants' social evaluation. These studies familiarize infants to the different ways in which two actors behave (e.g., helping vs. hindering, speaking a native vs. foreign language, imitating or not imitating), and then the two actors are displayed side-by-side, out of their action context, and infants are given some period of time in which to look at, reach for, or interact with them (Hamlin et al., 2007; Kinzler et al., 2007; Powell & Spelke, 2018b). Biases to look to or engage with one individual over the other may be taken as evidence of a social preference, though it is sometimes hard to rule out alternative, non-evaluative explanations for differential looking (see, e.g., Begus et al., 2016).

In older, more verbal children, studies of social cognition also examine expectations and social evaluation, but do so by asking children what they think or who they like or think is nice, rather than tracking their gaze (Flavell, 1999; Turiel, 2015). Such measures, while using simpler questions, resemble methods in adult social psychology and may also ask for other verbal inferences, such as which people are friends or who possesses other traits (e.g., intelligence, leadership). Furthermore, they may ask children to justify or explain their answers, sometimes providing insight into the cognitive processes involved. We give more specific examples shortly.

Early Positive Inferences

When put in the position of third-party observers, infants and young children already use patterns of imitation in their social inferences and evaluations. In general, observations of imitation seem to elicit positive evaluations and inferences of affiliation. In violation-of-expectation experiments, infants expect imitators to approach or smile at the imitated model, rather than to turn away from the model or approach a person the imitator chose not to model (Liberman et al., 2021; Powell & Spelke, 2018a). Two sets of studies find that infants expect imitators, relative to non-imitators, to behave prosocially toward the target of their imitation in other ways, by helping or comforting them (Kudrnova et al., 2024; Pepe & Powell, 2023). Infants also prefer to look at and reach for imitators over non-imitators, suggesting they judge them to be better potential social partners (Powell & Spelke, 2018b; Thomas et al., 2020). When 5-year-old children see a person choose to imitate one potential model rather than another, they explicitly report that the imitator likes the imitated model more than the non-imitated one (Over & Carpenter, 2015). Interestingly, younger children failed to make this explicit inference, though some data suggest they do when provided with more scaffolding while observing interactions (Over & Carpenter, 2015; Afshordi & Carey, 2019). Children across several cultures rate those who conform during an instrumental task—making necklaces—as more intelligent and more well-behaved than non-conformers (Wen et al., 2019).

One open question concerns how general early positive inferences from imitation are. Do infants interpret social imitation as evidence of the imitator's broadly prosocial disposition, or a more selective positive relationship between the imitator and model? Some evidence suggests the latter. In one study, infant participants saw their parent imitate one puppet and respond non-imitatively to another, and then heard a voice saying "Hi, [participant's name]!" while the two puppets were side-by-side on screen. When they heard their own name, infants looked more to the imitated puppet than the non-imitated puppet, indicating that they inferred the imitated puppet was more likely to know their name (Thomas et al., 2022). This suggests participants may have used their parents' imitation to infer that the imitated puppet was part of their particular social network. Additionally, in the studies referenced above, there was no evidence that infants' expectations of imitator prosociality extended beyond the imitated model to additional social partners (Kudrnova et al., 2024; Pepe & Powell, 2023). This possibility does raise the question of why infants themselves reach for imitators over non-imitators (Powell & Spelke, 2018b), if they view social imitation as reflecting the imitator's specific relationship with the model. This is a puzzle that ought to be addressed by future research; one possibility is that infants look for social partners who seem good at forming relationships, rather than those who are impartially nice to all.

Role of Imitation vs. Similarity in Inference

One alternative interpretation of the findings discussed above is that infants and children respond to similarity rather than imitation. They could generally expect individuals who are similar to be friends and positively evaluate individuals who are part of a group (Afshordi & Liberman, 2021; Liberman et al., 2014; Liberman et al., 2021; Shutts & Kalish, 2021). However, a number of findings suggest that infants base their inferences and evaluations on imitation, specifically, rather than similarity. First, infants track which individual is imitating the other, and expect this relation to remain stable (Bas et al., 2023). These roles shape infants' looking to approach actions in violation-of-expectation studies: though infants look longer when an imitator approaches the social partner they did not imitate over the one they did imitate, infants do not expect models to approach imitators over non-imitators (Fawcett & Liszkowski, 2012; Powell & Spelke, 2018a). This suggests that their inferences of affiliation from imitation are asymmetrical. Similarly, though infants preferentially look at and reach for imitators over non-imitators, they do not prefer imitated models to non-imitated individuals (Powell & Spelke, 2018b; Thomas et al., 2020).

Knowledge and intention also impact infants' inferences and evaluations in a way that suggests they are concerned with intentional imitative alignment, rather than mere similarity in independent choices. Six-month-old infants expect people who display the same food preference to affiliate, looking longer if the people look angry and turn away from one another instead. However, this violation-of-expectation effect is only observed if the people were together when expressing their matching preferences (Liberman et al., 2021). Preliminary evidence suggests 12-month-old infants only preferentially reach for imitators over non-imitators if those agents could perceive the model action they did or did not match (Powell & Spelke, 2017). These results are in line with experiments on infants' evaluations of puppets who do or do not match the infants' own preferences: 11-month-old infants only prefer a puppet with the same food or color preference vs. a different preference when the puppets' matching and mismatching are done intentionally, following the infants' own choice (Mahajan & Wynn, 2012). This indicates infants prefer those who imitate or align with them, rather than those who are merely similar.

Although infants seem to be attuned to social imitation, and not just the similarity that arises from it, children do come to expect some kinds of non-imitative similarity to predict social affiliation. By age 4, children expect others to have friends of the same gender and race, though they did not expect shared activity preferences to guide friendship (Shutts et al., 2013). In another study, 4-year-old children interpreted one person's agreement with another's preferences for food and toys as evidence of friendship only if the two people were together when stating their opinions, not if they stated them separately or another character described each one's opinions (King et al., 2023). However, older children thought people with matching opinions were likely closer regardless of whether those opinions were stated together or separately, in line with a number of other studies that children age 5 and older treat shared preferences and other similarity as cues to affiliation (Afshordi, 2019; Jordan & Dunham, 2021; King et al., 2023; Liberman & Shaw, 2019). Intriguingly, shared but independent preferences for food, specifically, may be treated as a cue to social affiliation somewhat earlier (Liberman et al., 2021). These findings underscore the importance of carefully teasing apart imitation and similarity as sources of early social inferences.

Negative Inferences

Another class of phenomena that suggest children continue attend to social imitation and the roles of model versus imitator is the negative inferences about imitators they begin to make in some circumstances. After observing imitation, children judge the model to be of higher social status than the imitator (Over & Carpenter, 2015). In some circumstances, children infer that imitators are antisocial. One such circumstance is when matching another's preference creates competition over a limited resource. Pesowski and colleagues told children stories in which one character had stated a preference for one kind of resource (food or art supply) over another. In some stories, there were plenty of the preferred resource. In those "resource rich" cases, children judged another character who echoed the first one's preference as nicer and more likely to be friends with the first character, compared to a third character that expressed a different preference. However, the judgments changed when there was only one of the first character's preferred resource. For those "resource limited" stories, children instead said it was the character who made a different choice that was nicer (Pesowski et al., 2023). A second circumstance in which children disapprove of imitation is when it involves copying someone else's ideas, or plagiarism. In a series of studies, Olson and colleagues found that children across several cultures disapproved of story characters who copied others' drawings, rather than drawing something different or making the same drawing by chance (Olson & Shaw, 2011; Yang et al., 2014). This disapproval may stem from an intuitive sense that copying ideas involves violating someone else's "ownership," or to use adults' language, their intellectual property rights (Shaw et al., 2012).

Adult Reasoning About Imitation

Outside of the developmental literature, a smaller body of research finds that adults also make social inferences from third-party observations of imitation. These findings are similar to research on children's inferences, though they suggest that the inferences from mimicry can more easily turn negative and, obviously, become more nuanced. In one study, observing social mimicry did improve third-party observers' liking of outgroup members who mimicked each other (Bretter et al., 2023). This finding matches the standard findings of generally positive effects of simple mimicry in dyadic, first-party interactions (Duffy & Chartrand, 2015). However, the research also revealed a variety of unfavorable inferences. In a finding that echoes the developmental finding about children assigning higher social status to models (initiators) over imitators (Over & Carpenter, 2015), adult participants perceived imitators as more submissive than their interaction partner who initiated the gestures (Genschow & Alves, 2020). Furthermore, not only are mimics rated as more submissive in comparison to models (initiators), the mimics are also rated as more submissive than those who respond with a non-mimicking gesture or who do not respond at all. Overall, this line of research clearly suggests that, at least from the perspective of third-parties, mimicry is not a universally good thing and invites concerns about the mimic's social status and independence (cf. derogatory terms for mimics such as "lackey" or "toady" or even a more neutral "copycat"). From that perspective, it is perhaps unsurprising that in some dyadic interactions, instead of mimicry, there is a counter-mimicry, with the responder producing opposite gestures, or opposite facial expressions from the model. Such counter-mimicry can even occur spontaneously and is typically seen in situations that involve some form of dominance contest or competition (Carr et al., 2014; Hofree et al., 2018; Weyers et al., 2009). One account suggests that social perceivers quickly learn and automatize inferences about situations in which regular mimicry does or does not pay (Cook et al., 2012).

But it is not only inferences of submissiveness that mimics should worry about. There are situations where mimicry can do reputational harm, at least from the perspective of third parties. One context where this occurs is when the model (initiator) is treating the mimic badly (e.g., by being condescending to them). In this case, third-party observers perceive imitators of the model's neutral gestures as *less* competent than non-imitators (Kavanagh et al., 2011). Importantly, control conditions show that this effect is not simply due to observers noticing similarity between the gestures of the unpleasant model and the mimic. This is because observing similar neutral gestures, without evidence that they derive from mimicry, eliminates the effect (Kavanagh et al., 2011). In fact, just like in the developmental literature, the adult literature highlights a key role for perception of intention behind imitation (cf., Powell & Spelke, 2017). Preliminary evidence for sophisticated incorporation of intention information was provided by a study in which third-party observers watched someone mimic or not mimic a model with a "bad" or "good" (un/trustworthy) reputation (Kavanagh et al., 2013). In this study, the third-party observers always knew the model's reputation (they heard favorable or unfavorable gossip about the model). Critically, observers also knew that some mimics were unaware of the model's reputation (did not know the gossip), whereas other mimics were aware of it (they also knew the gossip). The results showed that third-party observers only made negative (or positive) inferences about the mimics if they knew that the mimics were aware of the model's reputation. Notably, mimicry of a disreputable model did not negatively influence third-party observers' judgment of the mimic, if the observers knew that their mimicry was "innocent" (Kavanagh et al., 2013).

More broadly, U.S. adults rate children who closely conform to others as less intelligent than low conformers, but this finding varies across context and cultures. Adults from Vanuatu, a subsistence farming society in Melanesia largely disconnected from Western culture, rated high conformers as more intelligent (Clegg et al., 2017). Sanchez-Burks and colleagues also found cultural differences in inferences from observed imitation. When watching a video of a supposed job interview, U.S. Latino participants rated performance of the interviewee higher when the interviewer mimicked them compared to a no mimicry condition, while U.S. Anglo participants rated interviewee performance similarly, regardless of interviewer mimicry (Sanchez-Burks et al., 2009). Overall, there is less evidence that adults make positive social inferences on the basis of third-party observations of imitation, but this may vary substantially across cultures.

Summary

In sum, social inferences from third-party observations of imitation begin in infancy and persist throughout the lifespan. These inferences are shaped by developmental trends. First, infants initially seem to focus on imitation, specifically, as a basis for inferences about affiliation and prosociality: They resist inferences from independently arising similarity, and expectations and evaluations of the imitator are distinct from those for the imitated model. This yields to rising attention to general similarity, which may be the primary basis for inferences of affiliation in middle childhood. Children and adults do continue to encode the dynamics of imitation, and come to use it to infer status and submissiveness, though more attention should be paid to the emergence of cross-cultural differences which are apparent in adults. Children and adults may also use information about who acted first and who copied to make nuanced inferences and evaluations in cases of conflicting goals. Finally, they pay attention to intentions behind imitation, and to the knowledge that the imitator has about the model. In short, any account of the social cognition involved should be able to explain both positive and negative inferences from imitation and the phenomenon of asymmetric inferences made about imitators and targets. The account we discuss next does all that.

Adopted Utility and Reasoning About Imitation

Social connection between humans often involves shared interests or goals (Eisenberg, 2000; McCullough, 2020; Tomasello et al., 2005). This can involve one person helping or caring for another, two people cooperating toward a jointly desired outcome, or even just two people liking to listen to the same kind of music. We propose that people reason about the affiliative meaning of social imitation using the same kind of social cognitive inference mechanism they use to reason about this broad class of shared goals. This reasoning is, in turn, built on processes used to make simpler inferences about individual behavior.

Reasoning About Others Using a Naive Utility Calculus

People approach reasoning about an individual actor's behavior using a "naive utility calculus" (Gergely & Csibra, 2003; Jara-Ettinger et al., 2016). Observers assume an actor will choose the actions, or inaction, that will maximize the actor's expected utility, calculated as the difference between expected rewards and expected costs. These beliefs can be instantiated as a causal model of others' behavior, in which the actor's desires and affordances (i.e., what the actor can do in a situation, given some amount of effort or other cost) feed into a planning process that selects a behavior. Such a causal model allows observers to make both forward and reverse inferences about other people (Baker et al., 2017; Liu et al., 2017; Woodward, 1998). If you know what another person prefers and also how much cost or effort the available choices require of them, then you can make a confident prediction about their likely behavior. Conversely, if you see the cost someone puts into obtaining a particular outcome (e.g., how much they pay for concert tickets, or how early they wake up to go fishing), then you can infer something about how rewarding that outcome is to that actor, specifically. This calculus is a piece of a broader "intuitive psychology" that can also integrate reasoning about the actor's beliefs, emotions, and personality (Flavell, 1999; Wellman & Gelman, 1992).

Some actions, however, do not seem oriented toward the actor's own rewards. Consider one person, Anne, who helps another, Bianca, move apartments, first carrying heavy, packed boxes from the old apartment to a truck, and then carrying the boxes from the truck into the new apartment. Anne expends a lot of effort on this task, but she receives no direct reward. Instead, it is Bianca who experiences the reward of having all of her belongings transported where they need to be. An observer relying on a naive utility calculus framework can reason about actions like Anne's by inferring that Anne has incorporated Bianca's rewards into the utility calculations Anne uses to select which actions to pursue (Hamlin et al., 2013b; Jara-Ettinger et al., 2016; Powell, 2022; Quillien et al., 2023; Ullman et al., 2009). Adopting such an interest in Bianca's rewards could be considered evidence that Anne *cares* about Bianca. This does not demand assuming that Anne cares as much about Bianca's rewards as Bianca does, or as much as Anne cares about her own rewards; the value of others' rewards is often discounted to some degree relative to the actor's own (Jones & Rachlin, 2006; Murphy et al., 2011; Tooby et al., 2008).

Understanding that people sometimes consider others' rewards in their own utility calculations can provide a basis for reasoning about prosociality in the form of both dispositions and relationships. People who consistently incorporate others' rewards into their utility calculations would be perceived as "nice," and observers can infer friendship and other prosocial relationships from one person's consistent consideration of a specific social partner's rewards when making choices (Jara-Ettinger et al., 2016; Kahane et al., 2018; Powell, 2022; Tooby et al., 2008). In contrast, when an actor refuses to help another person or even causes them harm, an observer may conclude that the actor places either no weight or a negative weight on the other person's reward in their utility calculations. The observer may use this information to infer a negative disposition or relationship. These inferences may impact the observer's judgements about the actor's moral character or potential to be a good social partner for the observer themselves, though there are other factors that inform these judgments as well.

Utility-based inferences about others' pro- or anti-social relationships and dispositions can be the basis for observers' social evaluations, beginning in infancy. From around 6 months of age, infants preferentially reach for a helpful actor over a neutral or hindering one (Hamlin et al., 2007; Margoni & Surian, 2018; Woo & Spelke, 2023a). The preferred actor's helpfulness is typically demonstrated by the effort they put toward helping a social partner achieve a simple instrumental goal, such as going up a hill or opening a box. Importantly, this helpful effort does not need to be successful. Infants prefer those whose actions reflect a desire to help even if the helpee's goals ultimately remain unfulfilled (Hamlin, 2013; Woo et al., 2017). Similarly, infants' helper preferences depend on the perception that helpful actions were knowingly selected. If an actor does not know what another individual wants, then infants do not positively evaluate the actor for engaging in an action that helps the other person achieve their goal (Hamlin et al., 2013b). Conversely, if an actor has a false belief about another's goal (e.g., that the object the other wants is in Box A when it is really in Box B), then older infants will positively evaluate the actor for taking an action the actor would believe is helpful, even though it fails to promote the helpee's goal (Woo & Spelke, 2023b). This pattern of preferences is consistent with the hypothesis that infants use a naive utility calculus to figure out when actors value others' rewards, and that this caring—rather than the positive effect of an action—is the foundation of their social evaluations.

Adopted Utility and Imitation

Many social interactions do not involve situations in which an actor has the opportunity to help or reward their social partner(s). For example, if two friends meet in the hallway and have a conversation, there may not be a clear way in which either can act to materially benefit the other. However, an observer may still see evidence that each friend adopts the value the other places on actions and choices, through their use of social imitation or mimicry. Choosing the same postures, actions, words, facial expressions, and so on is relatively unlikely unless the imitator is noticing the choices the model made in these domains and upweighting their own value on those options as a result. For this reason, social imitation can reflect the imitator's habitual tendency to adopt concern for the things that others value. This can be a dispositional habit extended to all of the imitator's social partners or a feature of the specific relationship the imitator has to the model they align with. Thus, we propose that the same type of utility-based inference that people use to evaluate helpful actions forms the basis of inferences and evaluations from observed social imitation as well.

As noted at the outset, we use the term "social imitation" to refer to the variety of ways in which social partners may temporarily align with one another during an interaction. This includes adopting the same posture, engaging in similar movements, making matching word choices, or expressing similar opinions or preferences (Chartrand & Lakin, 2013). Social imitation of this sort reflects and enhances liking between social partners and increases when imitators are motivated to seek social affiliation (Lakin et al., 2008; Lakin & Chartrand, 2003; Over, 2020; Watson-Jones et al., 2016). Social imitation can be distinguished from imitation aimed at learning novel information or skills from others (Over & Carpenter, 2012). The latter is likely to take the form of a long-term adoption of behaviors or preferences associated with successful outcomes or individuals, and it continues in the absence of the person being imitated. In contrast, social imitation of the type we discuss here typically involves transient changes in behavior enacted in the presence of the social partner who is being modeled or other observers. Learning-oriented imitation does not need to involve any care for the goals or rewards of the model; it is motivated instead by the imitator's desire to achieve a better outcome for themselves. Social imitation typically does not result in any direct rewards for the imitator from the imitated actions themselves, however. Instead, we argue that observers perceive the motivation of social imitation to be based in adoption of the model's value function.

Adopted Utility Inferences from Imitation in First-Party vs. Third-Party Settings

Notice that this framework suggests that in dyadic interactions, one should usually observe positive effects of imitation on the model. After all, from the perspective of adopted utility, imitation suggests to the model that the mimic notices their action, understands the value function that led to it, and seeks social affiliation and even coalition by placing a similar value on those actions. From the perspective of the model, these are all usually good things and thus dyadic mimicry usually pays off—results in more favorable judgments. This is, of course, unless copying the model actually results in competition between the mimic and model, as when choosing the same limited resource or shadowing someone's movements to block their path (Naber et al., 2013; Pesowski et al., 2023). Or, it may be very clear that the intention behind mimicry is ingratiation, parroting, or parodying (Jones & Pittman, 1982; Kavanagh & Winkielman, 2016; Over & Carpenter, 2009, 2012). In fact, it has been argued that spontaneous imitation may be particularly valued and considered informative by models in dyadic interactions, and also by third-party observers. This is because spontaneous mimicry is harder to "fake" and thus provides stronger evidence that the mimic genuinely shares values with the model, and either is, or truly wants to be a part of the model's social group (Kavanagh & Winkielman, 2016).

However, from the perspective of the third-party observers, all these inferences are qualified by the fact that the observer does not directly benefit from the signal of affiliation. After all, the mimicry is not directed at the observer, but at the model. Thus, in evaluating the mimic, the observers ask additional questions and consider the character of the model and the mimic's knowledge about the model. The adopted utility framework thus easily explains negative inferences about the mimic (as opposed to non-mimic) of untrustworthy, or incompetent models. After all, the mimic "decided" to adopt (or spontaneously felt compelled to adopt) the model's utility, suggesting the mimic would like to affiliate with the model and is willing to share goals and values the observer may not approve of. Observers may also notice that a model is not responding positively to an imitator's alignment with them (e.g., in Kavanagh et al., 2011, the model continued to be condescending to the mimicking responder), and this could raise questions for the observer. Does the model have other reasons to dislike the imitator or question their motives?

Despite these opportunities for negative inferences, the prosocial, affiliative nature of imitation will often lead third-party observers to infer that imitators have positive traits that would make them good social partners. All else being equal, people would rather have social partners who are socially perceptive and interested in friendly, well-coordinated interactions or relationships. Loyalty is also a valued trait, which may help explain why children acting as third-party observers negatively evaluate individuals who do not conform to their in-group, even though the children themselves don't belong to that group (Misch et al., 2014; Roberts et al., 2017). Disapproval of non-conformity is strongest for individuals who choose not to conform due to their own diverging preferences, supporting the conclusion that children negatively evaluate individuals who are unwilling to support their group's values (Van Wye et al., 2021).

The adopted utility framework thus explains why imitation is sometimes but not always viewed positively by observers. Notice that this is a feature shared with evaluation of other typically prosocial behaviors, including helping. For example, the authors of helpful actions are generally liked, even if those actions are directed at others. However, they can be disliked from the third-party perspective, if their helping is directed at an actor trying to achieve an anti-social goal or known to be anti-social. This might be obvious when considering an example of adults negatively evaluating a person who has generously helped a fugitive murderer, but even infants prefer those who punish or hinder an actor who has previously acted antisocially, relative to those who ignore or help antisocial actors (e.g., Geraci, 2020;

Hamlin et al., 2011), and if a character has indicated their difference from an infant by expressing a contrasting food preference to the infant's own, then infants prefer an actor who hinders rather than helps the disagreeing character (Hamlin et al., 2013a).

Finally, this framework may be able to explain third-party inferences from another type of interpersonal alignment: empathizing. Empathy involves understanding another person's situation and feeling emotions congruent with their well-being and emotional state (Batson, 2010; Eisenberg et al., 2006). Recipients of empathy feel close to and supported by their social partners (Cramer & Jowett, 2010; Gable et al., 2018), but third-party observers can also make social inferences from observing empathy, or counter-empathy. One proposal is that observers do this by reasoning that empathizers experience shared or congruent emotions with the target of empathy because they care about the target's goals and welfare and thus appraise the target's outcomes similarly (Smith-Flores & Powell, 2023). New evidence supports this hypothesis. Infants and children expect others to empathize with their friends' or group members' outcomes, and children also infer social relationships from observed empathy or counter-empathy (Smith-Flores et al., 2023, 2024; Tompkins et al., in press). Children and adults both also typically positively evaluate those who comfort or empathize with others (Geraci et al., 2021; Wang & Todd, 2021). However, adults' evaluations of empathizers depend on what they know about the target of empathy: perhaps unsurprisingly, data show that adults don't positively evaluate someone who empathizes with a neo-Nazi struggling to achieve their goals (Wang & Todd, 2021). Thus, it seems that people may use observations of both social imitation and empathy to infer when a social actor has concern for the goals of their social partner, and that people judge these actors based not just on the affiliative or prosocial nature of that concern but also on their evaluations of the moral worth of targeted social partners (Kavanagh et al., 2013; Wang & Todd, 2021).

Automatic vs. Conscious Processing of Observed Imitation

Finally, how conscious are the underlying processes? Before we tackle this question about the observers, let us consider it in the context of dyadic interactions. After all, what makes dyadic imitation fascinating is its spontaneous, unbidden nature. We think the answer about automaticity depends on multiple factors. It is clear that some mechanisms of imitation relate to ideomotor processes (Chartrand & Bargh, 1999), fluency of embodiment (Carr & Winkielman, 2014), and perception-behavior action learning—the associative pairing of frequently observed action with frequently performed behavior (Heyes, 2011), but it is also clear that even automatic imitation is flexible and can, to some extent, incorporate goals and social variables (Cracco et al., 2018). Clearly, this depends on the nature of behavior. For example, automatic finger imitation can be insensitive to social variables, like power and status (Farmer et al., 2016), whereas facial imitation is sensitive to such variables (Carr et al., 2014). Presumably, the more novel, complex, slow, and controllable the behavior, the more higher-order inferences play a role. But even spontaneous and quick imitation can incorporate well-practiced goals, such as social affiliation, since, as mentioned, social perceivers quickly learn and automatize inferences about situations in which mimicry does or does not pay (Cook et al., 2012).

All this puts a young or old observer of imitation in a quandary. How much does the observed imitation reflect the imitator's social goals and beliefs versus other less intentional processes? Anecdotally, before we blame someone for spontaneously returning a dictator's smile or spontaneously meeting his outstretched hand, we may pause to consider whether the imitator was "tricked into it," did it out of politeness habits, etc. On the other hand, highly automatized behaviors are sometimes (but not always) deeply reflective of personal values, social preferences, and prejudices (Uhlmann et al., 2012).

One interesting, though yet unexplored challenge, also relates to the asymmetric knowledge of the imitator and the observer. Usually, the model's action is directly aimed at the imitator and may be more visible to them (e.g., leg crossing, hair touching) and thus is more likely to trigger an automatic process. The observer thus may underestimate the role of these constraints, as well as other constraints that contribute to the known asymmetries in actor-observer accounts of social behavior (Malle, 2014). Future research could explore these fascinating issues with both young and old observers, with an eye on systematic differences in how sophistication in understanding social relationships, as well as basic human psychology, changes the pattern of inferences from observed imitation (or lack thereof).

Conclusion

In this chapter, we reviewed evidence about third-party inferences from imitation across the lifespan, from infancy to adulthood. We then proposed that a simple concept of social affiliation, embedded in an intuitive theory of psychology, can account for basic, positive inferences from observations of imitation. We argued that as observers mature and acquire richer social knowledge, they can draw progressively more nuanced inference from observed imitation, incorporating the role of intention, mutual knowledge, social skills, theory of mind, as well as social strategies. They may even consider the extent imitation they observe is due to processes that are automatic and perhaps less under control of goals and beliefs. All this results in the rich tapestry of social judgments we see in our daily life.

References

Afshordi, N. (2019). Children's inferences about friendship and shared preferences based on reported information. *Child Development, 90*, 719–727. https://doi.org/10.1111/cdev.13237

Afshordi, N., & Carey, S. (2019). Preschoolers' recognition of and inferences from observed imitation. PsyArxiv. https://doi.org/10.31234/osf.io/zmsx3.

Afshordi, N., & Liberman, Z. (2021). Keeping friends in mind: Development of friendship concepts in early childhood. *Social Development, 30*, 331–342. https://doi.org/10.1111/sode.12493

Arnold, A. J., & Winkielman, P. (2019). The mimicry among us: Intra- and inter-personal mechanisms of spontaneous mimicry. *Journal of Non-Verbal Behavior, 44*, 195–212. https://doi.org/10.1007/s10919-019-00324-z

Aslin, R. N. (2007). What's in a look? *Developmental Science, 10*, 48–53. https://doi.org/10.1111/j.1467-7687.2007.00563.x

Baker, C. L., Jara-Ettinger, J., Saxe, R., & Tenenbaum, J. B. (2017). Rational quantitative attribution of beliefs, desires and percepts in human mentalizing. *Nature Human Behaviour, 1*, 0064. https://doi.org/10.1038/s41562-017-0064

Bas, J., Sebastian-Galles, N., Csibra, G., & Mascaro, O. (2023). Infants' representation of asymmetric social influence. *Journal of Experimental Child Psychology, 226*, 105564. https://doi.org/10.1016/j.jecp.2022.105564

Batson, C. D. (2010). *Altruism in humans*. Oxford University Press.

Bavelas, J. B., Black, A., Lemery, C. R., & Mullett, J. (1986). "I show how you feel": Motor mimicry as a communicative act. *Journal of Personality and Social Psychology, 50*, 322–329. https://doi.org/10.1037/0022-3514.50.2.322

Begus, K., Gliga, T., & Southgate, V. (2016). Infants' preferences for native speakers are associated with an expectation of information. *Proceedings of the National Academy of Sciences, 113*, 12397–12402. https://doi.org/10.1073/pnas.1603261113

Bretter, C., Unsworth, K. L., & Robinson, M. A. (2023). Watching the mimickers: Mimicry and identity in observed interactions. *Journal of Experimental Psychology: Applied, 29*, 398–413. https://doi.org/10.1037/xap0000462

Carpenter, M., Uebel, J., & Tomasello, M. (2013). Being mimicked increases prosocial behavior in 18-month-old infants. *Child Development, 84*, 1511–1518. https://doi.org/10.1111/cdev.12083

Carr, E. W., & Winkielman, P. (2014). When mirroring is both simple and "smart": How mimicry can be embodied, adaptive, and non-representational. *Frontiers in Human Neuroscience, 8*, 505. https://doi.org/10.3389/fnhum.2014.00505

Carr, E. W., Winkielman, P., & Oveis, C. (2014). Transforming the mirror: Power fundamentally changes facial responding to emotional expressions. *Journal of Experimental Psychology: General, 143*, 997–1003. https://doi.org/10.1037/a0034972

Chartrand, T. L., & Bargh, J. A. (1999). The chameleon effect: The perception–behavior link and social interaction. *Journal of Personality and Social Psychology, 76*, 893–910. https://doi.org/10.1037/0022-3514.76.6.893

Chartrand, T. L., & Lakin, J. L. (2013). The antecedents and consequences of human behavioral mimicry. *Annual Review of Psychology, 64*, 285–308. https://doi.org/10.1146/annurev-psych-113011-143754

Clegg, J. M., Wen, N., & Legare, C. H. (2017). Is non-conformity WEIRD? Cultural variation in adults' beliefs about children's competency and conformity. *Journal of Experimental Psychology: General, 146*, 428–441. https://doi.org/10.1037/xge0000275

Cook, R., Dickinson, A., & Heyes, C. (2012). Contextual modulation of mirror and countermirror sensorimotor associations. *Journal of Experimental Psychology: General, 141*, 774–787. https://doi.org/10.1037/a0027561

Cracco, E., Bardi, L., Desmet, C., Genschow, O., Rigoni, D., De Coster, L., … Brass, M. (2018). Automatic imitation: A meta-analysis. *Psychological Bulletin, 5*, 453–500. https://doi.org/10.1037/bul0000143.

Cramer, D., & Jowett, S. (2010). Perceived empathy, accurate empathy and relationship satisfaction in heterosexual couples. *Journal of Social and Personal Relationships, 27*, 327–349. https://doi.org/10.1177/0265407509348384

Csibra, G., & Gergely, G. (2009). Natural pedagogy. *Trends in Cognitive Sciences, 13*, 148–153. https://doi.org/10.1016/j.tics.2009.01.005

Duffy, K. A., & Chartrand, T. L. (2015). Mimicry: Causes and consequences. *Current Opinion in Behavioral Sciences, 3*, 112–116. https://doi.org/10.1016/j.cobeha.2015.03.002

Eisenberg, N. (2000). Emotion, regulation, and moral development. *Annual Review of Psychology, 51*, 665–697. https://doi.org/10.1146/annurev.psych.51.1.665

Eisenberg, N., Spinrad, T., & Sadovsky, A. (2006). Empathy-related responding in children. In *Handbook of moral development* (pp. 535–568). Psychology Press.

Farmer, H., Carr, E. W., Svartdal, M., Winkielman, P., & Hamilton, A. F. C. (2016). Status and power do not modulate automatic imitation of finger movements. *PLoS One, 11*, e0151835. https://psycnet.apa.org/doi/10.1371/journal.pone.0151835

Fawcett, C., & Liszkowski, U. (2012). Infants anticipate others' social preferences. *Infant and Child Development, 21*, 239–249. https://psycnet.apa.org/doi/10.1002/icd.739

Flavell, J. H. (1999). Cognitive development: Children's knowledge about the mind. *Annual Review of Psychology, 50*, 21–45. https://doi.org/10.1146/annurev.psych.50.1.21

Gable, S. L., Reis, H. T., Impett, E. A., & Asher, E. R. (2018). What do you do when things go right? The intrapersonal and interpersonal benefits of sharing positive events. In *Relationships, well-being and behaviour* (pp. 144–182). Routledge. https://doi.org/10.1037/0022-3514.87.2.228

Genschow, O., & Alves, H. (2020). The submissive chameleon: Third-party inferences from observing mimicry. *Journal of Experimental Social Psychology, 88*, 103966. https://psycnet.apa.org/doi/10.1016/j.jesp.2020.103966

Geraci, A. (2020). How do toddlers evaluate defensive actions toward third parties? *Infancy, 25*, 910–926. https://doi.org/10.1111/infa.12367

Geraci, A., Rigo, P., Simonelli, A., Di Nuovo, S., & Simion, F. (2021). Preschoolers' evaluations of comforting actions towards third parties in different relationship contexts. *Journal of Applied Developmental Psychology, 76*, 101315. https://psycnet.apa.org/doi/10.1016/j.appdev.2021.101315

Gergely, G., & Csibra, G. (2003). Teleological reasoning in infancy: The naıve theory of rational action. *Trends in Cognitive Sciences, 7*, 287–292. https://doi.org/10.1016/S1364-6613(03)00128-1

Hamlin, J. K. (2013). Failed attempts to help and harm: Intention versus outcome in preverbal infants' social evaluations. *Cognition, 128*, 451–474. https://doi.org/10.1016/j.cognition.2013.04.004

Hamlin, J. K., Wynn, K., & Bloom, P. (2007). Social evaluation by preverbal infants. *Nature, 450*, 557–559. https://doi.org/10.1016/j.cognition.2013.04.004

Hamlin, J. K., Wynn, K., Bloom, P., & Mahajan, N. (2011). How infants and toddlers react to antisocial others. *Proceedings of the National Academy of Sciences, 108*, 19931–19936. https://doi.org/10.1073/pnas.1110306108

Hamlin, J. K., Mahajan, N., Liberman, Z., & Wynn, K. (2013a). Not like me= bad: Infants prefer those who harm dissimilar others. *Psychological Science, 24*, 589–594. https://doi.org/10.1177%2F0956797612457785

Hamlin, K. J., Ullman, T., Tenenbaum, J., Goodman, N., & Baker, C. (2013b). The mentalistic basis of core social cognition: Experiments in preverbal infants and a computational model. *Developmental Science, 16*, 209–226. https://doi.org/10.1111%2Fdesc.12017

Hess, U., & Fischer, A. (2013). Emotional mimicry as social regulation. *Personality and Social Psychology Review, 17*, 142–157. https://doi.org/10.1177/1088868312472607

Heyes, C. (2011). Automatic imitation. *Psychological Bulletin, 137*, 463–483. https://doi.org/10.1037/a0022288

Heyman, G. D., & Legare, C. H. (2013). Social cognitive development: Learning from others. In D. E. Carlston (Ed.), *The Oxford handbook of social cognition* (pp. 749–766). Oxford University Press.

Hofree, G., Ruvolo, P., Reinert, A., Bartlett, M. S., & Winkielman, P. (2018). Behind the robot's smiles and frowns: In social context, people do not mirror android's expressions but react to their informational value. *Frontiers in Neurorobotics, 12*, 14. https://doi.org/10.3389/fnbot.2018.00014

Jara-Ettinger, J., Gweon, H., Schulz, L. E., & Tenenbaum, J. B. (2016). The naïve utility calculus: Computational principles underlying commonsense psychology. *Trends in Cognitive Sciences, 20*, 589–604. https://doi.org/10.1016/j.tics.2016.05.011

Jones, E. E., & Pittman, T. S. (1982). Toward a general theory of strategic self-presentation. In J. Suls (Ed.), *Psychological perspectives on the self* (Vol. 1, pp. 231–262). Erlbaum.
Jones, B., & Rachlin, H. (2006). Social discounting. *Psychological Science, 17*, 283–286. https://psycnet.apa.org/doi/10.1111/j.1467-9280.2006.01699.x
Jordan, A., & Dunham, Y. (2021). Are category labels primary? Children use similarities to reason about social groups. *Developmental Science, 24*, e13013. https://doi.org/10.1111/desc.13013
Kahane, G., Everett, J. A., Earp, B. D., Caviola, L., Faber, N. S., Crockett, M. J., & Savulescu, J. (2018). Beyond sacrificial harm: A two-dimensional model of utilitarian psychology. *Psychological Review, 125*, 131–164. https://doi.org/10.1037%2Frev0000093
Kavanagh, L. C., & Winkielman, P. (2016). The functionality of spontaneous mimicry and its influences on affiliation: An implicit socialization account. *Frontiers in Psychology, 7*, 458. https://doi.org/10.3389/fpsyg.2016.00458
Kavanagh, L. C., Suhler, C. L., Churchland, P. S., & Winkielman, P. (2011). When it's an error to mirror: The surprising reputational costs of mimicry. *Psychological Science, 22*, 1274–1276. https://doi.org/10.1177/0956797611418678
Kavanagh, L., Bakhtiari, G., Suhler, C., Churchland, P. S., Holland, R. W., & Winkielman, P. (2013). Nuanced social inferences about trustworthiness from observation of mimicry. In M. Knauff, M. Pauen, N. Sebanz, & I. Wachsmuth (Eds.), *Proceedings of the 35th annual conference of the cognitive science society* (pp. 734–739). Cognitive Science Society.
King, R. A., Jordan, A. E., Liberman, Z., Kinzler, K. D., & Shutts, K. (2023). Young children apply the homophily principle to their reasoning about social relationships. *Developmental Psychology, 59*, 928–939. https://doi.org/10.1037/dev0001517
Kinzler, K. D., Dupoux, E., & Spelke, E. S. (2007). The native language of social cognition. *Proceedings of the National Academy of Sciences, 104*, 12577–12580. https://doi.org/10.1073/pnas.0705345104
Kudrnova, V., Spelke, E. S., & Thomas, A. J. (2024). Infants infer social relationships between individuals who engage in imitative social interactions. *Open Mind, 8*, 202–216. https://doi.org/10.31234/osf.io/zuwpc
Kuhl, P. K. (2007). Is speech learning 'gated' by the social brain? *Developmental Science, 10*, 110–120. https://doi.org/10.1111/j.1467-7687.2007.00572.x
Lakin, J. L., & Chartrand, T. L. (2003). Using nonconscious behavioral mimicry to create affiliation and rapport. *Psychological Science, 14*, 334–339. https://doi.org/10.1111/1467-9280.14481
Lakin, J. L., Chartrand, T. L., & Arkin, R. M. (2008). I am too just like you: Nonconscious mimicry as an automatic behavioral response to social exclusion. *Psychological Science, 19*, 816–822. https://doi.org/10.1111/j.1467-9280.2008.02162.x
Liberman, Z., & Shaw, A. (2019). Children use similarity, propinquity, and loyalty to predict which people are friends. *Journal of Experimental Child Psychology, 184*, 1–17. https://psycnet.apa.org/doi/10.1016/j.jecp.2019.03.002
Liberman, Z., Kinzler, K. D., & Woodward, A. L. (2014). Friends or foes: Infants use shared evaluations to infer others' social relationships. *Journal of Experimental Psychology: General, 143*, 966–971. https://doi.org/10.1037%2Fa0034481
Liberman, Z., Kinzler, K. D., & Woodward, A. L. (2021). Origins of homophily: Infants expect people with shared preferences to affiliate. *Cognition, 212*, 104695. https://dx.doi.org/10.1016/j.cognition.2021.104695
Liu, S., Ullman, T. D., Tenenbaum, J. B., & Spelke, E. S. (2017). Ten-month-old infants infer the value of goals from the costs of actions. *Science, 358*, 1038–1041. https://doi.org/10.1126/science.aag2132
Mahajan, N., & Wynn, K. (2012). Origins of "us" versus "them": Prelinguistic infants prefer similar others. *Cognition, 124*, 227–233. https://psycnet.apa.org/doi/10.1016/j.cognition.2012.05.003
Malle, B. F. (2014). The social self and the social other: Actor-observer asymmetries in making sense of behavior. In *The social self* (pp. 189–204). Psychology Press. https://doi.org/10.1037/0022-3514.93.4.491
Margoni, F., & Surian, L. (2018). Infants' evaluation of prosocial and antisocial agents: A meta-analysis. *Developmental Psychology, 54*, 1445–1455. https://dx.doi.org/10.1037/dev0000538

McCullough, M. E. (2020). *The kindness of strangers: How a selfish ape invented a new moral code*. Simon and Schuster.

Meltzoff. (1990). Foundations for developing a concept of self: The role of imitation in relating self to other and the value of social mirroring, social modeling, and self practice in infancy. In D. Cicchetti & M. Beeghly (Eds.), *The self in transition: Infancy to childhood* (pp. 139–164). University of Chicago Press.

Misch, A., Over, H., & Carpenter, M. (2014). Stick with your group: Young children's attitudes about group loyalty. *Journal of Experimental Child Psychology, 126*, 19–36. https://psycnet.apa.org/doi/10.1016/j.jecp.2014.02.008

Murphy, R. O., Ackermann, K. A., & Handgraaf, M. J. (2011). Measuring social value orientation. *Judgment and Decision making, 6*, 771–781. https://dx.doi.org/10.2139/ssrn.1804189

Naber, M., Vaziri Pashkam, M., & Nakayama, K. (2013). Unintended imitation affects success in a competitive game. *Proceedings of the National Academy of Sciences, 110*, 20046–20050. https://doi.org/10.1073/pnas.1305996110

Olson, K. R., & Shaw, A. (2011). 'No fair, copycat!': What children's response to plagiarism tells us about their understanding of ideas. *Developmental Science, 14*, 431–439. https://psycnet.apa.org/doi/10.1111/j.1467-7687.2010.00993.x

Over, H. (2020). The social function of imitation in development. *Annual Review of Developmental Psychology, 2*, 93–109. https://doi.org/10.1146/annurev-devpsych-033020-024051

Over, H., & Carpenter, M. (2009). Priming third-party ostracism increases affiliative imitation in children. *Developmental Science, 12*, F1–F8. https://doi.org/10.1111/j.1467-7687.2008.00820.x

Over, H., & Carpenter, M. (2012). Putting the social into social learning: Explaining both selectivity and fidelity in children's copying behavior. *Journal of Comparative Psychology, 126*, 182–192. https://doi.org/10.1037/a0024555

Over, H., & Carpenter, M. (2015). Children infer affiliative and status relations from watching others imitate. *Developmental Science, 18*, 917–925. https://doi.org/10.1111/desc.12275

Pepe, B., & Powell, L. (2023). Infants' expectations for prosociality in imitators. *OSFPreprints*. https://doi.org/10.31219/osf.io/cjnkb

Pesowski, M. L., Powell, L. J., Cikara, M., & Schachner, A. (2023). Interpersonal utility and children's social inferences from shared preferences. *Cognition, 232*, 105344. https://doi.org/10.1016/j.cognition.2022.105344

Powell, L. J. (2022). Adopted utility calculus: Origins of a concept of social affiliation. *Perspectives on Psychological Science, 17*, 1215–1233. https://doi.org/10.1177/17456916211048487

Powell, L., & Spelke, E. (2017). The role of perceptual access in infants' third party evaluations of imitation. *PsyArxiv*. https://doi.org/10.31234/osf.io/63tyq

Powell, L. J., & Spelke, E. S. (2018a). Human infants' understanding of social imitation: Inferences of affiliation from third party observations. *Cognition, 170*, 31–48. https://doi.org/10.31234/osf.io/63tyq

Powell, L. J., & Spelke, E. S. (2018b). Third-party preferences for imitators in preverbal infants. *Open Mind, 2*, 61–71. https://dx.doi.org/10.1162/opmi_a_00018

Quillien, T., Tooby, J., & Cosmides, L. (2023). Rational inferences about social valuation. *Cognition, 239*, 105566. https://dx.doi.org/10.1016/j.cognition.2023.105566

Roberts, S. O., Gelman, S. A., & Ho, A. K. (2017). So it is, so it shall be: Group regularities license children's prescriptive judgments. *Cognitive Science, 41*, 576–600. https://doi.org/10.1111/cogs.12443

Sanchez-Burks, J., Bartel, C. A., & Blount, S. (2009). Performance in intercultural interactions at work: Cross-cultural differences in response to behavioral mirroring. *Journal of Applied Psychology, 94*, 216–223. https://psycnet.apa.org/doi/10.1037/a0012829

Shaw, A., Li, V., & Olson, K. R. (2012). Children apply principles of physical ownership to ideas. *Cognitive Science, 36*, 1383–1403. https://doi.org/10.1111/j.1551-6709.2012.01265.x

Shutts, K., & Kalish, C. W. (2021). Intuitive sociology. In *Advances in child development and behavior* (Vol. 61, pp. 335–374). JAI. https://doi.org/10.1016/bs.acdb.2021.05.004

Shutts, K., Roben, C. K. P., & Spelke, E. S. (2013). Children's use of social categories in thinking about people and social relationships. *Journal of Cognition and Development, 14*, 35–62. https://doi.org/10.1080%2F15248372.2011.638686

Sinclair, S., Lowery, B. S., Hardin, C. D., & Colangelo, A. (2005). Social tuning of automatic racial attitudes: The role of affiliative motivation. *Journal of Personality and Social Psychology, 89*, 583–592. https://doi.org/10.1037/0022-3514.89.4.583

Smith-Flores, A. S., & Powell, L. J. (2023). Joint reasoning about social affiliation and emotion. *Nature Reviews Psychology, 2*, 374–383. https://doi.org/10.1038/s44159-023-00181-0

Smith-Flores, A. S., Bonamy, G., & Powell, L. (2023). Children's reasoning about empathy and social relationships. *Open Mind, 7*, 837–854. https://doi.org/10.1162/opmi_a_00109

Smith-Flores, A. S., Herrera-Guevara, I. A., & Powell, L. J. (2024). Infants expect friends, but not rivals, to be happy for each other when they succeed. *Developmental Science, 27*, e13423. https://doi.org/10.1111/desc.13423

Stahl, A. E., & Kibbe, M. M. (2022). Great expectations: The construct validity of the violation-of-expectation method for studying infant cognition. *Infant and Child Development, 31*, e2359.

Stel, M., van Dijk, E., & van Baaren, R. B. (2016). When and why mimicry is facilitated and attenuated. *Social and Personality Psychology Compass, 10*, 561–574. https://doi.org/10.1002/icd.2359

Thomas, A. J., Saxe, R., & Spelke, E. S. (2020, July). Infants use imitation but not comforting or social synchrony to evaluate those in social interactions. *CogSci.*

Thomas, A. J., Saxe, R., & Spelke, E. S. (2022). Infants infer potential social partners by observing the interactions of their parent with unknown others. *Proceedings of the National Academy of Sciences, 119*, e2121390119. https://doi.org/10.1073/pnas.2121390119

Tomasello, M., Carpenter, M., Call, J., Behne, T., & Moll, H. (2005). Understanding and sharing intentions: The origins of cultural cognition. *Behavioral and Brain Sciences, 28*, 675–691. https://doi.org/10.1017/s0140525x05000129

Tompkins, R., Vasquez, K., Gerdin, E., Dunham, Y., & Liberman, Z. (in press). Expectations of intergroup empathy bias emerge by early childhood. *Journal of Experimental Psychology: General.* https://doi.org/10.1037/xge0001505

Tooby, J., Cosmides, L., Sell, A., Lieberman, D., & Sznycer, D. (2008). Internal regulatory variables and the design of human motivation: A computational and evolutionary approach. In *Handbook of approach and avoidance motivation* (Vol. 15, p. 251).

Turiel, E. (2015). Moral development. In *Handbook of Child Psychology and Developmental Science* (pp. 1–39). https://doi.org/10.1002/9781118963418.childpsy113

Uhlmann, E. L., Poehlman, T. A., & Nosek, B. A. (2012). Automatic associations: Personal attitudes or cultural knowledge? In J. Hanson (Ed.), *Ideology, psychology, and law* (pp. 228–260). Oxford University Press. https://doi.org/10.1093/acprof:oso/9780199737512.003.0009

Ullman, T., Baker, C., Macindoe, O., Evans, O., Goodman, N., & Tenenbaum, J. (2009). Help or hinder: Bayesian models of social goal inference. *Advances in Neural Information Processing Systems, 22*, 1874–1882.

Van Baaren, R. B., Holland, R. W., Steenaert, B., & Van Knippenberg, A. (2003). Mimicry for money: Behavioral consequences of imitation. *Journal of Experimental Social Psychology, 39*, 393–398. https://doi.org/10.1016/S0022-1031(03)00014-3

Van Wye, E. M., Wang, M., & Roberts, S. O. (2021). Explanations for norm violations affect preschoolers' judgments of norm violators. *Journal of Experimental Psychology: General, 150*, 1688. https://doi.org/10.1037/xge0000942

Wang, Y., & Hamilton, A. F. D. (2012). Social top-down response modulation (STORM): A model of the control of mimicry in social interaction. *Frontiers in Human Neuroscience, 6*, 153. https://doi.org/10.3389/fnhum.2012.00153

Wang, Y. A., & Todd, A. R. (2021). Evaluations of empathizers depend on the target of empathy. *Journal of Personality and Social Psychology, 121*, 1005. https://doi.org/10.1037/pspi0000341

Watson-Jones, R. E., Whitehouse, H., & Legare, C. H. (2016). In-group ostracism increases high-fidelity imitation in early childhood. *Psychological Science, 27*, 34–42. https://doi.org/10.1177/0956797615607205

Wellman, H. M., & Gelman, S. A. (1992). Cognitive development: Foundational theories of core domains. *Annual Review of Psychology, 43*, 337–375. https://doi.org/10.1146/annurev.ps.43.020192.002005
Wen, N. J., Clegg, J. M., & Legare, C. H. (2019). Smart conformists: Children and adolescents associate conformity with intelligence across cultures. *Child Development, 90*, 746–758. https://dx.doi.org/10.1111/cdev.12935
Weyers, P., Mühlberger, A., Kund, A., Hess, U., & Pauli, P. (2009). Modulation of facial reactions to avatar emotional faces by nonconscious competition priming. *Psychophysiology, 46*, 328–335. https://doi.org/10.1111/j.1469-8986.2008.00771.x
Woo, B. M., & Spelke, E. S. (2023a). Infants and toddlers leverage their understanding of action goals to evaluate agents who help others. *Child Development, 94*, 734–751. https://doi.org/10.1111/cdev.13895
Woo, B. M., & Spelke, E. S. (2023b). Toddlers' social evaluations of agents who act on false beliefs. *Developmental Science, 26*, e13314. https://doi.org/10.1111/desc.13314
Woo, B. M., Steckler, C. M., Le, D. T., & Hamlin, J. K. (2017). Social evaluation of intentional, truly accidental, and negligently accidental helpers and harmers by 10-month-old infants. *Cognition, 168*, 154–163. https://doi.org/10.1016/j.cognition.2017.06.029
Woodward, A. L. (1998). Infants selectively encode the goal object of an actor's reach. *Cognition, 69*, 1–34. https://doi.org/10.1016/s0010-0277(98)00058-4
Yang, F., Shaw, A., Garduno, E., & Olson, K. R. (2014). No one likes a copycat: A cross-cultural investigation of children's response to plagiarism. *Journal of Experimental Child Psychology, 121*, 111–119. https://doi.org/10.1016/j.jecp.2013.11.008

Correction to: Mimicry in Psychological Disorders and Psychotherapy

Maike Salazar Kämpf and Cornelia Exner

Correction to:
Chapter 15 in: O. Genschow, E. Cracco (eds.), *Automatic Imitation*, https://doi.org/10.1007/978-3-031-62634-0_15

The book was inadvertently published with an incorrect running head for one of the authors of Chapter 15.

"The original version of this book has been revised."

For this book, one of the authors of Chapter 15 has the below corrections:

The last name of the author M. Salazar Kämpf is incorrect and please find below the complete message from the Author: inside the chapter on the upper right corner on p.310, p.312, p.314, p.316, p.318, p.320, p.322, p.324, p.326, p.328 and p. 330 it says M.S. Kämpf. The correct way would be: M. Salazar Kämpf, as my last name is Salazar Kämpf.

The updated version of this chapter can be found at
https://doi.org/10.1007/978-3-031-62634-0_15

O. Genschow, E. Cracco (eds.), *Automatic Imitation*,
https://doi.org/10.1007/978-3-031-62634-0_17

Index

O. Genschow, E. Cracco (eds.), *Automatic Imitation*,
https://doi.org/10.1007/978-3-031-62634-0

The manufacturer's authorised representative in the EU is Springer Nature Customer Service Centre GmbH, Europaplatz 3, 69115 Heidelberg, Germany. If you have any concerns regarding our products, please contact ProductSafety@springernature.com

Printed and bound by CPI Group (UK) Ltd, Croydon, CR0 4YY
01/10/2026
02225858-0014